Operation Triple X

An Indian Spy-Run in Pakistan

DEDICATION

To dear Mayukh, Mainak and Puja.
Thanks for all the support.

Operation Triple X

An Indian Spy-Run in Pakistan

A Novel by

Maloy Krishna Dhar

Manas Publications
New Delhi - 110 002 (India)

MANAS PUBLICATIONS
(We Convert Fighters into Writers)
(Publishers, Library Suppliers, Importers & Exporters)
4402/5-A, Ansari Road (Opp HDFC Bank)
Darya Ganj, New Delhi-110 002 (India)
Off. ✆ 23260783, 23265523, Fax: 011-23272766
E-mail: manaspublications@ gmail.com
manaspublications@ yahoo.com

ISBN 81-7049-301-3
₹ 495/-

Designed at
Manas Publications

Printed in India at
HS Offsets, Delhi
and published by Mrs Suman Lata for
Manas Publications, 4402/5-A, Ansari Road
(Opp HDFC Bank), Darya Ganj,
New Delhi-110 002 (INDIA)

Author's Note

OPERATION TRIPLE X is the scintillating story of an Indian spy embedded in Pakistan, at a crucial stage of strategic relationship between the umbilical twins. Special sculpting has been carried out to merge the characters with the historical milieu of the time. The tradecraft essentials of the story are peculiar to intelligence agencies, which go in making spy-run in a foreign country a roaring intelligence coup.

I am grateful to many readers in India and abroad for making certain valuable suggestions on the story contour of the novel, which unveiled the personalities in Pakistan who filled their ego-bags and pockets at the cost of dismemberment of the nation.

Though a work of fiction, OPERATION TRIPLE X reflects true pictures of the political ambience and social milieu of the time. The readers may find shadows of some historical characters in the novel. Such similarity is inevitable as the spy-run story is based on contemporary relations between India and Pakistan, which did not end with the Indo-Pak war of 1971.

This near-real life classic story has not been lifted from any known spy-run by India inside Pakistan.

1

Nakshatra Lok (galactic abode), the awesome structure that carried the audacious name, housed India's super-secret spy agency, the National Security India (NSI). Located at a remote corner of Delhi, bordering the wooded banks of river Yamuna, alongside the Humayun Tomb, it presented the eerie spectre of a spiralling space station.

The architectural marvel of Nakshatra Lok created an illusory conjunction of amorphous and ethereal awe. It copied a star-war concept, stolen from the neurons of science fiction scribblers. The architect had translated the geometric designs and aesthetic concepts of a space station, envisioned by the chief of the NSI, Balachandran Nampoothiri.

Nakshatra Lok's structural ingenuity was craftily synthesized with its functional ethics. It was meant to be a business place, the serious business of national security and external intelligence affairs. Specially designed glass-encased tubular elevators, controlled by a master computer, connected the functionally and intrinsically independent modules. The reception area, cloned from modern business-house front offices, offered a soothing ecological delight. Green tropical plants, arranged with poetic imagination created a mirage of cool environs.

Nakshatra Lok was far from a cool niche.

Exceptionally beautiful women, all in the age group of twenty to twenty-five, operated the geometrically designed front reception cubicles. Glued to their chairs and specially designed desks they presented a monotonously titillating sight. But they were, however, not clones. Each one of them, fabulously charming, presented a cool impersonal appearance, distinct from their surrounding. Their chiselled features, sculpted frames, and honey-laced impersonal looks created the clone syndrome.

Monogrammed plastic boards, hung in front of each desk, proclaimed the names and logos of the companies they pretended to represent. These front decoys were wired to the access control system of the National Security India and entry to the surreal front reception was routed through basement parking bays, which were controlled by laser-hologram identity cards. Close circuit television cameras concealed beneath fancy lighting props monitored the front desks and peripheral bays. These were, in turn, connected to the master consoles of the security terminals. The charming dames mechanically placed the identity cards under scanner beams connected to a mainframe computer. A green flash elicited melted smiles and programmed welcome greetings. A flicker in red meant trouble, leading to segregation and polite but uncomfortable questioning and an occasional journey to a safe house for thorough screening and decontamination.

This nimble façade, succinctly symbolised the good, the bad and the ugly features as well as functions of the reputed, ridiculed and often cursed external intelligence agency of India.

*

One of the front desks, farthest from the right, displayed a miniature signboard, 'World Vision Infotech,' proclaiming supposed commercial activity in information technology, located somewhere in the fourth tower of the complex. That tower terrace housed the global communication network of the National Security India, connecting its stations in world capitals as also the capitals of Indian states and district detachments. An intricate Compact Communication Module (CCM), hooked to a PARAMA supercomputer, handled digitally secured data and voice communication that poured in over line, radio, and satellite facilities. The super secret communication monitoring facility, with an installed capacity to hook 10,000 inland and overseas telephone lines, was housed in the top two floors. The satellite communication-tapping hub, hooked to the major External Transmission Gateways and wired to the hubs, which tracked the footprints of the Chinese and the Pakistani satellite communication systems, supplemented the traditional physical line monitoring consoles.

Arrays of antennae, dispersed over two separate funnels, facilitated the reception and transmission modules for High (HF), Very High (VHF), Very Low (VLF) and Ultra High Frequency (UHF) radio stations. Radio wizards handled all secret and top-secret communications and trained mathematicians and computer buffs manipulated the complicated computer generated cipher traffic.

Internal communication linkages were skilfully segregated from the Public Service Telephone Network (PSTN). A nine hundred-line Electronic Private Automatic Branch Exchange (EPABX) system with automatic patching facility with the PSTN system handled the internal traffic.

The third and fourth towers also provided two mini-heliports, capable of handling four MI28 and Chinooks.

Two dedicated lines connected the office of the DINASIA, Director National Security India. Ten exclusive lines were extended to an underground bunker complex below the Raisina Hills that almost cloned the seat of power above the hills. A retractable roof camouflaged a helicopter landing facility. The arrays of bunkers below housed the Crisis Management Station (CRISMAS) and the Command Head Quarter (CHQ), two super secret entities, programmed to be activated in the event of a nuclear war alert.

The special NSI exchange wires were extended to another super-secret underground complex, located somewhere in Lutyens' Delhi that accommodated the Supreme Command Station (SUCOSON)—the emergency functional headquarters for the President, the Prime Minister and his War Cabinet besides the Chiefs of the Armed Forces. An underground tunnel connected the fourth tower with the SUCOSON and the CRISMAS.

*

Chapter 1

The Chief or the Director National Security India, DINASIA, occupied the fabled room number 0003, located at eleventh level of the fourth tower. Balachandran Nampoothiri, fondly called Balu and Balls by acquaintances and golf-turf buddies, was born in an orthodox Malayali Brahmin family. A policeman by training, he was inducted into the Federal Intelligence Bureau (FIB) soon after independence after the Muslim officers of the Bureau opted out for Pakistan.

Described as the coolest hawk, Nampoothiri worked his way up, much to the envy of his colleagues and Delhi's bureaucrat watchers, nicknamed *beauronthologists,* seemingly the first cousins of ornithologists. A glib talker and a social live wire, he had endeared himself to the top politicians and famous parlour creatures, who normally seeded India's political and economic clouds over soothing drinks and catty smiles.

Nampoothiri's thirst for the top intelligence slot, a lonely place at the pinnacle of the pyramid, had propelled him into a fiery race against another powerful contender, his colleague in the undivided Federal Intelligence Bureau, Kumar Anand Prasad, a wily Bihar *kayasth* (intermediate caste). Kumar didn't dither in mustering stronger propellants for out-racing Nampoothiri. This was a bitter blazing fight, a razing fire that refused to be extinguished by soothing Scotch on the rocks and contrived manipulation of facial muscles, often described as smiles. The silent peaceful war often rocked the agency and nation's security ambience. Nampoothiri believed firmly in the doctrine of fighting wars through peace.

In Ram Karan Prasad, the permanent Union cabinet minister, Kumar had a benign godfather. Both hailed from Pataliputra, the nerve centre of an ancient empire, associated with the name of Chanakya, the acknowledged Indian spymaster and strategist. What better credential could Kumar Anand claim?

However, a Nampoothiri, according to Hindu tradition, could not be wished away as a lesser Chanakya. In Kerala, wherefrom the Namboodris hail, people preferred to kill a Namboodri first before smothering a golden arrowhead cobra. Balu, friends and foes vouchsafed, wasn't as malevolent as his legendary caste kinsmen were portrayed to be. He used his own brand of lubricants, which Kumar Anand jokingly described as coconut butter, and polished his way up the critical cone of the external intelligence outfit. The reference to coconut butter critically reflected the NSI chief's glorious roots in the coastal state of Kerala. The allegation was not correct. Nampoothiri did not have a buttery brain; it was filled with solid commonsense.

Nampoothiri, his friends and foes agreed, was an accomplished spymaster with exclusive tunnels to the minds, thoughts, and perceptions of leading politicians. It was no mean an achievement. With the advent of Manjira as the prime minister after the tragic death of her predecessor Jung Bahadur Sharma, appointments to higher government slots depended on a single cardinal principle-loyalty to the chair. Manjira preferred a committed bureaucracy. She herself claimed to have been committed to the mission of rescuing India, a task she feigned to have inherited from her father.

Nampoothiri was a different piece of blade, adept in skilled fencing game. His adversaries didn't even winch after their heads were severed from torso. It required a whiff of Virginia snuff to make the severed crown sneeze and fall apart.

The capital's bureaucrats maintained a fearful proximity and distance from Nampoothiri for his alleged capability of staging a coup at the most unexpected moment. That was the reason why some of them preferred to call him Balls. They did not refer to golf-turf. They meant, the parts of the sex organs of the politicians, to which, they alleged, Nampoothiri preferred to attach himself.

That too was not the correct portrait of a person who waged mostly invisible and often visible wars against enemies of the nation—especially Pakistan.

He was, by far, the coolest cat in Delhi's power alley.

*

However, the morning chill of the 19th day of November 1971 could not cool Balachandran Nampoothiri. He was sweating profusely and uncomfortably in his 0003 den. A specially fabricated thick inner lead casing, for denying access to invasive electronic snooping, protected the dreaded and coveted room. The lead coating supplemented by soundproofing materials made the room impregnable.

The two other integral fixtures of his office–Jatadhari Garo, Nampoothiri's Man Friday, and Amrita Bhalla, his secretary cum alter ego–also sweated nervously. They had some idea of what had pushed the boss down the brink. But they were not sure. Jata and Amrita exchanged quick glances and asked mute questions.

A short introduction to these human machines may not be irrelevant. They existed because Balachandran ruled over India's external intelligence empire.

Nampoothiri could perhaps not be a complete intelligence boss without his shadow, Jatadhari Garo. The jet-black Garo tribal had almost dropped into Nampoothiri's life through the skies. In real life, Jatadhari held the rank of a junior superintendent of police. This tribal of Tibetan stock, six feet two inches tall, all muscle and no fat, was conjoined with Nampoothiri in course of a strange accident at Nathu La pass, one of the frontier outposts on Sikkim-China borders.

Balachandran Nampoothiri was on one of his many trips to Nathu La, heading a group of electronic specialists, for installing directional microphones and a Very High Frequency (VHF) radio-monitoring centre. The directional microphones were designed to pick up conversations of the Chinese army contingents, which occupied a lower shoulder, barely 300 metres below the ridge. Howling winds rolled up from the Chumbi valley below and thrashed against the peaks on the Indian side with wailing sounds. The windy pass frustrated all HumInt and TechInt efforts to record conversations of the inscrutable Chinese troops.

Challenges never disheartened Nampoothiri. He worked on the idea of installing directional microphones, drawing inspiration from similar CIA operations on the DMZ on North Korean side of the borders.

That January morning Nampoothiri stood facing the Chinese formations amidst early snowfall. The Tsangu Lake, on Indian side of the valley, was still full of rainbow trout and the graziers were yet to move down to the lower reaches of the rippling pastures. The Yak herds were roaming in the green patches dotted with Dandelion, Iris, and Tiger lilies. The Bhutia and Lepcha herd-tenders were busy in their Yak-skin tents cooking barley meals, roasting dry meat, and melting frozen cheese. Fresh coats of powdery snow covered the Rhododendron bushes that were trying to burst out of their wet white burial.

It happened suddenly. A Chinese soldier peeped out from his bunker, looked up at Nampoothiri, and fired two indeterminate shots in the air to express his disapproval of the presence of the Indian contingent just above his head. A perplexed Nampoothiri jumped back and the soft snow beneath his feet gave way. He slithered down the precipices, a sheer fall of 500 feet. By instinct, he grabbed at a Rhododendron bush and managed to hang precariously.

Before anyone could react, Jatadhari, all six feet of him, grabbed another Rhododendron bush, stretched down his long arms and jerked up Nampoothiri, as if he was tossing a tiny basketball. Nampoothiri fell on soft snow with a thud. The Rhododendron bushes wilted under his weight and his bulky figure skidded down to a grassy patch, a good 20 feet below.

In the process, Jatadhari slipped down the slope into a deep crevice. He was finally rescued with one leg and three broken fingers. The technical operation was temporarily abandoned and Nampoothiri airlifted the junior officer for treatment all the way to Delhi in a special AN 26, owned by Kalyani Air Lines (KAL), another super-secret adjunct of the Federal Intelligence Bureau. Nampoothiri himself was in the flight. He owed his life to the valiant tribal officer. He and Jatadhari became inseparable and emotionally interdependent. The bond of trust between them was more sacrosanct than the holy vow of a Hindu marriage.

Amrita Bhalla, a mid-ranking official of National Security Service (NSS), was there not for her chiselled body, aquiline beauty, and expertise in Karate and martial art. She possessed a vibrant mind with youthful bounty of humour and an inbuilt X-ray, which enabled her to discover the proverbial pig behind hungry human looks. Her father, a SAS trained Colonel of the Indian Army, was the hero of Bomdi La war against China. He did not leave his post until the last bullet was spent and scores of Chinese bullets riddled his body. Nampoothiri liked this steely beauty to guard his front office. She often acted as his mirror to remind that despite age he was the best sleuth around.

*

The heavy door slightly opened up. Amrita Bhalla glided in. Nampoothiri, busy reading a dispatch from his station chief in Islamabad, looked up.

"Yes?"

"Sir, Mr. Achariya is at the front desk. He wants to see you urgently."

Balachandran Nampoothiri wasn't pleased. He had just returned from a secret location where Triple X and his wife and child were housed after their unexpected arrival from Pakistan in a virtually hijacked mercenary flight. He was not ready to be bored by stale information and smoky anxiety of his desk officer.

Achariya, he presumed, was on a panic trip over the mysterious loss of contact with Harfan Bukhari, NSI's Operation Triple X, and Alamgir, India's most valuable long-term intelligence anchor inside Pakistan.

He had no time to waste for his panicked desk chief. Triple X, India's top-secret resident agent in Pakistan, had violated the final disengagement instructions and mysteriously landed in an Air Force base near Delhi. A South African mercenary, hired by Islamabad for ferrying weapons to East Pakistan, piloted the aircraft. The strange connectivity was scary. Totality of the oddities had befuddled

Nampoothiri. The greatest intelligence coup or fiasco of his time was likely to pour flammable fuels in the surcharged relationship between India and Pakistan. The volcanic drama was shoved behind a curtain of secrecy on orders from the Prime Minister. Only Nampoothiri and the Case Officer of Operation Triple X, Dhiren Bhagat, were aware of the hideout where the turbulent agent was housed.

The DINASIA expected Amrita Bhalla to turn Achariya away.

Nampoothiri squeezed his eyebrows, created a deep furrow on forehead, and smiled at Amrita.

"You know dear, I'm awfully busy."

"I know sir. I tried to shake him off. He refuses to drop out."

"Okay. Ask him to be brief."

Amrita glided out painting herself with extra courtesy and friendliness.

"How're you Robin?" Amrita asked smilingly, "anything gone wrong?"

"Big problem dear," Robin drew up a chair, "Triple X has disappeared."

"Oh dear!" Amrita started with a pout, "don't get worked up, agents come and go, like autumn clouds."

"He was important, dear to the boss." Robin smiled back, hoping to prolong the dialogue.

A faint blue light momentarily glowed on a screen hidden under the wooden panel of her table and Amrita stood up with a courteous gesture.

"Boss knows better. You can go in sir." She cleared the way for Achariya with a naughty twinkle. She always spoke these last words with a lilting and slurring accent. Some visitors interpreted it as a deliberate sexy finale. Others digested it as an expression of arrogance of a junior officer, with a bloated ego, because of her physical intimacy with the top man, a perception, that was not based on fact.

Achariya threw a smile and a wink and entered the room closely on Jatadhari's heels. As he occupied a thick cushioned moccasin upholstered chair, Jatadhari drew the heavy curtains on the window, and Nampoothiri switched on his music system at low bass. This was a normal practice, to create noise pollution, making it difficult for hostile snooping operations.

"How're things Robin?" Nampoothiri looked up at his anguished look.

"We appear to have run into problems with Operation Triple X. We're cut off for last couple of days. He should've been in London by this time, following your final instructions. Our efforts to activate the communication channels have failed. Agent Double X, I mean Qurban, is silent too." Achariya blurted out rapidly, his panic apparent.

"Where is Alamgir?" Nampoothiri.

"No contact sir. We've no contact since he left London for Islamabad. Kabul isn't able to raise him."

"Have you checked with his family in Berne?"

"Not yet."

"Has there been any distress signal at the pre-fixed radio frequency?"

"No sir. Our boys have been scanning all the three channels assigned to Alam," Achariya kept on staring at his boss, "as you're aware Triple X's radio was earlier decommissioned."

"That's correct. Have you checked with our man in Peshawar?"

"Peshawar is unaware of his whereabouts. Alam and Harfan have simply disappeared, it seems. I'm afraid, they may have fallen into the ISI trap."

Nampoothiri felt uncomfortable. Droplets of sweat appeared on his forehead. He wiped the back of his neck and forehead in repeated motions with a silk handkerchief and pressed the buzzer.

Triple X was not the cause for his anxiety. He knew where he was. Nampoothiri was puzzled over Alamgir. Alam's silence could trigger a domino effect and collapse India's pack of cards in Pakistan. He silently puffed the Havana. The pungent smoke helped in clearing the smoke of confusion. Achariya was genuinely concerned. He too was concerned, but there was no need to exhibit the wound before him. For a while, how long he did not know, he was required to suffer the loudness of silence of the approaching storm.

Nampoothiri's thought waves took a sharp inward turn.

Yes, he had spent two crucial hours with Harfan Bukhari and had pumped out sensitive intelligence about Pakistani plans of an aerial blitzkrieg against Indian targets that was to trigger off the third war between India and Pakistan. Triple X was dead accurate on that count. He was informed, minutes ago, by the Director of Military Intelligence (DMI), about strafing of a few airbases by Pakistani Sabre jets in the volatile western sector.

Harfan Bukhari, however, persistently dodged all questions on Alamgir. Nampoothiri didn't press either. It appeared Triple X had corked up certain chambers of his mind. He resisted friendly questioning. The Prime Minister had ordered a go-slow policy in respect of Triple X and the South African pilot, Vudurume. It suited Nampoothiri. The NSI, at this point of crisis, when Indian and Pakistani forces were in active engagement in the eastern and western theatres, was more concerned with the wartime task of gathering tactical intelligence. A detailed post-mortem of the spectral collapse of its intelligence network inside Pakistan could be carried out after the initial storm was over. The job required a levelheaded approach and calm analysis. No rush action, Nampoothiri had agreed with the Prime Minister.

In any case, he wasn't keen to share the nuts and bolts of the foxy riddle with Achariya. Pakistan related intelligence was his special turf and Operation Triple X was his own baby and he'd like to carry out a leisurely postmortem. Moreover, he did not like the entire bureaucratic world squirming at his seeming failure and demanding his scalp.

Nampoothiri licked his parched lips and looked towards Jatadhari. Jatadhari knew the drill well. The sweating forehead of the boss told him that some storm was tossing inside. He switched on the exhaust, picked up a Havana from a silver casket and flicked open a blue flame by pressing the Ronson lighter. Nampoothiri inhaled the smoke with a relish, like oxygen starved fish and looked up at Achariya.

"What about your Quetta LP (Listening Post)?"

"The Quetta LP and our OP (Observation Post) at Chaman haven't been able to contact Alamgir." He hinted at a top-level Afghan trader, who operated dozens of loan sharks in the Indian states of Bengal and Bihar.

"What about your auxiliary channel at Tashkent?"

"They're dry. I'm afraid," Achariya blinked peevishly with a naughty smile, "Triple X may have defected to Pakistan."

"That sounds improbable." Nampoothiri looked up with a stony gaze and mildly shook his head.

Robin Achariya nervously rattled his throat and explained that prolonged silence of Triple X, located at Jhumra near Faisalabad, worried him. This particular asset, turbulent and irrepressible, had the potential of exploding into a self-destructing blast. In the process, he could trigger off an avalanche of exposure, burying other intelligence operations in Pakistan.

"I can't agree more," Nampoothiri looked squarely into Achariya's eyes, "raise our MI6 liaison channel in Cairo. Not the River Channel. They may have some clues."

Nampoothiri wished him off and picked up a yellow phone, part of the exclusive in house communication network and asked Krishna Kumar, Chief of the cryptographic division, to rush in.

*

Nampoothiri harked back into memory lane.

Alamgir was a unique asset from day one.

He was an antithesis of copybook low-key resident agent. His flamboyance coupled with the traits of a bullfighter had created an aura of dubious reputation. These qualities had earned him wide spectrum of acceptability in the Pakistani establishment. He owned several business establishments at Peshawar Fort market, ostensibly selling dry fruits, and assorted merchandise.

Alamgir owned another establishment, an under-cover one, better known in Pakistan as GREG (Global Research Group). The shady outfit had levelled up smooth business relationship with the high and mighty in the Pakistani armed forces. In simple language, Alam Khan, a patriotic Pathan, and his honourable associates scouted around and procured arms and ammunition from world arms bazaars for the military regime. His marketing network was spread over Afghanistan and the Central Asian Soviet Republics, besides the lucrative arms bazaar in Europe and South American hotspots. The arrangement kept everybody happy. The reward packet was fat.

The dry fruit business had, over the years, metamorphosed into a convenient cover operation for international drug trafficking from the Golden Crescent to the dark alleys of Europe and the USA. The uniformed bosses and fringe politicians had found a convenient fall guy in the daredevil Pathan. They thrived merrily on human miseries and Alamgir craftily used the cover for deeper infiltration into the system. Delhi had turned a blind eye at his cover operations. What he did hardly mattered to them as long as their bird laid golden eggs.

Besides catering very high-level intelligence on Pakistan, Alam acted as Nampoothiri's personal emissary and handled shallow penetration Indian intelligence assets in Pakistan. New talents infiltrated by the Federal Intelligence Bureau, now the NSI, were supposed to go through the grilling sieve of this master spy. He enjoyed the total trust of the agency, especially its boss, Nampoothiri.

*

The discreet blue lamp glowed instantly and Amrita silently and respectfully ushered in Krishna Kumar.

A dry and matter of fact person, Krishna Kumar had no other interest in life, except sitting before computers and playing with intercepted coded messages. To him breaking enemy codes was as exotic and erotic as exploring the creases and contours of a beautiful woman.

"Transmit this immediately to Kabul, Tashkent and Moscow." Nampoothiri passed on a slip to Krishna Kumar.

The chief cryptologist glanced at the paper, brought out a compact briefcase from a cupboard, a High Frequency trans-receiver connected to the main transmission and receiving towers. The keyboard gave it a mini-piano look. The simple message had requested the auxiliary station chiefs to immediately direct Alam to get in touch with Sparrow, one of the several code names of Nampoothiri. The auto-encrypted message was burst transmitted in less than three seconds. Krishna Kumar received the 'roger' protocol and switched off.

"I want quick confirmation." Nampoothiri extinguished the cigar and sipped water leisurely.

"No problem sir, if the receiving stations have none."

Krishna Kumar replaced the trans-receiver in the cupboard, handed over the key to his boss, and left without even exchanging mandatory greeting.

*

Agent Taqdeer from Kabul reacted after four hours, via a special communication hub in Moscow. Operation Triple X had simply vanished into thin air. Taqdeer's emissaries could not contact his wife and child. Lahore police didn't confirm his death or arrest. Alamgir's usual communication hubs were silent. Crucial channels assigned to the top agent failed to raise him and his Peshawar den maintained a mysterious silence. These were virtually taken over by unknown faces, suspected Inter Service Intelligence (ISI) officials.

Taqdeer's input unnerved Nampoothiri. He had reasons to sweat in November chill. Alamgir wasn't a dime of an intelligence agent. He alone could demystify the riddles of the suspected collapse of the Indian network inside Pakistan.

The blue lamp on Amrita's desk glowed and Nampoothiri's voice came in.

"Can you come in for a minute?"

"Yes sir."

"What do you think of this Operation Triple X affair and Alamgir's silence?" Nampoothiri tried to pick fresh ideas from his secretary.

"Harfan must have been pushed to the wall," Amrita spoke in soft measured words, "I'm not sure how Alam handled the final disengagement ritual."

"Do you doubt Alam's integrity?"

"Pardon me sir," Amrita continued, "his latest reports on Triple X weren't unbiased. Your debriefing notes of Maulana Rizwan had indicated that. I fear they had developed incurable apathy."

"Probably you're correct dear. Perhaps I should've intervened," Nampoothiri lowered his eyes, probably in retrospection; "I suspected traces of incompatibility between Alam and Harfan. Double X had warned me. But that shouldn't trigger off a supersonic avalanche."

"Your presumptions are natural. But we don't know how much they had drifted. The desk officer should've smelt a rat. I think you're more worried over Harfan's sudden appearance in Delhi."

"Right you're dear. I hadn't expected the coup. Nevertheless, I'm more worried about Alam. He's silent and not responding to radio pulses." Nampoothiri picked up another Havana. Amrita flicked the lighter on.

"Thanks dear. I'm stuck in muck. Another India-Pakistan war is breathing down our neck and my top agent has disappeared. My intelligence edifice inside Pakistan has simply collapsed. That's no fun. The PM isn't going to be pleased. You know her."

Amrita knew little about the lady Prime Minister. But she knew well that the NSI would come under direct fire, if her boss failed to deliver the goods.

"Better go home and relax sir."

"No dear. Call up the Additional Directors, East and West, and ask them to send their SITREPS (situation reports) on the war front. I have to wait for some urgent feedback. Tell Jata to be around. You call it a day."

Nampoothiri, for a change, walked up to the window, opened the glass panels, and looked out at the waters of the river Yamuna. His mind was clogged like the polluted Yamuna. It wasn't moving in any direction.

What had gone wrong, where and why?

Nampoothiri had drawn blank while quizzing Triple X on Alamgir's status. The sullen agent maintained enigmatic silence. Preliminary debriefing could bring out scraps of information about Pakistan's deep penetration inside India's top bureaucratic hierarchy and nuclear research facilities. He repeatedly asserted that some top guns were serenading in Pakistani ears.

Yes, Harfan Bukhari was dead correct. There must have been a fatal intelligence leakage. Someone, well placed in the Indian decision making structure, had traded either with the Pakistani or with a third country intelligence operative.

In all probability, the ISI might have pricked a pin in the overblown balloon of Alamgir's cover and neutralised him. The ISI had scored on two counts, Nampoothiri reasoned. It destroyed an important Indian espionage network and proved its excellent penetration inside the Indian system, at the highest political and bureaucratic levels. However, no tangible conclusion could be drawn before Triple X removed the veil of diffidence and indifference and opened his treasure chest.

He closed the window, called in Jatadhari, and ordered another coffee.

"Sir," Amrita Bhalla spoke on the secured intercom, "Mr. Krishna Kumar is here."

"Haven't you gone home? It's ten p.m."

"I can't leave you alone when you're lost in an uncertain walk inside your mind."

"How do you guess that?"

"Too much unguided walk inside isn't going to help sir. You'd get lost. I think you require a focus. Shall I bring him in?"

"Perhaps you're correct, dear. I'm taking a disjoined walk and I feel I'm lost. Please bring Krish in."

*

Krishna Kumar walked in with a few crisp decoded reports. Nampoothiri's worst fears were confirmed as he quickly glanced through the papers.

Station Kabul reported, quoting Russian embassy sources in Islamabad, that Alam's bullet ridden body was recovered from Bhagatanwala airbase, about 150 km south-east of Chak Lala. He was killed, the report said, along with five other Pakistanis, one of them identified as Ibadat, a hotel employee. Jamanat Ali, a senior ISI official, was seriously injured in the shootout, allegedly carried out by an Indian commando unit. Their target, the Russian sources added, were two squadrons of improved version of Sabre jets, just flown in from Turkey, a virtual gift from Washington.

Shit! Nampoothiri scowled. He hadn't commissioned any commando raid. The Kabul report continued, citing some delicate sources in Pakistan, that the ISI had stormed the Jhumra residence of a suspected Indian linkman and lifted some of his contacts and acquaintances, which included a few notorious and notable arms traders. The ISI was tightlipped about the entire clean up operation. There was an ominous blanket of secrecy over the whole affair.

The Pakistani media, wrapped under wartime censor, maintained a ghostly silence about the disappearance of a Pakistani charter flight with a consignment of supplies for Dacca.

The media, however, blamed Indian commandos for the assassination of one of the patriotic sons of Pakistan and a few policemen. They attained martyrdom, but had succeeded in saving two squadrons of precious fighter-bombers. Some newspapers carried a photograph of Alam Khan, paying tribute to him in glowing words. These reports confirmed Nampoothiri's hunch that Alamgir's cover wasn't blown up by Triple X. Harfan didn't betray India. He wasn't a blowback operation of the ISI. Alam had died in a shootout.

Who had shot him? What was Double X doing there in the airbase? Was Ibadat helping Alam in a super-sensitive operation? What could that be? Delhi hadn't assigned any task to its agents at Bhagatanwala.

What was Alam doing at Bhagatanwala? Was he trying to prevent Triple X from fleeing Pakistan? Did Harfan kill his tactical handler?

The thought came back to Nampoothiri, as he lighted another Havana. He didn't rule out the possibility. After all, the fellow was a cold-blooded killer. His recruitment as a potential resident agent and his training process had presented plenty of pleasant and bitter surprises. Did he slip anywhere in selecting the target and moulding the raw material? Where did he go wrong as the Chief Operations Director of the Federal Intelligence Bureau way back in 1964? Did he fail to assess the intrinsic deficiencies in Harfan Bukhari?

Nampoothiri tried to unfold the pages of the fascinating story, the story of his tryst with Indian intelligence and tango with a turbulent agent, Ramendra Kaushal @ Harfan Bukhari @ Operation Triple X.

*

Destiny had not favoured the idea of wrapping Nampoothiri with sleep and rest. The phone rang sharp as he prepared to step out of his room.

"Huzoor, Dewan here. The lady wants your immediate presence." Rajendra Kumar Dewan, personal assistant to Prime Minister Manjira announced.

"Agenda?"

"Uncertain. Rush."

Nampoothiri rushed through sparse winter night traffic punctuated by movement of men and weapons laden army vehicles. The Prime Minister, seated on her rosewood chair with a pile of files, wore a serious look.

"I'm worried Balu. Pakistan has just opened up the first volley. It's war. I believe your guest from Pakistan suspects serious compromise in top places."

"He is emphatic."

"Talk to the FIB chief. Identify and neutralise all Pakistani moles. I don't want other Ram Karans to gnash teeth inside my government and the system. No compromise of our crucial nuclear programme and, I don't want any slackening of Operation Lotus. And remember, we've lots of lessons to draw from the Ram Karan affair."

Manjira's reference to Ram Karan was related to a political parasite who died sometime ago in a mysterious bomb explosion. Operation Lotus was clinically linked to the ongoing turmoil in the eastern wing of Pakistan. She exploited that Pakistani fault line in a coordinated and strategic intelligence thrust in East Pakistan. It has intractable linkages with the subcontinent's political and diplomatic developments.

The dramatis personae of the Bengali freedom movement were intricately connected with the Lotus concept, independence for the ethnic Bengali speaking East Pakistan. Her father, Amritlal, and her predecessor Jung Bahadur Sharma had nursed the precious concept with admirable patience and grit.

"I trust you Balu. Pakistan must meet its nemesis in East Pakistan. Hope your boys won't let me down." Manjira looked up with a faint look of appreciation.

"My loyalties are with you ma'am. The Lotus will bloom very soon. I want guidance on a thorny problem. What do I do with the mercenary South African pilot and his crew members?"

"What does he want?"

"He wants to visit his roots at Uttar Pradesh. I can arrange it, if you've no objection."

"Do it on the quiet. We don't even have diplomatic relations with the Pretoria regime. Put them on a flight to Bangkok. I've spoken to the Thai Ambassador. They've no objection to give him a visa. From Bangkok he can easily obtain a French visa."

"Thanks ma'am."

Nampoothiri stood up and left, closing the door silently behind him.

"One more point," Manjira looked up with an unusual charming glint in her eyes, "you can talk to Triple X personally. He has rendered a great service. He has more dopes on ISI penetration in our vital areas. I presume he has."

"Yes ma'am." Nampoothiri returned her smile with a pleasant nod and walked out of the room.

"That crook has emerged as a living martyr." He muttered under his breath as he entered Dewan's room.

"Did you say anything?" Dewan asked.

"No dear. It's my nemesis that I'm trying to figure out."

"Don't try. She comes stealthily and isn't regulated by government notifications." Dewan tried to thin the tense smog.

"Forget it, give me a fag."

Nampoothiri lighted the cigarette and stepped out into the well-lit courtyard. His mind was preoccupied with the events of past twenty-four hours sudden appearance of Triple X, Alamgir's death and identification of the dead body of Double X asset, Qurban. Only Harfan could throw light on the foxy puzzle. However, he was still in a sulking mood. That charming rogue was his personal creation and only he could unravel the mystery.

Nampoothiri again dived into his memory pool.

*

2

The X category forward intelligence operations were special, a clever synthesis of shallow and deep penetration intelligence thrust inside Pakistan. That was the brainchild of Rabindra Narayan Dutta, chief of the Federal Intelligence Bureau. He had spun around him queer threads of history and mythology, the history of the dreaded imperial intelligence establishment and the myth of his invincibility, which he derived from the first Prime Minister of India, Amritlal.

The Single X assets were shaped out of trans-border smugglers for gathering shallow tactical intelligence. The Double X agents were literally double edged. They were trained for penetration up to a depth of 50 miles. Some Double X talents, recruited from collaborating Pakistani nationals, offered a mixed bag of tactical and strategic intelligence. Some of the sharper talents were used for one-time dirty-trick operations like some bomb blasts, some acts of arson and mindless massacre. The messages transmitted were often brutal, matching the boorish and abominable acts of proxy war executed by the Inter Services Intelligence of Pakistan.

The Triple X concept was born very back in late 1964, long before the NSI achieved embryonic conceptualisation. The process started soon after Amritlal, the first Prime Minister of independent India, a hotchpotch democratic philosopher and a romantic dictator, expired barely after two years of a mismanaged war against China. The euphoria of universal friendship and the theme of *Panchsheel*, enunciated by Amritlal had received a white burial on the heights of the Himalayas.

Coinciding with Chinese attack Pakistan mounted proxy war operations in Indian North East. The border skirmishes in the Runn of Kachchh and speculations over another Pakistani offensive in Kashmir had prompted Dutta to dissect the espionage logistics inside Pakistan. The pot looked big with only a few grains inside to cook any intelligent collage. That's when he summoned two deputies, Nampoothiri and Kumar Anand Prasad, to scratch brains and evolve new formulae.

"Sir, the idea isn't new. We've done this in Operation Alamgir," commented Balachandran Nampoothiri, a Deputy Director in the FIB, "but, it's not easy to give foolproof cover to a Hindu and merge him in Muslim milieu."

"I never said it's easy, and you can't rest on your haunches with one Alam and a couple of X talents." Dutta shot back, "the job is tough. The PM isn't happy. The old man is furious and wants immediate action. He wants quick results, and I agree with him. Less of golf dear, concentrate on the Pak-turf."

An agitated Dutta, slighted by the PM's not so silent ire, screwed up his deputy, an avid golfer.

"Sir, it's easy for Pakistan to plant their agents in our country. Their pigeons can roost in sympathetic religious nests," commented Kumar Anand Prasad, the other Deputy, "we should pick up Muslim talents, especially from families having relatives in Pakistan," Prasad continued.

Dutta shook his head violently.

"Would you stop talking nonsense?" Dutta threw a nasty look at his second deputy.

"I want you to handle the project," Dutta pointed his finger at Nampoothiri, "I don't trust any Muslim and I can assure you, as long as this damn democracy doesn't force us, I'd oppose induction of Muslims in the Federal Intelligence Bureau."

"But sir, we need Muslim talents."

"I never said no," Dutta, quipped back, "raise as many informers and agents you can. No problem. But I can't trust any Muslim with secrets of the nation, can't afford to have these fifth columns in sensitive areas of state activity."

Dutta momentarily closed his eyes, an indication that the point was not debatable.

"But sir, in a secular country we should have some Muslims in the agency." Prasad reiterated.

"Over my dead body Prasad. Let the politicians extend lip service to secularism. It's nothing but another name of apartheid. I've a job to do and you all play by my rules. It's an unwritten state policy. No argument." Dutta snapped back sharply, thumping a clenched fist on the table.

"Let this project be known as Operation Triple X. Draw up a comprehensive training programme. Take a few crack officers. Apply the finest tradecraft. Yes, don't forget to involve Shyam Purohit, our Maulana Rizwan. I want him to convincingly convert the recruits to Islam and teach them everything that goes into the making of orthodox Muslims out of our targets." Dutta instructed his deputy Balachandran Nampoothiri, with a sanctified sermon from the pulpit.

"I want young, daring and daunting targets, capable of facing the impossible and living on the edges of life. The project requires young and offbeat talents with plenty of courage and a bag full of weaknesses for good things of life."

Young minds, he elaborated, were far more resilient than ossified middle-aged professionals. The old fogies, he believed, were incapable of thinking beyond having ritual sex with their spouses once a week, preferably on a Saturday night, and sleeping out the mandatory Sunday. They were too rigid, timid, and fossilised to bare any part of brain to challenging assignments.

Nampoothiri took the queue over from Dutta.

The company, he impressed upon a select group of talent spotters, was ready to foot the bills for all the grease that were traditionally used for trapping suitable targets. The slippery tracks of the game of espionage were coated with glittering gold, to some it symbolised the gold of patriotism, and to some others it was the Midas metal.

"Mount aggressive hunt," he advised the crack team. "the talents, once trapped, should not be able to escape. They should surrender to the seasoned blackmailers, their designated case officers....

"Offer them a price, each one according to his utility and corrode their original personality. Encapsulate them in an ideological cocoon. The cerebral cortices of the targets should suffer permanent lesions, changing their personality beyond redemption and restoration....

"A successful agent handler should feel happy," Nampoothiri emphasised, "only when his target had undergone a total personality transformation the edifices of his self confidence sufficiently subverted. A perfect spy should be like a hypnotised zombie, a human robot...."

"Any questions?" Nampoothiri asked the assembled Operation Triple X talent spotters, who stared at him with half closed pigeon-eyes.

"Good boys, as we understand in our daily lingo, may not agree to take up challenges of trans-border operations, sir." Dhiren Bhagat, a junior intelligence officer, stood up, after mustering great courage.

Son of a *chamar* (shoemaker), Bhagat had entered the hallowed precincts of the intelligence fraternity by dint of sheer merit. But, as was the vogue in Hindu society, Bhagat was a hated brat, catapulted to the high pedestal of a government job by virtue of the constitutional reservation policy. Caustic comments at his lowly origin and open discrimination were a part of his daily salt.

"I don't want saints", Nampoothiri smiled back, "I want gutsy boys. I don't mind if they're fringe criminals. However, they should be honest criminals. Not the double crossing and cross-cutting types."

"Roger sir." Bhagat replied with a dash of enthusiasm. He was happy to be tasked, for the first time, with a major operational responsibility.

*

Dhiren Bhagat's beat, his immediate superior decided, should be the difficult Delhi University circuit, the hottest hub of student activities. A whole lot of them, the socialists, communists and budding pro-Chinese extremists thronged the campus, its restaurants and pubs, and of course the lovers' corners in the manicured ridge park. It was a tough beat. The students hated the red turbaned police and the intelligence operatives, derisively called '*chipkalis*' (house lizards). The hatred was rooted in history.

These professions represented the long and strong arms of the colonial administration. They continued to play the same role even after independence, protecting and promoting the new rulers. For them nothing had changed. Only the wordings of the choir were substituted, singing in praise of the indigenous instead of the foreign masters.

Bhagat knew he was an object of hate in the university campus. What he did not know was that he was a lucky traveller.

Ramendra Kaushal, fondly called Prince by his acolytes, was the most shining star of the campus, and he couldn't be missed even by a fish-eyed mendicant. The Prince, with his wild macho personality, was present everywhere. A lady-hunter and a drug pusher, Ramendra Kaushal walked the very edges of crime and politics and was a virtual terror in the campus. The Prince honorific, his friends asserted, was a blood inheritance. He belonged to some obscure royal family of Jhunjhunu, in the fabled land of the kings and queens of Rajasthan. He lived the life of a giant sized prince.

Dhiren Bhagat, an intelligence ground rat, studied the susceptibilities of his strange target, Ramendra Kaushal. He trailed him for about a month and logged in a highly impressive dossier.

"Well, well." Rabindra Narayan Dutta said tapping fingers on the table. It was pretty unusual of him to betray excitement.

"Our friend is an all-rounder. Whisky, brawls, and oh my!" Dutta laughed heartily, "he likes his women."

"There are more attractive attributes, sir." Added Nampoothiri.

Dutta looked up, eyebrows squeezed in at the centre of his forehead, forming a deep vertical furrow.

"He is a close associate of Ram Karan Prasad, the minister, and fronts a petty drug pushing chain for him. And sir," Nampoothiri halted, "there is an unconfirmed suspicion of his involvement in a gruesome murder case. He carries a gun and a couple of knives on his person."

"Well Balu. Some politicians are necessary evils. We've replaced kings and queens by these creatures. But no saint would agree to be your spy. I like the target. My intestines tell me this one bastard will make a fine agent. With some clever trimmings and toppings, he can be shaped up as a daredevil deep-cover agent, a category Triple X agent."

Dutta glanced through the appended note on the Triple X target. Kaushal's parental background at Jhumra Valley in Pakistani Punjab, near Sangla Hills, made him especially invaluable. A real life prince, Ramendra Kaushal was the legal successor to the throne of the tiny kingdom of Jhumra. His mother was forced to flee Pakistan after his father, Raja Digvijay Kaushal, was killed by Muslim Niazi serfs and assorted tribes for refusing to merge his tiny sovereign kingdom with Pakistan. The big-ego potentate of Jhumra pretended that he could try out a bluff like the Nizam of Hyderabad and foolishly vacillated like the Maharaja of Kashmir. He had adopted a tough line of bargaining and had invited the wrath of the Muslim League and the landed Niazi, Mazari and Khan gentries. They coveted the fertile Jhumra valley land and wanted the Hindu king out. The inevitable course of partition-eve holocaust overtook Digvijay's ego. He died fighting a vain battle to protect his honour and kingdom.

"It's a good catch," Dutta passed his final verdict, "hook him and exploit his past background to weave a fine cover. Consult Shyam Purohit for developing the cover story. I think this rogue is a Triple X material."

Balachandran Nampoothiri agreed and summoned Ram Krishna Prasanna Banerjee, in short Ram Banerjee, the designated supervisor of the P7 desk and Dhiren Bhagat for briefing them on the proposed Triple X operation.

"Have you made direct contact? What were his responses?" Asked Nampoothiri.

"I met him twice under the cover of a bookseller, hawking books to college libraries. He didn't take interest and I didn't want to risk exposing my cover."

"What are his weak spots? Can he be blackmailed?" Nampoothiri didn't hide his impatience. This should have been examined before putting up the dossier to him.

"Sir," replied Bhagat, "he enjoys the privilege of a free pad at Divine Inn, a shady joint in Gole Market, courtesy Ram Karan Prasad. He takes his girls to the joint. Vidyasagar Suri, the inn manager, isn't happy with Kaushal, as he squeezes out weekly protection money and other frills."

"I find you've a good understanding of the target. But you haven't recorded these in your reports." Ram Banerjee, Bhagat's immediate superior intervened with a scowl on his face.

"Sir, this is my initial target priming report. I can't record unconfirmed observations." Bhagat quipped back.

Nampoothiri felt heat building up under his skin. However, this wasn't the correct time to intervene.

"Well! I think the first report is rather exciting," he looked at Banerjee and continued, "I want an operation appraisal plan by tomorrow. I'd prefer the use of blackmail bait to hook this cute bastard."

"Pardon me, sir," Bhagat submitted, "it won't be easy to hook Kaushal. He's close to some political leaders. He commands a brigade of ruffians, ready to kick up fight at the slightest provocation."

"Why don't we try some other targets?" Banerjee spoke in a measured voice, "blackmail isn't the best tool, I suppose."

"What brings you to that conclusion?" Nampoothiri shot back.

"A criminal can't make a good resident agent."

"Let's not split our hair so early in the day. When did we start mixing ethics and morality with intelligence?" Nampoothiri snapped back.

Ram digested the dig, but could not download the idea of a *chamar* Bhagat stealing the show and polluting his cultural and religious ambience.

"Have I made it clear?" Nampoothiri asked with a touch of finality, "show me your action plan tomorrow morning."

He pressed a button summoning Jatadhari. This was a loud signal for Ram. He quietly withdrew. Jatadhari poured coffee from an ornate glass percolator. He sipped the black brew, simmered out of golden Brazilian seeds, and looked up at Jatadhari.

"Jata, What do you think of this fellow Bhagat? Is he good? Can he be trusted with a delicate operation?"

The tribal from Garo Hills, Nampoothiri knew, carried in his genes the tributes of excellent Tibetan shrewdness.

Jatadhari knew his master well. When in confusion he preferred to consult him rather than talking to his wife and God.

"Sir, together we did a stint in Manipur. He did very well in anti-insurgency operations. And I understand he's very good in counterintelligence work." Jata replied in a confident voice.

"What damn good did he do in Manipur?"

"He did a lot. He is an icon of tenacity and rational thinking. He had, all by himself, tackled the movement of a Naga insurgent gang to Pakistan and had infiltrated right up to Sylhet. He returned in one piece with the photo-evidence of training camps run by the Pakistan Intelligence Bureau (PIB)."

Jata finished the sentence in one breath, and inhaled another lung full with an audible sound. A pragmatic intelligence operative and analyst, with his ears nearer to the ground, Nampoothiri derived pleasure in discussing operational matters directly with his juniors. The lowest seam in the shaft mostly yielded the best diamond. Their raw productions usually passed through several filters and lost its sheen and brilliance. Some intermediate filters were adept in credit grabbing, usurping the fine works of their juniors.

"Ask him to see me at my residence tonight and tell the fellow to keep his trap shut."

The hint was enough for Jatadhari. He had carried out similar errands in the past. Damn lucky fellow; Jatadhari silently congratulated Dhiren Bhagat. The boss was a fussy person and it wasn't easy to please him.

*

Dhiren Bhagat, an Assistant Intelligence Officer, a veteran of 17 years, was visibly shaken by the invitation to the lion's den. It was very unusual for the number three in the Company to invite a low caste untouchable to a social evening. In his strata of Indian society, the cardinal mantra of survival included the time-tested tricks of avoiding the frontal ire of a boss and the posterior fury of a wild horse. His wise father, a cattle hide processor and dealer, had survived all his seventy summers by scrupulously following the golden Indian social prescription.

Bhagat was more worried about Banerjee. The Brahmin nursed flaming hatred for a social insect like him. His friends in the Field Unit Zed (FUZ), the internal watch-dog, were sure to enlighten him on the odd meeting of an untouchable junior officer with the big boss. That should be a provocation enough to bring down avalanches of humiliation on him. The system didn't allow people like him to aspire for the top. Tradition and convention inherited from mythical times had twisted the social fabric. This was his first encounter with a real big boss. Moreover, he didn't know how to face it. He prayed silently. God should see him through this ordeal. Bhagat, immersed in his dark thoughts, walked along the pavement.

"What do you want?" Bhagat suddenly found himself accosted by an unarmed security guard from the other side of an iron gate.

"I'm Bhagat, Assistant Intelligence Officer. I'm supposed to see the boss at 9 p.m." He stood in front of the gate with excitement galloping through his veins.

"Wait." The duty officer talked on the intercom before opening the gate. He escorted Dhiren Bhagat to a flight of stairs leading to the living room, opened the door partially, and announced the arrival of the guest.

Nampoothiri, seated in one corner of the sprawling living room, was turning over the pages of the Time magazine, not really reading any item. He concentrated on the soft recital of *Darbari Kanada*, a Hindustani classical *raga*, played on the *Sitar* by maestro Alauddin Khan. He loved classical music, Western, Hindustani and Carnatic, besides Negro spirituals and open throated North American country music.

"Yes." responded Nampoothiri.

"Sir, the officer has come." Announced the duty officer.

"Oh yes." Nampoothiri looked at his watch. Two minutes past nine. He was impressed. He walked up to the door, opened it fully, and gestured at Bhagat to enter. Guiding him to a corner, he called for Jatadhari.

Jatadhari entered, pushing a trolley, laden with a bottle of Chivas Regal, neatly wrapped in a piece of pink cloth, a Belgian cut-glass decanter and an ice bucket, all in pink. He poured whisky with meticulous artistry, mixed soda, dropped two cubes of ice, and offered one to Nampoothiri.

"Have a drink." Nampoothiri offered the glass to Bhagat.

Dhiren hesitated, his eyes weren't meeting his boss's.

"Come'n. Have one with me. Forget office protocol. It's my home and you're my guest." He pushed the glass into the clammy palms of the junior officer.

Jatadhari served chicken nuggets in pink bone china plates. On Tuesdays, Nampoothiri preferred everything in pink. That was based on an astrological advice tendered by the holy saint of Sringeri temple, a shrine in the southern peninsula. Each day of the week was represented by a distinct colour code, synchronising with the colours of planets of the solar system. He followed the code scrupulously with a view to deflecting evil designs of the malevolent stars and planets. Though a perfect brown Brit, Nampoothiri had cultivated a fervent belief in astrology, herbal medicine, the occasional oil bath, and regular sea-fish dishes, cooked with Malabar spices and coconut milk. The permissible exceptions were Brazilian instead of Malabar coffee and imported Havana.

"Tell me all about this Kaushal fellow. Am I wrong to presume that we should resort to blackmailing the guy?" Nampoothiri kept on munching chicken nuggets in between words.

Bhagat suddenly felt a surge of confidence. He sipped the golden liquid and enjoyed the warmth flowing down his throat and firing up the capillaries around his heart. He always felt confident when it came to professional matters. He started on a brief resume of the target and dwelt upon his wild sex life. The target was courageous, capable of taking on the impossible and improbable, fond of imported whisky, easy cash, and women. He dwelt on the fringes of crime, drug peddling and hoped to climb the higher ladders in national politics.

"Most criminals do. Isn't it?" Nampoothiri added.

"Yes sir. His role model is Ram Karan Prasad."

"Understandable. If Ram Karan can manage to reach the top, why can't he?"

"He has access to Manjira, the junior minister."

"Don't worry. So far, the criminals have been helping the politicians to rule and loot the populace and extract their share of the spoils. Now is the time for the criminals to capture political power. Tell me if the target has any other weakness." Nampoothiri lighted his favourite Havana and settled for another serving of fish nuggets.

"He has an admirable umbilical attachment to his mother and he visits a temple on Tuesday mornings."

"I see. He has a hidden streak of religious leaning too! Why do you think that his attachment to his mother is a point of weakness?" Nampoothiri pressed the calling bell. Jatadhari entered silently, poured another drink, placed two fresh plates of fried fish nuggets and retreated.

Bhagat looked at his boss intently, slipped back on the sofa and replied, "perhaps he can sacrifice his girls to see his mother happy."

"Here you are. Behind the whirlwind, there's a placid lagoon of love. The man is capable of loving and caring. He can love and respect the job, if properly motivated. He's not a casual office clerk with no commitment." Nampoothiri grabbed pieces of fish nuggets, indulgently placed them in mouth, and came up with an idea.

"Here's the spot you can hit. He can't be blackmailed simply for sleeping with girls. His mother is the key. His love is the key. How do you want to proceed now?"

"Sir, as I understand," Bhagat spoke in a low decibel tone, "he has an indomitable lust for women. He is specially attracted to Hema."

"Who is she?"

"Daughter of the health secretary."

"Keep track."

"And sir, the target has a volcanic temper. He flares up at the slightest provocation."

"How does it help?"

"His criminality sir. That's the possible window for blackmailing. We've to send him a message, in due course, that he has reached a cul-de-sac."

"And the mother angle?"

"Once properly implicated, we can use the threat of exposing his misdeeds to his mother," Bhagat added haltingly, "one more point sir…."

"Continue."

"He often gets into violent fits, destroying everything coming his way. That's what I call a killer streak."

"I get you. Is it living by conviction rather than convention?"

"I should say more of conviction...his own brand of conviction."

"That suits me. Both conviction and convention can be manipulated, at least in our trade." Nampoothiri lighted another Havana and added its smoke with the philosophy he just enunciated.

Dhiren Bhagat sipped his whisky in silence and felt strange warmth rising up from his intestines to his front lobe. Below the scalp, warm streams of sensation stirred up his neurons, electricity travelling fast from one junction to another. The golden liquid was doing well. New neutron proteins were sending signals of innovation. For the next one-hour Nampoothiri and his junior carried out an exercise on the multi-dimensional aspects of Operation Triple X.

Nampoothiri admired the professional excellence of the junior officer and appreciated his grasp on the subject. But for a few professionals like him, the organisation would have gone to the dogs.

He felt confident that Operation Triple X should be a fabulous success story. The message should go louder to Rabindra Narayan Dutta that he, the one and only Nampoothiri, was the worthiest successor to room number 308, the top-secret hole of India's intelligence chief.

"Fine," Nampoothiri stood up, "follow the leads meticulously, note all the details. Every bit of information counts."

"What about his cover and motivation?" asked Bhagat.

"Let me think over it. Let me consult experts. We'd cross the bridge when time comes."

"Thanks sir. Good night."

"Get going. We're under pressure. This target must be prepared in record time. Good night and God bless you."

Nampoothiri felt mighty pleased. The fine evening was well spent, in good company and over good work, drink, and food.

*

3

Rajni Krittika Hemaprabha Rao carried a long but beautiful name. She was dusky like *Rajni* (night), scintillated like *Krittika* (a constellation) and radiated like a polished *Hemaprabha* (golden figurine). Rao was her clan name. In short, Hema was the cutest butterfly, which fluttered around Delhi University campus located amidst the sprawling greens of the Shivalik range that had witnessed several battles during the 1857 uprising against the rulers of the British East India Company.

Tall, slim and fair, with a Hellenic complexion, head full of curly hair and a youthful bust, Hema padded her charm consciously with a contrived Marilyn Monroe pout. A pulsating throb of the campus young hearts Hema was overtly conscious of her body and beauty and the status of her father, a secretary to the government of India. Her aloofness verged on contempt for the creatures around. A fluttering beauty like her hadn't graced the campus for the last two decades. That was the verdict of the veterans, some of them habitual students for the last one-decade.

Students from the post-graduate faculties drifted around the corridors and canteen of St. Stephens to have rare glimpses of the dream girl and to steal some whiffs of her biological aroma.

Hema ignored most of them, and at best, looked at some from the corners of her eyes, lips slightly curled in, either in contempt or willful arrogance. The electrifying oblique looks were more devastating than debilitating darts. Her aroma sprayed out a loud message: touch me not. She wàs aware of the biological theory of intricate linkages between smell and sex.

Hema used costly French perfume to camouflage her real body odour. She carried a spray in her crocodile-leather beauty pouch.

Bagging a Rhodes scholarship was Hema's family tradition. Her father was one. Sure of flying to London in another two years, for her Masters in Economics, Hema looked at the surrounding creatures as insects from wayside gutters. These baser animals weren't pedigreed enough to talk and socialise with her.

Though disdainful of the crowd around, Hema liked to dress to kill. She preferred a modified version of the Punjabi *churidar* suit lower portion clung to her slim legs, in cascading creases. The upper *kameej* (shirt) was tailored with deep cuts at the back and front, deep enough to reveal her bosom, displaying the rippling pink bulge of arrogance.

Just from below the bust line, it tapered down in a sharp fall, lifting the bosom provocatively. Hema didn't bother to cover her bust with a flimsy *chunni*, a silk scarf. Her lifestyle logic was directly borrowed from the pages of the western magazines and periodicals. Shying away from exhibiting her assets wasn't her cup of tea. Flowers didn't cover themselves up with foliage. Did they?

Prince Ramendra Kaushal's philosophy of beauty was poetic too, with a different perception and connotation. A flower was there to be plucked, enjoyed, and thrown out with the rotten memories of the exploits of a stale night. Didn't some people enjoy flowers fried in batter and fat? Pleasant tormentation under masculine muscle was the acme of appreciation of feminine beauty. Hadn't God created woman to enjoy the muscular spasm from the stronger male species? Well! history was the great witness to this unique footprint of creation.

No one, not even his staunchest admirers, took Kaushal seriously when he declared his intentions to tame the bronze-beauty and pin her down under his thighs. Kaushal didn't mind swinging away minor campus girls to his secret den at the Divine Inn. That was his usual style. But roughing up Hema was a different ball game. Her father's official status, as was the wont in the city of bureaucrats, had added an impregnable shield around her.

However, the torrent called Prince Kaushal was equally irrepressible. Ramendra Kaushal, the lady-killer, fondly called LBW—Ladies' *Bawarchi* (cook) and Waiter, by admirers and friends, was in a foul mood that morning. The Hindu Sangh candidates had defeated his boys in students' union elections. The scimitar of defeat had pruned his ego by a couple of inches.

"Fuck the bastards, those Sangh Nazis," shouted Kaushal, "I must spray them with bullets."

"*Ustad* (captain) don't take it so hard. If you want, we can finish off the Sangh bastards and go for fresh elections."

"Plan it out. I don't mind spending some dough on bullets. But, that bitch is...."

Ramendra stopped short of revealing his mind.

One of the cronies offered coffee to the boss in foul mood. Another one flicked open a packet of Players. They were uneasy with the sulking and fretting captain. Ramendra ignored the coffee, lighted the cigarette, and kept on looking vacantly at a patch of sky visible from his corner of the café. He looked somewhat pensive and withdrawn. That's what worried his cronies. His murderous mood normally witnessed broken glasses, china, and splashes of blood, if the fracas happened to be a minor one. They hadn't seen him enwrapped in melancholia.

The five jewels, Kaushal's permanent companions, were piqued by their General's unearthly mood. It was something more than just election discomfiture. If it were, the Prince would've stabbed few of his rivals by now, a few bombs would've gone off, and a few heads crushed.

Was it a love affair? Kaushal wasn't a love loony! If he liked a girl, he seldom let her go. Prince Ramendra Kaushal simply grabbed his kill. In the last two years, the campus roster recorded his three achievements. His fat wallet, audacious tenacity, and animal machismo helped him bluff his way through. Most girls landed up in the special room, reserved for the Prince in Vidyasagar Suri's Divine Inn.

"*Ustad*, any problem?" one of his sidekicks asked.

"The bitch thinks she's more beautiful than Marilyn Monroe. If I don't take her to bed in next seven days I'm not the Prince of Jhunjhunu." Kaushal turned the chair around and demanded another cigarette.

"Hey *Kancha* (a Nepali boy) get me a double chicken omelette with two toasts and lots of butter. Don't forget a dash of black pepper." Ramendra shouted at the waiter. He felt more relaxed and enthralled his gang by lighting another Player.

"*Ustad*, who's the new chic?"

"That bitch, that whore of a daughter of the secretary," Kaushal took a big bite of the omelette and continued, "she has the audacity of casting nasty glances at me! She calls me dirt, a goon. Am I a speck of dirt! No woman does that to me and rides her *doli* (post marriage ceremony) without being laid and fucked?" Ramendra Kaushal looked up, demanding an endorsement of his special philosophy of social relationship.

"Surely not *Ustad*," Brij, one of the tails, prodded up the spirit of his leader, "she must be humbled."

"Tell me a practical way, no filmy stunt. How do I get her to bed? She must pay for her arrogance and calling me names."

Kaushal expected some clever reply from Matang, his disciple from Bihar, and a habitual resident student for the last six years striving to grab a law degree. A worthy companion of the campus prince, Ramendra Kaushal, it was expected of him to flunk the exams this year as well. He was treated as the *Chanakya* (strategist) of the group.

"Why are you agitated dear? Every woman has a secret door to her heart." Commented Matang.

"I'm not bothered about her heartaches, I want her to suffer pain for insulting me."

"Yes *Ustad*," Matang slurred out the words while gulping down juices of *paan* (betel leaf) and tobacco, some rolling down corners of his mouth, "I've digested the essence of the problem. That bitch's father happens to be a secretary to the government. I think you should go for another cow. This one's holy."

Matang passed his judgment with the air of a kilned elder in wigs.

"Bastard," Ramendra Kaushal exploded. He thumped the table repeatedly and kept on shouting, "you Bihari rat, are you afraid of a secretary! You call her a cow! How dare you? She, this bloody Hema, must come between my thighs. I must snatch away that arrogant smile from her face, fucking her all the way."

"Do that. It's your peril you're inviting. Hell, why abuse me?" Matang, technically a senior to Kaushal, shouted back, "you asked for the advice. Go to hell and stew in your own juice." He stood up and made a motion towards the exit.

"Me? And go to hell? How dare you Bihari rat? Why do you think a secretary's daughter is inviolable?" Kaushal shouted back menacingly.

"Because he can hunt you down," Matang stuffed another betel leaf in his mouth, "this one fucking may prove fatal, for all of us. You better find another cow." The modern day Chanakya replied, chewing betel leaf and the words in a luxurious motion of his tongue and teeth.

Kaushal, in a split second, whipped out a pistol from his waistband and pointed it at Matang, waiving the barrel menacingly.

"You bloody Bihari, you can't talk like that about my girl. And you can't walk out on me like this. We've been together in too many crimes and you've to be with me, in this game too. Don't ever try to be a police informer. I'll split your head like a rotten melon."

"Don't be funny," replied Matang, "this cow isn't your wife. We know your worth. You can't even win a small college election and you dare challenging the might of a secretary to the government! I don't propose to rot in jail, because of your precious fucking."

"You Bihari trash." Ramendra rushed at Matang with the cocked pistol.

"Don't call me names and remove that toy. It doesn't frighten me. If you can't wait to fuck that cow go and have a go with your mom." Matang waved his hand trying to brush aside the dangling pistol.

"You scum," Kaushal erupted like a volcano, "you dare calling my mother a whore? How dare you insult my mother?"

He cocked the pistol in a swift move. Brij, another acolyte, stood in front of the barrel and pushed Matang back. He was privy to the weakest lesion in Kaushal's heart. A known woman eater, the Prince of Jhunjhunu nursed a profound regard for his mother. The very mention of her name worked like the flute-tune of a snake charmer. That was a sure trick for lowering the king cobra's hood.

"*Ustad*, what's happened to you? Calm down. And Matang, have you lost your mind? Why drag his mother into this? We're one in this game and we can't afford fighting like wild roosters. We can't break up our company for a silly girl." He turned to Matang.

"What the hell are you up to? And what's your worth minus our captain?" Brij, son of a Hanuman (Hindu monkey god) temple priest, recited a Sanskrit couplet from the holy Hindu scripture Gita, which meant: anger generated hallucination, leading to destruction of the faculty of reasoning, finally ushering in total annihilation.

"You bastard, don't quote from the scriptures," Kaushal threw a dirty look at Brij and took a chair, "I know, some day you scum will purify yourself with the holy water of the Ganges and occupy the chief priest's throne, in that bloody den of corruption, you call a temple. Tell that bloody Bihari to behave. Another mention of my mother's name and he's a dead rat."

"Listen carefully. There are outsiders around," Brij pointed to Dhiren Bhagat occupying a corner table, "I'm a pure Brahmin, I recite *Gayatri* (a sacred couplet in praise of the Sun God) five times a day. Don't breach the banks. I know that the best flower in the garden must be offered to the deity. But friend, have patience."

"Fuck you Brahmins, you bastard, a boozer and whore fucker, don't dare to hurl *mantras* at me. I'm also from the sperms of a Brahmin and at that a king. That doesn't make me a fucking Brahmin. I've no patience and I want her quick."

*

Ramendra Kaushal was not a man of patience. He was guided by impulse, and was not trained to count milliseconds before taking major decisions. No one, not even his indulgent mother ever tried to cork the jinni of ancient Kaushal kings in him. He imagined destiny as an ever smiling and obliging mistress of the brave hearts.

Dhiren Bhagat's calibrated prism had failed to detect this knotted twist in his target's character. He had failed to analyse the steam of carnal pressure that boiled inside the Prince. He had meticulously mugged up the family history of his target. Information gathered from diplomatic sources and archive records had helped him in building up a fascinating profile of Kaushal. However, the printed materials weren't the correct barometers to measure up the wild progeny of a wild king. The FIB field officer simply wasn't aware of the depth of the 'mother' syndrome complex Ramendra Kaushal suffered from. Women were playthings for him, but Kasturi was sacrosanct. The turbulent twister of the campus was scared of the saintly lady whose prayers flowed around him as a protective cocoon.

Bhagat's records described Ramendra Kaushal as the son of a Punjabi Brahmin royal, drawing more on the gene banks of his father, Raja Digvijay Kaushal, the maverick king of Jhumra, a principality on the banks of the Chenab, below Sangla Valley in Pakistani Punjab. Adulated and abused for his pro-British leanings, arrogance and impatience Digvijay Kaushal ran his hereditary grant with a whimsical cocktail of iron handedness and benevolence.

The grant, owned by a vanquished Niazi *sultan* (Rex), was bestowed upon Pundit Vikramaditya Kaushal, Digvijay's great-grandfather, for his services to the advancing British troops to the Wild West of India, the North-West Frontier Provinces. The British traders had grabbed India from the weak Muslim rulers. To stabilise the new gains they required Hindu support, starting from Bengali baboos to upcountry Brahmin and *Kshatriya sepoys* (traditional soldiers).

The Kaushals, a family of brave fortune seekers, didn't disappoint the British masters. Most of their kind didn't. It was a period of British bonhomie with the Hindu collaborators, against the just vanquished Muslims.

Digvijay's wife, Kasturi, daughter of a Kannauj (city in central India) Brahmin, was given in marriage to the young king. Daughter of a blue-blooded royal on the Ganges, Kasturi was declared barren, after she failed to bear an heir to the Jhumra throne. Digvijay direly needed an inheritor to keep the throne to his line. The Muslim nobility, he knew, wouldn't even wait for his ashes to cool, before they petitioned the Crown to revert the Jhumra throne to its original owners, the descendants of the deposed Niazi *sultan* of Mianwali.

Bhagat's records were silent on the miracle of Ramendra Kaushal's birth from the womb of a barren mother. Some vague reports mentioned of a Vedic sacrifice performed by the saints from the Himalayas, which helped in fertilising Kasturi.

The events around the apocalyptic Second World War had signalled the collapse of the colonial powers. Inability of the bankrupt Britain to keep its sprawling empire in leash had triggered off the inevitable process of chaotic transfer of power. London was in a hurry to abdicate its empire overnight, what had taken centuries to acquire and consolidate. Independence came to the subcontinent like the apocalyptic Great Flood. There was no Noah to save the millions of Hindus and Muslims who were guillotined in the stampede of Britain's Great Escape from India.

Digvijay wasn't brought up in the culture of heeding to pragmatic advices. He scowled at his friends and courtiers and politely brushed aside a subtle message from the Viceroy to agree to merge his kingdom with Pakistan. No. Under no circumstances would he agree to surrender his sovereign power to either of the contending monkeys, one Hindu and the other Muslim, both busy in a tug of war over an abandoned loaf called India.

Digvijay proclaimed sovereignty soon after the lapse of Paramountcy of the Crown. His was the second voice of defiance after that of the Nawab of Multan. The Muslim leaders, especially the inheritors of the Niazi *sultans*, refused to allow the Hindu usurper to assert unilateral sovereignty over a predominantly Muslim population. The inheritors of the conquerors of Hindu India were simply not ready to allow a tiny *kafir* princeling to fly his flag of arrogance and defiance.

Digvijay Kaushal decided to defend his territory. He precipitated the situation by leading a hoard of horsemen and foot soldiers burning down a few Niazi settlements. It was meant to be a warning to all! The Brahmin king wouldn't allow any act of stupidity by his Muslim subjects. He was wrong. Digvijay couldn't fight fire with fire. Fanatic gangs of Niazis, aided by northern tribals, liquidated most of his Hindu and loyal Muslim *rayats* (subjects).

On a fateful morning Digvijay led a final valiant charge to the top of *Jung Tikri* (hillock of war) against the combined force of police, tribals and armed Niazi feudals and died on the back of his favourite horse. In an uneven engagement, Digvijay was beheaded. Queen Kasturi and the suckling babe Prince Ramendra Kaushal were guided across to the safety of Hindu India by the loyal *khansama* (cook) and a *syce* (horseman). Kasturi had landed up at Jhunjhunu taking shelter with her brother, a court official in the *durbar* of a local potentate. Himself a childless Brahmin Kasturi's brother had adopted Ramendra as his son and legal heir.

With a view to giving Ramendra the best possible education Kasturi secretly encashed her gold *mohurs* (coins), which she had managed to bring from Jhumra. She wished to see him climbing the high chair of a Collector, an administrative position she understood best.

*

Dhiren Bhagat's diary ended there. His archives didn't contain the drama of charade and shame that took place behind the thick walls of the Jhumra palace leading to the birth of Ramendra Kaushal. He missed out other vital inputs too.

Dhiren Bhagat was yet to discover, believed that Ramendra Kaushal, he was a born ruler. For a ruler the slightest act of defiance by a courtier deserved capital punishment. The tiff with Matang was, therefore, a mighty provocation. The puny Bihari shouldn't have dared to advice him on his choice of a casual bed partner. A jackal never dictated terms to a lion on the preference of the kill, it should choose for mid-day meal.

Seated at a corner of Blue Dart restaurant, Bhagat ruminated over his thoughts and chewed his mutton cutlet garnished with garlic sauce. However, his eyes and the hidden camera had not failed to record the near fatal brawl. He didn't fail to capture Ramendra Kaushal puffing away cigarette after cigarette and eyeing Matang from the corners of his eyes. He wasn't exactly listening to Brij.

However, Brij's word of caution about presence of an outsider had alarmed the snake in Kaushal. Was he a police informer? Not unlikely. Ramendra had seen him earlier talking with a police inspector. That implied a latent link with the criminal investigation department. To top all these, Ramendra hadn't forgotten that this dirty Bihari had double-crossed him in a recent gold smuggling assignment and had tipped off the police. Kaushal teased his brains to put the pieces together and format the contours of an enemy sitting a couple of tables away.

Brij thought he had managed to diffuse the Blue Dart scuffle and things were back on the rails. He had reasons to believe. His captain threw up volcanic magma every second day. Such scuffles were as bitter as a few drops of Tabasco on a piece of medium cooked steak. He helped Kaushal to gently push down the firing pin and turned on his heels at Dhiren Bhagat.

"Hey lout, who're you?"

Bhagat, in the midst of chewing his thoughts and the mutton cutlet, didn't expect the fast turn of events.

"Sir," he stammered, "I'm a bookseller, from Midstar Publication. I sell text books."

"That I can see. Are you a Commie, a Chinese rat? What the hell are you doing here?" Kaushal joined Brij and lifted Bhagat up by his collars.

"Sir I'm a poor bookseller. I've nothing to do with Communists. I'm a regular visitor to this cafe. You can ask the people here."

"Empty your bag." Kaushal thundered.

Bhagat emptied the contents of a grey leather bag on the table, a few brand new books on English literature and Economics.

"Let him go *yar* (friend). He's an innocent rat, not a Chinese one." Matang intervened.

"Don't interfere in my affairs. I hate the Commies. They worship either Mao or Stalin as the Chairman of India."

Ramendra pushed Bhagat back to the chair, demanded another Player from Brij and wheeled back towards Matang. His eyes narrowed down to mere slits. Yes. He thought this one rat, Matang Singh, had exhausted his lease of life. He had become too big for his boots, too uncomfortable for the reigning lion of the University campus.

"Get lost. Remove your sticky ass from here. Don't dare selling Chairman Mao to us." He scowled at Bhagat, dismissed the meeting with warm handshakes, and promised to join them later near Khalsa College.

He wheeled back on his toes just before stepping out of Blue Dart, embraced Matang and apologised for the nasty incident. He was too depressed by the insulting looks and gestures of that stupid girl. And the election humiliation hung heavily on his psyche. Such a minor tiff, Kaushal explained, shouldn't spoil their camaraderie. He lighted a cigarette, put it in between Matang's lips, and loudly announced his intention to take a night bus to Jhunjhunu. He would be out for two days. Ramendra Kaushal jumped into his Morris Minor followed by his cronies and disappeared behind the next bend.

Matang kept on looking at the exhaust smoke, spat out red juice and leisurely walked towards the Ramjas college hostel, his abode for last seven years. He looked worried.

*

Bhagat heaved a sigh of relief.

Thank heavens! The Prince and his cronies had failed to notice the clandestine camera tucked in a corner of the bag. The camera with an auto-switching mechanism, embedded in the leather bag, had silently snapped all the developments at Blue Dart restaurant. The concealed tape recorder had recorded the dramatic conversations faithfully. He walked out leisurely and summoned a motorbike borne surveillance shadow positioned outside the restaurant.

"Follow the target. Be on air and keep reporting."

"Till what time?"

"Till I call off."

Bhagat took a bus ride to Dreamland, a cover name for FIB's Technical Laboratory, the secret hub of technical intelligence.

Bhagat's trained mind hadn't failed to notice murder in Kaushal's eyes, the reconciliation drama notwithstanding, Ramendra Kaushal couldn't be far from big mischief. His eyes had spewed fire and he had spoken in the voice of death, chillier than that of the ghosts from the depths of the black dungeon.

Matang Singh wasn't a saint. Bhagat's archive overflowed with records of his sins, which included a couple of gold smuggling and drug pushing cases and two murders. However, the budding criminal was no match for Kaushal in ruthlessness. The tactless Prince, Bhagat thought, should be kept under constant surveillance. The killer could do anything to get his dream girl and punish a renegade collaborator.

*

At the end of the day, Bhagat knocked the doors of Ram Banerjee, the immediate boss, and his designated proper channel.

Ram was in a furious hurry to take off for New Delhi *Kali* temple, to perform the special Saturday eve worship. This was a mandatory exercise, a ritual set by his mother, soon after he was born and reinforced by his wife, when he was married off at eighteen. After all, he, the only male progeny from his father's line, was born after his mother had offered special prayers at a *Kali* temple, presided over by a 19th century god man, Ramkrishna.

"*Ma Kali* (mother Kali), clear my promotion case." Banerjee chanted the words like a holy *mantra,* as Bhagat peeped in through the curtains.

The very sight of Bhagat, at the end of the day, meant inevitable stretching of hours beyond the needles of the clock. That low caste work-worm had perhaps no other pleasure in life. Banerjee muttered a curse. Nevertheless, professional, ethnic, and cultural decency prevented him from pouncing upon the gutter creature, elevated to human status after India's independence.

"What brings you so late Bhagat?"

"Sir, there are some interesting leads on the Operation Triple X target." Bhagat submitted meekly.

"You're late my friend. I'm supposed to go to the office of the Deputy Director, to pay my respects and to discuss an important operation. Come tomorrow."

Banerjee didn't wait for Bhagat's reply. He turned his bicycle towards the *Kali* temple. Oh holy Mother! He pedalled furtively. The most auspicious conjunction of Moon and Jupiter with constellation Virgo shouldn't pass by.

*

Bhagat felt flattened with frustration. The Blue Dart report required immediate assessment by senior officers. Premonition told him that the Prince of Jhunjhunu was up to greater mischief. He had seen murder in Kaushal's eyes. That ruffian wasn't made of stuff to suffer defiance and digest insult. Perhaps Matang's indiscreet use of the bovine epithet for Hema and the indecent dig at Kasturi had touched off some wild chords in him.

The churning of Bhagat's intestinal acid turned to gurgling sounds. Something continued to tick away inside ringing a warning bell. He could perhaps gather valuable lead on his target by placing timely surveillance. He required support from the wizards of The Dreamland, the FIB's technical intelligence wing. That required Banerjee or Nampoothiri's nod.

The thought of visiting the South Block office of Nampoothiri for consultations crossed Bhagat's mind. He abandoned the idea. It would be too much to walk straight up to the big boss. Banerjee wasn't going to like his jumping the gun. His gut feeling advised him to stop for the day.

Bhagat opted for a shorter route through a gap between the South and North Blocks, which led to the bus terminus. He entered the portals of South Block cutting across the corridors below the arches of the ornate gate. His steps were frozen by a lively reverberating shout, as he approached the exit gate, from where the long winding corridors forked out towards the Prime Minister's office. He turned around.

It was Balachandran Nampoothiri, walking down the corridor towards his office, a lighted cigar pressed between his fingers.

"So young man, what's the news?"

Nampoothiri was in a happy frame of mind. He had had an hour-long audience with the new Prime Minister, Jung Bahadur Sharma. The formal briefing on Pakistan was prompted by the Prime Minister's concern over loud noises made by the hostile neighbour. The briefing session went off very well. Neither he expected the new Prime Minister to listen to the number three of the FIB with rapt attention nor did he have high opinion of the intellectual accomplishment of the seemingly rustic neighbourhood politician.

Nampoothiri's encounter with the PM changed his perception. Contrary to allegations by political detractors Jung Bahadur understood the intricate functioning of the military regime in Pakistan. His perception of emerging ties between the USA, Pakistan and China was clear. The White House, he felt, was eager to configure India as a new punching bag, after the red or rouge nations like Vietnam and Cuba were punched and bombed. Washington was keener to build new bridges with China.

Why?

Sharma had smiled over the silly question from Nampoothiri. Wooing China was a major step towards cracking the iron curtain and pumping in hot air into the Cold War balloon. The uncanny fellow fortunately disagreed with some of his political colleagues and bureaucrats about the military intentions of Pakistan. A weak India, after humiliating defeat in the Chinese war, and the sudden change in leadership held out tantalising expectations to the adventurers in Rawalpindi. The men in uniform, in Pakistan, were planning dirty tricks in tandem with China and the USA, Jung Bahadur warned his deputy intelligence chief.

He advised Nampoothiri to sharpen India's intelligence tools and to build on penetrating assets. Pakistan wouldn't allow India a long breather, he warned. He smelt burning powder in the air.

The short wily fellow, had not forgotten to prick a pin by adding that the FIB should've been able to convince his predecessor about the perfidious intentions of the Chinese leadership. Intelligence was supposed to tender advice without fear and favour, without caring for the idiosyncrasies of the political masters. It was a subtle dig at Amritlal, his rouge-tinted maverick defence minister and Dutta, the FIB chief.

Nampoothiri was busy talking to himself, and recounting the observations of the Prime Minsiter. The smile hanging on his face displayed his happy frame of mind.

Bhagat returned the greetings with an uncertain Japanese bow and stood aside. The distant greeting of the boss must not be anything but a passing formality, he presumed. Very kind of the big boss indeed!

Nampoothiri was in a buoyant mood. He wanted to share his happiness even with the inanimate bricks of the cool South Block walls. He could sense a positive streak in the new PM. It should augur well in the forthcoming succession struggle between him and Kumar Anand Prasad.

"So young man, what's new with your Operation Triple X target?"

"Sir, there are some interesting developments."

He tried to keep pace with Nampoothiri's brisk steps. Perhaps he could brief the top boss about his intelligent guess, probably a hunch. Perhaps, sustained surveillance and technical coverage around the target could yield convincing leads.

"Is that so? Come up." Nampoothiri silently climbed the stairs.

"Tell me what's so interesting." Nampoothiri settled down in his chair, as Jatadhari Garo poured coffee in an ornate mug.

Bhagat narrated the story for next twenty minutes, in slow halting words, played the audiotape, and impressed upon him the need for mounting surveillance and technical operation. Ramendra Kaushal, he said, was capable of committing any crime. Killing came naturally to him and kidnapping a girl was part of his routine. Rajni Krittika Hemaprabha Rao was in grave danger.

Nampoothiri reached for the special red phone.

"Is it Dreamland? Hi Mitra, it's me. Is your mobile laboratory ready?" Nampoothiri talked to his Director Technical Laboratory.

"Yes sir. How soon do you want?"

"In the next one hour your lab should report to me." Nampoothiri replaced the handset on its cradle and gave instructions to Bhagat.

"Don't bother about the hierarchy. Get along, watch the fellow, and have everything covered. This is your chance to gather materials for blackmailing your target."

Nampoothiri wished Bhagat godspeed and reached for the red phone again. It was necessary to brief boss Dutta and discuss intelligence and military action plans along the Kachchh-Sind border.

Dutta had closed his eyes. His sensory organs were listening raptly.

"Ther'e a big problem Balu."

"What do you expect of me?"

"Visit Bhuj and supervise the intelligence operations. Direct your trans-border agents to run deep into Pakistan and ensure that the army units are deployed along the traditional dry routes through the salt desert." Dutta spelt out the task succinctly.

"Well sir, I'll take a KAL flight this afternoon."

Nampoothiri heavily weighed the professional advice but feigned to ignore the tangent prick in Dutta's words. He stood at the crossroads of a succession war for the top FIB slot. Coming few months were crucial. How could he allow Kumar Anand, a crony of Ram Karan Prasad, to grab the coveted slot? Nampoothiri spoke to himself that the biggest war of his life was in the trench ahead. What would he do in the FIB headed by that obnoxious rival? Well! that would be the time to hit back the coastal sands at Kovalam, his home turf.

As he left Dutta's room, and planned to board a Kalyani Air Lines flight to Bhuj, Nampoothiri simply forgot to call Alladi Subhash Chandra Rao, the health secretary. The secretary's daughter Rajni Krittika Hemaprabha Rao was in real danger. Ramendra Kaushal, if Bhagat was to be believed, wasn't going to digest the haughty demeanour of the impetuous fluttering Freya of the campus. He habitually managed to take his choice to bed. The journey to his bed wasn't always strewn with rose petals. Some of them were often unloaded at Ram Karan Prasad's pleasure spots, classy apartments, used as five star brothels. Others were often discovered by police as unclaimed dead bodies.

There were ample reasons for Nampoothiri to be amnesiac. The professional in him was under a severe tectonic crunch. The likely succession coup by Kumar Anand Prasad had fogged out his rational thinking process for a while. His dislike for Prasad and burning desire to step into the shoes of Dutta at the earliest opportunity had temporarily plugged the flow of signals from his neo-cortex. He was, for a few hours, being simply guided by the serpent, vainly hissing from beneath his medulla, buried deep, deep below his cranium. His neuron signals swung like an erratic pendulum.

Who could ensure his succession to the coveted top seat?

Jung Bahadur?

Perhaps not.

How long would he last! Perhaps, Manjira would protect his interest better. Amritlal's daughter had seen, from ringside seat, the serpentine political creepers around her father and grandfather. She wouldn't allow the diminutive earthy man to drive down his roots deep.

It shouldn't be difficult for a wily Nampoothiri Brahmin to keep the two Prime Ministers, the incumbent one, and the other impatiently biting her nails away, in good humour. As an ace intelligence operator, he had mastered the art of deception very well. The time had come to put his professional expertise to test.

Nampoothiri dozed off in a bumpy corner of the DC3. Bhagat, Hema, Ramendra Kaushal simply faded out into the slippery by-lines of disturbed sleep.

*

4

The Second World War vintage Willy's jeep, remodelled as a van, normally remained under a canvas wrap, inside a high-security garage, at a far end of the South Sunken Road, which connected the President's House to Dalhousie Road.

Kunal Kaushik, an assistant with The Dreamland, was busy giving final touches to the vehicle and chic electronic equipments. Adhesive screen-printed stickers bearing false number plates were put on the originals. Bold adhesive stickers reading MCD (Municipal Corporation of Delhi) were put on the rear and flanks of the van. Another sticker announced that the vehicle was on Emergency Service.

Nirmal Mitra, a wizard in electronics and communication technology, entered the van accompanied by Bhagat for final systems check. He switched on the VHF trans-receiver and spoke to operations control room.

"Wolf here," Mitra intoned, "how do you read me?"

"Roger sir, Lamb here. I read you five."

"All units standby, remain on air till you hear me next." Mitra ordered. He dialled a number and talked to the commander of the ZEBRA UNIT, the super secret arm of the FIB, deployed on selected operations.

The ZEBRAS, described as scavengers, wiped off telltale marks left behind by the vanguard operations team. They mounted counter-counter-surveillance on possible counter-surveillance measures adopted by the targets under cover. They performed daring rescue operations, whenever the vanguard teams ran into unexpected trouble. As well-trained commandos, the ZEBRAS, were legendary sharp shooters. They didn't have the licence to kill. But they did kill, only during extremely difficult rescue operations.

"I hope you have your orders to cover my team. No communication until we're in danger. Plug in and maintain silence. I'll give two beeps at every 5-minute interval. In case I miss two laps, rush to our aid. Got it?"

"Roger sir."

"Is your GPS in position?"

"All in tops sir. My boys have charged their automatics. Give them a chance tonight."

The remote voice chuckled.

"No dear. No fireworks. We're operating in the heart of the capital. Just follow my orders." Mitra sounded the final note of caution.

"Roger sir. Will comply." The ZEBRA commander switched off.

Nirmal Mitra went about checking the instrument panels. Night Video? OK. Infrared camera? OK. Night Vision Binocular? OK. Directional Microphone? OK.

"Kaushik," Mitra signalled his colleague, "handle the video camera. I'll handle the Infra, and Bhagat you keep the binocular. Signal me when to roll the cameras."

"Copy sir." Bhagat replied.

"What's your rendezvous?"

"The target, if I'm not incorrect, should come to his hunting hole." Bhagat replied and placed the MCD Emergency Service vehicle about 100 yards away from Ramjas students' hostel, the identified den of Matang Singh. He removed a manhole iron lid and hung a red lamp as a warning to drivers and pedestrians. Emergency maintenance works were on.

"Are you sure?" Mitra felt fidgety to position his chariot on a main thoroughfare.

"No problem sir. My boy is shadowing the target. I'm in radio contact with him." Bhagat trained his binocular on the hostel gate. No. There was no sign of Kaushal. He had perhaps taken the bus trip to Jhunjhunu. The Rajasthan bound buses normally left around 8 p.m.

Droplets of perspiration appeared on his forehead. A misfired operation at this crucial juncture could lead to devastating loss of credibility. His competence to handle such a delicate operation would be questioned.

No. No. He would deny that opportunity to Banerjee.

An old Fiat suddenly zoomed passed the van. Bhagat trained the binocular again.

Yes. A shadow was approaching the main hostel gate...perhaps.

Yes. The night vision binocular captured Kaushal's silhouette. Bhagat signalled Mitra and Kaushik. The reels started rolling and clicking silently. Kaushal parked his car at a distance and approached the hostel gates on foot.

The night guard saluted and opened the door.

The cameras stopped.

Mitra switched on the directional microphone.

Kaushal talked to the night guard in his usual cool murderous voice, passed on a few crisp notes, and ordered him to get lost.

The directional microphone picked up some of the words.

"How much do you earn?" Kaushal asked the guard.

"Only one hundred per month, master." The night guard with an oversized belly responded.

"Here are Rupees 1200, one year's pay. Get lost and I don't want to see your face in Delhi anymore. Look at the gun. Comply or else die." Kaushal's voice came in clear in the powerful microphone.

"*Huzoor mai baap* (master is the supreme boss). I'll be happy back in my village running a grocery shop."

The night guard walked out silently, pocketing the thick wad of notes. Mitra's face lighted up in satisfaction, the microphone was responding superbly. The first break was lucky.

In about twenty minutes, Kaushal emerged out of the gate, accompanied by Matang Singh.

"You're supposed to be in Jhunjhunu!" asked Matang.

"*Yar* (friend), I missed the bus," Kaushal replied, "let's see a movie. They're screening Hot Hot Woman."

"I don't feel like." Matang replied.

"Come *yar.* I owe you an apology. Give me a chance." Insisted Kaushal.

"I don't feel like." Matang resisted.

"Don't be silly. We're friends. You've the right to disagree and fight once in a while." Replied Kaushal.

They silently walked up to the car.

"Where did you get this Fiat? Is it stolen?" Matang.

"I borrowed it from friend Yaseen." Kaushal mumbled. Bhagat removed the red light and replaced the manhole cover. He winked at Mitra to follow the Fiat.

Kaushal stopped his car near the mausoleum of Mahatma Gandhi on the Ring Road, pompously named Raj Ghat, though the naked *faqir* (saint) had nothing to do with any Raj, either the British or the one run by his political inheritors.

"Why stop here? Where are we going?" Asked Matang.

"I've scouted out a fine *chuda* (night soil carrier) girl. She is a damn beauty and is a game too. Let's have fun." Suggested Kaushal.

"What about Hot Hot Woman?" Asked Matang.

"Come on *yar*! Surely, you want real kick from a warm blooded hot beauty. What's the fun in a celluloid one?"

Kaushal's luscious voice slightly turned to a whisper in the recorder, giving an impression that the vivacious beauty in bare skins was waiting in her waterfront shack. Matang's reaction to the luscious invitation remained mute, as the duo entered a narrow alley that led to the river waters. Bhagat whispered in Mitra's ears to follow them down the narrow deserted river front road. Mitra looked out thoughtfully and negated the request. The target could look back anytime, he warned.

"You take the Kodak and Kaushik will take the Video. Maintain a safe distance. Cover the red indicators on your cameras with black tape." Mitra cautioned Kaushik.

Kaushal guided Matang to a cluster of shacks, occupied by migrant labourers, hired for giving final touches to Shanti Vana, the cremation ground of Jawaharlal Nehru. Kaushal suddenly turned towards Matang, little short of the cluster, whipped out a huge Swiss blade, and in neat and fast moves stabbed him twice.

"This is for abusing my mother and this is for calling my girl a cow."

The powerful blows almost decapitated Matang.

Matang's burly figure didn't get any chance to react to the fatal blows. His half-lifted right hand slumped and he collapsed with a dull thud. His eyes were still open, whites glistening, as if asking Kaushal: was all this violence really necessary!

Kaushal folded the Swiss blade, wrapped it in a piece of cloth, and flung it with full thrust in Yamuna waters. The blood soaked knife made a mild sound on impact and settled down under the mud. He briskly walked through a patch of wild berry-bush, turned to the parked Fiat, and drove straight to the grounds behind the Red Fort. He leisurely alighted, emptied a canister of petrol on it, and threw a matchstick, after lighting a cigarette. Fire engulfed the small buggy, followed by an explosion. Ramendra Kaushal walked fast towards a lane leading to Jama Masjid. He didn't look back. A dead Matang and an exploded stolen car didn't matter much.

He was avenged.

Nirmal Mitra and Bhagat followed the sequences from their van, taking cover of the lush riverfront foliage. The video and still cameras rolled and clicked away merrily. Technically the operation was a copybook success. Mitra reclined against the passenger seat, lighted a cigarette, and picked up the mouthpiece of the radio set.

"Wolf calling Lamb, do you read me?"

"Yes sir. Any order?"

"Operation concluded. Returning to base. Instruct ZEBRA team to wind up." Mitra asked the driver to turn towards the Technical Laboratory.

"Sir, instruct the Lab boys to help me in processing the films and cassettes right away. The boss may like to see the inputs, first thing in the morning." Dhiren Bhagat requested.

"Rest of the night is yours. Just don't disturb me. I want a solid six hours of sleep.

"Anyways, I hope, we don't have to report this to the police."

"No sir. Our game is different."

*

Bhagat went over the events in his mind and felt happy that his target priming was progressing on the correct lines. The jackal was inevitably walking into his trap like cosmic particles sucked in by a Blackhole. The first physical contact, he presumed, should take place in another fortnight.

His Mosur (mobile surveillance) boys tracked Kaushal back at the official residence of Ram Karan Prasad, a palatial bungalow at 6, Race Course Road. He had chaperoned a young campus beauty along to plead her case for a coveted scholarship. Ram Karan turned out in an impeccably white hand-spun dress, characteristic of a particular political creed and summoned Kaushal to a corner.

"What do I hear about the murder of Matang Singh?"

"It's a mystery sir," Kaushal spoke in a steady voice, "I'm not sure what happened."

"I believe you had a quarrel yesterday."

"Oh shit!" Kaushal exclaimed, "who told you that? It was a minor argument sir."

"Whatever it is, you asshole. If you are caught, I simply don't know you. Hide in Suri's den and cover your trails."

"I need money."

"How much?"

"Five thousand."

"That's big. Anyways, Matang should receive a hero's funeral. Blame the Communists and Hindu Sanghis and gain sympathy for our party."

"Done sir. Please do something for this poor girl."

"Leave her behind. She'll leave this place none the poorer." Ram Karan summoned his Man Friday, Kalua Mushahari, and ordered him to make the girl comfortable in an adjoining room.

"Spare her." Ramendra pleaded.

"Sure," Ram Karan slurped up the flowing *paan* (betel leaf) juices and said in a mocking tone, "she's as safe with me as she was with you."

Ramendra Kaushal took the hint and left on his motorbike after collecting a bunch of bills from Kalua. He drove straight for his sanctuary, Divine Inn, minus the campus beauty. She stayed back for deriving inspiration from the veteran politician.

*

Divine Inn, a seedy joint, not far from the Mughal City of Sahjahanabad, Lutyens' Vice Royal palace and British Delhi's Piccadilly, the Connaught Place, was located at Gole Market, an upbeat shopping joint for the Indian baboos. The Inn had lost its glamour like most landmarks associated with the abandoned empire. The historic city was now under the occupation of a new breed of adventurers and invaders, the Punjabi refugees from Pakistan and the fortune hunters from the rest of India.

Vidyasagar Suri fronted the pleasure spot owned by Ram Karan Prasad, the seemingly permanent minister in the Indian cabinet. Vidyasagar was a repository of knowledge, different kind of knowledge, about alcoholic beverages and thinly clothed bar beauties. He had landed the lucrative job by virtue of his specialisation in marketing techniques for illicit drugs, narcotics, and fair-skinned barmaids, described by social bandicoots as call girls. He often acted as talent spotters for identifying and recruiting presentable and marketable lasses from the lost corridors of Delhi's burgeoning fringe dwelling social scum.

Ramendra Kaushal was not his trade-buddy. Ram Karan had forced his trusted lieutenant on him and had granted the macho ruffian the power to supervise and scrutinize Suri's operations. Suri hated the gutsy ruffian.

Ramendra Kaushal reached the Divine Inn trailed by Dhiren Bhagat's Mosur. He parked the motorbike behind a shrub and walked up to room 105, especially reserved for his pleasure breaks. Suri saluted the budding politician and followed meekly.

"I'm not here," Kaushal whispered, "understand?"

"No problem sir." Suri replied meekly.

"Send a Scotch and I don't want to be disturbed for next few hours."

"Anything else?" Suri asked with a grin hanging on his face.

"No thanks. Call up Prasadji. He has instructions for you."

"Some policemen had come looking for you."

"What the hell did you tell them?" Kaushal grabbed Suri's collar, ready to thrash him.

"Like you said yourself, you're not here."

"That's good." Kaushal banged the door on Suri's face.

*

The gatekeepers of sin often dare not challenge the keepers of law. Dhiren Bhagat didn't have to haggle much with Vidyasagar Suri, when he approached the innkeeper. His FIB identity card, some photo snaps of Suri's involvement in drug dealings and a bunch of currency notes to top it all, convinced VS that he was in mighty unpleasant company. The long arm of the law was just about throttling his jugular. He opened the door to the pleasure castle of Ram Karan with an obliging bow.

"What exactly do you want?"

"Leave the details to me. You want to even a score with Kaushal and we want our job done, no hitch and no hiccup. My men will come to install a few gadgets. Just keep mum. Okay?"

"Fine, but take care of my minister. It's his hotel. The area police chief already troubles me. He refuses to be bribed."

"There're many more surprises Suri," Bhagat consoled Vidyasagar, "that's why the country still breathes."

"Sir", said Suri cutting his tongue with big incisors, simultaneously touching his ear lobes, "by God! Mine is a honourable profession. I barely earn my family keep."

"Well, well! let God bless your family with more progeny like you. Take care. You know the consequences for a drug related offence and you know how cruel SITA is (Suppression of Immoral Traffic Act). You'd simply rot in jail for ten years."

"I'm your servant sir. Just take care of my security."

Vidyasagar bent down before Bhagat with folded hands.

He didn't feel comfortable with the idea of conniving with a FIB officer. Dhiren Bhagat, however, played the game cool, sending Himalayan chill waves inside Suri's bones. The *quid pro quo* was neat and brutish.

"Sir, take care that my inn isn't defamed."

"Don't worry about the chastity of your charge. We do often trample on the privacy of social pirates. Nevertheless, we do it scientifically. Everything is top secret with us."

Bhagat and his team were trained to be discreet, and very discreet, where honey traps were involved. Nirmal Mitra and his Dreamland boys operated for the next two days on rooms 105 and 106. Two pinhole video cameras and radio microphones were installed and synthesised with the video and audio tracks.

The super-secret technical operation was Nampoothiri's brain wave. With powerful political mentors shielding him, the police might find the going tough in slapping a murder charge on Kaushal. The Indian political breed was adept in blunting the edges of the law and bending the judiciary. They, Nampoothiri argued, belonged to a heavenly class and considered themselves above the Constitution and the statute books. Moreover, the police and politicians were the last items in his scheme of things. He preferred chiselled tradecraft evidence for blackmailing the target. The fear of his photographs in compromising position with women in bed reaching his mother could clinch the deal. Ramendra, as the records said, was more scared of his mother than himself. He didn't have, if Bhagat's archives were correct, any god to fear. His mother was his goddess.

*

The net was cast. However, the big catch was busy elsewhere dangling tantalising baits to the stunned and stupefied student community.

The university campus was in turmoil. The recovery of Matang's decapitated body from the back alley of Raj Ghat had created tumultuous commotion. Horrendously named in the memory of Gandhi, a person, who had little to do with any Raj, either the British or its successor, the Raj Ghat back alleys had been transformed into happy hunting grounds for drug and flesh peddlers. Ramendra took advantage of the roaring reputation of the horrendous place to deflect the cause of murder to the just concluded students' union elections. Police had no reason not to believe the top student leader.

Kaushal delivered a devastating speech blaming Hindu Sangh for the ghastly murder of the bright star of Delhi University. He blamed the Chinese agents for importing a nihilist culture to the peace loving country of Mahatma Gandhi. The students didn't clap. Ramendra's political filibustering was too incongruous and they were well aware of the deeds and black-deeds of the campus charlatan. Brij and his fellow acolytes looked at the sombre crowd and raised slogans.

"*Shahid Matang amar rahe* (martyr Matang be immortal), Chinese *chuhas murdabad* (death to the Chinese rats), kill the Hindu Nazis, Kaushal *tum age chalo, hum tumhare peeche hain* (Kaushal you advance we're behind you)."

Some students repeated the slogans and clapped indeterminately. Others walked out silently. Kaushal could not convince them. Brij too, couldn't drown his conscience under the din of tutored slogans, and wasn't carried away by the rhetoric. Matang, the ruffian from Bihar, was apolitical. He was deeply entrenched in criminal activities and believed that the highway of criminality was the shortest conduit to the exalted pedestal of national politics. Brij hadn't forgotten the tongues of fire in Kaushal's eyes at Blue Dart restaurant. He had seen that look earlier when Kaushal and Matang killed two gold smugglers from Punjab.

"How did it happen?" He gathered courage to ask his team captain, "are you hiding something?"

"Do you suspect me?"

"No. I don't. But there were other witnesses in Blue Dart. Some of them may sing under police torture."

"You bastard! Don't you dare betray me? I'll make mince meat of your dirty balls."

Kaushal slipped his hand on the cool comfort of the blue steel in his pocket.

Brij looked at the contour of the gun and softened his tone.

"Cool down boss. Sharpen your guard. You remember that Communist looking book seller in Blue Dart?"

"Where's that bastard? I'll squeeze out his balls too."

"Patience captain. Just cool down. Why don't you go home for a few days?"

Kaushal took out his hand and placed it around Brij's shoulder.

"You're my best friend Brij. Matang has paid for his *gaddari* (act of betrayal). Do you know that he tried to woo Hema?"

"Don't tell me!"

"I'm correct. He'd even written a love letter to her. How could he dare to touch my kill?"

"You still want her? Don't you?"

"Why not? She must pay for scorning my offer of love. No girl can do that to me. I can't go home before I humble her."

"Take care, boss. Things are too hot." Brij volunteered the advice after gathering plenty of courage.

Ramendra Kaushal levelled his cool eyes to Brij's uncertain looks. Brij nodded his head vaguely. That was a sure fire way of saving his skull.

"Leave my kill to me. I'll take her at my sweet will. Get busy with Matang's funeral. I want at least 30 vehicle loads of people. Get them from the nearest slums. It's politically important for us. Ram Karanji and Manjiraji have promised to come. Matang's funeral will be a major political offensive against the campus Commies and the Hindu Sanghis. We must put up a formidable show."

Matang's funeral turned out to be an impressive affair. Manjira arrived in style with a retinue of party cadre. Ram Karan Prasad followed her. Manjira's shrill speech reminded the students about the struggle carried out by her father against the Hindu Sangh and the Chinese invaders. Matang, she proclaimed, was a victim like Mahatma Gandhi, who was assassinated by rabid communalists. She announced donation of a liberal amount for installation of a bronze statue of martyr Matang. Her announcement was accompanied by Ram Karan's loud declaration that a gold medal would be instituted in memory of the martyr for the most brilliant law student from Bihar.

He loudly called upon the party cadre to retaliate martyr Matang's assassination by the conspirators of the Hindu Sangh and their Chinese collaborators. Ramendra Kaushal mastered a 100-vehicle procession to carry Matang's body to the nearby Nigambodh cremation ground and consigned it to the flames with the assistance of his grieving father.

*

5

The glowing embers of the funeral pyre were yet to cool down along the polluted waters of the Yamuna. The campus was yet to limp back to normal. Fear stalked the students ominously.

However, Matang's spectacular and politically correct funeral buoyed up Ramendra Kaushal's stature by a few more inches. His acolytes sounded loud warnings to the Hindu Sangh controlled Students' Union that the Prince of Jhunjhunu was still the uncrowned king of the campus. Kaushal too didn't fail to rub in the message with deliberate muscle flexing.

Kaushal's inflated ego and burning sensuality didn't abate with Matang's killing and the roaring flames of his funeral pyre. The fire of carnal desire to grab Hema turned to a schizophrenic vector and propelled his heart muscles with spasm of craving. This wasn't a fire that he could douse with liberal servings of Scotch, philosophical buffers, and cautionary signals from a balanced cerebral cortex. The captive fire continued to pour fat into Kaushal's blazing cauldron of desire. His twisted gene-cords were chemically so aligned that a mere infatuation often exploded into an infernal desire. He knew for sure that the ghost wouldn't dismount from his shoulders until he mounted Hema and punished her. The unseen hands of destiny had engineered him like this, he knew and he wasn't shameful about it.

"I must get her." He told Brij, while sipping coffee at Blue Dart.

"Wait. Let things cool down." The pragmatic son of a priest advised.

"What for? It's my way of life. I want her."

"It's a different case."

"What bloody difference does it make?" Kaushal grimaced with a nonchalant look.

"Wait for a few days," Brij commented, "I've to take my mom to Benaras for a pilgrimage. We shall talk again."

Brij didn't dare repeat his advice. A few days' tactical absence from Delhi should be a better act of discretion. The Prince was in no mood to wait. Patience was not his forte.

Kaushal was indeed not ready to wait for Brij's return from Benaras. He preferred to enjoy his women in absolute privacy. Hema should be his private kill. She was unique and a live encounter could alone douse the fire.

Kaushal kept on driving, rather absent-mindedly, imagining the likely expression on Hema's face after she was subdued. She might squirm and cry out in ecstasy. Some apparent cool cats often exploded on impact. A high-strung woman apparently abhorred sexual overtures. But they sure admired hot pulsating muscle. He felt sure that this one cool cat would feel electrified, once she was disrobed, and masculine fingers caressed her vital contours. Screech! Kaushal suddenly applied the brake. Hema's contorted facial muscles fleeted past his mind's screen. He licked his parched lips and looked into his own eyes in the rearview mirror.

Why not now? Yes, now. He should abduct her. This one cool cat wouldn't yield, unless she was forced to.

Kaushal parked his car near the mouth of the ridge road that faced Kashmiri Gate and lighted hashish filled cigarette. The magic-smoke electrified his neurons. He looked out impatiently for the black car, which usually dropped Hema at the college gate. It should've turned up by now. Perhaps, the bitch wasn't turning up today, Kaushal thought.

The hashish started acting slowly but decisively. Ramendra closed his eyes, responding to the slackening impulses of his brain. Perhaps the stars weren't propitious. Perhaps, his decision wasn't correct. Should he wait for Brij's return? What for? That son of a priest wasn't going to chant *mantras* while he pinned Hema down under his thighs. Kaushal closed his eyes. The hashish had started seeping into his blood.

For a split second, he nearly missed noticing the black Ambassador car approaching from the opposite direction. Kaushal ignited his car engine. In a sharp swing he placed his Morris Minor horizontally on the main road and forced Hema's driver to apply the brakes. Kaushal sprinted down to the Ambassador, dragged Hema out, and shoved her inside his Morris. Hema fought back and rained blows on Kaushal. Her fingers scratched his chest, drawing blood and flesh.

Kaushal freed his right hand and hit Hema's medulla in a swift karate chop, dumped her on the back seat and drove off at high speed. Hema's limp body writhed and convulsed for a few moments and turned still. Three vertebrae of her neck had snapped under the unmeasured blow.

Kaushal pressed the accelerator, concentrated on driving, and anxiously scanned the rear view mirror. He was soon out of reach of Hema's aging driver. However, he failed to notice his nemesis, Dhiren Bhagat, following his Morris in a posh Ford with a fake diplomatic number plate of a West-European embassy.

An alley cat of the walled city, Kaushal avoided the main thoroughfare and drove straight to Ajmeri Gate, took a turn to Connaught Circus and swung towards Gole Market. The vehicle entered straight inside Divine Inn and came to a halt under a huge banyan tree.

Dhiren Bhagat parked his car well away from the hotel and activated his VHF communication set.

"Tiger's in the den." He raised Mitra.

"Fine. Bait's ready." Mitra replied and activated the system.

"I'll join the party soon."

"Roger, no hurry. Take your time." Mitra hung up, switched on the pinhole video cameras, and concealed audio systems.

*

Kaushal's Divine Inn room was fitted with a small fridge, an air conditioner and was well stocked with the beer and whisky of his choice.

He dumped Hema's body on the bed and switched on the air conditioner. The damn compressor didn't whine.

Bloody bullshit! He summoned the room service.

"What the hell is this? Why isn't the AC working?"

"Sir I really don't know." The room boy trembled in terror.

"Go and call VS."

"Sir, he's out of Delhi."

Kaushal dialled the intercom and demanded immediate replacement of the AC. The floor manager politely informed that the compressor had blown off and it would take at least three days to get a replacement.

Kaushal kicked the room boy out, closed the door, and gulped a stiff whisky straight from the bottle. The liquid fire warmed him up as it travelled down the oesophagus, leaving a burning sensation all the way down.

The ancient ceiling fan rotated slowly and screwed into Kaushal's patience. Everything was going wrong.

The bloody bitch was still feigning unconsciousness.

Did he hit her very hard? Perhaps. At that anxious moment, he could probably not measure the momentum. Such a chop at the base of the neck could often lead to a fracture. Damn, damn! Damn the whole world! Did he carry a dead body all the way?

Kaushal gulped another drink and tried pushing a few drops into Hema's mouth, parting her lips with his thick fingers. The fairy girl didn't respond. Nevertheless, her rouge tinted cheeks, red lips and fine folds on the eyelids provoked Kaushal. Dead flesh couldn't ignite that kind of fire in him. Her body was still warm and it was driving him mad.

He slapped Hema's cheeks gently and kissed her lips. Kaushal picked a bottle of chilled water and sprinkled some on Hema's face and eyes. Was Hema dead? The mighty karate chop might have broken her vertebrae and a piece of bone had probably punctured a few veins travelling down from the brain. Kaushal's eyes betrayed fear as he unknowingly looked into the camera. An eerie feeling gripped him.

He wasn't ready to believe that his kill was dead before he had feasted on it. Her body was still warm.

Kaushal placed his ears on Hema's breast, trying to feel the beats. The bulging sacks of membrane were still warm. He couldn't feel the heartbeat, but the dying embers of Hema's body sent shivers of warmth down his spines. Kaushal was seized by a maddening impulse that ran through his spine and travelled down to the muscles of his genital.

He kept on caressing Hema's breasts over and over again, trying to draw warmth from the taut flesh. Hema's face, a wonderful sculpture in beauty and innocence, didn't react to his paranoid touches. She couldn't. The essence of life had deserted the body at least 20 minutes ago. But the neurons of her brain still pulsated, acknowledging Kaushal's touches. Her neuron proteins weren't in position to send instructions to Hema, to react. She, the living-kicking creature, was simply not there.

A strange frenzy gripped Kaushal. How could she dupe him? Nobody could. He undressed Hema, slapped her cheeks again and failing to get a response shouted out some obscenities. Undressing himself, Kaushal mounted the cadaver of Rajni Krittika Hemaprabha Rao and carried out the frustrating ritual of a sexual assault. A frustrating ejaculation sent a shiver of shame and guilt in him.

Ramendra Kaushal, for the first time, felt that he'd wronged an innocent girl. This one murder wasn't necessary, neither for his survival nor for his pleasure. He screamed out like a deranged lunatic. The bitch had defeated him, at the final moment of his victory. She had deprived him of the pleasure of making her beg for mercy. He had gone too far. He had killed Matang not for this dead idiot woman! He wanted her alive, submitting and begging.

Kaushal ran for the toilet, collected a mug of water, and sprinkled some on Hema, as if the liquid would wash away his sin. He developed a strange affection and aversion for the flesh, which used to be Hema, lying before him.

He felt haunted and scared. The face of his mother Kasturi shot across his mind in a flash.

"No mother, no. I didn't intend to kill her." Ramendra covered his eyes and shouted.

Kasturi's face kept on hanging. Kaushal sprinkled some water on his face.

"How could I kill a woman?" he cried out. He couldn't kill his mother. Could he? What a damn mess! His mother wouldn't ever pardon him, for raping a dead woman. A black cloud of guilt enveloped him.

"Oh Mother!" he cried out aloud, rushed to the toilet, picked up the water jet, and applied cold blast on his face and head.

Two frames zoomed in and faded out on the thin film of water, Hema's and Kasturi's. He threw down the water jet and screamed in anguish and frustration. This dead woman was reminding him of his mother's face. Why? Why did he see the image of his mother's face whenever he was in the company of women? Kaushal couldn't make any sense of it. Had a sin syndrome struck him? What sin? It wasn't his mistake. That idiotic girl shouldn't have resisted, compelling him to use the karate chop.

Kaushal muttered a few more curses and replaced Hema's clothes, as best as he could, and wrapped the body up in a bedspread. He straitened his clothes, momentarily tended to the bleeding scratches on his chest, combed his disheveled hair and picked up Hema's limp body. He disappeared from the monitor.

Ramendra placed Hema's body in the backseat of his car and zoomed out of Divine Inn. He drove past New Delhi Kali temple, took a right turn on to a small dirt lane that disappeared into the ridge forests. He parked the car by a huge weather beaten boulder, overlooking a depression that was covered with thick flowery foliage of wild lilies. Kaushal gently took out Hema's body and placed it on the ground. A few red-faced *langoors* (monkeys), expecting Kaushal to offer them eatables, tiptoed closer to Hema's body. Taking advantage of Kaushal's preoccupation with a cigarette, some of the daring simians pulled out the bedspread and grimaced at the bluish face of Hema.

One of the more daring, perhaps the herd leader, bent down and sniffed the cool skins of the once vibrant girl. No. It wasn't exactly an edible offering. The frustrated herd grimaced at Kaushal and climbed up the nearest banyan tree with loud sounds of protest. Startled by the queer behaviour of the simians, Kaushal shooed them away by hurling pieces of stone.

Stupid fools!

Kaushal lighted another cigarette, removed the bedspread, and for the last time looked at Hema's body. His eyes moistened up and a few drops of tears rolled down his eyes. He didn't want to kill the girl. This one accident was unintentional.

In a rare gesture, Kaushal folded his palms and prayed in silence, perhaps after ages. What did he do with his seeds of desire? The damn demon had sprouted into a sky piercing shadow of death. Could he, by any chance, change the shape of events that might ensue from this unintended act of wanton violence? No, he won't be able to drown this ghastly experience even in a sea of whisky. Perhaps the seeds of his desire would be finally incinerated with the mortal remains of the girl, whom he had picked up as a sex object and ended up developing aches in his soul.

Would he be able to have sex with any other woman? Perhaps not, not in near future. He looked deep into Hema's eyes and felt a sinking sense of guilt. He closed his eyes firmly, with a determined effort to wipe out from his memory cells the ghastly act of raping the dead girl. He lightly kissed Hema's dry blue lips. Had he started loving Hema? He had never loved any girl. He didn't know what love was all about. That lightening had never struck him.

Ramendra stood silent for a few moments, picked up the body, and rolled it down the grassy slopes. Hema's remains rested with a thud against a big stone, after rolling over thorny bushes. The thick greens covered up Rajni Krittika Hemaprabha Rao, in a final gesture of taking the dusts back unto them. The multi-coloured wild lilies parted temporarily and sympathetically wrapped up the beautiful naked body. It was a final floral burial.

Kaushal stretched his neck and looked down the depression. Hema's body, covered under the thick foliage of flowering lilies, wasn't visible from his position. A sudden burst of remorse seized him as his overflowing eyes glanced at the mocking lilies. He never had the opportunity of looking at flowers dancing under a lazy breeze. Ramendra Kaushal felt the beautiful blooms were taunting him by shaking their heads. The beauty, that he had wanted to torment, had defeated him and had just begun a process of tossing and turning his entire existence.

As he ignited the engine, Kaushal again felt two drops of tear rolling down his cheeks. What nonsense was happening to him? He didn't have any answer to that question. He wiped the teardrops and swore silently to atone this ghastly mistake. This one woman had shaken his world. Hema proved in her death that muscle alone couldn't open the door to a heart. What was it? Love? He hadn't bothered about that amorphous commodity all these years. He didn't know its meaning.

Perhaps he should should really go over to Jhunjhunu, to his mother and seek her blessings. She alone could put his mind on the rails again. Perhaps she could tell him what love was made up of. Perhaps she could transform the seeds of his desire to the seeds of creation. Only a mother could do that.

*

6

The assigned mission was successful, that's what Dhiren Bhagat thought. His calibration warranted hooking the target up for initial priming. However, Ram Banerjee thought otherwise. Like most Indian bureaucrats and deities, he reserved the right to break all the rules and laws and expected others to go by the statute books. He didn't see any virtue in the operational methodology adopted by Balachandran Nampoothiri to hook the Triple X target. Where was the need for such wanton sex, bloodshed, and excesses? The entire process smacked of unethical crudity. He wondered why Chief Dutta was in love with the target! Why did he give *carte blanche* to Nampoothiri and his stooge Bhagat? Didn't the organisation have any moral obligation and accountability? At the end of the day, the taxpayers footed the entire bill.

"Sir." Banerjee's woolly thoughts were broken by the sudden intrusive voice of Dhiren Bhagat.

"You wanted a briefing on Triple X."

"Give me the papers."

"I haven't drawn up a report yet. I thought you'd like to have a verbal report first."

"What makes you think that your verbal junk is so holy?" Ram shot back.

"There are some sensitive aspects. Perhaps, you would like to keep the technical operations out of the formal report." Bhagat tried to reason out, what he thought was the normal FIB practice.

"Well, I don't want any verbal briefing," Ram snapped at Bhagat, "I want a detailed written report, a comprehensive basic operational data-sheet, for discussion with the Deputy Director. And I want it by five today. No hedging and no monkey games."

"Do I put down all the details in black and white?" Asked Bhagat.

"What's your problem? As an intelligence officer you're expected to put down all the details on record."

"Fine sir, the job would be done. I just wanted to know if all the details of our technical operations are also to be incorporated."

Bhagat tried to remind his boss that his instructions flouted a cardinal principle of the FIB. It didn't allow its deeds to be recorded in black and white.

"Do as I say. To be frank, I really don't know the details. It's between you and the boss. If he wishes my presence, I can come in at the discussion stage. I can probably give a few suggestions on tradecraft matters, at the training stage."

He walked past Bhagat as carefully as he could, probably to avoid body contact with the latter.

Bhagat looked at the fading figure of Banerjee and lighted a cigarette. All that he could do was to silently curse his senior. Writing down an operational report wasn't as easy as filing a heated knife through a lump of frozen butter. Bhagat couldn't get his thoughts together. He couldn't establish smooth co-ordination between his training, service ethics, gut instinct, and cerebral signals. Banerjee was either playing a dodgy safe game or a deep and dirty conspiracy.

*

Bhagat decided to try his luck with the top boss.

However, reaching him wasn't easy.

Jatadhari could help, Bhagat decided to gamble.

To his consternation room number 187, at the turn of the corridor towards the Ministry of Defence, was buzzing with action. Nampoothiri was in the midst of a meeting with Major General Naveen Sahni, Director, Military Intelligence, and the intelligence chiefs of the Navy and Air Force. The Director of Military Operations, Maj. General Harbaksh, was there with his number two.

"It's a difficult day. He's too busy. A Hindustan-Pakistan war is about to begin. Sahibs are talking about the Rann of Kachchh." Jatadhari conveyed his helplessness.

Bhagat scribbled a few sentences on a slip of paper and begged Jata to show it to Nampoothiri.

"If I don't see him now, the boss is bound to face personal harm. It's more for him." Bhagat threw a psychological dart.

Jatadhari went in and Nampoothiri came out in a few seconds. He advised Bhagat to go home and meet him the next day at 7.30 p.m.

Should he write the report?

No. He should sleep and rest. He deserved it. Nampoothiri rushed back and called Ram Banerjee's number.

"Can you ask your officer Bhagat to see me?"

"Yes sir. It's my pleasure. He should be around."

Banerjee panicked. Did Bhagat directly approach the Deputy Director S—S standing for all security matters? That son of a *chamar* was capable of elbowing past his immediate boss.

Anyways, this wasn't the correct time to bray for Bhagat's blood. The bastard! Banerjee vowed to finish off the scoundrel, once Kumar Anand, the Deputy Director I—I standing for internal affairs, assumed command. He pressed the bell, rather a long one, adding his anger and frustration to the 220 volt AC current.

"You called me sir?" Bhagat entered the room peevishly.

"Is the report ready?" Banerjee looked up with a flicker of a butcher's smile below his butterfly moustache.

"Not yet sir, I suppose it should take another two hours. I'm yet to receive the technical report from Mitra sahib. Would you like to call him, sir?"

"Leave it. See the DD (S) first. Tell me if he has any new instruction."

Bhagat returned to Ram's room in ten minutes.

"Sir, he's busy in a meeting. He just told me that you may like to see him, tomorrow at 7.30 p.m. Until then, he said, no report should be drafted. He would like to discuss some important operational aspects with you."

"Okay. You can go. Prepare a check list of points for the discussion."

Banerjee dismissed Bhagat.

Very clever, eh? Banerjee turned and twisted his neurons again. How did that Keralite get to know his mind? That *chamar* must've short-fused him.

*

7

Next evening sharp at 19.30 Ram Banerjee shepherded the procession tailed by Dhiren Bhagat. Jatadhari ushered them in.

"Good evening sir." Banerjee greeted the boss.

Nampoothiri didn't respond. His eyes were glued to copies of diplomatic telegrams from Karachi and Rawalpindi on Kachchh war situation.

"So Ram," Nampoothiri shuffled the telegrams under a folio cover and asked, "what brings the gang here?"

"Sir, you desired a briefing on the Triple X target."

"Oh yes! What do you think? Is the target ready for recruitment?" Nampoothiri asked with a hint of a naughty smile.

"Sir, let's hear Bhagat first. He's the main handler or you may say the master chef." Ram replied, vainly trying to hide his discordant vibe behind the raw humour.

"Give me your assessment Ram. I depend on you totally." Nampoothiri spoke with an impish smile.

"What can I say sir?" Was he caught, pants down by the boss? Did this son of a *chamar* carry tales to the archrival of Kumar Anand?

"Let Bhagat speak sir." He added peevishly.

The story from the beginning to date was lengthy and intricately textured. The daring technical operation fascinated Nampoothiri. But a mist of gloom suddenly generated an ache somewhere in his heart. He rued with silent and deepest regret his colossal amnesia. He had simply forgotten to warn the health secretary, Alladi Subhash Chandra Rao, about the imminent danger to his daughter.

Nampoothiri begged to be excused and rushed into the toilet. He looked at the mirror. The wrinkled face and black shadows under the eyes reflected his tormented psyche. Did he commit a mistake? Was it deliberate? Perhaps yes. The smoking anxiety over the succession battle had burnt out his reflexes. Yes. The fire was still raging, burning him down to ashes. What the hell was he doing in this damn FIB? That bloody Kumar Anand was sure to walk away with the cake.

What was damn Banerjee up to? Was this Bengali *asshole* trying to implicate him in a devastating scandal!

Nampoothiri felt sorry for Hema. He wasn't perturbed over the moral implications of the operation. In his profession, moral scruples normally took the back seat. It was by far the most immoral profession, a few degrees on the higher side than professional prostitution. The latter had some occasional privilege of choosing a business partner. He didn't. To him a task was a task and no price was insurmountable. It was a war—a war of wits and conscience prick wasn't charted out as an ingredient of the tradecraft. Nampoothiri momentarily paused. Hema could've been saved and she needn't have died a grisly death. He splashed his face and eyes with cool water, perhaps to wash away the momentary pangs of guilt. He re-emerged from the toilet and called in Jatadhari and ordered coffee and Havana.

"So, where were we?" asked Nampoothiri.

Bhagat narrated the nuts and bolts of the story. He skipped details on the Matang Singh and Hema episodes.

Ram Banerjee felt ill at ease. The *asshole* was trying to protect his hide, as well as that of his super boss, Nampoothiri. Two murders and a rape had taken place with virtual FIB collaboration. What for? Just for the sake of an idiotic operation? His eyes suddenly crossed glances with Nampoothiri's eagle squint. He felt a dozen darting electrodes piercing his corneal film.

Nampoothiri didn't shift his gaze. He finished the coffee and concluded that the wily Bengali was acting as a limpet of his rival for the top post.

"Fine Ram. You may go."

Banerjee walked out as a limping lamb. He knew he was caught.

"Stay put." Nampoothiri said the words more through his eyes than his mouth.

Bhagat was unnerved by the sudden strategic move of Nampoothiri. How did he come to know the inner thoughts of Banerjee? Left to him the Bengali baboo would have allowed the XXX target priming rot in the morgue of his putrid psyche. Nampoothiri, he concluded, must have had planted pet cats among the unsuspecting pigeons inside the FIB. That's another name of the game of running an intelligence shop. His thoughts, however, did not flash up on his face.

"What do you feel?" asked Nampoothiri, "is Banerjee serious with the operation?"

"You know better, sir." Bhagat parried the embarrassing question.

"Fine. I don't want intermediary. Report to me directly. I want all the video and audiotapes and the still positives and negatives. Seal them in a cover and hand over to me by 9 p.m. tonight. Understood?" Nampoothiri directed Bhagat.

"Yes sir, the job would be done." Bhagat got the message straight. The boss was building up defences.

"And no one moves about in the organisation with leaking cans. There should be no juicy story about Triple X going about the place."

"No problem, sir. But how do we accost him now?"

"Use the direct approach. He's now a cornered scarecrow. Take precautions. I expect him to behave like a coward. A bully can't stand up to crisis. He generally fumbles and caves in."

"What about his political clout? Ram Karan may interfere."

"Leave that to me. I'll brief the boss and he'll take care of the political crust. Meet Maulana Rizwan and Colonel Pathania personally and brief them about the training aspects. I've spoken already."

Nampoothiri felt relaxed, closed his eyes. He tried to visualise his favourite longboat race on *Onam* (New Year) day, in the backwaters of Cochin. The feeling of smooth sailing, the splashing sounds of oars and lilting folk tunes slackened his eye muscles. He momentarily lapsed into a catnap.

*

Jhunjhunu, a sleepy town in Rajasthan, boasted of several exquisite marble *havelis* (old style houses) and a famous *Sati* (woman burnt alive in husband's funeral pyre) temple. The exquisite marble edifice, raised about seventy years back, attracted millions of Hindu devotees. They paid homage to *Sati Mata*, a fifteen-year-old bride, who was burnt alive in the funeral pyre of her eighty-year-old husband, just two days after her marriage. This ghoulish religious practice, fertile Brahmin minds ordained, was the ultimate offering to womanhood, whose status in traditional Hindu society oscillated between damnation and deification.

Jhunjhunu was also advertised in Delhi University campus as the most important principality in Rajasthan, the lair of its famous lion, Prince Ramendra Kaushal. His maternal uncle, Sukhram Chakrapani, well versed in English and Persian languages, was appointed *Dewan* (minister) in the court of a local king. A childless Brahmin, Kasturi's brother, and Digvijay Kaushal's brother-in-law, Sukhram Chakrapani had amassed fabulous wealth. His critics alleged that most of his wealth came from the coffers of an affluent Marwari businessperson, Seth Mangeram Chuniram Bagaria.

He owned several *havelis*, 500 acres of agricultural land, 1000 cows, and a few business establishments.

Bagaria claimed the presence of his ancestors under the same banyan tree, from where Job Charnok, the English trader and alleged founder of Calcutta, traded jute, silk and other assorted merchandise. Bagaria's fabulous business house was as ancient as the Company Bahadur's (East India Company) empire. His great grandfather was a banker of repute often rivalling Jagat Seth, who had befriended Robert Clive, the clerk turned General and the founder of British Empire in India.

Seth Bagaria, it's alleged, had persuaded Sukhram, to act as his dewan, managing his estates in Rajasthan and some of his banking interests in Surat. Sukhram Chakrapani did everything to make his employer happy. However, despite his two marriages poor Chakrapani didn't have a child of his own. His sperms simply did not have the capacity to fertilise the womb of any woman. He lost his wives in quick succession and after distressed arrival of Kasturi from Pakistan, he had buried the idea of having a third wife. Ramendra Kaushal, besides being the son of a deprived and deposed king, was therefore, the natural heir to the properties of his maternal uncle.

Jhunjhunu, on that balmy morning, was in a festive mood, observing a rare sacred festival after a gap of, may be, 70 years.

Seth Mangeram Chuniram Bagaria had expired three days back in Calcutta. The uncouth obese trader had died of a heart attack. Relatives, who loathed him for his treasure chest and business empire, however, didn't hesitate to whisper that Bagaria had, in fact, collapsed while trying to mount a bombshell of a beauty. She was imported all the way from Goa to give a live performance in one of the joints owned by the Seth. An excited but not aroused Bagaria gulped down a few extra pegs and finally collapsed on her body, even before he could position himself on the hot beauty. He didn't wake up.

Bagaria's body was flown to Jhunjhunu in a private Dakota for cremation at the bank of a pond, locally revered as *Sati Mai Ki Pokhri* (pond of goddess Sati).

Dhiren Bhagat had chanced to reach Jhunjhunu on an auspicious day. *Sati Mata's* mantle was being thrust on Bagaria's wife. Two brothers of Bagaria had roped in a few Brahmins, who passed an edict that Satirani, wife of late Mangeram Chuniram Bagaria, surprisingly matched hitherto undiscovered signs of the *Sati Mata*. She was destined to embrace eternity like the deified legendary Sati Mata.

Sukhram Chakrapani opposed the idea. He was exposed to modern ideas and had come in touch with the Brahmo Samajists of Calcutta. He supported widow remarriage and opposed child marriage. He had decided to prevent the villagers from committing this farce and even had petitioned the police. The value of muscle was not new to him. He hired the services of his nephew and adopted son, Ramendra Kaushal, to use his muscle and political influence.

*

Ramendra Kaushal, seated under the canopy of a gas station, was busy directing his goons to prevent people from participating in the bride burning ceremony. The gas station, next to Sukhram's house, was Ramendra Kaushal's favourite hunting ground. Ramendra wasn't bothered about the bride burning ceremony. He never bothered about sanctity of women. He was concerned with Sukhram's promise of some extra money, if the job was well done.

Kaushal noticed first the strange sight with a sense of disbelief. That Commie looking Blue Dart bookseller was standing under the portico of the *Shiva* temple. The trademark bag hung from his shoulders. The blighted bookseller had the temerity to follow him here too! What bloody book could he sell in the desert town of Jhunjhunu? Could he be a police informer?

My goodness! Kaushal recoiled like an injured snake and started scheming for self-defence. The insect must be smothered out, pulverised to dust and thrown to the mercy of the desert scorpions, better still, into the funeral pyre of Bagaria.

"Bhero," Kaushal called out loudly to a midget of a man, with a mismatched big moustache, "go, and fetch that bastard".

Bhagat obliged. He walked alongside the dwarf and coolly took a seat next to Kaushal.

"Haven't I seen you in Delhi?" Kaushal asked in a stern voice.

"Correct," Bhagat didn't remove his eyes from those of Kaushal, "perhaps we met at Blue Dart Restaurant, behind the Raj Ghat lane and Divine Inn."

"Get lost. I don't want to see your face here. This is Jhunjhunu, not fucking Delhi."

Ramendra Kaushal stared menacingly at Bhagat.

Bhagat, a rare smoker, took out a cigarette and offered one to Kaushal.

"I feel like smoking and don't feel like igniting the petrol tanks. Can we take a small walk?"

Bhagat's cool voice unnerved Kaushal. However, the snake inside wasn't yet ready to lower its hood. His eyes narrowed down to mere slits and his voice hissed.

"Don't put your hands in a snake-hole." In a quick move, Kaushal slithered his right hand into his trouser pocket and was reassured by the cold steel.

Bhagat followed his manoeuvre and spoke softly.

"Look across the street. Do you see two persons under the portico of the temple? They carry two pistols each and I've one. Between us, we've one hundred rounds to pump into your body. And for your information, we're from the Delhi Police." He produced a photo identity card, a fabricated one obviously, a deception often practised by FIB officials. Bhagat usually carried on his person half a dozen ID cards of various government departments.

Ramendra Kaushal suddenly shrunk back, like a leech bouncing against a salt pile. Nampoothiri wasn't far from the truth. A bully often behaved cowardly.

"Let's go out and see the fun."

Bhagat led Kaushal towards *Sati Mai ki Pokhri*, a big pond, around which the great religious perfidy of human sacrifice was being perpetrated. The place was now milling with crowd, singing and dancing in praise of Satirani. At a far corner of the pond, next to the temple of *Sati Mata*, a group of women, seated in circle, sang and swung to the beats of percussion drums and cymbals. One young woman, bejewelled and decked in a costly *lehanga* (skirt) swung her body in a circular motion, beating the ground with a green twig. She was supposed to have been possessed by the spirit of the fifteen-year-old girl, who was burnt alive and deified seven decades ago. A funeral pyre was decked up with sandalwood, pure milk fat and other holy ingredients, about 50 yards north of the temple.

Sukhram stood at the far edge of the pond, trying to mobilise some of his supporters. Most villagers avoided him and jostled with each other to snatch fat portions of the sumptuous food, a rare treat for the desert tribes. They hadn't had a royal treat like this one in their living memory. They were a motley crowd, high on marijuana and opium trip and religious intoxicants. Dhiren Bhagat followed by Kaushal and two other FIB sleuths proceeded towards a cluster of banyan trees, located on a raised ground that overlooked the pond and the funeral pyre. He lighted a cigarette and offered one to Kaushal.

"Why are you bothering me? What's your problem? How much money do you want?" Kaushal asked while fiddling with the cigarette.

"You can reserve that grease for your God. You know dear, you're the problem. We know and the law knows, what all you've done. A few murders and a couple of rapes and drug smuggling."

Bhagat flicked the lighter and helped a frozen Kaushal to light his cigarette.

"You've no proof. I've powerful friends in Delhi."

"We know. Ram Karan, you mean?"

"Not Karanji alone."

"Well. Manjira isn't in the habit of using a dirty napkin twice. They've seen the video and audio evidences of your heinous crimes. And Ram Karan knows when to drop parasites like you." Bhagat hurled a mighty bluff.

"You require proof to arrest me."

Ramendra Kaushal chocked out and spoke in a voice that seemed as if the last ounce of air was escaping his deflated rib cage.

"That's not what I intend to do."

Bhagat shifted to a smooth boulder, took out a bunch of photographs from his shoulder bag, and handed over to Kaushal.

Kaushal shuffled through the photographs with an ashen face and a dead fish look. These were black and white witnesses to his acts of crime, the murder of Matang Singh and the rape of Hema's cadaver.

"You can't blackmail me," Kaushal returned the photographs and presented a brave front, "these are trick jobs. You can't prove anything against me."

"You've only two options," Bhagat put the photographs back in the shoulder bag, and placed his right hand on Kaushal's shoulder, "either you come with me or I arrest you."

"You've no proof." Kaushal made a feeble effort to put Bhagat off.

"We've real video reels of all of your black deeds, and your political friends have already viewed these materials. We don't take false steps." Bhagat spoke firmly.

"Don't bluff."

"Well! Police has recovered Hema's body and I've the video footage of her rape and murder by you. Suri is ready to talk."

"I didn't want to kill that stupid girl."

"You mean you loved her."

"May be I loved her. It was an accident. What're you going to do with me?"

"We shall talk. Come along."

"Where are you taking me?"

"The first leg of the journey takes us to Delhi."

"Give me half an hour. I've to meet my mother. Please don't mention anything to her."

"Not at all. But my office has an envelope ready for her, if you don't co-operate."

Bhagat hurled across a tricky threat.

"Don't give her pains. I'm the man you want, and I'm ready to cooperate." Kaushal finally surrendered.

As they climbed down the shaded high ground, Bhagat heard the loud chanting of *mantras* (couplets from scriptures), invoking the Fire God and assorted deities. Amidst thundering applause, Satirani's relations dragged her drugged nimble body to the funeral pyre and forced her to sit on it with the head of Bagaria's cadaver on her lap.

Clad in a bright red sari, profuse red vermilion powder on her forehead and piles of marigold garlands around her neck, Satirani looked like a scared goat, under the butcher's crossbar.

She had reconciled with the inevitable. Amidst frenetic singing, loud drum and cymbal beats and the chanting of *mantras,* a Brahmin handed over a flaming torch to Mangeram's young son. It was the sacred duty of every Hindu son, to light the funeral pyre of his parents. He was fortunate, a *pundit* commented, to perform the last rites of both the parents, a rare opportunity sought after even by the saints and gods. The puzzled kid looked around, threw away the torch, and jumped into the pyre.

Satirani clutched her son firmly to her bosom and jumped out. Some Brahmins snatched the kid away, forced Satirani back on the pyre and lit the fat soaked wooden heap to flames. Yellow flames engulfed the corpse of Bagaria and his drugged wife with a loud bang.

The crowd, estimated at a cool 10,000, went ecstatic in delirious singing and dancing, under the influence of *bhang,* a concoction prepared out of green female marijuana leaves and flowers.

Satirani stopped flinging her limbs about and slumped onto the pyre. Some one from the crowd banged the burning bodies with bamboo rods, a ritual observed by the Hindus, for breaking the skull of the dead.

Bhagat looked on in silence and sighed. There was no use in intervening. The gruel ritual had intoxicated the crowd with human blood and fire, a primitive intoxication inherited through the process of evolution.

The *neem* (margosa) tree in front of Sukhram's *haveli* acted as a good cover for Bhagat. He whispered into Kaushal's ears to hurry back, as he entered the low ornate gate, leading to the inner courtyard. No dirty tricks, he reminded the caged typhoon. The officials of Delhi police had surrounded the house and they wouldn't hesitate to force an entry and accost his mother.

"Spare me the humiliation. My mother won't survive the shock." Kaushal pleaded.

"Just remember, no political skullduggery will help." Bhagat warned.

"You're blackmailing me."

"From now on I am in charge." Bhagat answered coolly.

Kasturi, prevented by her brother, had missed the chance of a lifetime to witness the holy soul of Satirani rising to the heavens, with the spiralling funeral pyre smoke and dust. She stood near the exquisitely carved window, opening on a small balcony and stretched her neck to catch glimpses of the ascending soul of the just burnt divine woman.

"Ma." Ramendra Kaushal meekly stood behind her and spoke in a purring voice.

"Come Ramu," she climbed down the stairs, "feeling hungry?"

"Yes Ma. But I've to leave for Delhi, just now."

Ramendra followed her to the kitchen.

"What's the hurry? You came just two days ago."

She served some sweet made out of grated carrot and condensed milk, fondly called *gajar ka halua.*

"I've got an excellent job offer, a highly paid one."

Kaushal spoke hesitatingly and with evading looks.

"Where? In Delhi?"

"No Ma. It's in *Vilayat* (England). I must report to Delhi tomorrow for the interview."

"I may not be able to meet you frequently. But I'll keep you posted."

He touched her feet in traditional obeisance and locked her in a firm embrace.

"Come home once before you go to *Vilayat.* I must perform a *yagna* (ritual sacrifice). Your father had performed one, before he went to see the King Emperor in England, soon after our marriage."

Kasturi reminisced briefly on the historic sojourn of her late husband, to attend a meeting of the Indian Princes with the King Emperor. That was a memorable journey, accompanied by cooks, valets, and Brahmins. He was forced to perform a penance for undertaking a journey across *kalapani* (high seas), banned for Hindus by the sacred Brahminic dictate.

Kasturi drew Ramendra's head closer, kissed his forehead and blessed him with some dried pieces of flower and green grass picked from offerings to the family deity. For the second time, Kaushal's eyes moistened up and tears rolled down his cheeks. Ramendra Kaushal wiped the teardrops and smiled faintly. His punishment and retribution had probably begun.

He shrugged. "Okay, fine!"

He would face the new life with grit and determination.

The widow of king Digvijay Kaushal raised her folded palms in praise of the Mother Goddess. Her son was sure to restore the family glory. She must convey this to Ramayani. The poor soul should have the pleasure of knowing that her son had really made it big in life, bagging a job in England at such a tender age. He was indeed cast in his father's mould.

That night, leaving an ecstatic Jhunjhunu and his grieving mother behind, Ramendra Kaushal boarded Dhiren Bhagat's car and the wings of an uncertain destiny.

*

8

A sharp buzzer snapped Nampoothiri's trip through memory lane. Dewan, the shadow voice of the Prime Minister, floated in.

"Hi brother, how are things?"

"What's this love chat about?"

"Ma'am has scribbled a note asking for progress of your investigation into the leakage of nuclear secrets."

"Give me a break brother. I'm on the job and don't excite her to take a jab at me."

"No fun dear. She's damn serious. Do something."

"Just wait for a few days, expecting a breakthrough."

Nampoothiri cradled the phone and thoughtfully pondered over the bleak prospects of having a miraculous breakthrough. November 1971 had presented the DINASIA with fantabulous surprises and shocks. His trained and rational thinking process were short-fused by Triple X, Harfan Bukhari's unexpected arrival in Delhi on the wings of blazing bolts. It sent Balachandran Nampoothiri into a spin over the sudden collapse of India's intelligence edifices inside Pakistan. His exclusive niche that had housed the brightest cluster of long-term resident agents in Pakistan had suddenly exploded. It had left Nampoothiri amidst the naked debris of his agency's tradecraft.

The developing war situation did not act as fig leaf to cover up Nampoothiri's woes. Prime Minister Manjira hadn't slackened her tough stand on the alleged leakage of information from yet to be identified 'higher echelons' of the government. Triple X, however, insisted that some whore, dough, and Scotch-loving guy was singing honey in Pakistani ears over India's strategic and nuclear secrets. Nampoothiri could not push the needle of suspicion at Ram Karan Prasad. He was blown to pieces by a mysterious bomb blast only a couple of days ago.

Blanket Mosur and TechInt operations had hit a blind alley. The NSI telephone monitors had given up hope of homing on to the blue moon, the suspect lines, that could lead to the one that sang into Pakistani ears. The targeted diplomats talked about dames, drinks, and distant smell of cordite. These normal telephone transcripts did not worry Nampoothiri. He was worried to the bones about the prospect of facing the PM with an empty platter. Dewan could only be a temporary buffer.

"Sir, can I come in?" Amrita Bhalla's voice chimed on the intercom.

"Yes dear, welcome."

Amrita entered with elegant but excited steps, with a headphone in her hand. She plugged the accessory to an embedded socket and placed it on Nampoothiri's ears.

"What's this?"

"Shh! Please listen first. The boys have hit a gold mine." Amrita took a seat and waited for the call to end.

"Amen, how's the day?" Patrick Goldman, Minister Counsellor in the US embassy, Delhi, whispered on the phone.

"Fine Pat," replied Amen Gurtoo, Principal Secretary to Prime Minister Manjira, "all work, and no fun, no weekend for me. You're damn lucky. What's cooking?"

"You Indians are work slaves and are damn clipped to the empire's gown-frills. Get past it buddy."

"Wish I could. My boss is a tough task master, oops...mistress... sorry, or should I say ma'am." Replied Gurtoo with a light voice and followed by his trademark, a shallow and hollow loud laughter.

"I envy you. You can laugh even at a dead corpse."

"As they say chum, laugh it away and fuck it away." Amen transmitted another volley of laughter over the phone.

"Drop in at my Sheryl Street den. Plenty of laughter and pleasure is waiting for you. Recall Maggie? She's just flown in from Islamabad. This one butterfly is still fabs if she hasn't added more colours from the rainbows and replenished her pod with sylvan nectar."

Goldman sounded extra smooth like 200-year-old Scotch, just salvaged from the depth of the Pacific from a sunken pirate vessel.

"Don't entice me pal. What about Joey?"

Amen cautiously enquired about Goldman's wife, a puritan lady from American Midwest.

"She's back home. Her mother's taken another divorce and plans to marry a Texan tycoon. She's there to celebrate her mom's third nuptial knot." Replied Pat.

"Fine. Expect me around eight." Amen disconnected with a happy chuckle.

"Thank you dear." Nampoothiri sprang back to life, "let's celebrate."

He pressed the buzzer and ordered Jatadhari to concoct two strong cappuccinos.

"How did you get the lead?"

"It's your top floor boy Zapurello Angami. He chanced to hit the line and I just patched it to your table." Amrita smiled back.

"Thanks dear. I must reward that Naga boy. He deserves it." Nampoothiri thought he had earned a celebration. The barren spell was perhaps over, he hoped.

Triple X had brought in damning reports about leakage of India's nuclear secrets and secret battle orders in the western theatre. A verbatim report of the CCSA (Cabinet Committee for Security Affairs) meetings, if Triple X was to be believed, had found its way to the table of the ISI chief.

A teleprinter intercept of the Pakistan High Commission's dedicated link to Islamabad had exploded another bombshell. The Mission had transmitted a copy of an NSI report to the PMO on Pakistani defence preparedness in the eastern sector. Agent Double X had procured the sensitive report, a few days before his death, from a well-placed chameleon in the Chief Martial Law Administrator's office.

Perhaps the Naga boy had picked up a lucky lead.

He lifted the red RAX communicator and dialled Dewan.

"Good evening, friend."

"What good is left of the evening? We've just walked into another war." Dewan replied in his usual jocular voice.

"Some wars are good and inevitable and war is just another form of diplomacy. Don't you fight with your wife when your charms fail you?"

"Well Balu, I'm a bachelor. You should know better. Girlfriends don't fight seriously."

"Curse me." Nampoothiri regretted his forgetfulness and added, "how is the PM placed?"

"Please hurry. She should leave for the President's Palace in another thirty minutes."

*

Manjira was busy in her camp office that was transformed into a war-ops room with maps and charts mounted all over the walls. The Director, Military Operations (DMO), was explaining the battle orders of the Armed Forces, punctuated on the grid maps with flagged pins and markers. What worried her most was the deployment of the ragtag Bengali freedom fighters. The motley-armed volunteers were practically leaderless and divided on ideological lines.

"How are you going to integrate these irregular formations with your regulars?" she asked the DMO.

"We've scattered them with our brigades and battalions deployed all along the borders. I think you'd like to see their linkages and assigned roles." The mustachioed Major General unfolded a sheet map and started explaining the nitty-gritty of deployment of the assorted forces of the *Mukti Bahini* (freedom fighters). Dewan peeped in and rattled his throat.

"Ma'am, Nampoothiri is here."

"I'm busy."

"He says it's important."

She looked up with an uncertain look and finally broke into a faint smile.

"Okay. Make him comfortable. I'm coming."

Nampoothiri explained the importance of the telephone intercept and asked her permission to investigate Amen Gurtoo, her Principal Secretary.

"What's special about this? It can be a social commitment." Manjira shrugged and brushed off her external intelligence chief 's concern.

"That's probable. But ma'am I suspect a classical intelligence sharing protocol between the CIA, ISI and MI6–long standing partners in the strategic security thrust against the USSR and the amorphous ghost of Communism around the globe. They are against our policy towards the Bengali freedom fighters."

"How do you go about nabbing the US intelligence chief in Delhi? The subtleties of diplomacy shouldn't be ignored. The war situation impedes us from adopting hostile stances towards the US."

"We can't trust them. They've been tilting towards Pakistan." Nampoothiri commented.

"I don't care about Washington's tilt," Manjira talked in a contemplative mood, "the US is insensitive to the problems of the largest democracy. They're suffering from Cold War obsession."

"If Washington leans towards Peking, Moscow should tilt towards us." Nampoothiri nodded in agreement.

"Leave that to me. You talk of matters inside Pakistan. I don't want an intelligence blackout there."

"Yes ma'am." Nampoothiri repeated monotonously.

"What about your guests from Pakistan? Have you started debriefing them?" Manjira hinted at Harfan Bukhari and Vudurume, the South African pilot.

"Your orders are awaited."

"Let me have a precise account of the weapon systems airlifted by the mercenary flights. It's urgent. And let me have an assessment of the damage suffered by your agency in Pakistan."

"The guests are cooperative. The South African pilot has spelt out precise details of some of the flights and I expect Triple X to come out with more sensitive disclosures."

"Fine. Go ahead." Manjira stood up and gestured moving towards her ops room.

"Do I investigate Amen?"

Manjira turned back, collected her thoughts for a few seconds, and gave a silent nod of affirmation.

Nampoothiri felt relaxed after the satisfying encounter with the PM. The nod from her had cleared the decks for a thorough interrogation of Triple X. Moreover, investigating Amen Gurtoo's links with the diplomatic Mission based intelligence officers should pose no great problem. The CIA station chief was too well recorded a client in the NSI's honour roll.

Amen wasn't a wayside urchin or a two-penny informer to be picked up for interrogation by the NSI agents. His 360-degree linkages inside the cocoon called India, infested with corrupt politicians, barons of industry, top-notch bureaucrats and media sharks had empowered Amen to spin around the entire intelligence bureaucracy. They survived on his mercy.

He could even wish away, by a single scratch of his pen, the Mount Everest from the geological map. Turning the black into white and the white into black were mere wish games for the top Indian bureaucrats, otherwise known as Permanent Government.

Nampoothiri's dilemma didn't end there. His men could mount covert Mosur operation on Amen and trace his movements to the doors of Patrick Goldman. That wouldn't prove anything. A whale of his stature could swim in any water. Accepting invitations from diplomatic Missions, provided the country wasn't listed unfriendly, was his privilege. An open meeting couldn't be construed as clandestine.

The mere clandestine nature of a meeting could also not be used to nail the coffin of a powerful bureaucrat. It required smoking gun evidence. That called for the elaborate use of Electronic Intelligence (ElInt), clandestine photo, and voice documentation. These evidences couldn't be produced by any Indian rope trick. It required a well-researched application of intelligence tradecraft.

That is what Nampoothiri thought he should go for. The short briefing session in his room was a snappy affair.

"Remember," he finally warned, "I demand the sky. You've got to fetch it. But we're dealing with an undercover US diplomat and the Principal Secretary to the PM. I'm keen, but I don't want any messing around. Is it clear?"

"It's a very difficult job sir." Robin Achariya pleaded.

"You don't have to remind me dear," snapped Nampoothiri, "it's a gamble. And gambling is a part of our job, and while gambling, I make sure that I hold the right cards," He snubbed Achariya.

"We attempt a break in." Suggested Dhiren Bhagat.

"Can't we go for parallel line tapping?"

"No sir. The US embassy phones are auto-scrambler equipped. We can use radio bug if the house is available for two hours."

"A good approach indeed. I can't assure you that luxury. What do we do?" Nampoothiri called in Jatadhari and ordered coffee. Jatadhari stepped in with a red folder. The red colour indicated that the subject matter required immediate attention.

Nampoothiri unfolded the cover and glanced through the contents. A faint smile passed across his face. He handed back the file to Jatadhari and asked him to talk to Amrita.

"Well gentleman! The meeting is over. Bhagat stay put."

"Sir, we'd give a try. I can't assure results. I also take your permission to abort the operation, in case of threatened exposure."

Bhagat, now a Senior Operations Officer, spoke with a tone of finality. He didn't leave any option open for the boss.

The guts of this officer as usual, amazed Nampoothiri.

"I appreciate that," Nampoothiri said, "but see that you deliver the goods. For your information Goldman's house will be available for one full day and your chance is day after tomorrow."

"That's a good break, sir."

"Try your luck. Don't litter the place with dirt."

Bhagat left after offering a smart salute. The shape of the operation was cooking inside his mind and he wanted to give final touches in consultation with the Dreamland boys. Nampoothiri summoned Amrita and instructed her to connect the Calcutta based NSI officer Vishram Satpore. Patrick Goldman and 20 other foreign diplomats were allowed by the Ministry of External Affairs to visit the India-Pakistan borders in the eastern sector. They were scheduled to visit a couple of refugee camps occupied by millions of East Pakistani nationals, who fled the bayonets and bullets of the Pak army. It was a godsend opportunity. He felt comfortable that Dhiren Bhagat would be able to utilise the spare 24 hours to implant the delicate bugs at the Sheryl Street home of the CIA station chief.

*

Dhiren Bhagat and his assistant, clad in ordinary clothes, carrying two slim imported telephone instruments, wires and tools, appeared in front of the well-secured Sheryl Street residence of Goldman.

"Who're you, guys?" Asked the Marine sentry.

"We've been directed to immediately repair the telephones of the Ambassador sahib." Bhagat replied.

"Nope. We haven't complained." The Marine scowled.

"Why don't you call the Chancery sahib? He called us."

The caretaker, an all-season domestic from Goa, confirmed that there was indeed a call from the Head of the Chancery to allow Indian staff to repair the lines. These had gone dead since morning after a speeding taxi hit a junction box.

Bhagat had played the neat tricks. A taxi belonging to his unit had hit the junction box and he had induced the telephone exchange supervisor to disconnect Goldman's residence lines for at least four hours. His next stop was a public call office. Introducing himself as a member of a breakaway faction of the Bangladesh Government in exile, he called the embassy front desk.

How could he reach Mr. Patrick's residence telephones, which appeared to have gone dead? He had come all the way from Calcutta to meet the *burra* (big) sahib. They were, he said, opposed to Sheikh Jainal and wanted a dialogue with Islamabad. The Chancery officials swallowed the bait and requested the telecom supervisor for speedy restoration of the lines.

The layout inside of the house wasn't familiar. Nevertheless, Bhagat, using common sense, asked the accompanying technical hand, to install a radio microphone inside the drawing room phone. The radio-microphone would keep transmitting signals at a pre-fixed frequency, until detected by anti-bugging operations.

The second radio microphone was planted, with two weeks power supply from tiny nickel cadmium batteries, behind the family portrait, hung over the master bed. A television camera, capable of transmitting images to a distant listening post complimented this equipment.

The operation took just about thirty minutes. Bhagat moved around the house with prayers on his lips and ticking mini-explosions inside the neurons. Anything going wrong would mean his dismissal from service and even imprisonment. His prayers were answered. The technical operation was a marvellous copybook success. The snooping electronic van, with a telephone department sticker, ostensibly on emergency duty, was parked two blocks away behind a telephone junction box. Bhagat and colleagues merrily recorded the audio and video signals from the implanted equipment.

*

Bhagat was happy. So was Nampoothiri. Quality of the audio and video intercepts was superb. Voices of Amen Gurtoo, Patrick Goldman and their common sex partner Maggie, Margaret Rose in real life, came in booming with shrieks of orgasm. The video images didn't leave anything to imagination.

Maggie was moulded in the tradition of the fair skin beauties shipped from *Vilayat* (abroad) for entertaining hungry soldiers of the East India Company, camping in makeshift cantonments, behind the Red Fort ramparts. Maggie, however, was one of the jet-setting pleasure objects, used for honey traps by the CIA, in stations like India, where fairer skins were worshipped as descendants of the fairies of the court of *Indra* (king of the gods).

The recorded dialogues were illuminating.

"Your NSI chief is a bloody gunk. The bastard talks for hours but doesn't reveal anything." Pat complained.

"Keep away from him. He's a bloody sucker. Never trust a Nampoothiri. In Kerala they're called snakes." Amen was more than charitable to the NSI chief.

"Yah. The bastard is an eel. No bait is good enough to hook him." Pat talked in a frustrating voice.

"Ever tried this fellow Ahooja, Kumar Anand's replacement in the FIB?" Amen suggested, "he should be useful."

"Well, gim'me an intro, call him over for lunch." Pat replied indifferently.

"Look Amen, Washington is keen to know about your nuclear programme. We're worried about Sikkim as well. How can she annex the protectorate? And what the hell is your PM trying to achieve in East Pakistan? Does she want to make it another Bhutan?" Pat sounded desperate.

"Your concerns are India's prime national policies. Moreover, you haven't told me anything about my sons. You had promised them scholarships at Harvard. They're rotting in Delhi. My daughter in Boston hasn't yet got her green card, and I'm short of money." Lamented Amen Gurtoo.

"Don't lose your pants. Consider my position. Washington has been pestering for details of India's nuclear programme and military build up. Tell me, how I can convince my people over there! It's after all a give and take game." Patrick built up pressure on Amen.

He broadly hinted at releasing some photographs.

Amen protested loudly.

"You can't do that. That'll ruin me." He implored.

"I too face peril Amen. Help me! I assure scholarship for your sons and green card for your daughter, within the next seven days," Pat paused, "and in another seven days we shall put your dough in your escrow account in the Bahamas. You cooperate, and things will be sugar and honey. I believe you're retiring next July. I won't fail to sound Washington out to fix up an assignment for you, may be with the World Bank or the UN secretariat."

The magic words electrified Amen. Employment with the World Bank was the ultimate dream of an Indian bureaucrat. He could do anything, minus fucking his mother, for that plum assignment. A veritable barrage of classified information burst forth from Amen.

For the next half an hour, he spoke non-stop, on the approximate timing of the possible atomic implosion and the blueprint for annexation of Sikkim. The grand lady was working on a set agenda and very few people had access to her mind. No. She had no agenda to annex Bangladesh. Her intention was to install Sheikh Jainal in Dacca. In East Pakistan she was busy cooking the goose of General Arif Khan, the Chief Martial Law Administrator and President. She was determined to Balkanise Pakistan by creating simultaneous unrest in Sind and Baluchistan.

Maggie's sound track came in superb in the videotape.

"Amen, you've been great," intoned Maggie's salacious voice, "when shall we meet next?"

"Any time you wish dear," Amen Gurtoo replied, "when are you back to the States?"

"I take a Pan Am flight in another four hours. Anything I can do for you?"

"I want to send $ 5000 to my daughter. You know the bloody hassles the Indian Reserve Bank creates. Forget the trouble. There's hardly any time."

"Don't fuss," Pat's voice came in dearly, "the bucks will be delivered and adjusted against your account. Give me the nuclear documents tomorrow at the golf turf. Don't forget the details of troop and armour deployments along the Pak borders, and the proceedings of last night's meeting of the CCSA. My diplomatic bag takes off tomorrow at 7 p.m."

*

Nampoothiri was more than pleased. On this rare occasion, he didn't insist on the retrieval of the electronic implants from Goldman's diplomatic den. CIA's sweeping operations were sure to detect these gadgets. The Mission chief was sure to lodge a routine demarche with the Joint Secretary, America Division. He had, in his thirty years with the spooky agency, mastered the art of deflecting such diplomatic protests with fudgy and incomprehensible notes. He wasn't in a mood to spoil this fine moment of victory and breakthrough.

He called Dewan around ten thirty p.m.

"Has the PM gone to bed?"

"Not yet."

"Should I come in now?"

"Is it urgent?"

"Yes, It can't really wait."

"Okay. Come in, right away."

Nampoothiri spent the next four hours with Manjira, playing audiotapes, and explaining the positives of clandestine photographs and other supporting reports. She had declined to view the videotapes, for reasons Nampoothiri understood well. After two hundred and forty minutes, Manjira leaned back on her chair, cupped her chins between the palms, and shot the first question at him.

"Are you sure there's no mistake?"

"I would be the happiest person if these were wrong ma'am," Nampoothiri spoke in a straight voice, "these are hard technical evidences; can't be ignored."

"What do you suggest?"

"I'm sure Gurtoo is the source of leakage. He should be taken out from your secretariat. My boys are about to locate and identify the suspected Pakistani moles inside our atomic establishments. And you may like to reorient our strategies in Sikkim and East Pakistan."

"The arrows can't be rolled back Nampoothiri. The nemesis is bound to strike Pakistan, may be Dacca first and Karachi and Quetta later. But, tell me what do I do with Amen?" Manjira spoke in a visibly distressed voice.

"I don't recommend any action under the Official Secrets Act. That would compromise your position. But I must share with you that Goldman has a direct line to the ISI station chief in Delhi."

"How come?"

"It cuts both ways. The link can be personal as well as at the agency level. The CIA has a well-oiled intelligence sharing protocol with the ISI."

"So where do we stand? You mean Islamabad will have all the dope on our nuclear secrets and war preparations."

"It's a natural conclusion. In fact, my boys have followed up leads given by Triple X, and they're on the trail of a major suspected ISI agent. I may soon have better news for you." Nampoothiri spoke with great relish as he watched the panicky movements of the PM's eyeballs.

"So where do we dump this idiot Gurtoo?"

"Perhaps you may consider giving him a diplomatic assignment, at a station, where he can't interact with his US friends."

"What about Mongolia?"

"That's a nice wilderness."

"I don't want any publicity. You take care of all the nitty gritty."

"Yes ma'am."

"Okay Nampoothiri, take care of the damages done by Amen." The PM wished her NSI chief out.

"It's a pleasure ma'am." Nampoothiri bowed profusely and left with a rare sense of satisfaction.

*

9

"Well friend," Nampoothiri tossed a coconut cookie into his mouth and spoke in a choked voice, "these are really nice."

He applied the old intelligence methodology of pumping out actionable intelligence and initiate hot pursuit action.

"Why talk to your lost baggage? You said you never claim."

Triple X refused to take cognisance of the stray dialogue. Kaushal wilted his lips and broke into a mild laughter.

"That's a cliché. Not to be taken literally. Are you laughing at the nice cookies, or at me?" Nampoothiri spoke with contrived hurt in his voice.

"Neither," Kaushal turned back from the window, "I've given you all that I had in store. Can I now go home to Jhunjhunu with my wife and kid?"

"Not yet dear. We're in the midst of hostility and the ISI won't spare any effort to locate and neutralise you."

"I can take care of them, at least on my own turf."

"Don't underestimate their reach. I don't think ISI will spare an Indian agent who has frustrated their designs. They can get at your wife and child."

"Jhunjhunu is a small place."

"No place is big enough to hide a twister like you," Nampoothiri stood up and walked down to the window, "the PM has congratulated you on the Amen Gurtoo catch. Now tell me something about the ISI plants in our nuclear establishments."

"Are you interrogating me?"

"Can't we talk minus the hiccups of your imaginary complaints?"

"My complaints are genuine. Alam and you condemned me."

"What happened to Alam?"

"No idea. Had no physical contact for over fifteen days."

"Fine. We'd talk later.Tell me about Ibadat's info on nuclear espionage. At least honour your dead friend, if not me."

"Have you checked at Jam Salaya near Jamnagar, Gujarat, and Dahisar in Maharashtra?" Harfan softened a little bit.

"No. What for?"

"The ISI often operate through the sea route for reaching India's nuclear installations in Bombay and Rajasthan."

"More details please."

"Sorry. Haven't any. All that I know is about the existence of a veteran ISI resident agent who has penetrated India's nuclear establishments. Ibadat had the details."

"He's dead." Nampoothiri spoke in exasperation.

"Sorry sir. I can only add that Dahisar is an important point of ISI operation. Ibadat had access to this channel of Pakistani operation and I had relayed this in my dispatches," Kaushal shrugged and lighted a cigarette.

"How do I get about at Dahisar?"

"Don't kid sir. You're the boss and you can monitor any phone you like. Isn't that correct?"

"Don't talk silly."

"Anyways, it's your baby. What are you doing with Vudurume?" He spoke about the mercenary pilot of South African origin, who had diverted the weapon laden Dacca bound Boeing 707 to Delhi and saved India from the catastrophe of chemical warfare by Pakistan.

"Don't worry. He'll be back home safe."

"Can I see him again?"

"No man. It's not done," Nampoothiri lighted his favourite Havana, "now tell me what should I do with this riddle?"

"Which one?"

"The nuclear installations."

"Merry hell! Scan the Muslim fishing community. Visiting birds nest in friendly coves." Kaushal glanced at Dhiren Bhagat and winked with a naughty twist.

Nampoothiri threw up his hands. The rogue was giving broad ideas, but not clear leads.

Well! He was, it appeared, a pawn in the hands of dame luck. He said goodbye to Kaushal. The fourth round of debriefing Triple X in an NSI guesthouse, where the agent and his wife and child were housed, proved frustrating.

"Well Bhagat," Nampoothiri shrugged, "try your luck with the inscrutable fellow. Try to get more dope on the fishing community. I know he knows a lot."

He left Ramendra Kaushal with Dhiren Bhagat for another spell of debriefing, especially on the yet unveiled mysteries of assassination of agent Alamgir and Double X at Bhagtanwala airbase.

*

The modular intelligence posts in the coastal areas of Maharashtra, Rajasthan and Gujarat had reactivated the sedimented, sloppy and sluggish units under repeated pressure from Nampoothiri. Rumour collectors fared better than these routine creatures flying tattered flags in strategic locations. The real break came from a chance observation at a non-family station in Rajasthan desert.

Sanchor, a desert station on the Indo-Pak border in Rajasthan, was an important strategic intelligence post with sub-zero temperature in winter and 50 plus Celsius in summer. However, the November ground frosts were heated up by war hysteria. Indian and Pakistani troops were holed up in eyeball-to-eyeball position inside sandy trenches.

Abhi Meena, a junior intelligence officer, had tuned his radio to the *ghazals* (sub-continental compositions) and film tunes broadcast by Radio Pakistan. His mind was elsewhere, busy dreaming of his wife's tender face, left at his village, just after fifteen days of their marriage.

The Pakistani announcer closed down with the usual *Khuda Hafiz* and *Pakistan Paindabad* greetings. Stratospheric noises crackled and disturbed Meena's dream. As he extended his fingers to switch off the set, a female voice came in from the same frequency.

"Majnu, Majnu, Majnu.... Meet Laila at Oasis20.... Meet Laila at Oasis20." She repeated the Urdu sentence thrice and went off the air.

Abhi Meena, a fresh product from NSI's training institute, brushed aside the lingering mists of his wife's contour and scribbled down the time, frequency and name of the station and the exact wordings of the mysterious broadcast. Next morning he transmitted a cipher to Delhi.

Meena's cipher gathered dust on Robin Achariya's table. He hurled a few of the choicest appellatives at the tribal officer at Sanchor and scribbled his valuable comments: *hallucination, the officer requires screwing up.*

Abhi Meena wasn't the lone listener to the silvery lovelorn voice calling for Majnu. In next three days, Achariya received four additional inputs. He finally sat up. Here was something intriguing. The distressed Laila was still wailing for Majnu.

"You've nearly damaged a wonderful lead," Nampoothiri shuffled the pages brought up by Achariya, "it must be the ISI, homing in for a specific agent."

"Why should they use an open radio frequency?"

"That's the easiest way of communication. The fellow must be somewhere in the arch area of reception of medium-wave signals from Radio Pakistan's Hyderabad station." Nampoothiri pointed his finger on a grid map of the Indo-Pakistan border and broadly indicated the arch of reception.

"So dear, as I was saying, that lady is no Laila calling her lover Majnu. She's conveying a message to an agent, with whom regular communication channels has snapped. This is a time-tested means of clandestine communication. We don't know the location of Oasis20. Get cracking."

"How do we go about it sir?" Achariya finally realised that his indiscretion had created a piquant situation.

Nampoothiri stood up, slowly walked down to the one and only window, and lighted a Havana. He opened it and looked down at the buzzing traffic below. A thought suddenly flashed past his mind.

"Cross check with the inputs I've shared with you. Study the hand drawn sketch. These were from a delicate source. Check with the FIB units in the arch area. Scan all the listed and active counter-intelligence suspects. Order blanket surveillance. Arrange local monitoring of phones at BARC location, Dahisar and a few other places in and around Ahmedabad, Surat, Rajkot and Bhuj. Don't neglect Jodhpur, Bikaner and Jaisalmer. If I'm correct some Majnu will try to contact his Laila."

"That's a vast arch."

"Yes. You're dealing with an efficient enemy intelligence agency Robin. Stop pissing in pants. Get cracking and now."

Nampoothiri almost shouted at his junior.

*

Nampoothiri's flash thought was corroborated by a piece of puzzle from Jodhpur field unit of the NSI. Security and counterintelligence suspect Mahesh Dube, fronting a grocery outlet at Central Road, Jodhpur Air force Cantonment, was mysteriously absent for over ten days. He was listed as a counterintelligence suspect, as he remained absent from his shop very frequently. Scrutiny of his records surprised Achariya.

Mahesh had appeared at Jodhour six years ago, married the daughter of a sweeper, and settled down with a grocery shop in the midst of the sweeper colony. His wife Phulan reported the missing report to police and the matter rested there.

However, a clever break in and scrounging of the shack of Mahesh and his wife Phulan produced a few pieces of paper with Urdu scribbling and some coded digits. Maulana Rizwan, the official Urdu specialist, deciphered the riddle. It contained the name of one Qamar, Gali Suiwalan, Jama Masjid, Delhi, and a Lahore phone number: 912 3089.

Qamar Ahmed had already found his way into the glorious gallery of the NSI. A visa agent by profession, he was listed as a forged passport and visa peddler and a well-connected linkman of the Bombay and Calcutta underworld dons. His reputation as a *hawala* operator had not gone unnoticed by the winking eyes and indulgent nods of the area policemen.

Junior consular officials of the Pakistan High Commission, who frequented his walled city den ostensibly for offering Friday prayers at the historic Jama Masjid, had befriended Qamar. He operated a mini brothel. Patronised by the Pakistan High Commission based intelligence officials, the shady joint acted as a fertile conduit for identifying and cultivating Indian targets. Qamar was a valuable local recruiting agent and a SAAD, Safe Accommodation Address, of the Pakistani intelligence operators in Delhi.

Nampoothiri's Mosurs tracked down Qamar and Bhagat's boys didn't take time to put the heat on. A taxi car, positioned at the fifth crossroad end of the Pakistan Mission's rear exit, observed Qamar peeping out of the High Commission around 8 p.m.

He walked into the trap only to be blindfolded and driven to the Madangir village safe house of the NSI. Two night's interrogation with scientific and unscientific tricks broke down his resistance.

Yes. Qamar knew Mahesh alias Safi Indrabi, a Pakistani smuggler, who had entered India through Jam Salaya sea route and was his houseguest for two weeks. He had accommodated Safi at the behest of Jamal Khatak, a consular officer in the High Commission.

Safi, Qamar revealed, had gone to Bombay to meet a fellow smuggler, Sikander Tandel, a fishing magnate at the sleepy minor port of Chiuchani, next to Tarapur, India's premier nuclear base.

At 3 a.m. sharp next morning, Robin Achariya's team swooped on the house of Sikander Tandel. Safi Indrabi, busy with a cosy woman, didn't get time to draw the pistol from under his pillow. Flown to Delhi in a special flight of Kalyani Air Lines Safi Indrabi was dumped in the dreaded interrogation centre.

Safi Indrabi's curricula vitae sounded impressive. A Signal Corps Major, seconded to the ISI, he was housed in India way back in 1968. His network in Rajasthan, Delhi, and Bombay had drilled gaping holes in India's security armours.

He was trained to absorb pain. He remained lock-jawed for two nights, but scientific application of exotic treatment breached the embankments of training. A clinching trick was used on the third night, by passing a miniature electrode through his anus, releasing a 220-volt charge in minuscule bursts. The frontiers of his training collapsed and he agreed to cooperate.

Given a bath, food and cigarette, Safi talked on the Lahore number: 912 3089.

"Majnu here, I got your message General," Safi talked to his boss in the Inter Services Intelligence, "I was away to target Buland."

It was a reference to Tarapur nuclear facility.

"*Rabba Khair* (let Allah help you). You bastard really scared me. Are you whoring around? Why were you silent for all these days?"

Major General Barqat Khan, in charge of Joint Intelligence Miscellaneous' India Operations Division, often referred as 'S' Division spoke loud and clear.

"Sorry boss," Safi replied, "first of all congrats for your promotion. The job had taken me to Buland."

"We called you thrice. Note down, next calls will be on Sundays from Multan station, 1430 kHz, at 23.50. What's the programme? When are they performing the marriage?"

"*Sagai pakki* (engagement ceremony is confirmed). But, the bride's father is yet to give the final nod." Indrabi replied, indicating the uncertain status of Indian preparedness with the intended weapons-grade nuclear enrichment. His contact in the Tarapur plant, a senior engineer, connected with the preparations, had indicated that India's programme had run into some problem. India was ready, but Delhi suspected some sniffing around by Washington.

"The Chinese say Delhi is ready for the big bang." Barqat lost his cool.

"Sorry boss, this is my precise finding. They'll wait for the war to be over. They don't want to provoke Washington on this sensitive front. Listen, I want more money for my Buland contact."

"Are you fucking around? Do you know what happened here? The NSI had run a riot in Pakistan. Our best friend Alam Khan is killed by Indian commandos and that bloody Harfanmaula has hijacked our plane and merchandise to India."

"Sorry boss. No publicity here. Boss, things are costly, even fucking has become costlier. And I had to pay my boys in the Punjab and Rajasthan borders."

Indrabi looked up at the pistol in Bhagat's hand.

"My friend here wants a fat amount for the drawings of the Kota nuclear power plant."

"Okay. You contact shop no. 106 at Meena Bazar, Jama Masjid. He'll pay whatever you require. The code word is *ILLAHI*. Call back soon. Listen," Barqat continued, "activate your Delhi friends, and ascertain details about one of our chartered flights, which landed there with important loads."

"There hasn't been much in the Indian media boss."

"Fuck the media. Ask your friends to burrow deep and get the details. We'll like you to locate and extinguish that fellow Harfan Bukhari. He may have a fucking Hindu name as well. Locate that South African pilot too. We need silencing him. We want them dead. Money's no problem. Understand?" General Barqat sounded vicious on the line.

"Got you sir. Please wait for three days." Indrabi replied from a text scribbled by Bhagat.

"Can't wait indefinitely. You're authorised to spend Rs. five million for the head of Harfan. Quick, we're at war with the infidels."

"Yes boss. Shall try my best."

"Don't get involved. Use hired butchers."

"Okay boss. Before I finish can I congratulate you again for your promotion?" Indrabi referred to Brigadier Barqat's elevation to the rank of Major General.

"Thanks buddy. Your promotion is overdue. Complete the mission and you're a Colonel."

"Thanks boss."

*

Nampoothiri's post-operation briefings on Indrabi affair fascinated Prime Minister Manjira.

"It's a puzzling game. You intelligence people are really crooked. It means Amen played havoc with our national secrets. We'd require some course correction," commented Manjira, "I'd take care of that. But Pakistan's nuclear quest worries me. Your Triple X had been consistently reporting about their frenetic efforts to borrow nuclear know-how."

"That's correct ma'am," Nampoothiri added.

"Now that Triple X is out of commission and you've suffered other losses, how do you propose to revitalise the system?" She asked her NSI chief.

"Asset creation process is slow ma'am," Nampoothiri replied, "we'll take at least another five years, if we're lucky, to regain the desired level of penetration."

"I suggest you accelerate your operations in Sind and Baluchistan. How are your friends Sartaj Jamil, Mengel and Mazari responding?"

"Their responses are satisfactory ma'am. But we are yet to achieve Lotus like penetration."

Nampoothiri elaborated his operational mechanism in the provinces of Sind and Baluchistan. Pakistan, he explained, had blunted Indian efforts of pushing weapons to the Sind rebels through the sea route. The Kabul, Kandahar and Mazar-e-Sharif routes used for pumping weapons to Baluch and NWFP tribal groups had achieved limited success. Absence of Alamgir, he apprehended, could dry up the USSR-Afghanistan pipeline.

"It's now your headache Balu. All that I want is Islamabad's preoccupation with its internal affairs. Mobilise all your X agents and get going."

Nampoothiri walked out of the PM house a worried man. The tantalising success in neutralising the double forked Pakistani thrust, involving Amen Gurtoo and Major Indrabi had redeemed some lost prestige. This small breather could be used to build up new assets. However, he was painfully aware of the impatient nature of the Prime Minister.

Nampoothiri delved back into his hidden neuron tissues, like a fond father with hidden weakness for a boisterous son. Tender thoughts overwhelmed his cautious and disciplined emotions. This young twister, Harfan Bukhari alias Ramendra Kaushal was indeed a loveable scoundrel. He hadn't come across a stormier agent in the 35 years of his intelligence career.

Now that the PM had given the clearance, his team would get cracking on interrogating the guests. He expected Triple X to come out clean. He was a patriot, and Nampoothiri hoped he would help the company to reassess and reorient operational modalities inside Pakistan. This one surviving link could help the NSI build anew on the past wreckage. Perhaps a time had come to recast the fundamentals of operational science and art. Contradictions inside the Pakistani Establishment could be exploited, like his agency had done with Operation Lotus in East Pakistan. Pakistan would not have the same geographical and ideological shape after the Lotus bloomed fully.

An independent Bangladesh was a near reality.

What fault lines could he exploit in the post-war scenario? Tap the Sindhis? Incite the Seraikis? Provoke the Pakhtoons? Arm the Baluchis? Exploit the Baltistanis? Turn the Afghans against Islamabad? How would the USA react to India's accelerated intelligence thrusts inside Pakistan? Should the Israelis be roped in?

Anyways, this fellow Harfan should be a gold mine for reorienting strategic and tactical approaches. He had been deep inside the system and could provide rare insight into the functioning of the ISI. Nampoothiri felt happy that his earlier deactivation order hadn't destroyed this valuable operation. Triple X enjoyed the proverbial nine lives, which a spy of his standing could seldom claim. He was turbulent from day one, Nampoothiri mused, but a likeable rascal.

He enjoyed the thrill of recruiting and training this asset. He was often outpaced by his fast and furious penetration inside the Pakistani Establishment. Now he was mystified by his daring escape from the clutches of the Inter Services Intelligence. Harfan Bukhari was indeed a fascinating asset, all the way superbly fascinating.

"Sir," Amrita Bhalla's voice flowed down the intercom, "you've a meeting with the high-powered delegation of the Government of Bangladesh in Exile at 10.30. You've just two hours left. You'd sure like to have a briefing from the desk officer. Wouldn't you?"

"Come in dear," Nampoothiri invited his secretary with an expansive voice, "let's have a small private celebration."

"What for sir?"

"I'm happy that I'm again right and wrong. Right, because the Lotus is blooming soon. Wrong, because I've been proved wrong. Have a seat and share my thoughts and pleasure." He ordered Jatadhari to concoct a strong coffee. Nampoothiri looked back fondly, intermittently chatting with Amrita and reminiscing over the stormy Operation Triple X episode.

This was the time for selecting the right seeds for sowing in the post-war fertile Pakistani soil. He hoped he would be able to exploit the November woes of Pakistan and expected Triple X to lead him through the right furrows.

"You know dear, it has been really a unique experience, recruiting and training that rascal."

"You love him sir."

"I don't know, there must be a rascal in me too. But he defies most tricks of the trade. He's really a freeborn creature. I'm happy he's free again. I'm happy that I've been proved wrong. Some spies do have nine lives."

Nampoothiri allowed himself to pleasantly surfing over the waves of his memory, waves that churned out Harfan Bukhari, Agent Triple X, out of a violent typhoon called Prince Ramendra Kaushal.

*

10

February 13, 1965.

The Second World War vintage DC3, operated by Kalyani Air Lines, a sleek cover for the air-wing of the Federal Intelligence Bureau's Special Aviation Force (SAF), circled over Sirsa airstrip nearly for 30 minutes, amidst a blinding sandstorm. The fuselage of the old warhorse rattled ominously. The landing approach to the sparsely used dirt-runway had simply vanished from the horizon. Dust haze had narrowed down visibility to a miserly 200 meters.

The pilot finally lowered the elevators, levelled the nose, and touched down almost at the end-edges of the strip. He applied emergency brakes and brought it to stationary position, at the farthest corner of the runway, overlooking some tented accommodation. The tented tactical HQ of the Second Infantry Division had sprung up a few days ago, in response to Pakistani incursions in Kachchh.

The DC3, however, wasn't braving the desert storm on any military mission. The Kalyani Air Lines generally flew air reconnaissance sorties deep inside Pakistan and China. It was sparsely used in a support-role for training, deployment and transportation of the Special Volunteer Force (SVF), a super secret security adjunct of the FIB, raised after India's China-war debacle.

The Dakota wasn't on SVF operation either. The sturdy bird dared the desert storm to accomplish a special assignment. It carried Ramendra Kaushal, blindfolded and hands tied at his back, escorted by Dhiren Bhagat and two armed officers in plainclothes. Their destination was a dilapidated fort, located behind a garland of undulated mounds and remnants of broken stone and mud walls. Locally referred to as the fort of Maharaja Agrasen, the structure was an archaeological fossil.

Agrasen, a *baniya* (businessman) by caste, had strangely opted for the sword, contrary to the historical practices of his ilk, which recognised better the wheels of money, rather than the wheels of canon carts. Fired by rare sparks of nationalism he had quit his moneybag at an uncertain period of Delhi's troubled and tortuous political history. He had carved out a short lived but glorious Hindu interlude.

The British, during the Second World War, used the abandoned fort of Maharaja Agrasen as a makeshift rest house for their senior officers.

Sirsa, located on the important artery between Delhi and the Indian North West, had witnessed the advances and retreats of many armies which descended on Hindustan in search of gold and manna, right from the Aryans to the Mughals. To the British Sirsa was a launching pad for the defences of the vital North West Frontiers, against the Afghan bandits, Tsarist Russia, and its Bolshevik successors.

Rabindra Narayan Dutta had simply taken over the property from Punjab administration, ignoring objections from the Archaeological Survey of India. To him the perpetuation of the memory of a *baniya* king was less important than running a special centre for training his agents in dirty tricks. The Sirsa School of Black Arts was a feared and dreaded training centre that didn't exist on FIB records.

Located in the midst of desert wilderness, Agrasen's fort wasn't even connected by a tarred road. Two high frequency trans-receivers operating at fixed schedules maintained bare minimum communications with Delhi.

Six underground rooms with modern facilities of civilised living were constructed a few years ago, well below the ramshackle surface and dilapidated façade. The undulating sand dunes, scrubs, and bushes provided a natural camouflage to the super-secret edifice. Karam Chand Pathania, a living legend in the FIB, had rooted himself well, in the hostile environment of the desert fort, like succulent cacti. An indestructible life force, he could root himself anywhere. A seemingly ageless person, with a head full of white hair and a dyed jet black moustache, Pathania stood six feet three inches on his bare soles. His muscular body defied the laws of ageing in his 68 eventful summers and springs. Pathania was the master of the place, training FIB's top agents, in the dirty tricks of intelligence tradecraft.

Pathania, retired First World War veteran, a Pathania had seen action in the Italian and French fronts and had picked up the coveted Victoria Cross. The Imperial FIB (IFIB) groomed him as an intelligence operative after the guns fell silent. He had served for years behind the forbidden walls of the Potala Palace, the holy seat of the Dalai Lama, running intelligence network aimed at the heartland of China. Tibet, in British perception, was a geographical and political cushion between its sprawling empire in India and the Russian Red Bear and the inscrutable Yellow Panda.

Pathania had raised and trained *FORCE TURAG* (horse), a formidable Tibetan commando force, following a silent tripartite agreement between London, Delhi, and Lhasa. But Dalai Lama's flight to India had cut short the adventures of the Lawrence of Potala, the nickname Pathania had earned for his daredevil forays against Chinese incursions in Tibet.

An innovative bulldog, Pathania was moulded into a ruthless trainer by the British SAS and the Airborne US Army Special Forces Group. He specialised in training agents in the classified crafts of stealing information from foreign territories, and carrying out acts of sabotage and subversion. Some of his creations were often endowed with the extralegal power to kill, in special circumstances, for protecting vital national interests. Pathania had mastered the art and science of silent assassination as a tool for promoting the progress of special agents inside and outside the national borders. Very few officers in the FIB were aware of his other acronym: *the butcher*.

*

Ramendra Kaushal was consigned to Pathania's underground hole for intensive tradecraft training, recasting, and remoulding his personality. His psyche required thorough scrubbing and removal of layers of scum and dirt, before he could be tailored for Triple X operations inside Pakistan.

"Where are you taking me? Why don't you remove blinds from my eyes?" Muttered Kaushal.

"We're on a picnic trip. You'll be free soon." Bhagat reassured his catch. From a mere talent spotter, he had graduated to being the case officer of Operation Triple X.

"You can't do this to me. My people in Delhi won't spare you. Let me talk to minister Ram Karan Prasad. He'll clarify everything." Ramendra Kaushal pleaded and threatened.

"You'll have chance to reevaluate Ram Karan. Now get into the jeep." Bhagat sounded sweet but stern.

The dusty road to the fort wasn't visible. It happened in Sirsa and adjacent areas. Drifting sand from adjoining deserts usually buried the road beyond recognition and negotiation.

However, driver Nafar Singh was a field bandicoot of the terrain. He sniffed out the route and guided the jeep immaculately to the foreground of the palace ruin, still guarded by two stone *Yakshinis* (female celestial beings) with two massive maces in their hands. High above the *Yakshinis*, glimpses of a dilapidated fresco of the Sun God driving a chariot, powered by seven multi-coloured horses was still discernible to curious eyes.

Karam Chand Pathania, seated on a cane chair, stood up, body rigid and erect, as Bhagat and the team entered the room. The cool air inside the dilapidated edifice, just after the scorching desert heat outside sent shivers of chill under Kaushal's skin. He still groped in the darkness, his eyes covered with a black scarf.

"Welcome to my nest Mr. Kaushal."

"What's this bloody welcome with my eyes blindfolded?" Kaushal retorted. Bhagat unfastened the blinds on Kaushal's eyes and unscrewed the handcuffs. The dim pale light pierced Kaushal's painful eyeballs with a thousand needles. He could hardly figure out the contours of the gigantic figure of Karam Chand Pathania, standing imposingly, flanked by two jet-black Terriers, which looked like devils incarnate. Slowly the kaleidoscope of blurred vision cleared up and he saw the imposing frame almost stooping over him. Ramendra Kaushal shuddered inside his bones. A strange cramp gripped his intestines. Though he couldn't coordinate his brain signals, Kaushal vaguely figured out that he was being readied for the frying pan.

"Welcome to my palace, Mr. Harfan." Pathania greeted his new charge.

"I'm Prince Ramendranath Kaushal." Replied Kaushal in a curt formal voice.

"That's the identity of your past life. I'm talking of your present incarnation, Mr. Harfan Bukhari."

"What's this rubbish?" Asked Kaushal, puzzled as he was, looking at Bhagat.

"We shall talk. Mr. Pathania is the boss of this place and you're his charge."

*

Dinner was delicious, cooked by Nafar Singh, chicken with plenty of spices and gravy, lentils and fried potato, served with *chapati* (flat bread) from a blazing oven. The food tasted like nectar in Kaushal's palate after 18 long hours of near starvation. However, the damp basement room scared him. He longed for a shot of whisky to fortify his resolve and face the odds ahead. Bhagat recommended a large dose of patience instead. Better times were ahead, he explained. There could be plenty of whisky, if Pathania endorsed. He was the master here and a legend in the non-existent underworld of the FIB, of which very few people, even in the organisation, were aware.

"Sleep early," Bhagat sounded a friendly note of caution, "Nafar will serve tea at 5. You're expected for the outdoor activities at 5.30. You'll find the morning gear in your room."

"What do you expect of me? Why should I listen? You can't keep me confined here. Inform my people in Delhi. Inform my mother." Kaushal gathered courage after a tasty dinner and two cigarettes.

"If you insist, I can only inform the police and hand you over to them. It'll take only three months for you to walk up the gallows. I don't mind, if you don't, and I've spare copies of the photographs for your mother."

Kaushal looked at Bhagat with fire-spitting killer eyes, muttered a curse, and crushed the third cigarette under his shoes.

"Good night. Don't act funny. The place is well guarded. They shoot first and talk later. If you're lucky to escape the bullets, Terry and Sparrow, the killer dogs, won't miss your jugular." Bhagat smiled and wished him good night.

Nafar Singh along with Terry and Sparrow on leashes guided Kaushal to his room. He closed the door behind him and unleashed the Terriers, patted them and spoke into their ears. He left Kaushal alone to think over the events of the last twenty-four hours, and snatch a few winks of sleep, if the elusive dame did agree to favour him. Kaushal's nerves were too raw, as if scratched by spotted leopards. Sleep wasn't the proper incarnation of time to numb his frayed and scared senses. His eyes itched and ached. He could barely close the swollen lids. Pain, shame, anger, and anxiety haunted him. He closed the eyelids hoping to snatch a few moments of rest. But his convoluted psyche was busy churning out the dark thoughts, which he thought he could wish away.

The snowy ashen face of Rajni Krittika Hemaprabha Rao appeared from nowhere, the moment he closed his eyelids and tried to disengage from the surroundings. Hema stared at him with an impish smile. That scared him. Hema did not merely taunt him, her looks conveyed a loud message; in her death she had vanquished the all-muscle campus-macho.

Kasturi's face suddenly fleeted in from cosmic vacuum with loaded questions in her eyes. Kaushal, since his adolescence, couldn't manage to face those looks and bluff his way out. She would know the truth somehow. Perhaps she had an X-ray vision, hidden somewhere behind her cornea.

Suddenly, a severed head, blood flowing in torrents faded in before his eyes. Was it Matang's head? No, it wasn't. Whose head was it? Kaushal couldn't figure out any sense out of the grotesque apparition. It faded out.

Kasturi's face faded in again.

He rubbed his eyes and jumped out of the bed. He stomped his feet on the bare floor, wishing to scare away the scornful smile of Hema, the gory head and the heavy eyelids of his mother, pregnant with imponderable questions.

Kaushal stood in front of a wall-mounted mirror and noticed profuse perspiration rolling down his cheeks, mixed with salty tears. His enemy, the memory bank, was haunting him. All these years he lived in present, now he felt, his past and future were mixing up in the memory-shaker. What a confusing broth it was!

"Ma (mother), excuse me. I'm a sinner." Ramendra cried out and covered his face with trembling palms.

The mirror echoed back his cry.

Nafar Singh tapped open the door.

"Good morning sir. Hot tea for you. The Colonel will expect you in half an hour."

He left the door open. Ramendra Kaushal peeped out. Terry and Sparrow were gone. Thank God!

He sipped the steaming tea and felt better.

In the quiet shadowy cools of the basement, judging the exact time by daylight was difficult. One had to go by the watch. The wall clock in the room chimed 6.15.

Dhiren Bhagat entered silently and stood by his side.

Kaushal ignored Bhagat's presence. He kept on squatting on the bed, head buried in the illusory safety of the warm niche of his knees drawn to his chest. He was, in fact, trying to use his fleshy thighs to block his eardrums. The echo from the mirror was still ringing inside him.

"What's happening?" Bhagat placed his hand gently on Kaushal's shoulder, "the Colonel is waiting for you."

"Hang your Colonel, whoever he is," Kaushal retorted, "I must be told, why have I been brought here? What do you expect of me?"

Bhagat drew up a chair, sat next to him and opened up in a low voice.

"I thought, I was doing you a good turn, saving you from the gallows and preparing you for a new life."

"What's this bloody new life? I'm a prisoner here."

"You won't feel so after a few days. You can't get back to the life you left behind. It's better you prepare for the new one. I assure you, it'll be exciting. You'll live to enjoy every moment of it." Bhagat spoke in a seducing tone.

"Enjoy what? What the hell are you talking?" Kaushal straightened his legs and put them down on the floor.

"I'm offering you the exciting career of an intelligence officer, and an opportunity to take revenge on your father's killers, the Pakistani Muslims. You can redeem the prestige of your glorious family. You, a real life prince and a patriot, can serve your motherland."

"That doesn't make sense," Kaushal bent down slightly, placing both elbows on his knees, "who told you Pakis killed my father?"

"It's history. Listen carefully."

After the storyteller finished his fascinating account of the life story of Prince Ramendranath Kaushal and his father Raja Digvijay Kaushal, king of Jhumra, a tiny but flourishing kingdom off Jhang in Pakistan, the caged tiger stood up. He paced excitedly across the room furiously puffing at a cigarette.

"All these days you've been stalking me just for trapping a prospective agent in Pakistan!"

"Well! You're correct. But, you've three points to score, in the bargain."

"What's that trash?"

"You're reborn. You escape the gallows, at least on two counts of murder; you get to take revenge on the killers of your father, and finally you pick up a glorious profession, with plenty of opportunity to destroy Pakistan. That's the country and those are the people, who had disinherited you from the Jhumra throne." Bhagat looked up and offered a cigarette to his client.

"Suppose I refuse to buy your story."

"Didn't they dishonour your mom?"

"I'm not sure."

"You never bothered to live with history. You lived with momentary pleasures. Your father was a part of glorious history. If you decline you lose on all counts. It'll prove that you aren't a worthy son of your dad and mom. You're a plain and simple criminal." Bhagat repeated the refrain of his story.

"No. I'm not a criminal." Kaushal shouted back.

"Your definition of crime can be different, but the facts remain where they are." Bhagat replied coolly.

"Are you selling me 007 trash?" Ramendra Kaushal looked up and asked for a cup of tea.

"No. You're lucky to be selected for the honourable task of serving the country, and you've your own scores to square up. I offer you a great opportunity."

"Don't confuse things," Kaushal rebuffed his handler, "I'd have been much better placed as a front line soldier."

"Correct dear," Bhagat continued the bombardment, "our job, in the realm of espionage, is more adventurous and honourable. You get the real thrill, cutting down your enemy too fine; not by a bayonet, but by intelligent action."

"Shall I be on my own?"

"You'll have the independence of action, subject to tradecraft guidance and control. That's necessary for your safety. We'll take care of your needs and those of your mother. You'll have nothing to fear from the law."

"Do you know the killers of my father? Ma never told me the details."

"You'll get all the dope, in good time. I'm here to prepare you for the journey ahead. It's a tough journey and I'm afraid, you've to rewrite your slate." Bhagat tried to assuage Kaushal's bruised ego.

Bhagat's psychological darts scored the bull's eye. He didn't have to chase Kaushal to wash, have a hearty breakfast, and turn up to the office room of Karam Chand Pathania. The old legend, the Terriers removed, was seated on a cushioned chair, behind a formidable table. Quarter inch grid maps of Pakistan occupied most of the walls, strategic locations marked by coloured flags and pins. Behind him, alongside the wall, a bright and polished brass Ashoka emblem buttressed two cross-mounted Tricolours.

Karam Chand Pathania started with the family history of the Kaushals, tracing the roots to Rishi Vishwamitra (a mythological Brahmin saint who, against Manu's edict, had donned the mantle of a king), the first ever Brahmin king of Aryavarta (habitat of the Aryans). He had defied the Kshatriyas (ruling warrior class) and rattled the gods in their heavenly abode.

Coming from such an illustrious lineage, the Kaushal kings had struck up a special relationship with the British, represented by the East India Company and the later day Viceroys in Delhi and layers of political agents and legions, in the Punjab. Pathania supported his story with the moth eaten pages of history. The Kaushal kings, like other loyal, pampered and spoiled potentates, had collaborated with the white masters, by leading numerous punitive campaigns against the turbulent Frontier Mazari, Bugti, Pathan, Pushtoon, and Niazi tribal warriors and marauding bands of Muslim *thuggies* (band of killer criminals) and dacoits (robbers). The Sepoy Mutiny of 1857, as the empire liked to call the first secular Indian revolt against the tactless and mindless rule by the East India Company, had left thousands of Mughal soldiers and other Muslim satraps jobless. The vanquished Muslims were the prime suspects. Hindu collaborators like the Kaushal kings and the English educated Bengali Baboos had emerged as fulcrums of the empire.

The Kaushals, like other Hindu peers, had become a feared and hated clan. In the heartland of the fierce Punjabi, Mazari, Bugti, Niazi, Pathan and Pakhtoon majority tract, Hindu kingdom of Jhumra was viewed as a festering sore. The advocates of Pakistan, a pure land for the followers of the Allah had given notice to Digvijay Kaushal in early 1937. Raja Digvijay Kaushal, the ruler of Jhumra, was never rated as a diligent student of history and current affairs. He defied the 1946 communal award and advocated the merger of his territory with India. The British Viceroy and his agent, the Governor of Punjab, didn't come to his rescue when hordes of fanatic Muslims attacked his palace and killed him in an unfair war.

Ramendra Kaushal, progeny of such a proud Hindu father, Pathania advocated, should dedicate his life to redeeming his family honour. And what's life for if it wasn't offered to the services of the ancestors and the nation!

*

Ramendra Kaushal's sensors responded grudgingly to the psy-war particles bombarded by Pathania and Bhagat. Bouncing from junction to junction inside his intricate modules, capillaries and the mysterious wiring system of his neurons, the particles of indoctrination gradually started sinking under the layers of his conscience. New emotions started replacing his carnal desire and bloated ego. The present gradually connected him with the known and unknown past and anticipated future. He felt stretched along the entire scale of time.

Pathania believed in the perfect synchronisation between neuronal and muscular responses. An agent, planted in enemy territory, required razor sharp responses and a flexible body, resilient in response and quick in neutralising the adversary. There's no fun killing with a knife or pistol. He gradually introduced Ramendra to a strong physical regimen of karate, unarmed combat and the use of sharp blades and precision shooting from small and medium combat weapons.

A new instructor arrived, after about a month, to teach fabrication and controlled explosion of improvised explosive devices. This was followed up by field demonstration of planting and disarming anti-personnel and anti-tank mines, use of RDX, PETN and home grown improvised explosives in highly delicate tasks of mass destruction. Mr. Gonzales, a tradecraft expert, arrived one night, to teach cryptography, encoding and decoding devices. The old wizard of mathematics turned out to be the toughest nut to crack. Kaushal went mad over the use of logarithms, random generation of numerical and alphabet groups. Gonzales's load was added to the tricky lessons in Morse operation, use of compact HF wireless for clandestine transmission.

Karam Chand Pathania declared, at the end of fourth month, that his extraordinary pupil had completed the basic course and he would be required to return to the facility before he was finally launched.

"Go ahead. Build up the cover story with care. I don't want any gaps. And his conversion to Islam is a must."

*

11

"I hope you aren't up to your old trick of catching me on celluloid, fucking another woman." Ramendra Kaushal laughed at Bhagat with a naughty chuckle. They were seated in a plush hotel room at Ludhiana, an industrial town in Punjab and were were cracking jokes.

"Forget that old shit," Bhagat felt embarrassed, "enjoy yourself. Don't trust the girl. She's a pro, use a condom. I've kept a packet in the drawer. Yes, in the cupboard you'll find a bottle of Old Monk rum. Tomorrow we take on the new job." He closed the door behind softly.

"Don't talk of tomorrow's job tonight." Kaushal lustily walked down to the cupboard and fished out the bottle, kissed and uncorked it.

"Good luck, I'm in the next room. Have fun and be ready for the job ahead." A professional, Bhagat wasn't known to cave in under emotional stress. His softness for the target wasn't personal. Temporary identification with the emotional vibes of the subject was part of a trade trick. In diplomatic language, they called it confidence-building measure. In intelligence vocabulary, it was levelling up with the psychological strata of the target.

Such levelling was often highly rewarding. The facade of mental levelling created an illusion of proximity and implicit trust in the case officer. Ramendra Kaushal carried no ideological bug inside his cranium. His psyche was still tangled with raw mammal emotions and reptilian responses. For Bhagat the job was rather difficult, swimming against the known current of the intelligence tradecraft. He was supposed to inject an ideological motivation into the target and make him respond to new stimuli.

Ramendra Kaushal wasn't sensitive enough to understand the subtle subversion game. His mind was focused on the blood soaked soil of Jhumra. He conjured up the facades of the lost kingdom's glory and steadily fastened himself to the dream of avenging his father's assassination.

Bhagat's success in creating an illusion of trust in Kaushal's psyche was another feather in his cap. The foundation of trust grew stronger day by day, as Kaushal developed an emotional dependence on his case officer.

Kaushal allowed a few seconds for Bhagat to settle down in the adjoining room and downed a few shots straight from the bottle. He felt fortified and looked down the hall, at the doll hired by Bhagat. She stood in her bare skins near the sprawling bed. He walked around the female, in slow unsteady steps, occasionally puffing a cigarette.

His eyes, narrowed into slits, examined intently the intrinsic quality of the product. The doll didn't transmit oscillating waves of desire and emotion. Ramendra looked at her face and suddenly stepped back. Rajni Krittika Hemaprabha Rao was staring at him with the same scornful looks, her lips drawn inside, and her eyes sternly rebuking him.

Oh God! Ramendra shivered for a while and again looked up.

No. The plump woman wasn't Hema. She looked straight at him with an amused invitation. He gulped another drink and took another round of the smiling doll.

Hema reappeared with her scornful looks.

No, he couldn't enjoy sex with this woman, perhaps with any woman, ever.

Ramendra asked the lady in nude to dress and quit. He wished her good night after pushing a bunch of notes in her clammy palms. He gulped another drink, brooded over the apparitions, but failed to connect the shadows with the undressed lady. The dumb face of the hired prostitute tormented him. The never-ending celluloid footage of Rajni Krittika Hemaprabha Rao's face and that of his mother kept on flashing past his mind's eye.

He did not sleep well and woke up next morning fully drained and exhausted.

"Did you like the girl?" Bhagat asked.

"She was fine, nothing special." Ramendra avoided a direct answer.

"Avoid stray women. That's not good for your profession. Your enemy in Pakistan, the ISI, would often use honey traps to neutralise you. Learn the tricks of controlling your responses."

"How do you do that?"

"I've friends in Delhi's G.B. Road red light quarters. I'd take you for a few learning sessions. Hot flesh shouldn't heat you up."

"Is this a part of your darn training?"

"You're correct. It's a kind of *yoga.* The training helps you to keep cool. There are more wonders to discover in this wonderful trade."

Bhagat smiled inscrutably and drove his car along the Grand Trunk Road. He branched off to an unpaved rural link road and reached the outskirts of village Faqira, situated below the spurs of the rail track that connected Ludhiana to Amritsar. He parked the vehicle behind a dilapidated mosque, neglected burial mounds, and asked Kaushal to alight.

"Why are we here? What am I to do in this darn place?" Kaushal felt intrigued and irritated.

"These are the remains of village Faqira, village of Harfan Bukhari. Seventeen years back, in 1947, he was a seven-year-old lad, studying in the village *madrasa* (religious school) and helping his father in his fields and in a ball bearing and minor auto parts factory...

"His father, Maqdoom Bukhari, marketed his products in Amritsar and Lahore...

"On July 5, 1947, the entire Muslim population of the village just vanished, barring a few elderly women. The Hindu and Sikh mob looted and put ablaze everything and raped every woman they could lay hands on. Maqdoom Bukhari's entire family was cut to pieces and thrown into a blazing fire. It was a mad time on either side of the border...

"Somewhere," Bhagat pointed his finger to a heap of brick rubble, nature's greenery spreading its soothing cover on the bygone blood and ash, "there was the house of your father Maqdoom Bukhari...

"Only your uncle, Shamim Bukhari, who happened to be at Amritsar, could take a train to Lahore. He didn't return to the village. He's now settled in Karachi, married to a refugee woman and running a factory, producing defence related spare parts."

"Didn't the Muslims deserve the carnage? After all, they did the same to the Hindus and Sikhs! They killed my father."

"It depends from which angle you would like to see the picture. Even the most horrendous criminals in history, say one like Hitler, have their own philosophy to kill people. Man can justify all his actions. His cerebral capabilities are flexible. Try to rise above the events and you'll see that, all of us are blind and helpless puppets in the hands of the puppeteer, called history."

Bhagat tried to explain the queer games played by history in the sub-continent.

"I can't agree Bhagat. Your reasoning is good for a Buddha. But we're raw animals, packed with emotions. How can I forget that they killed my father and hounded my mother out, in sackcloth and ash?" Ramendra Kaushal poured out his hatred against the Muslims.

"We're immensely influenced by incidents affecting our lives. At times you're required to rise above the skeletons of events and peep into the soul of philosophy."

"What's your bloody philosophy behind chasing me and turning me into a machine of destruction?"

"You and I are soldiers of a geopolitical war. That's different from individual wars. Your and my small wars are controlled by a national strategy. It's a trade, and not a crime. In our profession, we keep the individual buried. The nation gets priority." Bhagat explained succinctly the role of an individual in intelligence warfare.

"Why should I fight your war? I've my own war to fight inside Pakistan." Kaushal thundered out again.

"Yours is a special case. You've the freedom of pursuing your own agenda...So, as I was telling you," Bhagat continued, "for your cover, our story runs like this: Harfan Bukhari, the seven-year-old lad managed to escape the slaughter and was restored to his *phufi* (paternal aunt). A woman in her fifties, Harfan's aunt, and her husband lived in one of the blind lanes of the walled city of Delhi...

"Their nightmare wasn't yet over. Her husband was cut to pieces in the communal carnage of 1950 and she just managed to run up the stairs of the Jama Masjid, with you. The old lady had no means to bear the expenses for migrating and no neighbour was kind enough to pick her up. In the second exodus too, from either side of the gory border, each one was on his own."

"Didn't she get in touch with her brother in Karachi?" asked Ramendra.

"She didn't like to desert the memories of her husband, and Shamim's second wife didn't encourage her. The blackest nightmare came to an end, the blood and flesh were washed clean, and the old lady started a new life. She brought up Harfan, educated him, and died three years ago. Harfan, a bitter enemy of the Hindus and India, has now decided to go over to Pakistan. His goal is to trace out his uncle and live as an honourable and proud Muslim, in the country of his destiny."

"Why are you telling me this story?"

"This is your basic cover story, the story of Harfan Bukhari. Here are copies of few letters you had written to your uncle Shamim and his replies. These are your certificates from Aligarh Muslim University. Your uncle is keen to see you and wants you to join him in his business. Here's a pamphlet. This contains details of the Bukhari family tree. Mug it up."

"I didn't write any letter."

"We've done the job for you. You are now supposed to be a resident of Umerkot in Sind. Read the letters and keep yourself updated, your uncle is expecting you."

"But, I'm a Hindu! How can you forge my birth certificate, school documents and how can you change my physical features?" Kaushal looked up in disbelief.

"You'll be given all the training necessary to be a good Muslim. We'd take care. Here's another pamphlet. It contains all details about your real father's well-wishers back in Jhumra. Some Muslim families are still loyal to him."

"Who are these characters?"

"Find out for yourself."

"Mother never spoke about such people back in Pakistan."

"Don't quiz her if she hasn't. She can't be a privy to your new life and assignment." Back to the car, Ramendra Kaushal lighted a cigarette, inhaled a few puffs, and shot back.

"Suppose I decline!"

"Do you have any choice? Why try to slip back to times where you can't go back? Your old identity has been erased. You've a new identity. Destiny has provided a path of light for you to walk on."

"You talk differently Bhagat. I wish I knew you before I was trapped by Ram Karan's gang."

"Don't worry. Ram Karan is an enemy of the nation. You'll have opportunity to score even with him. You can achieve anything if you wish. Let's go. We drive straight to Delhi. Maulana Rizwan shall be waiting for you."

Bhagat opened the door and facilitated Kaushal, still smoking with an audible sound. He understood the game very well by now. In his new incarnation, Harfan Bukhari was supposed to walk past minefields in a new country and live a shadowy existence. One false step and he would be blown into pieces. No quarter was given to anybody in this game.

"Aren't the Pakis going to tear down my cover in no time?" Ramendra asked.

"We'll teach you all the tricks needed to merge in the new milieu. The Pakis can't get at you, if you live by the rules. That's important." Bhagat turned the wheels towards Delhi.

"It's scary."

"A soldier doesn't get scared of shadows. Get ready for the war ahead."

*

Shyam Purohit alias Maulana Rizwan, FIB's cornerstone in Islamic studies and agent moulding for Islam and Pakistan related operations, functioned from a nondescript building located in the wilderness of rural Delhi. The sprawling wooded farmhouse, camouflaged behind cowsheds, chicken coops, and a flourishing fruit orchard was the only human oasis in the midst of the sub-tropical Shivalik forest.

The stray shepherds and tribal hunter-gatherers knew Maulana Rizwan as an ardent religious Muslim *peer* (saint) and a humble owner of the poultry-cum-dairy farm. He usually dressed as a village *maulana* and flaunted a flourishing moustache and beard with a white mosque cap to match. Proficient in Urdu, Arabic, and Persian, Rizwan was an *alem, maulana* and *mufti*, all rolled in one. He took years to perfect the cover.

He frequented nearby Muslim villages to perform *nikah* (marriage) ceremonies and other religious rituals. He wasn't known as a social creature. However, he did not fail to show up for the Friday prayers at the historic Jama Masjid and *ijtema* (religious teaching) congregations organised by the Tablighi Jammat and *Rabita-al-Alam-al-Islami,* the Saudi based fountainhead of proselytising missions.

Shyam Purohit was both a legend and an icon in the FIB. Recruited way back in 1950, the genesis of his tryst with the intelligence fraternity had actually started very back in 1948. The FIB was presented with a giant-sized problem soon after the transfer of power. The Muslim officers had opted for Pakistan and those who preferred to stay back were shunted out of the prime intelligence edifice. Intelligence in post-partition India, as was with the Empire, was wedded to the ruling clique. The new masters meaninglessly parroted the slogan of secularism but weren't ready to trust the Muslims with state secrets. Communal hatred and distrust still haunted the noblest of souls, both Hindu and Muslim.

The Partition left the FIB almost crippled. The Muslims, a suspect community in Hindu majority India, had shut all the windows and the Hindus in turn treated them as poisoned cheese balls. The age-old communication links had snapped.

Rabindra Narayan Dutta had conceived the idea of creating Muslim clones in FIB's in-house laboratory. Enterprising talents staffed it. Shyam Purohit was one such early talent, trained to don a complete Muslim cover. Son of a Gujarat Brahmin and a promising officer, he learnt Arabic, Urdu and mastered the *Quran Majid* and *Hadith,* all the technicalities of *Namaj, Qalma* and intricacies of personal law. He passed the test of all tests by undergoing the process of circumcision.

Shyam Purohit trained as a hardliner Muslim fundamentalist had infiltrated deep into the targeted Islamic religious and political bodies. In his new incarnation, bearing the lofty name of Maulana Rizwan, he had accomplished the task of spawning several intelligence hatcheries inside the Islamic Jamaat. He had cloned himself through the process of rigorous training and helped the FIB in churning out deep penetration agents inside Islamic organisations.

Shyam Purohit fronted Mumtaj Farm, as a cover for his training facility. It existed beyond the realms of reality, marketing poultry, milk, and milk products and training officers of the FIB in special tradecraft. The cover was perfect and the trainer was impeccable.

Four trained Alsatian dogs came in with Muhim Khan, an assistant to Purohit. Muhim alias Gautam Rai was earlier infiltrated into the Deoband School of Islamic studies, the alma mater of the *Wahhabi Sunni* faith.

Bhagat was made privy to the existence of the special training facility only a day before he was supposed to escort Ramendra to the den of Rizwan. He had heard about the legend but had not met the legendary person. He knew Pathania but could make only shadowy conjecture about this wizard, who made Muslims out of Hindus.

*

12

Ramendra Kaushal wasn't the first open market talent to enter the clandestine precincts of Maulana Rizwan. But he was the most turbulent one.

The rickety motor van of Mumtaj Farm was the only means of transportation to Rizwan's secret hole. It honked at the outer gate at six in the morning, with Dhiren Bhagat and Ramendra Kaushal as additional passengers. Other usual passengers and loads included two coops full of broiler chicks, sacks of cattle fodder, chicken feed, and rations for human and canine inmates. Muhim Khan opened the gate, allowed the van in, and closed it with a bang.

Kaushal jumped out of the van cursing everyone, right from the elusive God above, to Dhiren Bhagat, standing next to him. This wasn't the way, he complained, for a gentleman to travel with chattering and foul smelling birds and assorted garbage. His protestations were drowned in the orchestrated high-pitched howling of the Alsatians, leashed to an iron pole. Kaushal jumped and took cover behind Muhim.

"Do you have to have these killer animals everywhere? And I don't think these animals are in any way a part of your damn training." He grumbled.

"I'm afraid you're correct, they are. But you must appreciate that, for coming to the farmhouse of *chacha* (uncle) there's no other transport available." Bhagat smiled feebly.

"You don't travel with your table bird." Kaushal repeated the complaint.

"All of us are fellow travellers. We all belong to the food cycle."

"Shut up Bhagat. I'm sick of your philosophy."

"Welcome to my *garib khana* (small place of a modest person). Sorry for the inconveniences." Maulana Rizwan greeted his guest as Kaushal dusted his trousers and shirt.

"Who're you?" Kaushal blinked his eyes at the unbelievably deceptive figure of Purohit.

"*Bande ko Maulana Rizwan kahte hain* (the modest person is Maulana Rizwan)."

"Why am I here?"

"Let's talk about that later. Breakfast is ready. Come." Rizwan invited his guests to the dining room.

Breakfast was sumptuous, flat bread fried in melted cow milk fat, fried potatoes, and roasted chicken nuggets, followed by glasses of buttermilk.

"*Beta* (son)," Rizwan spoke in a low voice, "I've heard a lot about you. Ordained by *Allah*, I run this place in my own fashion. In addition to me, you have Muhim, a black belt in karate and four Alsatians, all trained to kill intruders, who try breaking my fences. For your information, Muhim charges the iron mesh with 230 volts before he retires. I don't like intruders."

Kaushal looked at Bhagat with nervous eyes, for support.

"The van leaves at 8.30 sharp. Get ready," Rizwan spoke to Bhagat, "I don't like guests who overstay their welcome."

"When do I come next?" Bhagat asked.

"After two months, if your friend cooperates," Rizwan replied with an impish look, "that's the schedule for now. Keep touch with the boss."

The joint didn't impress Ramendra Kaushal. It wore a ghostly appearance. The brick building, located in the midst of nowhere, was surrounded by thick and wild growth of vegetation. The wooded farmhouse, lined with fruit and all-season flowering trees was girdled by a paved jogging track.

Kaushal, 25 years younger to Rizwan, ran slowly behind him followed by the Alsatians and Muhim. This was his morning routine, and he expected the trainees to honour it as well.

"Tired?" Asked Rizwan.

"Out of touch *Ustad* (captain)."

"Build up strength and stamina, you'd require a fit body and a super-fit mind." Rizwan advised.

He stopped, took a deep breath and turned to Kaushal.

"Are you religious?" He asked.

"What do you mean?"

"How deeply are you attached to your religion?"

"I've no religion. I'm a born Hindu, perhaps a born Brahmin. Why?"

"Just like that. To me, my profession is my religion. It's gratifying to note your status. I have to teach you all the tenets of Islam."

"I hate the Muslims."

"Why?"

"I hate them. They killed my father." Kaushal replied.

"Fine. But to fight a Muslim state you have to be one of them, you must respect and practice their religion."

"I can kill them from outside too."

"That's very difficult. To kill your enemy you must understand him. Practice their religion, customs and rituals. You win half the war, if you know your enemy well."

Muhim took over after breakfast with lessons in Urdu. The Alsatians snoozed under the mid-summer heat, intermittently sniffing Kaushal's exposed limbs.

"This is the most important part of the job." Muhim pontificated.

"Every bloody step is important. But remove these devils first. They don't help in remembering the queer alphabets."

"Try living with all odds, you'll start loving them."

"Stop pontificating. I hate dogs."

"Better give me a check list of things you don't hate. Hope you don't hate yourself!" Muhim retorted.

Kaushal's tangent look almost singed his tutor. Muhim smiled back and started a new lesson on the basic concepts of Islam.

As the afternoon lessons progressed, under an idle cloud covered sun, Maulana Rizwan slithered in silently from a corner. Before Kaushal could capture a glimpse of the profile of the intruder, Rizwan pushed in the needle of a syringe into his left arm.

"What the hell is this?" A shocked Kaushal tried to jerk his arm away.

"You require a little sleep and I'm required to perform a small surgery, *janab* (mister) Harfan Bukhari."

Rizwan, assisted by Muhim, carried Kaushal's limp body to a dining table, and took out a vapour emitting sterilised steel box. He slipped in latex gloves and shaved the areas around Kaushal's private parts, swabbed it with disinfectant and carefully carried out a microsurgery, removing the foreskin of Kaushal's genital. He bandaged the operated part carefully and administered a shot of antibiotic, a precaution against infection. Kaushal woke up after about two hours, only to find his hands and legs fettered to the table. His eyes were still groggy but he could hear Maulana Rizwan's booming voice.

"Welcome, Mian Harfan Bukhari. Sorry for the pain."

Kaushal tried to move on to his side and felt a biting pain in the general area of his crotch, his testicles burning from the effect of the operation.

"What have you done to me? I'm not Harfan Bukhari." He retorted in a sore voice.

"Don't forget your new name. It's going to stick to you for the rest of your life. Ingrain it. You've to live the new life of Harfan Bukhari," Rizwan explained, "I've just performed a small surgery and removed a little bit of skin from your genital."

"Why did you have to deceive me? Untie my hands and feet."

"You aren't my first student. Only one person before you agreed to undergo the circumcision willingly. I don't like cries of pain and resistance. Sorry for the pain, but I can assure that you'll be fit in two days and your sexual prowess will increase. This is an important part of the cover. Circumcision is an integrál part of Islam and Judaism."

"Hell with these fucking religions?"

Rizwan didn't reply. It was useless to argue with this Satan. Nampoothiri was correct about the turbulent nature of his student. He carried in a tray of hot coffee and some tempting cakes.

"Son, from now onwards I'll call you Harfan. You've to start living the cover, along with the learning process. Every bit of your personal life should look like that of a Muslim. A keen observer shouldn't be able to detect even a single grain of inconsistency." He spoke in a soft affectionate voice.

"Repeat after me: *Bismillah-ur-Rehman-e Rahim,* In the name of Allah, the Beneficent, the Merciful; recite with me, *La Ilaha Illa llah Mumammad-ur-Rasulu'llah*-There's no God but Allah, and Muhammad is his Prophet. Remember, this is the *Qalema-e-Tayeb,* the essence of all praises of the Almighty Allah and his Prophet, Muhammad, son of Abdul Muttalib, of the tribe of Qureysh."

He presented a *Mushaf* (copy of the Quran) and a copy of the *Hadith* to Kaushal.

"Read these books carefully. Muhim will help. These are the Holy Books and foundations of Islam. Master the technicalities of the Islamic rituals. These are *behesti jevars* (celestial jewels), like Hindu prescriptions of daily rituals."

"What's so great about these fucking rituals?"

Kaushal tried to provoke Rizwan on several points during the lessons related to *Namaj, Roja* (ritual Ramadan fasting) and prescription for studying the *Quran Majid.*

"Keep your precious views to yourself. Ingrain deep inside what I teach. These are essential for your survival. Remember that the Muslims, like the Jews, Christians and Sikhs are people of the Books, unlike the Hindus. Respect other's faith. Don't babble like a baboon." Rizwan chided his student.

"It's so difficult."

"I'm here to help. Tolerance is the name of the game. Don't be snappy. Read more. The *Holy Quran*, the *Hadith* and the *Sharia* are the pillars of Islamic faith. Read and practice these tenets carefully. Understanding your enemy is the only way to arm yourself efficiently."

"Oh shit!" Kaushal reacted vehemently, "anyways, I suppose I'm to enjoy the raping of my soul."

Rizwan smiled. He knew that behind the foul mouth there was a diligent learner. This one student had sprung surprises, outpacing him in the process of learning.

Sixty days flew past.

Maulana Rizwan, accompanied by Harfan Bukhari, reached the portals of the grand Jama Masjid, built by emperor Shahjahan, to attend the Friday prayers. He had taught Harfan all the nuances of *Fazr, Zohor, Asar, Maghrib, Isha* and *Jumma Namaj* rituals, with meticulous stress on the rituals of *Ruqu* (bending properly) and *Sizda* (obeisance in a prostrated position).

Standing next to his pupil, Rizwan appreciated the perfect and synchronised performance of the young devil. Behind his apparent foul and sharp tongue, he had a receptive razor sharp mind. Harfan passed the test right down to the last detail. He was now a real Muslim, in every sense of it. Even a seasoned *namaji* for forty years, with a black spot on his forehead, would not be able to detect any flaw. Harfan was a fast learner, a talented student.

*

Dhiren Bhagat took over from Rizwan soon after Kaushal alias Harfan Bukhari graduated out of the Mumtaj Farm seminary.

"You get just one month to acclimatise in an undiluted Muslim ghetto. Don't forget that you had a *phufi* (aunt) at Gali Qabristan, behind the *dargah* (burial place) of Dada Pir Bukhari, ancestor of the Bukhari clan."

"The history is fine, but what do I do there?"

"Acquaint yourself with the old city. Be a Harfan who grew up in that milieu for the last eighteen years. Learn the finer nuances of living like a Muslim. Live like a true Muslim..."

"In Pakistan, where you're assigned to, you'll be watched by everyone. You have to pass the vital tests, when you meet your Uncle Shamim Bukhari. The old man must be nursing many memories under his chest. All migrants do."

"I can't get into the roots of a life which aren't mine."

"Come'n Harfan," Bhagat cajoled his agent, "you've done it. Now just live like one. That's all. We shall be in touch. Remember my eyes shall all the time follow you. We meet again after a month."

Harfan Bukhari hesitated for a while and turned back.

"Suppose I run away and disappear?"

"I know you won't do that. Raja Digvijay Kaushal's son won't run away without avenging his death. Your destiny is waiting at Jhumra. Anything else? Want more scotch and girls?"

"Thanks. I don't feel like."

Harfan turned down his case officer's offer politely, boarded a cycle rickshaw, and proceeded towards his aunt's place at Gali Qabristan, literally meaning lane of the burial ground.

He lighted a cigarette and smiled uncertainly at the milling crowd he was passing through. Oh! What a damn tryst it was with witch doctors like Pathania, Bhagat and Rizwan? He had come to love and respect them. A dedicated trainer, Rizwan had devoted his entire life to the cause of his department, perhaps the nation. He believed in his cause and philosophy, like any orthodox Hindu or Muslim believed in their scriptures and archaic social practices.

Bhagat had, by now, become an inseparable part of his existence. The intimate association and levelling of psychological strata had brought about chemical changes. He didn't realise that his handler had started conditioning his neuronal impulses by subverting his psychograph.

For next thirty days, Harfan Bukhari lived at 1437/309 Gali Qabristan, off Turkman Gate. The final test was supposed to be very tough, living the life of a

Muslim in undiluted surroundings that had warded off civilisational changes for over five centuries. It was a frozen society, where life stood still behind the walls of the great ramparts of the massive mosque.

The nephew of Zubaida Begum, sister of Shamim and Maqdoom Bukhari, settled down in the new surroundings, as a young graduate from Aligarh Muslim University, ostensibly surveying opportunities to start a factory to manufacture ball bearings and auto accessories.

A real estate agent, an under cover FIB officer, chaperoned Harfan around the walled city, explaining the peculiarities of dress, food habits and the minute details of the peculiar accent of spoken Urdu.

"It's a different civilisation," he explained, "captured in the frozen city of Shahjahanabad, the capital city of emperor Shahjahan. Move around the small lanes, visit the *havelis* (old mansions) and markets. Get to know the people."

"In what way are they different?"

"The people here live in the past, both Hindus and Muslims. The later day British and Punjabi invaders haven't been able to change them much. You'll find the same frozen trends in the lanes and markets of old Karachi and Lahore. A unique rhythm runs through the veins of the people in these traditional settlements. You must discover this world, common to the people, living on either side of the border."

Bhagat's man wasn't far from truth. The walled city, immersed in the past, was pleasantly different from the imperial Delhi and the other Delhi built by the Punjabi refugees. It throbbed with life and pulsated with unique rhythm.

Harfan Bukhari patiently peeled off the apparent dirt and modern masks and slowly discovered the lost world of centuries old culture, preserved by generations of decaying and daring people. They dared the invasive British and Punjabi cultures, which doggedly knocked there dilapidated ramparts.

Thirty days passed by like wind-driven cotton flakes. Harfan didn't know when the *jinn* of hatred against everything Muslim, subtly yielded to deep channels of love for the people around him. He suddenly discovered that a unified flow of compassion had flooded the deep furrows in his mind. The seeds of life and love, he understood, always triumphed over the debris of death and destruction.

His new birth would have remained incomplete, Harfan felt, had he not lived in this unique world. The experience invigorated him with the life-essence of the people who lived in dark alleys, foxholes, dilapidated *havelis* and were enwrapped in the memories of emperors, warriors, courtesans and magicians.

Harfan's charmed stay in Jama Masjid area was terminated by a terse message from Bhagat. It was time to take a long journey to his final destination. He would be taken to certain border areas for acclimatization and dry runs. Another deputation for fifteen days to the fort of Colonel Pathania was designed to teach him the graphic ground realities of his area of entry, safe housing and personalities he was likely to be exposed. Harfan packed up his rucksack and followed Bhagat with thirsts of anticipation and expectations. But his launch to the designed orbit was delayed by unexpected developments.

*

13

The remote sensing satellite was ready for precise launching. That needed permission from the top. But some unforeseen hindrance delayed the final counting. The launching pad itself was not traceable.

Ram Banerjee followed by Dhiren Bhagat entered the room, fearfully described as the Den by the FIB officials.

"What's your plan?" asked Dutta.

"Sir, the product is ready. We've to infiltrate the talent to Karachi area. In the first leg of the operation he has to establish contact with his uncle, Shamim Bukhari." Banerjee enunciated the main task ahead.

"When can you get going with the operation?"

"There's a problem," added Bhagat, "our transborder facilitator Amrik Singh Johal isn't available at his usual rendezvous. We can't execute the operation infiltration till he's located."

"Johal can't simply disappear into thin air," Nampoothiri intervened, "he can't be out of business. Trace him out, I say, at the earliest."

"He has probably gone to Agra-Mathura area to procure export commodities." Bhagat submitted.

"Is he an exporter? What merchandise does he deal in?" asked Dutta.

"I'll explain later," Nampoothiri added and winked at Bhagat, "you get going and seek out Johal."

"Yes sir." Bhagat responded with a flourishing bow.

"Yes sir won't do," Dutta thundered, "I want urgent action."

"Sure sir."

Bhagat looked up and replied with an anguished expression. He had heard about Dutta's short spell of bad tempers. But to him the top boss appeared to be hanging on a very fragile tenterhook.

*

Amrik Singh's Hotel Capitol office fronted a travel agency, GUN-DEV TOURS, a Texan abbreviation for Guru Nanak Dev Tours. He was, in fact, a consultant and export-import promoter for Ram Karan Prasad, the evergreen cabinet minister. He was on an urgent business errand, a business of different kind and export of novel and fancy commodities.

Amrik represented the audacious second-generation Punjabi fortune hunters, who believed in making millions from thin air. Amrik wasn't the prototype of a hard working honest Sikh, earning his bread by sweating out the summer and suffering the winter shivers. He didn't believe in tough life; he believed in bucks–fast and big bucks.

Short of leaping into a galactic void, Amrik jumped his way up by corrupting everyone, right, left and centre. All that he required was enough grease for the palms of the power pinions and good-looking women for the politicians and bureaucrats. Those were the magic *mantras* for entering Aladdin's golden cave.

It didn't take time for Amrik Singh Johal to take a few frog-leaps to reach the diamond-studded world of mafia don Mardan Pathan of Bombay and his Delhi associate Salim Langra. They fronted drug, gold, and silver smuggling operations. Amrik was drawn to the orbit of a politician turned flesh exporter Ram Karan Prasad, Jung Bahadur's precious cabinet colleague, and an icon of the sub-continental social engineering that represented the stigmatised and dogmatised low caste masses.

Recruited by Vidyasagar Suri, Amrik turned out to be a superb talent. The immaculately dressed Sikh looked more like a beach gigolo, much more a sophisticated operator than the wild buffalo, Ramendra Kaushal. Ramen was a killer and Amrik an exporter.

Amrik was under great pressure from Mardan Pathan and clients across the borders. Starved of fresh supplies for brothels and guesthouses, the connoisseur market in Pakistan and beyond had started breathing fire down his chest. Troop movements on the border had choked his supply lines and the fertile fields in Nepal and East Pakistan had suddenly turned barren.

Only the Boss could extricate him from the crisis. That's how Amrik landed at the doors of Ram Karan Prasad with great temerity.

"What's your problem?"

Ram Karan Prasad spoke as he sipped usual morning tea, brewed with a queer concoction of holy *tulsi* (basil) leaves. The concoction tasted bitter and he too was in a bitter mood today.

The crazy PM had called a meeting at 3 in the morning, which concluded at 6. He was forced to miss an engagement to deflower a young beauty, kidnapped from Chamoli, up in the Himalayan heights. To top his misery, Raghu Chawla, the barnacle of a journalist, was seated right in his drawing room, for a report on last night's cabinet proceedings. He had to, Chwala said, keep a dateline with a Pak High Commission official.

"What bloody business, in the name of your blasted Guru, brings you here?" Ram Karan asked Amrik with a pungent grimace.

"Sir, we've run into troubles. This damn war has threatened supply of East Pakistani and Nepali women. They have diverted the traffic to Bangkok and Singapore markets. Your Umerkot friend Hassan Rathore has sent an immediate demand for 20 girls. We're late by twenty days."

"What the hell have you been doing? What about our agents in Calcutta, Kathmandu and Patna?" Ram Karan scowled.

"Sir, they're scared, because of the war hysteria. Bangkok market is paying higher premium."

"Fuck your mother. There can be war over the thighs of women, not in between." Shouted Ram Karan.

"But sir..."

"No but. Go and get the women from wherever you can." Ram Karan gulped the queer *tulsi* concoction and grimaced at Johal.

"But sir," Amrik replied in a confused voice, "how do we send our consignment across the border? There are soldiers everywhere."

"Have you got the stock?" Ram Karan was by now impatient.

"No sir."

"You good for nothing fucking asshole. Kalua..." Ram Karan Prasad shouted. In came a 6 feet tall sack of fat and muscle from Siwan, the hon'ble minister's home town. A rare family heirloom, Kalua, with a pitch-dark complexion and all white hair, looked like a *jinn* walking out of the Arabian nights.

Ram Karan had inherited Kalua from his father Kalika Kiran Prasad. Initially used as a catamite by Kalika Kiran, Kalua finally graduated as the killer arm of Ram Karan, leading his private army. It carried a glamorous name: Surya Sena (Sun Brigade). Bihar, one of the Indian tracts, lost in a Jurassic jungle, boasted of several such private armies. This private arm of Ram Karan plundered villages, grabbed land, abducted women and eliminated defaulters and dissenters.

On occasions, his Surya Sena fought bloody battles with neighbouring landlords and grabbed land from poor farmers, suffering from the infinite burden of loans that compounded at a galactic rate.

For Kalua, life had frozen under the moccasin of Ram Karan. He grew up biologically but the man in him had turned into a robot, a killing machine.

"Any orders for me sir?" Kalua entered the room, bending his body slightly.

"What's the size of your army at Siwan?"

"There are fifty. But, some may have gone to their villages for paddy transplantation."

"To hell with your fucking paddy," shouted back Ram Karan, "I want thirty young girls and soon. How long would you take?"

Ram Karan asked the question while plucking out a strand of hair from his right nostril and polishing well oiled white hair on his head.

Kalua stood silently for a few moments, scratching his baldpate.

"Sir, they require twenty." Amrik intervened.

"Shut up you fucking asshole. I require ten for local markets."

"You want all of them young and virgin?" Kalua asked.

"Young, yes, but not below 15. Customers are funny these days, they don't like young buds."

"Sir, it may take more than two raids," Kalua submitted apologetically, "the days are difficult. The Patna based journalists are a menace. They created big fuss the last time I raided Mohammadpur village."

"Don't worry. I'll call up the inspector general of police. There is a national emergency. He'll book the journalists under Defence of India Rules."

"Won't it be risky?" Amrik managed to butt in.

"A mother fucking idiot." He cursed.

"You mean me?" A surprised Kalua, who hadn't used his sex organ until now, for obvious biological reasons, asked.

"Shut up."

"Yes sir, can we proceed now?" Kalua bowed down like a black Burmese cane.

"Do whatever you like. Here's Amrik. He'll take a bus for transporting the merchandise. You get them at the earliest. Keep me out of it."

Ram Karan turned to Amrik Singh Johal.

"And you motherfucker, your problem is solved. Kalua will supply the merchandise. It's your duty to ship them to the destination. And remember delivery is strictly against cash."

"Where do I take the bus?" Amrik Singh wanted guidance that was more precise.

"Follow Kalua and report back after you've delivered the merchandise." Ram Karan Prasad dismissed Amrik. He called aside Kalua and talked to him in a slow and seductive voice.

"Kalua, I want all the girls young. No old haggard with sagging breasts. Scout around the low caste villages and impose your own curfew. Lift the girls and put them in Amrik's bus. Fire in the air to scare the villagers. Don't kill. Looting of women is a cool business. Handling of body bags is a difficult task. I don't want any complication. And keep Rs. twenty thousand. Pay the *thanedar* (police in charge) and others, if necessary."

Kalua left after being fully briefed by his master.

Ram Karan Prasad cursed his stars for being disturbed by Amrik. The disgust turned to a burning thirst for Scotch. The urge to have a stiff dose before he commenced the strenuous exploration of the Himalayan beauty, still chained to his ornate mahogany bed, propelled his steps towards the bar. He turned back halfway. That pain in the neck, his third vertebrae, and bloody Raghu Chawla was waiting in another room.

"*Sala* (a slang)." Ram Karan uttered a curse. These Hindustanis and Pakistanis have no business sense. What's the use of fighting wars? They should allow business to thrive and that should take care of all the problems. To him there was no difference between a Hindu and a Muslim woman. In bed, they were equally warm. In fact, given a choice, he preferred young Muslim women. They were more skilful than most soggy Hindu women.

Ram Karan walked in briskly to the room, where Raghu was biting his nails.

"Hi Raghu, what's the matter?"

"Sir, your obedient servant is waiting for last two hours."

"What the hell do you want?"

"Friend Mushtaq has requested for an urgent meeting."

"Tell him, I am busy." Ram Karan wasn't willing to put off the adventure of exploring the creases, heights, and depths of the Chamoli beauty. The thirst of an impatient explorer was violently gurgling inside him. Climb, he must.

"Sir, you'd better meet him, the friends are anxious, they want vital clarification on last night's Cabinet meeting."

Raghu Chawla hinted at the demand of a Pakistani diplomat, who used the budding journalist as a cutout to Ram Karan.

"Shit!" Ram Karan relented, "we can't meet in the open, you understand. We're at war now. Arrange a discreet venue and keep me informed. Take these documents and get the money for me."

He banged the door and hastily turned towards the chained Chamoli beauty. Oh, Mother Kali! he sighed. The life had become so complicated. Business was getting dull and this Jung Bahadur was making life miserable for him by summoning emergency meetings at odd hours.

"Kalua." Ram shouted for his father's pederasty partner.

"Yes sir." The jet-black *jinn* appeared from nowhere.

"Prepare the girl for me."

"Done sir."

*

Amrik Singh entered his office room with an exhilarating pace, humming a film tune. He didn't notice Dhiren Bhagat seated behind a huge Bartholomew globe and piles of files and smoking away his favourite brand, Capstan. He hated the guts and tenacity of this intelligence officer.

"Hello Amrik." Bhagat stood up with a stretched palm.

Amrik reciprocated and walked down to his chair.

"Hi Bhagat. What's new?"

"Nothing unusual," Bhagat shifted to a chair opposite Amrik, "ask for tea, been waiting for two hours."

"Anything serious?"

"Usual export matter."

Amrik lamented, as they sipped thick-brewed tea, about dull business and a wasteful war. Was it worth fighting foolish wars for nothing? His export-import business had hit the lowest patch.

"Well Amrik," Bhagat broached the business proposal, "war doesn't impede your business. Your merchandise appreciates all the time."

"It's very dull brother." Johal lamented again.

"Don't fool me. I know your tricks," Bhagat spoke in a firm voice. "I've a friend to cross over. It's urgent."

"It's very difficult brother." Amrik said with folded hands.

"It can't wait. Tie it up with your counterparts. We prefer the Gujarat route."

"My contacts have snapped." Amrik gestured his helplessness.

"Don't bullshit. Only 15 days back you received 100 kilos of gold. We keep our eyes closed but not our senses. You've to pay the price." Bhagat sounded a little formal.

"You know the border situation." Amrik tried to parry.

"Who doesn't? And who doesn't know that on either side of the border your ilk operates usual runs. Your breed thrives on war. You're the same, all over the world, war or no war." Bhagat hammered in his point.

Amrik smiled faintly. There was no way to get past the field rat. He would, no doubt, ruthlessly pursue his goal. Better, not irritate a man having his fingers on all the border outposts.

"I'll be out of town for about four days, but your job will be done," Amrik sounded extra sweet, "do me a favour."

"You want the right of passage?"

"Yes," Amrik lowered his tone; "I'll prefer the Gujarat lane. Hassan Rathore of Umerkot will receive the consignment."

"What're you trading this time?"

"The usual consignment of meat. Don't ask details. Do me that courtesy and I promise safe conduct for your man."

"Deal. When do I expect a call?"

"Can't say, for sure."

"Don't worry. But I want a firm undertaking."

"Spell it out."

"A safe passage for my man up to Karachi."

"I know Bhagat, one day you'd put the noose around my neck. Anyways, I don't mind being hanged for the nation, like martyr Bhagat Singh." Amrik mimicked a patriotic martyr from Punjab and raised hands in salutation to his Guru.

"Enough Amrik," Bhagat stood up, "reserve the jokes for your grave. I'll write a touching epitaph, in glowing Gurmukhi (Punjabi script), extolling the virtues of a fallen front-line warrior, that you are. Believe me."

Bhagat extended his hand. The business partners parted company with a warm handshake, presuming that each had scored a victory over the other.

Crime and intelligence, as the time watchers said, were perfect bed partners. Each one knew the rules of the game. Each one was aware of the sharp edges that he was required to walk on. They managed to smile behind their pains. It didn't come from within. It was another cool business deal as usual.

*

14

Kalua Mushahari's Surya Sena numbering over fortyfive had dutifully raided the villages of Bhangipada, Chamartola and Telitola under the snoring nose, blinking eyes and morphed mind of the police officers and conniving assistance of the village chiefs. They lifted over 35 young women and dumped them in the garishly decorated bus of Amrik Singh, which was parked outside the gate of Siwan police station. The banners and festoons described the bus as a vehicle of bounty gifted by Ram Karan Prasadji for *dalit* (untouchable) women making a lifetime pilgrimage to the holy city of Varanasi.

A loudspeaker blared out devotional songs, extolling the virtues of Lord Shiva urging Him to rescue the *Suras* (gods) from the clutches of the *Asuras* (demons).

Kalua wakened up the Station House Officer of Siwan police station from his beer-induced slumber. The obliging minion of law piloted Johal out of his jurisdiction, after pocketing another gracious amount of Rs. 5000. Amrik didn't mind the bargain. His net share out of the transaction, if completed, would be Rs.50000. Ram Karan should be left with a fat margin of half a million, if the merchandise was sold at Rs. 30000 per head.

"*Wahe Guru*" (hail the preceptor), Amrik prayed. Good sense should dawn upon both the warring sides and peace should hold for at least one more week. The blind politicians, *Wahe Guru,* should be bestowed with more wisdom, like Ram Karan Prasad had. Johal sighed agonisingly.

"*Saccha Padsa Wahe Guru*"(Guru is the true God). Amrik cast a glance at the wailing half-naked village women and closed his eyes for a brief catnap. Only that intelligence leech Bhagat worried him. He was sure to catch up near the exit rendezvous. He uttered another curse linking Bhagat sexually with his mother and muttered mechanically under his lips a couplet from the Sikh Holy Scripture.

*

"Mian Mirza Qasim is an important person. I want no meddling by the Border Rangers and the Pak Intelligence fellows." Bhagat caught up with Johal at Suigam, a sleepy town in northern Gujarat.

"Who is this fellow Qasim?"

"That's none of your business. He may be a Qasim or a Hashim. He's a notorious smuggler of Calcutta."

"Suppose Hassan refers back to Ram Karanji?" Amrik made a cautious query.

"Don't drag Ram Karan. It's very important and you'll be responsible if anything goes wrong. You know the consequences. I'll simply chop your fingers off."

"Understood sir," Amrik replied, "but Rathore might send in two this time."

"Smugglers or spies?"

"Can't say. That's your headache."

"What's the delivery point?"

"The Sufi shrine of Chishti at Ajmer."

"No problem. Who's the consignee?"

"Amir Khan, shop number 687, opposite the shrine."

"Fine. I'd take care."

"Don't embarrass me."

"Have I ever cracked your neck? You're a precious friend. Just take care that you don't sleep with the Pakis without my approval."

"Correct boss. Just see that this poor servant of the Guru remains unharmed."

"Shit! Since when you started remembering him?"

Bhagat, however, felt mighty pleased. He should get plenty of head-time to exchange pleasantries with Amir Khan of Ajmer and cook a fine curry out of the new Pakistani spies. However, his immediate concern was the successful exfiltration of Harfan Bukhari and housing him in Karachi. His task stretched that far. The second stage of propellant, beyond Karachi, was to be provided by the Indian Mission based FIB operatives.

*

Suigam, an active theatre of Kachchh skirmishes with Pakistan, was a sleepy hamlet, thriving on cross-border smuggling. The British brokered peace was tenuous. Indian and Pakistani border guards usually mounted intensive patrolling on camelback and just for the heck of it, opened fire at each other.

The petty border runners were not deterred by the grandiose ideas of war and peace. They smuggled in camel loads of gold, silver, and foreign fabrics. They carried back foreign made Indian liquor, *pan* (betel) leaves, *bidi* (leaf-wrapped indigenous cigarette) and acetic anhydride, which was very much in demand in the heroin refining industries of Afghanistan and Pakistan. Most of the carriers did a bit of intelligence scouting both for India and Pakistan. They took refuge with their caste-folks and Peer Pagaro devotees. Indian and Pakistani vote-begging politicians wooed the Peer, a religious cult leader, having a large following on either side of the border.

The Pagaro followers were pay rolled by Sardar Illahi, a drug baron at Pakistan's end of the tunnel, who resembled the likes of Ram Karan on the Indian rim. They determined the destinies of the border dwellers and trans-border traders. Intelligence and security officials on either side of the border were on their payroll. A conventional war was too insignificant a disincentive to deter their thriving economic activities.

However, the Suigam field officer of the FIB unexpectedly put a cork on Bhagat's well-oiled tunnel. He illuminated Bhagat on the hitherto hazy areas of the operation.

"Is it a shallow run?" the officer asked.

"May be a deep one, I really don't know, I presume so."

"For infiltrating a deep run, if you don't mind sir, I suggest, you avoid Johal's gang, at least this time."

"Why?"

"Hassan Rathore has links with the Pak Intelligence Bureau and his own brother Major Usman Rathore is with the Sind Border Rangers." The local officer shared his ground knowledge with Bhagat.

"Hassan is Ram Karan's friend."

"Must be, but Usman is not. The Pak army and the Rangers are everywhere. We should have an independent channel for infiltration."

"You make sense. What's the army deployment like?"

"Some massing of troops has been reported from Diplo. Two squadrons of Patton tanks have been sighted there. Nagar Parker has the presence of two companies of the Baluch Regiment, for rearguard support to the Sind Rangers. Some complements of *Ansars* (armed irregulars) and Pagaro's *Hur Laskars* have been deployed in depth."

"What's the state of border vigil?" Bhagat wanted more details.

The energetic field officer pulled out a paper and drew a sketch of the route: Suigam>Kuwala on camelback> bus ride to Nagar Parkar> train journey to Tando Adam and Hala>crossing the Indus by boat and finally a local train journey from Rajri to Karachi Cantonment station.

"Why do you prefer this route over the one controlled by Rathore?" Bhagat asked.

"Rathore's drug cartel is shared by the top Pak army brass. I don't think you'll like the Army and ISI drug traders to share your secrets. Ram Karan is a politician and he can get away with an act of treason. We can't take risk."

"Are you sure?"

"Yes."

"Who'll carry our load?" Bhagat asked.

"*Chacha* (uncle) Radu Nagar. He's a legendary figure on this route. And he's a paid agent of the FIB. Won't open his trap."

"How do you get him over to our side?"

"He should be here tonight with his *kafila* (caravan)."

The logic was very transparent. Bhagat wasn't aware of Amrik's precise connections with the important cogs in Pakistan's ruling military clique. Well, ground realities changed very fast in this fast-track domain of trading in drugs and live flesh. He thanked the field officer and transmitted a cipher to Nampoothiri seeking a modification in the original plan. Nampoothiri's call came at 2 a.m. Dot, dot, dash, dash—the wireless set hummed for the next twenty minutes.

The new route was approved.

*

The next task was more delicate. Bhagat had to offload Amrik with a convincing explanation. His neurons were not connected to the precious human characteristic called conscience. A veteran in flesh trade he wouldn't hesitate to sell off his own mother. Locating Amrik wasn't a big task. He was busy guarding his merchandise in a shabby warehouse, surrounded by high walls. The joint was used for storing red chillies and salt, before the consignments were put on railway wagons. He was singing a lullaby to the Siwan women.

"Look sisters. Back home, you owned nothing but poverty, bone-grinding work, and indignity. You're treated as bonded labourers." Amrik spoke in slow Hindi. The womenfolk stared at him, fear writ large on their faces.

Another agent of Ram Karan spoke fluently and friendly in Siwan dialect.

"You have nothing to fear. I'm a fellow *chamar.* Trust me; I only have your welfare in mind. I'm making arrangements for good jobs that will fetch you all a neat Rs. 1000 per month. That's a minimum guarantee, and then there is free housing, running water, and electricity too. Imagine, you can send a minimum of Rs. 500 to your homes every month." He paused.

"Don't you trust me? Take this," He took out bunches of crisp notes, "I'm giving each one of you Rs. 20 as a goodwill advance. It's your money. keep it. Merwa was a nightmare for you with daylong toiling and tolerating heaps of insults. I offer you independence from slavery."

"My sisters," added Amrik, "trust me. I swear in the name of Mother *Kali.* You're absolutely safe. Treat me as your brother."

Some faces lighted up. Many of them hadn't seen a full rupee in their life. They didn't understand the meaning of one thousand rupees. It must be a lot. They couldn't imagine what twenty rupees could fetch for them.

"How much is twenty?" Asked a married woman.

The tout took out a bunch of crisp one-rupee note, counted out loudly up to twenty, and handed them over to the woman.

A strange light flashed past her eyes. She clutched the notes, her fingers quivering. She started counting, using her fingers. She lost count midway, felt confused and suddenly laughed out aloud. She felt happy. The money felt warm, the crisp papers held out many promises.

"How many *saris* (apparel used by women) can I purchase with this money?" She asked.

"Ten." Replied the tout.

"Ten? How many saris make ten?" Asked another voice.

Amrik took out ten ordinary saris from a jute bag, and placed them one over the other, in front of the teenaged girl.

She counted them slowly and asked, "How can I send money home, to my blind parents?"

"Don't worry. You can send it by money order. Don't bother about the details; your employers will arrange everything." Amrik added. He smiled. The ice was melting very slowly.

Dhiren Bhagat witnessed the charade for a while and summoned Amrik out.

"What time do you start?" He asked.

"Tonight. Rathore's guide has crossed over. The police have been tackled. Where's your man?"

"There's a slight change of plans," Bhagat whispered, "my man hasn't turned up. The bastard has perhaps escaped."

"I can't wait," Amrik gestured helplessness, "I now have with me a minute to minute programme."

"What do I do if my man doesn't turn up?" Bhagat feigned helplessness.

"What can I say brother! My part of the job is going fine. I'm always at your service."

"I can see that. Can you give me a return lift?" Bhagat asked.

"Perhaps." Amrik weighed the word alphabet by alphabet. He wasn't in a position to alienate Bhagat. He knew too much.

"Wait for me even if you're delayed by a day. Think of a proper cover for me. And be sure you don't talk to the Pakis about my failed mission. I have my eyes and ears in Pakistan too." Bhagat left, leaving Amrik in a quandary.

Hassan Rathore wouldn't like the idea, he knew. The Pakistani guests might protest as well. But, Dhiren Bhagat knew the colours of the marrow of most of the operators in his line, including Ram Karan Prasad's.

Well! Let the moment of truth come, he'd tackle the problem astutely. Amrik resigned to the uncertain prospects and muttered—*Wahe guru*. Why should such nagging problems dog him? *Sat Nam Wahe Guru*, Amrik sighed out loudly.

*

Bhagat faced the moment of truth that night itself. Radu Nagar, the key Pakistani carrier, had reached village Barduva with a caravan of five camels.

"Are you sure your man is reliable?" Bhagat asked his field officer.

"I'm putting my job on the line," he exuded confidence, "I know lay of the ground well."

Only a motorbike could approach Barduva. There was no defined road. Even if there was one, frozen waves of shifting sands obliterated it. The villagers didn't pester the authorities for one. It was better that way, for their business. A tarred road often offered tempting invitations to the police and revenue officials.

Radu Nagar usually camped at the residence of Jiva Koli, a border trader for generations.

"No, this won't do," Radu looked at Mirza Qasim alias Harfan Bukhari, as if he was evaluating a woolly camel, "your dress is too foreign. You require a proper

Sindhi dress. With this kind of *angreji* (English) dress you'll get roasted in the Rann sand blast."

Radu directed Harfan to drink a few glasses of water, salt and sugar added. Retention of fluid was necessary during the long trek, particularly in the saline desert tract between Suigam and Kuwala.

"Do you know Sindhi?" asked Radu.

"Very little, rather elementary. Urdu is my mother tongue." Replied Harfan.

"Help Jesu! Keep your trap shut. Between this place and Karachi, no one speaks Urdu and Punjabi. Avoid talking to the locals. It's my job to dump you at Karachi. After that it's your own ass that you have got to cover."

"*Chachaji* (uncle), take care that my man isn't intercepted by the Rangers. Your boys should safely take him to Karachi." Pleaded Bhagat.

"*Sant* (saint) Bhit Shah willing we'll cross all the barriers," Radu took out a small dose of cured opium from a plastic vial and put it carefully under his tongue, "It'll cost you Rupees twenty thousand." He spoke in a whispering tone.

"That's unreasonable. Isn't it *chacha*?" Asked Bhagat.

"It includes incidental expenses. Policemen aren't saints. I've to grease their palms, both the Indians and the Pakis."

"Agreed *Chachaji*." Bhagat accepted the pure and inevitable logic of Radu Nagar.

He guided Kaushal to a corner and fished out a silver chain with a square pendant from his pocket, "hang this around your neck."

"What's this?"

"This is the sacred thread of your trade," Bhagat opened the sealed pendant, took out a charm written in Urdu along with four bluish capsules, "the Urdu charm is real. It's a couplet from the Quran. Devout Muslims carry this for protection from evil forces." He said.

"What's in the tiny capsules?"

"Cyanide powder. Use these only when the pain of torture breaches the limits of your training and physical capabilities."

"You're arming me with death." An eerie laughter throttled out of Harfan's mouth.

"It's an arm of defence. It's part of the trade. You've been taught how to die gracefully and how to kill impeccably."

"It's nice you reminded me."

"It's always nice to die on one's own turf. Bye brother. Bon voyage." Bhagat slipped the necklace around Harfan's neck and turned back.

"See you back in Delhi." Harfan waved.

"Sure. I'll be there to receive you." Bhagat waved back.

To utter a few meaningless sweet words at the point of take off had become a ritual with Bhagat. These were dry and futile gestures. Most of them, these *resident agents* didn't come back home to heroes' welcome. They were routinely detected and summarily executed by the Inter Services Intelligence and the Pakistan Intelligence Bureau. He didn't expect Harfan to break the jinx. But somewhere inside he felt a tinge of remorse. He had come to like the jackal.

*

The caravan left Bharduva well past midnight. It skirted past Suigam and took a detour due southwest. Harfan was gracefully allowed to sit on a spare camel, not for too long, he was warned, only up to Gidhni Bet, a small green oasis amidst the saline sandy desert. That's where the last border police post was located. It was blessed with a sweet water spring, a scarce commodity, often costlier than gold.

"Whose *kafila* (caravan) is this?" The lone Indian police constable on duty at Gidhni Bet challenged.

"*Bade Baap* (big father), it's your poor son Radu." The veteran smuggler replied with molten humility.

"What're you carrying?"

"*Huzoor* (sir) inspector sahib, you know all. Here's your *salami* (offering). We shall leave in ten minutes. Can we have some water please?"

Radu passed on a bunch of Indian currency notes, about Rs.3000. That was the normal rate for small caravans. Another Rs. 3000 would be paid to the Sind Rangers at Junjo Bet post.

The caravan reached the Pakistani outpost at Junjo Bet, around five in the morning.

The Rangers' sentry wasn't satisfied with the customary offering.

"Who's this fellow? He wasn't there when you crossed over last." He pointed a finger at Harfan.

"*Khudaband* (representative of Allah), he's my nephew Jafferi, coming to our side in search of a bride. We Christians don't have many eligible grooms in our community. That you know *malik* (master), for sure." Radu tried to convince the constable with glib talk.

"You donkey of an *Issai* (Christian)," the Ranger proclaimed, "if you want to marry a Pakistani girl you must pay us taxes."

Harfan was ready with the cash. He fished out Rs. 3000 and passed it on to the minion of security.

"This is not enough. I want a big wedding party." The sepoy patronisingly slapped Harfan's back.

"*Huzoor*, leave this to me. You have to come to the *nikah* (marriage ceremony). Without you the priest won't perform the rituals."

The Ranger, mighty pleased with the cash and the prospect of an invitation, allowed the caravan to pass. Radu was a known face and a good milking cow. The Border Rangers did not mind these petty *sawaris* (passengers) promoting petty trade. His likes kept the economy moving in the absence of a formal trade agreement between India and Pakistan.

Around the same time Amrik Singh Johal's merchandise crossed over to Pakistan, about 5 km below a point chosen by Radu's caravan. Kartik Dushad, a low caste Hindu from Bihar, a caste crony of Ram Karan Prasad, received them. Kartik's job was limited. He was to shepherd the women to the bidding platform across the border. Rathore's men armed with rifles and assorted weapons joined Kartik, soon after the convoy crossed over to Pakistan. They lined up the Merwa women, hanging between hope and despair, in a sprawling mango grove. Experts carried out detailed examinations of the merchandise to determine market value for each.

The rating process depended on physical features, looks, and attractiveness. The younger ones were segregated. Each one of them would fetch Rupees one hundred thousand. The rest were put in a separate group, meant for the Karachi brothels, each one selling at a lower premium.

A few young and attractive ones, who were expected to fetch a fabulous price of half a million each, were earmarked for markets in Afghanistan and Iran. The rest would find their way to the Northwest Frontier Province, Sheikhdoms of the Northern Territory and even to the tents of some desert Bedouins.

The haggard belles from remote Merwa weren't even aware of their market value. They didn't even know that the female species was the prime carrier of genes, all over the globe, in all civilisations. Perhaps two generations later some Uzbeg, or some Kazakh would carry the chromosomes and genes of the Merwa women, resulting in the queer mixing of the Central Asian strain with those of the Austro-Negrito stock. Johal's merchandise was taken in a separate tarpaulin covered trucks and driven to the forward destination at Mirpur Khas. The final auction would take place, in a remote village, where Rathore was camping with the prospective buyers from foreign and domestic markets.

The innocent Merwa women joined Kartik Dushad in frivolous jokes and some of them even tried to find out the nature of their prospective jobs. Kartik, an articulate entertainer, had managed to titillate their imagination and expectations. The path ahead, he added, was rosy and money was about to rain down on them, more torrentially than monsoon pouring.

Some of the belles, in their abundant excitement, started humming rhythmic tunes, as if they were ceremonially dancing along to the weekly village market.

It was a celebration time, of some sort.

15

Radu Nagar and his half brother Mukhtiar lived in *bhangikhola* (scavengers' living quarters), a shanty corner of Nagar Parkar, in ghettos assigned to the low caste sub-humans ages ago by the Hindu kings. Succeeding Muslim rulers had used their blades for proselytising the scavenging class to Islam. Worthy Christian missionaries had followed with greater zeal to save the souls of the scavengers. Radu and Mukhtiar never realised that their souls were saved. But they were vaguely aware of their Christian status, being the followers of Jesu Masiha, Jesus the Messiah.

They finally succeeded in fusing the tenets of the *Shariat*, the *Bible,* and the *Manu Samhita* into a thriving border smuggling syndicate. On this well-oiled ground, all of them coexisted, transcending all taboos, prejudices, and sanctions of the Books. *Bhangikhola* had assumed a unique character, a rare confluence of the three major religions, an ancient amalgam of animism and Hinduism, Islam and Christianity.

However, the lowest of the low followed their own brand of social and religious customs and continued to process raw animal hides and carry night soil. It made little difference if they carried head-loads of Hindu, Muslim, or Christian night soil. Time passed by. They were imprisoned in curses hurled by a million witches, some calling themselves sacred Brahmins, some Pak (pure) Mullahs and some Fathers and Priests.

Mukhtiar, a practicing Christian, was no exception. He had, over time, mastered a few tricks to win over the local police and civil officials. The likes of Mukhtiar and Radu knew well the tricks of the illegitimate border trade. The smuggling syndicates could not do without them. Radu and Mukhtiar's caste relations in India were too many and they knew the tricks prevailing on the other side of the international border.

Harfan Bukhari, Radu Nagar's guest, was consigned to a dark dinghy room, at the far end of Mukhtiar's outhouse, next to his pigsty. Since his arrival he hadn't ventured out; a strict curfew was imposed on him by Radu.

Harfan didn't resent the rotten smell and dampness of the room. By now, he had learnt to live with all odds. His chemistry didn't explode any more at the slightest provocation. The psychological buffer assiduously created by Maulana Rizwan and Dhiren Bhagat had helped in developing a detached outlook towards the ambience.

Harfan wasn't asleep. His mind flipped over the pages of events during the last six months.

Shit! He laughed at himself. What funny turns his life had taken? What a life it was, that of a freewheeling macho Casanova, murderer and a drug peddler! And what a life he was stepping onto!

Surprise of surprises! His body and soul chemistry had added on new salts. He didn't miss the booze and bumpy female contours. His endocrinal glands triggered off a strange secretion at the very thought of women. An acute sense of aversion crept in, accompanied by flashes of the face of Rajni Krittika Hemaprabha Rao. That was a big foolish girl, too dumb and mighty stupid. The heavens would have not come crashing if she had shared his bed.

Harfan again felt a ghastly shiver running down his spine, at the thought of raping Hema's cold dead body. He spat out a lump of saliva at a dark corner of the room and coiled up on the cot in a spring action.

Shit! He wasn't a vulture to feast on a dead body. The stupid woman had left a deep scar on his psyche; she had defeated him in her death.

Mukhtiar Masih slithered in like a seeping shadow.

"Qasim Mian, wake up. We've to start at eight tonight to take the bus for Tando Adam."

"*Ji* (yes), where is Radu *chacha* (uncle)?"

"Gone to Umerkot to meet Mian Farooq." Mukhtiar replied.

"Who is he?"

"He's our boss, the right hand man of Hassan Rathore and his boss Sardar Illahi. In this side of Pakistan, he's the law. His men are everywhere, in the police, Sind Rangers, army, and civil administration. Rathore's gold, silver, and drugs flow freely into India and in many parts of the world. Not the yellow, but white and brown gold." Mukhtiar's face lighted up even in shadowy darkness.

"What's this white and brown gold?" Harfan felt an urge to have a glimpse of the intricate tunnel.

"Opium derivatives, made in the tribal areas by everybody, whoever can dupe and rope the law in, and anyone who can keep the army happy. They've their own cartels. On your side, the boss is Harubhai Dasani, a fabulous business tycoon in Bombay. And his big boss in Delhi is said to be a powerful minister."

"Who's that blessed fellow? Ram Karan Prasad?"

"We're too small to know all that."

"It must be him." Harfan muttered under his breath.

"Forget it. These are matters of our bread and salt. You shouldn't be concerned. Radu will turn up any moment. He's tying up the loose ends for your safe journey to Karachi. Put on these clothes of a Sufi ballad singer, a follower of Shah Latif of Bhit Shah. That's your cover, till you reach Karachi." Mukhtiar explained the props and dialogues for his next act.

"Who's this Shah Latif?"

"A revered *Sufi* saint in this part of Pakistan. His followers have free access, even in restricted areas."

"Tell me one thing," Harfan offered a cigarette to Mukhtiar, "have you ever heard the name of Ram Karan Prasad?"

"Does uttering this name make you any richer? Hurry and dress up. And don't forget to have your dinner." Mukhtiar tried to silence Harfan.

"You didn't answer my question."

"You don't push over death by learning to spell the word. Get ready." Mukhtiar left in a huff.

Harfan Bukhari alias Ramendra Kaushal concluded that Ram Karan Prasad was the counterpart of Illahi and Rathore. It must be him. Ram Karan's class wasn't concerned with war, Kashmir, Kachchh and any other aspect of the bloodiest relationship between the two umbilical adolescent antagonists. And people like Vidyasagar Suri, Ramendra Kaushal and Amrik Johal were sucked into the slick world of easy money, free booze and occasional women. That was the eternal Indian motto: everything was done under the veil of a fake philosophy...*Bahujana Hitaya,* for the good of the greater majority. Shit! The parasites!

*

Radu Nagar arrived at about seven, accompanied by a tout, Liaquat Masih, a native of Bohri Bazar, Karachi. A frequent visitor to Delhi, Liaquat was a legend in clandestine border crossing.

"We travel up to Tando Adam by bus and take a train to Hala. We cross the Indus by boat. After I put you on a train at Rajri, you'll be under the care of my friend Liaquat. The train will take you to Karachi Cantonment station."

Radu Nagar described the route on a piece of paper and destroyed it in the flame of a matchstick.

"And keep this." Radu handed over a photo identity card to Harfan with a distinct number, which certified his permanent residency at Umerkot.

"Keep this card carefully. Liaquat charges Rs. 5000 as professional fees. Do you have the cash?"

"Yes."

"Good. Get ready. Don't forget to don the costume and carry the *Sufi* tambourine."

The rail and road journey to Hala was monotonous, except for the occasional police searches. A glib talker, Liaquat kept on entertaining the fellow passengers, mostly army sepoys, with juicy stories about the defeat of Indian forces all along the border. He and Harfan managed to sing a rural Sind tune, in praise of *Allah*, beseeching the Lord for a miraculous performance by Pakistan against the heathen Indians. Like the Tughlaks, Lodis, Khiljis, Ghoris and The Great Mughals, the new nation shall bring the *kafirs* under Islamic rule and fly the Crescent Flag on the ramparts of the Red Fort.

Some soldiers, high on intoxicants, danced to the catchy tune and dropped coins in the bowl of the followers of Shah Latif of Bhit Shah.

Liaquat and Harfan danced past the Karachi Cantonment railway platform. Once out of police cordon, they hired a *tonga* (horse cart) and made straight for Nazma guesthouse at Khazoor Bazar. The first floor dinghy room overlooked shanty shops selling, piles over piles of dried fruits, to the accompaniment of symphony orchestrated by the oscillating wings of bees, flies and numerous other winged creatures. The usual crowd milling around was from rural Sind and neighbouring Baluchistan, who forayed into the city seeking good bargains and pleasure in the red-light areas.

"Qasim Bhai, do you know the Shehnaz guesthouse in Delhi's Ballimaran?" Asked Liaquat.

"Yes. How do you know that nice place?" Harfan felt surprised and apprehensive.

"I'm in your trade, smuggling gold and brown sugar. I've been to Delhi five times, carrying white powder and *hawala* (illegal cash transfer) cash. *Yar* (friend), I can't forget Yasmin. She gave me heavenly pleasures." Liaquat's eyes flashed happiness reminiscing the good times back in the alleys of old Delhi.

"Yah, some of them are as pretty as fairies. Perhaps I've seen her." Harfan lied.

"Have you seen her? Did you ever sleep with my beauty?"

"No friend. I've my young wife at home and she hovers over me like a mother hen." Harfan lied again.

"Tell her, when you go back, that her dream is my cherished treasure. I'll be back to Delhi once this bloody war is over and bring her home to Umerkot."

"*Insha Allah.*" Repeated Harfan.

*

On his third day in Karachi Harfan moved around the markets and selected a public telephone booth at Bartan Galli post office, next to Bombay Jewellery Mart.

"Is it the Indian Embassy?"

"Yes. It is the office of the Consul General."

"Can I talk to Irfan Cowasji, your driver?"

"Who's there?"

"I'm Farzan Tyrewalla, his cousin from Lahore."

"Hold on."

"Hello brother Farzan," the voice of Irfan, a Pakistan based driver of the Indian Consulate, boomed on the phone, "when did you arrive?"

"A few minutes back. How do we meet?"

"Where are you calling from?"

"Bartan Galli."

"You *motherchod* (motherfucker), is it a question to ask? Take a *tonga* and ask him to fly you to my Nishat Road residence, next to Jubilee Market. Reach there by six."

"Six should be fine brother. *Shabba khair.*" Harfan disconnected.

Irfan Cowasji, a Parsee by descent, was a vital link in X Operations. A local employee of the Indian Mission for the last 10 years, Irfan was an important asset, an undercover FIB operative, holding a non-diplomatic rank. His prime task was to spot prospective contacts from among the Pakistani visa seekers and arrange their exclusive meetings with the consular officer.

The Jubilee Market residence of Irfan was an elaborate affair. The ancient house, a 6-room *haveli* (mansion), a legacy of the colonial past was the ultimate in urban luxury. Irfan's joint family lived in the midst of urban and ancient Karachi, enjoying the rural bounty.

"So brother Farzan," Irfan initiated the talks, "from now on you're Harfan Bukhari, nephew of Shamim Bukhari."

"How do I get to him?"

"Your uncle lives near Memon Masjid, off Jodia Bazaar." Irfan described Shamim Bukhari's residence in graphic detail.

"How do I get introduced to him? Don't remember when I saw him last. For him, I'm as good as dead."

"Leave this to me. Your main problem may come from his young wife and her two brothers. They're waiting for the old man's final journey to the grave."

"You mean a nephew from nowhere will upset their melon cart!"

"Right brother. Tackle them carefully. And you won't be in Karachi forever. Consul sahib will brief you. In the meantime, I'll get the necessary papers for you. Give me your Umerkot identity card, and I want 10 copies of your photograph." Irfan spoke in short sentences.

"How much money do I give you?"

"Don't bother, Consul sahib will take care. You require a passport, citizenship card, ration card and being war time, a movement warrant as well."

Irfan's style of talking worried Harfan Bukhari. In the endless maze of bureaucracy, someone somewhere might raise eyebrows and start burrowing holes like adamant rodents. Could they be pacified by mere offerings of currency notes? Yes. The rituals were the same, in Pakistan too, assured Irfan.

Irfan's matter of fact approach impressed Harfan. The man exuded confidence and knew his way about the loops and tunnels of the Pakistani bureaucracy. He was as foxy as his counterparts in India.

*

Irfan broke the news to Shamim Bukhari with a dramatic flourish. He had scouted out the old *muhajir's* prayer patterns at *masjid* (mosque) *Anjuman,* a small place tucked inside the busy market place. Shamim never missed his Friday prayers and giving away alms to the milling beggars.

That Friday too he turned up on the dot and physically bumped into Irfan Cowasji, who stood next to a pomegranate vendor's stall.

"*Assalaam-u- wale kum* Bukhari sahib." Irfan startled Shamim by the intimate greeting.

"*Wale kum*...I couldn't place you *janab*."

Shamim's words froze as he looked at the young face standing next to Irfan. It was a replica of yet another faded memory, that of his brother Maqdoom. Is he Harfan, the only surviving member of his brother's family? Or was he dreaming? He had been receiving letters from the lost nephew for some time; some posted from Delhi, some from Aligarh and a few from Umerkot. He expected him at Karachi, but not now, when a war raged on the borders.

"How's the day? Going for prayers?" Irfan fired a volley at the confused and perplexed Shamim.

Shamim couldn't speak. His eyes were glued on Harfan's face.

"*Wale kum asalaam mian*," he managed to react, "who's this fellow and who are you?"

Irfan dragged Shamim behind a movie hoarding and whispered into his ears.

"I'm Khaliq, a border trader. That's enough you should know about me. Here's your long lost nephew. Don't mind the small drama. We're at war with Hindustan and I'd to take tremendous risk to smuggle him into Pakistan. Don't advertise his arrival."

"How did he come? Police CID are everywhere."

"Allah has listened to your prayers. The *sawari* (border trader) who helped him cross over is my cousin. I thought I'd favour you by arranging a discreet meeting."

"What're your charges?"

"It's a free service to a fellow *muhajir*." Irfan turned on his heels towards the mosque, his hands rose in prayer, "my family is from Baroda." He added.

"It's all willed by the *Allah*," Shamim replied, "his face had scared me. It's a replica of my brother's face. Indeed he is my nephew." Old Bukhari embraced Harfan and wept like a child.

The reunion with Harfan sent fresh, delighted but painful streaks of light into the clogged labyrinth of Shamim's memory. Harfan was just a toddler when he had seen him last. His mother, daughter of a former officer with the Patiala State Army, a blue blooded Syeed, carried real Arab blood in her veins.

Shamim couldn't remember what had exactly happened to his nephew. He was presumed dead. Those weren't the times to shed idle tears. He alone had managed to cross over to Pakistan, leaving behind his wife and others to the mercy of the wild hyenas.

"Don't let emotions betray your precious nephew, Mian Shamim," Irfan lighted a cigarette and offered one to him, "*Allah Tallah* has many miracles and wonders in store. He can make a dead alive, and call a living soul back unto Him. Truth isn't always the truth, though it seems to be true. Dreams often take on real shapes."

"*Subhan Allah,*" chanted Shamim Bukhari, "the wishes of the Almighty shall prevail."

"*Chacha*, one final word of caution," counselled Irfan, "take him home tonight. Don't beat your excited drum. He's crossed over from India without a visa, and a war's going on. Guard him carefully, until I get his papers ready. Pass him off as your nephew from Hyderabad, for the time being."

"Don't you think the police will ask questions?"

"Not really, unless you blabber out. He has genuine Umerkot papers with him."

"Why should I? He's my only male inheritor."

"Guard him from your wrestler brothers-in-law. They won't like a strange nephew dropping in on their dinner plate right through the roof."

"I needn't be a burden on you uncle. I'd better stay in a guesthouse and look for a job." Harfan spoke for the first time. He wasn't enamoured with the idea of being confronted by Shamim's brothers-in-law and pretended inheritors.

"Don't be silly son," Shamim hugged him again, "my own blood can't rot in a guesthouse. And you're an educated youth. My friends Jung Sher Khan and Mian Israr Sharief would be too glad to employ you."

"Not so fast Shamim sahib," Irfan intervened, "let the kid relax."

"That's fine Khaliq *mian*. But I know they would lap up my nephew. They're the leading military contractors and suppliers."

"As you wish *chacha*. But take care, I've retrieved your lost diamond." Irfan took leave with a discreet wink at Harfan. He had other commitments to attend to.

"*Allah meherban* (Mercy of Allah). He's a real diamond, the *Koh-I-Noor* of my clan."

Shamim saluted Irfan and entered the mosque, followed by Harfan, for Friday prayers.

16

Karachi's summer air was a continuous bath to Harfan's skin, very different from the dry desert air of Jhunjhunu. It burnt, itched, and oozed out body fluids in a steady stream of sweat.

He liked the city, a bit mixture of Bombay and Calcutta. Variety was the soul of the people in Karachi too. They came from everywhere, Punjab to Waziristan, Chaman to Kanjarkot.

On the sixteenth day, Irfan sought out Harfan at Bartan Galli market, at a pre-fixed rendezvous.

"The honeymoon is over. The boss wants to meet you."

"Where?"

"Memorise the map, take a bus, and reach Makli Hill. It takes about 2 hours." Irfan brushed past Harfan, who was apparently busy in examining a silver trinket. The meeting took place after three days, under the shadows of the graveyards and ruins at the Little Mecca, the Makli Hill.

"Meet our Consul sahib, Mr. Dagar." Irfan introduced Harfan to the Consular official, under the walls of the tomb of Isa Khan Tarkhan, a Governor in the Mughal courts.

Makli Hill, the world's largest necropolis with a million graves, mausoleums of the unknown, gave Harfan a scary feeling. A graveyard for the nearby town of Thatta, the ancient capital of lower Sind, Makli Hill had seen dynasties after dynasties being buried, layer upon layer. The haunted chambers stood as mute witnesses to the glories and foibles of a retreating Alexander the Great, the Tarkhan and Sammah Kings and the other lesser ruling families.

"What's the brief for me?" Harfan asked.

"Listen carefully. Leave for Lahore day after tomorrow. A room has been booked at Azam guesthouse next to Dabbi Bazaar. Memorise the sketch and destroy it. Irfan will receive you there and give onward directions."

"I believe, I'm on my own after that!"

"Not really. This is your last meeting with me. Don't contact Irfan or me again. Irfan will evaporate after settling you at Lahore. He'll give you some money to set yourself up at Jhumra. Start your business and merge with the background. One

Alam will contact you on the 28th of this month. He takes over from me and hereafter will be your link with Delhi."

"Who is he?"

"He is Delhi's man."

"How do I recognise him?"

"He'd recognise you."

"What about my papers?"

"Irfan would take care. These are as genuine as money can buy. Take care of security drills."

"How do I go back?" Harfan asked Irfan.

"Take a bus ride to the city. Your initiation has begun." Irfan cautioned Harfan.

"I presume so. Who's this Alam?"

"Don't ask questions." Replied Irfan.

"What do you mean?"

"You'd learn soon. Listen and obey him. That'll be good for your health." Irfan cautioned the new talent.

Shamim didn't like the idea of his nephew moving over to Lahore. The only surviving male member of his dynasty, the Bukharis of Ludhiana, he wished, should settle down in Karachi, and take over his business.

"Don't move to the uncertain waters of Lahore. It's not a good place for business. I'd take you to Jung Sher Khan, the biggest military supplier. His friends can fix a steady job for you. Business isn't the best option in a new place." Shamim suggested.

"I can't be your inheritor. Your wife and her brothers won't agree. I can start a factory, in due course."

"The idea is fine, but Punjab is a choppy sea for we *muhajirs*. The Jats hate us. Take up a job and try your luck. Jung sahib is an influential person and Alam sahib will be glad to help."

"Who's this Alam?" Harfan was confronted with this mysterious name for the third time. Delhi hadn't briefed him about this intermediary.

"He is a big contractor in our line of work, with good links at the top."

"Hope he'd find me useful." Harfan pretended to be skeptical about the idea of seeking a job.

"Leave that to me. Jung sahib is a powerful man. I supply spares to his factory. He can offer you a comfortable placement."

Shamim reassured his nephew and informed that Jung Sher Khan had already sorted out the minor problem. He had found a nice start up job at Sangla Hills, in the defence accessory production factory of Israr International. The elder scion of the Sharief Empire, an influential army supplier and a burgeoning steel manufacturer, needed a young marketing executive and a liaison manager.

*

The journey to Lahore city station was monotonous, except for the guttural and intestinal noises produced by soldiers, some limping back home, and others marching to the forward trenches on the Indian borders. A few soldiers abused Hindu India and a few others wished to consign the mothers of the Pakistani military leaders to the red light abodes in the nearest towns. They were happy and they were bitter. Some felt happy as the war provided an opportunity to fight the *jahil* (ignorant) Hindus and the others were bitter, as they knew that another victory for Islam over India was impossible. The kaleidoscope of emotions charmed Harfan.

However, the anxiety of alighting at a strange place was taken care of by Irfan, sporting a Pathan suit, with a colourful headgear to match.

"Hotel? Do you want hotel accommodation brother?" The voice was familiar, though the body was attired in strange apparel.

"Follow me." Whispered Irfan.

A taxi took them to Azam guesthouse at Dabbi Bazaar. The room was booked in a fake name.

"You get full fifteen days here. Acclimatise with the people and the place." Irfan suggested.

"When do I report to Israr Sharief?"

"Wait for Alam. He's the man to fix your orbit. He'd decide your fate henceforth."

"Is he another *Paigambar* (the Prophet)? How can he decide my fate?" Harfan fired the sentence forcefully.

"Look brother," Irfan looked straight into Harfan's eyes, "I don't know what *masalas* (ingredients) are used in the making of a messiah. But I know for sure that, this man Alam is very important in your present and future laps of the race. Keep this money, Rs. 20,000. Get Punjabi clothes stitched. Avoid talking in Hindi, use Urdu and Punjabi. It's 13th day of the month. Alam would come on the 28th. Go by his advice." Irfan delivered quick instructions and prepared to leave.

"How do I get to Alam?"

"Don't bother, he'd search you out."

"Are you so scared of him?" asked Harfan.

"Find out for yourself. Alam has deep conduits to people like Israr, Jung Sher Khan, and the Generals who rule the country. Ask questions silently and discover solutions loudly. That's the order from Consul Dagar sahib."

Irfan left in a huff. He was supposed to take a truck ride to Karachi, avoiding train and long distance bus services. His clandestine visit to Lahore was unofficial, even without the knowledge of the Head of the Chancery.

*

The Azam guesthouse room, barely 8x10 ft, hung low and made Harfan feel claustrophobic. The walls, he felt, were being pushed by a giant hydraulic machine for pulverising him down to a few grams of dust. Lack of space within him and out in the dingy room choked his emotions and breath. Fear of the unknown and the anxiety of facing a mysterious Alam had filled in his space within. Conflicting emotions had begun puncturing his dream bag, the dreams of a perfect launching at the desired orbit and the grand finale of avenging his father's death. The spy-job was a mere platform. His Pakistan mission was very private and intimately personal.

He opened the window.

A whiff of fresh air disengaged his mind from the claustrophobic gloom inside. The open piece of sky and the cloud formations hanging above the trees suddenly transcended his wildest imagination. A massive tunnel, dark, but momentarily brightened up by pale blue tongues of fire, followed by rumblings of thunder flashed past his screen. Yes, it was definitely an uncertain tunnel. He had himself burrowed deep dark tunnels underneath the lively pulsating world above, just like a wingless hymenopterans insect. Could he ever fly out into the open skies, to his freedom? Perhaps, he had crawled past one tunnel, wading through blood, rotten flesh, slime, and grime of all the misdeeds of his own making. Now, he was about to enter another tunnel, colonised by his supposed exterminators. That was a nameless and faceless world of surreptitious activities, a kind of contradictory existence, full of deceit and deception.

Why did he shape his life so wild? And how did he walk into the FIB trap? Was it necessary to kill and rape that innocent girl?

The rumblings inside his stomach gurgled loudly.

It was indeed foolish of him. No, he wasn't born out of killer seeds. The tunnels he crossed were nightmarish. His will to live and wish to grow new wings of freedom should materialise soon. No. He wouldn't accept another phase of tunnel crawling. He must fly free, like the birds, yes those tailorbirds weaving their nests in the trees below Azam guesthouse. Harfan turned away from the open piece of sky, ordered coffee, and lighted a cigarette. His struggle with the conflicting images and emotions, the invitation to the open piece of sky, the birds, and nests continued to flutter their rainbow wings around him.

Harfan decided to escape the confines of the messy and mossy smelling room and take deliberate and calibrated steps beyond the old curtains. It was time he prepared for the new role; he was supposed to play in the sub-continental drama, scripted by the spymasters in Delhi, and orchestrated by his destiny.

*

Next few days, attired in a Punjabi suit, and a mosque cap to match, Harfan ventured out to breathe in the pulsating spores of Lahore life. He visited the Badshahi, Wazir Khan, and Sunheri Mosques, all in the old city. The intricate woodcarvings and frescoes by craftsmen from Chiniot, the neighbouring district, amazed him. Wasn't Chiniot a part of his father's kingdom. Yes it was. Kasturi had narrated the fascinating stories of the enslaved Chiniot artisans, whose exquisite artistry had given shape to the Taj Mahal, the love-dream of emperor Shahjahan.

Harfan brushed aside the thought and moved around the throbbing market places and small lanes that were impassable even on foot. The entire space was crammed with all sorts of vehicles, *tonga*, hand and ox driven cart and cycle-rickshaws. Harfan enjoyed the pulsating life around him, which exuded a unique vitality. They weren't different from the honeycombed shop cluster of shops in the charmed and vibrant lanes behind Delhi's Jama Masjid. The same people, the same ecstasies, and the same oriental friendliness fascinated Harfan. He didn't find any difference between the rhythm of life in the dingy Lahore markets and those back in the myriad alleys around Jama Masjid.

"Sir, may I borrow your matchbox?" Harfan's charmed introspection was interrupted by a whispering voice.

The slightly built young person with a lush beard, long hair and a rat-tail moustache standing before him looked quite ordinary, except for his deep-set eyes, which weren't really looking for a matchbox. Harfan's auto-reflex pressed the alarm bell.

A police informer?

An ISI agent?

A Pakistan IB agent?

He offered a cigarette and lighted it for the stranger. The vaporous shallow person inhaled a lung-full of smoke, exhaled leisurely, and opened up a small conversation.

"New to Lahore?"

"No. I'm from Karachi, hoping to take up a job here."

"A nice place isn't it! Like the walled city of Delhi."

"Can't say. Haven't been to that grand city of the Mughals." Harfan parried, "Lahore is an *aftab* (sun) by itself."

"Like to meet *chandni jaisi* (moonlight like) girls?" The x-ray eyes of the slightly built person twinkled with a naughty smile.

"Thanks friend, not really looking for one." Harfan was now sure that the stranger was a pimp, looking for hungry wolves, at a fat commission.

"Real beautiful one, film starlet."

"Thanks for the offer."

"Don't worry. I'd get her cheap...only for you."

Harfan abruptly disengaged from the strange character and briskly walked towards a vendor selling *sherbet* (drink). He looked back. The slightly built pimp was gone.

Thank God! No, he had no appetite for any woman, after the Hema episode. Enough was enough.

The task ahead was stupendous and he was just about to be launched into a strange orbit. This was no time for brooding over a bad dream. The realities yet to be faced, he expected, should be made of sterner stuff.

Harfan hired a cycle-rickshaw, usually driven by East Pakistan Bengalis and left for the Sunheri Masjid to attend *johar namaj* (afternoon prayer).

He went through the motions of bending and prostrating immaculately like a religious Muslim. His mind wasn't in it. He didn't believe in religious rituals, either Hindu or Muslim. But, in Pakistan, as a good Muslim he should be seen more in the prayer gatherings than in the social circuit.

The rituals over, he hired a *tonga* and asked the driver to take him to Lahore Fort, another Mughal marvel, built by Akbar the Great in 1560.

Another few hours to kill, he thought, before he returned to the guesthouse for an insipid mid-day meal. Harfan took a cosy seat on a marble platform in front of the Sheesh Mahal (palace of mirrors).

"Like me to be your guide sir!" Harfan was awakened out of his thought by a familiar voice. The same pimp stood before him, a slight mocking smile lingered at a remote corner of his face.

"Thanks."

"It's a wonderful place sir," the faint voice persisted, "no charge sir. I'll guide you free of charge."

"Thanks brother," Harfan bridled his galloping temper, "leave me alone."

He walked past the nagging pimp towards a vendor dispensing small eats and drinks. The rumbling stomach signalled that he was hungry. The intestinal juices were almost eating at the walls, creating a sensation of pain and cramp. As he turned around to approach the hawker, two *burka* (veil) clad women edged past him and ordered cold drinks.

Harfan stepped back to wait his turn, lighted a cigarette, and tried to concentrate on a gang of child beggars. His eyes didn't miss the vaporous pimp standing under an old canopy.

His roving and suspicious gaze suddenly hit a pair of fabulous liquid blue eyes, which were exploring him. Yes, they were exploring him. The blue eyes oscillated in quick movements like a pair of summer swallows crisscrossing the skies in search of raindrops.

Harfan's eyes were auto-locked to the pair of unknown bottomless blue eyes. Black corneal moons centred light azure blue, nay light marine blue eyes. Harfan simply plunged into the azure depths. He lost his way.

The vapour of suspicion that hovered over the slightly built pimp suddenly gave way to a serene calmness. He was unable to unlock the gaze from the bewitching blue eyes.

The owner of the fabulous, young, liquid and infinite eyes too didn't shift her gaze. She lifted her veil partially and made a vain motion of sipping the canned drink with indeterminate effort; her lips wide open. Her eyes were in a gridlock with those of the unknown youth with aquiline Greek features.

Oh God! What eyes! What could be behind these eyes? Behind the *hijab* slits, the aquamarine eyes, lined with dark black lashes and pink skin invited Harfan to splash in. The miniature seas, tender and apprehensive liquids rippling uncertainly appeared to be a sure invitation to death.

Harfan couldn't move. Glued to her gaze, his entire consciousness started burning silently like scented camphor, emitting an imperceptible fragrance. It wasn't the mammal response he used to get from the hidden chambers of his cranium. No, his sex organs didn't wake up, pulsating through his veins and sending a tingling sensation to his temples.

The rippling eyes, for a change, were transmitting strange signals. The fluids from the blue eyes were about to transport him to a domain, which was perhaps called love and caring. His neurons transported him far beyond the ghostly apparition of Rajni Krittika Hemaprabha Rao. What was that heavenly invitation for? Sinking and dying? Soaking and attaining nirvana?

What was it? Was it love? Or was it the old itch? Harfan could not discern clearly, what was happening inside his chest cavity. He did not like to believe that the old Delhi campus itch had revisited him. It was surely not that fleshy urge.

The alarm bell, which was primed by Bhagat and Rizwan, rang again automatically inside his head. No. He shouldn't succumb to frivolities. The allurement of unknown blue eyes could be the harbinger of an intelligence trap.

Harfan decided to hang to the orbit worked out by the launch directors in Delhi. He was too well burnt a brick in the alleys of desire and lust to fall in love with an unknown pair of eyes. Harfan made educated efforts to remove his looks with a deliberate jerk of his head. But his eyes refused to move. They were still locked with the strange apertures of the scintillating life force standing ahead.

Was he in love, with those ravishing doe eyes? Harfan Bukhari stood frozen under the blazing sun and for the first time felt a faint pain somewhere in the undefined domain called heart.

What was happening to him?

The second lady, perhaps an elderly one, didn't miss the two pairs of eyes lost in each other, fathoming the language of their hearts.

She pushed her younger companion with a slight movement of her elbow and pulled down the eye-strip of her *hijab.* They moved out in elegant strides and advanced towards the main hall, a string of nine rooms with latticed marble screens. They moved on for a while behind the fine latticed marble curtains.

Harfan moved like a shadow, on the other side of the marble screens, trying not to loose sight of the owner of the fabulous eyes. Fleeting images of the frail and fragrant figure kept on attracting him like a galactic magnet.

The elderly woman escorted her charge out and hired a *tonga.* Harfan didn't miss the younger un-ethereal figure turning her face, perhaps to capture another look at the fair, robust young man, with a fascinating Greek complexion, deep blue eyes and an aquiline nose.

Harfan's effort to board a cycle rickshaw was obstructed by a man standing next to him. He grabbed the cart and threw a benign smile at Harfan. Holy hell!

It was the same pimp. Was he following him? The fear that the pimp could be a Pakistani intelligence operative rattled his bones again. But the urge to follow the *burka* clad beauty prompted him to board another rickshaw and follow the *tonga.* The horse cart, after traversing several lanes stopped near Masti Gate, once used as the main gate of the fort and named after the mosque of Maryam Zamani, a Christian wife of the Muslim emperor, Akbar the Great.

The *burka*-clad figures skirted an octagonal battlement and entered a narrow footpath. Harfan stopped short of the lane, fearing the unknown. For the first time he felt that, to follow a woman, as he was doing now, was an indecent act. It could highly embarrass the owner of the fascinating eyes.

Pursuing a woman, in a blind lane, was against the rules of the game, ingrained in his brain by Bhagat and his Company. Fascinated sure he was, but there was no use jumping into the wild and unknown waters. Fathoming must be done first, like a good sailor. What about that pimp? The thought came back like an adamant fruit-flea. Was he an ISI operative? Must be. What for, otherwise, would he follow so doggedly? The mixed bag of emotions helped Harfan to put his mind on two distinct rails. The pimp, he concluded, wasn't a Pakistani sleuth. The ISI, whenever in doubt, pressed the trigger first. The dreaded Company would have given him a ride to nowhere by this time, if they had the slightest doubt about his identity. That fellow could as well be a genuine pimp, looking for some easy money.

However, the other experience filled his mind with a mysterious fragrance. For the first time he felt a strange feeling in the depth of his heart. It wasn't the intestinal juices that stirred up the feeling. The gastronomic fluid had stopped troubling him since he first locked eyes with the fathomless blues of the unknown beauty.

Today he didn't feel the old itch. Biting desire didn't trouble him. The animal in him had elevated itself to a newer plane. His biological chemistry had given way to something new. Harfan couldn't define what it was.

The zephyr left behind by the tender beauty intoxicated him, no doubt, but it also infused a strange strength in him. The frozen, mummified blue face of Rajni Krittika Hemaprabha didn't scare him. She fleetingly appeared in his mind's screen like a goblin. Harfan catapulted the image away, by using superior mental strength. No, she wouldn't scare him any more.

The sensation was different this balmy afternoon. The strange doe-eyed gaze had penetrated his corneal films and entered the intricate jungle of neurons seated deep below the cortex. Signals from those eyes had scintillated his body cells. It was love and only love.

He was surely in love, Harfan felt, with the eyes and obviously with the frame and mind behind that *burka.*

He moved towards an eating joint and ordered roasted chicken and thin hand made flat bread. For the first time, after arriving in Pakistan, Harfan enjoyed a hearty meal.

The shopkeeper, a migrant from Nuh, Indian Punjab, was sharp enough to notice Harfan's peculiar Urdu pronunciation.

"A Hindustani Mussalman?"

"Yes," Harfan looked up apprehensively, but retrieved his composure quickly, "Now from Karachi, looking for a job."

"Which part in India?"

"Ludhiana, Punjab."

"Say so. Your Urdu has a distinct HIndustani flavour."

"Brother I'm looking for a room. I want to start a business. Is there anything available in the lanes around?"

"Brother, the lane in front is known as Masti Galli, historically the homes of the *mujrawallis* (danseuses and singers). They've been here since the *shahi* (Mughal) days. Interested?"

"Don't really know." Harfan finished the lunch with relish, licking the bowl of lentils.

"The biggest house belongs to Zahoor sahib, a big businessman. One of the ladies you just saw is his daughter." The shopkeeper gave him a sufficient hint that he had noticed the enchanted gazes of Harfan following the belles in *burka*.

"I don't understand you." Harfan shrugged out the nascent distress signal.

"Mian, eyes can hide murder but not love." The man from Nuh again laughed.

His eyes twinkled with naughty sparkles.

"That's nonsense," Harfan hedged his emotions, "I'm from Karachi and looking for business opportunities. Accommodation near the main markets would be convenient." He added.

"Welcome. Love and business aren't strange companions. I'll scout for you, both a *makan* and a *makanwali* (A house and the lady who makes it home)." The shopkeeper offered a cigarette and a *pan* (betel leaf) free of cost.

"Take it Mian, fresh from India."

Harfan accepted the offer and looked out for the pimp. He was not there. Must have gone scouting for other customers. He hailed a cycle rickshaw and boarded it leisurely. As the cart started rolling, a middle-aged person jumped in and sat beside him.

"Can I hitch a lift with you?"

Harfan looked at him in pale horror. Perhaps this was the beginning and end of his intelligence career in Pakistan. Perhaps that pimp had returned with the ISI goons. He darted an oblique glance at the stranger. The fellow was enjoying his predicament. He puffed a cigarette loudly and chewed scented tobacco. His multi-coloured beard blew wildly in the soggy late summer breeze.

"What's the time?" The stranger asked.

"It's four p.m."

"What's the date brother?"

Harfan looked up at the face of the stranger and again at his own watch. Oh God! It was the 28th of September, the date on which he was to meet Alam.

"Drop us at the taxi stand." The stranger ordered the rikshaw puller.

He hailed a taxi and guided the chauffeur to Orient Hotel, McLeod Road.

Harfan followed like a mesmerised lamb.

"Name of this servant of Allah is Mian Alam Khan."

The stranger whispered.

Harfan didn't require any further introduction. He knew it by now.

His nemesis had arrived.

Another thought fleeted past his mind. Was that pimp an advance scout of Alam? Was he maintaining a lookout to ensure that Harfan was not contaminated by ISI surveillance?

Whatever it was, Harfan locked his mind and mulled over the dialogues he expected to have with the master spy, India's Alamgir in Pakistan.

*

17

Orient Hotel was Alam's favourite joint in Lahore. It provided a bird's eye view of the residential and bustling business districts off Nicholson, Dil Mohammed, and Montgomery roads. It overlooked a sprawling park, Bagh-e-Jinnah and further to the north, the Race Course Park. Scenic beauty was not Alam's cardinal consideration. The choice was tactical. Located next to Lahore city railway station and bus terminus, it provided easy access and exit for the Indian intelligence anchor in Pakistan, who masqueraded as a military supplier and international trader.

Mian Alam Khan preferred travelling by road. His Mercedes could make a steady 60 km in the hill section, and he enjoyed the flexibility of making detours, to suit his extraordinary job assignments.

"*Salaam* Alam sahib." Harfan wished Mian Alam Khan with trepidation as they settled down in the hotel room, "sorry I couldn't recognise you."

"*Walekum*, Mian Harfan. You were not supposed to," Alam clicked a pistol shaped lighter to light a Marlborough, "I'm supposed to discover and brief you. Like to have a drink? It's chilled beer time." He poured a mug for himself and expectantly looked at Harfan.

"Don't hesitate. People back home may have branded drinking a vice item," Alam poured one large glass for Harfan, "take them seriously, but use discretion. No harm in drinking a beer or two in good company."

"You appear to be an Indian." Harfan commented as he sipped the drink.

"What makes you think so?"

"Your wonderful Hindi."

"Don't be curious. Curious cats don't enjoy nine lives. Never try digging my turf.

You'd find mines and not mushrooms."

Alam sounded terse. He felt embarrassed, being ticked off by his understudy, for his indiscreet use of Hindi. This one guy, Alam noted, was hell of a clever client. Caution! Alam took a long breath to hide the enormous irritation that welled up within.

"We should know each other, if we've to work together."

Harfan made a probing comment. He hadn't forgotten the warnings of Irfan Cowasjee about the mysterious reputation of Alam Khan.

"We won't work together *ad infinitum*. However, we'll work in close collaboration. I'm here to brief and launch you."

"Thanks, sir. For a while I was unnerved by your sudden approach."

"You did fine. Your grit and guts amaze me. Reserve these qualities, you'd require plenty of these in Pakistan." Alam didn't hide the sarcastic intonation and continued the briefing session.

"For you, I'm like the Hindu *Atman* (soul). I exist and don't exist. I know everything and when you're inside the nutcracker, I'd disown you. Know this much, that I'm your anchor in Pakistan. Don't try to probe beyond this. That way we're safe. Remember, I'm a patriotic Pakistani and you're on the threshold of becoming one." Alam transmitted the message with a razor sharp smile.

"No problems, if you feel so strong about it."

"That's okay."

"Fine with me. Let's talk business."

Harfan changed tracks. He didn't want to annoy the big man, in their very first meeting. Important he sure was, perhaps an undercover senior officer of the FIB. But the air of arrogance around Alam didn't escape Harfan's receptacles. His aggressively superior attitude sounded an alarm bell. The initial chemical handshake didn't blend well.

"You seem to have liked the girl. Not bad. Nevertheless, there's no need to turn lovesick. As part of your cover you've to marry a Pakistani girl. Your choice is good. The girl's name is Jamilla. Her mother was a Lucknowi court singer…once upon a time. She'd left the profession after marrying Zahoor Choudry, a flourishing businessman." Alam poured another drink for himself.

"Is she from Lucknow?" Harfan wanted to know more.

"Don't panic. Keep your cover intact."

"I was bothered by that pimp."

"Worried? How long have I been trailing you?" Alam offered a cigarette, "not a bad beginner, barring a few minor lapses. I appreciate your handling of the pimp."

"I could smell rotten fish. He was crude."

"That's fine. Some crudities are designed. Keep the address of Zahoor. Ask uncle Shamim to send a proposal for your marriage once you're firmly on the saddle. There's no hurry. Go ahead only after I give clearance. Let's have food. You've a long session ahead."

"What cover do I take in Jhumra?"

"These things have been sorted out. Let's have dinner first."

Dinner was sumptuous; saffron treated *biryani* with lavish chunks of meat, roasted chicken, and beaten curd, laced with shredded cucumber.

With a delicate Benarasi (from the city of Benaras) sweet *pan* (betel leaf) in his mouth, Alam eructed unique fragrance of the spices. He appeared full and contented.

"Ah! If there's *Allah Tallah,* it's in the Benarasi, after a good meal. What do you say Mian?" Alam was in an expansive mood.

"And that should be followed by the warmth of a loving woman. Right? Are you married?"

Harfan took another chance with Alam, who by now was in a relaxed mood.

"No, no dear. No personal question. Keep in mind the lessons of restrictive security."

Alam snubbed Harfan.

"Now listen carefully. Open up your cranium and store what I've to say. Any missing step can lead to disaster," Alam lighted another Marlborough, and said, "hope your vibes with Karachi uncle is perfect!"

"No problem, I'm his dear nephew."

"Fine. Take care that his end of the cover remains intact," Alam continued, "you'll be located at Jhumra, seat of a former Hindu principality. Look at the map. It's just at the base of a triangle formed by Sangla Hill, Faisalabad and Chiniot. Take a train from Lahore; it'll reach you there in three hours. It's before Faisalabad, the west of the territory is locally known as Jhang Maghiana. It was once a strong domain of the Hindu Punjabis, basically Khatris and Aroras (caste classifications) and assorted trading castes....

"Take a *tonga,* avoid a taxi, go past the airstrip, and next to the reserve forest and by the side of a tributary of the River Chenub, you'd find the old palace of Raja Digvijay Kaushal. It's now a hotel, Hotel Royal Palace. Get a room there. Got it so far?"

Harfan's mind suddenly sprouted wings and floated away from the physical surroundings around him. That was his father's palace. He had seen photographs of its facade and interiors and heard so much about its grandeur. Left blind folded, he could probably walk through its corridors.

"Are you listening?" Alam asked.

"Oh yes. I've been trying to store the information." Harfan didn't like betraying his very private emotions. It was obvious that Alam hadn't read those few pages of the Kaushal dynasty. Perhaps, Delhi didn't tell him everything after all.

"Register as a visitor from Karachi. Next Monday hire a taxi and go towards Sangla Hills. After about 10 kilometres you'd find an industrial estate. Ask for Israr Sharief, the managing director, and give him this letter." Alam handed over a sealed cover to Harfan.

"From whom?"

"It's from Jung Sher Khan, an important military contractor of Karachi. Israr supplies defence spare parts for tanks and aircraft through Sher Khan. Sher is also a big importer of defence items."

"Yes, uncle had spoken about him. But how do I justify my intimacy with him?"

"Your uncle's ball bearing and gasket manufacturing units fill in Sher's pipe line. These are used in the maintenance old Sherman tanks, the mainstay of the

Pakistani cavalry. Don't bother about these details. I've already briefed Sher Khan and Israr's a trusting type."

"What's the nature of the job with Israr Sharief?"

"Basically he wants a roving marketing manager."

Alam kept on evaluating Harfan with a piercing squint look. He hoped that the new talent would be able to assimilate the complicated brief.

Harfan coolly puffed away his cigarette and smoothly repeated back the instructions quoting Alam verbatim. Alam hadn't expected so much.

"You've been well trained." He congratulated Harfan.

"Thanks for the compliment," Harfan added, "any more dope on Israr Sharief?"

"Your job is that of marketing and liaison officer. It'd take you all over Pakistan. You'll have access to cantonments and restricted defence areas." Alam continued the briefing, mostly in Urdu.

"Israr enjoys enormous goodwill and his identity card is respected by the military bosses. People like Israr and Sher Khan give hefty cuts to the top Generals, both on domestic products and imported items. The glue of money binds them together."

"Is there no security verification process, like we've back in India?"

"Barring the slogan of two nations, we're all the same, on either side of the artificial line," Alam continued, "Israr and Sher Khan are well respected by the Chief Military Law Administration bosses and the President. But avoid his brother Nawab Sharief. He's unscrupulous. Don't ever get trapped by him."

"Any more details?"

"The elder Sharief, Mian Mumtaz, had built up a big industrial empire. Israr, the son from his first wife, has inherited the major share. The younger son, Nawab, is from his second wife, an Afghan lady. He's a single man demolition squad, who believes more in wrecking than making."

"A real charlatan!" commented Harfan.

"Put any sticker you like. He's politically ambitious and is close to Izaz Afroz from Sind, the former foreign minister. He has his own conduits to the armed forces and the intelligence fraternity. In the whole pack, which you're likely to face, Nawab is the most untrustworthy."

Alam continued briefing Harfan throughout the night. The priority target areas were delineated with meticulous care: coverage of the KANUPP nuclear plant at Karachi, penetration of the top army brass and deployment of formations, missile batteries and repositioning of cavalry formations.

The most important target, Alam stressed, was the den of the Chief Martial Law Administrator. It was the vital pump house of Pakistan's political and administrative lungs and heart.

"It's a tall order." Harfan demurred.

"You've been designed for these tasks. I'm briefing an important Indian resident agent. Delhi wants quick results."

"I'm afraid I'm not a designer creation, Alam sahib." Harfan shot back in rapid fire.

"I'm afraid you're. A trained agent is custom made for specific intelligence needs. He's a robot in flesh and blood."

"That's funny."

"Well! There are more surprises than you can imagine." Alam poured himself another drink. Harfan noticed that his supposed anchor in Pakistan was a connoisseur of drinks. He had downed six pegs of whisky by now.

"India's internal political situation is fragile. The bosses would like you to monitor the sensitive aspects of decision making in Pakistan, relevant to internal matters in India and the security threat to very important persons."

"Why? Is there any assassination plot?" Harfan asked.

"War and espionage are extensions of diplomacy. War indicates the bankruptcy of statecraft. Pakistan today, and I think tomorrow and the day after tomorrow as well, would pursue the profane policy of open and proxy wars."

"It's hard on the people of Pakistan."

"Don't worry for them. Keep this list with you."

"What's this?"

"Brief notes on some important personalities. Memorise and destroy." Alam doused his cigarette in the whisky, gulped it, and advised Harfan to relax and not to worry about getting up early. It had been a long day, a really long one. They shared a nightcap and said *Khuda Hafiz*

Alam started snoring straight away.

*

Harfan couldn't sleep.

The haze created by Alam's bombarding faded away and the liquid salty eyes floated in. He was happy to have a name for the persona behind the eyes. Jamilla's mellow looks enveloped his conscience. His inner eyes tried to fathom the warmth of her looks. Was there love and curiosity in her eyes? Did fate bring him to Jhumra! Had he met his destiny at the Lahore Fort? Did that mysterious force called God or whatever it is, design it?

Harfan had a disturbed sleep. Jamilla appeared and disappeared like patches of rainless autumn cloud. Suddenly the silhouette of the Jhumra palace, the seat of his father's kingdom popped up like a remote galactic blinker, appearing and disappearing with faint pulsating burst of light.

The shadowy montage of his parents hovered over the elegant edifice for a while. His father suddenly appeared on a horseback, decked up in war regalia, charging enemies with an open sword raised above his head.

Harfan cried out in excitement as his sleep snapped abruptly with unsaturated expectations.

Alam, by now fully dressed and geared up for the day, woke him up with a steaming cup of coffee.

"*Barkhurdar* (dear young person), had a bad dream? I'm ready to hit the roads. You can't reach me. In case of real emergency, call Quetta number 76989 and ask for Intikhab. This is the number of Farah Restaurant, at Jinnah Road. In case Intikhab responds, tell him that Alam's nephew would like to talk to him. Don't reveal anything else on the phone. I'll install the communication facility once you set up home at Jhumra."

Alam took out a fat bunch of Pakistan currency notes.

"You're my nephew too. Keep the cover that way. I've nothing more to add. Expect you to live the cover. Keep this money, rupees fifty thousand. It's for your upkeep and professional expenses. Check out, after you've had breakfast. I've taken care of the cheque. *Khuda Hafiz*."

Mian Alam Khan picked up his safari bag and left the room.

Harfan slithered out of the bed leisurely and lighted a cigarette. His mind was preoccupied by the mysterious appearance and departure of Alam. The Quetta safe house phone number, Harfan mused, must only be a cover for the master operative. Could he be an officer of the FIB operating in Pakistan under deep cover? That was the most plausible explanation, he concluded. How else could the master Indian spy agency trust another resident spy like him to handle sensitive operations in a hostile foreign country? Well! A jackal on the prowl should know the neighbouring jackal well. That was essential for his safety and security. Harfan decided to explore the idea at an opportune point.

He pushed back the curious thought to a backburner and took a leisurely shower, enjoyed a sumptuous breakfast and checked out before eleven.

*

Harfan Bukhari skipped lunch, hailed a rickshaw, and asked the puller to proceed to Masti Gate. A mysterious force inexorably drew him towards the blind alley behind Mariyam Zamani mosque. He alighted near the eating joint of the Punjabi from Nuh and ordered a cup of spiced tea.

"Hello Mian *Ludhianvi* (from Ludhiana)," the jolly Nuh man offered him a cigarette and continued, "your *huri* (fairy) hasn't come out today."

Harfan feigned he wasn't interested. He supplemented the order of tea with a plate of reshmi kebab, garnished with garlic and mint sauce.

"I've news for you, brother," the vendor continued in an excited tone, "she is Jamilla Bano, daughter of Zahoor Chaudry, a man of means and status."

Harfan kept his cool. This was stale news. Moreover, he didn't want to betray his emotions. He wasn't sure how safe it was. The intelligence sleuths, for tidbit information, tapped the street corner vendors like the friendly Nuh Punjabi.

"Brother let's have a walk inside the lane. Let's see if we can locate a suitable accommodation." Harfan spoke while crushing the kebabs between his tongue and upper palate.

"Sure. You can even visit a *faqir*. He lives in the ruins of an old Christian church."

"Don't bother. Show me around. I'm told there are remains of an old Mughal time church in the lane."

"Brother *Ludhianvi*," the Nuh fellow added jocularly. "Lahore has many surprises. But the church of Begum Mariyam is no more there. The land sharks have eaten up the bricks. Come I'll show you around Zahoor Chaudry's palace."

"Not interested. Just show me the area. I'd take a home if I like the area."

Zahoor Chaudry's magnificent mansion faced a small park, skirted by the Mariyam Zamani mosque. The main approach to the mansion was from Circular road. The approach from Masti Gate was a shortcut, a remnant from the historic days.

Harfan, with the Nuh friend by his side, settled on the park greens. He kept expectant eyes glued on the balcony of the house.

"Come. Let's go to Anees *fakir*'s (mendicant) abode." Harfan's companion stood up.

"Who's that?"

"He's a holy person and can fulfill all your wishes."

"Shh!" Harfan silenced his companion.

His wish, the owner of the enchanted pair of eyes, appeared at the edges of the balcony of Zahoor's house.

She was real. Those were the very eyes. From a distance of about 100 yards, Harfan could recognise the azure blue shade, wonderfully long and black lashes and creamy creases around the diamond cut wonders. Yes. The wise *fakir* Anees or not, she was there, his dream had materialised. Her slim vine-like body was draped in a light pink *salwar-kameez.* She appeared as fresh as a dewdrop on a pink rose petal, dazzlingly bright, a refreshing breath of air. She leaned against the wooden railing and looked out, probably at the stratus cloud formations, hanging low over the horizon.

She sprang back suddenly like a tender flowery cane, in an electrifying swinging move. Yes. It was the same face. Those were the same eyes. His pinkish Greek face, with the lavish growth of black beard looked sad, beaten by many summers. Yet, it looked innocent, starving for love and care.

In a final retro-swing action, she came near the railing, leaned against it, and turned her head, swirling her huge cloud of dark hair and disappeared inside. To Harfan it was an invitation to jump from the parapet and land before his dream maiden.

Electrified, he stood up.

The Nuh friend pulled him down.

"Keep cool Mian. Love has infinite ways of expression. Reserve your responses for better days. Let's go. It's not safe to loiter in the park."

"Wait for a few more minutes."

"No brother *Ludhianvi.* The day's tour is over. Sleep with your dream. *Allah* willing she'd be yours soon."

He pulled up Harfan, licked by the remote thunder-current that emanated from the swirling cloud like hair of Jamilla. They walked down the lane, the shopkeeper guarding Harfan's rear.

Jamilla, the music of the name kept on bouncing inside Harfan. The space inside his frame was flooded with the sweet fragrance of the belle he had left behind at the enchanted lane.

What was it? Love?

Harfan didn't know what love was. He had never cared to know.

In what way was it different from desire?

He managed to get whatever he desired, dead or alive. Could he force Jamilla to love and care for him?

An inexplicable feeling told Harfan that his ribs were singing like enchanted reeds. His body and soul strings told him in so many fragrant tunes that he was in love. And love just happened. It could not be earned or looted.

Was Jamilla his destiny? Perhaps. Otherwise, why had he traversed all the way to Pakistan and met her in a lost corner of Lahore?

A conviction that God had especially created her for him started rooting somewhere deep inside him. A mysterious force kept on ticking and telling him that this dream belle, in this unknown corner of Lahore, was simply made for him, perhaps by God, perhaps by destiny.

Well! His Nuh friend was correct. Wait he must.

The inner churning slowly settled down and Harfan felt slightly relieved. He had discovered a new star. She was sure to guide him to a new destiny, giving a new lease of real human life. Harfan didn't feel that he was a mere intelligence robot, crafted by Delhi. The human inside had just discovered that for the light of love and life had not yet extinguished with the cadaver of Hema.

He packed up and prepared to catch the 7 a.m. train to Jhumra, a small station connected by meter gauge rail, about three puffing and panting hours from Lahore Cantonment station. He spent the rest of the night listlessly, tossing between the shadows of Jamilla and the besieged palace of Raja Digvijay Kaushal. Two passions tormented him. The probability of winning Jamilla's hand appeared to be uncertain and he didn't know what to expect at Jhumra?

*

Jhumra railway station wasn't a big affair. However, military requirements had changed the strategic importance of the sleepy station. A big supply base had sprung up between Sangla Hills and Jhumra that supplemented the forward bases behind Lahore. The Khyber Express, which mostly carried men and materials for the war front, slowly rolled onto the platform with a cacophony and finally stopped with the engine-exhausts releasing clouds of steam. A few reluctant hawkers leisurely loitered past the platform vending cigarettes, tea, and small eats. Harfan brushed past the milling crowd of soldiers and squeezed past the ticket checker.

Harfan hailed a *tonga* (horse cart) for over two kilometers long journey to Hotel Royal Palace. The *tonga* cantered past the huge wrought iron gate of the palace of Raja Digvijay Kaushal. The well-manicured garden, lined with bottle palms, spruce, acacia, chinar (maple family) and ornamental trees and bushes looked fabulously elegant. The entrance arch, lined with hazels and dwarf magnolias, was covered with sweet smelling flowery creepers. The pathway, paved with yellow

Jaisalmer stones, meandered through a well-mowed lawn, ended up below the ornamental portico, still decorated with carvings of Hindu gods, nymphs, and well sculpted male and female figurines. An oversized receptionist flaunting a huge moustache and wavy beard looked up with fatigued eyes.

"You want the King's or Queen's rooms? None are available, already booked for an American group. I can offer you a room originally used by a concubine of the king."

"What's her name?"

"Who cares? *Janab,* who cares for dead kings and their concubines! Didn't they maintain a harem full of whores, these kings and nawabs?"

The bored receptionist wasn't interested in continuing the dialogue.

"Any room will do," Harfan put a lid on his emotions. "I'm here for a few days. Can you give me a river facing room? That'll be a great favour."

"Done sir, you get room number 16. Ibadat!"

He yelled at an employee, who stood at a distance with his eyes glued to the front desk. The face appeared to be familiar, minus the beard and rat-tail moustache. Was it that of the pimp at Lahore? The resemblance was astounding.

"Have I seen you earlier?" Harfan asked.

"Sir, your servant is a poor employee in this hotel, haven't been out of Jhumra all these years. Your servant is called Ibadat."

"So Ibadat you're a hotel employee?"

"Any problems sir?"

"No. Show me to my room."

Harfan silently analysed the probable relationship between Alam, that rat-tail mustachioed pimp and Ibadat. Was he acting as Alam's lookout at Lahore? It was too early to dissect the anatomy of a suspected intelligence operative. However, Harfan coined the coincidence carefully and stored in a live chamber of his mind.

*

The southwest facing room, with a high ceiling and Greek windows, offered a pleasant view of the river and virgin woods that tapered down along the uneven contours of small hillocks. Whiffs of fresh air filled Harfan's chest. He stretched out to look beyond the woods. Two moderate huts, tucked in a remote corner of the verdant greens appeared inconsistent with the mosaic. So was the sari clad elderly lady, lighting an earthen lamp below a bushy plant.

"Who's that lady?" Harfan asked Ibadat, still waiting with his baggage.

"That's really nobody, a leftover from the former royal retinue. She lives in a hut near the riverbank and offers worship to the family deity of the Raj family. What you see now is a daily ritual, lighting of the lamp under the *tulsi* (mint plant sacred to the Hindus) bush." The porter replied.

"Is she's a Hindu?" Harfan added, "doesn't anybody object?"

"Sir, she's a lonely heart. People have accepted her as part of the ancient vegetation."

"Why?"

"The Hindus were very powerful in this part of Punjab," Ibadat offered an explanation, "their spines have been broken, and the new masters aren't disturbed by this insignificant woman."

"Are you also from the former regime?"

"Your humble servant is the son of the chief chef of the former king."

"You must be privy to a lot of inside stories about the king and the queen. Did they have a child?"

"My mom knows a lot sir."

"Interesting! I think I should meet her one of these days."

"You're welcome sir."

Harfan lapsed back to his memory bank and recaptured the fascinating stories Kasturi had narrated about the loyal and brave cook. She hadn't mentioned anything about Ibadat, his son. Perhaps he wasn't born before she left Jhumra. Even if he were, a queen wasn't supposed to know of the existence of a cook's son.

Back in bed, Harfan looked vacantly at the roof. Greco-Roman figurines flanked the ornate canopy with an inverted lotus of Persian design. The kings of Jhumra had indeed liberally borrowed from Hindu, Persian and British styles of architecture. He concentrated on the core of the lotus and ruminated over Delhi's choice of Jhumra, as his launching pad. Something very personal, something very dear and very sacred to him was mingled with the dust and grass in this backyard of Pakistan.

Cool, cool!

Harfan collected himself. It was too early to declare a war. The enemy must be sighted first. There was no need to charge like a pine-headed Pinocchio.

Cool. Cool! He smiled and walked up to the window.

Harfan took a deep breath. He must wear his cover snug and prepare for the war ahead, the war to destroy the evil Niazis of Rasulnagar, responsible for his father's assassination. He recalled Maulana Rizwan's contemptuous description of Muslims as *Ahl-e-Kitab,* people of the book, blind bigots. What a Book it was!

Harfan walked over to the window. The swift flowing currents of a tributary of distant Chenab broke into a rhythmic lullaby, just like Kasturi's soothing voice, humming the enchanting message of peaceful sleep.

Not very far, across the silhouettes of trees and bushes, faint lights flickered in the rippling breeze. It must be from the hut of the lone-hearted lady, living under the shadows of the palace of her former employer.

He felt tempted to walk down to the source of the light. This lady must be an interesting character, privy to the exciting drama of the last days of his parents at Jhumra. She must have known the killer of the former king.

Harfan lighted a cigarette and turned towards the door.

"Going out sir?"

Ibadat appeared like a ghostly apparition.

"Yes. Just for a stroll." Harfan stepped out under the portico.

"Very fine night sir," Ibadat followed, "but don't move out in the dark. There are wild animals around."

"What bloody animals?"

"Wild hogs, cheetah, and varieties of serpents."

"Shit!"

Harfan felt a surge of irritation. He felt he wasn't a free agent and couldn't make any move without the master resident regent's permission. Was this fellow a puny mole of Alam?

"I saw a faint light from the quarters of that old lady, you talked about this evening."

"Oh! That light? She's a lunatic, doesn't sleep most nights."

"Insomniac?" Harfan commented.

"Sir, her life is queer."

"What's it all about?"

"Sir," Ibadat led Harfan back to his room, "most of us are victims of some acts of some drama scripted by *Allah*. Who knows whom he casts in what role?" Ibadat said *Khuda Hafiz* and left.

Drama? Yes, he too was a character in the drama scripted by *Allah*, goddess *Kali*, whoever He or She was. Well! He was ready to play his role, but not according to Mian Alam Khan's and his stooge Ibadat's script. They sure weren't his designated master puppeteers. A Kaushal was capable of scripting and directing his own act.

Well! There was no need to fret and fume. He evaluated the scenario coolly and realised the limitations he suffered from. He could free himself from the domineering personality of Alam only when his own channel of communication to Delhi was established. Delhi, he sighed, was too far and too scary and the master scriptwriters there couldn't be reached on the wings of wish.

*

18

The scriptwriters back in Delhi were too busy with their own acts. This drama wasn't scripted by the unknown entity invariably described as Ishwar, Allah, and God. The dramatis personae were very much mortal.

They were busy honing their axes. To some, the question of succession to Amritlal was still an unfinished agenda of the transfer of power from the Windsor to the Amritlal dynasty. Jung Bahadur wasn't destined to play the main character, some of them, especially Manjira believed. How could he? God had chosen her, the only child of Amritlal, to stretch the dynasty's span beyond the limits of history.

The FIB chief was highly perturbed by the drawn daggers and gashing teeth of the politicians on the issue of India's acceptance of the UN sponsored ceasefire formula between India and Pakistan and the proposed talks at Tashkent. As the intelligence chief, he had no doubt that both India and Pakistan had reached the tether's end and could not stretch national resources even for another fifteen days to bring the war to the limits of victory or defeat.

However, he was more engaged with an emergency call from his deputy Balachandran Nampoothiri on the intercom.

"Yes Balu?"

"Alamgir was on the High Frequency channel. Some interesting messages require your immediate attention."

"Okay. Bring it up."

Nampoothiri presented the exciting decoded cipher from Pakistan, transmitted through Kabul hub.

**DOUBLE QUOTE: Reproduced below is the copy of communication from BHC (*British High Commission*) in Pakistan ** SINGLE QUOTE: Personal from HoM to PM. Source close to Pak President confirms a late night meeting between Lee Fang, Chinese Ambassador Plenipotentiary, and top Presidential aides, which took stock of the war situation. Pakistan's gain of Indian territory is substantial. Pakistan may not accept any agreement if India doesn't return Haji Pir and areas across the CFL (*Cease Fire Line*). The Chinese have agreed to deploy troops opposite Ladakh, NEFA and Sikkim and pressure India. The Chinese may move one Division plus an extra Brigade to Nathu La and Jelep La gaps bordering Sikkim....

"The PP (*Pak President*) has access to top secret medical reports on the precarious heart condition of Jung Bahadur. Pakistani doctors have opined that another cardiac attack was imminent and could be fatal. The PP has been advised by Izaz Afroz (*foreign minister*) to stall the talks...SINGLE UNQUOTE** The source is reliable, inside BHC, Islamabad. ADD=the consignment has reached destination. Will take another two weeks to settle down. Shall contact him and install the device. Material good. May shape well. DOUBLE QUOTE. EOM. ALAM **

R.N. Dutta looked up with loaded questions.

"Analyse it word by word," Dutta asked Nampoothiri, "I want a complete analysis by eight a.m. The PM must be briefed before he meets the CCEA (Cabinet Committee on External Affairs)."

"And you," he turned to Kumar Anand, "investigate the leakage of the PM's health report. Identify the mole. We can't allow Pakistan to run riot inside our government secrets. Identify the bastard and finish him off."

"But sir, its too short a time to tackle such a big problem." Prasad protested mildly.

"The Tashkent talks are at stake. Those who can reach the report can easily reach the man physically and take a pot shot. I hope you understand the stakes involved." Dutta looked at the wall clock, picked up the red phone, and requested the PM's secretary for an urgent meeting.

"Do you think it's fair?" fumed Prasad, "detecting a serious leakage isn't a quick-fix job."

"Try your best. That's all we can do." Nampoothiri replied casually, without lifting his eyes from Alamgir's message.

"Balu, you're being unfair. This is a needle in a haystack case and you're giving me a sermon." Prasad lamented in an anguished voice.

"Well Kumar, as they say, if you can't resist, enjoy the rape. What choice do you and I have? I've to burn midnight oil too. Can I help?"

"Thanks for the nasty joke." Prasad walked out leaving behind not too mute vibes of hostility.

Nampoothiri smiled and rushed back to his room. He summoned Jatadhari and instructed Amrita, his secretary, to fetch the master file on Operation Alamgir. Jatadhari Garo knew well the order of sequence of the chores he was to follow when the boss was visibly at a bind. He prepared a stiff black coffee, served it without sugar, and brought out a Havana.

Nampoothiri inhaled the pungent smoke and appreciated the texture of the coffee. His mind raced against time, trying to piece together the entire spectrum of Indo-Pak relations, British interests, and Chinese postures. He was planning to tie and stitch together remotely related patches of intelligence, assessment reports, and raw tactical and strategic information, for presenting a logical collage to the

PM. Nampoothiri naturally reposed intrinsic trust in Alamgir. He was involved, from day one, in recruiting, motivating, and training the officer. It was a unique success story of the FIB.

Nampoothiri had picked up Jiwan Bahutule, an orphaned Marathi Brahmin, from a batch of twelve trainee-officers for the top-secret assignment in Pakistan. He had displayed uncanny aptitude for deep undercover operations from day one. Way back in 1949, after completion of training, young Bahutule stunned his course mates by kicking his job and declaring his intention of pursuing Islamic studies in Egypt. He embraced Islam and studied theology at Deoband for one year. He disappeared from India, spent two years in Cairo, and finally landed in Kabul, travelling all the way through Iran and Afghanistan.

From Kabul to Peshawar wasn't a difficult journey. His marriage to the daughter of a Pathan chieftain of Mian Khel sanctified his cover with all the trappings of a genuine Muslim trader, keen to set up his establishment in Pakistan.

Nampoothiri's Operation Alamgir had flourished over the years and the FIB achieved unprecedented success in creating a number of Double XX category agents inside Pakistan. Alam, as the designated handler of these operations, had become the eyes and ears of Delhi in the neighbouring hostile country. He enjoyed the unique status of running almost a subsidiary unit of the FIB inside Pakistan, without any interference of the High Commission based under cover operatives. Nampoothiri treated Alam's reports with utmost seriousness. He was a trusted officer and agent, a rare combination of tradecraft experimentation.

Alamgir's special cipher, on the eve of the Tashkent negotiations, following the second drawn war between India and Pakistan, was a precious input. Nampoothiri wanted to add his best analytical inputs to the gold nugget. Indian response to Islamabad and the Western capitals would definitely be conditioned by these excellent pieces of gems and diamonds pilfered from the high security vaults of the British High Commission in Pakistan.

Nampoothiri had a personal stake in processing the information to the finest level of perfection. He was named as a member of the Prime Ministerial delegation to Tashkent. That was the best opportunity to impress Jung Bahadur. The time for naming a successor to Rabindra Narayan Dutta was around the corner.

*

Prime Minister Jung Bahadur was busy with his strategic preparations for the Tashkent summit. Crosscurrents of diplomatic shenanigans and internal political kirsch slashing had bound him down to higher realities of real politick. He did not have time for fishy manipulations by Ram Karan. The worthy colleague was busy promoting the idea of an immediate succession by Manjira. How could a nobody be the successor to the House of Windsor? Mahatmaji had nominated his political heir, and heirs only produces heirs.

Nampoothiri, as a designated member of the Tashkent delegation, was busy drafting notes and strategy papers and Dutta was lost in the undergrowth of interdepartmental cold war on various internal and external security issues, which arose out of the drawn war with Pakistan. Alam Khan was out on another arms procurement errand for the Pakistan army. They did not have time for the Triple X talent counting vital minutes in his temporary shelter in Hotel Royal Palace at Jhumra.

The Triple X asset in Pakistan was virtually marooned. Incessant early autumn rain and the surging floodwater from the upper catchments had breached the banks of the Chenab and its tributaries. The Jhumra plains and Sangla foothills were heavily inundated. Disruption of rail and road services had put life completely out of gear.

Ibadat maintained a cool distance. No hurry, Harfan thought. The ice should melt soon enough. A little more biological and psychological warming should do the magic. The lobby television was, however, broadcasting plenty of heat. Izaz Afroz, the Foreign Minister, harangued over the idiot box trying to pump more blood in the sagging hearts of Pakistani people.

The transmission ended abruptly with a sudden power cut. Harfan looked around.

Burning time wasn't as easy as burning cigarettes. He threw the burnt out stub and looked around for Ibadat. He was apparently sleeping, reclining on a chair, at the far end of the reception area. This should be a good time to have a sneak preview of the palace compound, all by himself.

Harfan walked past the ornate portico and peeped through the screen of green vegetation. A faint mist, rising out of the flooded Chenab, had enveloped the palace and the surrounding orchards and forests. The soft beauty beckoned him with wet-whispers. Harfan ventured out, wading knee-deep floodwaters.

The front lawns of the hotel and the Chenab beds had merged under the floodwater, creating an illusion of a watery vastness. Small islands of lush green trees and bushes swayed in the cross winds, like beautiful maidens swinging their hair, after a leisurely sauna.

The earth, trees and grass, soaked in flood and rainwater, oozed out a cocktail of strange sweet fragrances.

Harfan Bukhari, bathed by the pristine nature, felt a shiver of joy. How did he manage to ignore so splendorous beauty around him, in Jhunjhunu, and in Delhi? Why did he keep his sensory organs shut all these years?

He took in a few deep breaths. The aromatic air sweeping the palace compound, the vegetation around and the earth enriched by his father's blood injected exciting sensations into Harfan's cortices. He felt buoyant and sprinkled his hair with a fistful of rainwater. Harfan concentrated on picking up the ethereal sounds that emanated from the trees, the raindrops, and the air that encapsulated him. They were whispering his name; Harfan liked to imagine. He raised both his arms and felt the wet air dancing past. He felt like dancing, like the rainbow-coloured peacocks, back at Jhunjhunu. The magic in the misty air dragged Harfan along the trail leading to the orchards, beyond the palace lawns. The distant groves invited Harfan, swinging their twigs and dancing with the rhythm of gusty winds. He lost himself in a charmed trance.

"*Janab*," Ibadat moved closer in silent steps, "I feel you like this place."

"Why? What's your problem?"

"No problem sir. Our Jhumra is unique."

"I think so. What kind of a king Jhumra had?"

"Sir, he was a king, valiant, proud and fearless."

Harfan didn't like the idea of entering into a debate.

"Look at the eastern skies," Ibadat pointed his finger, "it's time for the sun to paint rainbows in the skies."

Harfan stretched out, standing under a magnolia grove, its pale white flowers swaying in rhythm with the light breeze. The cloud cover was fleeting past under a strong north easterly wind. The mist had dissipated. The steel-grey clouds hanging low over the western horizon were being painted in bountiful rouge.

Yes, Ibadat was correct. Suddenly the eastern sky started glistening with a scintillating seven-coloured rainbow, buttressed by a shadowy, fainter rainbow, nearer to the horizon.

"*Janab*, have your coffee." Ibadat kept on stirring the contents intermittently.

"How do you know when the rainbow's going to show up?" Harfan asked in an amazed tone. He'd never bothered to understand the intricacies of nature all these years. He didn't have the time for these tender things of life.

"*Janab*, this is rustic wisdom," Ibadat opened up again, "our Jhumra is a wonderful place. My mother used to sing about the sun going to bed, all wrapped in a red quilt, after a spell of rain and coming out next morning with a riot of colours."

"Should we walk to the green bushes over there. I feel like." Harfan handed back the empty cup, folded up his trousers, and ventured out, wading through ripples of floodwater. Ibadat followed.

Harfan noticed a raised ground at his right, covered with shrubs and plants. Beyond the fruit orchard, behind the clusters of banana groves, he noticed two brick huts. Curiosity dragged him along.

The same Hindu lady emerged out with a silver plate on her left palm as he approached the huts. A bright brass oil lamp burnt at the centre of the plate, some white rice, green grass, and red vermilion powder placed around it. Harfan's steps made splashing sounds in the rainwater.

The lady looked back, her gaze locked on Harfan's face. She covered her head and stood motionless, turning her back to the stranger. Harfan couldn't see her flooded eyes; the saline sea inside overflowed the banks of her clogged emotion.

"Excuse me, who's this lady?" Harfan whispered at Ibadat.

"We know her as Ramayani. I think you'd seen her through the hotel window. Mom says that she was a companion of the former queen. Let's go to the other side of the palace compound." Ibadat made a feeble attempt at diverting Harfan's attention. The name wasn't new to him, though his Delhi brief-masters were silent about her existence. Kasturi had briefly mentioned the name, while explaining the frail figure standing by her side, in one of her wedding photographs.

"*Adaab*," Harfan saluted the old lady, "how do you feel?"

The emaciated body visibly shivered for a few seconds. She stood like a piece of frozen stone, though the sudden storm in her chest kept on swirling and surging, forcing out tears. She didn't reply. A few moments lapsed before she turned around, trying to control the streams of saline flow. She looked straight into Harfan's eyes, her mouth wide open, in gasping disbelief.

Harfan could see, in dim fading light, her wide eyes hungrily exploring his face and body contour. Her sad and salty looks, like the reverse arrows of time, probably bent back, trying momentarily to connect herself with the events of yore. For the first time Ramayani realised that her present world was nothing but a chunk of the frozen past. The young man standing before her was a clone of King Digvijay. His live apparition had suddenly materialised straying from its orbit around another time wrap.

Large teardrops rolled down her cheeks. Muffled sobs sent spasm of shivers all over her fragile body. Ramayani paused for a split second, ran into her hut, and gently closed the door behind.

Harfan peeped through a lattice and found her seated in front of an image of goddess *Kali*, her cheeks moist with flowing tears.

He turned back, questions drilling deep in his mind.

What was she looking for? Was she trying to discover something from her past? What else could be her problem? Did his presence torment the old lady? He must probe this. It won't be prudent to sleep with the shadows of the past, which had the inevitable habit of catching up with the present.

"Why was she weeping?" Harfan asked.

"She's deranged. You may find her laughing next moment," Ibadat brushed aside the question, "let's get back. It's getting dark. You sure don't want to be beaten by cobras."

"Cobras?"

"Yes, king and queen cobras. Plenty of them."

Ibadat turned his steps towards the hotel. Harfan followed silently. He wasn't sure if Ramayani was mentally deranged. Her looks were sane and steady. Her eyes didn't betray her spasmodic mind. Her eyes were digging for some missing gems.

He must explore the mystery of those flooded eyes, Harfan resolved.

*

Ibadat's meteorological forecast was accurate. The morning dawned bright and glorious. Harfan stared amazingly through the large Gothic window, at the huge red disk hanging and pulsating over the horizon and kissing the endless expanse of floodwaters. Distant sparkles on the water brought back to his mind the liquid looks of Jamilla.

Oh, heavens!

Why was the soggy face of Ramayani appearing in his vision? Harfan buried his face in a pillow and tried to float in that unknown expanse, of the inviting looks of a fairy called Jamilla. He didn't want to see any other face, not now. Jamilla returned. This time her wavy hair sprayed a whiff of fragrant air on his face. Harfan momentarily travelled back to the cascading hair that had numbed his mind with electrical impulses.

Ibadat's knock pierced the dream diaphragm.

"*Janab*, tea." He entered the room with a tray in hand.

"To hell with you," Harfan looked at Ibadat in mock anger, "you don't even allow your clients to enjoy their dreams in peace."

"Excuse me sir. You've a new dream ahead." Ibadat placed the tray on a bedside table.

"What's that?"

"You've a date at Sangla. Isn't it, sir?"

"*Hai Rabba* (Allah)! I'd forgotten. How's the flood situation?"

"The Chinese and the Americans have left for their respective work places. You've to take a taxi. It's more convenient."

"Can you arrange one?"

"No problem sir. The hotel van will drop you if you don't mind the charges."

"Thanks brother. Better do that."

*

Israr Sharief dressed in a usual Punjabi suit and routine looks didn't carry the air of an important tycoon. He glanced through the letter from Jung Sher Khan and spoke in chaste Punjabi.

"So, you're the nephew of Shamim Bukhari! Please make yourself comfortable." Israr ordered tea.

"As you know, mine is a prime industry in Pakistan, which produces vital spares for the armed forces. We specialise in the field of night-vision field equipment, nickel-cadmium batteries for shoulder-pack field-communication sets, special alloys used in the manufacture of gun barrels, and high altitude clothing and kitchenware. I scout around for weapons systems in international markets. The war has opened up better business opportunities. Several contracts are in the pipeline," Israr added.

"I'm grateful for the briefing sir," Harfan replied politely, "where do I fit in?"

"Get a feel of the production lines first," Israr advised, "I'd like you to work in my marketing division and take care of my national and international commitments. That's an expanding market and I can't manage it alone. I'll help you to get into the grooves of the Army establishment and bureaucracy. They're our main providers."

"You can trust me. I'll give my best." The sincere briefing of his employer impressed Harfan.

"A few more points that you should know about," Israr paused for a while, "my half brother and business rival Nawab is after my business and blood. I hope you'd understand him better as you get to know my business affairs."

"Anything special?"

"He's ambitious, more than he can manage. And he's unscrupulous."

"Must be a powerful person."

"He aspires to be one. He's close to Izaz Afroz, the foreign minister. He's close to the intelligence fraternity and the drug mafia. I'll tell you later how to get past these lusty jackals."

Israr advised Harfan to pick up the tricks of special business management. Grease, he explained, worked better in Pakistan than any other established business school stratagem.

"I've some important business collaborators. Count Jung Sher Khan and Mian Alam Khan amongst them."

"How important is Alam Khan?" Harfan tried to probe about his immediate handler.

"Well! He's important," Israr displayed a meaningful smile, "he's close to the Principal Staff Officer (PSO) to the Chief Martial Law Administrator (CMLA) and several Corps Commanders, who control the drug pipelines. He has fabulous connections with international gunrunners and the US and British intelligence operators." Israr was liberal in his comments on his business collaborator.

"How important is he for your business?"

"Valid point. We're competitors. But we depend on each other. The arms market is a close-circuit theatre. My company works in tandem with Alam and Sher Khan."

"Is the competition nasty?"

"Yes and no. We jackals in the arms bazaar do not mind backstabbing, if that's important for promoting business interest."

Israr Sharief explained lucidly his business relationship with two other important suppliers to the Pakistani armed forces.

"Settle your personal affairs fast. Sangla isn't a good place to set up home. You can scout out a fine living quarters at Jhumra. Some elegant old houses are available there. Not much of a distance from here."

"Yes. Jhumra appears to be a nice place."

Harfan agreed with his boss. That was his pre-destined theatre, which he missed out by a quirk of fate. Fate had again tossed him back at the battleground of Jhumra.

*

The job kept Harfan busy; the cover enveloped him comfortably. However, he couldn't stop dreaming of the beautiful eyes he had left behind in the rusty Masti Gate of Lahore. However, dreams alone were not good enough to get home a bride.

A matrimonial proposal would require Alam's approval. The big shark, he presumed, would in turn seek Delhi's nod. A low-key local marriage was a tradecraft adjunct of his assignment, obviously a station marriage, minus the hiccups of the heart. Some sort of a sailor's wife! Shit! The idea of taking a sailor's wife bounced violently inside his mind.

To hell with Delhi and Alam! Jamilla was his dream girl. He wouldn't deceive her, never ever. Harfan pushed the thought aside and hurled it back to the copybook of Dhiren Bhagat, from which he first came to know about some famous and infamous 'station wives.' He didn't require any. Jamilla, if he happened to marry her, would be his life partner, not a 'station wife.'

The other thought relating to briefings in Delhi and by Alam crept into his mind like a caterpillar. He wondered if he could live up to the expectations of his launch masters. What about his personal agenda? How would he assimilate the three equally important and conflicting strains of expectations?

Seated on the grassy slopes of his backyard that tapered down to the very edges of murmuring waters of the Chenab channel, Harfan kept on throwing small pebbles into the placid waters. He watched the tiny ripples rising up and dissipating in to the blue vastness of the fast flowing stream. The blue below his feet transported Harfan to the fathomless blue tinged hazel eyes of Jamilla that invited him inexorably from beyond the clouds, remote verdant hills and the hidden sack of pain, very close to his heart. He felt like singing aloud.

The trained spy in him advised caution. The song was perhaps immature, a figment of imagination. His lonely dream wasn't good enough to conjure up a palace in the sky. How could he get into Jamilla's dream?

Should he?

Would that peel off his cover?

No raw nerve should be hurt. Feline curiosity was surely a spy's forte, but he didn't have the proverbial nine lives. His love shouldn't jeopardise his professional security! Harfan's professional caution was, however, overwhelmed by songs of joy and melancholy. Autumn had silently walked into the fall, lending a riot of colours to the cherry, chinar, almond, and apricot trees. The greens suddenly yielded to multi-coloured hues.

The subtle changes enchanted Harfan. He'd never observed the nature pulsating around him, flourishing in seasonal blooms and changing colours. He was indifferent to human invasion on nature, grabbing and destroying the essence of life inch by inch. The nature quietly seeped into his molecules. A strange realisation, that the hands and souls of some unseen artists were busy in frenzied activity, injecting subtle chemical changes in his mind. He could hear strange tunes emanating from somewhere within. His singed and rugged psyche was submerged under cathartic fluids of joy and pain. Harfan looked up at the cloudless early afternoon blue sky. A few kites and thrush were lazily gliding, perhaps just for the fun and love of singing to the ethereal void. A piece of cloud drifted in from Sangla Hills and a red-breasted robin swooped in from nowhere. Her mellow whistle and deep black eyes opened up another tunnel. Jamilla's eyes flew in through the clouds. They were fathomless, placid and deep, deeper than the distant blue of the rippling Chenab, breaking into soft murmurs.

*

"*Assalam- u- Alaikum*. Where have you been Mian Mirza Ghalib (a famous Urdu poet)? Dreaming of Jamilla?" Alam approached Harfan from his right flank.

"*Wale Kum*... Sorry I didn't notice you. When did you come by?" Harfan felt intrigued, looking at the grey *mehndi* (herbal dye) tinged lush growth of beard on Alam's face. He presumed that Alam had reasons to move incognito.

"Don't be surprised young man. I'm on a mission. But your reflexes are slack. Be an alert cat. Crouch for your kill, but don't ignore the hunter's dart."

Alam headed towards the front room clutching under his arms two bulging brief cases. Once inside the house, he set himself to surveying the accommodation, inch by inch. He softly hammered the walls to feel for the hollows and cavities. There were none. He examined the wooden floor meticulously. The windows, with opaque glass panes, drew his attention and appreciation.

"A fine home and very tastefully done up." Alam settled down over a cup of coffee, took out a pint-sized bottle from his brief case, and sprinkled the contents on a wooden window panel.

"What're you doing?"

"I'm putting it on fire."

"Why?"

"There has been an electrical short circuit."

"No. You're damaging the nice woodwork."

"What do you do when there is an electrical fire? You replace the wires and do some repair work. Your place is old and a short circuit is but natural." Alam explained that these common electrical items weren't going to trigger off any suspicion.

"What do you need these for?"

"I'm installing your communication set. Fetch some Black Labels from the hotel and order home delivery dinner."

Harfan dropped by the hotel and informed Ibadat that his uncle, third removed, had suddenly arrived from Karachi with a marriage proposal. The old crook required at least five stiff pegs before he went to bed. Would he be good enough to deliver two Black Label bottles at his residence!

A trifle of a smile rippled past Ibadat's left eye. He liked Harfan's thin efforts to guard the secrets of Mian Alam Khan. It was a fine effort indeed. He displayed a mask of happiness, offered home delivery of a few plates of kebab, and roasted mutton nuggets. He would take care of dinner as well, Ibadat assured him.

*

Dinner over, Alam removed his wig, quick fix beard and moustache and set himself to work. He sawed off parts of the wooden floor, near the base of the bedroom fireplace. It took the shape of a hidden sunken chamber that was reinforced with leak proof cement and chemical compounds. He dug up the old brick wall, laid an insulated hidden electric connection, and completed the circuit for an external aerial, by running a length of thermal coated pipe through the fireplace exhaust.

On the second night of stay, Alam closed all the doors and windows and opened his brief cases.

"This is your communication set, Barrette 530-D, from the latest NATO inventory. In fact, this is the standard High Frequency trans-receiver for clandestine operations."

Alam unwrapped the packing and explained its features.

"It operates on 1.6 to 30 MHz, requires 15w to 125w power input. Basically, it operates on SSB system, though there's provision for Amplitude Modulation and CW system. Hope you understand the technical jargon." Alam asked.

"No problem," Harfan asked, "can I use it for VT (voice transmission)?"

"You can. That's technically possible, but there's a total embargo on VT."

"Now look," continued Alam, "the system has twelve memory caches, scanning facility, a remote control panel and a auto-alarm device. With power on it will activate a diode in your wristwatch, which I've given you. The set weighs just 4.1 kilograms. There's a built in error correction facility and you can transmit in continuous as well as burst modes."

"Does it require an external antenna?" Harfan enquired.

"Yes, that's very important. A unidirectional antenna will do. Don't hang one on the roof. We require a camouflaged device."

Alam opened another small bag and took out a crescent moon crafted out of sensitive alloy that was designed to pick up weak radio signals. He fished out a few miniature minaret shaped ceramic insulators.

"These are materials for the high gain antenna. We'd mount these tomorrow and synchronise with the trans-receiver set."

Alam explained, over a drink, some of the unique feature of the trans-receiver set. Communication wasn't possible until the two ends reached an electronic handshake. This feature minimised the risk of detection. The burst transmission facility, he explained, should guarantee against snooping by Pakistani monitoring stations. Alam displayed a miniature auto-encryption accessory that could be jacked to the main trans-receiver.

"All that you're required to do is to key on the message and push the auto-encryption button. Push the burst transmission button after the handshaking diode flashes blue. Your message will reach Delhi in a fraction of a second." Alam explained.

"For reception, switch on the memory button, activate the deciphering key and switch on the printer. The deciphered message will be ready in 2 minutes." Alam kept on narrating the intricacies like a wizard.

"That means I don't use the cipher pads."

"Good question. Something is wrong with me." Alam poured another whisky and lighted a cigarette.

"The auto-encryption ensures low grade encoding, which the enemy can break easily. For all communications to Delhi, use the OTP (one time cipher pads). Here's your supply for one year."

On the third night Alam keyed in a trial message.... "Fish in water, swimming well." That was the pre-determined code for the post-installation communication with Delhi.

Alam explained the schedule protocol.

Harfan should expect calls on 3rd, 13th, 23rd of every month, in 002.007 or 18.009 MHz bands. He should expect calls between 0200 and 0210 hrs. Monitors of Pak Intelligence Bureau, Joint Intelligence Signals of the ISI and the Signals Research Bureau of the Army normally inter-changed their frequencies during this thin margin. That was a part of standard security drill.

For transmission, Alam explained, Harfan should use a random schedule. *Behest*, the designated master hub in Delhi, would be on air round the clock.

"Your station nom-de-plume is *Huri* (fairy). In case of emergency, you switch on at will and seek protocol with call sign *Khalis*, over 23.46 MHz." Alam warned Harfan that the *Khalis* channel was to be tapped only in an emergency, involving his personal security and security of India.

He replaced the wooden floor panels and finally put back the Cashmere carpet on top of it. The camouflage was perfect.

Harfan was introduced to the functioning of an electronic signal scanner that was capable of detecting intrusive snooping devices. Every week, he emphasised, Harfan should carry out electronic scanning of his house, top to bottom; all walls, crevices, behind the wall hangings, undersides of tables, chairs etc, etc. The enemy enjoyed advantage in its home turf, Alam emphasised, and was steps ahead of an intruder like Harfan. The best way to fox the challenger was to maintain communication ambiguity, spare use of telephone and never for professional talks. All professional talks, which can't be avoided, should be carried out from lonely and safe PCBs (Public Call Booths), never from the same one. Use of the clandestine radio was strictly prescribed for special communications that required the immediate attention of Delhi. Harfan was advised to hone up his Drop, Brush, Dead Letter, and Live Letter Box (DLB and LLB) drills.

"And set up a lab for preparing microdots. Use the FIB prescribed invisible ink, in between innocuous black and white writings. Use interesting topical writings in prominent magazines for hiding secret messages. Post your mail to the London cover address, the River Channel, from different towns. Never use the Jhumra post office." Alam refurbished some of the tradecraft lessons earlier imparted by the trainers in Delhi.

"What if I fail and commit mistakes?"

"Don't kid. No loony can survive in this game of walking the razor's edge. If exposed, you're either at the mercy of the Pak intelligence or the FIB executioners." Alam replied without blinking his eyelid.

"No protection from the Company?" Harfan asked in a wounded voice.

"Sorry friend, this is a one way plunge into the black hole. If you happen to emerge at the other end, it's *Allah's* grace. Don't expect any mercy." Alam poured another drink and lighted a cigarette.

"The Agency should've some responsibility for its agents".

"Relax. Intelligence is a raw fire walk sans the magic insulation and rope tricks. Your innovative skills are the only assets you have to live with."

"Any special dope on the power structure at the top?" Harfan enquired about the lay of land in the Armed Forces' hierarchy.

Alam's comments traversed through a virtual minefield of intrigue and tense power struggle. President Field Marshal Akbar Khan was already sucked into the whirlpool of internal and international conspiracies. A pawn in the hands of USA and China, he was mindlessly playing their geo-political games.

"Is he unpopular?" Harfan asked.

"Yes and no. The drawn war and his acceptance of the UN brokered peace have irked the politically ambitious leaders and Generals."

Izaz Afroz, Alam explained, and a few top Generals were involved in multi-layered conspiracies. They vied with each other to plunder Pakistan and stash away its wealth to their foreign bank accounts.

The men to watch out, he said, were Lt. General Sarfaraz, General Hyder Bux, the ISI chief and the Corps Commanders of Karachi, Quetta, Chak Lala, Peshawar and Lahore. They controlled, besides their troops, the fabulous drug cartels. It's they and not the system that decided Pakistan's fate. They were the Establishment.

"Any link with Indian drug barons?" Harfan asked.

"Yes. But don't wreck your head over it. It's out of your orbit. Tread cautiously," Alam cautioned his probationer, "it's worse than a minefield, and I won't be there to push your pram around."

"I'm no toddler." Harfan replied.

"So happy to hear. Bye...." Alam turned back, "yes. I forgot to tell you about linkages between Nawab Sharief and Izaz Afroz. This slimy character moves in and out of power-grabbing conspiracies. His present strategic ally is the Chinese ambassador in Islamabad."

"What about the President?"

"Last of the Pakistani troika, he is a terminally sick person. He has lost the will to fight back...may call in the Chief of Army Staff to step in. Take care." Alam stepped into his car. Before igniting the engine, he summoned Harfan.

"I approve of the girl, an excellent choice. You must know that the girl's mom is a close friend of the most prominent social elite, Begum Jahanara."

"Who's she?"

"Heart throb of many and nemesis of a few prominent Pakistani fortune hunters."

"A seductress?"

"Well! Keep off her charmed circle."

"Thanks uncle."

"Call uncle Shamim. He may like to formally sound Zahoor Chaudry."

Harfan nodded happily.

"And don't forget to inform Jung Sher Khan and Israr about the match. Bye." Alam pressed the accelerator. The car zoomed out bathing Harfan and Ibadat in a thick shower of dust.

Harfan kept on gazing at the receding silhouette of the car and realised that he was finally placed at the designated orbit. It was a delicate and dangerous orbit, spiked with meteorites. He would have to spin along an impossible booby-trapped apogee and perigee. He recalled the cynic advice of Maulana Rizwan. A spy lived only once and not many of them witnessed a second life. What choice was he left with? None. He should live it dangerously, like a cliffhanger, as long as it lasted. That was the secret survival mantra.

Harfan, however, didn't relish the last few words of Alam, which he remorselessly spoke like a professional killer. Neither Bhagat nor Rizwan had given him any inkling of this one-way journey to the abattoir.

Well! He was now inside the ring. Why should he worry about the executioners and stop living and enjoying life! He would face them like he faced the seemingly perils in Bhagat and Rizwan. The executioners won't find him a sitting pregnant duck.

Ramendra Kaushal, the fiercest Delhi University jackal, wasn't yet dead. The butchers of Delhi and Rawalpindi should find their going very tough. Harfan looked back at the distant murmuring river.

Well! He had a dream to pursue, a Jamilla to woo and a new life to live.

*

19

The fine-tuning of Triple X, as a deep penetration resident agent was a part of the task assigned to Jiwan Bahutule alias Mian Alam Khan. His job wasn't over with the ignition of the rocket. It required the firing of micro-retro rockets to place the agent in its desired orbit.

Over a span of five years, the PIB and the ISI had busted six out of ten previous Indian launches. The remaining four were nestled in peripheral areas and had failed to burrow deep inside the establishment. Nevertheless, Harfan Bukhari, Alam calculated, was made of different stuff. The audacious, moody, and daring youth was sure to go places. He seemed to be a man of ready wit with gift of the gab.

Employment with Israr Sharief had provided a snug second layer cover. That coup had added a certain level of respectability to the high gear resident agent. His marriage to a local girl, coming from the social strata of Zahoor Chaudry, should harden the outer shell, argued Alam. Zahoor wasn't a bad choice for a snug cover. The shipping and export tycoon and a sort of industrialist, he was well connected to the top military leaders. His wife Sayeefa was a steady friend of Malika Jahanara, the queen bee of music and pleasure. Jahanara's fabulous friendship with General Arif Khan, the next choice for the post of COAS of the Pakistan Army, had added an aura of heavenly charm to her mysterious personality. Malika Jahanara was trying to mould herself in the cast of the glorious historical mistresses.

With Harfan's proposed marriage to Zahoor's daughter, Alam expected a quantum jump in his personal business dealings with Jung Sher Khan, Israr Sharief and the hungry and scheming bosses in the CMLA. That should offer opportunities for gathering golden hay even on the rainy nights in the Pakistani polity.

Alam threw his dice after meticulous calculation and pleaded forcefully in favour of an early nuptial tie for his understudy.

Nampoothiri vacillated. Yes. Marriage sure was a good cover. But marrying Zahoor Chaudry's daughter could generate professional impediments. Zahoor, he argued, was a high profile businessman and his wife Sayeefa had become a culture-totem in Pakistan. A famous durbar dancer and singer of yesteryears she moved with ease and élan in the highest social strata.

"But he's nose-deep in love with that girl." Alam pleaded.

"I don't approve of it. A Triple X agent shouldn't acquire that kind of social prominence. Ask him to settle for a low profile homemaker. I know him; all that he wants is a female companion. It should be purely a temporary arrangement." Nampoothiri was firm in his views.

"Boss," Alam pleaded, "I think much water has flown down the Indus since he landed in Pakistan. I find many changes in the robot. He has a mind of his own. Moreover, circumstances have placed him in Pakistan's privileged circle. Marrying a nitwit nobody won't fit his cover."

Nampoothiri finally caved in after Alam explained the advantages of penetration of the inner circle of the arms dealers and suppliers and the higher echelons of the military brass. This one Triple X, he reasoned, should climb up high and very fast.

A word of final warning, Nampoothiri said, Harfan Bukhari should be advised not to develop emotional hang-up for the Pakistani girl. It should simply be a marriage of convenience. He required a station-wife and that's all Delhi could concede.

Alam had decided not to stonewall the proposal. He stood to gain out of the match. Shamim Bukhari was pleased too. The marriage was sure to give him better access to the cartel headed by Israr, Jung Sher Khan and Alam. He travelled all the way to Zahoor's Lahore residence and sought Jamilla's hand for his nephew.

Zahoor Chaudry, financially a stronger person, but socially inferior, was flattered by the proposal, initiated by Jung Sher Khan and Israr Sharief. He couldn't imagine that all his money could buy a Bukhari for his daughter, offspring of an estuary tribal and a danseuse.

Sayeefa, a woman of modern values, insisted on a pre-marriage meeting between the boy and the girl, a condition unheard of in their social milieu. Zahoor, a Mohana tribal, was transformed to a heavenly angel by the love, compassion and caring of Sayeefa. He had also developed a healthy respect for her human values. Zahoor was a different kind of male, who was not a miserly in stretching the limits of respect for womenfolk.

Sayeefa didn't like to throw her daughter to one more male pig. She abhorred the idea of forcing Jamilla to enter a blind marriage. She didn't want another *mullah* (priest) to lead her daughter to a blind nuptial knot that could be nullified by three repeat utterances of the eternally anti-feminist dirty word, *talaq* (divorce). Zahoor, like all good husbands, hardly disagreed with his wife. He knew Sayeefa well. She would have her way, in any case.

The glitterati and chatterati of Lahore turned up for the grand social evening arranged by friend Jung Sher Khan. Mian Israr Sharief, the *muhajir*, the Punjabi elite, and the big bosses in uniform led the cheer groups. The nostalgic surroundings of the Faletti's, an old imperial heritage with a majestic structure, arcades, and manicured gardens, were decked up elegantly for the occasion.

Nobody talked about the marriage. Pleasant talks, sober drinks, whiffs of French perfume and delectable snacks filled the light hearts.

Sayeefa played a neat trick.

"Here's Harfan. Perhaps you'll like to meet him."

She guided the young hearts to a corner and whispered into Jamilla's ears. She melted into the crowd, leaving Harfan and Jamilla in a storm of silence swirling around them. Harfan's imagination failed to comprehend that the frame of the owner of the deep blue eyes, now clad in a pink *salwar-kameej* and a matching light-rose *dupatta* (scarf), could be so unearthly and ethereal.

Her cascading long hair sparkled like the silken slough of a queen cobra. The colour of her skin was a mysterious mixture of fully blossomed Bengal *champak* (michelia champaca) and the light pink Bukhara Rose. The heavenly glow, he thought was borrowed from the late evening clouds, hanging low over the horizon. The sun, the master artist, went to sleep after painting the clouds with a tender brush. The colour remained frozen on Jamilla's skin and soul.

The blue eyes, now free from the restraints of the *burka* slits, rippled amazingly, with small waves of endless questions piercing Harfan's frozen frame, which was rooted to the marble floor.

Harfan Bukhari was no novice with women. He always felt a strange thirst and depression after every wild orgy. The thirst came, perhaps, from the genes of Raja Digvijay Kaushal and the melancholy was perhaps a gift from his mother.

However, the shiver of joy pulsating through his existence transcended the paralysing moments. Harfan felt a benign glow lightening up his senses with a million-volt charge. He didn't feel the thirst and the melancholy was nowhere near. He felt like he was floating on the waves of an unknown sea, a very blue one, reflected in Jamilla's eyes. The silent waves mesmerised him. Harfan was incapable of opening his lips, the words having lost their way deep inside his neurons. The left hemisphere of his brain was momentarily stupefied.

Jamilla recognised the young eyes and now the complete features of the man. Yes. It was he, the lost Bedouin with Greek features. The eyes, light brown, deep-set behind thick brows looked sad; like a captive pool of liquid, struggling to breach its banks. The eyes were asking mute questions, not perfectly coordinated with his speech organs. A strange and mysterious smile momentarily appeared in the left corner of her slightly pouted lips, with a matching vibration in her eye fluids.

"*Allah kasam* (by God). *Khuda banaya use meri liye* (by god. He has made him for me)." Jamilla silently spoke to herself.

Harfan reciprocated with a silent reply. The vibrations of his eyes matched those of Jamilla and conveyed the magic message.

"By God! *Tum meri hi ho* (you are mine only)."

Pulsation inside two sets of arteries and veins levelled down with the unuttered resolution. The eyes disengaged. Jamilla drew the scarf on her head and flew in the direction of a chattering group of young girls.

Back home Sayeefa sounded Jamilla about the young man she had met in the party. Did she like him? Would she like to make him her life partner?

"As you wish."

Jamilla covered her face with a book. Her face, bright pink with delight and glow of love had failed to hide the inner feelings. Sayeefa, the mother, understood the signals and gave the final nod to Zahoor. She liked the boy. Jamilla too had approved the choice. He could now call a *Kazi* (magistrate) for the ceremonials and rituals. She was sure the two would make a fine pair. The boy was accomplished and oozed out an aroma of aristocracy. He wasn't another male pig.

*

The brief honeymoon at Nathia Gali, a scenic and solitary hill resort next to Murri, was an experience in heavenly bliss. The cosy retreats of Pines Hotel, long walks along the grassy Dunga Gali ridges, ecstatic touches and burning flames helped the mingling of their souls, like an ethereal fragrance loosing its identity in the thin galactic void. Wild exploration of the body and eternal penetration in each other's amorphous consciousness had exploded Jamilla's existence. She reached the pinnacle of a new realisation and resolution. She loved the man. It was beyond physical love. She cared for him. Harfan felt like a born-again person. A strange faith had burst forth into a new sunrise. He realised that love wasn't an act of madness! It meant caring and silent emptying and mingling with another soul. By emptying himself in Jamilla's love, he felt enriched. Her spring of love had filled in all the crevices and depressions of his singed psyche. The bliss was more than heavenly, if that state of situation existed anywhere. Jamilla was only for him. God had specially crafted her and put a wonderful soul in the delicate frame, only for him. Her love transported Harfan beyond his second incarnation, a programmed Indian spy in Pakistan.

He felt a strange transcendental force pushing him through a tunnel, to a third incarnation, a new existence, far removed from that of Ramendra Kaushal and Harfan Bukhari. This was indeed a tunnel to freedom, freedom from fear. She helped him break the glass-cage erected by Bhagat and Rizwan and reinforced by Alam. God alone could say wherefore had He gathered all these primordial elements to create this angel of love! It wasn't her outer beauty; something divine in her had mesmerised Harfan.

Harfan stood near the window ledge and again looked at the contours of Jamilla's body, wrapped in a silken blanket. The sleeping beauty again reminded him of the unique *Shakti* (female power), created by the elemental gods.

A couplet from the *Murti Rahasyam* (mystery of the image) of the Hindu scripture *Chandi* came to his mind…"This goddess is golden coloured, her apparel is golden, and her body is adorned with the finest golden ornaments. She has just stepped out of the dazzling golden morning sun!"

Harfan smiled for having picked up a couplet from a Hindu scripture to describe his Muslim wife. How funny life could be? But, he felt helpless. Jamilla's beauty could only be described by reciting the classic couplet. No other poet had yet conceived another woman, so beautiful, so energised and so resolutely poised against the evils of the universe. This eternal beauty transcended religion.

*

The dream journey to Nathia Gali concluded abruptly. Israr Sharief wanted Harfan urgently back at Sangla. A Pentagon team was flying into Rawalpindi for peddling military hardware. His company was short-listed by the government for attending a meeting with the visiting team.

Israr was not final spoil-pleasure. The worst jolt came from Sayeefa.

She poured tea from an ornate hand-painted china pot and spoke in a whispering tone.

"I believe you've hired a heritage home at Jhumra."

"It's a fine place, bang on a tributary of the Chenab."

"I've been there. Oh! That was good two decades ago."

Harfan silently sipped the spiced tea. He knew she was there, in his father's *durbar* at Jhumra, around the fateful days of partition of India.

"That's a lonely place I believe." Sayeefa looked up at Harfan.

"Yes, splendidly solitary."

"You see my intention isn't to separate you two," Sayeefa spoke in her usual low voice, "Jamilla is just 21. You're most of the time out on business tours. It's not good for a kid to live alone in that splendidly lonely place."

"But...," Harfan tried lodging a mild protest.

"Jami is a good student. She stood first in her honours and you'll obviously like her to complete the higher course."

Harfan couldn't protest, though the very idea of living without Jamilla tormented him.

"You're new to the job and it's a responsible position," Sayeefa continued, "your business involves frequent travel. She'll feel miserable, all alone at Jhumra. You understand the problem." Her argument was irrefutable.

"When does she start her new course?" Harfan managed to ask.

"Next month. You come over and stay with us whenever you're off from Israr's work," Sayeefa poured fresh tea for Harfan, "you're our son, as dear to us as Jamilla is."

The short spell of bliss of being with Jamilla, Harfan realised, was too sublime to be mired by the prolonged interlude of separation. For the first time he discovered the divine pain of separation. There was pain as well as pleasure in it. He glossed over the circumstances that surrounded him.

As a resident intelligence agent, he was required to walk the razor's edge all the way. No tilt, no slip. An insignificant miss could blow up his cover and push him to the gallows. A neutralised agent in foreign soil mostly took a one-way journey behind the walls of high security prisons. Never could he expect to crawl back to Jamilla's love nest. Very few in his class ever did. The jackals growled all around for their pounds of flesh. He wasn't the knight to tame them, not yet.

Harfan finally Okayed Sayeefa's suggestion, but insisted that Jamilla should visit his new home, for a few days at least. The home, without her touch, would just be another wilderness.

Sayeefa understood and agreed.

*

Harfan's idyllic heritage Jhumra home nestled on the wooded banks of a tributary of the Chenab. The fall colours and lush green vegetation around bemused Jamilla. She hated the mere thought of returning to Lahore, leaving her dream man alone. The threads of her life were textured with those of this strange person only a few days back. It seemed like they had known each other from eternity and had been travelling together on the same arrow of time, never separated from each other.

A new dream had enveloped her. *Insha Allah* let this be the eternal dream!

"Why don't we spend a night in the royal chamber of the hotel?" The idea first hit Harfan's mind.

"It doesn't make any difference. Wherever you are I'm your queen and you're my prince." Jamilla replied.

Jamilla's reply infected and intoxicated Harfan. A prince he was and Jamilla was his queen of hearts. He couldn't suppress the desire of spending a precious night with her at the royal chamber of his parent's abode, now a heritage tourist hotel. He always felt the amorphous presence of his father, the clanging hoofs of his stallion, and shuffling clothes of his courtiers.

Hotel Royal Palace enchanted Jamilla too. The sheer charm of the place propelled her to take a walk to the edges of the palace compound, beyond the orchards that traversed the undulated ground and disappeared inside the riverbed.

Brought up in the honeycombed clusters in a narrow lane, she felt like spreading herself on the grass and embracing the trees, some of them broadcasting a distinct aroma. She enjoyed the walk.

Walking down with Jamilla Harfan had lost count of their pace and direction. They talked about the river, distant glistens from its blues, the twittering birds, and the enchanting fall colours. He suddenly realised that they had reached the edges of Ramayani's huts. The frail old lady, seated under the shade of a huge banyan tree, was busy feeding her pet goats with tender green grass and leaves.

She noticed the couple approaching her hut. There was no mistake, she murmured. He must be Ramu, Ramendra Kaushal, her son, and son of the late king. She had nursed him in her womb for nine and a half long months. This must be her own drop of blood. She hadn't committed any mistake on their first encounter.

Yes, she was sure. She had kissed and loved an exact replica of this very face, decades ago. The pain and pleasure of bearing the child, as a surrogate mother, was rewarding, but at the cost of permanent silence. She was administered the vow of eternal silence, before the goddess *Kali* and a raging sacrificial fire, never to claim her own drop of blood. But her vow of silence couldn't plug the memory lane. The dark magic box of old wounds and pleasures opened up spontaneously. Her thoughts floundered on the rocks of doubt. Perhaps she was dreaming and conjuring up a truth, which she liked to believe to be true. Kasturi's mail hadn't mentioned anything about their son visiting the lost kingdom. He had taken up a job in *Vilayat*. Why should he be here, in this heartless country, which had mercilessly killed his father?

She was intrigued on the first encounter itself, to see the face of the young Maharaja implanted on the body of the strange visitor. The lower part of the face was a replica of Digvijay's young feature. His lips too were slightly curled at the edges and there was a deep fold at the centre of the upper lip.

She had no doubt about the strange similarity. Harfan's lush growth of beard couldn't deceive her eyes.

They were just a few paces away. Ramayani noticed through the corner of her eyes.

"Here's Ramayani," Harfan introduced Jamilla, "my wife Jamilla Bano."

"A Hindu?" Jamilla whispered.

"Yes, a legacy from the old kingdom. They didn't kill her. She's deranged, I'm told."

Harfan stretched the introduction.

Ramayani stopped feeding the goats, entered her hut, and came out with a silver plate on her left palm. White rice grains, green blades of grass, and an ivory box full of red vermilion powder flanked an oil lamp at the centre.

She surprised Jamilla by putting a large vermilion mark on her forehead and in the parting of her hair. She showered the young bride with blades of grass and a thimble full of rice grains. Jamilla looked with innocent astonishment. She didn't know how to react. Harfan moved in to protest, but Ramayani surprised him too by placing some blades of grass and grains of rice on his head. She unfastened the knot of her sari end, took out two gold coins, with the impression of a distinctive Hindu goddess on one side and a strange crowned head on the other.

"What're these? British coins?" Harfan asked.

"No," Ramayani spoke for the first time in a slow but firm voice, "these coins were minted by Maharaja Vikramaditya Kaushal, grandfather of the late Maharaja, on the occasion of his accession to the Jhumra throne. Keep this. This'll bring you good luck and happiness."

"You know we're Muslims and our ladies don't put on the Hindu style vermilion marks." Harfan spoke haltingly.

"I know son," Ramayani continued, "I'm a mother and I know only my kind of ritual. Don't mind. You've come for the first time with your wife to a mother's abode. I thought, I must greet the *bahu* (bride) in my own way."

"But lady, I've nothing to do with the old regime and your religion. We're Muslims…." Harfan tried a feeble protest, but his words were lost inside his oral cavity.

Ramayani's looks puzzled him. Her disturbed gaze oscillated alternately between Harfan and Jamilla, drops of tear hanging at the edges.

"I understand son," Ramayani replied, "forgive me. Please keep the coins. This'll bring you good luck."

She pressed Jamilla's palms with a message of earnest request.

"Daughter, keep this. The symbol of the Kaushal family will augur well for you. May the goddess bless you with many children! Let your husband live for a hundred years and may you be loved by him infinitely."

The old lady broke down in tears.

Jamilla, highly embarrassed, wiped her cheeks, and promised that she would never part with the lucky gold coins. She didn't bother about the ritual. But something strange about this lady touched her inner chords. She looked like an eternal mother. It didn't matter if she was a Hindu.

Jamilla saluted her in customary Muslim style.

An alarm bell, however, kept on ticking inside Harfan. He was, by now, aware of the strange glimpses in Ramayani's looks. What was she exploring? Was she trying to discover the image of Digvijay Kaushal in his face?

Her looks did not exude love alone. Her eyes and words were trying to convey some hidden message. That would be too close a call, simply disastrous. His delicate cover would be at a tremendous risk. He couldn't afford to be emotional. Harfan resolved not to venture again to this part of the palace, which harboured a killer umbilical to his past. He whispered into Jamilla's ears and turned back to the hotel.

*

Ibadat served food in the royal chamber's anteroom. Delta prawns fried in garlic sauce, tender smoked chicken nuggets; potato stuffed with minced meat, with thick gravy to match and *tandoori rotis* (flat bread baked in a special oven) made the savoury dinner exciting.

"She's very kind and peculiar, isn't she?" commented Jamilla, still mystified and enchanted by Ramayani's demeanour.

"*Bhabiji* (sister-in-law), don't mind her queer ways. She's somewhat deranged." Replied Ibadat.

"Didn't look like one." That's all Jamilla could whisper back. It would be rather impolite for a newly wed bride to enter into an argument with a hotel cook.

"She's taken a fancy for brother Harfan." Ibadat laughed while serving the pudding, a real English one, with brown caramel topping, "this has been specially baked by my mother, for you *bhabiji*."

Jamilla appreciated the pudding.

The excellent food did fill Jamilla's stomach. But the ecstasy of body and mind reminded her that the night itself had inclined on the horizon, excitingly chasing its love, the bright rouge coloured dame, daybreak. It was time for her to chase her dream. She decided to keep awake, stretching the dark hours, and keeping Harfan busy, in her own way. She must make him compensate for the impending separation. The pleasure of the two bodies coming together, in an ecstatic search for the peak of sublime satisfaction, and pangs for not having been able to reach the peak, had warmed up her mind and body. She wanted Harfan alone, all to herself. She stretched her left hand under the table and pinched Harfan's thigh, with a twinkle in her eyes. The signal was inviting and tempting.

Harfan led his bride to the royal chamber, once used by his father and mother. Jamilla was the angel of love, of his life, and he would like her to conceive their first child in this very bed.

The kingdom wasn't anyway coming back to him. History created through enormous bloodshed couldn't be undone without much bigger blood baths. He was perhaps not another epochal hero to put the clock back. But he could sure make a new beginning. Jamilla, winking at him, was history in the making. And he should thank his stars, if he could create a new identity for himself.

Harfan, the spy, he hoped, could be segregated from the man just sculpted by an artist called Jamilla, with the sublime chisels of her love and imagination. He wouldn't like to endanger this pretty gift of God. Harfan picked up Jamilla and smilingly walked up to the bed.

*

20

A tiny blue diode flashed intermittently in Harfan's wristwatch. It was an invitation to go on the air. A tiny processor in the spy trans-receiver activated the diode whenever *Behest* wanted him to be on air for special transmission. There hadn't been many such emergency flashes and special calls from *Behest* so far, except for a solitary tasking on the likely Pakistani strategy at Tashkent. It was a low-key task, rather a probing one. A surface scrounged reply was highly appreciated in Delhi. It had corroborated the Mission based reports and inputs from Alamgir. Delhi's calibration of the diplomatic needles at Tashkent was heavily dependant on these reports.

However, tonight's diode flashes surprised Harfan. He switched on the set and established electronic protocol.

The recorded printout was crisp.

"30978. GR12. XOURTH 6A10X8. WPERT KMHCG OUREF SPIQW CZXYY KLHXX QOMPT RMOZZ WOULL BDFRE WNYST BPKTS LONTX UOTRS YWQQO SLRTH. EOM. 0XTL1."

Harfan fished out, from a hidden cavity, a card-sized one-time pad and deciphered the message, using the key XOURTH 6A10X8.

"Require immediate report on Operation Mardan. Is it a part of OP-Bakhtiar? Pak HQ spoke to Dacca on Mardan."

Harfan secured the set and the accessories, burnt the used cipher card in the washbasin, drained the ashes, and settled down in front of the fireplace with a large whisky. Delhi's first formal request intrigued Harfan. The ISI and the GHQ had scripted Operation Bakhtiar in tandem with the Special Services Group, as a multi-layered corollary to Operation Gibraltar and Operation Grand Slam. It was conceived as a strategic mixture of limited frontal and long-term deep penetration guerrilla warfare in the chicken neck area of Indian Bengal and the eastern Indian States of Assam and Tripura. Removed from the main arch of war theatre in the western sector, Assam and Tripura offered strategic advantages to the Pakistan Army. It was a standby contingent plan for swift penetration, in the event of Indian forces knocked at the doors of Lahore and Sialkot. The UN brokered ceasefire and the Tashkent talks had forced the establishment hawks to stash away Bakhtiar to a temporary chill-tray.

Operation Mardan appeared to be a red herring. The usual boisterous army mess birds normally babbled their hearts out in drunken stupor and vain brawls. They too didn't react to Harfan's clever probes. His conscious and sub-conscious assets in the CMLA establishment and the GHQ hadn't indicated any fresh military venture against India.

Could it be a super-secret war game planned by the new military junta that had inherited the mantle from President Akbar?

How could Pakistan embark upon another adventure?

The White House had sounded clear signals that the Pak-US honeymoon was chilling down. Pakistan's burgeoning strategic ties with China had generated vapours of suspicion and distrust. Washington had played down President Akbar Khan's state visit with subtle diplomatic noises.

The new junta couldn't risk another war, either of the Gibraltar or Bakhtiar type. Senior Generals in Chak Lala cantonment and Rawalpindi GHQ didn't talk in terms of another war. They talked, in hushed voices, about augmenting Pakistan's military infrastructure. That's where Israr International and its cartel partners Jung Sher Khan and Alam Khan appeared. They solicited the Chinese, the undercover European adventurers and rogue-CIA operators for supplementing the inventory of the starving Armed Forces. Fat slices of drug-money were rolled back into the arms bazaar. Harfan knew well the thinly papered clandestine conduits. He himself was a major player of the team headed by Israr International.

The butchers of democracy needed sophisticated weapons more for scaring and silencing the Pakistanis than fighting the infidel Indians. The new sets of dramatis personae were not in the best of shape for another bout of war.

What else could Mardan mean? Could it be a revised concept of low-key proxy war against India, in a new theatre?

Harfan felt tempted to call Alam's Quetta number to solicit guidance. On second thought, he aborted the idea. Demystifying the cobwebs of Operation Mardan was his first major task. Failure would put a question mark on the career of a highly rated agent. Harfan decided to trek the lonely furrow all by himself. The Kaushals never shied away from challenges. A job was as sacrosanct as his faith and love. He must explore the usual conduits used by Israr Sharief, for reaching the grooves of the top Generals. That alone could unearth the Mardan mystery.

The final resolution made Harfan happy. He lighted a cigarette.

A contradictory stream started bubbling up as the whisky mixed with his blood. Was it necessary to stick his neck out? The pendulum inside oscillated nervously and advised Harfan to look beyond Delhi's brief. Why couldn't he buy a new life? Why couldn't he and Jamilla start a new life in London?

No. That was impossible. Harfan gulped the liquid, squeezed in his facial muscles, and moved his head violently. A Kaushal wasn't a finicky colt to bolt the front trenches. His father didn't. Why should he?

Harfan didn't feel like finishing the drink. He threw the liquid on the dying embers. The flames leaped high for a few seconds. The momentary dance of the fire further melted the neuronal membranes, hurling Harfan into a spin. The earth below, the sky above and everything else started spinning like a churning wheel. Harfan felt he was in a trance.

Kasturi appeared first, out of the churning vortex. She stood over a pool of blood; a child clung to her breast, covered with a blood-soaked piece of cloth. An elderly person, whom he didn't recognise, Ramayani, Ibadat and a white-skinned British guarded her flanks.

One tall young Pathan, with a pockmarked face appeared next. He brandished a sword, blood dripping all the way from its sharp edges. He carried a huge round metal plate on his left palm, covered with a blood soaked silk bandanna. Fanged hyena laughter crackled out of his throat. He walked up to Kasturi and with a jerk removed the bandanna cover.

Harfan could see a severed head, the brown eyeballs starkly staring at Kasturi with pain, anger, and compassion. Whose head was it?

The ghastly scene changed to a grislier one.

Harfan suddenly found himself armed with a curved knife and chasing Ramayani. She ran across the spice orchard and shouted at the top of her voice.

"Yes, you're Digvijay's mirror image. Who'll pay your blood debt? You're not a Muslim, you're my son." She disappeared.

A galloping horse faded in, with the beheaded body of Digvijay Kaushal mounted on it. The horse abruptly stopped, splashing warm blood on Harfan's face, mouth, and nostril. The salty taste prompted violent nausea.

The headless body passed on an unsheathed sword in his hand; before he could react, King Digvijay's lifeless body slumped onto his blood soaked lap.

The dream celluloid suddenly snapped. Harfan jumped out of the sofa, switched on the lights, and inspected his nightclothes.

No. There was no blood anywhere. He looked at the toilet mirror. No blood.

Yes, his upper lip was swollen, slightly scratched at the edges. He smiled. It was a parting gift from Jamilla.

Where from had this ghastly buried dream come? Did he like to invent a new set of events for his past? Or the scenes were captured in the molecules of his very tender brain, a mere child of two? Possible. Perhaps the events had taken place as replayed in his dream! Who could predict what picture would be engrained at what stage of life?

He moved closer to the mirror.

Was he really a mirror image of his father? Had Ramayani recognised him? What nonsense did she shout in his dream? The old lady had betrayed her emotions. Some hidden embers must be burning in her blood that had excited her frozen emotions. What made her greet Jamilla in that peculiar fashion?

The alarm bell kept on ringing inside Harfan's serpent brain and the wild days peeped out of the gene bag. He must take care of the old lady. A silent liquidation would not be bad!

Harfan abandoned the idea of returning to bed. Anyways, without Jamilla it was as hot as a sand dune. What about these horrible footages from his past? Had he become a prisoner of history, of his past?

No. He wouldn't into any prison. The idea of living in history was good, but he was here, in Pakistan, to create a new history.

He made coffee, lighted a cigarette, and mulled over the haunting apparitions. Did he ever think of killing Ramayani to permanently shut one window to his peril? Did he ever think of eliminating Ibadat, the probable second window?

These thoughts might have crossed his mind as an auto-defence mechanism. The neurons inside played their strange chess game, even in his dreams, casting an advance shadow of events, still in the womb of the future.

What about that pockmarked face holding his father's severed head on a platter?

Had it really happened? His mother had never mentioned about the grisly event. The fleeting image of passing on the sword flashed past his mind. Yes. He owed a blood-debt to his father. His son couldn't bolt the arena without liquidating the assassins. That black memory would simply not allow him to escape to the cocooned world of Jamilla.

The dreams were real. The mirror of history wouldn't allow him to sleep in peace. The war ahead was more of a personal than a proxy war he was supposed to fight for the FIB.

The war this time was on the holy soil of his birth. He must fight it and pay back the debt of blood.

*

The bright sun brought with it a glorious morning and a nasty headache and hangover. He must stop these drinking bouts, Harfan reflected. Weakness for intoxicant could land him in immense trouble.

He lighted a cigarette and started walking towards the orchard area of Palace Hotel, along the trail to Ramayani's huts. Some hidden force dragged him to that obscure corner. After the initial struggle, he let his steps follow their natural rhythm. What was happening to him? Why was he pushing himself to the quagmire of own memory? Was he a prisoner of his dreams? No. He couldn't allow this to happen. The rear-view mirror was necessary, for smooth piloting ahead. But he wasn't surely a creature of fossilised memories.

Harfan's confused rumination and scattered concentration was broken by the sounds of quick footsteps behind him. He turned around.

Ibadat, Harfan noticed, slowed down his pace with a deliberate effort, like a snail drawing its snout in. What was he anxious about? Was he watching his movements, under orders from Alam, or the Pakistani intelligence?

"*Salaam* Ibadat sahib," Harfan wished him with contrived warmth in his voice, "Taking a stroll, good for digestion!"

"*Walekum janab*," Ibadat replied nervously, "I wanted to catch up with you. Thought, you might like to have a conducted tour of the palace compound."

Did Ibadat have a brief to keep him away from Ramayani? Did the brief come from Delhi, or from Alam?

Harfan concealed his anxiety.

"An interesting place, isn't it?" He graciously allowed Ibadat to maintain the tenuous cover. He had no doubt that, this son of the former royal cook, was an integral part of Delhi's networking in Pakistan.

"You're so correct sir," Ibadat continued, "Jhumra and the surrounding areas of the Chenab basin are exquisitely charming."

"So interesting! You must give me company for hiking in the hill tracts and the lush forests, one of these days."

"That's great. Let's move on. I'll show you the *Jung Tikri* (war hillock)."

"What's that?"

"That's where the former king had fought his last hopeless battle with the tribal invaders."

Ibadat led Harfan away from the old lady, who was apparently busy caressing an all white goat-kid.

"Is that so?" Harfan felt the heat of anxiety building up inside. Last night's gory apparition of king Digvijay reappeared before his mind's screen.

Ibadat led the way, through waist high shrubs and bushes, high above the slopes, towards a raised ground. A few dilapidated stone and baked brick structures were still fighting a losing battle against the advancing nature that covered them up with creepers and tall grass.

"These were the advance battle positions of the king's army, the main defence parameters of the palace. The Kaushal kings had fought many battles from these ramparts, their own battles, and some for the British masters....

"Look down below. Can you see the broken stone and cement walkways, lost in river sands?"

"Yes."

"The river, even ten years back, used to flow below these ramparts and the galleys and boats of the former kings used to berth there."

"Where has the river gone?"

"They've raised a barrage upstream. It's now navigable only in monsoon." Ibadat replied and sat on a broad stone covered with dried up moss. Harfan followed him silently, lighted a cigarette, and inhaled a few eager puffs before he spoke.

"Tell me more about the king, his queen and his people."

Ibadat spoke, in a low lingering tone. Harfan failed to keep count of time. But the descending darkness and the sudden wing fluttering of a flock of nesting peacocks and their shrill homecoming calls brought him back to the present surroundings.

"Thanks for the fascinating conducted tour," Harfan stood up and started climbing down the broken track, "you must tell me more." He added.

"There are more stories, the stories of the last war the king had so valiantly fought."

Ibadat followed Harfan.

"Some other day." Harfan started descending the rough slopes of the hillock. His mind had flown out of his body cage, following the misty contours of his parents, painted by Ibadat's sedative narration.

No. He couldn't run away from Jhumra. Some rabid Niazi tribal had killed his father, in an unfair battle and a brave cook saved his mother. He himself owed his life, probably to Ramayani and Ibadat's father. He had many people to pay back. Visit to the family battleground, infused new life force in Harfan. The visit to *Jung Tikri* added a new dimension to his mission Pakistan. The vague personal stake had taken a concrete contour. He must fight. He wasn't a mere spy. He was an avenger.

Harfan shelved the idea of deserting his mission. The cover given by Delhi was unique and he thanked his FIB friends, for relocating him at Jhumra. Jamilla, his dream, was his soul. He loved her, was ready to turn the world around to protect her. But he would, under no circumstances, abandon his mission, the mission of destroying Pakistan.

"Mind coming in for some coffee?" Ibadat asked, as they approached the hotel.

"Wouldn't mind a cup."

Harfan perched himself on a couch and Ibadat followed with a pot of coffee.

"Coffee please." He poured the brew, casting a sideways look at Harfan's stiff facial muscles. A brief smile crossed his eyes and face. The visit to the ramparts had worked as a tonic. He could see the taut muscles on Harfan's face and the jaws grinding against his teeth. He must share the new chemical changes in Harfan with Alam.

Harfan kept on sipping the coffee, but his mind was lost in a piece of sky, visible through the window. The resolve to fight the secret wars kept on generating steam. He lighted another cigarette, thanked Ibadat and slowly walked out. His love and his war beckoned him. The war had just begun.

Harfan told himself loudly. The mute words bounced violently inside his cortices. The stiff climb to his pilgrimage at Jhumra had just started.

Why look back? Ahoy! The enemy was ahead starboard and astern.

*

21

Journey to Islamabad, along the historic Grand Trunk Road built by Sher Shah Suri, the upstart Afghan fortune hunter, took Harfan about four hours. He was on a hunting mission, hunting out a likely target in the Pakistan Army for eliciting vital intelligence on Operation Mardan.

Hotel Khyber, next to the railway station, off Shahrah-e-Islamabad, a posh upcoming neighbourhood, was a respectable address with reasonable charges. Harfan checked in there. It offered two distinct attractions.

Anar Begum, a queen bee in Israr's business operations, who usually warmed the beds of top army cats, lived just three blocks away. The Defence Supply Corps office, which was headed by Brigadier Habibullah, could be reached in ten minutes.

Habibullah epitomised the success story of the sub-continental elite. A successful harvester of the Pakistan Army, he had harvested millions of rupees in the name of *Allah* and *kafir* India. *Allah* was the ultimate acid that purified the dirtiest misdeeds and *kafir* India was the glue that kept together the building chips of Pakistan. He owned, among others, a posh palace at 6th street, Markaz Ramna 7, off Fazlul Haq Road, a Central London apartment, and 5000 acres of farmland at Nurpur, off Shahiwal. It was rumoured that his numbered Swiss account was no slimmer than $ 200 million. Besides his paltry salary and a 3% cut in all defence deals, Brigadier Habibullah earned on the side, what was known as sugar money, money earned from peddling refined brown sugar.

An integral part of the top brass controlled drug cartel, Habibullah acted as a conduit to the Lahore and Karachi based dons, who smuggled out the precious consignments, processed in Afghanistan and the Frontier Provinces. India, a porous transit territory the was used by his mafia-cousins for forward trading with American and European destinations.

Habibullah was an important cog in this mighty machine. His forward and backward linkages ended with a few dreaded names in the drug cartel. He was aware of the Indian luminaries who shared drug nectar with their Pakistani brothers-in-trade. The identities of Ram and Allah, Hindu and Muslim did not queer their pitch. On either side of the border, they played cricket with human skulls and bones.

Habibullah didn't lose his sleep over their identities. A queer military officer without political ambition, he had opted for the soft role of a clever facilitator. He greased the tarmacs up and down and plundered the coffers of the fabled forty thieves. A true Aladdin he was.

Habibullah didn't care for confidence building or demolishing measures. The big bosses lived above cloud nine and were beyond the reach of warfront bullets. They never faced the stinking cadavers of soldiers. From their exalted position, like high priests around the sacrificial fire, they offered human blood and tissues to the altars of rabid nationalism, fermented in the cauldrons of hatred and religious bigotry. Habibullah and his breed believed in the Hindu dictum: *Vasudhaiva Kutumbakam*—all creatures inhabiting the planet were friends. Sages anonymous had sung this eternal message thousands of years ago.

However, Habibullah's love did not radiate beyond his pockets. He demanded and grabbed a flat cut of 3% in all major defence purchases. In army conclaves and social circuits, he wasn't unnecessarily known as the 'three percentage Habib'. He didn't care for the appellatives. What mattered at the end of the day was the glittering dough. He believed in universal happiness, and shared the extra crumbs strictly according to the rules of *Hadith*, to each one according to the sharpness of his teeth. The *Allah* was no exception. He was liberal in doling out *zaqat* (charity) to the needy, during Ramadan month.

Known for his well cushioned catty sense of survival, Habibullah cajoled and humoured people to achieve what he wanted, and what he felt was his rightful claim. The richest creation of the *Allah,* according to him, was the circular golden wheel called money.

His next preference were *sharab* (wine) and *shabab,* fair looking experienced women. No deal or contract could be finalised without fattening Habibullah's pocket and warming up his bed with a '*hum bister*' (bed partner) of his choice.

*

Israr Sharief had discovered Begum Anar, a *ghazal* (genre of poetry) singer and a bit of film actress, during one of the international conferences of the Pakistan Export Promotion Council. Women of the class of Anar are hired all over the world as integral décor of international conferences, especially conferences where big business deals are struck.

Israr, a devout Muslim, didn't consider the idea of hiring Anar's services as an act of blasphemy to clinch a fat deal with a Japanese party. In war and business, such innocuous contamination was permissible. It was nothing but a kind of capital investment. In any case, he had not warmed up his own bed with Begum Anar's biological heat. Even the Paigambar (pbuh) had managed to receive fresh directions from *Allah* to accommodate the idol worshippers. Business, after all, was a deal, whether it was the *Allah* or Anar.

Harfan's offer of another liaison job, therefore, didn't surprise Anar. Israr was a respectable client. No problem, she would be available, but for the usual fees. Each successful engagement would cost Rs. 50,000, and for an aborted deal, her compensation package would be Rs. 20,000.

"This job's different," Harfan informed Begum Anar, who was busy choosing the right eye-shade for her evening engagement. "our business depends a lot on this information."

"What's the big deal?"

The Begum threw the words out casually as she exhaled clouds of smoke. She didn't think any job was unachievable, if it concerned male pigs, born out of a mother's womb. She was fond of boasting scornfully that, so far, no male born out of nonsensical and imaginary Immaculate Conception had dared to walk out of her bed.

"What's your target? For how many nights?" The Begum talked in a straight professional voice.

"You see," Harfan introduced the subject hesitatingly, "our army has adopted a new war game, Operation Mardan. They'd require plenty of new defence supplies from abroad. Israr wants to bag the contract. Get me the details of Mardan. The Brigadier, I'm told, has full knowledge, as he had visited China recently, as a member of the Mardan planning team."

"It's a very tall and a risky order, *mian*," pouted the Begum, "how much are you offering?"

"The usual fees."

"No dear," the lady spoke with a tone of finality and continued stroking her cheeks with a sable brush, "the job's risky, it will cost you Rs. 100,000 straight." She averred.

"It's pretty high." Harfan pleaded helplessness.

"Let's call off the deal," Begum Anar dismissed the meeting, "this Habib bugger is a bull, he will do it for a minimum of five times and leave me half dead. And I've other engagements. The younger Sharief, Nawab sahib, has an assignment for me. He's paying one grand." She parted a shot.

"Who is the target?"

"Don't bother. These are trade secrets. Each bit of additional information would cost you an amount equivalent to the original contract money."

"Okay, you get the money, but only after completion of the job. We must get the contract of supplying 100,000 pieces of snow boots, and 100,000 pieces of fur-lined parkas, in addition to the Mardan details." Harfan argued.

"Getting the contract is your headache. My job is facilitation. For Mardan you've to cough out extra dough."

"Fine. Contact me in my hotel, after you're through with the Brigadier." Harfan left after paying the customary advance.

That was Anar's style. She worked for compensation package. After all, she was required to take the trouble of using her body, intellect and other skills she had acquired in seducing men, and making them breach the banks of their senses and spill out, what they were oath bound to protect.

After two nights of successful fishing, Begum Anar reported back to Harfan.

His company would land the deal, provided Israr transferred Habib's share to his Swiss account, well in advance. This was a fat contract involving 100 million-dollars worth of German small and medium weapons and Swedish snow boots and high altitude clothing. The Mardan story, Anar declared with an animated pout, had nothing to do with another war. Pakistani armed forces weren't capable of fighting another war so soon. In fact, they would require another five years to match up to India's military inventory. Hectic searches were, therefore, on.

Izaz Afroz and General Arif Khan, during one of their *shikar* (hunting campaign) at Larkana had worked out a strategy to bleed India white. The Chief of Army Staff had embarked upon a new war strategy. It was a diabolical game, taking the proxy war inside India's inner belly and bleeding her to a slow death.

He had drummed up support from the Inter Services Intelligence and the Special Services Group (SSG). Habibullah's visit to Peking, Anar disclosed, was partly related to Mardan. China had blessed the new strategy in an exclusive meeting between the Deputy Chief of the PLA and Izaz Afroz. The Special Service Group, besides the Pakistan Intelligence Bureau and the Inter Services Intelligence were working in tandem with the Deputy Chief of Staff of Intelligence for the Chinese People's Army. They had set up shops in East Pakistan for training and arming India's tribal insurgents. Begum Anar had a long story to tell over three hours of debriefing. It was a fascinating story, impugning India's internal security.

Operation Mardan, in simple tongue, was a top-secret plan to support, sustain, and promote ethnic insurgency in India. India, she hoped, would be made to pay for the losses suffered by Pakistan in the last war.

"Thanks Begum," Harfan counted the money, Rs. 1,50,000 in crisp bills and asked, "would you like to add anything?"

Anar counted the bills and settled for a cigarette.

"Oh yes. I had forgotten a vital point. The ISI has hired the services of some rogue Palestinian commandos to train a specialised group of Pakistani army men for highly sensitive operations inside India."

"Any details?"

"Habib wasn't forthcoming. These experts specialise in target killing and planned use of explosive devices."

"What kind of target?"

"You're an impossible person Mian Harfan. Target killing could mean an important person or an unsuspecting group of persons."

"Thanks Anar. I may have another assignment for you soon."

"You're welcome." She picked up the fat packet and lighted another cigarette. Harfan Bukhari's blind hunting had produced precious results.

He composed a concise cipher and raised the emergency call sign *Khalis*. Operation Mardan, as the ciphers exchanged between Rawalpindi and Dacca, indicated a new strategic thrust against India's North East. The smouldering tribal belt, he elaborated, was likely to be on fire. Ethnic insurgency was about to explode with catastrophic bangs. The PFLP factor, he mentioned, would require deeper probes inside Pakistan and in the Middle-East stations.

The crisp cipher requested Delhi to retrieve an urgent mail from River Channel, London, to assess the threat potential of the latest Pakistani design.

A major task well concluded, he slept well and next morning took a train to Lahore. Israr allowed him a short break. The just married young executive deserved it.

*

The deal clinched by Anar Begum and Harfan, however, infuriated Nawab Sharief, Israr's celebrated half-brother. Anar wasn't his private property. His advance investment of rupees one million in the private account of General Hyder Bux, the Inter Services Intelligence Chief, wasn't gift wrapped with Anar. He was slightly late in understanding that Pakistan's war and drug lords were equally hungry for live flesh as they were for cash and golden liquid.

He wasn't pleased to be outsmarted by a puny *muhajir* executive. Nawab traced Harfan back to Zahoor Chaudry's cove.

"You've put your hands in the snake pit." Nawab hissed on the phone.

"I don't follow you Nawab sahib." Replied Harfan.

"Anar is my territory, you've to pay dearly for the intrusion."

"Sir," replied Harfan politely, "a public lady is common property. We're in business. Sometimes you win her favour, sometimes we."

"I never lose. Tell brother Israr. And be ready to pay for it." He banged the phone down.

Israr didn't lose his shirt. Nawab thundered frighteningly but rained miserly, he explained.

"Don't panic. I'd tackle him."

"But he sounded vicious."

"I'll speak to *abbajan* (father). Don't forget, we've warmed the pocket of Lt. General Sarfaraz. He's a better shield."

"I hope he won't go for my jugular."

"It's better you watch your steps. Brother Nawab normally stabs from the back. Anyways, I'm here to protect you. Breathe easy and get ready for the trip abroad."

Israr advised Harfan to prepare for the business trip abroad for negotiating with the German and Swedish companies. He could take his bride along. The presence of a charming woman often helped in clinching tricky business deals. Jamilla deserved the treat. The just clinched deal was sure to make Israr International richer by rupees fifty million and Harfan was entitled to 2% of the gross profits.

*

The cipher that Triple X had transmitted after debriefing Begum Anar and the subsequent River Channel mail shook Delhi out of its usual stupor. His first major report, with devastating implications rattled Dutta and Nampoothiri. Operation Mardan was indeed a bombshell.

"Text Begins," the communication continued, "Mardan is a multi-layered intelligence and military concept, crafted by Izaz Afroz, the ISI and the GHQ, in tandem with the Chinese intelligence. It has three segments; each to be handled by designated groups....

"Part one: Indian intelligence is suspected in the pro-democracy movement in East Pakistan. The GSO-1 (ML-3) has been tasked to smother the movement....

"Part two: (1): ISI, SSG and DMI are involved in the Lushai Hills insurgency. Camps set up in Chittagong Hill Tracts and Tangail for training them. The rebel leaders have met the ISI and the Chinese State Security Bureau officials in Dacca...

(2): China is training Naga rebels at Kunming camps. Expect two groups of 500 each leaving this winter. Naga Liaison Office functions at Bara Mugh Bazar, Dacca. Expect a Naga gang of 400 reaching Pakistan in December, for lifting weapons, diverted from CIA's Vietnam inventory....

(3): Four leaders of Garo and Khasi Hills are in Dacca for consultations. Two of them, Provost and Wynndale, are planning insurgency there as well....

"Part three: The ISI has hired Palestinian experts to train special commando groups for target killing in India. The ISI has floated front organisations: Markaz-ul-Farhan, Inquilabi Mujaheedin, Quami Fidayeen etc., to foment communal carnage in India. The Markaz have plans for assassination of important Indian leaders. EOM."

"What do you make out of this loaded message?" Rabindra Narayan Dutta asked.

"There's an avalanche of information. Our Operation Mardan intercept has turned out to be a mine field." Replied Nampoothiri.

"Requires verification. Check with Alam," remarked Dutta, "and I think we should seek corroboration from North East stations."

"Do we inform the Prime Minister?"

"We should. Operation Mardan is a spin off from the just concluded war. Pakistan is about to embark on a different kind of war, more bloody, more painful than Grand Slam." Dutta favoured immediate consultations with the Prime Minister.

"But I'm more worried about the Garo-Khasi and Lushai Hills. We must prevent Pakistan from cutting off the Brahmaputra Valley. That'd give tremendous strategic advantage to China and Pakistan. You take care of this contingency." Dutta left the fine-tuning of the job to Nampoothiri.

"It's a difficult job sir," Nampoothiri submitted, "we can't keep the North East by mere fire fighting action. It's high time the nation takes a comprehensive view."

"I agree. However, you and I are basically fire fighters for the policy makers. Let's do the job we're supposed to. Ask our stations in Egypt, Lebanon and Syria to confirm the Palestinian involvement with the ISI."

"Why should the PLO help Pakistan?" Nampoothiri asked.

"I don't think the PLO is involved. It could be the breakaway Al Hijaj group of the PFLP. Better get back to the CIA and MI6 friends. Is your Mossad channel open?"

"I can talk to a few top guns on personal level."

"Do that early. Only Mossad can deliver the goods."

"Perhaps we can go for a counter kill."

"What do you mean?"

"We take a nod from the PM to sharpen up Operation Meghna in Dacca." Nampoothiri made a strategic suggestion.

"That's a good idea. Weigh the consequences and come up with a format of the operation. If Pakistan hurts us in the North East we should injure it in East Pakistan."

Dutta advised Nampoothiri to use his discretion as long as he did not ruffle the secular feathers of the politicians.

Alamgir's follow up cipher, transmitted through Kabul confirmed, in essence, the Triple X report. A subterranean movement, he added, was indeed gaining ground against the ailing Pakistani President. His future would be decided by the Tashkent outcome. Izaz Afroz was busy manoeuvring the derailment of the USSR hosted talks. A high level Pak delegation, headed by Afroz, had indeed recently visited Peking. The delegation included the Deputy Chief of the Misc. (iii) section of the ISI, which worked directly under GSO-1 (ML-4), of the Department of Martial Law Affairs. Alam's message was silent about the Palestinian factor.

Triple X, Alamgir conveyed, was likely to be out of the host country on a business trip. Someone could debrief him on Mardan in London, his transit lap to Germany and Sweden. Triple X had agreed to call London River Channel for confirmation of a safe rendezvous.

*

22

Operation Triple X's first major communication alarmed Nampoothiri. It was viciously accurate and it spoke volumes of the degree of penetration achieved by the talent. It was possible for a blindfolded amateur to shot an arrow and be crowned as a victor by the law of averages.

"I think you should debrief Triple X personally." Dutta told Nampoothiri.

"Alamgir is there. We can trust him."

"No problem with Alam, Balu," the seasoned spymaster continued in his usual soft voice, "I think we've planted Triple X as a long-term agent, with an independent agenda. He has the potential of emerging as another Alam. No agent is immortal. Moreover, Harfan is not the type to submit to another overbearing intermediary." He cautioned.

"What's bugging you sir?"

"I'm keen to know what tradecraft was applied by Triple X to achieve such precise penetration. Did he use a short fuse to get to the core? Doesn't his approach smack of recklessness? Such temptations aren't uncommon even in seasoned agents."

"Do you want a direct debriefing by us?"

"Yes Balu. Don't leave him at Alamgir's mercy. I've better ideas for Triple X. Alam has been in Pakistan too long. Don't you think he has sprouted innumerable shoots like an ancient banyan tree? It's but natural. Develop an independent agenda for Harfan."

"You mean we may have to dump Alam."

"Why get hurt Balu? In our trade we require reserve pools."

"What gives you that feeling?"

"A good chef knows his curry."

Nampoothiri reflected on the small crisp sentences of Dutta. The old man often displayed a prophetic insight. He couldn't be ignored.

Yes. The chemistry of the message from Triple X contained some salts of conscious revelations by the root source. It wasn't a sub-conscious or unconscious leakage. The chief, he appreciated, reasonably wanted to have a clear picture of the forward and backward linkages of the chain established by Harfan Bukhari.

Perhaps the new-babe hadn't taken a one-way jump from the precipice, to satisfy the bosses in Delhi. The desperate exhibitionist as he was, Harfan could as well have done that. He shouldn't have direct access to the intricacies of tradecraft adopted by Triple X.

Alamgir was Nampoothiri's personal creation. Alam was assigned the task of directing the operations of a few Double X talents. He was supposed to provide initial booster to Harfan. Dutta, the wizard of Indian intelligence, wasn't in the habit of making casual comments on serious business of agent operations in hostile territories. Was he thinking in terms of creating a second Alam out of the Triple X talent? Nampoothiri partially rationalised the suggestion of his boss and called in Amrita Bhalla to dictate a small note on the probable new guidelines that he would like to share with Harfan during their meeting in London.

*

London, River Channel in FIB lingo, was a neutral rendezvous for the cold-war spymasters. Delhi favoured the jaunt for briefing and debriefing ultra-sensitive agents operating in Pakistan and China. The hotbed of international intrigue was, therefore, the natural choice for establishing direct contact with Operation Triple X. That's how Dhiren Bhagat landed up in London, as an appendage to Balachandran Nampoothiri. Being the case officer, he was considered the best litmus to decipher attitudinal changes in the sensitive agent.

Daylong wait in an apartment, off the busy junction of Kensington High Street and Holland Road, however, drilled in pounds of boredom into Bhagat's patience. Rented by the High Commission based FIB station chief, the safe house apartment was apparently occupied by a non-diplomatic India based employee. For operational reasons Bhagat was alone today, expecting a call from Harfan Bukhari. The mellow chime of the phone around 6 p.m. interrupted Bhagat's slumber.

"Hello, 473-2207? Is it Cashmere Carpets?" Harfan asked hesitatingly.

"Yes sir."

"Can you show me some exotic varieties?"

"Oh yes! We hold special Cashmere stock, just flown in from the valley." Bhagat shared the pre-set code.

"When can I see the samples? I require both woollen and silk carpets." Harfan replied.

"We're next to The Mother's Recipe, close to the Council Housing estate, about three furlongs south of Hounslow tube station."

"Can you arrange a preview tomorrow this time flat?" Harfan asked.

"Sure sir. See you tomorrow."

Thank god! The bloke had finally called.

Bhagat hailed a cab and enjoyed an escalator ride to Nampoothiri's tenth floor Hotel Wilson Plaza room, a small affair, and two blocks due south of the Harrods. His orders were specific, no telephonic contact. Bhagat played by the rules. Nampoothiri had reasons to play safe.

He was no novice to the complicated love-hate relationship between India and Great Britain and the paranoiac policy perceptions of the Foreign Office mandarins in London. India, though not rated Red, was rouge enough to attract attention of the MI6. Monitoring suspected and identified Indian intelligence officers on British soil were also prompted by the Cold War compulsions. Delhi had adopted an orbit, closer to Moscow, rather than London and Washington.

The Indian High Commission was under selective electronic and human surveillance of the MI6, the external intelligence outfit of Her Majesty's Government. The Indo-Pak war and the Soviet initiative to broker the peace talks hadn't pleased the British Foreign Office. The Westminster had earlier brokered fractured peace talks in the Kachchh skirmish, between India and Pakistan and expected Delhi to kowtow their line in Kashmir too.

"What's your impression?" Nampoothiri asked Bhagat.

"He sounded intimate and observed the code-protocol immaculately."

"You think it's safe to see him! Suppose he's trailed by the High Commission based ISI sleuths!"

"I don't think he has come under cloud."

"He is engaged in a highly competitive business of arms supply to the Pak army. His corporate rivals may trail him."

Nampoothiri, the veteran sleuth, wanted to play it by the book.

"I see no problem, sir. Let's adopt the usual counter surveillance measures. I'll enter the den first. You take a round about route and walk down the last two furlongs. If you wish you may put on a bowler hat and carry your stick and no cigar." Bhagat suggested another copybook recipe for shaking off possible shadow mounted by the ISI and Israr's business competitors.

"Well boy. Why target my cigar? Not a bad guile anyways. Expect me in time. Sanitise the room and activate the recording devices. Don't follow me. Take a separate tube."

Nampoothiri gave a few more security instructions and approved the rendezvous. Understandably, he took extra precautions in moving to the rendezvous location. He rented an old Bentley and drove around a few busy shopping malls before taking the motorway to the Iona Terrace safe house, off Kensington High and Holland Road. He left the car at a pay parking lot and walked down two blocks.

Bhagat did some shopping at the Mother's Recipe eating joint and idled out pretending watching a cricket match at a nearby school ground. Harfan was sighted after good fifteen minutes. Bhagat refused to recognise the sensitive agent. He surveyed the ambience with great care and was convinced that his contact-man was uncontaminated. He took two rounds of the apartment block to make sure that the safe house wasn't under observation of the unfriendly agencies and entered the designated den after good ten minutes of entry by Harfan Bukhari, the Triple X agent of the FIB.

Debriefing of Harfan, as planned by Nampoothiri, was as detailed as the examination of microbes under an X-ray microscope. It encompassed all the key features of his assignment, starting from the day he crossed over to Nagar Parkar to the tradecraft mechanism that he had adopted to procure the Mardan information.

"What about Irfan? Are you in touch with him?" Nampoothiri asked.

"No, not since he helped me with the lodging in Azam guesthouse."

"I believe he's left the job and joined a Sufi *dargah* as a *khidmatgar* (volunteer). Has he embraced Islam?"

"It's possible. His wife is a Muslim." Harfan didn't understand why Nampoothiri should be worried about Irfan changing his religion and adopting a spiritual life.

"Don't you think he should be silenced?"

"Better ask your men in Karachi. I don't think I can do that."

Nampoothiri made a mental note. Alam should be tasked to permanently silence Irfan. He had out lived utility as a local talent spotter. He knew too much. It required a minor accident, so common to Karachi.

"You should not have jumped into a marriage so soon," commented Nampoothiri, "what was the hurry?"

"It gives me an excellent cover. Her father is well connected and respected in the military circles. Alam must have had consultations with you."

"You brought tremendous pressure on us. I feel you should've marked time. There was no reason to rush." Nampoothiri explained that he should've allowed room for more acclimatisation.

"You're missing the positive story." Harfan reiterated.

"Hope your vibes with Alamgir are okay?" Nampoothiri changed the topic.

"A fascinating man. Full of himself..."

Harfan avoided debating the issue. He hated Alamgir. Perhaps one of these days they would clash. This intermediate wheel was superfluous. A spy, as he understood, couldn't afford to be polygamous, handled, and fondled by several masters. Alamgir, behind the facade of friendly patronisation, often irritated Harfan. Delhi didn't acquaint him with the training to enjoying the insufferable rape of his conscience.

"Hope you don't keep on hopping bed." Nampoothiri cautioned the agent.

"What makes you feel that? Don't you believe in evolution?" Harfan shot back, "I love Jamilla. I've powerful relatives having access to important business houses and top military bosses. Zahoor Chaudry's name sells well in the market crowd. Don't you think it's the best cover?"

Nampoothiri changed tracks. Harfan's reaction to his opening remarks convinced him that Triple X loved his wife and wasn't callous about his cover. The fellow was dedicated, by all means.

"Is Anar Begum a safe tool of the trade?" Nampoothiri hurled a drilling question while debriefing him on the tradecraft mechanism Triple X had used for collecting material for his last cipher.

"Well! She's a recognised business facilitator, as honest as a bread earning whore can be," Harfan shrugged wantonly, "your query was on Operation Mardan, and she was the most convenient tool to unscrew Brigadier Habibullah's nuts and bolts." Harfan's witty reply amused Nampoothiri.

"How sure are you about the ISI floating front organisations for carrying out special tasks in India? What's their charter?"

"The information is correct. The Palestinian training camp has been located at Isha Khel, in the NWFP. The ISI has started two training centres at Mian Khel and Matti near Peshawar and one at Muridke, near Lahore. The talents, called *mujahideen* (revolutionaries), are recruited from *madrasas* and *tanjims* (religious congregations) and trained in the black arts of sabotage and subversion. Several core groups have been infiltrated into India."

"Any possible area of identification?"

"No clue."

"What about this assassination story?"

"No clear idea. May be a new tool to create void at the top."

"Any big targets?"

"Not that I know." Harfan shrugged.

"Keep your antenna open." Nampoothiri suggested.

"Hope I'm done with!"

"Wait," Nampoothiri lighted a Havana and spoke slowly, "listen carefully. Exploit your contacts for penetrating targets near Izaz Afroz."

"Why give so much of importance to him?"

"He's the minister for Atomic Energy. The SWG (Special Working Group) created by him for making the Islamic Bomb is very important. I want all the dope on Izaz's nuclear initiatives."

"These are tall orders."

"Indeed they're. Make graduated efforts. Penetrate the KANUPP reactor facility and the Atomic Energy Department." Nampoothiri continued.

"That's okay. You should be more concerned with the likely political changes in Pakistan. President Akbar, all said and done, is a stable person, not as erratic as Izaz Afroz and General Arif are. I sense cordite in the air." Harfan gave his point of view in clear terms.

"Is it going to be a violent coup?"

"Possibly. Much will depend on how developments shape up at Tashkent and what views are formulated in Washington."

"I appreciate your views. Keep tactful watch. Keep this list of Pak nuclear scientists. Mug it up and destroy. Try to penetrate a few of them."

"It's very risky. They're under ISI and PIB watch."

"You've been trained for the job. And one more point. Now onwards Alam fades away from your life. You should contact him only under special circumstances. For emergency money supply, use this number in Karachi. It's of Adamji Pestonji, a *hundi* operator (money launderer). Give us three days' notice, your demand will be home delivered." Nampoothiri stood up to leave.

"Anything else?"

"Not much. Just take care. Evaluate each and every step. Don't take blind jump. We don't advertise and reclaim lost property."

Nampoothiri stood up, walked to the door, and turned back.

"Check, if the ISI front organisations have any plan to assassinate our top political leaders, other than the Hindu protagonists."

"No news as yet, I'd keep the windows open."

"Here are some names of Islamic fundamentalist leaders, having close links with the Middle-East terrorist groups. Memorise the names and destroy the paper."

"What do you expect me to do?"

"Just keep an eye on their linkages with international terrorist groups. Assassination and hijacking of aircrafts are their trade specialisations."

Nampoothiri walked out after instructing Dhiren Bhagat on the safe dispersal drill, for shaking off the possible MI6 tail and probable ISI watchdogs.

"What did he mean by not reclaiming lost property? Am I a piece of dirt? Don't you have any loyalty to your men?"

Harfan accosted Bhagat as soon as Nampoothiri left.

"It's his way of talking, don't take seriously. You're accountable to us and we're to you. He just reminded you of the security drills. That's all." Bhagat didn't sound convincing enough. He wasn't too good at imbibing the supreme philosophy of the FIB: discard the compromised assets with no tears and no nice funeral.

"It leaves a bad taste in the mouth. I'm not a garbage carton, that you'll discard at sweet will." Harfan complained.

"Don't read too much in his words. That's a cliché."

"How's my mother?" Harfan changed the topic.

"Fine. My boys gave me a firsthand briefing before I left."

"Can I write to her?"

"Let me consult the boss." Bhagat reacted cautiously, fearing a sharp reaction from Harfan.

"Fuck him," Harfan betrayed his anger, "is he the possessor of your mind?"

"Don't be nasty. I can't take that decision."

"I'm not your bonded serf. Tell me more about my mother."

"Fine brother! We'll meet before you take off for Berlin. Let's move now. It's time we disengage."

Bhagat tried to placate the man, whom he had started liking, simply for his guts and capability of absorbing waves of life and death, as they came his way. Harfan Bukhari was no cheap two-penny intelligence contact. Here was a super-sensitive man who deserved compassion and careful handling.

The high profile briefing had left a flunky stale-beer taste in Harfan's mouth and a deep scar in his mind. Nampoothiri's 'lost property' dig continued to bounce from neurons to neurons, inside his psyche. A strange chemistry started cooking inside; increasing the gap of emotional attachment with the job, he was assigned to. Bhagat's vain patch working didn't help much.

What for was he risking his neck?

For Mother India?

Did India really care for him?

Was he really serious about settling a personal score against an enemy country?

Was Pakistan the real enemy or the history that gave birth to it?

Could he fight against history and turn back the needle of time?

Harfan couldn't cull out the correct response from the spiralling cloud of confusion. Caring was a mutual concept. But the big FIB boss was cruelly callous with his top agent's security problems. He didn't even have the courtesy to wish Jamilla! Well! Harfan shrugged. He should develop his own philosophy towards the assignment.

Should he not?

*

23

Alamgir's priority call from London surprised Nampoothiri. Alamgirl wasn't supposed to make a line call, not through the under-sea telephone cable, except in real emergency. Delhi had taken that vital decision after Washington's refusal to deactivate the CIA planted deepseabed telephone cable bugs off Bombay High. Installed in 1962, in the wake of the Chinese aggression and as part of a short-lived honeymoon between the FIB and its US counterpart, the bugs were still alive. These gadgets transmitted data to the US warships stationed in international blue waters of the Arabian Sea.

Washington's clear tilt towards Pakistan and accelerated bonhomie with Peking had clouded its bilateral relations with India. Delhi had, therefore, designated its sensitive agents, especially Alamgir, to communicate either through the Kabul-Delhi diplomatic bag or encrypted high frequency radio message. The deep cover FIB officer, rooted in Pakistan for last the 16 years, was a top grade asset. Nampoothiri rated the operation as his personal triumph.

"Hearing after ages, sir. Hope things are fine." Alam came alive on the line.

"Been busy with the changeover here, you know the circumstances. Still fluid."

Nampoothiri avoided entering into specifics.

"Any impact on smaller fries like us?"

"Fortunately not. The new boss is vastly interested in your family affairs. How are things over there?"

"Hope there's no change in policy. I'm always apprehensive of political changes at home."

"How is your home front?"

"Back at home we too expect a change."

"How do you rate the new baby?"

"It's a downhill journey all the way. The Indus fox is on rampage and the new man on the horizon is busy with his newest flame and holy waters from Paisley."

"What? Presley?"

"No sir. I said golden malt from the Scottish city of Paisley."

"Sounds encouraging," Nampoothiri laughed rather loudly, "who's the newest flame?"

"The soprano. Like lady luck, she loves to shower smiles only on the brave and daring. She bets only on the winning horses." Alam chuckled and continued.

"Can't you explore her?"

"Impossible. She's the personal property of the boss man. Need a meeting. Something startling from Triple X. It's a spin off from your last fishing venture to the River."

"Would the Lake be good for fishing?"

"No problem. Plenty of Bass." Alam disconnected. He knew the drill. Nampoothiri would send his itinerary through the diplomatic bag.

Lake, the preset code for Kabul, was agreed upon between the spymaster and his top embedded agent in Pakistan.

*

Alam had raised Nampoothiri from London after he picked up a Quetta Live Letter Box coded message. The crisp message from Triple X had simply mentioned about a consignment of dry fruits having been received in putrid condition. The message didn't conform to the previously agreed communication code. What could have gone wrong with Harfan Bukhari between his visit abroad and fresh eruption of fluidity in the Pakistani establishment?

Israr Sharief was enchanted with his new executive and Zahoor Chaudry had just sent a letter inviting him to the first marriage anniversary of his daughter. Things were hunky-dory with Triple X.

Pakistan was shaken up by the post-Tashkent turmoil. In *Allah's* own Pakistan the uniformed politicians had converted the nation to a mutual benefit fund of the Armed Forces. It didn't matter if a Colonel Hotchpotch replaced another General Abracadabra.

The inveterate fish-curry and rice bowl revolutionaries, the East Pakistan Bengalis were, however, spoiling the army bosses' appetite. Sheikh Jainal, leader of the Peoples' League, had cast a magic spell on the Bengali psyche and raised the bet for a better share of the spoils. However, these earth-shaking events had no ostensible bearing on Harfan's routine. For him any goose that laid eggs was good enough, be it a Colonel H or a General A.

The absence of a plausible correlation between the LLB message and the developing events intrigued Alam Khan. He called Harfan at Israr's Sangla office from a pay phone at Rawalpindi's traditional joint, Hotel Shalimar.

"How's the weather?" he asked a sounding question.

"It's fine here. Little bit cloudy, but no rains. Can we meet for dinner and discuss about the rotten consignment?" Harfan used the pre-set code, giving an all-clear signal.

"What's the extent of damage?"

"Can't assess. Require your help."

"No problem. Hotel Pilot, Pindi." Alam gave clearance for the meeting as he sensed that the coast was clear.

Harfan checked in at Pindi Club and took a taxi to Pilot Hotel at the other end of the city.

"What's the problem?" Alam asked in a patronising tone, "I'm out of bounds for you. You know Delhi's advice."

"It's serious, couldn't inform the details to Delhi without consulting you."

"Cough it out."

"My friend says that Markaz-ul-Farhan and Jammat-e-Mujahideen, two important fronts of the ISI, have been working on a project to assassinate the Indian PM. Musa Company unit of the SSG is coordinating the details."

"Possible. The ISI had hired some Palestinian experts to train a special commando force."

"That's admitted. But some special inputs point the needle of suspicion at an important political figure."

"Spell it out."

"I'm told that Izaz Afroz is working in tandem with the ISI chief and the chief of the Markaz, Mullah Basir. Special commandos are being trained at Attock for the precise execution of the plan.

"You should've informed *Behest*. Delhi is the point to contact, why summon me!" Alam was visibly annoyed.

"Don't be funny," Harfan retorted, "friend says that an attempt on the life of the Indian P.M. is surely on the cards. Her execution, they feel, is the shortest route to sniff out the Bengali separatist movement. Hope you understand the seriousness of the information!" Harfan disclosed his source of information in the Directorate of Military Intelligence, an officer in the Cabinet Division of the GSO-I (CA-I), the all-powerful segment of the Chief Martial Law Administrator's outfit.

This information, Harfan argued, could be a test drop, to draw out and compromise him. Planting of such misinformation wasn't uncommon. The information was too good to be true. He wanted Alam's help in fine-tuning the information. This could be done by independent sources. The crude lump of information was too raw to be communicated to Delhi. He didn't want to press the panic button.

"Make it clear," Alam tried to pump out more details, "I'm yet to know how your friend in the DMI came across this startling piece of intelligence. If it is the Markaz boys, the operation could be a babe of the Joint Intelligence X of the ISI and not the DMI. They aren't the dirty boys of the trade."

"Fine boss. My friend was travelling in a private plane operated by Joint Intelligence X Division, from Isha Khel, the training centre manned by a joint team of the ISI and the Palestinians. These flights normally lift refined heroin from isolated factories in the remote tribal areas. Two Markaz boys travelled with the consignment, providing security to the operators."

"Why Markaz boys and not the ISI regulars?"

"I'm told that the big bosses get their dirty jobs done through these non-government operators, for a price of course."

"That makes sense. But that's second hand info."

"That's why I need your help. I don't have access to the Markaz HQ at Muridke."

"What about your SSG friend in Dacca?"

"That comes next. The primer is in Muridke and in the ISI HQ. Do you have any access to Mullah Basir?"

"No. However, I get the point."

Alam finally softened his tough posture and appreciated Harfan's argument. Yes. His story had all the ingredients of a bubbling potboiler and he did well by not shooting a cipher to Delhi. The input required independent corroboration. Alam promised help and advised Harfan to explore the possibilities of verifying the information from the office of the Colonel G-II, in the DMI headquarters. 'Section Q' of the Joint Intelligence X, which exclusively handled such delicate operations generally imitated CIA technique. Nothing would be planned for that volatile part of India without their clearance.

"It's a tough job, I'm not sure." Harfan expressed reservations. He could perhaps not press his luck too far.

"Try beginner's luck, it works," Alam shared the usual sundown whisky with his apprentice, "Do your bit. Let me try as well. Take care. The lady in Delhi is very sensitive and suspicious in nature."

"Do you think the agencies can plan such an action without consulting the CMLA?"

"They can. The CIA and the ISI often pursue parallel state policies. The Establishment in Pakistan is different from its people. It has its own mind, independent of the people and even the government of the day."

"But that's not diplomacy."

"Diplomacy is a fig leaf with the ISI. Innumerable Pakistani stalwarts including a premier had fallen prey to these goons. The CIA has tried this very trick in the Latin American and African banana republics. This is a rogue but tested statecraft ethos."

"Do you think the ISI will stoop down so low?"

"No harm, if you operate through front organisations. Don't forget Congo, El Salvador, Chile, and scores of other theatres of CIA operations. The ISI has only one prime target, the destruction of India, and reassertion of Muslim hegemony over the subcontinent. The use of front-paws like the Markaz is a strategic weapon."

"Thanks. Let's remain in touch." Harfan prepared to leave.

"Can you try at the Dacca end?" asked Alam, "that could be the final launching pad."

"Perhaps. Israr International had supplied some small weapons for the SSG battalion and spares for the F8 fighters." Harfan replied tentatively. He did not mention the names of his Dacca based friends Major Anjum Mani of the SSG and Group Captain Ahsan Khondokar. He could depend on them.

"That's a good opening. The SSG often operates as the execution arm of the Establishment. Try your luck. Take care. The matter is too sensitive."

*

Alam left Harfan blindfolded in a dark alley. He hadn't even mentioned about his scheduled visit to Kabul for briefing Nampoothiri. He was left to execute a tall and edgy order. The feasibility of corroborating the information through an independent agent was remote. Talents in such exclusive clubs of killers and hunters were hard to come by. Toughened and baked intelligence operators could take years to penetrate their security diaphragm.

What about starting with a trip to Dacca?

Israr had no problem. The Martial Law Administrator (MLA) over there had floated tenders for one hundred motorboats for coastal and river patrolling. He needed the crafts urgently. Sheikh Jainal had upgraded the language movement to provincial autonomy and restoration of democracy. The Indians, the Martial Law Administrator suspected, had started pumping in weapons, and were plotting an armed insurrection.

"Have a nice trip and tap your contacts in the MLA's office. We should bag this contract worth $ 20 million."

"No problems. Can you pursue Begum Anar to fly into Dacca and lodge in Hotel Rangamati?" Harfan asked with a naughty twitch.

"It's your game. Play it as you like, but play cautiously. Some of these Bengalis are funny moralists."

"Don't bother. In bed most animals respond uniformly."

Israr laughed and relented.

However, Harfan's Dacca sojourn wasn't a roaring success. Begum Anar harvested tidbits from Major Anjum Mani over two nights' of sweaty adventures. The Markaz boys, he averred, were being trained by a special contingent of the 15 Baluch Regiment, at a forward camp near Rajshahi. Anar also confirmed that a contingent of non-Bengali youths was undergoing specialised training in the camp.

Harfan confronted Anjum Mani on the third evening after Anar had watered the grounds.

"For the contract you approach Commodore Jilani. We're not taken into confidence."

"What's the problem?"

"They don't trust us Bengalis. Things are getting tougher. Keep in touch. We are heading for a crash." Anjum Mani confided in Harfan.

"Why?"

"The Sheikh is determined to demand the pound of flesh we have been denied all these years. We support him. A lot many officers of East Pakistan Rifles and the Bengali officers of other regiments support him. We're on the verge of an undeclared war against Pakistan. Nevertheless, you're welcome. I'm ready to help if it weakens the junta rule. Don't supply the boats. Don't supply deadly weapons. All these are meant for killing we Bengalis."

"If we don't, someone else would. You've a friend in me. I can share the secrets."

"Fine. Let's remain in touch. You're a brave fellow. Luck would sure favour you." Anjum Mani departed with an optimistic note in his voice.

*

Dame luck didn't favour the braves alone; she often smiled on the adventurers, pushing some on top of the Everest and some down a thousand leagues below the Pacific. Harfan, by birth a Hindu, believed in luck. In fact, the elusive lady had rescued him out of some intractable screwy jams. He had walked past the minefields of crime and optimistically winked at the lady. She hadn't failed him so far and he expected her to be profusely benign in this new tryst with destiny.

Alam wasn't wrong. Lady luck or witch misfortune, whichever sticker one liked to stamp on the inevitable femme fatale, virtually knocked at Harfan's door. Nawab Sharief, Israr's half-brother, and variously sketched as a two-legged viper and a Satan-on-the-rock paid a surprise visit to Jhumra and invited himself to a lunch with Harfan.

"Bukhari sahib, you're a genius. Since you joined Israr, my brother hasn't looked back. His business is flourishing. Why don't you help me? I'll double up your compensation package. Keep this blank cheque." Nawab pleaded over frothy beer and exquisite food at the Hotel Royal Palace.

"Money can't buy everything." Harfan replied in a flat voice.

"I believe you've bagged the Dacca contract as well. Well! It's indeed gratifying to see that Anar Begum keeps your company these days."

"Don't spread canards. She's your asset. We've used her on payment of professional fees. Hope you're not jealous. She never slept with me, I can assure you."

"Well. The Zahoor family won't relish the story."

"Stop blackmailing. Don't mix vengeance with business."

Nawab digested the dig. He had reasons to.

A ruthless omnibus trader, from military hardware to toilet tissues, Nawab believed that everything in *Allah's* creation had a price tag. The expansion of a business-empire and the storming of Punjab's political citadel were the deadly propellants, which powered his wings. Ambition often used the fodder of jealousy, to keep the fire smouldering. His jealousy towards Israr had turned to a scathing hatred for Harfan. How could a puny *muhajir* dare spiking his route to the top? He was snatching live meat away from tiger's mouth.

Nawab wasn't in the habit of masking his feelings. Nevertheless, he chose to hang an extra sweet smile on his face. He required the services of Harfan for a queer purpose. This *muhajir* had built up enormous contacts with the Indian Diaspora in London. One of his contacts could do a simple job for him, back in India.

He direly needed to please the most powerful lady of Pakistan. Malika Jahanara, the reigning soprano of millions of Pakistani hearts and the very heartthrob of

General Arif Ali Khan, the new *Sadr-i-Ryasat* (President) and Chief Martial Law Administrator, was in need of some vague medicine for an undefined ailment. The damn medicine could only be had from *vaid* (medico) Dhanwant of Dehradun, a Himalayan foothill town in India.

The war had snapped old linkages. No patriotic Pakistani dared doing business with the Indians. Who in Pakistan would risk midnight knocks from the ISI and scientific torture in its Badr interrogation centre?

However, the future of the rupees 2000 million Army contract depended on a favourable nod from the mighty lady. Nawab Sharief couldn't afford to miss the bus again.

He surveyed Harfan with a squinted Black Widow eye and hoped that a little pressure should help him in wrapping up this prey in his gooey net. The procurement of medicine for Jahanara and a few top guns in the CMLA could be entrusted to Harfan. There wouldn't be any adverse publicity. He could deflect all possible flaks at Harfan Bukhari and elder brother Israr. That would be a sweet revenge. Demolition of Harfan was sure to clip his umbilical tether, tied to Pakistan's commercial fortune. And a charmed Jahanara, he expected, was sure to shower him with the multimillion-dollar contract.

Harfan had not missed Nawab's spider-squint. He was mighty worried and intrigued by the sudden surge of love and affection showered by the legendary arachnid. Could it be in preparation for offering his neck to the noose?

A close cohort of top Generals and intelligence bureaucrats, Nawab boasted of his capability of unleashing packs of establishment hounds after his enemies; police, income tax authorities and of course the omniscient and omnipresent ISI. Harfan did some quick thinking.

This one was to be a spot decision and a correct one. He couldn't afford to antagonise the merciless double-edged saw blade called Nawab Sharief. His fascination for fellow human beings was no better than the love and affection of a butcher for the animals packed in abattoir corridors.

"Anything else?" Harfan asked, breaking the momentary silence of his guest.

"Let's enjoy the drink. What's the hurry?" Nawab smiled and slowly sipped the draught beer. His guts told him that the catch was just about swimming inside his trap.

Harfan stole a sneak view of the scheming eyes of Nawab and decided to play the game as long as he was not caught inside the pincer.

"Hope the Anar episode is over. Anything else you expect of me?" Harfan played it cool.

"I've a small job. I'm not asking for the moon." Nawab offered a cigarette and helped lighting it with a pistol shaped lighter.

"I can't do anything without Israr's knowledge. I'm his employee." Harfan tried to probe the intensity of Nawab's reaction.

"Look brother," Nawab picked up a largish drumstick and buried his teeth in the juicy flesh, "nobody says no to Nawab. My offer will give you an opportunity to go closer to the woman, who sleeps with the top man. It's her problem. If you help her, she'll help you and me. No dirty feather will touch brother Israr. The Generals run this country, but this lady makes their phallus pulsate."

"Who's she?"

"Begum Jahanara."

"Whoosh!" Harfan chuckled loudly.

Begum Jahanara, the reigning Aphrodite, was the heartthrob of the nation. The senior army officers, who looked at the country through amber Scotch, served in Belgian cut glasses, compared her with a *behesti huri* (divine fairy). They were her permanent parlour guests.

"It's an easy job. You've better access. Why should I get involved?" Harfan argued.

"Don't act smart," Nawab snapped back, "don't I know the dirty games you and Israr play by hooking up Lahore film stars? Don't ask me to believe that you'd flown Anar to Dacca for a pilgrimage. Don't compel me to go public on your trade secrets, the way you two keep on bagging lucrative army contracts. What difference does it make if you hook Anar or Malika?"

"Anar is a market commodity. Malika is not. Big money uses easy women for lubricating business deals. It's no trade secret. You're in the game too."

"Harfan Mian, don't compel me to go public about your mom-in-law's shameful background. You know well that, before marrying that *mohana* fishing tribal, she was a dignified whore." Nawab Sharief spewed fire.

"Don't exceed limits Nawab sahib. Don't invite a sound thrashing. I don't care your riches and clouts." Harfan stood up, forgetting that he wasn't having coffee in Delhi's Blue Dart Restaurant and that Nawab was no Matang Singh.

"Cool down Mian. Nobody in Pakistan dares talking like this to the future Chief Minister of Punjab. Don't kid around. History is the abode of truth and you can't ignore it."

"Why drag my in laws? We're talking business and not family matters. Don't compel me to spill the beans about your mom's background, the so-called Afghan parlour danseuse from Herat." Harfan retaliated with a forceful voice.

"Harfan Mian," Nawab replied coolly and climbed down, "lets bury the slandering match. The top lady has some medical problem; at least she feels she has. She wants help."

"You started it. Say you're sorry."

"Okay. I'm sorry. Let's do some business."

"How can I attend to her medical problems?"

"I know you have good Indian contacts in London. Perhaps your Indian contacts in London could tap *vaid* Dhanwant of Dehradun, who is supposed to be a wonder medic. Only he knows the correct medicine. Perhaps you can help in soothing her ruffled psyche." Nawab described the job to Harfan.

"It's a long shot. Why me? You've many friends in London and Colombo."

"I've never traded with Indians."

"I don't know any Indian." Harfan reacted sharply.

"I mean Indians settled in Britain. Your last German and Swedish deals were routed through a.prominent London based Indian, the Sindhujas. Am I correct?" Nawab shot back.

Harfan held his breath for a while. Thank God! Nawab didn't call him a Hindu Indian. He muttered a silent curse under his breath and managed to hang on his face a faint smile.

"What's wrong with the Sindhujas?"

"Nothing. But many in Pakistan are aware that the senior Sindhuja had negotiated India's submarine deal with the French. Does it not mean a compromise of our national security? The ISI would sure be interested in probing into this queer business connection." Nawab spoke menacingly, grinding each word with the roasted chicken flakes.

"You're distorting issues. Sindhuja is a British citizen."

"A Hindu is always a Hindu; it doesn't make any difference if he's a British Singh or a Fijian Patel."

Harfan sipped the beer slowly and tossed the heavy feather around in his mind. It was no good to allow this dirty beaver to dig deeper. His conclusion was quick.

"How do I get to her?" Harfan asked, while he managed to hang on to his face a feeble smile.

"That's good. Leave it to me and don't tell the big brother. Don't involve your mom-in-law. They are good friends." Nawab slapped Harfan's back.

"When do I see her?"

"In a day or two. And I won't cheat you. You get Rupees fifty thousand if my job is done. *Khuda Hafiz*."

Nawab left with a broad smile on his face and a deep curse under his breath. This two-penny *muhajir* dared to cross his path and threaten him! Did he threaten to expose his mother? Yes, he did.

Well! Nawab wouldn't allow this lackey of brother Israr to escape unscathed. He was, however, happy with the minor encroachment into the microcircuits of his brother's business empire. The point of this needle would one day surely become as deep and wide as the Suez, good enough to drown brother Israr.

Harfan signed the bill and listened to the murmurs of Ibadat, who spoke into his ears.

"It's not a good sign sir. This man is a serpent. He can harm you."

"How does he manage to know my business contacts in London?"

Harfan asked Ibadat, who was busy gathering the plates on a tray.

"Nawab has long arms. He can mobilise the ISI resources to promote his business interests. He fronts a Leasing Company for the ISI. He launders money for the agency. He's the Agency's choice for the top political slot in Punjab."

"That's interesting!"

Harfan restricted his reactions willfully, but decided to make deeper probes into Nawab's linkages with his London based ISI operatives. He wondered if the viper had snooped over his last London meeting with Nampoothiri and Dhiren Bhagat. Hoary hell! He should be more careful in meeting his professional friends, if he was to survive in Pakistan.

*

Begum Jahanara, the mercurial sex kitten, did control not only the libido of the CMLA and President, but also his business interests. All government expenditures required final approval of the top General, who called himself the President of the Islamic Republic of Pakistan. And his signature was a costly affair. It could mean millions, depending on the size of the deal.

Nawab Sharief had lost cool after waiting at Jahanara's doorstep for a few diamond-studded signatures from the boss on vital files related to Air Force contracts. The signing ceremony depended on clearance from the high priestess of pleasure. His social flirting wasn't warm enough to penetrate her exclusive and mysterious diaphragm of privacy. She required, some army birds chirped, an *ayurvedic* medicine (Vedic medicine system) from India, for an unknown disease. Nawab had promised the moon to the Aphrodite, on the prompting of General Hyder Bux, the ISI chief. The General, past his menopause, also wanted some nerve tonics from the same medic. A lot depended on her smile and fattened pockets of the Generals, many of Nawab's business interests.

Nawab didn't mind applying the strange grease. The multi-million dollar deal would leave a profit of one hundred million. That dough was adequate to make him stand taller than elder brother Israr. But he simply didn't have the correct ladle to spread the cheese.

Harfan shuddered at the idea of earning a few bucks at the back of Israr, the person who provided iron cast covers for him. Israr's reaction to the Jhumra episode did not kick up dusts of panic, but he was of the confirmed view that Nawab was unscrupulous and Jahanara was a live minefield. The man-eater tigress of Islamabad was on the prowl, for man and money. Her gooey net had become a hub for intrigue and conspiracy. A few powerful Generals were trying to malign the President and the Chief Martial Law Administrator, by spreading juicy stories about his escapades with the soprano. Inspired leakage to the media had fabulously increased the daily circulation of some yellow rags.

There were wheels within the wheels, Israr added. General Naim, the Pakistan Intelligence Bureau chief, was a real brother of the President. There was a running feud between him and General Hyder Bux, the ISI chief. Lt. General Sarfaraz, the Personal Staff Officer to the CMLA, stood somewhere in between. Most of these drug-money rich Generals carried curved kirsches under their sleeves.

The uncanny duo, Israr revealed, Generals Hyder and Sarfaraz, had cobbled up one layer of conspiracy. The 'Larkana Shikar (hunting) Club,' headed by Izaz Afroz, the unscrupulous sycophant from Sind, and a couple of Generals formed another layer. Izaz was mixed up with another gang, the inner coterie of the CMLA, ostensibly for saving the soul of Pakistan. He was busy hurling all and sundry darts in the hope that one of those could hit the bull's eye.

"Where does Nawab fit in?" Harfan asked.

"He's an all-season bird and doesn't have fixed nest. He is close to Izaz Afroz, who has charmed him with the promise of the top political slot in Punjab. I smell another dirty coup," Israr whispered, "being cooked in the cauldron of the stinking power structure. Steer clear of these jackals."

"What about co-operating with Nawab?"

"You're left with no option. Nawab can go to any extent to destroy both of us. He can let the Army and the ISI goblins lose to draw our blood." Israr cautioned his manager.

"What do you say? Do I do his job?"

"I don't think you've handled the viper tactfully. For heaven's sake this should be your last engagement with the viper."

Anything could happen in the military durbar. The highest bidder earned speedy access to the right ears and wrong orders, from the CMLA directorate. One such order could mean facing the firing squad on charges of treason and sedition. He mildly reminded Harfan of the prolonged incarceration of hundreds of political and tribal Baluch leaders under trumped up charges.

The prospect sent chilled shivers down Harfan's bones. Caught in the forked edges of Pakistan's murky politics he was left with no other choice. He didn't know if he was kissed by lady luck or stung by a whole colony of bees. But he was aware that neither Alam nor Delhi would appreciate his fleeting but dangerous liaison with Nawab Sharief. He remembered his family deity, perhaps for the first time and sent up a silent prayer.

*

Begum Jahanara lived in a sprawling mansion off 57th street, at the crossing of Nazimuddin Road and Ataturk Avenue. The mansion, gossipmongers whispered, was bequeathed to her as a special favour by SIV Division of the CMLA office in recognition of her cardinal contribution to Pakistan's art and culture. She was carted to the sprawling bungalow from her modest Kashmir Road house in Rawalpindi, ostensibly to run an academy of fine arts.

Harfan was not surprised when armed guards stopped his old Nissan at the outer gate. He was not a security-vetted visitor. No respectable Pakistani, in right frame of mind, would choose to turn up at the temple of the Aphrodite, in a self-driven dilapidated car. They came, if they did, in chauffeur-driven Mercedes and assorted made cars in the USA and Japan.

This was expected. Nawab Sharief had briefed him of the possible stonewalls at the front gate. Harfan Bukhari fished out his entry ticket, a letter from Nawab, and handed over to the guard commander.

A smart attendant, a six feet tall *habshi* (slave of African stock) in whites, took over from the armed guards and escorted Harfan to the inner sanctum of the mansion. Jahanara, sporting a bright red headband, which held her carelessly coiffured hair, was resting on a divan, imitating her aeons old predecessor, Cleopatra. Her head, partially resting on delicate right palm, moved slightly towards the door-curtain, as it rippled under the palms of the castrated *habshi.* No hotblooded male, possessing the gifts of full masculinity, was permitted among the personal staff. Jahanara followed the good old medieval monarchic *harem* code.

"Yes?" she crooned in a commanding tone.

"Ma'am, the visitor is here." The *habshi* replied from behind the curtain.

"Bring him in."

Jahanara lifted her finely sculpted body, artistically uncovered in see-through white lingerie, all her feminine assets declaring their presence, rather provocatively. She didn't, as a matter of fact, treat her personal attendants as fully evolved humans and therefore, didn't take the trouble of dressing up adequately. Didn't her pet dogs and cats often see her in the raw? It didn't make any difference, if her body was seen and appreciated by naives and fools. That should increase the pumping paces of their otherwise morbid and stagnant hearts. Better blood circulation could help in improving the electric currents in their underdeveloped cranium.

Her eyes licked up Harfan with the appreciative look of a tigress sizing up her late afternoon kill. Yes. Here was a fine young and robust body, charming but confused.

"Ask Miriam to send in some wine and eats." Jahanara dismissed the *habshi.*

She stood up. Her imposing frame and dress amused Harfan. He wasn't the type to put on blinkers and ignore a thing of beauty. In his ten years of active sex life, Harfan had derived great pleasure in forcibly undressing feminine bodies and often pinching their bosoms and bottoms, in fits of violent passion.

However, this witch appeared to be dressed and undressed to kill. Harfan took a deep breath, and counted to sixty, a yogic discipline taught by Maulana Rizwan. He gradually released the trapped air and steadied his agitated nerves. He transported his mind back to Lahore, to Jamilla, the fairy that had flooded him with swirling and incandescent love. The sudden surge started levelling down. However, Jahanara was just another name of a rare typhoon. Her chiselled bust, inadequately arrested by an undersized red bra, protruded through the see-through lingerie; like mist covered early morning mountain peaks, inviting the initiated climber. She didn't believe in sporting a bikini around her waist. The curvature of her body and static electricity attracted the fine fabrics of her lingerie to her pink skin. She looked like she had just stepped out of a steaming bath.

Jahanara dismissed the lady attendant, who had just entered, pushing in a cart of wine and eats. She left, closing the door behind. She poured vermouth from a Belgian decanter, offered one to Harfan, and picked up the other.

"I believe you require some herbal medicine ma'am." Harfan asked.

"Enjoy the drink first, have some kebabs, the finest in town." She held the stem of the glass between two finely chiselled and manicured fingers.

She placed two pieces of kebab in a fine bone china and sprinkled a few drops of Tabasco. The kebabs prepared with Kashmiri saffron and several aphrodisiac ingredients were rare items in Jahanara's parlour, meant for only a few privileged visitors and favourite kills.

She liked such tender moments to be rendered softer by a touch of instrumental music. She tuned on the Akai system, rather loudly. The tape played a *Sarod* (a string instrument) recital of *raga vasant bahar* in a fast beat, depicting joyous reunion of young lovers.

The vermouth, a fortified wine, treated with a fine concoction of cocaine and shots of amphetamine, drained down his gullet to the intestines and warmed up Harfan's young frame. The kebabs, melting under his tongue, travelled faster to the stomach stirring up a strange sensation. He felt the sleeping jinn rising up again, defeating Jamilla's love-shield around him.

His eyes could now see only the bulging breasts of Jahanara, the red bra contrasting fabulously against the whites of the lingerie.

Harfan jerked his head in a voluntary motion to get out of the foggy mist. It was perhaps a perfect trap to compromise him. The use of honey-trap was a common tool of the intelligence trade. He had foolishly walked into it, believing in the trash story of Nawab Sharief, a friend of the ISI chief. He regretted the decision to visit Malika, the ultimate temptress.

Jahanara, an expert reader of male demeanour, noticed the sudden change of colour in Harfan's face. The fellow must have been scared to stand so close to the radiating flesh of the virtual first lady of Pakistan. Most war veteran Generals melted down before her biological radiation, in predictable manner. And this was a kid of about 30, may be 27. She tried to assess the greenness of the new kill.

"I've a problem," Jahanara turned her back to Harfan and continued, "darling Nawab told me that some of your clients have good links in India, and you can perhaps get the medicine from *vaid* Dhanwant."

"I could tap some Indian business contact." Harfan managed to reply and heave a discreet sigh of relief; it was, after all, not a trap.

"See for yourself." Jahanara, in a magic twist of her body, dropped the upper portion of the lingerie, exposing her back and breasts, inadequately caged in a red brassiere. Harfan could see a few large white patches on her back, around the right shoulder blade, which travelled along the blue capillaries towards the breast.

"Have you seen it?"

"Yes ma'am."

"It's the white patches," she turned around, "I started getting these five years back. Doctors say my body pigment mechanism is loosing vital melanoma and these patches may spread fast."

Before Harfan could react to the provocative sight of the protruded pinnacles, Jahanara unhooked the bra and shed it in one swift move.

"Look at my bosom. The cursed patches have started appearing here too." She, now fully in the raw, held the red and blue capillary lined audacious sacs of membrane for Harfan's inspection.

Yes, a few patches did appear on the breasts and abdomen too. These patches, Harfan thought, looked like blossomed jasmine, on the pink vine of her body.

"I used to get *ayurvedic* medicine from this Dehradun medic. But India's Pakistan war has disrupted the treatment. New patches have come up in the last six months."

"Perhaps the Indian ambassador could help."

"I can't request the CMLA to bow down to the Indians for me. He hates that beak-nosed lady."

"She's pugnacious."

"Correct you're dear. Some one should take care of her. I'm told your London friends can get tne medicine."

"Yes Malika. My London clients have connections in India. Perhaps they can help." Harfan suddenly felt that the inner linings of his oesophagus were cracking up, like wild squirrels scratching at it. He felt a burning thirst and tried to clear his throat by coughing out, what appeared to be a stubborn piece of phlegm. He must get out, before the enchantress trapped him. Israr's warnings kept on vibrating inside him. Run. Run faster.

"Have a drink." Jahanara poured some more wine.

It aggravated the burning sensation.

He felt a steady stream of heat, radiating from the naked frame of Jahanara, was enveloping his senses. He felt the tongues of fire singeing his skin as if he was standing in front of a lump of weapon grade processed plutonium. No. This wasn't correct. Not fair to Jamilla. She had inundated him with love and this temptress couldn't enchant him by blatant display of naked assets. He emptied the glass and tried to make a move towards the door.

"*Khuda Hafiz, mohtarma* (mademoiselle). I'd get back as soon as the medicines are available." Harfan stood up and saluted her.

"What's the hurry dear? The door's closed and the *habshi* is standing guard outside. No use shouting. No help will come. And dear, a hot blooded man never gets out of my den without partaking the nectar." Jahanara picked Harfan by right hand in a sudden move, dragged him to the bedroom, and banged the door behind. Harfan thought of shaking her hand off by using a mild karate chop, but resigned from the decision. This tigress, desperate for young flesh, could create complications. Who would believe him, in Pakistan, ruled by men in uniform! They would go by distressed sob story of the virtual first lady and hang the impetuous young man who had tried to molest their Aphrodite. Holy hell! The noose was perfect.

Next 45 minutes Harfan tossed and twisted in the storm of Jahanara's passion and finally exploded in a violent surge. She screamed out and held Harfan tight to her slithering body, like a primitive Anaconda. Her limbs relaxed, it seemed after eternity, and Harfan managed to inhale some fresh oxygen.

"You're the most wonderful man I've enjoyed in years." Jahanara, now dressed in decent attire, sat at the edges of her bed and increased the music volume.

For the second time, Harfan felt guilty after having sex with a beautiful woman. Jahanara's wasn't a cool dead body. This body was made of molten lava. But he was again burnt inside. The buried feeling of remorse resurfaced. It made him sick to the stomach. To hell with it!

Harfan tried to down the involuntary guilt with a few sips of water. He felt steady. Why not take advantage of the situation? He shouldn't have to suffer the sex kitten for nothing. He had an urgent job to do. He spun the story carefully.

"I've some problems in contacting the Indians." Harfan reverted to the subject, for which Nawab Sharief had pushed him in the tigress' den.

"What's that?"

"You know the fall out of the war. Trades have been suspended. That stupid Manjira is rabidly anti-Muslim. We should do away with her." He threw a pebble in the steaming pool of Jahanara's still buoyant mind, just out of the stormy and torrid encounter.

"I don't blame our people." Jahanara pulled Harfan gently and seated him next to her. She pressed a bell and ordered the maid to bring some coffee.

"This witch has been trying to dismember Pakistan. Haven't you heard of Indian collusion with the Peoples' League and Sheikh Jainal?" She poured coffee in a transparent hand painted bone china cup.

"No Malika," Harfan sipped the coffee and felt some relief, "I normally don't bother about political news. Simply don't get time."

"Be a good Pakistani dear. Keep track of what happens in our neighbouring country."

"Any idea what's cooking?" Harfan moved closer to Jahanara.

"Look love," Jahanara nudged in closer, trying to feel the snug heat, "I'm in the thick of happenings in Pakistan. The *Sadr* (President) and his Martial Law Administrators won't do anything without consulting me. They rely on my astrological acumen."

Harfan almost blurted out that it wasn't her astrological power but sexual prowess, which dragged people to her parlour. He resisted the temptation.

"Really?"

"Give me your hand." Jahanara fondled Harfan's right palm and talked about his troubled childhood, his propensity for violent actions, capability of charming women and success in career.

"You're great," Harfan titillated Jahanara by shifting closer, "what's your forecast for our great nation? Are we going to give a final drubbing to the Indian dogs? I've no doubt that our *Sadr* (President) is capable of giving a bloody nose to that lady."

"You're correct dear, he's the man of our destiny. There'll be a final and decisive war with India; Manjira will fall to the bullets of assassins; the traitors in East Pakistan will be eliminated; Kashmir will be ours, and Hindu India will again come under Islam." She spoke as if she were in a trance.

"You mean the Indian PM will fall to assassins' bullets."

"Most likely, very soon, not later than October this year."

"That's a good forecast."

"Keep to yourself. It may happen in Delhi itself. She's playing with fire in East-Pakistan and our people aren't nincompoops."

"You mean our leaders?"

"There are people to carry out the assignment, these are the Markaz and Jammat people. You know they're friends of General Hyder Bux, the ISI chief." Jahanara opened her eyes. She wasn't exactly in a trance. She was enjoying the soft touches of Harfan on the exposed parts of her belly and getting ready for another bout of lovemaking.

"Our people must be working on concrete plans."

"The commandos are ready for the job, the Markaz people, trained by the SSG."

Jahanara's hand steadily crawled towards Harfan's private parts.

Harfan disengaged and stood up, intending to make a move.

"I think I should go now," he looked at his wristwatch, "please tell Nawab that your job is done."

"Don't bother about that pig," Jahanara stood up, drew Harfan closer, kissed him lightly and said, "this is an incomplete visit dear. Come again and again. Keep coming. I need the medicine, don't forget."

She kissed him again, this time driving her tongue deep inside, engaging the root of Harfan's tongue.

"And you're a great medicine yourself, you know that."

Harfan promised to activate his London friends, to get to the Dehradun *vaid* and to visit her at the earliest opportunity.

The castrated *habshi* took over. Harfan was escorted out in the same fashion and security ritual.

Jahanara's hungry looks followed Harfan until his figure vanished behind a cluster of dwarf chinars. She turned to the music system and increased volume of the *Sarod* recital, now playing a tune set in *raga malkaush*, which reflected a delightful mood. She hummed the tune and prepared to step into the sauna. She should be ready to receive her lover boy, General Arif Khan, the President and the CMLA of Pakistan.

*

The enchantress was, however, blissfully ignorant that the loud instrumental music had saved the day for her. Noise pollution had obfuscated the sound waves and blunted the electronic receptacles of the tiny radio microphones implanted all over her place.

General Arif Khan was ignorant too of the deep games played by General Hyder Bux, the ISI chief, and Lt. General Sarfaraz Lodi, his Personal Staff Officer. They had initiated afresh, another domino game, a conspiracy to topple General Arif Khan, who had deposed his ailing predecessor and imposed himself on Pakistan.

General Sarfaraz, hero of many wars, wasn't amused by the silent putsch. Hyder Bux too nursed a multi-tongued fire in his chest. Why couldn't he, a scion of the family that pioneered the Pakistan movement, put on the crown? He had better claim on the lurching animal called Pakistan, bled white by soldiers and bureaucrats. Two tongues of fire, that of Hyder Bux and Sarfaraz, had mingled at a common burner that sought live roasting of General Arif. The planned infringement of the premises of Malika Jahanara and the bugging of her rooms were part of a super-secret Operation Red Rose.

General Arif spent more of his time in the pleasure abode of the Aphrodite than in his designated office and official residence. His wasn't the platonic thirst for Jahanara's nectarous voice. A sick mind escaped to his self-designed quagmire of fantasy.

What better joint could the intelligence sleuths seek out for collecting incriminating evidence against the Head of the State?

Harfan too didn't expect bugs in the enchantress's den. Even if he had anticipated, as he should have by training, he could help precious little. One could simply not afford to grimace at a lioness after entering her den, hoping against hope to frighten her away. She was determined to have her late afternoon meal and Harfan was definitely a delicate piece of live meat.

*

24

Harfan didn't raise *Khalis* to transmit what he considered the most sensitive piece of intelligence. The queen bee herself had sung in his ears and that sweet music confirmed what was initially gathered from acquaintances in the DMI and the SSG. All indices indicated the strong possibility of trained commandos infiltrating India from Rajshahi side of East Pakistan, lodge in Delhi, and carry out the assassination of the century. It was as potent as a threatened nuclear attack on the Indian nation.

A radio transmission was more vulnerable to interception than waylaying a well secured live drop and pick up. He opted for the live courier drill and concealment tradecraft device.

Harfan carefully removed, using a fine surgeon's scalpel, about an inch thick chunk from a cake of London Beauty bathing soap. He secured the ciphered text in a waterproof plastic film, tucked it inside the cavity, and replaced the top chunk. He obliterated the incision marks by light brush strokes, dipped in a mixture of melted fat and water. The soap was restored to its original shape and factory finish gloss. He examined the cake under a magnifying glass. The job was excellent enough to fox a trained eye! He placed the soap box in an assorted gift pack, marketed by the Harrods of London, and inscribed the name and address of the receiver: Miss Nazma Akhtar, c/o. Dr. Saleem Akhtar, Main Market, Kabul, and delivered the packet to a cut-out in the Indian Consulate, Jalalabad.

The Consular officer, an undercover operative of the National Security India, personally carried the gift packet to a safe house behind Shakar-Darah, where Balachandran Nampoothiri was anxiously waiting for it and for a pre-arranged rendezvous with Alamgir.

His mind leapt out in excitement when Harfan's gift packet was delivered. Triple X's dispatches naturally triggered off Nampoothiri's imagination. An agent of his quality was rare to come by. He was sharper than veteran Alam, in many ways. And he had surprised this veteran of many intelligence intrigues and encounters one too many times.

Jatadhari opened the packet.

Layers of shredded papers and a foam buffer had protected the lovely gifts of soap, perfume, and eau-de-cologne. Must be for the family, Jatadhari presumed. Nampoothiri directed his shadow to leave the packet and remember to pick it up while returning home. The gifts were from a relation of his wife.

Nampoothiri walked into the anteroom and took out the contents of the gift packet one by one.

No. The perfume spray canister couldn't be used for concealing a message. It must be in the soaps. He placed the soap cakes, one by one, under a magnifying glass and looked for fine incision marks.

It was there, in the sixth soap. The circular incision carried out with a diamond cutter's precision didn't escape his trained eyes. Nampoothiri folded an absorbent tissue paper, soaked it, and placed on the soap with a gentle pressure of thumb. Two impatient minutes later, the mystery was unravelled.

The circular incision mark surfaced in sharp contrast. He applied lever-pressure with a thin steel knife and removed the upper crust, cut like a diamond that created a minuscule hollow chamber beneath.

It was there, the most important piece of paper, wrapped in a light blue waterproof plastic film.

Nampoothiri carefully lifted it using steel tong, removed the protective cover, and unfolded carefully the message from Triple X. He pressed the bell, ordered coffee and asked Jatadhari to bring in his car.

"Ambassador sahib," Nampoothiri called the Indian ambassador, "hope you aren't in bed. I'm coming down to the embassy. Please reach there immediately. Get your strong room keys along."

The ambassador opened the wall-embedded safe and took out the special OTP, one time cipher pad. Together they spent two hours in deciphering the 130 odd numerical groups with zero error.

The three-page report deluged Nampoothiri with vital details of inner contradictions in the CMLA set up. Devoid of any meaningful co-ordination with the traditional civilian administration, the military brasses were busy in apportioning the Pakistani loaf to their private breadbaskets.

Important of all, the cipher confirmed existence of a sinister plan, hatched by the Markaz-ul-Farhan, for assassination of the Indian PM. Their links with the ISI and SSG were incontrovertible. The message ominously concluded…"The Special Services Group in Dacca is busy synthesising the Markaz-ul-Farhan and chosen commando groups. *Operation Janbaaz* (daredevil), assassination of the Indian Prime Minister, was the name of the game. The most likely venue: the heart of the nation-Delhi.

Action Time frame: September-October 1969….

Source…Impeccable…

Action…Self-following up. Rest—*chacha* (Alam) will explain. Shall revert back… ."

The ambassador, a career diplomat, bubbled up in excitement. He had never handled such hot stuff.

"It's a live bomb." He went almost pale.

"Yes. It is." Nampoothiri destroyed the used pads by burning them and washing down the ash and settled for his favourite Havana, "Come to my hotel. I'll serve the best Brazilian coffee." Nampoothiri was hard pressed for time.

Alam was supposed to meet him at 11 a.m. the meeting rendezvous was at a remote corner of the capital city in a nameless and faceless guesthouse behind Kabul University.

"Just forget the message." Nampoothiri advised the ambassador, as they drove down to his hotel, "You haven't seen anything, got it?"

*

The explosive message from Triple X was too good to be true. The veteran sleuth in Nampoothiri was tempted to churn it with plenty of salt before coming to an intelligent conclusion.

But Alam's follow up briefing at a Kabul safe house assured him of authenticity of the information. Harfan was accurate, almost like an atomic clock. His source was impeccable, the Aphrodite herself, the ringmaster of the top players of Pakistani circus.

"How discreet is she?" Nampoothiri asked.

"Indiscretion isn't one of her problems. However, I understand she is an epicentre of an impending political quake. Izaz Afroz and a few Generals want to use her linkages with the President for scandalising him."

"Is it safe for Triple X to get any closer to her?"

"It's safe as long as she isn't targeted by the ISI. I expect the conspirators to cast nets in her steaming pool too."

"How soon?"

"Depends on how things shape up in East Pak. The President enjoys US and Chinese support. That's what is holding back the sharks."

"Any new input on the VIP security angle?" Nampoothiri asked.

"Yes. It's slated for one of her public engagements. I understand two experts from the Special Services Group have been selected to co-ordinate the action plan.

"They're experts in sniper-shooting and the use of explosive devices," Alam revealed his cards.

"Any idea about the Indian collaborators?"

"No specifics. The Markaz boys have been trained for the job. Local collaboration is possible. Harfan is on a brief business trip to Dacca. He should be able to extract more resin out of the poppy pods there." Alam came out clean, in his flowery Urdu.

"Can we take him seriously?" Nampoothiri repeated the latent fear of a seasoned intelligence officer.

"We should," continued Alam, "but sir, I think he should run at a slower pace. In our game a fast runner often doesn't touch the finishing line."

"Some are born to run faster, the spin is almost predestined, buried deep in the genes. Take care of your own security. Harfan's indiscretions shouldn't endanger your cover. Ask him to steer clear of the enchantress."

"Why do you feel so?"

"I don't want him getting embroiled in Pakistan's chronic power struggle. If I were the conspirator, I would've targeted her first, before slugging lead into the old man's bones." Nampoothiri closed the discussion.

"One more point. Ask Triple X to disengage from the Israr-Nawab fratricidal fight. Our man in New York has noticed Nawab orbiting around an important official of the CIA." Nampoothiri cautioned Alam in measured and precise words.

"You're correct sir. Nawab is close to the ISI chief and Izaz Afroz. They're trying to install him as the chief minister of Punjab."

"That's not important Alam," Nampoothiri added, "Nawab is known to us for fronting the ISI in certain operations across our borders. He's related to an important drug cartel too."

"Ram Karan?"

"Yes. I'd like some concrete dope on that crook, and very fast."

"Anything urgent?"

Nampoothiri didn't react. His silence spoke volumes. Ram Karan was very high on his agenda. That stinking skunk should be prevented from fouling up the high office of the Indian Premier.

"I'm worried about the PM's security. Do you have any details, other than what Harfan has supplied, on these SSG commando experts? Can you specify their movement pattern? Any profile?"

Nampoothiri preferred to revert to his current concern.

"Again to quote Triple X, they've been camping in Rajshahi area under cover of an *Ijtema* (religious congregation) camp, fronted by *Islamic Chhatra Jihad* (students' crusade)." Alam elaborated the information.

"Can you monitor their movement?"

"With pleasure. I shall be in touch. As you know, a few companies of the Special Services Group have been raised in Dacca recently. I've some friends in the Military Law Administrator's set up, but Triple X has better contacts in the force."

"How?"

"His company regularly supplies field hardware to the force."

"Why don't you visit Dacca? It's important."

"Let's leave that part to Mian Harfan. I suggest you consider taking help from your Israeli friends. These commandos were also trained by a breakaway group of the PFLP."

"That's worth considering. Keep in touch."

"Don't worry. We'll do our best."

*

Amrita Bhalla's weary face lit up as the rotating chopper blades generated a dull humming noise above the fourth tower of *Nakshtra Lok*. It was time for Nampoothiri to land on the rooftop helipad, at the end of his long journey back from Kabul.

Keeping late hours wasn't new to her. She had calibrated her vibes with that of her boss. They understood each other well.

Jatadhari stirred the coffee silently and left the steaming mug on Nampoothiri's table.

"Brother," Nampoothiri picked up the hot line to the PM's office and called Rajinder Singh Dewan, "I need an urgent meeting with ma'am."

"Bad, it's a bad evening," Dewan replied.

"Please squeeze in a few minutes, the matter is urgent."

"Brother, it's never a few minutes with you. You've a long love chat planned out all the time. Hold...." Dewan walked down to Manjira's room and came out immediately. The PM preferred to give top priority to her intelligence chiefs. Their reports often fascinated her. In this exercise, she found a remote echo of her juvenile errand brigade that she had run for her grandfather's political party. She had learnt the tricks more from her mother, a dignified lady, who silently combated a hostile world around her, inside and outside her family.

"You're lucky," Dewan informed the anxious NSI chief, "Come at 10 p.m."

Seated in a rocking chair Manjira gently asked her external intelligence chief to relax and talk.

The NSI chief slowly read out the Triple X message.

"Do you act on the basis of a single report?" Manjira asked, her eyes still closed.

"No ma'am. We don't. But this agent is special, and I've personally visited Kabul to seek verification through another top agent."

"Give me a detailed report on the contradictions among the dramatis personae in the military regime, along with personal profiles of the junta leaders. Don't miss the provincial governor and Martial Law Administrator of East Pakistan." Manjira spoke in a flat voice.

"That can wait ma'am." Nampoothiri noted down the point.

"Tell me how serious is this *Janbaaz* threat?"

"Our other sources of information corroborate this Triple X report. We feel the threat is genuine and serious."

"What do you propose?"

"Please allow me to take some assistance from my Israeli friends."

"Why Israeli?"

"Perhaps you won't like the USA to know what its rogue ally is planning at their back. And the Israelis have the right type of equipments to assist my boys. And I'll require a few experts also to operate those gadgets."

"You want to hang me politically? Do you understand the adverse political fall out of public access to this secret? My Muslim support base will disappear."

"It won't. You're more important than political squirming."

"Okay Balu. Be discreet and keep me informed."

*

A Boeing 737 of Kalyani Airlines touched down at Sarsawa Air Force base in the wee hours of a late August night with a lone passenger and a liaison officer of the NSI. They were received at the taxi bay and taken to a waiting helicopter. It landed on the fourth tower helipad of the NSI and the passenger was whisked away to a super secret rest house of the agency. The lone passenger was Joseph Dayan, a retired Major General of Israeli army, and a front operator of the Mossad. A personal friend of Nampoothiri, he often rendered assistance to the Indian agency against considered compensation packages and with assurance of total secrecy. The occasional deals implied foreknowledge of head of state of both the countries, still un-bridged by diplomatic relationship. Nampoothiri was present to receive the expected guest.

"Hi Balu, what's the big crisis?"

"It's a real crisis and I've a long shopping list."

The two veterans sat down over cognac, coffee and cheroot and explored the contours of the threat perception and equipment needed to track down the band of assassins deputed by the ISI, through its front paw, the Markaz-ul-Farhan.

"You can't plant tracking bugs on the persons of targets. You don't even know them."

"Yes."

"You don't know the route they would take from East Pakistan. You don't know their camping site."

"Look Yossi. I don't run a grocer's shop. My boys know where they are. See this map. This is Rajshahi next to River Padma or Ganga. The camp is in a forested area at Jafarpur. The likely crossing point is between Char Majher on our side and Panchbaria on Pakistan side. They may catch a train either at Beldanga or Palashi for Calcutta. The final destination is Delhi. And we've identified five modules of the Markaz in Delhi. Most likely, these modules would be used to house them. Look at the map."

"Excellent Balu. I'm impressed by the data. You know the geography and history. Don't disturb them at Jafarpur. I'll provide a drone to keep surveillance in the area. Alert your police to tighten security along the suspected crossing points and to leave three pockets unguarded. They would prefer to use a less secured route. Have my gadgets installed at the railway stations. The Markaz boys will look strikingly different from your normal Bengali Muslims and Hindus. Am I okay?"

"Empty your bag first."

"Install a few of my secret cameras in Delhi stations and near about the suspected modules. If you know the geographical location of the assassins, my boys can play wonders with remote cameras, telephone and wireless monitoring. Wherefrom would they get the weapons?"

"There are many routes Yossi. The ISI can use Nepal, Kashmir and Punjab routes."

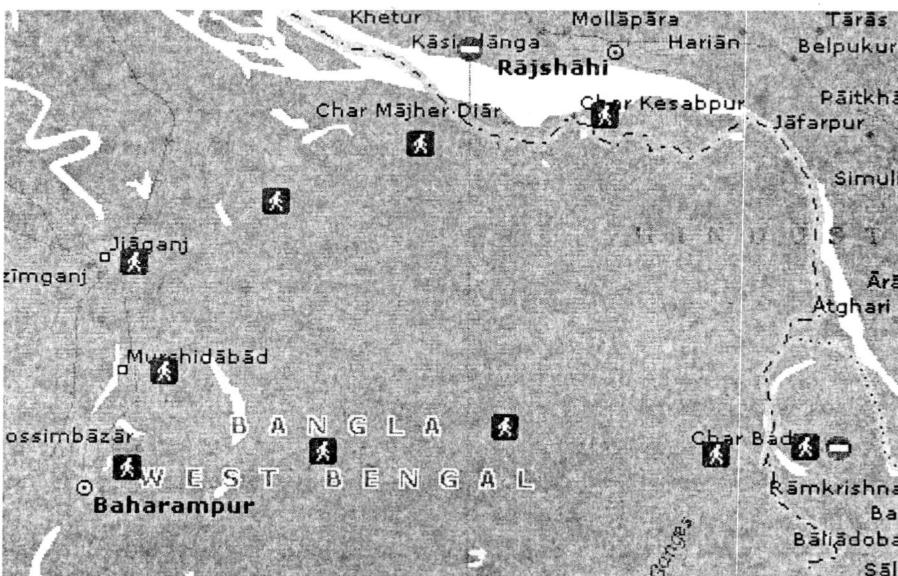
Khetur
Mollāpāra
Tārās
Harian
Belpukuri
Rājshāhi
Char Mājher Diār
Char Kesabpur
Pāitkhā
Jāfarpur
Simuli
Jiāganj
Atghari
Murshidābād
B A N G L A
WEST BENGAL
Baharampur
Rāmkrishna
Bāliādoba
Ganges

"Intensify checking of cargo and passenger traffic at the suspected points. Are you sure they won't use containers which are normally offloaded in the very heart of Delhi?"

"Oh, hell Yossi. That had escaped my mind. We've a huge container dumping station next to the Old Fort."

"Keep check there. I don't say they'd use this channel, but what's the harm in looking under the lamp."

"I get you. I'll take care of these points. When can you start the operation? What all you propose to give us?"

Joseph Dayan drew up a list of hidden radio cameras, thermal imagers, portable X-Ray machines, handheld explosive detectors, invisible infrared ground movement detectors, a remote controlled drone and digital HF, VHF wireless monitors and line and wireless telephone interceptors. You'd provide the operators. My men would only handle the wireless and telephone monitoring consoles and the thermal imagers."

"Okay Yossi. When can you supply the logistics?"

"Give me three days. Ask your men to pick up the merchandise from Phet Buri near Bangkok. The drone will be disassembled in a big packet. Ask your man to contact a restaurant run by Dussolf, a German settled in Thailand. He would supply the hardware. Fly these in your own aircraft and don't get caught by Thai customs."

"I know the tricks Yossi. What's the price tag?"

"Five million if you keep the tools. Half a million less if you return. Normally we don't carry back loaned tools."

"Dear friend, and pray for me. Don't charge for training my boys."

"Nope. Business is business. I've to pay the trainers. Why don't you bomb these Pakis?"

"Sorry pal. Even during war, we're supposed to be in peace. Big brothers are breathing down our necks."

Joseph Dayan took a special flight from Sarsawa next night and Balachandran Nampoothiri got down to the usual business to ensure that the assassins did not perforate the body of his Prime Minister and souls of millions of Indians.

The length and breadth of the story boiled down to a minor shootout between Nampoothiri's Special Volunteer Force commandos and three Markaz assassins somewhere in Delhi, a place called Sarai Julena. One of the assassins was killed on the spot and the captured duo sang like monsoon canaries filling Nampoothiri's bag of information. Intelligence archive of the nation was richer by tons of intelligence, an assorted collection of sophisticated security equipment and poorer by a mere five million dollars. A vital stretch of Delhi, within three kilometers of the President's Palace, was rid of container piles and a new commando force was born, for exclusive protection of the Prime Minister and a few other important national mortals, aspiring to be immortal.

Triple X did not receive a note of thanks and Balachandran Nampoothiri was not decorated with a national award. However, the print and electronic media carried the story implicating an intelligence agency of Pakistan and certain lunatic religious congregations. Nampoothiri's leaking bag, Robin Achariya, briefed the hungry media on the lines he was briefed to carry out measured leakages.

The Prime Minister went on her daily chores with a smile, Pakistan wondered what went wrong and the intelligence community in India was wisened by furlongs and miles.

*

25

The attempted assassination saga was a unique experience for Nampoothiri. Indian intelligence and security fraternities were accosted, for the first time, by a foreign inspired assassination plot. The compulsions of dirty geopolitics had borrowed heavily from the mafia games of the Wild West and the violent tools refined and perfected by the terrorist groups in the Middle East. A new wave of state-sponsored terrorism had hit the sub-continent's shores. The rabid anti-India forces in Pakistan had transformed the democratic values it had inherited from the West Minster to crude weapons of mindless violence. The ISI, a first cousin of the CIA, Nampoothiri thought, had diligently copied the craft of proxy-war. Its calibration of terrorist strikes against important foreign political targets borrowed heavily from the dirty-tricks department of Langley.

The most precious lesson, he reasoned, was the sudden discovery of gaping holes in the security parameters of the nation. It lacked a well-defined intelligence infrastructure, political awareness, and application mechanisms for combating Pakistan's novel war-strategy. It was high time for the NSI to introspect and introduce course correction measures. A new vista of possibilities had been opened up by the aborted assassination attempt. Nampoothiri also realized the need for self-sufficiency in technical gadgetry and requisite training.

Nampoothiri zeroed in on the decision of formulating a comprehensive report and discussing it personally with Manjira. Sensitisation of her mind was important, because in the Indian system the PM was the final authority to decide the intrinsic inputs that should go in for refurbishing the haggard colonial edifices of the intelligence and security edifices of the country.

"Sir, Mr. Dewan is on the line. Would you like to talk?"

Amrita Bhalla's voice on the special phone, that provided special connectivity between his and the Prime Minister's office, broke Nampoothiri's indeterminate dalliance with the thoughts of the future contour of the intelligence fraternity in India.

"By all means," Nampoothiri pushed a yellow button that activated the scrambling protocol, "hello brother, how are you?"

"I'm just earning my bread. Come sharp. Ma'am PM is in a very foul mood."

"Am I on the guillotine?"

"Don't joke. She wants you immediately."

Dewan disconnected the line leaving Nampoothiri with barely 10 minutes to reach the residence of the Prime Minister.

Dinanath Taploo, Manjira's principal secretary, a man of impeccable integrity and razor sharp intellect, was a welcome departure from Amen Gurtoo, whose wayward ways were terminated by the NSI in a superb intelligence operation. He welcomed the participants and introduced the subject.

"Let me make it clear," Taploo spoke in his low bass voice, "what we discuss here is absolutely informal. No record should be kept in any office, except in the office of the NSI. The honourable ministers are requested to keep away from the media. The subjects we're gong to discuss will also remain out of bounds for the Parliament, till such time the PM thinks it's necessary to take the august body into confidence." He looked at Manjira for an approval of what he had just conveyed to the small gathering in the exclusive office of the PM.

"I want you all to listen seriously. The attempt on my life has exposed the audacious and unorthodox approaches of the military rulers in Pakistan. They have imposed two wars on us. They have patronised our disaffected ethnic groups in the North East and now they have come down to target assassination. I was saved by timely intelligence catered by Balu's boys."

Manjira spoke rather in an agitated voice.

"Now apply your mind to what I've to say," Manjira paused momentarily, perhaps to gather her thoughts, "I don't see any reason for Pakistan to survive as a nation. It must be broken into pieces."

The small gathering was stunned by the Prime Minister's pronouncement.

"How do we go about this?" Manjira's minister for interior affairs, virtually a political nonentity, reacted first, "Pakistan is backed by the USA and China."

"I don't care," she turned towards Nampoothiri, "Balu brief us about *Operation Meghna* and blooming of the Lotus. I think we should start from there."

Nampoothiri was not prepared to discuss the top-secret intelligence operation that had received the blessings of two Prime Ministers before Manjira. His professional ethics militated against the concept of discussing operational matters with all and sundry government ministers, until that was cleared by the PM.

"I think we can proceed. I hope all of you understood well what Taploo said to start with."

Manjira winked at Nampoothiri, clearing the way for him to make the vital disclosures.

"Meghna is the essence of our diplomatic and intelligence thrust against Pakistan." Nampoothiri continued in a slumberous tone…

"Our blueprint incorporates the concepts of providing moral and material assistance to Sheikh Jainal and other leaders of the People's League and convert the disjointed language and autonomy movements to a focussed confrontation between the Bengali dominated East Pakistan and the Punjabi ruled West Pakistan."

"This will break up Pakistan." Commented the external affairs minister.

"Well minister," Manjira threw a sharp rebuff, "I'd do that even if I'm the first to break up an Islamic nation after the World War Two."

She took over from her external intelligence chief. She wanted her minister for external affairs to work on a scheme to pump in clandestine funds to the People's League leaders with a view to strengthening its striking capability.

"Would we not incur displeasure of the US and China?" Manjira's minister for interior affairs joined his voice, seeking clarification from the NSI chief.

"I presume the US and China wouldn't endorse our game plan. But Pakistani leadership is in disarray. Several Generals and political leaders are involved in multiple power grabbing conspiracies. Militarily Pakistan can't match us, though Islamabad is frantically scrounging the arms markets for procuring modern weapons of war. *Operation Meghna* is a clever admixture of diplomatic, intelligence and military thrust. The Punjabi elite is in no mood to accommodate genuine Bengali aspirations. It's the best time for us to proceed with the plan."

"Please don't enter into a debate. If you can't help, get out. Two of you coordinate with the NSI chief and the COAS. No publicity. I also want astute mobilisation of the world media towards plights of the Bengali patriots and excesses committed by the Pakistani establishment. Dinanath will coordinate with the information and broadcasting minister."

Manjira made almost a conclusive statement demanding total support from her ministerial colleagues.

"And Balu," Manjira addressed her NSI chief, "I want the self-rule movements in Sind and Baluchistan to be propped up carefully. Activate your boys. Speak to me soon."

"Okay ma'am."

"Anyways, I want regular briefing on Meghna, Sind and Baluchistan. I expect better results."

"Yes ma'am."

Nampoothiri nodded in agreement.

Dinanath Taploo took over from Manjira and recanted the security drill. This top secret meeting, he reminded the elite gathering, was informal and off the record. They should take further direction from him and consult Nampoothiri as and when required.

As he stood up to walk out of the room Manjira asked Nampoothiri and Taploo to stay put.

"I want simultaneous activation of the Sind and Baluchistan nationalists. You meet them in London."

"I'm on the job ma'am. However, my meeting important leaders like Sartaj Jamil won't go unnoticed. Please allow me to use a dependable officer. I'll get back to you with concrete proposals."

"Okay Balu. Dinanath will coordinate the operations. Meet me once again to discuss the details of my talks with the USSR ambassador."

"Fine ma'am. We'd require their help in Baluchistan."

"Get going Balu. We must act decisively this time. I've had enough of their bullshit."

*

Nampoothiri was flabbergasted by Manjira's audacious and unexpected exposition on *Operation Meghna*. He personally handled this delicate operation through his Calcutta representative Vishram Satpore. In fact, linguistic and ethnic nationalism amongst the Bengali speaking people transcended the narrow interpretation of cultural and political nationalism. That's what worried the Punjabi dominated junta of Pakistan and ego bags like Izaz Afroz.

Personally, he did not think that the correct time had come to precipitate another war with Pakistan. Direct interference inside East Pakistan, in collaboration with the volunteers of the People's League, could precipitate another all out war. He preferred intensifying the tools of subversion and supply of weapons through indirect channels. To implement that scheme he required aggressive intelligence tools and supply of such weapons and explosives those could not be traced back to the Indian armed forces. However, his narrow bureaucratic views were not compatible with the wider strategic views nursed by his Prime Minister.

His agency excelled in novel tricks of the trade, but wherefrom would he resource silent supply of sophisticated weapons which could match the firepower of Pakistan army? Should he turn to the KGB? Or should he break the Indian political taboo of boycotting Israel and take a few lessons from the Mossad?

He ruled out the KGB. The Soviet Union was deeply interested in firming up its presence in the eastern wing of Pakistan. The KGB, in spite of Russian bonhomie with Delhi, would not like India to jump straight into the troubled waters of East Pakistan.

China too was propping up a parallel group through a revered maulana. The Red factions were working at cross-purposes and often impeding the main body of freedom fighters fighting under Sheikh Jainal's leadership.

Well! Why should he not try the Mossad? Joseph Dayan and his New Star Global Fuel had rendered invaluable services only a couple of months back. They wouldn't mind to procure and supply weapons to the Bengali freedom fighters.

The Jews were discrete business partners and they won't surely run up to Pakistani windowsills to serenade the beauty of its strategic importance. With all its umbilical ties with Washington Tel Aviv was far from being chummy with the Islamic nations. Perhaps he could do some serious business with his under-the-rug friends in Tel Aviv.

Nampoothiri picked up the intercom and summoned Amrita Bhalla.

"Do me two favours dear."

"Order me sir." She stood silently with the calculated knowledge that the boss was cooking up some broth in the ever-blazing hearth of his mind.

"Recall this fellow Yossi?"

"You mean Joseph Dayan, the Israeli arms supplier, who fronts an oil exploration outfit and who was in Delhi recently?"

"Correct dear. Wasn't he a good friend of your late father?"

"Yes sir. They were trained together in the UK."

"Yes. I know they were SAS trained buddies. Set up a discreet meeting at hotel Novotel in Bangkok. I'll like to reach there day after tomorrow. Book two rooms in the name of Mohammad Yasin, a garment importer of Bombay, and *mohtarma* Nasira." Nampoothiri ordered.

"Who's she?"

"Not my girlfriend. You're accompanying me."

"Why me?"

"A pretty face like you would provide a nice cover for this old haggard. May be you can pass off as my fourth wife."

"Mind your words sir."

"Sorry dear. I need a cover and your dad was a friend of Yossi."

"He is a former Mossad General. Isn't it?"

"I know dear. That's why you're fixing up the meeting at Bangkok. Use our channel in Rio de Janeiro to contact Yossi."

"I've a point to make."

"You don't want me to go to Bangkok. Am I correct?"

"Correct. Bangkok is a deep alligator-pit of international espionage. The American adventures in Korea, Vietnam, Laos, and Cambodia have turned the quiet Siamese capital to a cesspool of intrigue and a high profile intelligence watchtower. The CIA and its friends wouldn't miss your arrival." Amrita Bhalla kept her point of view succinctly.

"Perhaps you're correct. However, Yossi is a fussy jackal. He wouldn't like to meet anyone else."

"Why can't you depute Alamgir to meet him?"

"The idea isn't bad. However, Alam is a trusted arms supplier to the Pakistani armed forces. The Mossad won't trust him. You better change our rendezvous to Singapore."

"Hotel Ambrosia, I believe?"

"Now call that fellow... What's his name!"

"You mean Bhagat?"

"Here you are dear. I don't know what should I do without you!"

"Well sir," Amrita shrugged, "I'm here at your service."

Bhagat turned up pronto and left in a huff. The brief was short and specific. He was to rush to the airport to catch a flight for Kathmandu. An important call from Triple X was on the pipeline.

*

The Royal Nepal Airlines flight reached Kathmandu late in the evening. Bhagat hired a taxi and reached hotel Swapnalu at Maharajganj market. The nondescript hotel was a favourite hole for budget Indian tourists. He called Triple X at a mutually agreed telephone number indicated by Nampoothiri. Harfan received the call at Pearl Continental hotel, located in a proud corner of Sharah-e-Quaid-e-Azam, a distinct landmark in Lahore.

"Your uncles are happy here." Bhagat talked in an even tone without betraying anxiety.

"Thanks *mamu* (maternal uncle). We must take our nephew abroad for treatment."

"Can't you get him treated at Riverdale Clinic?"

"No. Best treatment for damaged pancreas is available only in Canada. I'll take him to Ottawa next week. My passage is booked via JFK. Can you make it? Our nephew wants to meet you," Harfan enquired.

"Can't say for sure. I'll get back same time tomorrow. Anything else?"

"Call tomorrow, our nephew can't wait indefinitely." Harfan disconnected.

Dhiren Bhagat visited the residence of the under cover First Secretary of the Indian embassy and made a call to Nampoothiri to discuss if he could convey Delhi's approval to his visit to Canada. Within seconds, Nampoothiri unfurled the green flag.

"Come down home. I've urgent consultations."

"Yes sir."

Bhagat's brief visit to Kathmandu was task specific. He returned with loaded apprehension. Facing the tornado called Harfan in a strange land could mean inviting turmoil and endless wool-ball pursuit of intelligence tasks. What could be the next surprise?

*

Dhiren Bhagat travelled to Ottawa, under cover of a special diplomatic courier, with a diplomatic passport, carrying a personal message from the Indian PM, to her Canadian counterpart. The letter was a genuine one; on the Indian interpretation of the grandiose plan of a *'supreme government'* enunciated by Sardar Niyamat, the mercurial leader of Indian Kashmir. Niyamat had written, many political observers alleged, at Pakistani prompting, to important world leaders, enunciating his perception of the panacea for the troubled state of Kashmir. Sympathetic Canadian voices had staged a couple of rallies before the Parliament building demanding the free world's intervention in the Kashmir imbroglio. The Indian PM explained the ground realities and professed Indian adherence to the UN resolutions.

Bhagat was lodged at Hotel St. Bernard, a few blocks away from the Parliament building, overlooking the small French-speaking town of Hull and River Ottawa, which was known in aboriginal Indian vocabulary as River Outaouais.

"Hello *mamu*," Harfan called over the house phone, "how are you today?"

"Fine. Where are you?"

"At Chateau Laurier. Relatives are with me, can't meet here. Let's meet at Tandoor restaurant, next to Riverside Boulevard."

"How do I get there?"

"Take a taxi. Avoid an Indian driven one."

Food by candlelight, over strong Miller beer, was slightly hot, hot enough to titillate the palate and warm up the body.

Late October snow flurries had chilled the air down, cool enough to scare the summer swallows.

"What's the big game?" Bhagat asked.

"It's big. But, tell me how is my mother?" Harfan's eyes looked deep into Bhagat's.

"I didn't personally meet her, but one of my boys had delivered your last letter."

"Did he talk to her? How did he find her?"

"Look brother, she's well, but misses you. All these years she has been living counting the footsteps of your father. Now, I presume, she's counting yours. She knows you're alive and you'll soon be back." Bhagat's sappy voice didn't amuse Harfan.

"Didn't it occur to you, that you should meet and talk to her personally?" Harfan sounded bitter.

"I'm a government servant. I can't freelance. My man had talked to her. She is okay and worried."

"Can I return to her?" Harfan involuntarily touched Bhagat's hand.

"Why not? You'll return to a hero's welcome once your mission is over." Dhiren poured beer in Harfan's glass.

"Don't bullshit! Suppose I'm caught."

"Don't think negative. Spies are caught and they're periodically exchanged as security prisoners. This is an eternal game, all over the world. Haven't you heard of periodical exchanges at the Berlin Wall? There's always an element of professional risk. You know all that."

Bhagat reminded him of some of the training stuff.

"What about my wife and kid?"

"*Yar* (friend), don't imagine things. You're our top man and the PM herself is handling your matter. Trust me, we can spirit your family out to London and from there to India." Bhagat gently tapped Harfan's arm.

"What brings you to Canada? Who's the other fellow with you? Why couldn't we transact this business in London?"

"Patience brother," Harfan replied coolly, "my cover brings me to Ottawa. Clear? The other fellow happens to be my boss, Israr Sharief. Our company has bagged a defence contract for supplying anti-tank missiles, amphibious boats, small and medium weapons and armoured personnel carriers. Four Canadian parties have been short listed."

"You called me all the way to freezing Ottawa just to tell this!"

"No. There are more. The CMLA has access to information of the existence of a joint battle order, between the Indian Army and the ragtag volunteer forces of

Sheikh Jainal. He had in his pocket concrete proof of NSI's involvement with Jainal."

Harfan added that both the USA and China had shared with Pakistan their critical assessment of India's strategic intentions in East Pakistan.

"Keep this. It's a Xerox copy of a report of ISI top agent India, Aftab, stolen from the records of the CMLA office."

"Authentic?"

"Hundred percent."

"What's your suggestion?"

"None. All that I know is unless you keep Pakistan busy, General Arif will launch *Operation Khyber.*"

"What's that?"

"That's what I was hinting at. Keep these papers. These are the blueprints for Pakistan army action in East Pakistan. They have a sinister plan. You can expect a crack down on the Peoples' League movement any time. The CMLA is in touch with Washington and Peking and his guardian angels have endorsed the tough line."

"Why should Washington and Peking be interested in a full scale Pakistani genocide in Dacca?"

"Tell the boss to take care. China wants groups loyal to it should head the movement, and the US doesn't want Pakistan to go the Bhutan and Sikkim way-becoming just another Indian protectorate."

"Hold your breath," Harfan prevented Bhagat from interjecting, "the ISI has plans to come up with more dirty tricks for scuttling the scheduled Indian polls. Aftab and a few other political bosses have been tamed and a number of media persons have been hooked. A lot of drug-money is in the pipeline. Ask Delhi to be watchful in Kashmir. The sleuths are preparing to stage a spectacular show."

"Be specific." Bhagat demanded.

"That's what *Khyber* is all about. More armed Islamist gangs will be exported to Indian Kashmir, like they did in 1948 and '65 for triggering large-scale violence. They may hijack aircrafts to divert attention from the flu of democracy. I've received specific proof about one Aftab, an intelligence asset of the ISI, operating from inside your political structure." Harfan looked at his watch and stood up abruptly.

"Who is Aftab?"

"I've no doubt that he's my college-campus boss Ram Karan Prasad."

"Why Ram Karan? Are you serious?"

"You know the meaning of Aftab? It's the dazzling Sun. Remove your opaque bureaucratic glasses and you'll see the truth behind the dazzling disk. I suppose he was a British pawn, a crony of the Muslim League and now an agent of the ISI."

Harfan replied mimicking a couplet from the *Upanishads* (classical Sanskrit works) and begged to be excused. Israr Sharief, he said, would be expecting him for a briefing session.

"How do you unmask this Aftab?"

"Now you're being ridiculous. You're the spymasters, you should know better. All that I know Pakistan is pumping in huge funds to some politicians and media persons. They want Manjira's defeat and Jainal's demise. Only Ram can be the logical master conduit."

"Noted; now tell me more on the nuclear programme."

"Sorry brother. I'm on a tight schedule. Here's a write-up. Read it. You'll discover the real philosophy of Pakistán's nuclear quest," Harfan continued, "Izaz Afroz is the father of the programme. He has an unmitigated hatred for Hindustan and Hindus and he thinks he has been created by the *Allah* to destroy the Hindu *kafirs*."

"That's strange."

" Strangeness is not a stranger to geostrategic policies. Take care of the documents and contact *vaid* Dhanwant of Dehradun. I want these medicines to be delivered to my friend in London by next week." He passed on a piece of paper to Bhagat.

"What are these medicines for?"

"Some skin disease caused by the absence of melanin, the pigment which gives colour to our skin. The other is some queer aphrodisiac concoction. The *vaid* is supposed to be good. His clients in Pakistan are anxious to avail of his services."

"Who requires the sex-stimulants?" Bhagat asked.

"Don't forget that most of the Generals in my host country are past 50 and they're used to extramarital affairs. Contact the *vaid* on behalf of a London based Indian. Your hands should not be seen at all."

"Can I take help from a neutral journalist?"

"Go for a trusted Muslim one."

Bhagat promised to arrange delivery of six month's supply of medicine at the London contact point. He passed on a leather pouch to Harfan.

"I appreciate."

"Do you think the Americans will intervene?" Bhagat requested for elaboration.

"Seek answer from your own company. All I know is that both America and China have taken lease of Pakistan. Short of starting a war they would oppose India tooth and nail."

Harfan's briefing amazed Bhagat. The streak of defiance apart, Triple X had shaped up beyond his wildest expectations.

"It's been an excellent meeting Ramen," Bhagat added, "I take a morning flight to JFK and on to Delhi."

"I've to stay put. Israr is expecting a meeting with the Chinese Trade Minister at Toronto."

"What for?"

"A high level Chinese defence delegation is scheduled to arrive in Islamabad in another four months. We expect to bag a fat contract for picking up Chinese military supplies from a third country base."

"Military hardware?"

"Yes."

"You mean Peking will support the military regime's dirty deeds in East Pak." Bhagat asked.

"Oh my god!" Harfan searched his jacket and brought out an envelope, "keep this. It's a classified document from the CMLA secretariat. Tell boss that General Arif and Izaz Afroz are building a secret bridge between Washington and Peking."

"How come?"

"No details. It could be a flank attack against the Red Bear, a strategic Cold War gamble."

"That's a queer cocktail."

"That's real geopolitics for you now. And tell Papa that Aftab Ram Karan requires his immediate attention."

"I think you've a Ram Karan fixation."

"You know the Satan well only when you lend your soul to him."

"Hope life with Jamilla is very rosy." Bhagat asked to give a personal touch to the professional meeting.

"Yes. I'm happy. I wish this life lasted forever."

"It's only a part of your cover Ramen. I believe Zahoor sahib is a very influential person in Sind. Do you think he can help us?"

"Look Bhagat," Harfan clicked his cigarette lighter and blew off the blue flame, "Zahoor is a part of my cover too. I'm here under your guillotine chopper. Don't drag them under it."

"There's no need for the rhetoric. I just wanted to know if he takes interest in Pakistani politics."

"No. He's an apolitical businessperson, and nothing else. Close this topic." Harfan fished out a cover from his chest pocket, as they started walking along the gangway and passed it on to Bhagat.

"Please give it to my mom. There's a letter and some Indian currency in it." He begged Bhagat.

"You're taking a huge risk. It's not done in our line." Bhagat reminded Harfan of the security requirements.

"Don't be cruel and I don't bother."

Bhagat struggled for a while for the correct words. He didn't have any. He stood motionless at the wooden gangway leading to the parking lot. Only the ripples of the lake waters added some sad notes to the silence of darkness.

"Would you take care of my Jamilla and Pervez if they shoot me?" Harfan asked again.

"You don't have to ask Ramen," Bhagat replied, "I stand committed to you and your family. I'll take care of them."

"You've helped me regain my human traits. I trust you. Take care of my Jamilla and Pervez and my mother." Harfan moved closer and hugged Bhagat.

"Don't despair. You're on top of the situation." Bhagat added in a rather hollow voice.

"Yah, I know that. I've to build each stair, brick by brick, before I take the next precarious step." Harfan laughed and lighted a cigarette.

He picked up the bag, walked down to his rented Ford, and started the engine without looking back. In his job, he could look back with nostalgia, but a revisit was very rare, if not forbidden.

Bhagat felt a streak of pain and anxiety stirring his guts. This pain arose out of the knowledge that the NSI didn't normally reclaim a compromised spy. However, his immediate task was to rush to the High Commissioner's residence and avail of the cipher facility of the Mission. He had very important materials to convey to Delhi before he visited Boston for call on Sartaj Jamil, the veteran Sindhi leader.

*

26

Sartaj Jamil, the aged Sindhi leader from the lower Sind interior feudal belt of Tando Muhammad Khan, was a man of courage and conviction. A person with Arab ancestry, he claimed his lineage to the legendary Arab conquerors who had hit the shores of Sind in the 8th century A.D. One of his ancestors, according to family tradition, was revenue official in the court of later day Abbasid Caliphate.

The Jamil family was highly influenced by Lal Shahbaz Qalandar, the famous Sufi saint of Sehwan Sharief, once a dazzling seat of the rulers of lower Sind. At heart, Sartaj was a Sufi too. He believed in human values and cherished the values of sharing and caring. But the spirits of Sufism had also taught him the values of standing up against injustice and oppression.

Educated in Bombay and Karachi, Sartaj had left his lucrative job as the Deputy District Collector in the NWFP to join the Khudai Khidmatgar (Servants of God) movement of the Frontier Gandhi. During the freedom movement he had aligned with the Indian National Congress. His closeness to the Communist leaders from Punjab and Bengal had made him popular to the proletariat masses of Sind, Baluchistan and Punjab. At one point Moscow had evinced keen interest in him as a likely spearhead against the British.

By the age of 40, when he spearheaded the Quit India movement in 1942, in the province of Sind, Sartaj had already spent eight years in British jails at odd places like Bannu, Dera Ghazi Khan, and Peshawar. He was again incarcerated in 1942 and was finally released from the dinghy district jail at Mianwali only in December 1946. By then the retreating British masters and the tired Muslim and Hindu leaders had decided to cut India into pieces to create a geographically incongruous Muslim nation called Pakistan and a vaguely secular country called India.

Sartaj did not approve of the civilisational vivisection of India. However, the combined bureaucratic and military leaders had persuaded Sartaj to join the Sind provincial cabinet in 1960. The diehard Muslim League fanatics and the landed feudals from Punjab soon pushed out the secular and democratic leaders from Sind, Baluchistan and the NWFP.

By 1962, Sartaj Jamil and a few of his secular friends in the exclusive Muslim nation of Pakistan had reached the end of their journey to disillusionment. Sartaj's clouds of woes were darkened by the sudden rise of Izaz Afroz in the political firmament of Pakistan. The maverick and self-styled messianic scion of the Afroz feudal family from Larkana had spent most of his time in Britain either as a student or as a playboy.

The military-bureaucratic rulers had suddenly discovered that this flamboyant Sindhi was ready to dance to their tune. A pathological sycophant, he danced to the tune of the military rulers and had taken upon himself the task of punishing those leaders of Sind who cherished the dreams of having better say in national matters.

Izaz was allergic to the flu of democracy. The PIB and the ISI were made to manufacture a few damning reports implicating Sartaj with the Indian intelligence agencies, which aimed at balkanising Pakistan. Izaz could not keep him behind the bars indefinitely. The influential Pir Pagara and the elder brother of President Akbar Khan persuaded the supreme leader to reconcile with the lower Sind leader before he went through the exercises of promulgating a new constitution and holding elections to the National Assembly. Izaz did not like the idea of sharing power with another Sindhi, but decided to mark time till he took over from ailing Akbar Khan.

By the end of 1963, Sartaj Jamil had built up a strident movement for better economic and political rights for the province of Sind. His volunteers had started building up resistance groups with minor arms supplies from Baluchistan and the NWFP. His linkages with the Indian leaders had opened up another vista of mutual support for securing better rights for the people of Sind and Baluchistan.

Rabindra Narayan Dutta, the Federal Intelligence Bureau chief, did not have much difficulty in persuading and convincing Amritlal, the Prime Minister, to allow him to oar around in the troubled waters of Sind. The events in Kashmir and the North East India had convinced him that the subtle wars of sabotage and subversion were to be taken inside the belly of Pakistan, and the sick nation had its own fault lines, which could be exploited by his agency.

Operation Meghna had already started taking firm roots in the eastern wing of Pakistan. Dutta targeted Sartaj, Sherdil Khan, and Aliullah Mengel and others in the west. Sartaj was a prized catch. By 1963, the disillusioned leader firmly believed that the military was in no mood to transfer power to the elected representatives of the people and the sycophants like Izaz were bent upon destroying Pakistan by alienating the majority Bengalis. That fiend of a politician was obsessed with the idea of ruling Pakistan with an iron fist and inviting the deluge after him.

Sartaj had his first meeting with a cabinet colleague of Amritlal, who had shared common political platforms with him during the independence movement. His second meeting was with Amritlal in London. The Indian PM in a subtle move introduced him to Dutta and Nampoothiri. The liaison between the FIB stalwarts and the alienated Sindhi leader thereafter flourished steadfastly.

Operation Qalandar, another heated needle in the troubled flesh of Pakistan, was conceived as the second aggressive clandestine front against the military regime. Dutta's views were clear. He could not allow Pakistan to enjoy undisturbed sleep and export its proxy war to the underbelly of India in Kashmir and the North East at the same time. Qalandar was a favourite baby of Nampoothiri. He had struck a personal rapport with Jamil, Mazari and Mengel and had assisted them with the sinews of oft-violent civil unrest through conduits in London, Paris and Frankfurt. India's forward moles like Alamgir were scrupulously kept away from the Qalandar operation. Briefing and debriefing were conducted either by Nampoothiri personally or through designated embassy based under cover diplomats.

The choice of Dhiren Bhagat, rather a junior officer, to contact Sartaj Jamil at Boston was deliberate. His sister and her husband had set up home in a residential area behind Columbia Road. Both of them worked in an insurance company. A small detour from Ottawa to Boston looked natural.

Sartaj Jamil's daughter, married to a white American, taught astrophysics in the MIT. They had set up home at Starraw Drive, behind Boston University. Jamil's presence in Boston for an urgent medical check up for his heart ailment did not arouse suspicion of the Pakistani and American spooks.

His movements in New York, Washington and high profile cities were meticulously covered by the ISI. The CIA and the FBI too monitored his movements because of his alleged linkages with the Indian and Soviet Communist leaders.

Sartaj's visit to Boston synchronised with the political turmoil in Pakistan. President Akbar Khan had surrounded himself with a band of sycophantic courtiers, whose activities were orchestrated by his son, a retired junior army officer. Izaz Afroz, Sartaj's tormentor and Akbar Khan's hatchet man, had distanced himself from his one time mentor and busied with the impossible task of putting together a ragtag opposition. He conveniently donned the garb of socialism too to satisfy the left oriented democratic forces.

He assiduously cultivated a few top Generals, including General Arif Khan, who was appointed as Chief of Army Staff by a beleaguered President, simply on consideration of his easygoing lifestyle and his weaknesses for wine and women. General Hyder Bux, the ISI chief, and the Corps Commanders of Peshawar, Lahore and Karachi and the Air Chief as well were his special targets.

They formed a coterie, which had shifted loyalty, like the seasonal sand dunes of the Thar Desert, from Akbar Khan to Arif Khan, after the exact political implications of the Tashkent agreement dawned upon the Pakistani people, especially the Armed Forces. Only Lt.General Sarfaraz Lodi, the most important commander of the Chak Lala AHQ Reserve Corps, maintained a fearful distance from the Jackal of Larkana, as he preferred to call Izaz Afroz, behind his back. Sarfaraz firmly believed that Izaz had goaded President Akbar Khan to launch the disastrous Kashmir war of 1965. The Pakistan army was not ready for a full-scale war against the superior Indian Army. As the Chief of Staff to the former Army Chief, he knew rather too well the weaknesses of the Pak army. Moreover, he nursed a secret ambition to take over the reins of Pakistan at an appropriate moment.

The east also was in ferment. The President had released Sheikh Jainal, an accused in the trumped up conspiracy case, with the fond hope of bringing round the malcontent political forces to a round table conference.

Sartaj Jamil and his friends like Sherdil and Aliullah were disenchanted with Akbar Khan and his coterie. They were also not inclined to trust the highly idiosyncratic and hypocrite Izaz, who was busy cobbling up a political opposition. Sartaj had his own agenda. He wanted to free Sind from the clutches of the Punjabi military rulers and the milling *muhajirs*, who had encroached the economic interests of the ethnic Sindhis and Baluchis.

Sartaj's game plan was simple. He expected India to pump in more money and weapons for his supporters. The trickling support that he was getting from Delhi was inadequate. His band of followers among the ethnic Sindhis and Baluchis were fighting pitched battles against Pakistan army in isolated pockets of resistance. Their antiquated weapons were no match for the ruthless army, which freely used napalm and cluster bombs and air to ground rockets on the defenceless civilian population.

He expected the Boston meeting to be decisive, but not as decisive as the Boston Tea Party of 1846.

Bhagat's low profile appearance on a chilly evening disappointed Sartaj. He expected Mr. Balachari (code name for Nampoothiri) to come down for discussing the nitty-gritty of the scheme of collaboration explained to him by no less a person than the High Commissioner of India in London. The lakefront courtyard of the house of Sartaj's daughter was surrounded by thick vegetation. Sartaj, seated on a camp chair, did not stand up to greet his guest. His straight gaze was fixed on the placid waters of the sprawling lake.

"Sir, I'm Laxman Singh," Bhagat braved the chill reception, "I've a communication for you from Mr. Balachari."

"I expected Balachari to be here. That's what I was given to understand," Sartaj extended his palm hesitatingly, "you Indians are not decisive players. You lack the killing instinct."

"He is busy with the events at home," Bhagat digested the dig, and offered an unconvincing excuse, "lots of things are happening there."

"Yes. I'm aware of the developments in Delhi. That does not deter you people from supporting the Bengalis in East Pakistan. The army fiends in Islamabad are bleeding the Baluchis and Sindhis. You don't care even if hundreds of my countrymen are butchered by the Punjabi thugs."

"I'm sorry sir that you carry that impression," Bhagat decided to come straight to the topic, "Mr. Balachari has requested you to consider the following points."

Bhagat spoke with an air of confidence. Delhi, he said, was worried about the fractured nature of the Democratic Alliance of Pakistan (DAP). The rise of Izaz Afroz was also causing concern. The 'Ceylon Tea Party,' Izaz Afroz's secret coterie of some of the power hungry Generals, was in no way friendly to the resistance movements in Sind and Baluchistan. They were working on a different agenda. Much would depend on mass mobilisation, subversion of the police and paramilitary forces in the two provinces and support from key constituencies like the students, trade unions, and the intellectuals. Delhi was unable to decide upon a firm line of action in the absence of significant control of the leaders of the resistance movements on mass psychology.

Nevertheless, Mr. Balachari, Bhagat elaborated, was keen on supporting the movement. Kabul would continue to be the main supply base. Additional routes would be opened up through Gujarat and Sind land borders. A possible new supply route, Bhagat explained, should be the age-old Dhow (mechanised country boat) channel between Indian Jamnagar and Kati Bandar and adjacent minor ports in the estuary of the Indus. Much would depend on the leaders of the resistance movement. They should be able to mobilise a fleet of trusted dhow operators to lift supplies of weapon from the international waters.

"Mr. Balachari wants to know if you can arrange safe transit through the sea route." Bhagat finished his exposition with a relish.

His impeccable Sindhi vocabulary and style of expression had softened Sartaj. It was time for him to stand up. He walked up to the waterfront, picked up a few pebbles and threw them on the placid water. The small circular ripples mingled up with his agitated thought process. The daring suggestion of sending arms shipment through the sea route posed several challenges. He knew one person who could help him in mobilising a couple of enterprising Dhow operators. He was Zahoor Chaudry, the famous *mohana* tribal, who made it big in shipping industry. He lived in far off Lahore, a bastion of the Punjabi entrepreneurs. He was a thorough apolitical person. Sartaj was not sure if Zahoor would agree to exercise his influence on the fishing folks of Kati Bandar and the adjacent minor fishing ports.

"Tell Mr. Balachari," Sartaj turned towards his guest, "the Kabul and Gujarat routes should be activated immediately. I will soon get back on the other proposal."

"Fine sir."

Sartaj continued his soliloquy in as placid a voice as the placid water mass before him. He conveyed that Izaz Afroz should be prevented at any cost from capturing the seat of power in Islamabad. He was not capable of toppling the ailing President. The armed forces were not yet ready to hand over power to the civilians, that too to an untrustworthy jackal like Izaz. There were indications that the new Chief of Army Staff, General Arif would eventually depose the old man. Arif was incapable of leading the tottering nation. Izaz had already cast a spell on him and he was sure to lead him up the garden path. Izaz disliked Sheikh Jainal and his hatred of the Bengalis was pathogenic. It was the best time for India to hit back and help the oppressed people of Sind and Baluchistan.

"But sir," Bhagat made a sleek intervention, "Izaz appears to be riding the crest of popular support."

"It's a myth he will like the world to believe Mr. Laxman Singh. He and his band of rabble-rousers are trying to get on to the top with the help of the army Generals. You people in India should know that Izaz is as good a democrat as Hitler was." Sartaj Jamil poured out in an emotion filled voice.

"Sir, I'll convey your views to Mr. Balachari."

"Do that. And if it is possible request him to convey to Prime Minister Manjira that Sheikh Jainal is an alter ego of Izaz Afroz. Between them, they are bent upon destroying Pakistan. Jainal is an agitator and not a consummate politician. She would require a sound politician in East Pakistan. Tell her that I, as a colleague of her late father, want her to intervene in Sind and Baluchistan as passionately as she is helping the East Pakistani leaders. We Sindhis and the Baluchis have better democratic and secularist credentials than the Bengalis. It's they, who had conceived the Muslim League."

Bhagat understood that he had completed his mission and the old man had nothing else to tell except venting his frustration. He stood up and saluted the veteran freedom fighter in pure Sindhi, the mother tongue he inherited from his parents.

"You speak very good Sindhi."

"Yes sir. My parents, belonging to the untouchable Kahar caste, had migrated from Sind. In India our family had adopted the high caste title of Singh."

"That's a good news Singh. We two Sindhis can do better business. By the way, ask Balachari if he is familiar with the name of Zahoor Chaudry of Lahore."

"Anything special sir?"

"Zahoor is a *mohana* Sindhi. He owns a flourishing shipping line and some of his dhows ply between Karachi and the minor ports in Gujarat. He must be having linkages with the Indian dhow operators."

"Sure sir. I will mention this to Mr. Balachari. These are valuable suggestions sir. I don't think Mr. Balachari will have any difficulty, if you can firm up the loose ends in Pakistan."

Bhagat left the old soul alone to cook an infinite broth out of his dreams of attaining a better political status for Sind and Baluchistan. His mastery on the political history of Sind and Baluchistan was confined to the textbooks and he did not have any precise idea about the intrinsic interest of India's intelligence operations in these two provinces.

Bhagat ruminated over his exchanges with Sartaj Jamil. He took a mental note to send a cipher to Nampoothiri from Ottawa. He framed the sentences of the cipher in his mind and focussed on the formulation that under no circumstances Zahoor Chaudry should be allowed to get involved with *Operation Qalandar*. Rest of the aspects, Bhagat knew, would be decided after close interaction between the PM, NSI and a few other key ministers.

*

27

Izaz Afroz did not nurture very high respect for General Arif Khan, the new Army Chief of Staff, and the Chief Martial Law Administrator, who was handpicked by Akbar Khan. The President, more of a political conjuror than a war-hardened soldier, appreciated more the carnal qualities of his new COAS than his proven cranial credentials. General Arif blended contradictory qualities. A battle hardened soldier, he was not averse to democratic rule. However, an indecisive person, he easily succumbed to feudal pressure of the Punjabi elite and bumpy women and bouncy bottles.

Akbar Khan did not trust Lt. General Sarfaraz and the most respected Corps Commander Lt. General Hamidur. The minor fries like General Tarakki and Hyder Bux did not have the capability of conjuring up another coup. They simply did not have support of the Corps Commanders and the most respected soldier of the country, Air Chief Marshal Rahmat Khan, and universally loved Naval Chief, Admiral Shauqat. However, President Akbar had underestimated General Arif.

General Arif, like most Pakistani soldiers, harboured some vapour of ambition under his chest and considered Pakistan as the unprotected treasure chest of the people, which could be plundered at will like his illustrious warlord predecessor Nadir Shah did. However, he did not know the vanishing tricks to plunder under illusory smoke screen. He had not honed up the techniques of the alchemy that turned a mere soldier to a crowned king.

His first serious lesson in political banditry came from elder brother Maj. General Naim, who, as an intelligence technocrat, had the opportunity of peeping into the wonder world of power game dominated by the witchy combination of senior bureaucrats and ambitious soldiers. Arif finally gathered courage, gave the ultimate push to President Akbar, and crowned himself as the new ruler of Pakistan.

However, Izaz Afroz, the Pakistani incarnation of Prince Otto Von Bismarck and Charles Andre Joseph Marie De Gaulle, had other ideas in mind. He had sized up General Arif with the precision of an expert goldsmith and concluded that the time was not opportune for him to ascend the throne. There were still a couple of obstacles; the fishmonger Bengalis were as archenemy of his as the army brass were.

In Izaz's view, Sheikh Jainal was the most important challenger to his ascension. 'That half educated son of a farmer' was no match for him. He carried blue blood in his veins and had coated himself with the civilisational fineries of the west. He, and not that bumpkin from Dacca, was destined to lead Pakistan to greater glories. Majority alone was not the hallmark of democracy.

Izaz always nursed a dream, his canonisation as the second Quaid-e-Azam of the Muslim nation. Izaz's precise and latest rationalization boiled down to two priority tasks. President Akbar deserved rest. He had plundered Pakistan for over a decade and a half. General Arif, with the connivance of the 'Ceylon Tea party,' coterie of Generals, had taken over the reins of the drifting nation. It was important for him, Izaz rationalized, to attach himself to the tail end of the blundering bacchantic and his intimate circle of hungry Generals. They should, in the final count, act as his stepping-stone to the throne of Pakistan even if it meant a truncated Pakistan.

The second task evolved around the idea of teaching historic lessons to the pernicious Bengalis, like Hitler had dispensed loud lessons to the horrendous Zionists. These two races, Izaz rationalized, were irrelevant to the passage of human history. Nothing serious was going to happen if the Bengalis disappeared from the face of the earth and the Jews were buried under the desert sands. But, to drown the Bengalis in the Bay of Bengal he required the services of General Arif. A nice noose should be tied to his nose for driving Pakistan like a blind camel in sandblasted desert.

With all such revolutionary ideas in mind, Izaz Afroz picked up the phone around eleven in the morning, to call up General Arif Khan. The itch to call the new President had been scratching his mind since early morning. However, the call could not be made any sooner. His friend General Hyder Bux, the newly appointed chief of the ISI, had tipped him off about the daily routine of the *Sadr* (head of the State).

He spent most evenings at the sprawling residence of Begum Jahanara, the celebrated classical Hindustani music exponent. The power-lobby grapevine had painted Jahanara as the illusory lady luck, who favoured only the brave and the bold. She had mastered the uncanny skill of attaching herself to the ruler of the day. Begum Jahanara was not a petty pickpocket. She knew well the art of robbing the high and mighty of the land by using the finest craft of singing and the best gift of the God, her sizzling beauty. The rumour mill was agog with the bounty of luck that Jahanara had showered on the new strongman of Pakistan, General Arif Khan.

General Arif, besides losing himself in the fathomless beauty of Jahanara, often remained preoccupied with important matters like jackal shooting in the interiors of Sind and Punjab and walking the golf greens once in a while. Izaz Afroz therefore selected the appropriate needle of time to call up Pakistan's new man of destiny.

"Izaz this side. May I speak to the President?"

"Sir," a hesitant voice replied, "the President is busy. Can you call later?"

"Listen to me, whosoever you are, a captain or a colonel. I want to see the General immediately." Izaz tried to bamboozle the aide d' camp of the President.

"Sir I'm Colonel Munir here," the voice replied politely, "the boss is just getting ready. Hold on. I'll connect him."

"Hello Izaz sahib, *kaisa mizaaz* (how is the mood)?"

"It's both good and bad General. The good is that you're the rising star and the bad news is that the sick man of Dacca is haunting the nation. Can I come over?"

"Now?"

"Yes Mr. President. It is urgent."

"Come over. I'm getting ready for a chilled Heineken. Hope you'll like to share the nectar?"

Izaz Afroz lived four blocks away from the official residence of the Chief of Army Staff, who was yet to shift to the official residence of the President of the nation. It took over half an hour to get past the array of Patton and Sherman tanks, numerous armoured personnel carriers, barbed wire fences and armed pickets. The unprecedented security paraphernalia were lined up to meet contingencies arising out of the civil strife against the deposed unpopular President. General Arif was yet to crack down on the mob that had paralysed the nation.

Afroz emerged out of his Ford Classic with a great flourish. Colonel Munir conducted him to the shaded forecourt verandah, where the General was seated amidst a pile of files, a glass of frothy Heineken, and a lighted cigarette between his fingers.

General Arif did not bother to rise to greet the former minister and the architect of the 1965 war against India. He knew this jackal very well. He only wondered which axe of the Larkana jackal required urgent grinding. Izaz's machete was merciless. He had used it unscrupulously in the past to promote his political career and he would not hesitate to axe another General if he were offered the slightest chance to ride the tiger of fortune again.

"What brings the brightest star of Pakistan to my modest home?" General Arif offered a seat to Izaz and ordered Munir to pour beer for the honoured guest.

"Serious matters of the nation General," Izaz Afroz settled down and looked up appreciatively at Munir, who waited with the beer mug, "I hope you know that President Akbar is plotting a counter coup. How can he maintain secret links with traitor Jainal? Are we going to be ruled by another illiterate Bengali?"

"Cool down Izaz sahib. Let's not forget that we had chosen to attach ourselves to the Bengali majority at the dawn of independence. It's they who had championed the Muslim League concept."

"Shit!" Izaz squirmed his lips with disgust, "these Bongs are half Muslims. We can't trust them."

"I agree. Please be sure that I won't allow another Bengali to rule over the nation. We had enough of them. Anything else?"

"Oh yes. I wanted to brief you about my visits to Washington and Peking. There's good news for you. The White House thinks that you're the right leader to takeover from Akbar Khan."

"What about Peking?" General Arif asked with a squinted look at his maverick visitor.

"They appreciate your dynamic initiative in arranging the ice breaking ceremony that augured in a meeting between the US Under Secretary of State and the Deputy Premier of the Peoples' Republic of China. It's a momentous diplomatic initiative after the Cold War stalemate."

Izaz spoke with his eyes fixed on the rotund face of General Arif. He knew that this foxy bait was sure to hook the knave General.

"Look Izaz," General Arif spoke in a straight voice, "I'm a soldier. I know best how to solve a situation by pure military means. You're a politician. To you, yes means no, and no means yes. I can't indulge in double speaking. I'm waiting for this evening's meeting with the senior commanders. I'll take corrective measures after they endorse another brief spell of guided democracy under the Armed Forces. But I'll finally go by the wishes of the people of Pakistan."

"That's what I'm pleading for," Izaz spoke ebulliently, "you're the man of destiny. I'm here to support you to put down the Indian inspired civil unrest in East Pakistan."

"Let's speak about this later."

"Fine General," Izaz took the blunt hint rather nonchalantly, "but I've a couple of points to discuss."

"Fire quick. You've precise twenty minutes to empty your clip. But don't deliver another UN type marathon speech."

Izaz Afroz took the blunt hint and started with his deep-rooted suspicion about the Indian inspired movement for greater autonomy in Sind and Baluchistan. The unholy forces commanded by Sartaj Jamil, Farooq Jatoi, Sherdil Khan and Aliullah Mengel, he said, were emulating the pattern of civil unrest in East Pakistan. President Akbar Khan had tried in vain to woo these traitors. Their seditious activities could be contained only by firm military action.

"What proof do you have against them? How can you implicate Delhi?" General Arif wiped off the froth that had nestled in his bushy moustache and asked Munir to help him with a cigarette.

"You can talk to General Hyder Bux and General Naim. The ISI and the Pak Intelligence Bureau chiefs should know better. But, as the former foreign minister I can assure you that Prime Minister Manjira has adopted a double pronged strategy to destabilize Pakistan."

"I don't disagree with you," General Arif scaled down his voice, "tell me how can we get to know the precise working of the mind of that woman?"

"I know a few sure shots. Ask General Naim, if you so like, to activate Ram Karan, the Indian minister. He is our man in Delhi. My next trump card is the immediate revamping of *Operation Mardan.*"

"What's that?"

"This involves accelerated supply of weapons and resources to the tribal insurgents in the Indian North East. I have discussed this issue with our friends in

Peking. They are willing to invite a few Naga and Mizo groups to the PLA managed camps at Kunming."

"Why was *Mardan* suspended?"

"Can't say. I presume the ISI needs a little prodding."

"*Insha Allah,* we shall discuss this in a couple of days," General Arif spoke in a condescending tone, "tell me one thing straight. Will you agree to serve in a civilian government that I may put together as an interim measure?"

"Pardon me General. Possibly, I can't do that. I'm at the forefront of the Movement for Restoration of Democracy. West Pakistanis have started trusting me. You'll require a buffer between the East Bengalis and Pakistan, I mean our part of Pakistan."

"I get your point."

"I've another important point, General."

"Shoot out."

"You're the best judge of the present fighting fitness of our armed forces. We can't take on India even for a week long war if Manjira decides to hit us back at this point of our national crisis." Izaz lowered his voice as if he was discussing a matter of great conspiracy.

"I agree. But the US and its friends are not yet ready even to replenish the losses we suffered in 1965. They're harping on the conditionality of implementation of the terms of the Tashkent agreement, and some European powers have started raising the bogey of violation of human rights in East Pakistan. Do you have an answer to our problems?"

"There is a catch General," Izaz leaned towards the right ear of General Arif and spoke in a hushed tone, "the US is alarmed by the growing entente between Delhi and Moscow. They're worried about the poaching forays by the Soviet fleet in the Pacific Rim and the Indian Ocean region."

"You mean the White House will agree to supply hardware to us."

"Yes and no. They're agreeable to examine an inventory. And the supplies will have to be airlifted from friendly third country bases. Probably they will like to use some CIA front organisations to do the job."

"That suits me. What about the Chinese?"

"They too are ready to supply against hard cash in green bills. But there is a catch."

"Cough it out, clear."

"They are disinclined to deliver the merchandise at any Pakistani port. You've to tie up with a friendly Gulf government and arrange for airlifting by private cargo carriers."

"Izaz sahib," General Arif stood up, "I'm getting late for a meeting with the leaders of the religious parties. Shall we resume the discussion, say after three days?"

"No hurry General. But I want to mention that Nawab Sharief, whom I'm projecting as the next Chief Minister of Punjab, has excellent business contacts with the Pentagon and the crown prince of Sharjah. Probably you can consider him for airlifting of weapons to East Pakistan."

"These are unofficial supplies by the CIA and Chinese front agencies. Can Nawab be discreet? I believe he's a town crier."

"That's not correct General. It's a canard spread by his brother Israr."

"But, my information came from an impeccable source Izaz. Anyways, ask him to see Munir. They can discuss the preliminaries." General Arif extended his hand towards Colonel Munir for support.

"One last point General. What about joining me over a *shikar* (hunting) party at Larkana? We've plenty of pheasants, spotted deer and rare quails over there. I'm expecting both the American and the Chinese ambassadors."

Izaz threw the last bait with a shrewmouse pout in his mouth.

"Well," General Arif weighed the offer and in a split second came out with a reply, "I don't think I should disappoint the eagle and the panda, I mean the US and Chinese ambassadors, if they're willing to drink from the same pond. Hope you're taking care of the entertainment."

"Well put General! Nawab is lining up the cream of the female cine stars of Lahore. Perhaps you'll like to invite Mohtarma Begum Jahanara Sahiba also."

"Let me see Izaz. I'll sure be there if the affairs of the state allow me."

General Arif disappeared inside the sprawling bungalow through the main door. Izaz Afroz lighted a cigarette and displayed a broken smile like a happy hunter, who had just laid perfect bait for his kill. He should be able to mesmerize the lousy General by his intricate knowledge of international diplomacy and his inside knowledge of the orbital tilt of the US leadership to engage China in strategic parlays. He should be able to walk up to the throne of Pakistan over the rubbles of another military regime, the one headed by General Arif.

His pout turned to a rascally whistle when he recalled the just made remark on Nawab Sharief. Hell with it! Jahanara, the bumpy bitch, must have poisoned General Arif.

*

Afroz's other worry was the tilt-nosed Prime Minister Manjira. She had managed to consolidate her political base and her grip on Sheikh Jainal was almost complete. If his information was correct and if the CIA were to be believed, Manjira had been pumping millions to the coffers of the People's League. Izaz was not really sure about the scheming lady in Delhi. He was not an accomplished learner. More of a conjuror he thought most people around him were nitwits and he could raise tsunami of slogans and create a crescendo.

His traditional rival Manjira believed in attuned orchestration and jugglery with finesse. She was in a sulking mood that gloomy and rainy evening. It was not the rain and the slush that made her fume. A couple of juggling balls had started misbehaving. Her political adversaries had planned an audacious coup to defeat her in the forthcoming parliamentary elections. She was scheming to take them on.

A briefing by the Soviet ambassador had struck discordant notes in her inner cords. Washington and Peking were building a new geostrategic axis. Izaz Afroz, she was told, was spanning the bridge. The last thing she wanted was a diplomatic bridge that spanned the USA, China, and Pakistan. She was not disinclined to confront and demolish the jackal of Larkana. She had had enough of him in a couple of encounters in the United Nations. She would not allow that demagogue to damage her vertebrae.

She was ready to take on Izaz at a historically opportune moment. Nevertheless, her immediate strategic priority was pegged at the unorthodox idea of keeping the Pakistani Generals busy in their own home turfs, both in the east and the west. They should not find spare space to disturb her rocking political boat. The political sharks at home surrounded her ominously. She did not want a stable hostile neighbour pointing its guns at her and the nation she piloted.

Manjira was not very hopeful of the success of the movements spearheaded by Sartaj Jamil and his colleagues in West Pakistan, though she was assured of steady supply of arms by Nampoothiri's contacts in the KGB. The movement was simply not picking up. The armed forces and the religious parties had also ganged up to maim and murder the separatist activists in Sind and Baluchistan. Izaz Afroz was making common cause with the Punjabi junta. She believed that the landed Jat gentry and the Generals, who nursed harboured suspicion about the integrity of the Sindhis, would dump him sooner than later.

She naturally pinned better hopes on the movement in East Pakistan. This one weapon, if fired properly, was sure to hit the bull's eye and give her enough breathing time in the troubled North East.

The juggler Manjira often lost cool. After her meeting with the Soviet ambassador, she felt like transmitting her ire to East Pakistan with the heels of the marching army. Why was Nampoothiri dragging his feet? He could have his compulsions and she appreciated his allergic response to the Russian patronage to the Communist faction of the freedom fighters. Nevertheless, he must explore other alternatives. Some third party should be tapped for supplying weapons to the volunteer forces of the People's League. She was in no mood to give a long lease of life to the military rulers in Islamabad.

"Dewan," Manjira summoned her personal secretary, "call Nampoothiri."

"He is here ma'am, in my room."

"What's he doing here?"

"He came to personally hand over a special report. Shall I send him in?"

"Yes."

Nampoothiri's unannounced visit to the camp office of the PM was prompted by his failure to secure an early appointment before his visit to Singapore. The brief report contained only a few paragraphs about his intended meeting with Yossi Dayan, the former Mossad General, and a scrounger in the arms bazaar. He sold weapons to everyone, right from the rebel leaders in Congo to the diamond bandits in Rwanda and Burundi. His weapons reached even the drug mafia in Columbia, Peru and Panama. His deadly supplies spurred the civil wars in Peru, Haiti, and Guatemala. Yossi was a lone ranger. His corporate entity was a single man show. He did not believe in taking partners in his unique entrepreneurship.

"Did you call me ma'am?"

Nampoothiri walked into Manjira's small office room.

"Yes Balu," She removed her spectacles and rested her head on the high back chair, "did your man contact Sartaj?"

Nampoothiri gave a succinct account of Dhiren Bhagat's encounter with the elderly Sindhi leader at a Boston suburb. His request for weapons and other resources were being processed and a team of experts was examining the sea route from Gujarat to minor fishing ports in the estuary of the Indus. He did not think, Nampoothiri informed the PM, that it would be prudent to involve untested Pakistani talents like Zahoor Chaudry. Manjira nodded in silent agreement.

The Kabul route was being exclusively used for Baluchistan. That part of *Operation Qalandar* had run into trouble. The Pakistan Army had neutralized certain conduits selected by Alamgir for activating the underground tunnels to the rugged terrain of Baluchistan. Some elements of the Yusufzai tribe had betrayed the leaders of the renegade movement.

The National Security India had abandoned the Alamgir route for operational safety. A new Tajik talent had taken up the assignment in collaboration with a Mazar-e-Shariff based warlord.

"No Balu," Manjira shook her head in disapproval, "I'm not happy with the progress with your *Qalandar* operation. See this report from Moscow."

Nampoothiri collected the paper from Manjira's extended hand and silently went through the text, an unsigned note, most probably personally handed over by the Soviet ambassador in Delhi.

"Yes ma'am," Nampoothiri looked up straight into the eyes of Manjira, "I don't entirely agree with the report. I've reliable reports both from Alamgir and Triple X about the double game being played by some of the Parcham party (pro-Soviet Communist) leaders. Some Pushtoon elements in the Parcham are collaborating with Pakistan army."

"How come?"

"In that terrain," Nampoothiri continued, "tribal loyalty is stronger than ideological bondages. The Russians are overrating their followers in Kabul. The Afghan warlords are a united and dedicated lot like the Vietnamese."

"What do you suggest?"

"Our Tehran based agent has activated some smugglers from Kandahar and Herat, for delivering supplies deep into the Baluch tribal territories. Iran isn't unwilling to cooperate."

"Can we trust the regime there? It's not stable."

"Instability of the regime offers us opportunity to exploit the fortune seekers. All that you can tell Moscow is to foot the bill and our men would manage the logistics."

"I appreciate. What about your mission in the East?"

"That's a tricky problem ma'am," Nampoothiri spoke in an apologetic voice, "some of the supplies to *Meghna* by our Border Police Force from Indian ordnance factories were intercepted by the Pakistan army. These have been exhibited to the diplomatic corps and foreign media in Dacca."

"That's embarrassing."

"Yes ma'am. I'm shortly leaving for Singapore and here is an unsigned note on my new approach."

Manjira glanced through the brief report and gave it back.

"Is this man Yossi reliable?"

"None of them are. Nevertheless, he helped in our last operation against the Markaz-ISI plot to assassinate you. Yossi has a reputation of delivering the goods at the doorstep of the receivers. He is a time-tested supplier in the international trouble spots."

"What're his linkages with the CIA?"

"None. He is an independent operator."

"That's a queer world market. Explain your mechanism."

Manjira settled for a brief exposition by Balachandran Nampoothiri. She opened her eyes and asked a piercing question at the end of the fascinating narration.

"Do you think that Jainal's ragtag volunteer force can handle these sophisticated weapons?"

"I'm sure they can't. But our Mountain Division and the Special Volunteer Force experts have set up camps for training Jainal's Mukti Bahini (freedom fighters)."

"That's okay Balu. Advise Jainal to subvert the East Pakistan Rifles, the East Pakistan Infantry, and the National Service Battalions. He requires a group of trained fighters, who can take on the job of leading the Mukti Bahini. His ragtag fighters alone can't face up to the Pakistani forces. Ask Vishram Satpore to work in this direction."

"Yes ma'am."

"Does Jainal require money? Do you think he's a committed fighter?"

"I don't think he fancies monetary gains. He believes in genuine freedom for the Bengali speaking Muslims of East Pakistan. He requires weapons and seasoned fighters."

"Engage your trusted men to subvert the key mid-formation Bengali army officers and the top police officers. And take care that your Israeli link is not compromised. I have that damn Muslim problem at home and abroad. My forthcoming visit to Egypt and Iran should not be clouded by your operations. Do what is required to be done, but don't get caught."

"That's well understood ma'am."

Manjira gave an affirmative nod. Yes. Nampoothiri could unzip his bag of dirty tricks.

*

28

Nampoothiri, accompanied by Amrita, boarded a JAL flight to Tokyo that very night. He had ruled out the suggestion of taking a direct flight to the Straits Island. Prying eyes and minds were sure to ask inconvenient questions if the NSI chief flew into Singapore, tucking under arms his vivacious secretary. Her presence was sure to enliven Delhi's gossip-glitterati, some of whom were regular booze-clients of foreign missions, Pakistan included.

The deception was well calibrated. Amrita's presence would give, he thought, a natural cover of a holidaying husband-wife duo. She would look more natural than a Thai or Chinese holiday-paramour grid locked with aged western social laggards. He had planned to take a third country flight, the Garuda International, from Tokyo to Singapore, scheduled to land at the Changi airport around four in the morning.

Yossi Dayan was seated under a miniature palm grove at Singapore's Grand Capthome Waterfront hotel. He was feigning to watch a group of lively American ladies sunbathing at the poolside. Women did not enthuse him anymore. He had lost his mother at an Austrian concentration camp. He was forced to see the rape of his sister by a bunch of drunken Gestapo soldiers, who later consigned her to the gas chamber. Those horrific memories had prevented him from settling down in married life.

He had dedicated his life to the newborn country of the Jews, after his US army tenure ended with the fall of Berlin. His bizarre arms bazaar business was not a simple death peddling entrepreneurship. Income generated by Yossi was canalized to two Jewish underground outfits, which were committed to fighting the Islamic forces of Al Fatah, the PLO, and the freelancing terrorist groups headed by Abu Nidal. Securing Israel against the marauding Islamic forces had become a passion for him.

Balachandran Nampoothiri's cryptic message delivered through the Rio de Janeiro station of the NSI had immensely intrigued Yossi. The Indian rulers had imposed on themselves the funny diplomatic logic of ostracizing the Jewish nation with a view to pampering the Muslims at home and abroad. They even refused to engage the valiant people of Israel in any meaningful dialogue. What was then the call from the NSI chief for? Was there another crisis in Delhi? Did he require additional eavesdropping devices? Doubtful. The NSI chief was not required to travel all the way to Singapore for a minor job.

Yossi's concentration was broken by the light footsteps of Amrita and Nampoothiri.

'Hello old boy," Nampoothiri greeted the Israeli General with usual gusto, "what're you doing here?"

Yossi looked at the approaching figures and stood up to greet them. He hugged Amrita and planted a kiss on her forehead.

"How have you been dear?"

"Fine uncle. How have you been?"

"Not bad. Globe trotting and selling weapons."

"Aren't you going to rest?"

"Rest? Why not dear? But I've some civilisational serpents to take care. Anyways, I'm happy that you could come."

"Who're these serpents uncle?"

"They are the Islamists. They've been plaguing my nation from day one and it continues to plague all its civilisational ancestors, including your Hinduism."

"Oh no uncle! That's perhaps not correct." Amrita was aghast at the suggestion of Yossi.

"It's fine child. You're too young to understand the inner meaning of civilisational conflict."

"So General, can I sit down? Hope your family powwow is over?"

"Sorry Balls," Yossi profusely apologized and drew a chair next to Nampoothiri, "I'm really intrigued. What brings the Indian intelligence chief to an Israeli outcaste? Hope no more assassination bid by the ISI."

Nampoothiri took out a small radio set from his pocket, set the needle to a music station, and actuated the volume at a high pitch. He was not fascinated by the lilting Chinese tune. He required the ambience noise before he opened his mouth. He spoke at a monotonously low voice.

"Can you take up an assignment from me?"

"Me? Why not? But spell out the damn job."

"It's a complicated job. You've to supply a good quantity of small and medium arms, ammunition and spares and demolition materials."

"Fine. That's how I earn my bread. But tell me more about the target area."

"You've to deliver the supplies at St Martin, Sandeep, Bhola and Bibir Char islands, all located off the coast of East Pakistan. Here is a map of the target landing sites, this is a new terrain and the people are new. Do you want to take the risk? There is good money in it."

"So you want to fuel the fire in East Pakistan? No problem with me, if these damn Muslims get another drubbing. However, I will deliver the goods only to the people accredited by you. I prefer confidentiality over profit."

"No problem Yossi," Nampoothiri lighted a Havana and spoke through the cloud of smoke, "the whole operation is top secret. I'll advance half a million US dollars. Collect the cash from my man at Rome. Start delivering the consignments by September end."

"Fine. Will some Vietnam surplus suit your job?"

"I understand you want to use the Aranya Prathet and Phuket bases of Thailand. Am I correct?"

"Correct. Don't fear the CIA bogey. My suppliers are a few American Generals, who are in the habit of making quick bucks out of the miseries of the people of Vietnam. They've no ideological loyalty to the Pentagon and the White House. They'll supply to Pakistan if you refuse to take their stuff on damn moral grounds Give me your inventory."

"I don't carry one. My Rome man will hand it over to you. Don't disappoint me."

"Cheer up old boy. My record is impeccable, you know that", Yossi lighted a cigarette and spoke in a gutsy voice, "tell your navy not to buzz my boats. They should maintain radio silence even if they detect my trawlers. The CIA should not get any whiff of the transaction. They're sure to rush in a couple of destroyers and frigates from Diego Garcia and Singapore to thwart your design."

"No problem. I suggest you hire some Thai trawlers and assign some codes to them. Give me the details of your flotilla and their codes. My man at Bangkok will liaise with you."

"Fine Balls. But I wouldn't like to contact him in the Indian embassy."

"No need. Keep this Nana Road address. His name is Parijat Rao, a man who moves at the fringes of flesh trade."

"You keep nice company Balls!"

"In your and my trade the quivers are always full of strange arrows."

"I'll like to see you in London before the first consignment is shipped."

"No. London does not suit. Meet me in Paris. I am supposed to attend a meeting there in another 15 days," Nampoothiri stood up, his eyes restlessly scanning the visible vicinity, "I'll share with you the profile and photographs of the people designated to take delivery of the hardware. Ensure that the correct people contact your men."

"Okay friend. It is a deal. Alert me if there's any change. See you dear." Yossi hugged Amrita, "take care. See you soon."

Nampoothiri, followed by Amrita, slowly drifted away from the seafront.

"A nice person, isn't he?" Nampoothiri made a vague comment.

"Sure sir. And a deadly man too."

"Well dear," Nampoothiri gave a lungful puff at his Havana, "life itself is a deadly game. I've to play it by the rules set up by the Prime Minister. She wants to cook the goose of Pakistan and I'm supposed to be her kitchen assistant. That's how the games of strategic diplomacy are played. It's another name for war, indirect and direct."

"Wait a minute sir," Amrita took out a small receiver set from her unusually largish vanity bag, "there is a call from Delhi."

"Who is calling?"

"It's a message from Robin Achariya. He wants you to talk to him immediately." Robin, Nampoothiri's Pakistan desk analyst, was not supposed to use the emergency channel. That was preserved for his number two, Bhagirath Banerjee, and Dewan in the Prime Minister's office.

"Okay dear. Let's rush to the Robinson Road office of the Indian trade representative."

"Would you not like to go to the Grange Road office of the High Commissioner?"

"No dear. The Robinson road fellow is my cover man. I can use his communication facilities. Those are safer. Grange road fellow is a loud mouth drum beater." Amrita hailed a cab and asked the inscrutable Chinese face to take them to the residence of George Dayal, the Indian trade representative.

"Hello Robin," Nampoothiri locked himself inside the small communication cubicle and spoke to his desk analyst, "what's the big problem?"

"Sorry for intervention sir," Robin Achariya spoke slowly over the secured phone, "there is a special dispatch from TX."

"Go ahead."

"He wants another live session for consultation."

"Fine. Ask him to hold on and wait for activation of the Mountain channel."

"Okay sir. I'll shoot a cipher." Robin disconnected.

Nampoothiri emerged out with a smile painted on his face.

"Okay dear," he smiled at Amrita, "we take a flight to Tokyo tonight. I've an appointment at Geisha Sukimoto's teahouse."

Amrita smiled back. She knew well that her boss was not made of the stuff to spend his leisure at a Geisha teahouse. This small ruse was intended to befool George Dayal. Amrita was not new to such crisp jokes from Nampoothiri. That's what kept his old body and young heart going steady even at the gravest point of crisis.

She concluded from his demeanour that Nampoothiri was anticipating another storm, perhaps a stranger, and stronger one.

*

Kathmandu's hotel Pashupati, located at the southern suburb of the dusty capital city, was a nondescript lodge, mostly used by hotchpotch pilgrims. Named after Lord Pashupatinath, Nepal's presiding deity, the hotel was shunned by the tourist crowd with bulging pockets.

That suited Dhiren Bhagat, who arrived at the lodge accompanied by his real life wife. The quiet homemaker was dragged out for providing a convincing cover to the sudden visit to the Nepalese capital.

Bhagat woke up around midnight, whispered something into his wife's ears, and walked down to a phone booth operated from a shack next to the temple. This rare facility was installed by the Durbar (royal court) for facilitating the believers, who came to cremate their near and dear ones at the bank of river Bagmati, down below the temple.

After a couple of futile attempts, he finally accessed the Lahore number of Triple X, at hotel Mughal-e-Azam, a small establishment with a big name.

"Mamu (maternal uncle) here. Am I speaking to my nephew?"

"Yes Mamu," Harfan replied using a pre-fixed code, "my sister's *nikah* (marriage) has been fixed. The boy is from Sahiwal. I want some monetary help."

"No problem. But you have to personally pick up the money. I can't get out. Your aunt is unwell. How much would you require?"

There was a short pause.

Bhagat's code was meant for inviting Triple X to the Nepalese capital, and the numerical digit of the amount stood for the days Triple X would take to reach Kathmandu.

"Can't you come to the River?"

"No. As I said your aunt is not well."

"Okay Mamu," Harfan replied in a cautious voice, "I'd like to have a loan of Rs. 40, 000."

"No dear nephew," Bhagat replied, "I can't spare that much. I can afford only two."

"Three?"

"No. Two. That's final. Call me at 46097."

"Okay."

Harfan Bukhari, the roving executive of Israr International, arrived in Kathmandu on the second day after his coded conversation with Dhiren Bhagat. The Royal Nepal Air DC 10 flight from Karachi touched down at 19.00 hrs at the Tribhubhan airport. Harfan availed of a stage carrier to reach Hotel Sagarmatha (Everest). He moved out well after midnight with a north Indian headgear and a prominent red lipstick mark on his forehead. The genuine Hindu guise was necessary to hide his Muslim identity. He hailed a taxi and drove straight for the Pashupatinath temple.

Bhagat, attired in *daura-surual* (traditional Nepali dress) was seated on the stairs that winded down to the narrow stream below. Funeral pyres burnt all around, amidst loud recitation of *mantras* and occasional outburst of cries from the grieving family members.

Harfan did not take time to locate Dhiren Bhagat. Attired in ordinary shirt and dhoti he did not look different from the surrounding crowd. He sat down next to Bhagat and asked if the time and place were propitious enough for lighting a cigarette. Bhagat gave an affirmative nod and extended his fingers for a fag. He also felt the urge to smoke. The ambience scenario and the smell of burning human flesh had sickened him. Nevertheless, he had chosen the safest rendezvous for eluding the prying eyes of the ISI operatives, who had already established safe havens in the Nepalese capital.

"It's a nice RV. Isn't it?" Bhagat asked.

"Yes. It's the place of ultimate truth. We all end up here, eventually. Aren't you worried that some day someone will burn your body in one of those piles of wood?"

"No, not at all. That's the way we have to go," Bhagat tried to size up the expression on the face of Harfan, "what's the big story?"

"Big enough to warrant a meeting in this bizarre crematorium," Harfan spoke in a hushed voice, "I'm scared of this place."

"It's the safest place. Tell me the story. I've to fly back tomorrow."

"It's an interesting story. Listen carefully."

Harfan's story was fascinating indeed.

Pakistan, he said, had become an unfathomable whirlpool of conspiracies. President Arif Khan was conspiring to consolidate his position in collaboration with Lt. General Hamidur, the Corps Commander of Chak Lala, and the garrison chiefs of Peshawar, Lahore and Karachi. They favoured installation of a puppet civilian government and a sham election to the revived National Assembly. They were hopeful that some fringe political and religious groups could be manoeuvred to gain workable majority both in the eastern and the western wings. With a titular PM in position, the armed forces could run the show for at least another two decades.

Inside the armed forces two more factions, one headed by Lt.General Sarfaraz Lodi, the Principal Staff Officer (PSO) to the President and the Chief Martial Law Administrator (CMLA), and the other spearheaded by Lt. Gen Hyder Bux, chief of the Inter Services Intelligence, were vying with each other for staging another coup. They waxed and waned in a love and hate relationship. They were not against a limited collaboration, but were highly suspicious of each other.

General Naqibullah Sayeed, the chief defence advisor to the CMLA, headed another nucleus of conspirators. He expected support from a faction of the junior officers, especially from the artillery and cavalry regiments. His efforts to rope in Air Marshal Rahmat and Admiral Shauqat were yet to succeed. The Air chief nursed his own ambitions and he was mostly seen fraternizing with Izaz Afroz and a few more politicians from Punjab and the North West Frontier Province.

"Where does Izaz stand?" Bhagat asked.

"He is everywhere," Harfan continued his story, "he thinks he can manoeuvre the CMLA and obstruct Sheikh Jainal from capturing the prime ministerial slot. The CMLA is not averse to the idea of playing up Jainal and Izaz against each other."

"It's a fine ring circus."

"Yes. But Izaz is the most ambitious of all the trapeze artists. He thinks he can jump in the void and land on the laps of both Washington and Peking."

"A nice analysis Harfan. It's all known to our desk officers, I presume so. Where is the meat?"

"So, you think that history has no meaning in the evolution of a nation?"

"When did I say that?"

"You're too impatient Bhagat. I'm coming to the meat, a lot of it." Harfan started with the revealing story of secret parlays between General Arif, the US President and the Deputy PM of China. These top-secret contacts were being developed in collaboration with Izaz Afroz in Pakistan and the Secretary of State in Washington.

"That's real big news."

Bhagat pinched another cigarette from Harfan who too lighted another and continued briefing his handling officer.

"Yes. Here is copy of a secret note smuggled out of the office of the CMLA. Tell Papa that Washington now wants to engage Peking with a view to opening up trade and to explore the feasibility of weakening the flanks of the USSR."

"Where does Pakistan stand in this strategic shift by the USA and China?"

"General Arif thinks the USA and China will guarantee his continuity and they will resume supply of much needed military hardware."

"That's a cute arrangement."

"Yes, both cute and ugly. My friends say that Peking has agreed to supply Pakistan ground to air and air to air missiles to balance the Russian supply of SAM missiles to Delhi."

"That's not cute."

"Yes. And the other ugly story is that Izaz is trying to extract some promise from Washington and Peking, that in the event of a tie between him and Sheikh Jainal they should support him. I believe he has been given some assurance by the US Secretary of State."

"So, Pakistan is in for a big fun!" Bhagat leaned back against the pillar of the structure that resembled a sacred bull.

"Yes. But a funny Pakistan may turn out to be highly indigestible to Delhi's stomach," Harfan spoke in his usual flowery language, "Israr International, my company, and a few other big money grabbers have been sounded out by the CMLA office to submit estimates for airlifting military hardware from the Gulf countries, Saudi and Turkey."

"Why are they using private operators?"

"Simply because neither Washington nor Peking wants to be caught red handed in this power balancing game. They've resumed playing dirty geostrategic games in our region. That should worry Delhi."

"Are you sure of grabbing the contract?"

"That depends on a number of factors like humouring the seemingly first lady and greasing a number of key palms. My bossman is an expert in this field."

"Thanks for the.briefing Harfan," Bhagat made a move for disengaging the rendezvous, "What is your schedule?"

"I meet the Nepalese defence minister, may be in another two days, and submit a tender for supplying 3000 small weapons to the Royal Nepal Army."

"What are the details?"

"Sorry Bhagat. This is a trade secret. I'll let you know when we start supplying the toys. Don't force me to compromise on this and ask Delhi not to raise a hue and cry till the supply line is uncorked."

"Well, you understand...."

"I understand Bhagat. Nepal's acquisition of 3000 pieces of small weapons will not endanger India's strategic security. Tell papa that from Kathmandu I will fly to Dacca and return to Karachi via Bangkok."

"Any special significance?"

"Little bit. Israr International has grabbed a contract for shipping half a million metric tons of rice from Thailand to Chittagong. Nothing to do with your trade."

"I'm afraid Harfan," Bhagat brought out a piece of paper from his pocket and focused a pencil torch beam on it, "have a look at it."

Harfan examined the list carefully under the torch light beam and returned it to Bhagat.

"Yes. It's a list of a few important Bengali followers of Sheikh Jainal in Pakistan army and air force."

"Hope you know them?"

"I intimately know only two."

"Here is a micro tape. Consume the contents in the confines of your hotel room and destroy it. Give a feedback after your Dacca visit is over."

"Fine. Don't ask me to stretch too much. The People's League leaders are treated as Indian agents. I don't like the idea of being identified with them. That's a security risk."

"It's a one time job. Give us a response on the feasibility of subverting some Bengali officers of the EPI, EPR and other formations."

"Okay. But this should be my last assignment in East Pakistan."

"Any whiff of danger?"

"Not yet. I think my boss's rising fortune has caused heartburns in high places. Business competition has degenerated into gangsterism over there."

"Another point Harfan," Bhagat brought out another piece of paper from his pocket, "here is a list of senior Generals of Pak army. Boss wants an independent assessment about their potential."

"Potential for what? Are you thinking of a counter coup?"

"I really don't know. Deliver the material at our River contact point."

"Okay. But listen carefully. The main tussle is between General Sarfaraz and General Hyder. The joker of the pack, however, is Izaz. He has the capability of giving an uncertain spin to the events in Pakistan."

"Are you in touch with Sarfaraz?"

"No. He is a big shot, the hero of Samba and Khem Karan wars against India. I believe Alam is in touch with him. Watch this General out."

Harfan stood up and fished out a closed envelope from his pocket.

"Reach this money to my mother."

He turned on his heels after a quick glance at his watch. The needles told him that it was past three in the morning. The busy crematorium had also went into a slumber, except a few dogs, which were sniffing around for left out unburned human flesh.

"You know Harfan..." Bhagat tried to protest.

"I know Bhagat. Your work ethics does not permit you to reach the money to my mother. You also know that you'd do that. Good night...I mean good morning."

"You're impossible. Yes, contact your London friends. The Dehradun medicines should reach in a couple of days."

"That's great. Thanks for the help."

Harfan, Delhi's Triple X walked up the stairs, stood before the image of Lord Pashupatinath, and briefly prayed for Jamilla, their son Pervez and Kasturi, his mother. Bhagat noticed the queer behaviour of his trained agent and smiled. The charlatan of Delhi university campus had undergone vast transformation. Ramendra had matured in a big way. But he was not yet sure about the continued placidity of this bottled typhoon. He waited for a couple of minutes and turned his tired steps towards his den, and hoped he should find the warm body of his wife more inviting than the drudgery of witnessing the last journey of over a dozen of human souls.

*

29

Lt. General Sarfaraz Lodi, Principal Staff Officer to the President and the Chief Martial Law Administrator, often suffered bouts of black depression. Joy and melancholy, ambition and despair fleeted past his psyche like early spring light and shadows. The embers of ambition burnt incessantly, somewhere inside, but the fragrance of lady luck always eluded him. This was a childhood trait, which was imprinted as a permanent scar after his mother deserted her husband and eloped with a tycoon. Success always slipped out through his fingers. In short, Sarfaraz was an edgy person. Never could he grab the lustrous locks of lady luck.

That bout of despair revisited him once again. His mental focus delved deep inside and told him that frustration and misfortune had cast evil shadows on his life and career in a cosmic conspiracy. His depression wasn't simply a post-fifty hormonal disorder. Something was wrong with his stellar configurations.

A decorated officer of the 1942 North African campaign and a shining star of two wars against India, General Sarfaraz suffered from the nagging feeling of being star crossed. It was only five years ago, during the 1965 war, when his cavalry and infantry columns had penetrated up to Khemkaran, deep inside the Indian territory. Amritsar, his birthplace, was within the reach of his tank artillery. But for the command headquarters he would have celebrated his birthday at the old residence at Galli Jallianwala Bagh. *Allah* alone knows for what reason the GHQ dithered and allowed the Indians to open up new fronts, threatening Lahore and Sialkot. His cavalry had to beat a hasty retreat. Dame destiny had betrayed him again. A Cancerian, he should have been at the peak of power by this time; but for this imbecile General Arif Khan, the Peshawari rank impostor.

Why should President Akbar Khan hand over power to the bumbling General Arif! Why not him? That incompetent bundle of contradictions mostly frittered away the nation's time and money by serenading the flaming beauty and soprano, Malika Jahanara.

The imbecile Khan, with indulgent support from a few drug-baron Generals and the Sind fox, Izaz Afroz, whose opportunism out-smarted Opportunity itself, had transformed Pakistan into a pocket borough. They were eating out the very fibre of the nation.

Trrr...ring...ring...

The intercom buzzed.

"What the hell's happening? Why are you disturbing?" Sarfaraz shouted back at his secretary, as his woolly thoughts suddenly snapped.

"Sir there's a call from General Hyder Bux..." the secretary paused for a while.

"Okay. Put him through."

"Hello sir," Hyder Bux, the ISI chief, came alive on the line, "I need your time.

Something urgent has come up."

"Come on in." Sarfaraz disconnected.

Sarfaraz travelled back to his dark tunnel.

The Peshawari General, Sarfaraz uttered a curse, had managed to win over the support of a few key Corps Commanders and had mastered the art of pitting the power hungry and myopic politicians against each other. Their foxy rancour had buoyed up his stranglehold on the nation. He cared less if the Generals and their political hyenas gnashed teeth at the life and soul of the nation.

Only *Allah* knew what the Americans and the Chinese had seen in this man, whose upper limbic portion was devoid of grey material. But for the tacit support of the CIA and the Chinese State Security Bureau, this nincompoop would have been wallowing in the gutter of oblivion.

Hell with it! He should fly at once to London and consult Pundit Uma Shankar. That Hindu astrologer alone could decipher what the stars and planets had in store for him. He couldn't openly go to a Hindu pundit in this damn country. There were none around. Even if there were one, his devout Muslim colleagues would construe that as a sacrilegious unislamic act.

He was indeed surrounded by the bloody pack of pseudo religious wolves. Yes. This arms peddler Alam Khan was, perhaps, not wide off the mark, when he advised him to drift closer to the CIA bosses and the leaders of the Pakistani lobby in the US Senate and the Congress. A little wink from Langley, Pentagon, and the White House and even a passing nod from 10 Downing Street should be good enough to jump for the throne of Pakistan.

They should understand that only he could stall Russian consolidation in the Central Asian Republics and Afghanistan. The dogma of Communism could only be fought by Islamic resurgence. Only the Islamic forces of Pakistan and the *Ummah* (Pan-Islamic fraternity) could tame India, a keystone of the arch of Red Evil. He was the only competent Pakistani, capable of destroying the votaries of that satanic arch.

The cerebral light focused on his inner self. Yes, he was a lonely traveller. And a lonely traveller mostly ends up as an anonymous traveller. Sulking alone, without powerful alliance inside the establishment would lead him nowhere. Real politics was a different ball game, and Pakistan had, in the true sense of the term, become a soccer ground for the Chinese and the American power strikers. To kick the ball past the net he required borrowing their shooting skills. The local chieftains like Hyder Bux and Izaz Afroz could not be ignored. They had their own rules for kicking Pakistan around.

General Hyder Bux and Lt. General Amanullah, GOC in C of the 3rd Corps, were potential allies. However, each one of them, Sarfaraz suspected, harboured sky-skimming ambition below their chests. It was a dog-eat-dog situation.

What about Izaz Afroz? Thank heavens! The wily Sindhi, though rabidly anti-Bengali and anti-Indian, nourished his own political agenda. The super-sycophant, a suspected US stool pigeon, wouldn't stop at anything to realise his ambition, which was the gilt-edged throne of Pakistan.

Major General Hyder Bux, a puritan Muslim, rather a *mullah* in uniform and a thorough professional, besides other compelling commitments, had managed to keep the discreet alleys to the doorsteps of the boss-man well greased. The spymaster didn't, Sarfaraz knew, act in harmonious orchestration with the Intelligence Bureau chief, elder brother of the CMLA. No General in uniform, nursing even a thin vapour of ambition under his chest, would trust a colleague. Not in Pakistan.

Could he trust Hyder? A colleague could perhaps never be a friend, at least not the ISI chief. Trained by the CIA and British SAS, Hyder had his roots well embedded both in the ISI and the SSG. How could he trust the master of the black arts? Lt. General Sarfaraz lighted another cigarette and looked up at the front wall. The room was garishly decorated by restricted operational maps occupying three of the four walls. He tried to identify the location of the Corps Headquarters and important cantonments. Well! General Omar, Chief of the Armed Forces, Sarfaraz knew quiet well, was aligned to the wavelength of the Sind fox. In the event of a decisive putsch against General Arif he would require the support of the key loyal formations. That required, Sarfaraz mused, a contingency plan, to neutralise the Chief within the first few minutes of the coup. Could he count on the support of Lt. General Hamidur? He took a mental note to explore that horizon.

Well! He would need the SSG chief General Shaukat Ghori's help for securing a remote guesthouse somewhere in the hills for comfortable incarceration of the Army Chief and a few Generals loyal to him.

"Sir," the young Captain, Sarfaraz's aide de camp, saluted smartly and parroted hastily, "The President's military secretary says that he's busy and can't see you today."

"Am I pleased to hear this, young man?"

Sarfaraz interjected jocularly. His frustration stemmed from the hide and seek played by the Head of the State. The boss preferred to remain enchanted by Begum Jahanara's biological flames. Even pressing affairs of the State couldn't eject him out of the pleasure hole for days together. He knew the reason for such extreme pre-occupation, snoring away his time between the thighs of that bitch.

The last four days had been very excruciating. The US ambassador had called twice seeking an urgent appointment with the President. A Saudi delegation was cooling heels in a five-star hotel for strategic discussions. But the CMLA refused to respond.

"And sir," the young Captain reported, synchronising the clicking sound of his boots and voice, "Mr. Izaz Afroz is here. He says it's urgent."

"How urgent? Can't it wait unzipping of the fly?" Sarfaraz threw the innocent joke at his junior, "okay. Don't blush like a virgin sixteen. Bring him in."

*

Izaz Afroz, immaculately dressed in an all white three-piece suit and jet black Gucci, entered with a flourish.

"Hello General." Izaz extended his hand, but placed just the fingertips in the warm wide palm of Sarfaraz. It was just a ritual body contact, not even transmitting the slightest of warmth. He hated these creatures in uniform, half-witted, and mostly illiterate with bottomless thirst for power and money. He had seen enough of them, starting with Pakistan's first tryst with military rule. One tenth of his palm was good enough a gesture of greeting for these creatures.

"How're you Izaz sahib? Please be seated." Sarfaraz, not a less wily jackal, wiped his palm with a napkin, threw it in a dustbin and asked politely, "what can I offer you?"

"*Takalluf mat kijiye* (*d*on't take the trouble)." Izaz looked doubtfully at the discarded napkin.

"It's a pleasure. I'm your admirer and fan. I'm simply mesmerised by your speeches in the U.N. I'm convinced that you're a greater orator than Burke and Disra...."

"Don't joke Sarfaraz. I'm a common Pakistani. Why embarrass me?"

Izaz scrutinised the wall map and continued, "What're you doing with that Indian spy, Sheikh Jainal? Why is the President soft on him? Why can't he be hanged?" Izaz Afroz expressed his anguish in impeccable English with a few mispronounced Urdu words thrown in.

"What can I do Izaz sahib? The President has no access to professional advice."

"Don't you see, these Bengalis had started this damned movement way back in the sixties? They're half-bred Muslims, mostly converted low caste Hindus *ajlafs*. Why don't you advise the President to shoot that rabid Jainal?"

"I appreciate your views Izaz sahib."

Sarfaraz added that the situation had taken difficult turn. The professional civil servants had lost access to the President. He believed that the previous martial law administration had failed, because they had trusted too much the civilian sissies. The civilians had goofed up but the military faced the flaks. This time around, he was determined to do everything and take the credit too.

Sarfaraz hoped Izaz would understand the dig. It was he, who, as the Foreign Minister, had pushed General Akbar to launch Operation Gibraltar and Grand Slam against India in 1965. He did everything except lead the forces at the front.

"Do you agree with this shit? Don't you think that the permanent bureaucracy have some virtues? They shouldn't be kept outside the decision making loop." Izaz sipped coffee slowly and posed the questions at Sarfaraz, looking straight at his face, almost in a hypnotic trance.

"I'm not in a position to judge the intrinsic merits of the decisions taken by the CMLA. I'm a technocrat and not a politician like you." Sarfaraz gestured with a feeling of helplessness using his fingers and facial muscles.

"I'm told that the CMLA thinks that my party and that of traitor Jainal aren't likely to secure absolute majority and he can install a puppet government by cobbling up a rag-tag coalition of the political scum." Izaz exploded in a full-throated condemnation of the election assessment of the CMLA.

"Izaz sahib," Sarfaraz again shrugged, "these assessments are done by the PIB and ISI, you know better."

"Yes. I know General Naim, the celebrity elder brother, and Hyder Bux, related to another bed-hopping film starlet, is no better. Do you ask me to buy their sob stories? Anyways, take it from me, there can't be any constitutional solution without me."

"I'm not really aware if the President has received any election assessment. I think it's too early." Sarfaraz tried to avoid the politician, whom he considered unprincipled and unscrupulous.

"Anyways Sarfaraz, I'm not here to debate the national elections. I know the mood of the people. They want me. It's me or deluge. Help me by fixing a meeting with the President."

"Izaz sahib," Sarfaraz spoke politely, "I thought you've free access to the *Sadr*. As you know, I don't fix his appointments. You've to call his military secretary or better call Col. Munir."

"I've been doing that since I returned from Peking." Izaz spoke contemptuously, "there are important messages both from Washington and Peking."

"Must be. Can't we talk over that?"

"Sorry Sarfaraz," Izaz winked at the PSO, "certain things can't be shared even with the PSO."

"As you wish," Sarfaraz lighted another cigarette, and spoke through half parted lips, "all that I can do is to send a note to the *Sadr* stressing the urgency of your message."

"Please do that, and tell him that the US Secretary of State should be in Islamabad next month. And the Chinese Foreign Minister wants to transit through Karachi on his way to Cairo. These are important visits."

"Certainly these are, Izaz sahib! The CMLA must be aware of this," Sarfaraz tickled the former foreign minister on one of his usual ego trips, "you alone can get the tiger and the cow lick salt at the same hole. I believe, besides shooting rabbits, you and the top boss had a good meeting at Larkana. Is there any possibility of postponement of the polls?"

"Look General," Izaz spoke patronisingly, "that was a strategic *shikar* (hunting) outing. The President had good exchanges with the US and the Chinese ambassadors."

"I understand so. Are there new strategic directions from Washington and Peking?"

"Well Sarfaraz, East Pakistan has become a playground of that stupid woman, Manjira. Both Washington and Peking are highly suspicious about her moves in East Pakistan. We can't trust these Bengali fishmongers any more. I don't know why the CMLA has agreed to a one-man one-vote formula. The fucking Bongs are too many and they would simply inundate us."

"There I agree with you. We in the West are aligned to the Islamic mainstream. The eastern Muslims are fakes. How can we allow them to rule over us?"

"That's what some of you don't understand. Join and support me. I know how to drown these fishmongers in the Bay of Bengal." Izaz waived his hand vaguely.

"Anytime Izaz sahib. That'll be an immense pleasure." Sarfaraz flavoured his words with a sharp whistling.

"That's a promise?"

"Promise."

"Get your khakis starched, and get your gun oiled. We'll need you soon." Izaz Afroz extended his palm and held the fingertips of Sarfaraz in a firm squeeze. He left the room, leaving behind tons of airs from his leaking ego-bag and exotic French perfume.

"Fool!" Sarfaraz uttered a curse, "the Bongs are better than this Indus marsh jackal. My foot! I won't even go for a decent guesthouse to detain him. A small hole in Dera Ismail jail should be good enough for the ego-bag."

*

The young aide de camp entered again with a metallic click of the heels and a palm shaking salute.

"Sir… ."

"What's next?"

"General Hyder, sir… ."

"Show him in… ."

General Hyder Bux entered from a side door, offered the customary salute, and settled on a chair that faced the PSO.

"A stormy and perfumed visit indeed…" He alluded to the aroma left behind by Izaz Afroz, who was in the habit of using a costly brand of French perfume.

"Yah.... He wants us to join his brigade. Shit! What do you think of him? Can he be trusted?"

"Sir, don't trust any Sindhi. This womaniser is from the womb of a Hindu mother."

"Oh Hyder!" Sarfaraz laughed, "You intelligence people are impossible. I'm concerned with his ambition and not his women. Women are fleeting clouds, they come and go. Izaz is our competitor. You can't shoo him out."

"Don't worry sir. If I can't shoo I can shoot. I'll make him walk the planks before he climbs the throne. Pakistan is ours and we'll share it, between you and me."

"Well said, Hyder. Tell me, what can I do for you?"

"I've some audio tapes. These are from Jahanara's bedroom and will give you a fair idea of the *Sadr*'s state of mind."

Hyder Bux fished out two tapes and placed before Sarfaraz.

"Be discreet Hyder. Slight leakage will cost our necks. We can't afford to have an out of leash tigress roaming the streets of Islamabad. She will eat us raw."

"It's the only shortcut to many of his secrets. That's what had given us definite clues on the boss-man playing the Izaz card to stall the rabid Bongo, Jainal. We've to build up a case against him before we shoo or shoot him."

"Take care. The elder brother, the PIB chief, is counter-snooping on you and me. Izaz is a fleeting ghost. His visits are ominous. How far are you from making a demon out of Jainal? Under no circumstances should the boss-man play his game." Sarfaraz whispered into Hyder's ears.

"Don't worry. I'm keeping a tab on General Naim too. I've tapped Izaz through a different channel. The Chinese friends will ensure that he sabotages all rapprochement efforts between Jainal and the boss." Hyder whispered back.

"That's fine. Any political settlement, with either Izaz or Jainal on the throne will mean our sacking or imprisonment. Anyways, what's special about the tape?"

"I suspect she has picked up a new lover...some Harun, may be Hanif; not sure. Noise pollution was really frustrating."

"That infinite hole can take on anything. However, take care. She's all eyes and ears. She guards the *Sadr* like a mother eagle and hardly allows him to fly out."

"Another point boss," Hyder whispered, "General Tarakki...you know the doormat... He's gaining importance. His wings require clipping."

"Don't worry. Keep Tarakki's links with Izaz under watch. These two can give us real headaches. We've to get Tarakki implicated in controversial acts, may be in Dacca. And ensure that the boss does not make up with General Hamidur. We've to isolate him from the important commanders."

"Consider it done. Bye, I've some urgent matters to attend."

"Just one more point Hyder," Sarfaraz brought his lips closer to Hyder's ears, "keep an eye on General Omar, the Chief of Army Staff. I think he's playing a different symphony."

"Don't worry. He's fully wired up. I've tapped two key Corps Commanders. We can count on the cavalry regiments and the Vice Air Chief will fly with us. Just take care of the timing and keep my interests in view."

"You're the new Chief of Army. That's what *Allah* has ordained."

"*Amin* (so be it). *Khuda Hafiz*."

General Hyder Bux offered a smart salute and left through a side door.

General Sarfaraz pondered over the brush contacts he had with Izaz and Hyder. Two distinct hangmen were loitering around him with fancy nooses. None of them could be relied upon. Could he even use them as props? Were not they too slippery props? Perhaps they were.

The intercom buzzer snapped his concentration.

"What's again Adil?"

"The *Sadr* is coming on the line, sir."

"Okay. Relax." Sarfaraz waited anxious 30 seconds before Jahanara crooned over the line.

"Hi sweet darling! How is dear Asma?" A reference to Sarfaraz's estranged wife.

"Fine *mohtarma*. How have you been?"

"Come any day and see for yourself. Talk to the *Sadr*."

"Yes sir."

"Sarfaraz, I'm told that the Saudi and US delegations are in the capital. I'd like to see them tomorrow. Take care of everything. And I intend to attend office tomorrow."

"Fine sir. I'll get back after the timings are finalised."

"One more point Sarfaraz. I'm not happy with what's being done to that widow in Delhi. Why can't you think of something radical?"

"Shall we discuss this tomorrow sir?"

"Well, call Hyder and others. I want something big in Kashmir."

"Let's discuss sir."

*

Lt. General Sarfaraz accompanied by two Brigadiers, who handled Martial Law and Civil Affairs in the CMLA's central fort, entered the spacious Cabinet-room of the President, exactly at five.

The ISI and PIB chiefs, as well as three senior secretaries of the departments of Home, Defence, and Cabinet Affairs were advised to wait in the anteroom. They would be called in when required.

He greeted the Head of State, seated behind a mahogany table, with a smart salute. The President and the CMLA didn't respond. He feigned being busy reading a fat file.

"Good evening sir." Sarfaraz saluted again.

"What's cooking Sarfaraz?" The President, immaculately dressed in full regimental regalia, finally spoke. He was spruced up with a neat haircut, close shave, and a facial massage. Layers of fatty skin hung loose from his face and thick balls of fat dangled below eyes.

"Sir, I want a little of your precious time. Important policy matters require your immediate attention." the PSO submitted ceremoniously.

"Quick fire. Any big deal?" The President didn't appear to be too pleased with Sarfaraz.

"As you said we're more concerned with India's suspicious maneauvres. The latest despatch from our High Commissioner mentions about frenetic Indian war preparations." Sarfaraz replied.

" What're our agency reports?" General Arif asked in a fumbling tone.

"They agree." Sarfaraz submitted.

"What about that minister in the cabinet of that woman, Sarfaraz?" General Arif chuckled loud, "ask him to justify the salt he licks from our plate. We should teach India the bitterest lesson to date. That widow won't dare challenging our army." General Arif waived his hands vigorously, dismissing his PSO's apprehensions.

"*Insha Allah*!" Sarfaraz vigorously nodded his head to appear visibly supportive of the views of the boss.

"Has Aftab been able to sabotage her election prospects? Or have we just frittered away a few millions?"

"I think the ISI and PIB chiefs should be able to brief you better."

"Carry on. Mind some coffee?"

"It's welcome sir." Sarfaraz replied.

He ordered coffee and hoped that the fat ball, seated across, would soon explode in a catastrophic self-combustion. If not, he was there to activate the short fuse.

"So, what were you saying about Dacca?" General Arif sipped the coffee leisurely and asked.

"Sir, there is impeccable proof of Indian involvement with the Peoples' League. Sheikh Jainal is an Indian mole." Sarfaraz concluded the sentence with a tone of lingering continuity.

"We all know that. Tell me how can we neutralise these forces. In the eyes of the world, they're in majority and have a right to demand their share. Are we ready to give that?"

The President changed his posture and an attendant, at his signal, flick-opened a gold cigarette box. General Arif picked up a stick, lighted it, and inhaled a lungful of smoke.

"That's a vital decision. How can we trust these Indian agents?"

"You can't. But what the hell is that woman up to?" He exhaled the smoke leisurely, "we should teach her a few lessons in statecraft."

The brave dig was directed at the Indian Prime Minister, who was a common hate object in Pakistan.

"It's overdue sir. However, before we embark upon any action against that widow several policy matters are required to be discussed." Sarfaraz played along.

"Wait Sarfaraz. I must pin her down in Kashmir. What's happening with Operation K2? Where is the ISI chief?" The President reacted with a deliberate knee-jerk response. His focus shifted from the main issue.

The Brigadier Martial Law briefly went out and shepherded in Generals Hyder Bux and Naim, the PIB chief.

"Tell me Hyder," the President spoke while fiddling with his thick eyebrows, "what're you doing with Operation K2?"

"Sir I want to bring to your notice some related developments." The ISI chief started in a meek squeaky tone.

"Skip the skin, reveal the meat. Tell me about the operation and I want to know what can we do in Kashmir. That's where I want to hit her big." Gen. Arif firmly indicated the parameters of the briefing.

The ISI chief slowly elaborated the nitty-gritty of Operation K2, named after the highest Himalayan peak in Pakistan. Fabricated soon after the 1965 drawn war, K2 was aimed at achieving Pakistan's unfinished agenda in Kashmir, through a clever combination of subversion, ethnic insurgency, and Islamic *jihad*.

This was a new approach, vastly different from what Pakistan had tried in 1948 and 1965. The experiences of the Islamists in Lebanon and Palestine had proved that war wasn't simply a clash of two armies. An intractable war could also be won by other means, by employing the strategy of Islamising the political issues. Religious bigotry could win a battle that could not be clinched by weapons.

The Philosophy was important to bring the people of Kashmir into conflict with the Indian system. Distorted *Sufi* traditions were to be supplanted by *Sunni Wahabi* fundamentalism. The calibrated escalation of terrorist violence and fundamentalist indoctrination were sure to subvert the lotus and saffron eater *Sufis* of the Vale of Kashmir. Islamisation of the *Sufi* Kashmiris was the surest weapon to escalate spontaneous revolution, a perpetual *jihad* against the *kafirs*- the Christians, the Jews and the Hindu.

"Sir, the Al Fatah and Kashmir Liberation Front boys are ready to stage some spectacular action," Gen. Hyder affirmed, "some of them have been tempered in the fire of Islamic *jihad*. It won't be necessary to repeat costly ventures like Operation Gulmarg, Balakot and Gibraltar. We'll overwhelm India through Islamisation of the Kashmiris."

The President, his eyes closed, mechanically lighted another cigarette and twisted his eyebrows. He gestured at the ISI chief to continue. He was ready to listen and wasn't displeased, as yet, with the narration.

"Don't forget Hyder," General Arif spoke in a prophetic voice, "Islam is the biggest weapon we have. Look at the Iranians. Very soon Islam will emerge victorious over there."

"You're correct sir. There are two other layers in the operation. We've generated enough friends in the Organisation of the Islamic Countries. They're ready to support the Kashmiri Muslims. The World Muslim League has promised financial support. Libya and the Lebanese Fatah leaders have agreed to train some of our special commandos."

"*Shukria*. Sounds fine. But what happened to the US promise of training our boys at their School of High Altitude Warfare?"

"The SSG, under supervision of the US School of High Altitude Warfare, has made a beginning at our High Altitude Training Centre at Gilgit. But that would take time."

"What about the Indian Kashmiri leaders?" The President sounded impatient.

"Our efforts to penetrate Sardar Niyamat, the chief of Indian held Kashmir, are progressing satisfactorily. He now rues Delhi's game of deception." General Hyder added.

"He should, if he's a good Mussalman. Is he ready to play my game?"

Hyder's open-ended operations could wait, General Arif pointed out. His immediate objectives were the scuttling of the Indian Parliamentary polls, generation of communal violence and corner the Indian Prime Minister. She should not be given a freehand to meddle in the affairs of East Pakistan.

"No, no Hyder, I'm not happy with K2. Niyamat and Manjira should fight. I want changes in the Kashmiri psyche. They should realise that they're Muslims first and Kashmiris next. Muslims have no other option but to be loyal to the Ummah and Pakistan. We're not a part of the damn East. We're an integral part of the Middle East." General Arif, in a rare display of cerebral excellence, stunned his officers.

"In fact sir, we've switched over to this strategy. The Islami Jammat has been funded to induct *khalis* (pure) *alems* (religious teachers) and seasoned Islamic preachers from Deoband, Lucknow and Bihar to teach real Wahabi Islam to them. Their so-called *Kashmiriat* (Kashmiri culture) is the main psychological barrier."

"Crush their ignorance under your boots. Train and arm them. Bring some of them for training to our camps." The President talked with a tone of finality.

"Sir, these operations require a long gestation period." Added Hyder Bux.

"Fuck your operations, I want quick result. I want a burning Kashmir. Show me some fireworks, pump in more money."

"I follow sir. Wait for a few days. The boys in Kashmir are sure to stage a big show. They're planning aircraft hijacking." Hyder assured the Chief Martial Law Administrator.

"Do it early. I hope you won't let me down. What's your plan for the Indian elections?" Gen. Arif asked.

"Sir, we've injected liberal doses of finance to our targets in the friendly community. They should, encompassing the Congress, Communist, and some regional parties, be able to return over 50 parliamentarians. That's a good pressure group. Aftab should be able to come back with 25 members," replied General Hyder.

"Do something Hyder to scuttle the elections. Can't you think of any other earthshaking event?"

"The last attempt by Markaz had failed."

"That was a foolish plan. Think in terms of a huge communal conflagration."

"That's not a problem sir. Let me consult Naim. We'll come up with a scheme."

"So brother Naim, what all have you done so far? Is that woman's popularity on the wane?" General Arif asked in a flamboyant voice.

"I'm afraid sir, she's much too clever to let that happen. In fact, she has emerged stronger than ever." The PIB chief started his briefing with a disappointing note.

"What the hell have you been doing all these days? What in hell's name Aftab is doing?" The President didn't appear to be happy with what his elder brother had to say.

"Sir, Aftab is active. According to him Moscow has forced the Communists to support her. She has been using the commies for cultural intrusion in East Pakistan. Hundreds of books and pamphlets extolling Bengali nationalism have been distributed free. India is financing rural drama groups, which spread the messages of an independent Bangladesh."

"Why are these not reflected in Hyder's reports from Dacca? Don't you and Hyder have any coordination?"

"Not exactly sir. We've activated Aftab." General Naim submitted peevishly.

"What's that bloody Aftab doing?" the President repeated impatiently.

"Sir, his talents are active in several states. The gangs controlled by him have been deployed for unleashing anti-Hindu violence and random killing."

"But I haven't heard a single bang."

"A few mosques and temples have been desecrated and some reports of communal flare ups have been reported."

"Some won't do Naim. I want big fire. Hindustan should burn. Tell Aftab to play our game and he won't find us wanting. Tell him that he's our choice for Delhi's next Prime Ministerial slot. Washington and its allies would endorse him. Tell him on my authority," General Arif spoke expansively and continued, "ask him for a detailed report on the Indian involvement with the Peoples' League and that traitor Jainal."

"Yes sir."

General Sarfaraz was not inspired by the frivolous trends of discussion. The *Sadr* had not even discussed the burning issues involving East Pakistan and rebellious activities of the Bengali police and army personnel.

"Shall we discuss some reports on Dacca sir?"

"What's new happening?"

"I understand you want me to go over to Dacca for a meeting with Jainal. Before that we must neutralise some of the traitors in the police and armed forces."

"Just hang them."

"But that place is burning sir. We've to adopt subtler approaches," Lt. Gen. Sarfaraz intervened mildly.

"Look Sarfaraz," the CMLA continued his monologue, "these Bengalis aren't real Muslims. Let them go to hell. Finish them off."

The President lighted another cigarette and exhaled a thick cloud of smoke, perhaps to show his PIB chief the thickness of the smoke he had just referred to.

General Arif shifted in his chair impatiently as if he had ran out of steam. Lt. Gen. Sarfaraz was alarmed to see fresh wrinkles and creases on General Arif's face. Was it scotch time for the chief?

"Should we break for a drink sir?"

The President raised his right hand towards the door. His cerebral cortices weren't exactly oriented to absorb the complicated and thorny diplomatic issues. He felt a griping sensation in the gullet. It needed the soothing flow of his favourite Heineken. General Arif aimlessly moved both his hands, in synchronisation with his inner thinking. To hell with diplomacy! He was basically a soldier and wouldn't hesitate in pulling the trigger at the correct moment. That was his exclusive prerogative. As the procession prepared to move to the adjacent living room, Lt. General Sarfaraz moved closer to the President.

"Sir, I've a hunch; Aftab has been compromised."

"I've seen your reports Sarfaraz. In case he betrays, smoke him out. A compromised agent is a dead agent. He lives as long as he is useful. Hyder should take care of that rogue."

"One more point sir."

"Go ahead."

There are sure-fire evidences of blatant Indian support to the Bengali traitors.

"They've completed the training of several Mukti Bahini (freedom fighter) formations." Sarfaraz submitted.

"Well Sarfaraz. You have my authority to pack up the top leaders and drown them in that...what's the name of that river."

"Buriganga."

"Whatever it is. Shoot them all and drown in the damn river."

"That will be ensured."

"Call a meeting of the CMLA Divisional Heads and the three Chiefs. Inform the US ambassador. I'd like to receive him tonight, over a drink. And summon...." The President stopped short of completing the sentence. He was hesitant to mention Izaz Afroz's name to his overzealous PSO. That was a different strategy he was pursuing. It was a game in which Washington and Peking were discreet partners.

General Arif returned a feeble smile. In his Pakistan, no one should get too curious. No. Not this highly decorated officer, regarded as a possible alternative to him by some doubting Toms and Harries in Washington and Chengs and Chings in Peking.

"Well Sarfaraz, bring up operation cleanup proposal in an exclusive meeting. Ask Hyder and Naim to be present. Let's have a drink now." He dismissed the PSO.

General Sarfaraz shrugged. If the top boss was interested in booze and food, who was he to talk shop about the treacherous Bengalis! Whimsical maiden fortune and the puppeteers in Washington and Peking had catapulted the brat to the highest slot. The intricacies of politics and diplomacy were beyond him. Hang him!

Sarfaraz opened the door with an agile move, smiled lavishly, and said, "Sir, would you prefer a beer or something else?"

General Arif looked up at the PSO, breathed out a loud silent curse, and settled for a chilled Scotch, as a starter.

"My favourite Scotch, Sarfaraz, lots of ice please."

*

30

“Malika.” Harfan’s voice vacillated like the erratic needle of an overcharged oscillograph.

“Yes, darling.” Jahanara replied in a sweet flat voice.

“Your medicine from the Indian *vaid* has been procured. Nawab sahib will deliver it.”

“Hang that parasite. I’ve a recital commitment in Lahore. I should be there on the 15th. Come personally, check up with hotel Faletti’s.” Her voice sounded faint, disturbed by loud background instrumental music.

“Perhaps I can’t come to Lahore, my job takes me to Karachi.”

“Come over. I need the medicine urgently.” The soprano crooned in a lilting tone. Jahanara didn’t want her latest acquisition to visit her home in the capital.

“Perhaps you would like Nawab sahib to deliver the packet. It’s he who really organised it.” Harfan suggested.

“No dear, I told you. That lousy fellow is a soggy jelly bag, good for nothing. Does he chew raw asafoetida? He eructates the smell.” Jahanara insisted.

“Can’t say ma’am, I’d deliver the medicine if you insist.” Harfan disconnected.

*

General Hyder Bux examined carefully the insignificant piece of Operation Red Rose transcript produced by Brigadier Barqat’s boys in Section S of the Joint Intelligence Bureau Division. Operation Red Rose, the grandiose nom-de-plume assigned to the electronic surveillance operation on Malika Jahanara, often offered interesting insight into the affairs of the State.

A femme ‘fatale’ of infinite virtues, she had gathered admirers all over the country. The President apart, she received kaleidoscopic visitors and conversed with rainbow personalities, who decided or pretended to determine the fate of Pakistan.

What intrigued Hyder was the use of the direct bedroom line of Red Rose by the caller. Only a very few people reserved the privilege of calling her bedroom number. Only the *Sadr* had exclusive access to it, a sort of honeyed hotline. Her pet attendant, the trusted and castrated *habshi,* attended all other calls.

Questions were who could this Harfan be, and how did he access the bedroom number. Was it Harfan or Irfan? Is he a new lover boy? An under-the-carpet pet mice, a new competitor for the presidential hotline! A red herring?

What links could he have with Nawab? Nawab and medicine...from *vaid* Dhanwant of Dehradun! Did he say so? Hyder re-winded the tape and listened to the faint male voice. Yes. This bugger, whoever he was, had spoken about the Dehradun medic and medicines.

'*Hai Rabba*'!

Had he not asked the younger Sharif for some energy-boosting medicines from India? Hyder gently massaged his eyes and bushy brows with left big and middle fingers and concentrated on the transcript. Yes. He did.

By *Allah*, who could this Harfan be? Did he ever bump into any Harfan, in a Pakistan Chambers of Commerce annual dinner? Or was it at a meeting with the Consortium of Defence Suppliers? Did he figure in any earlier tape?

How could a petty nobody have access to the big man's hotline? Was Malika entertaining a strange lover? Did it have the potential of a new scandal involving the *Sadr*? Well! juicy scandals were welcome. These should help him in driving in the last few nails on the coffin of the usurper, General Arif Khan.

Perhaps the city editor of the *Dawn*, Najibullah Aksari, could help. He moved around the defence beat and maintained steady connection with the affluent suppliers and contractors.

"Hello Najib," General Hyder called the *Dawn* representative, a resourceful journalist, "do you know any Harfan? He is probably a defence supplier."

"Salaam General," Najib was gratified to receive a direct call form the top intelligence boss, "yes, I know him. He's not really anybody, a mere employee of Israr Sharief and son in law of Zahoor Mian, the shipping magnet. What's the matter?"

"We're short listing some major suppliers. I could not hit on the correct name. I know Zahoor and Israr. Come over for coffee. We have a lot to discuss."

"That's great General. Keep a slot free for tomorrow."

Hyder finally plugged in Harfan to his current memory cells. Perhaps he had met this Harfan. Yes. He might have met him at a social gathering in Lahore. Nothing extraordinary. He had just accepted his greetings and had probably said *Insha Allah* or *Khuda Hafiz*. Such creeping climbers among the business executives were a dime a dozen. He had encountered many of them in his long career in uniform. But?

Hyder Bux wasn't able to quench the raw thirst of a seasoned intelligence officer. The urge to drill deep into the root of the mystery pushed him inexorably. The mystery of a nonentity calling the direct bedroom number of the seductress kept haunting him. Was the lady involved in another major defence deal? Was the *Sadr* involved in another scam? Why should an Israr employee take orders from Nawab, his archenemy?

Hyder paused for a while and thought he should stop worrying over a nonentity.

However, he couldn't help pressing his mental drill bits in.

What medicine could this Harfan procure for the presumed first lady? Was Nawab trying to short-circuit his ISI patron and establishing a direct line to the Aphrodite? Did he push Harfan into the tigress's cage to strike a bargain with the *Sadr*? It was eminently possible. Why should Jahanara get medicines from India? She didn't suffer from frigidity. Even if she did most of the medical experts in Pakistan, in all branches of the science, would like to prostrate before her and lick the dust of her alley walk. He had, in his personal custody, the medical records of the President and his lover girl.

No, no. He could not allow this lead to go unexplored. Nawab could not be allowed to change boat. He was yet to pay up $ 50,000 for the last favour showered on him. Hyder Bux decided to accost Nawab first. A seasoned politician of Nawab's stature was not likely to make an uncalculated move.

"Brother Nawab...*salaam,* Hyder here." He called the redoubtable fat tycoon and sleek operator.

"*Janab...walekum assalam,"* Nawab replied, "any service for your servant?"

"Don't joke. How're things on the political front? Hope your preparations are complete?"

"Politics is an endless wool-ball. You can't get perfection, Hyder sahib."

"Any help from me?"

"How can I do without your help sir? Elections are costly."

"Don't worry. I want to see Punjab in your safe hands. Fund is not a problem. By the way, do you know a guy called Harfan?"

"Harfan?" Nawab chewed the alphabets and spoke again, "yes. I know a Harfan. He is my brother's business executive."

"Is he trustworthy?"

"You can't trust any one these days. Even the Prophet did not trust his own followers. Any special job?"

"It's not that. Anything else can you add?"

"He's a Karachi based *muhajir.* Has good connections with London based Indians."

"Find out a little more."

"Give me some space...something should come out...wise guys say that the queen has developed *ishk* (love) for this rag picker."

"Don't tell me Nawab. The big man will tear him up."

"How does it matter?"

"That would harm brother Israr."

"I don't care. Israr is spoiling my business and this *muhajir* is playing a big role in pushing down my margins."

"So you're the ring master who threw the kid into the tigress's den?" Hyder spoke in flowery Urdu, "but I'd told you to get some medicines for me too. Hope you wouldn't go to the town hanging me."

"*Tauba tauba janab*. Who'd do that to the mighty Chief? You're not alone sir," Nawab replied with a relish, "the mighty PSO is also a client of that Indian medic. Don't worry. I don't open my mouth as long as my interests are not harmed. You can cook the goose of brother Israr and that *muhajir*. I don't mind."

General Hyder was intrigued by the suggestion.

Was this Harfan being sacrificed by Nawab to harm his brother? Was he being used as a conduit to some Indian contacts by the CMLA? Which Indians? The Sindhuja one? Or the one headed by Hirubhai Dasani? Political and intelligence professionals? Was the CMLA planning new tricks, which he didn't know? Had he opened up a track II dialogue with the Indian PM?

Hyder didn't rule out the possibility.

The Sindhi fox, Izaz Afroz, was constantly bombarding the neurons of the President with queer political ideas. The poor old man was more baffled than a circus buffoon was. The ambitious Red Rose was known for running odd political errands for the top man and Afroz.

Was she using the Harfan conduit to Delhi, via the London tunnel?

Which tunnel? The creepy idea foxed Hyder.

The boss man too had a couple of crooked tunnels open to Delhi. Yes. His course mate Lt. General Dhillon was still around, leading a command in southern India. The *Sadr* could use him too.

That would mean the de-seeding of the war clouds and easing of military stand off and return to civilian rule. The next natural step would be to invite Sheikh Jainal to take over the reins of the country. It did not lead him, General Hyder, the claimant to Pakistan's throne, anywhere.

Hyder Bux couldn't imagine that a two-penny whore would scuttle his plans. He would fix her and hang that bloody Harfan. No one could stand in his way, not even Sarfaraz. He must immediately stonewall all possible tunnels to Delhi. Only a devastating war could expose the rotten hide of General Arif. The Pakistanis would not hesitate to accept him, a blue blooded Jat, as the next military ruler, if he could conclusively prove Arif 's clandestine Indian connections.

He required at least half cooked evidence against Arif and his ladylove. General Hyder pushed the intercom button and summoned his most trusted officer in the super-secret Section S, directly functioning under him.

"Barqat show me the list of calls received by Red Rose on her bedroom hotline." The officer returned in five minutes. The data was ready. In fact, Barqat updated it religiously.

Yes. She had received ten calls, from friends and admirers, in the last thirty days. Two calls were from Izaz Afroz, the former Foreign Minister. No big surprise. The President often used Malika for intimate dialogues with that possessed politician, with bags full of hatred for the Hindu neighbour and East Pakistan Bengalis. The PSO called once. Not significant. One call was from the PIB chief, General Naim, requesting her to pass on to the President a top-secret report on Izaz Afroz's latest French mistress. Well! Well! The top boss wasn't really a buffoon. He was aware of certain amorous activities of the ambitious Sindhi leader.

That's a precious input. Izaz should be made aware of Red Rose's special love for him; may be at an opportune moment. Why not? In his quest for power, he might require the services of the Sindhi sycophant. He wouldn't be a bad bargain as against messianic Sarfaraz.

The only odd call was from this Harfan, a wild dark horse. Unfortunately, the contents of the call were polluted by ambient noise, loud instrumental music. Did this ring a strange bell?

An earlier audio snooping in the nympho's living room had probably thrown up the name of this dark horse. However, Hyder's experts weren't sure. That irritating *sarod* recital, with loud accompaniment of the percussion drum, had polluted the audio quality.

"Barqat," Hyder asked, "did your boys ever pick up this man's trail?"

"No sir. He's new in our roster of honour."

"Do you think he's a new star in Red Rose's life? These artists are peculiar animals. They often pick up wayside lovers to satisfy their insatiable desire. Loved and admired by all, they often feel lovelorn, deserted and lonely." Added Hyder.

"Perhaps it's not a romantic affair sir," Barqat replied, "if I'm not incorrect, they talked about some medicine and Nawab being the initiator. I can investigate this fellow."

"Look Barqat," General Hyder spoke in a whispering tone, "this lady's chummy with the CMLA and I don't want to get axed for any act of indiscretion by your boys. Neither can I trust that jackal Nawab. Anyways, I'd like to consult the PSO. There may be a latent security angle to it."

*

General Hyder did not want the clue to go by. Diamonds are often struck from dead rocks. A great survivor, since the days of the former President, Hyder never relished the idea of jumping into a black hole, all by him. He wasn't the type to commit solitary suicide. Good company was always welcome, which left the opportunity open to walk up to *Allah's behest* (heaven), in strides with good friends.

Investigating of Harfan could lead his boys to the bedroom of the virtual first lady. The soprano was most likely to scream out for his blood. Hyder faced another dilemma. He could not authorise, all by himself, sensitive clandestine intelligence operations involving the highest in the land. The Joint Intelligence Bureau, the domestic wing of the ISI, was brought under supervision of the PSO after several high level political figures complained against roughshod treatment by ISI sleuths. The President was also peeved by a complaint from the US ambassador about the ISI Mosurs (mobile surveillance) tailing his car, whenever he went to meet political leaders. How could Hyder do that?

It was safer to consult Lt. General Sarfaraz, the listed number two. He was the designated authority to sanction a specific sensitive internal intelligence operation. It wouldn't take him moments to vitiate the ears of the CMLA, in murderous cacophony with the soprano. He would, in all probability, be shunted out to an insignificant diplomatic assignment, if not summarily shot. Bullets came cheap, often free, from Uncle Sam's inexhaustible caches.

The eerie thought rattled Hyder's bones.

General Hyder Bux picked up the phone.

"Sir, Hyder here. There's something interesting. Can I come?"

"Is it very urgent? I'm expecting the US Under Secretary of State at five."

"I'll drop in, just for a few minutes."

Hyder left in a jiffy.

*

"Let me tell you Hyder," Sarfaraz offered special Sri Lanka tea to the ISI chief, stirring the brew with a silver spoon, "don't fiddle with that bitch. She's the top man's property. He won't buy any excuse and won't hesitate in putting your neck under the chopping block. You know what happened last time you snooped on the US ambassador."

"That Yankee was trying to contact Sartaj Jamil and some Baluch leaders."

"I understand. However, America is our provider. We might be able to survive without the *Allah*, but not without America."

"Sir," the ISI chief sweated under his crisply pressed three-piece angora suit, "we've some delicate feedback about a possible Indian penetration of the security bubbles around the lady. You know her connections with a thespian of the Indian film industry."

"That's a dead story."

"But, our sources are impeccable. That temple of love is vulnerable. Who can prevent the Indian NSI from poisoning the *Sadr*'s food and drink?" Hyder used one of the hackneyed clichés of the intelligence community, VIP security.

"It's a filmy story."

"See the advantage sir," Hyder winked at the PSO, "this is a juicy story. We should develop it as a possible weapon against the *Sadr*."

"Simple juice isn't good enough to stew him Hyder. You require an infernal fire."

Sarfaraz muttered a curse under his breath. The smart bastard was trying to rope him in for a dirty operation. What for? Was Hyder showing a red herring, for implicating him in a bad jam? India, he knew, was the bedroom ghost; every Pakistani political player would like the common people to be scared of.

"This Harfan affair could light a big fire. He appears to be a lover boy of the lady."

"Why do you think this Hanif...er....Harfan is such a mighty *harfanmaula* (Jack of all trades)?"

"He figured in the first tape that I shared with you. Now this second tape is devastating. He has spelt out your and my name in his conversation with that bitch. Don't you think my junior staff may carry the tale to Izaz or anyone having the ears of the President?"

"What do you gain by hanging this minor chap? That may infuriate the lady."

"That's why I want to inject the security angle. Anything can pass through that eye of the needle, even a mountain. That's our holy ghost." Hyder opened up his cards rather frankly.

The seasoned PSO wasn't convinced.

"Developments in East Pakistan have rattled the President, he's a nervous wreck. He dreads the goblins and *jinns* of democracy. Don't provoke him if you can't kill. The infant may start shooting wildly. You and I can get hurt." Lt. General Sarfaraz spoke rather philosophically.

"His days are numbered. Let's kaput him at the earliest possible opportunity."

"Hyder," Sarfaraz finally said, "in our game we should be patient. We can push him out only after the war that we're sure to face soon."

"Why not now? He's wrecking the country in tandem with master demolisher Izaz."

"I'd like to. However, Washington and Peking won't be charmed by our moves. They want Arif to bridge the East-West chasm…a new Cold War strategy. What can you and I do without the US backing?" Sarfaraz advised caution and got back to his pet obsession.

"Don't you think, sir, by allowing him time we're helping Izaz? He'll take advantage of the emerging Islamabad-Washington-Peking axis."

"It's not an axis Hyder. The US wants to open a new front against the USSR. I'm worried that fresh arms supply by the US and China will help the old man to consolidate his position. How can we stop this?"

"Do you really want to? We need the supplies for East Pakistan. India is at our throat."

"That's the biggest dilemma. We've to act decisively before the President and Izaz can conjure up new tricks," Sarfaraz spoke with a twitch in his eyes, "let's heat things up for them in Dacca. We may start with purging the top Bengali army and civilian officers. Give me a list of the traitors, who deserve neutralisation."

"You want them in concentration camps!"

"Jokes apart Hyder," the PSO spoke in a definitive voice, "the movement in Dacca will gather momentum once we start weeding out the Bengali elite. These traitors should be buried alive. Why waste national wealth by feeding them free?"

"That's not an impossible task," Hyder added, "I get your point. Aggravated skirmishes between Jainal and Izaz will help us. The President, I presume, will be badly caught in the scissors' cleaves. I'd like you to consider mass destruction of the Bengali rats. Jainal has polluted and subverted their loyalty."

"A good point. The boss is considering General Tarakki for the hatchet man's job in Dacca. It suits us. Tarakki should be kept away from Izaz."

"That's our common goal. The Bengalis must perish, if we want Islam and Pakistan to survive. I think we should jointly brief Tarakki before he emplanes for Dacca. But allow me to explore this chap Harfan. He could lead us to some big scandal involving the lady. Why miss on something that could be important?"

"Are you serious? Do you think the *Sadr* can be beaten by that stick?"

"It's not impossible. We play up the whole affair in Pakistani and world media." Hyder twitched his moustache hoping that the weighty input would floor the PSO.

"I know that's possible."

"What's the harm in giving a minor twist to it? We stand to gain."

"Fine, if you feel so strongly about that employee of Israr. But I won't give permission in writing. Keep it informal. Keep away from Malika and the President. Treat it as a security exercise and not an internal operation." Sarfaraz sounded a final warning.

"Thanks. In office note I'd mention that you were consulted."

"You want to hang me! Israr pays the boss well. Take care that he's not hurt," Sarfaraz paused, "let's meet in two day's time, and finalise the list of the Bengali rats. I like your idea. These buggers have to be eliminated and Tarakki is the best choice." Sarfaraz concluded the last sentence with wrinkles of contempt that contorted his face.

"Let's wait for details from Dacca station, keep the date flexible. Don't worry about Malika. My boys will be very discreet. And as you said it's a security operation." Hyder replied and walked out triumphantly. Half the battle was won. The Bengali fixation of Sarfaraz had done the trick.

Back in his office, Hyder used the exclusive number to Barqat and summoned him.

"Trace down this Harfan, I want a run up on this creature. Be discreet. Put the best boys. No tampering with Red Rose. Explore the possibility of this Harfan brat having a link with Izaz."

"Yes sir."

"Ask Dacca station for two lists, one of the Bengali officers, both civilian and uniformed and the other of the intellectuals. They require a realm of higher wisdom, the wisdom of the grave."

"You mean we give them a quiet burial."

"Burial yes, quiet or stormy, I don't as yet know. That we'd decide after Tarakki takes over."

"How urgent is this sir?"

"The PSO is serious and I think the boss is keen too. Let's keep the powder dry. Ask your Dacca boys to activate the Mosur and Tesur (technical surveillance) teams on the short listed Bongo suspects."

"Consider it done sir. The University and Dhanmandi areas have been placed under blanket Int. coverage. We've quite a few singing pigeons in our cage." The Brigadier replied gleefully.

"That's OK. As you said, I want a total footage of the Dhanmandi residence of Jainal. You can task Major Khalikujjaman."

"It'll be done sir," Barqat shared additional information with his boss, "we've completed the dossiers on all the important People's League leaders and their

Indian contacts. In fact our Calcutta boys have snapped Jainal's meeting with Vishram Satpore, the NSI's Calcutta Bureau chief."

"That's excellent. Let's keep it under the sleeve for a while. Don't even share this with Sarfaraz."

"I'm your officer sir. I'd do as you dictate."

"That's superb. That would accelerate addition of stars on your pips," Hyder affectionately patted Barqat, "tell me how're you going to cover the Lahore rendezvous?" Hyder asked.

"A technical operation is the easiest way out."

"Do it with finesse. I want all the dope. Use the best boys you have. I don't want any stinking shit. Deploy the best ElInt (Electronic Intelligence) and TechInt (Technical Intelligence) boys."

"We've to treat her hotel room and that of Harfan." Barqat added.

"Go ahead, do it on the quiet. Don't leave dirty droppings behind." Hyder winked and smiled.

Barqat personally dialled Hotel Faletti without routing the call through his secretary.

"Is it 303660?"

"Yes please. Hotel Faletti. May I help you?" the petite receptionist replied in a silken voice.

"May I talk to your manager?"

"Anything I can do at the front desk sir?"

"I'm Brigadier Barqat from ISI, in charge of President's security. Call the manager fast."

Barqat felt irritated. These minor dolls, standing behind the counters, often pretended to dispense favours to their customers.

"Yes sir, Tahir here. What can I do for you?" The manager spoke after offering the ritual apology.

"This is about VIP security. My men, headed by Jamanat Ali, will report today. Give them all the help they require." Barqat preferred to be brief.

"Yes sir. Be sure of our sincere cooperation."

"And the name of the game is discretion. No one should get wise about what my boys do there."

"Don't worry sir. We understand your orders."

"That's better." Barqat felt happy after successfully intimidating the hotel manager.

*

31

The Air Force Fokker F-27 landed at Lahore airport two hours later, with Jamanat Ali and his team of ISI sleuths, carrying a few vinyl portmanteaus stuffed with electronic equipment.

The veteran sleuth did not have to persuade the manager to peg room 406 for Jahanara, instead of her standing choice of room number 306. The soprano preferred the third floor room that faced the old Charring Cross and overlooked the Bagh-e-Jinnah. She had developed an infatuation for this room, her detractors surmised, because it's walls were mute witnesses to many of her early life escapades.

Jamanat Ali, Barqat's anchor in the Special Operations Cell, was a veteran hunter. He wasn't the kind of tiger to raise its paw and fawn upon his prey. Harfan was the target rabbit, but he couldn't be boiled in a vacuum. Jahanara was the canvas, against which the target was to be probed and evaluated.

Why should that unislamic bitch be spared? These infidel western clones were greater enemies of the country. The *Quran Majid* and the *Hadith* had never prescribed such frivolous singing and dancing. Jamanat's prejudices and religious inclinations matched his professional excellence.

Suite 406, flanked by rooms 405 and 407, was treated with radio microphones and two micro-video cameras. With radio transmission facility built in, the motorised cameras were capable of sweeping wide spectrum angles. A few radio microphones were carefully installed in room number 407 too. The room phone was treated with a miniature radio transmitter.

Jamanat's team waited patiently for their kill. The charming lover boy was sure to walk straight into the ISI interrogation centre, Badr, located at the basement hideout of the agency's sprawling building. Very few were born with extra luck to come out of that honeymoon chamber, as they liked to call the dreaded hole.

*

Jahanara arrived late in the afternoon, accompanied by the inevitable *habshi* and a posse of security personnel. As expected, she raised a storm over change of her favourite suite. The suave manager politely explained his compulsions. Only two nights back a young Gujranwala couple had committed suicide in the room. He was under police orders not to open the lock, until the investigation process was complete. He begged for Jahanara's understanding and expressed total helplessness. Perhaps she would understand and pardon him. The management wouldn't like to allot the special room to her until it was fully redone.

"Why don't you keep the room permanently booked for me?"

"As you wish ma'am. It'd be done after the renovation work is complete."

"Isn't it foolish?" Jahanara commented with a sexy pout, "it's a pity that these days foolish lovers prefer to die at the slightest pretext. What's the fun in ending life, even if society doesn't approve of an affair?"

"You're correct ma'am," Tahir, the young manager synchronised his words with horizontal movements of his head, "they're pretty foolish."

"Exactly so, dear. Life is for living. Enjoy every moment of it." Jahanara licked up the strong and charming frame of the manager with the look of a hungry lioness. This man was promising enough for a warm nightcap.

"Thanks young man. You must come up to my room for a drink."

"That should be a honour ma'am."

The manager escorted the seductress to her suite, followed by a retinue of bearers and attendants, herded by the imposing *habshi.*

*

Harfan arrived next morning.

He wanted to make the visit brief and spend the spare time with Jamilla. He was not afraid to face the seductress, but his professional discretion told him to tread cautiously. The whole affair, as he later coolly analysed, smacked of a tricky plot by Nawab Sharief. That viper, a close associate of Izaz Afroz and Hyder Bux, could blow up his cover any moment.

He alighted from a tourist taxi at a road intersection, about 150 yards off the main gate and walked down to the hotel foyer. That was the normal anti-surveillance protocol he preferred to practice. These lessons were vital for survival. The receptionist processed his request for a room after several manipulations of the computer. Finally, she looked up nervously and whispered in the ears of a male colleague.

"Sir, welcome to the Faletti," the male receptionist replied, "sorry for the delay. I can give you only room 407. We're, otherwise, fully booked."

"That'll do. I require it for a couple of hours." Harfan brought out his wallet and prepared to complete the formalities. The petite receptionist looked askance at another close-cropped egg-headed male employee. He sprinted in the direction of the lift. The bellboy fearfully saluted him and opened the door.

Harfan watched the crude drama, performed by amateurs.

They must be cops, not trained for merging with the posh hotel milieu. Harfan produced his visiting card with a faint smile in a remote corner of his lips. The ivory white thick card proclaimed his identity as the marketing vice-president of Israr International.

"Any problem with the rooms?" Harfan enquired.

"Pardon me sir," the confused young receptionist spoke, nervously fiddling with a pen, "as I said, other rooms are already booked. You'll like room 407. It's a historical room sir. The Governor of undivided Punjab used to stay there. It was his personal preference. And for an honoured guest like you, we offer a 20% discount."

"Oh great! It's a rare honour. Why not? Bill it to my company. Okay?"

Harfan pretended to be overwhelmed by the gracious offer.

"That should be fine sir." The receptionist summoned the bellboy and asked him to help Harfan with his carry bag.

As he entered the lift, a bellboy who looked like a cop, followed him carrying his overnight carry bag. He opened the room, courteously ushered in Harfan, and even managed to say 'have a good day sir'.

Harfan thanked him profusely and offered a fat tip. The bellboy's hand coiled back in hesitation. Harfan forced the bucks into his clammy palms and casually closed the door behind him.

He realised that the bellboy was no boy with a gong-sized bell, and the intelligence rat in him was loudly aroused. Was the show exclusively for him or was it a part of the security measures for the virtual first lady of Pakistan?

The ISI or the PIB?

Why?

Harfan lighted a cigarette and coolly assessed the situation.

He was definitely expected here, but by which agency?

What could have gone wrong?

Ibadat? Ramayani?

Nawab Sharief?

Malika Jahanara?

Harfan couldn't hammer the nail on any spatial correlation. The process of elimination, encompassing all the aspects of his deep-cover glimpsed past his sensory scanner. No. Except Jahanara and Nawab Sharief he couldn't put a marker on any other bull's eye.

It must be the lady, the reigning beautiful bitch.

The intelligence reception team was either a part of her security or a piece out of the ISI's intricate operation, woven around General Arif 's Aphrodite. He was just an irritating additional fixture in the frame. Or was he minimizing the threat? He could as well be the target.

Holy heavens!

Harfan silently smoked the cigarette and tossed his thought in his trained bowl. What if the ISI targeted him? Nawab Sharief might have instigated the ISI sleuths. Or was his visit to Jahanara's house had generated suspicion in the highest quarters?

Thank heavens! Harfan shuddered to think of the prospect of being cooked in the cauldron of Pakistan's raging power struggle. He wasn't unaware of the gathering clouds over General Arif 's rocking boat.

To hell with Jahanara and her lover boy General Arif! To hell with Pakistan! He wouldn't allow ISI the pleasure of trapping him. Not any more, like Bhagat & Co had wrapped him up in celluloid at Divine Inn. He decided to play safe by the rules of the game.

Harfan enjoyed a sumptuous breakfast, took out a tiny electronic sensor, and meticulously searched all conceivable corners and crevices in the room. He fished out three tiny radio-microphones, made in USA, with 72 hours power supply.

Well! Well! It was an elaborate reception indeed!

He was very much a target of the agency! Not just a sideshow. Perhaps he'd picked up the virus from Jahanara's mansion. The Prima Donna must be under the prism. Which pinion of the military machine could be involved? The Pakistan Intelligence Bureau, headed by the celebrity elder Khan wouldn't dare bugging the soprano's room. He owed his office to her pleasure and that of the younger Khan.

The DMI wouldn't stray into the minefield of civilian intelligence.

It must be the ISI.

Well! With the Big Brother around, he had reasons to worry.

Harfan decided to play cool, and squeeze himself, if the nutcracker closed on him. He picked up the phone and called Jamilla.

"Hi darling!" He pumped in, as much sweet juice he could muster, "how're you? I'm here in Lahore chasing an elusive lady."

"Who's that witch?"

"Oh darling! She is the one and only *mohtarma* Jahanara."

"What're you doing with that whore?" Jamilla screamed on the phone.

"Wait darling. I'm not here by choice. It's Nawab sahib, my boss's younger brother. He wanted me to get some medicine for her, the PSO, and the ISI chief from an Indian medic. The consignment has arrived via London, and I'm here to hand over the medicine to her."

"Don't get entangled with her."

"Sure darling. I can't chase a bad dream when the best dream is etched in my heart."

Harfan whistled lightly over the line and wished Jamilla good luck. He tried to figure out the facial expressions of the wired up ISI operative. Must be furtively logging on and tracing the call.

Well! The call to Jamilla would keep them guessing for a while. The words-PSO and ISI chief-were sure to make them scratch their heads. They should be mighty foxed with the names of the two pillars of the junta figuring in his brief love-talk.

Harfan pried opened the phone using a screwdriver. Yes. An expert technician had implanted a radio microphone inside the resistance coil, below the dialling mechanism, a cute device with infinite life and having a range of 100 metres. The transparent scenario rattled Harfan. Both he and Jahanara were under ISI surveillance. The spooks had wired up the entire room. He had unknowingly walked into the minefield of political intrigue that involved the power brokers of Islamabad. The ISI operation could only be an extension of a conspiracy against the President.

By whom? It must be another set of hungry Generals, the ISI chief included. This was good fun! Harfan lighted a cigarette and refitted the screws with a slow and careful clockwise motion.

He dialled the private number of Israr and informed him about the likely late arrival of the Chinese team. The yellow arms peddlers were expected only next week. It was an important rendezvous. The Chinese side headed by Lin Ziao Zing, the Deputy Defence Minister, was to meet his Pakistani counterpart, General Naqibullah, in short Naqi, the Defence Advisor to the President. The Chinese were likely to conclude an agreement for supplying tanks, field guns, mortar batteries, and MBRLs (multi barrel rocket launchers). All against cash and through United Arab Emirate based intermediaries. Israr International, Harfan added, could expect to bag contracts for airlifting this military hardware to Sargodha and Karachi.

"But sir," Harfan dragged the dialogue, "why are we getting the Chinese? We should turn to the Americans."

"There's a problem. The US Congress has put an embargo on weapons supply to Islamabad after the March 25th crackdown in Dacca."

"That's dangerous for Pakistan."

"Don't worry. We're expecting a US delegation too, in another two weeks. The Turkish, Saudi, and Jordanian windows will open up soon. Anyways, keep General Naqi in good humour. We're basically patriotic Pakistani businessmen. Aren't we?"

"Sure sir. What should we offer him for clinching the airlifting contract?"

"Start with 3%. Go up to 7%. That's the upper limit."

"Are you coming?"

"No brother Nawab may be there. But raise the butter-bucks if he chips in more commission."

"Will ten percent be fine?"

"No problem, if that's absolutely necessary."

Harfan called Nawab Sharief next.

"*Assalam-u-alaikum* Nawab sahib, Harfan here," he spoke rather loudly, "are you coming to the concert of *mohtarma* Jahanara?"

"*Wale kum assalam*," Nawab replied, "no *yar*, I'm stuck up here. Have you got the medicines?"

"Yes sir."

"Deliver to her personally."

"Don't be unfair to me sir. I'm a tiny fry. You had sent me to *mohtarma. I* managed to get that medicine from the Indian medic. Better you give it personally to her."

"That's okay brother. She needs the medicine. Deliver it and mention my name."

"Sir, I thought you'd like to do it personally. It's you who had commissioned me to get the medicines."

"Don't be silly. I'll call her to say that you're representing me. Don't be scared, she's a fine lady." Nawab was lavish in his praise for Jahanara.

"And sir," Harfan continued, "the nerve tonics for the respected PSO and the ISI chief, procured from the Indian medic are at my workplace. Hope you'll personally deliver it."

"Leave it to me. I'd tackle them. Hope you haven't told brother Israr about this."

"No sir."

Harfan disconnected the line and connected Jahanara's room over the intercom.

As usual, the castrated *habshi* answered.

"Who is there?"

"*Janab*, Harfan Bukhari here. Can I talk to *mohtarma*?"

"Does she know you?"

"Not really. I'm speaking on behalf of Nawab Sharief sahib."

"Okay. Hold on."

Jahanara came on the line after a good two minutes.

Begging the indulgence of her exalted highness in sweetest Urdu, Harfan requested Jahanara's permission to come down to her room for delivering a packet from Nawab Sharief. He didn't fail to mention that some undelivered packets were meant for Generals Hyder Bux and Sarfaraz.

The dialogue baffled Jahanara. She was looking forward to a warm night, with Harfan's bare body setting fire to her flesh and soul.

What the hell was he talking about?

Harfan's strange telephone calls had baffled the ISI operatives as well. Jamanat Ali threw the earphone away and uttered a Punjabi slang, graciously linking Harfan in sexual relationship with his mother. The bastard was either a damn fool or a highly trained agent. He must have gathered the whiffs of his boys and bugs. Hell with it!

It clearly dawned on Jamanat that his electronic operations were either compromised or he was led into a serious trap by seemingly wrong judgment of his bosses. This guy Harfan was either a clean fly or he was a highly trained intelligence agent. The trained counterintelligence salts in him gradually catalysed in favour of the assessment that Harfan was too clever for his boys. Some army egghead might have betrayed nervousness.

The next possible scenario terrified Jamanat Ali. Who could prevent Harfan from leaking out the ISI covert operations against Begum Jahanara? The mercurial lady was capable of getting him skinned for her next pair of sandals. It was possible in General Arif 's Pakistan. Simply no one was going to come to his defence. Not even General Hyder Bux.

Jahanara wasn't trained to hide irritation.

She dialled Harfan's room.

"What bloody medicine does Hyder require?" She asked contemptuously.

"*Mohtarma*," Harfan drawled his reaction, "I don't know. Nawab sahib told me that the General required some tonic." He hastened to add.

"And what's that PSO looking for?"

"*Mohtarma*," Harfan talked with trained hesitation in his voice, "I've no idea at all. I just collected the packets on behalf of Nawab sahib."

"Tonic or aphrodisiac? They should come to me for picking up a few lessons in mid-age sexual bliss. Anyways, you're welcome to my room any time." Jahanara banged the phone on its cradle with a vicious sense of delight.

Harfan leisurely walked down the corridor to room 406. The *habshi* opened the door and stood guard outside.

Harfan stood behind the curtain, peeped in, and looked for Jahanara. She was seated before a mirror, busy applying her favourite eyeshade, with delicate brush strokes.

As she turned towards the door, Harfan placed his right index finger on his lips and signalled her to be silent. He respectfully walked down to the centre of the room and handed over a packet, in full view of Jamanat's video cameras.

"*Mohtarma*, here is your medicine from Nawab sahib."

He made a move to leave.

"Thanks, please convey my best wishes to dear Nawab. I'm so thankful for the medicines. *Khuda Hafiz.*"

Jahanara, perplexed as she was, wondered if General Hyder Bux had bugged her room. It must be him. She was baffled by the turn of events. Was she a suspect in the eyes of the *Sadr*? Did Hyder snoop her last escapade with Harfan?

Or was Hyder snooping for evidence against her and the President and cooking up evidence to justify a coup?

General Naim, the elder Khan, wouldn't dare.

Possible. The ISI only the ISI could do that.

She smelt the burning cordite of another coup-plot. That's what finally happened to military rulers—one coup overtaking the other, a coup within coup. Arif did it to his mentor. Why should not Hyder do it to him?

Bloody heavens! With General Arif's exit, these hungry Generals would fuck her to death. She must be on guard and speak to the big man in private. General Hyder, Naim had informed her, had ganged up with Sarfaraz and the Sindhi jackal,

Izaz. What had kept her lover boy hanging onto the fragile twigs of power was the Chinese and American support. Minus their support, the hungry pack of wolves would've made a hearty meal of his flabby flesh.

Why had they bugged Harfan's room?

Did Hyder bug her bedroom too? Did he have any evidence of Harfan's presence in her bedroom? Oh heavens! That could explode like another Krakatoa! It couldn't be anything else. She was the barrel, through which Hyder's bullets would reach Arif 's heart.

Jahanara thought of calling General Arif 's Islamabad number, picked up the handset, and hastened to place it back. She recalled Naim's warning. Hyder had perhaps hooked up the phones of the President to his trick boxes.

She ordered her *habshi* to pour a large measure of White Horse and settled down after lighting a cigarette.

Well! Well! A coup was nothing new in *Allah's* own Pakistan. She couldn't probably prevent another General thrusting down the gullets of dear Pakistanis, another stiff dose of patriotic rule in uniform. The Pakistanis were accustomed to these brats in boots, like they were with the annual monsoon and periodical locust visitations. She ordered another whisky and decided to probe the minds of the two most powerful men in Pakistan, Hyder and Sarfaraz.

Minds of men?

Shit! It existed in their libido and in a particular organ. She had tasted scores of them. Hyder shouldn't be an exception, if he really had the right balls between his thighs.

"Hello. Is it the number of Gen. Hyder?" Jahanara dialled the ISI chief. The young Captain on duty was floored at the mention of her name and immediately connected her to the boss.

"Hello Cher Hyder," the soprano spoke in melted-cheese Urdu with a few French usages thrown in, "Oh là là! haven't seen you for ages. *Bhai* (brother) *kabhi to meri gali me aaya karo* (stray into my lane once in a while)."

Hyder momentarily lost his bearings, but immediately composed his thoughts and replied in equally charming Urdu.

"*Wale kum assalaam, mohtarma.* Am I lucky enough to tread the pathway to the most beautiful woman and the reigning soprano of Pakistan? At times I feel you're greater than that *malika-e-tarannum* (queen of melody), Begum Nurjahan!"

"Don't compare me with her Hyder. How can a street singer from Calcutta be my equal? I've pure *ashraf* Arab blood in my veins."

"I entirely agree *mohtarma*. But unlucky me, I don't find spare time to visit your charmed musical sessions."

"No one's born with luck Hyder. Come and see if luck is waiting for you, may be, between my bosoms." Her whisky-numbed tongue slurred over the words mischievously.

A highly embarrassed Hyder managed to murmur that he would surely chase dame luck to her doorsteps one of these days. He assured Jahanara that her scintillating audio records usually filled his precious leisure. *Insha Allah*! They would surely meet one of these days.

"You know Hyder," Jahanara fired a fatal bullet at him, "I'm told that the Indian medic at Dehradun is very good. Can you get me some medicines from there?"

"*Mohtarma*, our links are totally frozen. Any problem? Can I help?"

"Well Hyder, who else, but you, can help me? Your presence itself is medicine for my parched soul. Come over, I really miss you dear."

Jahanara disconnected the line and loudly cursed the ISI chief. She cried out at her *habshi* and ordered another stiff measure of White Horse.

The bitch! Hyder cursed Jahanara hurling an obscene Punjabi slang, which normally described a woman as a bed-trotting whore.

He was too small a person to receive her attention. What was this open bosomed invitation about? She normally undressed for likeable and fat-purse creatures. She used her Urdu like she was fencing with the sharpest sword.

Barqat's Lahore operation must have run into some nasty problem. The bitch must have detected some flaw in Jamanat's EIInt operation. Jahanara was one of the greatest survivors in the high social circuit. However, the instinct for survival did not necessarily endow her with the crafts of detecting a delicate electronic operation. Did the imperial brother, the PIB chief, tip her off? Well! Nothing should be taken for granted. This bloody Naim could stoop down to the darkest crevices of a melting pot, if that boosted his service prospects.

General Hyder Bux was more worried of the sword, precariously hanging over his head. The slimy lady wouldn't hesitate splitting the beans to her lover, with saline-tear and venom-tartar sauces. And the CMLA wasn't known to be the Paigambar of mercy. He was sure to face the guillotine and hit the ditch.

What should he do? Perhaps it was time to take cover behind the PSO's shield. He was correct. Needling Jahanara was a risky game.

Jahanara was too seasoned a nymph to swim along Hyder's meaningless paean. She was aware of the ruthless character of this Jat Punjabi. As a commander of the 26th Jat regiment, he had wiped out over 15,000 rebellious Baluchis in their mountain hideouts. He carpet bombed the villages and rained fire from helicopter gunship. He was better known as the *Qasai* (butcher) of the Pakistan army.

Her temperature still scaled past the boiling point. She wondered if that creature of shadow realm did have all the organs at right places. The S.O.B was too clever and perhaps the only military brass to escape her charms. Perhaps no juice was left in his haggard balls. That's why he cribbed for a supply of aphrodisiac from India. A pug-nosed brat! Jahanara cursed the ISI chief. He deserved a sweet death. Gen. Hyder Bux must pay for his audacity. *Insha Allah*, she would squeeze his balls out, for his audacity of bugging her room and spoiling two wonderfully planned evenings with her new lover boy, Harfan.

What next? Should she check out the other pretender?

"Hello General, how have you been?" Jahanara dialled General Sarfaraz.

"Fine *mohtarma*, as fine as these bloody Bengalis and Indians allow us to be."

"*Allah rakhe aapko* (let Allah protect you). You must come one of these days and taste the best wine and kebabs in the city. I know you require relaxation, and darling, you know, that I'm the best for it. You know it." Jahanara's voice sounded inviting and salacious.

"That'd be a privilege."

"Sarfaraz darling, I've a nagging feeling that some one is tapping my phone. I haven't spoken to the *Sadr* as yet. Would you like to look into this? Would you please darling?" Jahanara threw a probing pebble.

To Sarfaraz, the pebble was reminiscent of devastating volcanic explosion, which rocked him with violent tsunami waves. The bewitching soprano wasn't a nitwit. The bumbling ISI brats must have blundered again.

"Anything special *mohtarma*?" The seasoned PSO tried to fathom the crest of the killer waves.

"Nothing much darling. I keep on receiving ghost calls and there are silly noises. I was reading a book on the CIA, and I'm told that their sleuths often bug the White House phones too."

"Who would dare doing that in Pakistan?" Sarfaraz came out with loud protestations.

"Oh dear," Jahanara sighed sweetly, "in our blessed land no one seems to be safe, not even the highest."

"That's preposterous ma'am. All of us are loyal to the *Sadr*." Sarfaraz replied in the sweetest possible Punjabi.

"Dear, dear!" Jahanara's voice recoiled, paused and fired at a new target, "how is Chère Ashma?"

A fond reference to Sarfaraz's estranged wife.

"She's fine."

"You know dear, in order to have a child you must consult that Indian *vaid* from Dehradun. I get my medicines from him regularly."

Jahanara's blazing meteorite this time hit Sarfaraz straight on the face.

"We're almost at war ma'am. I can't think of contacting Dehradun."

"Dear, dear! What a pity! Come over, I can probably give you a few tips. Life isn't as difficult, as you imagine it to be. There are more hidden treasures beyond the affairs of the State."

Sarfaraz lost his cool.

These ISI gunks must've littered the market with their gooey operations! Bloody Nawab Sharief! Confiding in a serpent was a biblical mistake, but a lively mistake, which spanned on to creation. But confiding in Nawab Sharief could normally lead to the firing squad. How did that nympho know about his requirement of aphrodisiacs? Nawab must have carried the tale. This double dealer, Sarfaraz muttered a curse, should be smothered at the earliest opportunity.

Well! Most middle-aged men required some props to fortify sex prowess. He needed it more for his family peace. Wife Ashma had almost become a psychological wreck, because of his inability to impregnate her. His sperms, doctors had opined, didn't have the capacity to swim the uterine pacific and reach the ovarian isles of his wife.

Sarfaraz dipped the pin of his suspicion on General Hyder. He was the real culprit, an African baboon. The stupid had no business to bug her Lahore hotel room. He had forewarned the baboon adequately.

What a massive disappointment!

Jahanara's verbal bullets weren't less lethal than the fireballs hurtling down from the skies. The bumbling beauty was sure to sing into the ears of the CMLA and he was perhaps hours away from the 'Badr' dungeon of the ISI or the dark chambers of the interrogation centre at Chak Lala cantonment.

Was he being sucked into a trap laid by the ambitious ISI chief? That crook was capable of fabricating a parallel coup and diverting some anonymous bullets to shatter his skull. Lt. General Sarfaraz paced up and down the confines of his office room. He must get out of this mess and quickly.

Was it safe to cross the bridge with an unreliable Hyder Bux? He could blow up the planks beneath his feet midway. Thank heavens! Nothing prevented Hyder from telling a sob story to the President about his authorising the telephone tapping operation. Sarfaraz *Amritsaria* must survive. He did survive the partition holocaust. Didn't he?

Why not now?

He must throw the blazing meteorite back into Hyder's court, and not allow him to gang up with that manic Sindhi. That should buy him a survival-insurance. The resolution kept on gurgling inside Sarfaraz's smouldering psyche. Could he do it alone? No. He must have vital allies. Major players in the junta should side with him.

What about that fellow Alam Khan, the arms peddler? He had secured well-oiled tunnels to the CIA, MI6, and the Pentagon. Alam should be tapped. He could influence some key opinion makers in the US Congress and Senate and around the President. Peking would accept anything, once he assured the yellow Reds about Pakistan's eternal hate-commitment against Hindu India. That elixir alone had kept Pakistan's brittle bones together.

*

32

General Hyder Bux didn't remain idle either. He could ill afford to do that. Who could prevent Sarfaraz from ganging up with Jahanara and Naim and ambush him at the next street corner?

As a commander of a mountain division, he had mastered the art of ambushing enemy at the most unexpected spot. He must, Hyder concluded, activate his own spider web, Izaz Afroz, General Naqi, General Hamidur and the Air Chief. He could even fall back on the Chief, General Omar. Why not? He could blunt the malfeasance of Sarfaraz conclusively.

Why not Nawab Sharief? He might have in store new stories on the bitchy witch and that dark horse business executive. Was that boy Harfan really involved? Or did Nawab use him to oil his passage to the inner chambers of the seemingly first lady? That decent boy, married to a distinguished couple's daughter, had never come to his agency's notice. Israr Sharief was a clever businessman. He was not interested in politics. Why should he give such higher rating to Harfan? Well! Nothing should be left to chance. Pakistan was a tricky quagmire. Any false step could be fatal. He must fathom the depth of the muck first, created by Barqat's boys at Lahore.

"Barqat," Hyder thundered at his deputy, "what the hell have you done to Red Rose?"

"No word yet from Jamanat sir. I presume everything's going well."

"Bullshit! I don't think so. Take the Cessna; fly immediately and check for yourself. I think the operation has misfired."

"*Hai Rabba!* (Allah) I'd given Jamanat a meticulous blueprint. And he's our best counterintelligence operator."

"Don't waste time. I think we've hit a hidden rock, more formidable than your planning and Jamanat's expertise."

General Hyder Bux despatched his deputy post-haste and turned to the array of phones. He must call his partners. Sure, he wasn't going to offer his neck on a platter. It was now or never. He must make it to the top.

"But sir..." Barqat made a feeble attempt to justify his action.

"Now get lost and repair the damage."

Hyder Bux brushed past Barqat, boarded his car, and asked the driver to rush to the office of the PSO, Lt.General Sarfaraz Lodi.

*

"No, no Hyder, you got it all wrong. Why did you bug her room?" Sarfaraz was surprised to receive the visitor at an odd hour.

"Not at all sir," General Hyder sounded mighty officious and lied all the way. "My boys had treated Harfan Bukhari's room. He's the security suspect. I told you so."

"Hyder, let's not pretend that your boys are *sufi* saints. How can you pass Harfan as a security suspect? Simply because he spoke to the lady? Don't forget that he loudly announced Nawab's and our names. If you want to hang any one, that's Nawab."

"Can we touch Nawab? He's politically powerful in Punjab and is a crony of Izaz. I'm not gunning for that Harfan. I want to use him as a bait for that lady. We're supposed to cross the bridge together sir. Let's not walk in different directions." Hyder sounded an indirect warning to the PSO.

"You can't use that cliché all the time Hyder. We've lots of explaining to do, to the boss. I've gone through the audiotapes. That boy sounded innocent."

"It was done with your foreknowledge. Has she spoken to the CMLA?" Hyder scaled down his voice.

"I hope she hasn't. Nevertheless, she has unfurled the red alert. She buttonholes you and me. It's a mighty warning. Have your boys found any incriminating evidence?"

"No. Apparently not."

"It's highly embarrassing Hyder. The entire world needn't know that you and I require some nerve tonics," Sarfaraz shared his frustrations, "this lady will now compose a ballad on our sex virtues."

"Sorry sir. I'll try to control the damage. Leave it to me."

"You'd better do that Hyder, and do that pretty fast, before she sings into boss's ears. One more word of caution, don't try your usual disappearance trick with Harfan."

"Let's talk about it later, sir," General Hyder stood up, "we're together in the juicer, in our game of toppling the *Sadr*. You alone can't escape the churning blade."

"You can't blackmail me and I can't support all your misadventures."

Sarfaraz shot back firmly.

"There can be a genuine mistake. I run an agency and I've the mandate to probe reasonably suspicious leads. I can't take chance with the security threat to our VVIP, the President and the CMLA."

Hyder smiled with a slight squirm.

"You think you can sell that story!"

"In the intelligence game it's possible. Security is our Holy Ghost. That's our plausible alibi. You can sell any shit to a scared crow. Arif will buy anything if we're not caught red handed. I'll play up this aspect in the print media, highlighting suspected joint Indian and Peoples' League conspiracy to assassinate our President."

"Who would buy that story?"

"Don't forget sir, the Indians had played up the Delhi incident beyond all proportions. We had to do a lot of explaining to Washington and London. Why can't we do the same? The war environs will provide an azure backdrop to our story."

"You've some real hard selling to do."

"Don't worry. I will send across a few fabricated Int. reports. One from Aftab should point the needle of suspicion at Harfan." Hyder smiled as he stood up.

"And you want me to put up those to the boss as genuine reports!"

"That's correct."

"You've a real crooked brain Hyder. But how does it help? Are you not sacrificing an innocent man, this son in law of Zahoor?" Sarfaraz smiled with a sense of relief.

"That's what intelligence is made of. It's crooked all the way. And you require a crooked partner, in our common game," A sly smile crossed Hyder's face, "Harfan is not our target. Demolition of Jahanara is a part of our game. We shouldn't suffer from conscience fever if he is demolished in the process."

"I think I should call the media and brief them about unearthing of an Indian NSI plot to kill our *Sadr*. But who'll be the Indian ghost? Harfan?" Sarfaraz added in a hushed relaxed tone.

"As the Book says sir, *Allah* will guide us through darkness! Don't bother about details. In Pakistan, we can name anyone and shoot. Our uniform gives us licence. I don't mind if Harfan is the convenient dog." Hyder smartly saluted the PSO and prepared to leave.

"Well Hyder, shoot with a silencer, if you have to," Sarfaraz stood up, lighted a cigarette, and said, "that should buy us a breather before we administer final blow to the old toad."

"A...a...a...min."

Hyder saluted again and left with a satisfying smile on his face. His twenty-eight summers in the army and three-year stint in the ISI had taught him well the tricks of survival. Any plausible intelligence story could be sold to the *Sadr*, especially at a moment when he was befuddled by the developments in East Pakistan. The ISI could sell anything in the name of 'that widow in Delhi.' It would be too late for him when he discovered the intelligence charade. By then, he would either be shot or incarcerated in a state guesthouse.

*

Howling hell!

Sarfaraz's mind was not lulled by the crooked assurances of Hyder. No one should repose complete trust in an intelligence chief. He stood near a window and looked with squinted eyes at a funnel of dust and dry leaves being sucked up by whirling wind. His mind raced fast. Spiralling contradictory currents thrashed their heads against his chest.

Why shouldn't he take advantage of this mess and roll down the coup ball? Media blitz, as suggested by Hyder, should help in building up a congenial backdrop. A few pot shots at the drunken blabber ball by some paid assassins would fit in snug with the media hype.

Why not? Delhi had one hundred reasons to bump off the *Sadr*. Putting a mad dog sticker on a faceless fellow like Harfan, and shooting him shouldn't weigh heavily on Pakistani conscience. No one would cry for his wife.

It wouldn't be difficult to sell the story to Washington and Peking. After all, what they needed was an obliging Cold War bed partner, a client state. It mattered very little if Arif or Sarfaraz prepared the bed. That should be a separate sub-plot, distinct from the one hatched between him and Hyder. He could probably hire some Baluch or Frontier desperadoes. What about a fanatic Waziri? They were good killers. Best would be his friend Diljahan Farghani, a drug baron of Waziri descent. He was discreet and his men could get past the tough security curtain. There could be two separate plots, the Hyder one and the one executed through Diljahan.

Some quick fence mending would be essential.

Sarfaraz dialled Hyder's secured personal number, "Hyder there is an additional point I wanted to mention. Do you have the voice implantation technology?"

"What's your game?"

"Can some people fake Jahanara and Harfan's voices?"

"Technically it's not impossible."

"Erase all traces of reference to our names and add some incriminating dialogue between the two. Can you fake a story of Harfan's linkages with some Indian leaders?"

"Well sir," Hyder commented with a jackal like broken dry smile, "you're a better intelligence crook than I'm. Let me see. I'll get back with the finished product. But I don't think such intelligence culinary would be necessary to shoot an suspected Indian assassin."

"No harm if we've additional armour."

Sarfaraz felt slightly relieved. That neat trick should be a mighty weapon for public consumption, if he was ever needed to proffer a public statement after the takeover. Nevertheless, he must prepare for that historic event.

The Waziri drug lord lived not far from the Chak Lala cantonment. However, contacting him was a tricky job, trickier was the risk of leakage. He was not keen on any political post. All that he expected from the army was *laissez-faire* for his drug trade. The top brasses obliged him smilingly as parts of his sugar-money flowed into their pockets.

Would he do the job? At what incentive?

Why not grant him freehold of all the tracts in Waziristan for poppy cultivation and running a couple of refining factories? In any case, men like Diljahan brought in precious green bills to Pakistan.

Diljahan was a discreet person and not a minor killer. A normal social figure in *roja-iftar* and *Id* parties no one suspected his presence in the sprawling lawns of Sarfaraz amongst the milling glitterati of the capital. Plenty of food, female fragrance and fashionable chats about cats, dogs and foreign visits kept everyone busy and happy.

Diljahan slipped out of the party and briefly met Sarfaraz in his bedroom.

"There's an important job Diljahan."

"Ready to do it if there is a right price."

Sarfaraz spoke into his ears for good five minutes and looked at Diljahan with expectant eyes.

Diljahan spoke into Sarfaraz's ears, just for a minute.

"That's too costly Dil."

"The throne of Pakistan isn't cheap sir. You transfer the money to the Man of Isle and the job is done. Both the *Sadr* and Hyder will become the dearest of the *Allah* in one go. And you know sir, I'm not a singer. I don't sing ballads."

"Well Dil. I agree. I'll give you only seven days' notice."

"Good enough. You'll get three days to transfer the dough. Come sir, let's celebrate the *Id* over sumptuous food."

"Okay Dil. It's a deal."

"Deal sir."

The two conspirators walked out through different exits and merged with the milling, smiling and feigning crowd.

Diljahan was not the only camel that could carry Sarfaraz to the throne. Yes. He could only partially negotiate. He required a smiling nod from the Pentagon, Langley bosses, and the White House. They should be made aware of the blueprint of Pakistan's succession riddle. He must strengthen his ties with the real owner of Pakistan, the President on the Potomac.

Perhaps Mian Alam Khan could help. That jackal of an arms peddler knew of numerous subterranean highways to the strategic planners in Washington, London, and other European capitals. It was high time he activated that channel.

*

Hyder, by designation the tallest intelligence executive in Pakistan, rued the self-inflicted holes on his palms. Those holes, he knew, would by no means make him a holy martyr. He should have not given *carte blanche* to Barqat and Jamanat Ali, the policeman turned counter intelligence operative.

Khuda kasam (by God)! He should save his skin, by any means. The loud sounding tape faking suggestion of the PSO might help. However, an immediate cleanup operation was very important.

"By hell! What have you done Barqat? Did I tell you to bug her room?" Hyder fumed like a wounded *cheetah*.

"Sir, it wasn't intended that way. I'm not sure how this lady got scent of the bugs, the way she did. It must be that Harfan fellow. Only a trained agent can adopt such countersurveillance measures. He must have unmasked some of our blundering baboons." Barqat explained.

"Did he tamper with your equipment?"

"I don't think he did. No tampering signature. Clever turn of screws can't be detected."

"I can't put my neck on the line for your blundering baboons. Give me an urgent damage control fact-sheet. Remember, the PIB chief is loyal to the *Sadr*. He won't take time to make the old guy wiser."

"Copy sir."

"Good. Draw up a few blockbuster reports about Indian threat to the person of the *Sadr*. Joint Intelligence X will produce a few matching reports. Your station in Delhi should manufacture something from Aftab, pointing fingers at Delhi. I want these in a couple of hours."

"Yes sir."

"Dig up Harfan's cupboard. I want a few skeletons unearthed, real or dummy, pretty fast."

"He appears to be a clean chap. Should we frame him?"

"Do what I say. The truth isn't what it appears to be. It's what you make it out to be. I know the higher truth. You follow my truth and climb up the ladder very fast. Is that clear?"

"Yes sir." Barqat replied meekly.

"Fine. Get going." General Hyder dismissed his trusted deputy with a firm warning. No more aimless angling, he had to manufacture smoking gun evidence.

*

Jamanat Ali had no explanation for the Lahore flop show. There must have been a mix up, he agreed. Only a well-trained agent could detect the hair-thin fault lines in his operations. How could anyone detect the bugs without an electronic debugger? It was beyond Jahanara to detect the bugs. Harfan Bukhari must have tipped her off. His telephone dialogues sounded like well-researched scripts of a Hollywood movie, full of clever ploys and plenty of misleading drops. The bastard must have had used a scanner to detect the bugs.

Plausible. Barqat agreed. He had other doubts.

Did Naim's men play spooky ghosts? Did the *Sadr* play up the PIB against the ISI? Did the CMLA suspect the ISI chief for piloting a coup? It wasn't a new trick. General Arif 's predecessor had used the MI Directorate and the ISI against the PIB for its suspected links with his political detractors. He had brought in a trusted SSG crony to the highest PIB post. That's how the elder Khan happened to grab the coveted seat.

Allah Mian! What should he do? Barqat sweated under his shirt and switched on the ceiling fan. Perhaps Jamanat was correct. Everything was possible in Pakistan. It was difficult to fathom the intricate crosscurrents and measure the arches of conspiracy against the President. Probably his chief too was mixed up in the odd ball game. A whole load of shit!

Anyways, why should he offer his neck to the chopping block by refusing to see the truth of Hyder Bux? If he was to serve him, he must perceive his master's truth as well. A few botched up fabricated reports would not necessarily shake the orbit of the earth. The boss and *Allah* were the most potent forces to reckon with.

Barqat transferred the Red Rose documents to his 'transit morgue' as he fondly described his personal record room, a concealed locker embedded in his office room wall. He initiated a file–Operation Salamat–scribbled a detailed note on Harfan Bukhari and flagged in four reports that he had drawn up to spell out the highest degree of physical threat to President General Arif Khan. A few reports from JIX and Delhi station were also dog-eared with red markers.

He called in Jamanat Ali.

Recruited in the Central Intelligence Bureau in 1935, Jamanat, hailing from the Frontier Province, headed a section in the India-Special Operations Cell under Section S. Known better by the endearing sobriquet, 'bulldog,' he was respected in the intelligence community as an uncompromising professional.

"Track down the horoscope of this Harfan, from the day his mother had conceived him," Barqat ordered.

"Fine sir," Jamanat clicked his heels, "that would please me most. The bastard had tricked us at Lahore."

"Are you sure? Or was it the PIB spooks?"

"My guts say it's him. He must be a trained agent."

"But your boys had goofed up."

"I regret it sir. But I can smell a counterintelligence suspect from a mile away. The PIB boys don't have that kind of finesse."

"Fine. However, be discreet. It's purely an in-house exercise. Nothing official. I want it to be a steady but low-key probe. Don't put these pig-headed army rejects on the job. Use some of the professionals."

"I get it sir. Do I use our Karachi resources?"

"What for?" Barqat asked.

"I've been getting some whiff of the air around this chap, a distant smell of a rotting rat. This creature Harfan is a fake. Give me time to chisel off his enamel." Jamanat's enormous moustache danced in tune with his beaming smile.

"How come?"

"Nawab Sharief feels that this chap could be an impostor, an Indian agent."

"Isn't he spitting venom to spite his brother?"

"May be. But Nawab's story is a helpful prop."

"Hook up his phones. Take care of his uncle in Karachi. Gather tidbits. But don't be intrusive."

"Fine sir. I'll put Karamat Suri on the Karachi job. He was posted there for four years. "

Jamanat clicked his heels sharply and offered a palm shaking salute.

*

33

Ibadat did not receive many phone calls at his Hotel Royal Palace desk. The small town received very few tourists. The American technicians working at the nearby Mianwali power plant were the regular customers. The Chinese had started visiting the place recently to install a backup radar station at Jhumra and for upgrading the nearby airbase at Jhang Marghiana. The squint-eyed guests did not bother Ibadat. Two cooks accompanied them and most of their cooking materials were flown in from Mainland China. The pungent smell from their kitchen, whenever they cooked dried fish, made Ibadat hostile to the very idea of testing Chinese culinary products.

That cloudy evening he was seated at a far corner of the lobby in a pensive mood. In fact, he was delving deep into the incidents that resulted in the assassination of the former king. His father too had died at the battle of the Jung Tikri while trying to protect the king. His mind was focused on Harfan Bukhari. Mian Alam did not spell out that the former king's son had returned to Pakistan with some special mission. Did he hold back the information deliberately?

There was uncanny physical and behavioural resemblance between the former king and Harfan. Ramayani's queer behaviour at the first sighting of Harfan had erased most of his doubts, if he had any.

Should he probe her a little more?

Ibadat shelved the idea. His mother had reassured him about Harfan's physical resemblance to the former king. She could not be wrong. She had sworn Ibadat not to disclose the secret. These human bondages, she emphasised, transcended the narrow religious and sectarian considerations. Human bondages, she believed, were even above divinity.

The sharp ringing of the telephone snapped Ibadat's concentration. He picked up the instrument and replied mechanically.

"Hotel Royal Palace here."

"Brother," a voice whispered on the line, "I'm Karamat Suri."

"Hello brother Karamat," Ibadat responded warmly, "how're things?"

"Fine with me. Please inform *ammi* (mother) that I'd be out to Karachi for a few days."

"Are you leaving today?"

"Not today brother. Probably I leave in another two days. A big operation has come up."

"Can we see a movie together before you go? You'll like the classic movie Mughal-e-Azam. Can you come down to Lahore?"

"I was in Lahore only a few days back. That's another fascinating story. *Allah* knows what's happening to Pakistan!"

"Come down for a few hours."

"Well brother," Karamat agreed, "tomorrow is Sunday. Meet me at Sabina restaurant, at the Model Town bazaar. You know that place behind the bus terminus. Is not it?"

"Yes, I know. I'll be there before lunch. Let's have food together. Don't worry about your *ammi*. She is fine and I'll visit her tonight."

"So nice of you brother." Karamat, a native of *mohalla* (locality) Rajora of Jhumra town, hung up the line.

The former king had exclusively assigned the Rajora habitat to his Muslim employees. Karamat's father, Qalam Suri, served Raja Digvijay Kaushal as a *subedar* (junior commissioned officer) and had laid down his life at the battle of Jung Tikri, in the wake of the earth shaking post-independence events.

The Suri family title was a distant linkage to Karamat's Afghan ancestors, who had migrated to Jhumra from Delhi. His family claimed to be the direct descendants from the lineage of Sher Shah Suri, the short Afghan hyphen in the prolonged Mughal rule over India.

The Jhumra kings followed the time tested tradition of maintaining a mixed army of Muslims and Hindus. Digvijay was especially fond of the Afghan and Pathan fortune hunters. These mercenaries helped him in keeping the turbulent local Muslim subjects under leash.

A junior commissioned officer in the 7th Northern Light Infantry, Karamat was seconded to the ISI and was attached to the Special Operations Cell, headed by Jamanat Ali. He and Ibadat had developed a special relationship. Their fathers were loyal employees of the former Hindu king. Both of them had fought valiantly to protect the king and queen. They were also motivated to fight the marauding Niazi, Mazari and other tribesmen with a view to protect their fertile land, granted to their families by the Kaushal kings. The raiding hoard did not stop after killing almost all the Hindus. They raided the Rajora habitat of the royal employees, plundered their homes, and raped their women.

Ibadat had not joined Alam's network for the love of money alone. He hated to be treated as a spy. But, he hated the new masters too, who had killed his father, dishonoured his sister and usurped his fertile agricultural land.

Karamat, a childhood friend, and a compulsive talker emotionally depended on Ibadat. Together they nurtured the secret plan to rout the Niazi usurpers, reclaim their valuable land, and take revenge against the killers of their fathers. In the process, Ibadat discovered that in Karamat he had a subconscious agent inside a very sensitive area of the Inter Services Intelligence. He did not fail to exploit the opportunity.

Lahore's Old Model Town market was a replica of the markets behind Delhi's Jama Masjid. It bustled with life and catered to almost all the needs of the frequenters right from wet merchandise to bumpy women. A contraption called the cycle rickshaws, which were mostly pedalled by Bengali Pakistanis, could only negotiate the narrow lanes. Ibadat hired a garishly decorated rickshaw and asked the driver to take him to Sabina restaurant, situated next to the wet market that exclusively handled fish, meat, and vegetables. Left to him Ibadat would have never chosen Sabina for a rendezvous. But Karamat liked the spot. It was conveniently located at the backside of a long distance bus terminus and the railway station was only three furlongs away. It was an important transit station for his journey to Islamabad from Jhumra.

Karamat arrived slightly late. He did not brook any delay in opening his mind. Ibadat hated the highly spiced food but relished what Karamat had to say about his interesting mission in Lahore and the forthcoming visit to Karachi.

"Brother Ibadat," Karamat opened up, "there appears to be another military coup in the offing."

"We just had a peaceful one," Ibadat added, "which one you're talking of?"

Karamat's logic was incontrovertible. How could the ISI mount an elaborate electronic surveillance on Begum Jahanara and her boyfriend Harfan, if the bosses were not sure of a change in the guard? She was the reigning queen of Pakistan. Ibadat gasped in disbelief.

"Did you say Harfan? I believe the lady is a personal friend of the President. Who is this Harfan?"

"Did you say a friend of the President?" Karamat continued to talk excitedly, "she's the queen of heart of the top boss. That's what we keep on talking in Islamabad. And to be frank I don't know who this Harfan is."

"Must be a big chap. Otherwise why should your company put him under surveillance?"

Karamat looked around to be sure that no one overheard him and continued his story in a whispering tone. This fellow Harfan, he said, was a clean guy. He had a brief love talk with his wife. His talks with Begum Jahanara and Nawab Sharief had simply mentioned about some medicines he had procured from an Indian *vaid* for the big lady and more surprisingly for his own boss and the PSO.

"Why should he go to India for medicines? We're fighting an undeclared war with India." Ibadat provoked his friend.

"Oh no," Karamat made a guttural sound to express his disagreement, "he got it from London on the prodding of Nawab sahib."

"That's a small matter. Why should you be so excited?"

This provocation was too much for Karamat. He alone was not excited; Karamat took a deep breath as he spoke. The entire ISI was in virtual turmoil over the incident. Begum Jahanara, he disclosed, had chanced to discover that her hotel phone was bugged. She did not spare his boss and the PSO and had pulled them up with nasty words.

"Brother," Karamat displayed a victorious smile, "the matter is not so simple. We're now investigating this fellow Harfan in a big way."

"Why? What is his fault?"

"Jahanara has tightened the screw on my boss and he's now trying to screw her and this fellow from Karachi. I'm going there at the head of a team to make secret enquiries about his uncle."

"Are you coming home tonight? There is a train at four p.m. Perhaps we can talk about your marriage with Alma."

"I feel tempted. She's a fine girl. But brother I've to take an early morning flight to Karachi tomorrow."

"It appears you're a big boss now."

"It's in line of my duty."

"Okay. Keep me informed about the big coup plot. I hope the next General will be a better one. Who's the likely next hero? Do you have any idea?"

"Very difficult to guess brother. But Jamanat sahib says that ultimately Izaz Afroz will win," Karamat brought his mouth nearer to Ibadat's ears, "but I can tell you for sure brother, it's going to be either my boss or the PSO, General Sarfaraz. He has put the phones of Jahanara and the President on tap. He knows everything."

"Presume you'll have a better time if he wins the race!" Ibadat provoked his friend further.

"Nothing will happen to me. But with the change I want to see that *randi* (prostitute) dancing nude in the Ananrkali market."

"Do you mean Jahanara? Why? She hasn't wronged you."

"I am a poor JCO. What can she do to me? She makes every one dance around her. I would like to see her dancing in the nude. You can't stop me expressing my wish."

"Let *Allah* fulfill your wish. Take care and keep me informed about the likely coup. Let's now go for the movie."

"No brother," Karamat declined the offer, "I've to report back to my unit for a briefing session. *Khuda Hafiz*."

Ibadat said goodbye and rushed to a pay phone booth at the inter-state bus terminal.

He dialled a Quetta number and waited for the other side to respond.

"Allahbux here. Who is on the other side?"

The voice at the other end boomed out.

"Is it Allahbux of Masjid Ghorewali?".

"I said so."

"*Janab*, (sir) I am the personal servant of Alam sahib. Will you please tell him that his pet dog is sick? It needs doctor's attention."

"You're a strange person Mian. Here I don't have the time to pray to the *Rasul* (representative of God) for human beings and you're worried over a dog!"

"What can I do *alem* sahib (the learned one)? I'm informing you as the dog is very dear to my master."

"Fine. Rest well. Your message will be delivered."

Ibadat disconnected the line and boarded a bus for Jhumra. Karamat's story had baffled and frightened him. He did not expect Harfan to get embroiled in the vortex of power tussle in Pakistan.

He was not sure about the reaction of Alam. That man often behaved strangely. Should he use the reserved communication channel to Delhi? Ibadat thought over it for a while and decided to wait for Alam's arrival.

Ibadat recalled the innocent face of Jamilla as the bus speeded through the green-forested area between Sangla and Jhumra. The distant waters of the Jhelum River reminded him of another tragic face, the weather beaten face of Ramayani. The bygone saga of the Kaushal kings, as he heard from his mother, glimpsed past his mind. Well! Ibadat exhaled a deep sigh. Why should Harfan Bukhari, whatever his Hindu name was, land up at Jhumra and excite new dreams in persons like him, Ramayani and Jamilla?

Strange were the ways of *Allah.*

*

34

Seated at a far end of the banquet hall of Lahore's Hotel Pearl Continental, Harfan allowed his mind to spread wings. The aborted Lahore rendezvous had rattled him. He flew over the open canvas of Pakistan's power politics and the possible contours of the net that the ISI was likely to cast for him. The collage appeared confusing and no light was visible at the end of the tunnel. He thanked his trainers, Col. Pathania, Maulana Rizwan and Dhiren Bhagat. The training rigors were more refined than the crude ISI ElInt techniques. The ISI boys were simply not equipped to manage a difficult target in a classy hotel like the Falleti.

Superior training in counter-ElInt tradecraft had earned him a reprieve. But the breather must be a transient one. The ISI was definitely not going to sit on haunches and allow their suspicion to sprout Mexican beans.

He must have caught the ISI flu from Jahanara's mansion. Or was he simplifying the threat? Perhaps. Why should the agency pursue him doggedly? Was it an accidental contamination? Or was he a logged suspect of the ISI? Whatever it was, he must deepen his trenches and strengthen his foxholes. Harfan went back in time and scanned all the events since his clandestine entry into Pakistan.

Had he committed any serious mistake?

Perhaps he had.

His indiscreet visit to Jahanara's mansion must have triggered off panic in the brittle citadel of the power brokers.

The ISI might have logged the visit.

Nawab Sharief could be another source of trouble.

Israr was correct about the raging struggle inside the Chief Martial Law Administrator's powerhouse. The ambitious Generals were gunning for the President and he, poor Harfan Bukhari, had inadvertently strayed into the minefield, spiked for the top man's favourite girl.

Anyways, he mustn't stray into that lane again. He did not expect any rescue team from Alam and Delhi.

So? He was there, on his own, in Wild West Pakistan.

Would Jamilla stand by him? Would she like to flee Pakistan with an Indian agent, who wasn't even a born Muslim?

Perhaps she would agree to take a walk over the razor's edge. She loved him. Her love had transformed his life. She had infused a new desire to live in him. The buck stopped with Jamilla. Yes, he must live for Jamilla, their son Pervez and for himself, of course. He wouldn't allow the butchers of Delhi and Islamabad to put his neck on the chopping block.

Harfan lighted another cigarette and tossed the idea of quitting Israr's job and take up some other assignment. He could go over to London for higher studies. Would the NSI agree? What if they gunned him down? Harfan looked around with a nervous look.

A young Captain, seated across the table, suddenly intruded into Harfan's private dream. He borrowed a cigarette, lighted it, and concentrated on his drinks. Harfan, lost in his dark thoughts, hadn't noticed the young officer. He appeared to have fogged out or lost in the spacious ambience of the banquet hall. The fellow fiddled with the room keys, and looked vacantly at the ornate ceiling, not exactly admiring the marvellous frescos.

Captain Ayub Suhrawardi, attached to the office of General Naqibullah, the Defence Advisor, was in fact, cursing his immediate superior, Brigadier Fateh Khan of Division L III, in the CMLA's office. That brute had forced him to attend this damn meeting in Lahore.

What for!

Just to copy minutes and prepare a detailed report for General Naqi!

Shit! An army Captain wasn't supposed to work as a stenographer! He wished he could hang the imbecile Generals, whose priorities were concentrated in their balls and foreign accounts! That's why the bloody Indians could maul them in successive wars.

"To hell with the yellow punks..." Captain Ayub blurted out.

"Did you say something?" Harfan looked at the seemingly disoriented officer.

"Sorry. It's not you. I'm cursing the Chinese midgets."

"Any problem? Can I help?" Harfan offered another cigarette and helped him light it.

Yes. There were problems galore. Captain Ayub opened up like a talking and Weeping Willow. The venue of the important defence liaison meeting was shifted to Lahore without any rhyme and reason. The wrap of secrecy was meant for befuddling India. New Delhi had lodged several protests in the UN Security Council, on the suspected induction of Chinese and American weapons to the killing fields of East Pakistan. They had managed to steal minute details of the Army and Air force supply inventories. The DMI and the ISI were still scratching their heads over the security leaks.

Shit! One of these days, Pakistan was sure to rue its friendship with these pork-eating yellow *kafirs*. They were simply using Pakistan against India. They weren't friends of Islam. Didn't they treat their Muslim minorities as desert insects?

"You mean India has positioned agents in our defence forces too!" Harfan asked.

"Oh dear friend!" The young officer stood up almost ceremoniously, "I'm Captain Ayub Suhrawardi from General Naqi's office."

"Glad to meet you," Harfan poured a drink for Ayub, "Harfan Bukhari here, representing Israr International."

"Did you talk of Indian agents? Why not? They're everywhere. The Hindus are our civilisational enemies." Ayub downed his drink, neat.

"Wish I could meet one." Harfan steadied his gaze on Ayub's face. No. There was no reaction.

"To hell with this war! To hell with the warmongers." Captain Ayub blabbered out the curse, through his half hanging lips.

"Don't worry. We've powerful friends in America and China."

"Don't ever be foxed by the Yankees. They aren't anybody's friend, not of Pakistan and nor of Islam. Damn Christians and Jews can't measure up to us Muslims."

"You appear to be upset." Harfan threw an anticipatory pebble.

Yes. He was. He had reason to be, Ayub blurted out.

Attached to General Naqi's office, he was literally forced to accompany the Pakistani delegation. The disturbing order was handed over at his leave address, only a day after his marriage to college day fiancée, Reshma. The Brigadier had mowed down his entreaties for exemption. His only argument was that Pakistan was on the brink of a war with the *kafir* Hindu country and all patriotic Pakistanis were required to come to the Fatherland's rescue.

Did he say that he was yet to consummate his marriage? Fucking a virgin hole could wait for better days. His immediate superior, Brigadier Fateh Khan had dismissed him unceremoniously.

"Wasn't it unfair and vulgar?" Ayub asked.

"Sure it was. The bosses can often be heartless." Harfan played along.

Two junior participants, Ayub from General Naqi's office and Harfan from Israr International were seated on the same table, at the farthest corner of the banquet hall; almost near the military band, playing a low decibel Chinese score. Harfan didn't take time to size up the young officer, doodling over drinks. Lost in his soured dreams he was a loose talking tree, rather a green sapling.

Ayub gulped another drink and suddenly turned towards the high table.

Funny creature! The chatterbox corked himself up.

Harfan offered another cigarette and volunteered information about his company trying to clinch a deal for airlifting defence equipment from Phuket to Dacca, in chartered flights.

The ice melted a little bit.

"It's not chartered flights friend." Captain Ayub responded in an agitated voice.

"Pardon!"

"You don't fly to Phuket. The fucking Yankees, I mean the CIA is arranging that leg of the operation. In their covert flights."

Well! Harfan rearranged the tools of his trade. The young kid appeared to be a hidden piece of precious diamond bearing rock. He geared up to drill the young Captain cautiously.

"You mean direct CIA flights! But the US Congress has banned weapons supply to us."

"That's for the matinee show. The late night adult shows start with Phuket and stretches up to Jeddah, Amman and Istanbul." Ayub flaunted a victorious smile.

"Weapons supply by proxy? Where do we stand then? I thought we've bagged the contract."

Harfan spoke in an injured innocent voice.

"Well brother, you may have bagged the Sargodha-Dacca sector. There are more surprises in heaven and earth than you can imagine, Hora…what did you say your name is! Whatever, it is Horatio…the Yankees have real long arms. They're the real owners of Pakistan and we're so dependant on three 'A's."

"It's Harfan. Horatio or Horace was a Roman poet. What're the three 'A's?

"America, Army and Allah, all in that descending order."

Ayub lifted his empty glass and looked around for another drink. Harfan summoned a straying waiter, poured a few extra ounces in Ayub's glass, and helped himself to one.

The Captain unfolded his wounded heart as the whisky started sinking. The Indian dogs deserved exemplary punishment. Weren't these heathens lorded over by Islamic monarchs for hundreds of years? They deserved another spell of purification, under the Islamic rule.

Harfan managed to say that history had the habit of often repeating itself. Another spell of Islamic rule over Hindu India wasn't improbable.

"Hell with them," Ayub flexed his fist, "before they try any misadventure, the Kashmiris are hell bent on giving them a bloody shower."

"I couldn't agree less. Hope we aren't walking into another war?"

War it was, Ayub displayed a tired smile, a slow and steady war, which would bleed India white. The Hindus must be penalised for their involvement in East Pakistan. This dogged and fierce proxy-war would be fought in Kashmir and all over India. Every Muslim home in India would be converted into a forward citadel of Islam.

Captain Ayub stopped his monologue as the heads of the delegations stood up to deliver speeches, highlighting bonds of friendship between their ancient countries. A toast to the good health of the two Heads of State was raised, followed by speeches. Captain Ayub Suhrawardi was in no position to stand up to raise the toast. He stared askance at the crowd around and tried to lift his body up. Like a battered scarecrow, cap on the floor, hair disheveled and limbs numb, Ayub collapsed. Harfan propped up his body and cautiously dragged him out of the ceremonial dining hall.

Back in the room, Harfan sprinkled water on Ayub's face, unfastened the uniform buttons, and removed his shoes.

"Did they see me in a drunken stupor?" He made anxious enquiries.

"I don't think they did."

"Thanks pal. You know the stress I'm in." Ayub explained.

"No thanks required and no excuses, friend," Harfan added, "these bloody Indians are screwing us all. They've ganged up with that traitor Jainal to tear our nation apart."

"To hell with the Indians", Ayub screamed out, "the Kashmiri boys are planning a big show. They may blow up the residence of the *Sadr-e-Ryasat* (Head of the State), hijack, and blow up Indian planes and the *Fatah* boys may even bomb that hornbill-nosed Indian PM."

"Like to have a black coffee?"

"So kind of you."

"To be precise," Ayub's drunken rambling continued, "my former colleague in the CMLA, a veteran of the ISI, Col. Akram and his colleague Mirza Baloch, both cover diplomats in the Pak High Commission, Delhi, are in touch with the Kashmiri boys."

"Forget it, have the coffee first. It'll help." Harfan poured the black concoction into two cups.

"The visit of the Chinese delegation isn't an end by itself. The President has already played an ace to ensure the US support. Serious talks are on between Washington, Rawalpindi and Peking for making a diplomatic breakthrough." Ayub sermonised with another victorious smile, "they're highly suspicious of the mysterious shuttles between Delhi and Moscow. Wait for the new axis to emerge. We'll give India a bloody nose."

"Hell with the Indians. But brother, are we in a position to contain the bloody Hindus?" Harfan asked innocently. He was more than delighted to have accidentally hit the jackpot.

"Another cigarette please. As I said, the CMLA and the President, the Chief of Army Staff and their advisors are totally seized of Indian designs in the East," Ayub continued, "Operation Kalam has been worked out, to blunt the Indian offensive."

"What's that?"

"The operation plans include depopulation of the border villages. The Bengali dogs would be housed in new village groups, guarded by our armed forces. All routes leading to India would be sealed."

"That's a nice strategic move," Harfan quipped, "it's sure going to thwart the evil designs of the Hindus."

"The troops have been directed to detect the Indian thugs and their Bengali collaborators, latest by May 15. The Indian stooges are to be executed. The ISI has prepared a comprehensive list of these Indian agents."

"Yup," Harfan responded, "once they kill the rabid intellectuals, it won't be difficult to silence the rest of the ruts— the enemies of our nation. How do they dare dining on the same plate with the Hindus in the name of secularism?"

"Correct. That's why General Tarakki has been posted to Dacca," Ayub poured out more of his knowledge. "the British had committed a big mistake by exposing the Bengali baboons to liberal education. Take their language away and they'll be as good as dead rats. It has been a mistake all the way, not imposing Urdu and pure Islam on these half Hindus."

"How correct you are!" Prodded Harfan.

"There you are," Ayub jumped on his bed, "we in Pakistan have committed a big mistake by trusting these Bengali *kafirs*."

"Now sleep," Harfan said, "*Insha Allah*, we'll drown the Indian rats in the Arabian Sea and the Bay of Bengal."

In drunken delirium, Ayub burst into hysterical sob.

"Don't cry. You should be back to your wife in another two days." Harfan comforted the lovelorn young Captain.

"To hell with the bosses. I'm stuck *yar*."

"Come on Captain, don't feel small," Harfan screwed in the nut, "a senior always gets preference over a junior. You'll get your turn."

"No friend, the buggers in the operations directorate may push me out to the front by the time I finish with this assignment." Ayub picked up a cigarette and walked down to a window, exhaling the smoke with a loud sound.

"Why should you move to the front so early? That's not fair." Harfan tightened the screw a little deeper into Ayub's psyche.

Ayub didn't disappoint him.

Pakistan, he blurted out, was on the threshold of another war. The military regime was biding time to replenish war-field hardware. The build up after the '65 drawn war was appallingly inadequate. The American pipeline was still clogged and the main source of supply was China. That was the mystery behind the red-carpet treatment to the Chinese defence delegation.

Peking had promised major help. The Chinese team was scheduled to discuss with the Military Law Administrator in Dacca the quantum of need of the East Pakistan Garrison. The saddest episode of the drill, Ayub commented, was his forced deputation with the Chinese delegation.

The grand finale of Ayub's intellectual oration involved stories of successful interception and deciphering of an Indian Army signal to its front formations. The cipher had advised readiness for an all out war with Pakistan in the third week of November, perhaps the day of the Eid, the auspicious 20th November.

"You've amazing knowledge." Harfan commented innocently.

"Naqi's office is a big clearing house. He's supposed to be the next President of Pakistan. He gets to know every bit that concerns our national security."

"Must be...you'd better get some sleep. We've an early morning flight to Dacca."

*

Harfan said *Khuda Hafiz* to his milking cow. He burnt late night candles to encode rather a long message. He did not forget to highlight the new contact's unconscious inputs on breaking of an Indian cipher. He went a step ahead to suggest that Ram Karan should be kept out of all strategic meetings. He could be the source of leakage. Islamabad was in a position to blackmail and hang him. After securing the DLB drop in a locker of Lahore railway station, he called Alam from a pay phone and trudged back to his hotel room. It was time for him to call Israr and share the good news with his employer.

"Morning sir, sorry to disturb you. There's good news. We may have bagged the contract for Sargodha-Dacca sector."

"Congratulations. General Naqi had called. I've finalised his part of the deal. Thank you for the astute negotiations." Israr responded in a happy mood, profusely thanking his junior.

"There's a catch. I believe the CIA is loaning two carriers for the Phuket operation. Perhaps we've to negotiate again with the CMLA's office. And I learn Nawab is putting a spanner."

"Thanks for the tip. I'd talk to General Sarfaraz and the Army and Air chiefs. Wish you a safe journey. Bon voyage."

"Listen sir. Nawab is pushing his claim through the ISI chief."

"I'd take care," Israr assured his executive and added, "I suggest that while in Dacca you meet Sarwar Illahi, the chief of East Pakistan police."

"Anything special sir?"

"He is a good Bengali. I am expecting a large order for small weapons, motorised boats and wireless equipment."

"I have never met him. Please call him up."

"Don't worry. Agree on a 5% commission if he insists."

"Understood sir."

Harfan hung up and threw himself on the bed, hoping to steal a few moments of sleep. He couldn't.

The shrill crowing of neighbourhood roosters snapped his snoozing slumber. He looked out. The huge bright crimson disk of the sun was just hanging over the tall trees of Bagh-e-Jinnah. It momentarily painted his windowpanes with a fast moving brush. The innate Hindu in him forced Harfan to fold his palms together, in the direction of the rising sun. He recited a Sanskrit hymn, in praise of the Sun god, seeking the safety and well being of his wife and son. They were his final anchors. Nothing existed beyond them. No NSI, no ISI, no Bhagat and no Mian Alam Khan.

The sun, as it always did, reminded him of the stark reality. Another day had come, another piece of bread was to be earned and to plan wearing better armours against the ISI. It was time he got ready to accompany the merchants of death to Dacca.

*

35

The Boeing 747 flight to Dacca, a charter from the Gulf Air Lines, with a technical halt at Colombo was boring. Harfan missed the delightful company of Ayub Suhrawardi, who was seated next to the Chinese delegation. He and another Chinese knowing Colonel from General Naqi's office made frenetic efforts to humour the inscrutable yellow faces. In between their incessant chattering in Chinese the members of the delegation asked the Colonel once in a while about the strategic Indian presence in the Andaman and Nicobor Islands. Some of them moved their heads both horizontally and vertically and took copious notes.

Finally, the huge bird flew low over the Narayanganj and Tungi industrial areas, plunged deep over the Buri Ganga valley and landed at Kurmitola Air Force base. Harfan was not a part of the official delegation. He was scrupulously kept out of the discussions between the Military Law Administrator (MLA) and the Governor and the Chinese delegation. Harfan was not unnecessarily worried about the contents of the closed-door discussions. His talking tree, Captain Ayub was around to fill in the gaps.

He took out time to seek an interview with Sarwar Illahi, East Pakistan's chief of police, and a scion of the former *nawab* family of Dacca. The meeting with Sarwar was brief. Israr had done the spadework. Harfan was just required to sign the tender papers on the dotted lines. The police chief waived the formalities of canalising the papers through various departments and pushed up a note to the MLA and the Governor for approval of the proposal on emergency ground. Harfan was not amused by the successful conclusion of the deal. He was acclimatised to the concepts of cuts and commissions and the philosophy of keeping everyone happy. That's how the wheel of the nation moved.

Harfan was not invited to the official dinner at the Governor's house in honour of the Chinese delegation. Holed up in his 7th floor room of Hotel Ichhamati he was bored by distant howls of jackals from nearby paddy and jute field marshes on either side of the river Buri Ganga. The pungent smell of dried fish that emanated from the nearby fishermen's colony irritated his nostrils. He switched off the TV and tried to concentrate on a book. This noble effort also was pleasantly disturbed by a lilting Bengali tune that came out from a nearby family quarter. He liked the pathos of the tune, which most probably fluttered its wings in search of a separated lover, but did not understand the language. He tried to train his ears to the craving tune when the unexpected call came in.

"Is Mian Harfan there?"

A whispering voice enquired as Harfan picked up the receiver.

Harfan tried to figure out the identity of the caller. Who could it be?

It could be another ISI trap.

"Are you there?"

"Who's there?"

"Mani this side. Come down, keep to your left, and walk past the hotel block. You will find a green Nissan waiting opposite a small mosque. Don't get into the car. Walk into the mosque straightaway."

"Is it safe?"

"You're safer with us than in the company of those Chinese louts. Come on in. We've important business to discuss."

Major Anjum Mani of the 3rd battalion SSG hung up.

Harfan gave a brief thought to Major Anjum Mani's invitation. He was already under the ISI scanner. That unfortunate visit to the pleasure house of Jahanara and his Lahore rendezvous had thickened the air of suspicion. Should he take another chance?

The intelligence bug got better of Harfan. He recalled Bhagat's tasking at Kathmandu and decided to take a chance. He changed over to jogging suit and track shoes and pulled the hood on as he walked passed the reception counter. The bored receptionist looked at the crazy jogger and closed his eyes again. These foreign guests were queer. They were adept in doing the most unexpected thing at the oddest hour. Harfan looked around and located the faint silhouette of the mosque two blocks on his left. He jogged slowly and caught a glimpse of the green Nissan as he sneaked past the wicket gate of the mosque.

"Open your shoes before you enter the precincts."

As a sharp beam of pencil torch focused on his face, Harfan looked up and tried to determine if he was in the correct company. Yes. Major Anjum Mani dressed in camouflage fatigue, but bare footed, stood before him.

"How do you know I'm in Dacca?"

"We've eyes and ears. The whole city knows you've accompanied the Chinese rats. Why are you doing this to us?"

"Am I doing anything wrong? I'm here to finalise a supply contract to East Pakistan Police and Israr International has bagged the contract for airlifting some Chinese supplies to Dacca."

"You're pumping in weapons of death for the Pakistani butchers. Stop it."

"Don't be unfair brother Mani," Harfan pleaded, "I'm a business executive. I don't preside over the fate of Pakistan. Are you alone?"

Harfan asked the question, as he smelt presence of strangers inside the mosque. He could see a group of people seated in a circle in the main prayer hall and discussing something animatedly.

"No. I'm not alone. There are few officers from the East Pakistan Rifles, East Pakistan Infantry, and other formations. We seek your help."

"Spell out."

"Brief my friends about arms supply from the US and China."

"I don't have a ready inventory. But I can tell that the supplies are meant to give the Pakistani armed forces a minimum of 15 day's battlefield and support logistics against the Indian invaders."

"Are you going to deliver all the consignments at Dacca?"

"That's my brief."

"Come, meet my friends."

Harfan did not reject the suggestion. He recalled the Kathmandu session with Bhagat. He was supposed to identify a few senior officers who could be independently contacted from Agartala, the capital of the Indian state of Tripura and other convenient points. Obviously, Delhi was keen to exploit the disgruntled Bengali officers.

"Come on in."

Major Mani prodded Harfan.

"I don't think it's safe. I've briefed you. You can share the details with them."

"Don't you believe me? Don't you believe that Pakistani butchers have already killed one million people?"

"The media in Pakistan is silent. There may have been excesses, but you are exaggerating."

"Don't live in fool's paradise. The army and its stooges like the Rajakar, Al Badr and the Jamait have wiped out hundreds of villages. Our women have been raped and our homes burnt. The Rajakar goons killed my own brother inside Dacca University. What more proof do you damn Pakistanis want?"

Major Mani wept like a kid in pain.

"Okay. I'll meet the others if it helps you."

He walked behind Major Mani and entered the main prayer hall, where about a dozen men in uniform were seated.

"Have you brought him?"

Asked a young officer who donned the rank badges of a Captain of the East Pakistan Rifles.

"Yes Rashid. He is here."

The Captain stood up and spoke to Harfan brusquely.

"Are you a Punjabi?"

"No."

"A Sindhi?"

"No brother I am a *muhajir* from the Indian town of Ludhiana. Why are you worried about my ethnicity? I am a Mussalman like you're and I earn my bread by honestly serving my master and the *Allah*. Can I help?"

"Paki Mussalmans are killing us. Islamabad is going to kill all the serving Bengali officers of the police and armed forces."

"You've the right information," Harfan replied with a steady voice, "and I can share with you another information. They've planned to kill all the Bengali intellectuals."

"And...?"

"And they're about to arrest and whisk away your supreme leader to Islamabad."

"How is it that you are friendly to Mani?"

"Can't two good human souls befriend each other? You could also be a good friend if we had the opportunity to meet earlier."

Suddenly a tall young man with a stubby beard jumped on his feet.

"He must be a Pakistani spy. Finish him here."

"Stop Tiger," Major Mani stood like a rock in front of Harfan Bukhari, "He's a good friend. He can help us."

"How?"

"He has promised to keep me and Wing Commander Khondokar informed about all the military supplies airlifted by his company to Dacca. That'll help us to plan our strategy. I hope you all agree."

There was a murmur of consensus.

"Look, killing me is not the solution. Are you Bengali officers' corps ready to fight? If you are, get in touch with your Indian friends. I hate what the junta is doing. Many Pakistanis don't endorse. But they're helpless."

"Your point is well taken. We're determined to fight to the last man and bullet. We've ceased to be Pakistanis," The Captain spoke in a friendly voice and added, "Let's know, if you can, when Islamabad plans to launch the final push."

"Wait till Washington and Peking give the final nod. It won't be very long. *Insha Allah* we'll be in touch. Can I ask you a question now?"

"You're free to ask."

"Why have you picked on me? I'm just another Pakistani. Why don't you contact the Indians directly?"

"As you said," Major Mani picked up the thread of the exchanges, "It's me, who wanted to convince my brother officers that we've a reliable friend somewhere in Islamabad. We expect you to drop messages at the phone number of this mosque and another number in Dubai, whenever you have useful information to share."

"Hope I too can fall back on you for help?"

Harfan asked the question involuntarily.

"Any time friend. We Bengalis are better friends than the Punjabis are. Just drop in and you're our honoured guest."

"It's time to go. I have to join the team for tomorrow's journey back to Karachi."

Harfan prepared to move out.

"What about the Chinese delegation?"

"They're flying to Rangoon in the first leg of their journey back to Peking."

"Wait for a minute. I've a query. Why is it that Indian minister advising low caste Hindus not to cooperate with the freedom fighters?"

"You've asked the wrong person. You should ask Delhi."

"It is difficult to reach them."

"Well brother," Harfan shrugged, "I shall help wherever I can. Let's go."

"Wait. Tiger please go out and see if the coast is clear."

The angry young man in civvies went out briefly and returned in five minutes.

"All clear. You may go now."

He joined his colleagues to say *shabba khair* to the visitor.

Harfan Bukhari looked back at the congregation of young officers of the Pakistan army and police and jogged out of the mosque after taking cover of the green Nissan. He looked back intermittently as he took the short jog to Hotel Ichhamati. The Nissan followed him until he reached the foyer of the hotel. It must be Mani's man, under instruction to ensure his safety. He liked the silent gesture and resolved to honour his commitment to the people who were struggling to free themselves from the bondages of the thugs in West Pakistan..

The lingering words of Anjum Mani about the Indian minister intrigued him. That charlatan must be his former political boss Ram Karan Prasad, the self-styled messiah of the oppressed and depressed classes of the Indian sub-continent. Harfan decided to include this precious input in his next cipher to Delhi. He felt satisfied that the night was well spent, though he could barely steal two hours' sleep.

*

36

Ram Karan Prasad, the legendary fixture in Delhi's political inner court, had suffered a bleeding nose and lighter pockets under the new Manjira dispensation. Media reports speculated about his backstabbing of Manjira's election efforts at the behest of a foreign power. Nampoothiri's reports about his Pakistani connection had impressed the Prime Minister. She had seen through his crude games of deception. Prasad had negotiated with her opponents for the top slot in South Block, on the ill-placed calculations that his 70 odd fledglings would waddle buoyantly to the Parliament floor, through the electoral slush. Only three injured ducklings came home to roost. His powerful allies had taken a sound beating at the hustings.

Manjira's astounding electoral success had changed all equations. Incarceration of Sardar Niyamat, the Kashmiri satrap, hijacking of an Indian Airlines plane by *Al Fatah* terrorists and the sabre rattling over developments in East Pakistan had generated new realities in the sub-continent and in certain world capitals.

Other developments in Delhi also moved ominously at faster pace. The most important circuit-connector and rising media star, Raghu Chawla, had retracted the Ram Karan bridge. His friend in Pakistan embassy had conveyed Islamabad's annoyance with Ram Karan and he was exiled from the new ministry headed by Manjira. Raghu, an ardent fortune hunter, had cast anchor of his rocking boat in the power wharf of Shankar, the rising son of Manjira. The rising son and rising star kicked well.

Ram Karan, he estimated, had metamorphosed into a stinking political corpse. The stigma of his questionable Pakistani connection had added a new stink to the existing fishy and fleshy smell around him. In Delhi, the city of winners, no one touched a political outcaste. Like the Hindu divine rodent, carrier of Lord Ganesha, Raghu believed in burrowing holes under the throne of the winners.

However, Raghu had underestimated Ram Karan's life force, whose voice ominously whispered on the celebrity scribe's exclusive unlisted phone seeking an exclusive dinner meeting.

Raghu arrived precisely at 9 p.m. in his just imported Toyota Corona, a new chariot gifted by a Bombay industrialist.

The drinks were silky, the dinner soothing and the dessert smooching.

Ram Karan broached the core theme over luscious food. With his billions, he did not deserve to be in political doghouse. He was ready to pay whatever it required to please lord Shankar.

"Wait it out Ram Karanji. You're under scanner of the NSI and the Pakistan embassy. They doubt your bona fide."

"Are you blackmailing me? Haven't you been my partner? Your links with the Pakis are well known."

"Don't bullshit," Raghu whispered, "I am a journalist. I can go and meet any diplomat. You can't nail me for simple information hunting."

"Don't threaten me. We're in the same boat. Now follow the strategy I suggest."

"I'm not threatening you. We may have been in the same boat Karanji, but now I've a new anchor. I'm no longer your protégé. Equations, like weather, change."

Raghu Chawla delivered the dialogue in a slow but piercing voice. He was no longer afraid of Ram Karan, now that he had tied his rope at the fishing wharf of Shankar.

"Take care," he continued, "the ISI often eliminates its sour assets. And I want you to know that my friend in the High Commission is mighty unhappy."

"What's his problem?"

"You had taken a couple of millions from them, for ensuring Manjira's defeat in the parliamentary polls. You know what happened."

"I've mended my fence with them. My followers are no more supporting the People's League."

"That's another problem. Don't meddle in East Pakistan. Manjiraji will make you disappear like a magician's rabbit. Your billions can't save you." Chawla winked at the former minister to measure up his reaction.

Ram Karan skirted the issue and guided Raghu back to the main theme.

"Please build a new bridge to Shankar."

"You can't build that bridge with small money. It takes millions."

"That's real big money."

"Not too big for a coat of saintly paint over the Pakistani taint. And what's my cut?" Raghu forked in a slice of broiled mutton in his mouth and continued, "I must be compensated adequately."

"You're a crook Chawla," Ram Karan laughed, "you won't even spare your mother in bed."

"I won't play the role of Indian Oedipus, Ramji. Certain holes are divine. Even to a crook like me."

He produced delectable sounds from his tongue, in appreciation of the seasoned mutton kebab.

"Have you seen the Marble Arch complex on Bhagwan Das Road?" Raghu Chawla continued.

"That costs a fortune. Don't blackmail me. I've given you two homes, a farmhouse and three petrol pumps."

"Karanji, I've a big family and one can't stop harvesting as long as shrimps are aplenty. Arrange for an apartment at the Marble Arch."

"Raghu, you're a great explorer. You never tire in your quest for money and fortune." Raghu now moved over to the dessert, a rare blend of milk pudding with Kabul raisins and Riyadh dates.

"Okay. It's a deal, but you've bled me white," Ram Karan wailed out, "please see that these NSI goons don't paste the Pakistani sticker on my back."

"They won't dare to. You've purchased a Shankar insurance."

"But the apartment costs a fortune."

"Karanji, the sea doesn't miss the mere theft of a few gallons of its liquid. Arrange ten million and tell me when you're ready. I'll meet Shankar tonight."

Final harvesting of the hunting operation had found a berth for Ram Karan in the hottest and richest compartment of the government–the railway ministry. Ten million, Ram was advised, was only a goodwill amount. Millions more should rain as the trains chug across the length and breadth of the country. Ram Karan was elated to climb the money-tree, but many others were not.

*

Balachandran Nampoothiri was not amused by the news received from Amrita Bhalla over a scrambler phone at Cairo's Hotel Alexandra. He was in the city of pyramids and sphinx on a mission to meet one of his assets at Ankara. The rendezvous was fixed after her Moscow friends warned Prime Minister Manjira about arms pile up in different military airbases in eastern Turkey by the USA and China. The mysterious build up could not be interpreted by Moscow in the light of its own geostartegic concerns. China had not yet cut its umbilical with Moscow and the USA obviously did not require piling up battlefield weapons in Turkey for mounting a surprise attack on the USSR. The thicket of suspicion gathered more opacity after two serving Generals of Pakistan were noticed holidaying with their wives in the general area of the suspected joint Chinese and US maneuvers.

An NSI asset in Turkish army confirmed the worst fear of Delhi. Both Washington and Peking were stockpiling battlefield weaponry for replenishing Pakistan's inventory. Most of the weapons were bought by the CIA agents from eastern block countries, the supposed surrogates and allies of Moscow.

It was indeed a bad news, but an expected one. Amrita's call, therefore, irritated him. How could the Prime Minister get that enemy of the country back to her ministry? The NSI had catered precise proof of Ram Karan receiving Pakistani fund for his election efforts. Nampoothiri was not a sulking babe. However, a sizeable agitation in his cranium was occupied by the latest Ram Karan coup. The Turkish jigsaw puzzle was solved but he failed to understand the new one involving Ram Karan Prasad. He drove straight to the residence of the Prime Minister from the airport.

By no stretch of imagination, Manjira could be credited with the qualities of a patient listener. She believed that she was born to talk to others. An acute sense of inbuilt insecurity pushed her all the time to suspect, even the mildest act of protestation. The Turkish part of the briefing cast a pale of gloom on her face.

"So you agree with Moscow that Pakistan is the end beneficiary of the stockpile."

"I've no doubt."

"Do you agree with these?" Manjira produced a bunch of papers.

Nampoothiri browsed the papers, one containing an unsigned note on Ram Karan's telephonic conversation with a Dubai based person, simply named Tariq. Tariq had confirmed transfer of rupees 50 million to a Ram Karan crony in Bombay. A footnote described Tariq as Colonel Taufiq Ahmed, an officer of 8th Brigade Pakistan Cavalry, on a cover diplomatic assignment in Pakistan embassy at Dubai.

The other paper was signed by one Muzammil Ahmad, a member of the Bangladesh Government in Exile alleging circulation of an audiotape containing Ram Karan's advice to East Pakistan Hindus not to flee to India under People's League provocation.

"That's what I have been exactly telling you ma'am."

"I don't disagree with you Balu. You're a security expert and a strategist. I'm a politician. Can I afford to beat drum proclaiming my political colleague as a Pakistani mole?"

"I don't suggest that, but you've the reports and these are impeccable."

"That's a political war Balu. Leave the matter to my political judgment. I can't alienate millions of Dalits and backward classes by hanging Ram Karan now. His face is acceptable to residuary Hindus in East Pakistan. The nation is facing a war situation. I wouldn't like to invite fresh trouble by branding my minister a spy. I require him for mobilisation of a vast segment of East Pakistani low caste Hindus. Moreover, I want to send him to Islamabad for a much-awaited CBM exercise pressed upon by Washington. They want me to have a dialogue with that fat General."

"That's an important aspect. But ma'am...."

"Well Balu, anything new you want to add?"

"I'll suggest attaching a senior officer with him."

"I appreciate that," Manjira smiled with a terse look from a remote corner of her eye, "I've assured the British PM that I would be the last person to preside over Pakistan's break up. The world communities aren't likely to support me if Pakistan is dismembered and India is perceived as the villain of the drama. The Ram Karan mission is important for me. He can help in throwing up a smoke screen."

Balachandran Nampoothiri knew he faced a layer of granite in Manjira. Her perception of the international political drama was impeccable.

"Thank you ma'am."

"Don't be upset Balu. Trust me. I'll take care of Ram as soon as I gain better elbowroom in East Pakistan. Ask your boys to watch him and his cronies."

"You mean Raghu Chawla?"

"Yes I'm worried about Chawla's closeness to Shankar. I don't want him to fill my son's cellar with scandals."

*

Captain Ayub, back to his seat after a short furlough, felt less forlorn. He exuded effervescence, having managed a short and cosy week with his wonder fairy, Reshma.

"Come Harfan." He gestured warmly as Israr International's executive entered Ayub's room. By now, he had developed a liking for the dashing salesman.

"Just dropped in to convey a message for Gen. Naqi. Hope you had a warm holiday."

"*Yar*, she's fabs," Ayub's happiness exploded in a warm order for coffee and lighting of cigarettes, "these Indians are rotten duds." He followed up with a spatial comment.

"What's new with the enemies of Islam?"

"The fools first send a minister, who's well known to our hooded people, and tops up the mistake by adding an intelligence officer as his appendage." He politely passed on the coffee to Harfan.

"Funny, who's this blighted gunk?"

"Some bloody Sagar...may be Heera (diamond), may be Moti (pearl). He was specially tagged to keep an eye on the minister."

"Stupid. These Hindu bums are incorrigible." Harfan tickled Ayub's not too latent hatred for everything Hindu.

"Serves them right. The delegation had plenty of wining and dining and very little meat." Ayub continued his narration.

"Sad *yar*. To hell with the bloody Indians! Tell me how was your furlough? Hope you had a swell time. Have you brought her along?"

Harfan initiated a feeble furrow into the fertile and brittle psyche of Ayub, and expectantly settled down over the coffee.

"No *yar*. She's back to her parents. Its some funny social custom to be observed there."

"That's cruel! Hope things are okay with your boss man." Harfan pelted an anticipatory pebble. He was not dismayed.

"The boss is fine. Work is fine."

"So when do we start the airlifting operations?"

"Can't say for sure. Washington is loaning two Boeing 707s, which are owned by a Mexico-based undercover CIA subsidiary. These birds will ferry weapons to Dacca. And watch out, we're going to pin down the Indian Army in its North East."

Ayub continued emptying his knowledge of the nation's secrets. He really felt big, when he unburdened his chest.

"That means Israr International is out!"

"Better check on that. Naqi should have the details."

"Any sabotage by our rivals?"

"Not sure. He was approached by the ISI chief, on behalf of Nawab Sharief." Ayub graciously offered the vital information.

"Thanks for the dope *yar*. Do you think the USA will like to take an open plunge?"

"That's the snag. But, we've other options. Don't worry. This time around we're sure going for the ramparts of the Red Fort."

Ayub reassured Harfan with an expansive sweep of his hand, as if he was only a furlong away from the fort built by Shahjahan.

Harfan smiled, shared a cigarette, and bade adieu.

"Hi buddy, aren't you from Jhumra?" Ayub startled Harfan by the unexpected question.

"Yea, I happen to live there, but I'm from Karachi." He replied in an assertive voice.

"That's what I meant *yar*. I'm flying to Bhagatanwala, accompanying an Army Signals team, from my parent unit. That's not far from your den."

"It's just an hour's drive. Come over for dinner at the fabulous Hotel Royal Palace."

"Can't make it dear. The team is moving in that area with an array of Direction Finders."

"What's that?"

"Oh brother! Direction Finders are used to locate clandestine radio transmission. The Joint Intelligence Signals of the ISI has detected some unauthorised transmission from the general direction of Jhumra. The Military Signals team is moving in to intensify the search." Captain Ayub explained the working mechanism of the Direction Finders with a flourish.

"How do you fit in?"

"I was trained with the CIA's signal intelligence outfit. I'm an expert DF handler."

"Hell with these brain teasing riddles. I'm happy with my two-penny business. See you later." Harfan said *Khuda Hafiz.*

"Well brother!" Ayub continued his dialogue, "There's more. We're locating the 3rd Corp at Chak Jhumra."

"That's next to my den." Harfan wasn't surprised with the information. It must be a part of the war preparations.

"Lt.General Shahbaz will be stationed there."

"Give me an intro to him. I can probably sell a few more boots and belts to his formation."

Harfan smiled back.

"Don't joke *yar.* I'm happy because it'll give me the opportunity to visit your exotic home."

"Come and spend a few days over there with Reshma."

Harfan extended his arm, pumped Ayub's palm and said *Khuda hafiz.*

Back to his nest, Harfan burnt late night candles and transmitted a short message to *Khalis,* incorporating some of the strategic disclosures by Ayub. He emphasised the need for lodging protest with the USA for its reported loaning of aircraft to Pakistan. The Direction Finder story and the deployment of the 3rd Corp were also highlighted. He conveyed his decision to switch his station off. Alam, he requested, should dismantle, and remove his trans-receiver set post-haste.

*

Latest inputs from Alamgir and Triple X about frenetic Pakistani scrounging of the world arms market had enormously disturbed the Prime Minister's strategic calculations. The CIA's involvement with mercenary flights to Dacca was sure to embolden the military regime. And that's what she dreaded the most. Stockpile of battlefield hardware in Turkey, Cairo, and Riyadh had worsened her concern. The mercenary flights were an indicator that Washington could even decide to land its Marines off the coast of Chittagong and position its Pacific Fleet in the blue waters of the Bay of Bengal.

That's what she did not want to bargain for. She was, nonetheless, determined not to allow the luxury of such perfunctory pleasure to the US President. He had precious little regard for her personally, and the nation she led. Their mutual apathy was pathological.

Dewan's shuffling feet disturbed Manjira's surfing of the international canvass.

"Yes?"

"Nampoothiri is here."

"Send him in."

"What do you think of the likely US response? What're the chances of their naval fleet intervening?"

Manjira fired the question even before her intelligence chiefs took their respective seats.

"The US Congress and the Senate are divided on this issue. Some Democrat lobbies are opposed to any US involvement." Nampoothiri replied promptly, as if he had anticipated the salvo.

"But the CIA is providing mercenary flights to Islamabad."

"Yes ma'am," Nampoothiri spoke with a chuckle, "the Foreign Secretary has conveyed our concerns to his counterpart in Washington and Friends of India, the New York based Democratic lobby, has written to the President."

"That's encouraging. The US won't hesitate in ordering its Marines to rub shoulders with the Peoples' Army in the killing fields of East Pakistan. They've ignored the genocide by General Arif and Tarakki." Manjira opened up with caustic remarks, which was very unusual of her.

"We need balancing support from the USSR and countries of the European and South American continents. The Islamic world should be made wiser about the Pakistani massacre of the unarmed Bengali Muslims." Nampoothiri added, expecting the PM to prolong the topic. She turned sideways in her chair and talked almost in a soliloquy.

"The Bangladeshi leaders are so divided, even at this hour of colossal crisis. I'm baffled."

"Yes Prime Minister," Nampoothiri responded, "some of them are talking in terms of reconciliation with Pakistan."

"Well, that's the last menu I want on my plate. Isolate the pro-Chinese and Muslim League elements in the government in exile." Manjira responded in a jerky voice.

"Let's ignore them for now. Warfront unity is important. We'll take care of that if Jainal succeeds in making the lotus bloom." said Nampoothiri.

"Sounds fine Balu," she changed tracks, "I believe the US is trying to divide the Bangla freedom fighters. What're your reports?"

"You're correct ma'am. The US consulate officials have had 7 clandestine meetings with some Bangladeshi leaders. Our monitors feel that the State Department is desperate to arrange a dialogue between them and General Arif."

"It won't happen. I won't allow them to catch us napping again," Manjira addressed Nampoothiri, "give me a brief on Colombo. I believe the US embassy is pressing them for smooth passage of Pakistani armaments. How much pressure can we put on them?"

"It's pretty difficult to guess. The island nation is seething with anti-India hysteria. The US embassy is working overtime to obtain transit facilities for Pakistan. The logic is simple; if Pakistan is truncated today, Ceylon can't be far behind." Nampoothiri summed up the prevailing anxieties in the island nation.

"Dewan." Manjira called for her secretary.

"Connect me Colombo, I'll like to speak to the Prime Minister," she ordered, but amended quickly, "tell the Foreign Secretary to talk to their High Commissioner in Delhi, before you connect me."

Dewan, as instructed by the PM, received the call and advised the personal secretary of the Ceylonese PM to hold on; the Indian Prime Minister would personally take the call.

Manjira took the line first and requested the secretary of her counterpart to connect his boss. This calculated diplomatic ploy was meant for pandering to the Ceylonese PM's ego.

She sugarcoated her well-rehearsed deliveries. How could she ignore the centuries' old cultural ties between the two nations, Manjira hastened to add! She would like to visit the wonderful sites at Kandi and Anuradhapur at the first available opportunity. Didn't her dad and mom select Ceylon for holidaying, even at the peak of their involvement in India's independence struggle?

Pleasantries over, Manjira cautiously unfolded her heartaches over the ghastly happenings in East Pakistan. Could the Ceylonese PM use her good offices to persuade Pakistan to resolve the issues through mutual discussions? She hoped that Ceylon would facilitate all civilian flights between Islamabad and Dacca and take care that the weapons of death and destruction weren't ferried through its territory.

"Is there going to be a war?" The Ceylonese PM asked.

No. She was against all wars. She'd be the last person to start any war with Pakistan. How could she, being a true follower of the Mahatma?

Yes. She would definitely remain in touch and exchange notes. Indeed, she was deputing her External Affairs Minister to Colombo to reassure her about India's stand on the developing situation in East Pakistan. Manjira profusely thanked the Island nation's chief executive.

She turned around and asked Dewan to connect her to the Indian ambassador in Moscow.

The ambassador, probably dragged out from a vodka-induced sleep, couldn't comprehend what Manjira was trying to convey. A shrill shout made the message clear to the diplomat in slumber.

He should immediately seek an appointment with the Soviet Premier, Manjira added. She would like to personally talk to Mr. Anatole Dobrynin and Mr. Wataloo; her foreign minister, would personally carry a message to him and the General Secretary of the CPSU.

The important calls over, she turned to Dewan.

"Ask Foreign Secretary to invite the Soviet ambassador tomorrow. I want to see him"

"Yes ma'am."

"The FS should be at hand for consultations. And call up the President's office. I'd like to see him tomorrow at ten a.m."

"Yes ma'am."

"Nampoothiri, don't you think we should do something about Ceylon? Why can't you take charge of the more vocal Tamil segments? We should prop them up, train and arm them and keep Colombo busy." Manjira suggested opening up of a new front.

"There's a problem ma'am. Most of the Tamil tea labourers are hopelessly divided. Give me a few weeks. We're in touch with some friends in the Jaffna area. The Tamils will be activated," replied Nampoothiri.

"Keep the pressure on. Ceylon cannot get away by supporting Islamabad," Manjira added, "alert your agents in Colombo, and I want precise feedback on all Pakistani flights using Ceylonese territory....

"Identify the politicians who are likely to support my pro-Tamil policy in Ceylon, and give me an assessment of likely impact of the growth of a militant Tamil movement in Ceylon, and on the common Indian Tamils. I don't want them to get infection." Manjira cautioned her domestic intelligence chief.

“We’ll come up with a detailed report.” The NSI chief assured.

“And Balu, I’d like your boys in Pakistan to come up with precise details of the CIA funded flights from Karachi to Dacca, carrying men and weapons.” Manjira’s ebullience coincided with the speedy flickering of her left eye. She was bubbling with enthusiasm.

“Tell them, I want photographic evidence. That’ll expose the US duplicity in full measure.”

“It’ll be done ma’am. Our top boys will be deployed for this special task.”

“Keep track of other mercenary flights as well.”

“Yes ma’am.”

“I want concrete evidence on meetings between the US diplomats and the renegade Bangladeshi leaders. Your reports aren’t convincing enough.”

“It’ll be done, ma’am.”

“I want to confront the Secretary of State with concrete evidence. And what do I hear about the flesh trade racket in the refugee camps in Calcutta?” Her eagle eyes pierced the NSI chief.

It was a difficult question to answer. Nampoothiri had in his pocket reports of the flesh business transacted by Ram Karan’s stooges. They had infiltrated the camps in the guise of relief volunteers. His pimps, promising them dream marriages, were luring the Bengali belles away from the refugee camps.

“We’ve some reports ma’am. Perhaps you may like to consult Ram Karanji first.”

“I wouldn’t have tasked you, if I could depend on him. Get me the details. And talk to Shankar, he has lots of information on this sordid affair.” She vented her utter disgust and started walking out of the room.

“Shall we pick up his pimps under Suppression of Immoral Trafficking Act?”

“No. I don’t want bad media. Shankar knows how to silence the scoundrel. Just keep him informed.”

*

37

Nampoothiri's intestinal churning was all the more aggravated by the last part of the cipher from Triple X. What compelled him to terminate HF transmission? Who could have deployed the Direction Finders at location Jhumra? Who could have peeled off Harfan's cover? Could it be the Inter Services Intelligence?

What else could that mean?

Direction Finders, consisting of sensitive rotating antenna and High Frequency receivers, could home in to the approximate location of a suspected radio transmitter. The frequency identification, pattern of Morse and cipher analogue, periodicity and strength of signals could lead the sleuths to the exact location of the source of energy emission. The ISI wasn't a novice in Signal and Electronic Intelligence, and advanced NATO gadgets recently replenished their arsenal. That meant real big danger.

Nampoothiri sat up with a sting of chilling horror and asked Jatadhari to brew another coffee. Something had terribly gone wrong. The clandestine High Frequency radio set of Triple X must have come under the scrutiny of the SigInt experts of the ISI. The trained tenacious hounds, as they were, wouldn't easily miss a blazing trail.

Holy heavens! Triple X was in imminent danger. His most productive resident agent in Pakistan was in trouble and the counter-intelligence canines were just about sniffing and licking the droplets of blood. Homing on to the location of the clandestine HF transmission station was just a matter of time, a very thin margin of time. Did Triple X commit any security breach? Was he careless? Nampoothiri buzzed the bell for Amrita Bhalla, his glamorous evergreen secretary. He required immediate consultations with his Signal Intelligence experts.

"Yes sir." Amrita dressed in a printed silk sari with a matching blouse and fascinating coiffure looked devastating.

The killer look wasn't really for Nampoothiri, she knew him only too well. This seasoned spy was perhaps never interested in sex. If he were, he should have been able to produce at least one child by now. However, Amrita enjoyed his clean appreciative looks. He was a fine connoisseur of beauty sans the ugly x-ray.

"Summon Achariya, Gogoi and what's his name!" Nampoothiri started scratching his head, trying to retrieve the name of the third person, through the follicles of his receding hairline.

"You mean the Joint Intelligence Officer, Dhiren Bhagat?" Amrita correctly anticipated the name.

"There you are! I wonder, why didn't you come to my life 28 years ago, my dear?"

"I couldn't sir. I was born just three years before your desired date of marriage. Too tender, even for a child marriage." Amrita never felt tired of listening to this compliment, meaninglessly uttered by her boss for countless times. He really didn't mean anything.

Nampoothiri enjoyed the reply. This vibrant girl always carried a whiff of freshness about her. They laughed, in a controlled fashion. The old man, Amrita knew, didn't like loud giggling. His scheming grey cells could perhaps not conjure up anything but spies, dirty tricks, and the black arts of intelligence.

She wondered what could be the latest crisis!

Dacca? Perhaps not. Achariya didn't handle the eastern wing of Pakistan. He was responsible for operations in the western wing.

*

Robin Achariya arrived first. That was a dream corridor for him, not because of his devotion to Nampoothiri. The rendezvous offered him rare chances to devour the trim, firm, and steely physique of Amrita Bhalla, at least with his moist and hungry eyes. His efforts to escort her to a dinner date always met with warm but meaningless giggles. She usually buried his hungry looks in her sweet rippling of laughter.

A leech, Amrita could compare Robin's looks with the probing snout of the eternal elastic blood-sucking creature of the undergrowth.

"You may go in." She pressed the button activating the electrically controlled door. She had the licence to do so.

"Presume, you've seen the last cipher from TX," Nampoothiri opened up the discussion, "what do you read into it?"

"The ISI is perhaps trying to locate signals emitted by some unauthorised stations. The triangulation mechanism may have brought them nearer to the station at Jhumra."

Replied Gogoi, the technical division chief.

"Can they home in easily on Harfan's den? Explain the technical drill." Nampoothiri requested.

"Modern homing devices can bring the SigInt people as near as one km of the suspected station. The rest is a matter of establishing the pattern of transmission and physical search. The same routine is followed by our SCSB (Signal Communication Security Bureau)." Gogoi replied.

"Hmm." Nampoothiri hummed with a worried expression on his face.

"Is there any way to shield the energy leakage?"

"We've provided a thick lead shield in the underground chamber. This can minimise radiation, but can't eliminate. The main radiation takes place from the antenna. The rotating Direction Finder antenna picks up direct signals and signals reflected back from the stratosphere. That's how the operators measure the general location of a clandestine set. I feel Triple X's set should be dismantled immediately." Gogoi offered a coherent technical explanation.

"Thanks Gogoi. You can go now." Nampoothiri dismissed the technical chief.

He wasn't supposed to share privileged operational secrets with him.

"Sir," Robin Achariya spoke, "contact Qurban has reported the presence of mobile units of the Corps of Signals in Triple X's location. I feel our man may have violated traffic discipline."

"Your conclusion is premature. Gogoi does not agree."

"What are your views?" Nampoothiri turned to Bhagat.

"Can't say, sir. No contact after my last meeting. I think we should dismantle the station first and have a face to face briefing session."

"Any new inputs from Alam?" Nampoothiri turned to Achariya.

"No sir. He just hinted likely involvement of Triple X in weapons airlifting operations to Dacca," replied Achariya.

"How do we debrief him on this sensitive issue?"

"Kabul is the nearest place." Dhiren Bhagat commented.

"Correct. Leave the details with me. Get ready to visit Kabul." Nampoothiri advised Bhagat.

Nampoothiri dismissed the meeting and called the Command Information Centre, a top-secret communication hub, reinforced to take severest pounding by enemy bugging and bombing.

"Raise Kabul." Nampoothiri startled the CIC-in-charge by his sudden appearance.

The operator closed the thick soundproof glass door of the cubicle and raised Kabul by manipulating the computer keyboard. The monitor screen displayed presence of Kabul, as light blobs flashed the assigned digits—7910-QMSRI. A blue light blinked, indicating that the station was in receiving mode.

"The station is ready sir," the operator said, "any message?"

"Is it safe on auto-scramble?"

"Yes sir."

Nampoothiri dictated a small message for personal attention of the NSI station chief at Kabul.

"Give me a tinkle when Kabul gets back."

Nampoothiri retrieved the piece of paper and walked out.

*

Alam was startled by Nampoothiri's surprise message. An Attaché of the Indian Mission in Kabul delivered it at his Peshawar residence, which doubled for his business den. The cryptic message had directed him to meet Bedad Aslam, an emissary of the chief at a Kabul safe house. The personal messenger of the NSI chief was carrying a special communication. Bhagat was perhaps the second NSI officer to meet Alam in person. The legendary resident agent, a fabled mystery, always evoked admiration in the informed NSI coterie. Perhaps only two NSI officers, besides Nampoothiri, were aware of his existence.

Bhagat flew all the way to Moscow by an Aeroflot flight and endured another long haul to Dushanbe and on to Kabul, which landed at the ill equipped airport around 9.30 p.m. amidst a freak snowstorm. The looped routing was chalked out by the NSI for protecting his identity. There was no emissary from the Indian Mission at hand to receive him at the ungodly hour. He passed through the immigration and ventured out to look for a taxi to take him to Hotel Hasina.

"Do you require a taxi sir?"

An Afghan, covered from head to foot in woollen clothes and a balaclava approached him with a whispering voice.

"Yes, I do. Are you a private operator?"

"Sir I'm Jaffar and I'm looking for Mr. Bedad Aslam."

"Has the apricot tree flowered?"

Bhagat asked Jaffar to reassure that he was in the correct company.

"Yes sir. There are 900 flowers."

"You've got the correct customer Mr. Jaffar."

"Thanks Allah," Jaffar Agha, a covert friend of the under cover NSI representative in Kabul spoke slowly, "Mr. Rawat, the First Secretary, has deputed me. Please follow. You're not lodging at Hasina. He has arranged a private guest house for you."

"Pleased to meet you Agha sahib. Please take me to the arranged den." Bhagat embraced Jaffar in the typical Islamic way and followed him to a waiting Lada, an ugly looking Russian car.

After a quick dinner, Bhagat was driven to another corner of the city and dumped in front of an ornate building.

"Aslam sahib," Jaffar spoke out, "You've reached the destination. Go in. Omar, a servant of the household, will receive you. Identify yourself as a trader from Dushanbe and ask to meet the householder."

"Aren't you coming in?"

"I disappear from here. Call this number when you are through."

Omar, a tall but stooping person, opened the gate with a squint-eyed welcome.

"Aslam here from Dushanbe. Is the householder in?"

"Step in."

He guided Bhagat to a second floor room, where the designated householder was seated on a rocking chair. This was Bhagat's first meeting with the master spy.

"Aslam here sir, *assalam-u-alaikum*."

"That's fine. Hope you know the rules of the game?" Alam accosted Bhagat in the confines of the safe house.

"Yes. I've not seen you and met you."

"And you visit Mazar-e-Sharif consulate with a diplomatic bag, before returning to Delhi via Dushanbe and Moscow." Alam added.

"That's how it is, sir."

"Okay. What's the big panic?" Alam asked.

"The boss is highly concerned over Triple X's security," replied Bhagat, "deployment of DF in Jhumra area is an ominous development. The boss feels that the any exposure of TX shouldn't lead to your compromise."

"Do I have the authority to neutralise TX?"

"I can't comment. Here's a sealed cover from the boss. I understand you've to take a spot decision."

"I understand, but you, as the case officer should know him better. Have you noticed any streak of indiscipline and defiance in him?"

"He's a complex person, aggressive, acerbic and argumentative. But he has a loving nature too." Bhagat added.

"That's what worries me, his love for life and his dear ones. I suspect he's too attached to his wife and child, much beyond the needs of his cover. He's too egocentric a person."

Bhagat didn't relish the terse comments. The pungent smell of hostility betrayed Alam's professional cover. However, he did not butt in and contradict the top Indian asset. He wasn't on a debating mission.

Alam went through the letter, scribbled a reply, and sealed it personally.

"Hand over this to the boss. Keep your trap shut."

"Roger sir," Bhagat stood up to leave, "I've been briefed by the boss personally."

"That's fine. Keep it that way. In our profession silence is the golden rule." Alam dismissed the meeting.

The mysterious Jaffar silently picked him up and asked Bhagat to remain ready for an early morning *ruksat* (journey). His flight to Mazar-e-Sharif was scheduled to take off at 06.30 hrs.

*

Meeting Bedad Aslam at Kabul was a surprise. However, for the second time Alam was surprised in quick succession. He hadn't expected Jamilla and Pervez at Harfan's Jhumra nest.

Ibadat had given the all-clear signal. The assorted team of Army Signals Corps and the Joint Intelligence Signals of the ISI had finished scanning the general area. They couldn't pinpoint the safe house that sheltered the clandestine wireless station. The only new thing that happened to Chak Jhumra was the arrival of the 3rd Corp. General Shahbaz was a friend. Alam had traded with him, on usual terms, when he had headed the AHQ Task Force that supervised short listing of the new weapons systems.

The brief meeting with General Shabaz at Hotel Royal Palace confirmed Alam's suspicion that the SigInt sleuths were chasing some unidentified wireless station.

The Pakistan army was developing Chak Jhumra as the tactical reserve command post for the Lahore front. The new radar formation was designed to give arraying capability to the existing radar stations at Sargodha.

"It's tough time Shabaz," Alam spoke with an anguished voice, "it is unfortunate that India is imposing another war on us so soon."

"Well brother," Shabaz spoke in his buoyant military style, "we must fight a final war with Hindustan. Islam must again rule over that *kafir* country. And personally I welcome another round of war. War means fattening of our coffers. You supply the weapons, I get my cut, and you get your commission. It's business as usual"

"Busines is okay, but I'm concerned about the innocent lives."

"Ha! Don't make me laugh Alam. It's you who peddle the weapons of death. You should not cry over the body bags. Look, this war is going to be decisive. The Bengalis will cease to exist as an ethnic entity."

Shabaz threw up his hand in excitement and summoned a junior officer, who stood guard near the entrance.

"Have the Signals boys arrived Wasim?"

"Not yet sir. I believe they are reaching in another two days."

"Fine. Tell Major Wadood to see me straight away, before he redeploys his DF monitors.

"Copy sir."

The young Captain saluted and affixed himself again near the entrance.

"Are you expecting more troops General?"

"No Alam sahib. These SigInt boys have created a fuss over some clandestine signals, which, they say, were originated from Jhumra."

"Oh shit. It's an additional headache."

"It's nothing. You can't differentiate one signal from the other. No one affixes trademarks on the carrier waves. It could be from my unit and even from the Bhagatan base."

"It's a great pleasure to meet you again General. I was here to finalise some supplies to the Bhagatan base. I should drive back to Lahore tonight."

"When are you crossing the Atlantic again?"

"Very soon, may be in another fortnight. Any service for me?"

"It's a minor matter. My daughter is in Virginia. She requires some cash."

"How much?"

"It is about $ 5000. I'll return it in Pakistani currency."

"Don't bother General. We'll adjust it in another deal. Let the young kid enjoy."

"So nice of you Alam. *Khuda Hafiz*."

"*Khuda Hafiz*."

Alam said goodbye and brushed past Ibadat, who had approached the table with a decanter of water in his hand.

"I'll see you soon."

"*Ji* (yes)." Ibadat saluted the General and politely asked if he would require some more water. General Shabaz tipped him lavishly and signalled at his aide de camp, the young Captain, who stood affixed near the entrance.

"Let's make a move, boy."

"Yes sir."

The General's convoy zoomed away after raising clouds of smoke.

*

Harfan had expected Alam's sudden visit, his illusive uncle from Peshawar. However, Jamilla wasn't pleased to have a houseguest. She wanted Harfan all to herself. The pangs of unquenched thirst burnt like fragrant camphor. She missed Harfan's unique love play, which turned her wild and propelled her to an ecstatic journey, transcending physical limits. Harfan's proximity sublimated the physical desire to an amorphous pining, which created a void somewhere within. Jamilla simply wanted more and more of Harfan. All the layers of her consciousness were shrouded by the unique love-chemistry.

She was worried too over the rumour radios that had started broadcasting stories about Harfan's links with Malika Jahanara. Pakistan wasn't a big place and Malika Jahanara wasn't the dullest sex kitten around. Harfan's casual contacts with Malika, like all bits of gossip around her, didn't take time to travel down to the lanes behind Lahore's Masti Gate.

Nawab Sharief, beaten by Israr in the arms lifting contract, had taken personal care to drop the gossip in Zahoor Chaudry's intimate circles. He wasn't known unnecessarily as an invisible viper that lurked below the skin. Words travelled faster than light to Zahoor's inner courtyard. Jamilla didn't believe in what she had heard, through the remote and distorted transmission by Nawab. Nevertheless, she didn't want to take chance. No, she couldn't. Harfan was too dear and precious to be left alone to the mercy of an enchantress. Well! Who wouldn't like to seduce Harfan, the finest flesh and spirit fleeting around! She was his mooring and anchor and she wouldn't allow him to be uprooted by any freak storm, Jahanara or Nawab. Her love, she knew, would be a protective shield around Harfan.

Alam completed the meaninglessly warm formalities of greeting Jamilla and Pervez and walked back to Hotel Royal Palace.

"What's the problem with Harfan?" Alam asked Ibadat, his Operation Qurban.

"My friend in the ISI tells me that they picked up his trail from Malika Jahanara's pleasure abode."

"Who is he?"

"The information is authentic. The ISI has started a probe."

"That's a disaster. Has he been dancing around her?"

"Not exactly. She's in the eye of the storm of intrigues and conspiracies."

"How did he walk into her trap?"

"At his level of operation he couldn't avoid it. And Nawab, Israr's brother, is after Harfan's blood. He thinks he can destroy his brother by neutralising Harfan." Ibadat argued his case with a straight face.

"What about the Direction Finders?"

"They had stationed one mobile scanner near his house a few days ago. Another station has been installed three miles down south, towards Mianwali."

"Anything specific?"

"They suspect clandestine transmission."

"How the hell did he get mixed up?"

"Can't say sir. The only important development in between has been a mysterious visit by Nawab Sharief, and his exclusive meeting with Mian Harfan."

"Fucking hell. Why did he get involved with that crook?"

"Can't say for sure. Nawab was heard threatening Mian Harfan with dire consequences over some business deal. Perhaps it has something to do with an airlifting operation and hiring of some German aircraft. I'm not sure."

"Didn't you try to find out?"

"I thought I'd better not."

Alam didn't like the terse reply, but decided to digest it.

He was posted with the developments in General Naqi's office. The General had awarded the airlifting contract to Israr International after the CIA backed out from loaning two Boeing 707s. The Democrat Congressmen and the Senators had stiffly opposed any open CIA involvement in the East Pakistan imbroglio. Israr had greased Naqi's palm and Harfan Bukhari had warmed up the pockets and bed of Habibullah. Nawab, on the other hand, had depended on Generals Hyder Bux and General Amanullah, and had poured money into their thirsty gullets. But Israr won the battle, thanks to General Naqi's direct access to Begum Jahanara.

"Why is Jamilla baby here?" Alam lighted a cigarette and asked.

"They're husband and wife. What's wrong in it?"

"Everything is wrong," Alam fumed in anger, "this was a marriage of convenience. We didn't want to write a sob love story script."

"We're dealing with a human being, not a machine, sir. I think he should be helped to get out of the mess created by Nawab Sharief." Ibadat suggested in a soft voice.

"Agents are controlled machines. Don't ever try to inject emotion into your work." Alam sounded a warning.

"Keep your antennae open. We can't afford misfire. The missile has to be shot down if it deviates from its flight path." Alam spoke coolly, but looked at Ibadat with burning eyes.

A rattled Ibadat served coffee silently, spilling some. Alam's last few words spoken coolly through his teeth almost carried the debris of the aborted missile.

"*Kyon mian* (what's the matter)?" Alam looked up.

"Sorry, I lost control of the pot."

"I don't want to lose control on Harfan, remember that." Alam sipped the cream topped coffee with relish.

"Keep an eye on ISI surveillance teams. I'm expecting Israr sahib. Receive him courteously and serve the grandest lunch you have in your menu."

"Don't worry. I'll take care. Please enjoy the drink meanwhile."

For Israr, the luncheon meeting with Alam was as welcome as the appearance of the Gabriel, from the cosiest niche of *Allah's* very private heavenly abode. They shared frothy beer, spiced Mughlai food, and discussed the predicaments of Israr International. His company, Israr revealed, had clinched the contract for airlifting war materials from Sargodha to Dacca, via Colombo.

The CIA chartered cargo aircrafts for ferrying men and weapons to Dacca were abruptly withdrawn following furore in the US Congress. CIA's Phuket based airlifting operations had also been suspended after stiff protests from the Kremlin. Israr informed Alam that the Indian intelligence had gathered precise evidence of direct CIA involvement in the East Pakistan imbroglio. New Delhi had circulated a few colour photographs of CIA cover-flights, operated by a fictitious Ohio based aid organisation, apparently flaunting the banner of World Wide Charity, which provided relief to the victims of hunger and plague.

The Indians, like elusive cygnets, had done a thorough undercover job, distinctly disturbing the placid White House poodle. The Secretary of State, according to Israr, had stoutly denied the US involvement and blamed the Indians for obstructing humanitarian services in cyclone-ravaged East Pakistan. But the photographic evidence circulated at the United Nations by the Friend's of India, a Delhi funded organisation of Indian Diaspora, had nailed Washington's lies.

The CIA friends had asked Rawalpindi GHQ to hire private chartered flights. Funds, they said, would flow in from Fort Knox.

Israr had roped in a West-German company to fly the war materials. However, the flights were grounded before they could take off. India had tipped off the West-German human rights groups, through their Socialist International conduit. Brother Nawab, Israr lamented, had played a dirty game. Beaten in the airlifting bid he had leaked out the information to Izaz Afroz. The maverick politician didn't take minutes to broadcast it in his public speeches.

"Nawab's tricks are understandable, but why Izaz Afroz?" Alam Khan asked.

"That sly fox plays his own game. He keeps egging General Arif on to crush the Bengalis. But his subterranean strategic moves are directed at denigrating the military ruler. He hopes, I think, to pick up his *Koh-i-Noor* from the debris of a devastated Pakistan." Israr spoke eloquently and succinctly.

"Yes, I understand Afroz's compulsion," commented Alam, "he's one of the Trinity, bent upon destroying Pakistan. The other two are, I believe, General Arif and Sheikh Jainal."

"Is that his end game?" Asked Israr.

"Haven't you heard of the Larkana Tea party?" asked Alam, "it's speculated that General Arif and Izaz have reached an understanding to abandon East Pakistan and defeat India in the western front."

"That's too dangerous."

"Who bothers Sharief *bhai*?" Alam lighted a cigarette, "We, in West Pakistan, haven't tolerated any Bengali rule over us. P-A-K-I-S-T-A-N, as coined by a Muslim Cambridge scholar, doesn't have the alphabet—B-for Bengal. It's a remote colony of the Punjab. Izaz will be the last person to allow Jainal of B to preside over his holy P for Punjab and S for Sind."

"Why?"

"Leave it Israr sahib. We Punjabis and Pathans are still haunted by the ghost of Hindu domination. The Bengali Muslims are three-fourth Hindus, worse than the Indonesians, where Islam is still shrouded by the Ramayana and Mahabharata."

"But, I've serious problems. Perhaps you can help," Israr pleaded.

"It's always a pleasure, order me sir."

"Can you arrange a few chartered flights for my operations?"

"Where is my nephew?" Alam asked in his usual booming voice, deviating from Israr's sob story.

"He's a gem of a manager. His untiring efforts have brought us several new contracts and *Insha Allah*, my company will register rupees 500 million in profits this year." Israr was effusive in his praise of Harfan Bukhari.

"I suggest you get him involved with the airlifting operations." Alam pitched in for his protégé.

"That's precisely what I want to do. But, I need two Boeing 707 cargo planes to carry the merchandise. The Germans and the French have reneged at the last moment."

"You shouldn't go to the West with such problems. They have mighty problems with the law and the so-called human rights. I've some South African friends, who would be ready to help out at a higher premium, about 10% more. Can you live with that?"

"Excellent! No problem. The bucks, anyways, come from Langley. They aren't so fussy about apartheid. How long would you take?"

"The mercenary flights are risky. The carriers have to be given a proper cover, a fresh coat of paint, call signs, and the registration details. Dacca isn't another Khinzagane, lost somewhere in the African forest. The Indians are present everywhere in East Pakistan. These formalities will take a few days."

"I can't wait indefinitely."

"Hope you've consulted General Naqi and Sarfaraz." Alam lighted another cigarette, scratched the back of his smooth hairless pate, and continued, "sending international relief items for the cyclone victims should look as the most plausible ruse. That's what the CMLA wants to project. Isn't it?"

"Great idea. Give it any plausible cover. The GHQ is desperate. They want immediate augmentation of military hardware in Dacca. Call your South African friends immediately." Israr handed over a cordless phone to Alam.

"Who takes care of the Turkey and Egyptian sectors?"

"The CIA cover flights are doing a fine job. We're worried about Sargodha and Dacca sector."

"Why can't the PAF do it?"

"You know Alam sahib, India keeps on lodging protests with Ceylon everyday and howls at the United Nations."

"That's natural, when the weapons are used to kill civilians. Don't mind the killing but don't use phone lines in such sensitive matters. There are still several Bengalis in our telecom services. Better, use a captive wireless set. Have you got any?" Alam asked.

"No. They won't give licence to a private operator." Israr replied.

"Ask Naqi. I can get one from Darra Adam Khel market, if he has no problem. That's a wonderful place to make fascinating purchases. Got an operator?"

"General Naqi may agree. The circumstances are favourable. I'll require a trained operator."

"Talk to Naqi and confirm your requirement. I'll take at least a whole day to get the set and another one to install. No questions asked. Tell Naqi that private German and South African operators own the cargo charters. They're mercenaries. They carry men and materials to various troubled destinations. Our bosses shouldn't suffer soul pricks about apartheid."

"Don't bother. Pakistan isn't concerned about apartheid."

"It's your ball Israr, at the post. Catch it or allow it to go past the net to Nawab's lap."

"It won't be Nawab, in any case. Come to Sangla with me. I'll like to discuss a few details with you." Israr closed the discussion and picked up the phone to make an urgent call to General Naqi, Defence and National Security Advisor to the CMLA.

*

38

Alam accompanied Harfan to his Jhumra residence. As he drove silently, Alam grilled him like a veteran criminal lawyer.

"I hear you got hooked up to this lady Jahanara." Alam remarked in a loaded voice.

"I'm no hookworm and there was no hooking up. However, I had sensed the ISI watchers stalking me. I noticed it first, when my stay in Lahore's Faletti coincided with her stay in the same hotel. You know rest of the story involving Nawab and the Dehradun medic." Harfan explained in simple words. He didn't like to elaborate his intimate visit to the den of the enchantress.

"What about the Direction Finders?"

"I was first alerted by an insider friend. Ibadat had seen a few antenna fitted vehicles moving in the general area of Jhumra."

"That's bad. I'm going to decommission the set. Hope you've secured the electronic devices adequately."

"Not yet. But I can give you a location drawing of these gadgets."

"You should acquire a better knowledge of the history and geography of Pakistan. Before you jump into the ring be sure that you know the dramatis personae well."

"What're you gunning at?"

"Before you walked into Jahanara's den you should've known that the Generals are at each other's jugular. Malika is in the eye of the big twister."

"I just met her once, courtesy Nawab Sharief." Harfan replied in a straight voice.

"Remain miles away from that plague. He isn't happy with you and Israr. He's a hungry Tasmanian Devil."

"I don't think we've reached that critical stage yet."

"Don't be so optimistic. Ours is a one way journey."

"Don't repeat the doomsday forecast too often. I hope I've some liberty to innovate. That's essential for my survival." Harfan was tired of hearing the stale warnings once too often and decided to hit back.

"You can't jeopardise the security of the agency." Alam retorted.

"Both are equally important." Harfan replied with a tone of finality.

"What family? You've no family. It's only a part of your cover. Take it from me dear. Don't develop roots in this country."

Alam replied curtly. He concentrated on smoking, but displeasure was written all over his face. He was surprised. The mechanised doll, Harfan, the secret agent seated next to him, had started developing a mind of his own! That was simply an invitation to disaster.

How could he think of a permanent family in Pakistan? The fool should know that in his trade such families were mere props, to be changed at short notice. Jamilla was nothing but a station wife. He must warn Delhi. It was high time to reassess the security grading of Triple X. The devil had started living beyond his brief, accepting the mirage as real. He must be chastised and disciplined before it was too late.

*

The dinner, served by Ibadat, was excellent. But the ambient was as chilly as at point zero in the North Pole. The taut facial muscles of both Harfan and Alam and the distant vacant looks in their eyes had alarmed Jamilla.

"Any problem uncle?"

"Not at all baby. Harfan has to take up a delicate mission to Dacca. That's what we're discussing."

"Dacca isn't a safe place anymore."

"Don't worry dear. He's not required to visit the countryside. Just run a few air sorties and get back to usual job. *Insha Allah* things will be okay. Sleep well dear. Let me brief my nephew." Alam fondly and smilingly stroked the flabby cheek of Pervez and wished them good night.

Jamilla excused herself and retired with Pervez after exchanging customary pleasantries. Alam and Harfan sat over a drink and reviewed the developments, which had possibly put the ISI on his trail. He snubbed Harfan, in a hushed voice, for walking into Jahanara's trap. Sensational reports could wait and be missed. Life of a spy wasn't as romantic as the fiction authors would like their readers to believe. Indiscretion could endanger his life and love, his wife and son. Was he ready for that? The ISI wasn't likely to drop the trail of a suspected spy, they never did. The intelligence fraternity scarcely slept over their targeted goals.

"Look Alam sahib," Harfan opened up, "it's but natural for the ISI to target counterintelligence suspects. I feel there's more to it than what we perceive. It is more than likely that Malika is the target and not I. The powerful Generals and Izaz Afroz want the President out. I'm just a part of the side show."

"That's what I told you. It makes the situation more vulnerable. You can't afford to be sucked into the vortex of Pakistani power politics."

"It's not possible to completely distance from the happenings around, when I'm required to move, eat and sleep with them." Harfan explained the inbuilt jeopardy he suffered from.

"I'm talking about your neck. And where's the need for you to stick it out?"

"I don't identify with the crowd around. My business cover takes to them."

Alam expected the high profile agent to genuflect before him. Harfan disheartened him. Well! It was time to deactivate this agent. He would become, if he hadn't already, a plague-spreading rat, once the ISI succeeded in perforating the thin diaphragm of his cover.

His own security would be in jeopardy. Alam decided to guard his hide. He had a longer race to run.

"Take it from me Mian Harfan," Alam spoke tersely, "your bravado comes out of your immaturity. Remain out of sight for sometime. I suggest you take up the airlifting operations to Dacca. Israr is a game."

"Will it help?"

"For sometime. Remain out of circulation and let me try to diffuse the crisis."

"I don't mind," Harfan replied.

"Okay. General Shabaz also gave me to understand that the SigInt team is likely to return in another two days. I'll dismantle the radio set. The ISI should draw a blank on this front, and I've found another use for this machine. Thank God, I did."

Alam suggested a short outing for Harfan and Jamilla. A trip to Muree, at least for two days, that should give him enough time to dismantle the set and cleanse the house of all electronic gadgets.

On his return, he would receive instructions on alternative communication channels. Things should look normal. No feathers should appear to have been ruffled.

"Don't commit mistake, let no emotion or attachment weaken you. You're a lone traveller." Alam lighted a cigarette and spoke expansively.

"Don't frighten me. Am I not giving my best, my life, for the country?"

"Don't be a fool," Alam whispered, "in this trade nobody reclaims a loser. You've to earn the right to your tomorrows." Alam's voice reminded Harfan of the lost property simile used by Nampoothiri.

"What security do my wife and son have? Why should I go by your orders?"

"That's what you've been planted in Pakistan for. You can't plough a different furrow. Your orbit is well defined."

"That's not acceptable. My wife and son are more important than your bloody work." Harfan nearly revolted.

"Sorry Mian Harfan. A spy never falls in love at the cost of his trade. They're a part of your cover. Rest is hallucination. Enjoy it, as long as it lasts."

"Withdraw me, if you're so panicky." Replied Harfan.

"It all depends on Delhi's final assessment. They're the people to decide your new cover."

"What's new about it?"

"Your cover is like the seasonal slough of a cobra. You shed it periodically for regeneration and survival. Make it a part of your life as long as your profession needs it." Alam gestured a message of finality.

The phone rang sharply as Alam finished admonishing his junior partner.

"Hello Alam," Israr came alive on the line, "they agree on both counts, South Africa and the communication set, with one condition."

"What's that?"

"The operator will be theirs."

"It's your problem. What about my share?"

"What share? We're doing it for Pakistan." Israr replied in an injured voice.

"Don't get hurt dear. We're all patriots, but we're businessmen too. Tell me one good reason, why should you and I, two honest businessmen, not expect our risk money? The Generals don't pay, the bucks flow in smoothly through the Potomac to the Indus."

Alam made his point with a deliberate emphasis on *risk* and *Potomac*. It was no joke to get involved with the South African mercenaries, most of who could as well be hardened war criminals of the Third Reich.

"You've a point. We'll take care of that. What's your expectation?"

"It's reasonable, I'm not expecting the moon," Alam lowered his pitch to a conciliatory decibel, "the HF set will cost rupees three million. For the airlift I claim 3% of the total hiring charges."

"That's rather high. If you take three, the CMLA sharks will take another five. Where do I stand?" Israr expressed his helplessness.

"You take another 4% over the usual 3% commission. That's a fat cut. You'll be the largest beneficiary of this military stand off between Hindustan and Pakistan. And that won't make any dent on Fort Knox either." Alam assured Israr about the soundness of his arithmetic.

"It's a drain on the country." Israr still tried to project his patriotic concern.

"Sharief sahib," Alam made a final effort to free Israr's conscience of the patriotism bug, "the Army and the politicians are fucking the country anaemic. We, poor businessmen, should honestly expect what every businessman around the world expects, nothing more, nothing less."

"Okay. When can you finalise the deal?" Israr shelved his wounded patriotism.

"Give me a day for the wireless set from a delicate supplier at Darra Adam. Wait for my next message, your eggs will be in the right basket, at the right time. Tell the bosses."

"That's fine with me and General Naqi," Israr replied.

"Tell the bosses that the pilot, co-pilot and crew may not have impeccable character sheets. They don't have, in this line of philanthropic mission," Mian Alam chuckled. "my friends don't accept crew from the end users, it's their trade specialty. Who'll liaise? Don't trust too many barrette tops."

"That's an important point. Harfan suits me."

"I hope Naqi won't have any qualms!" Alam asked.

"I don't think so. He wants a chic cover operation. And I'll get it cleared from Sarfaraz."

"I hope the ghostly shadows of the CMLA office wouldn't raise any objection."

"Do you mean the ISI? Forget it. Naqi is very secretive about his dear Operation Millat, that's the *nom de plume* he has assigned to the airlifting exercises."

"I'm happy. Hold on a second, Harfan wants to say something."

Alam advised Harfan to seek permission for a short break to Muree. Israr welcomed the idea. With Jamilla around, he should recharge his batteries and be prepared for a tough job ahead, working out the nitty-gritty of the chartered flights.

Harfan bade *Khuda Hafiz* and left Alam to go about his job. In the darkness of the bedroom, his mind focussed on a slice of the moon that peeped on Jamilla's face. She was fast asleep, her hand placed on Pervez. This face of Jamilla, saddened by a thick cloud cover, was new to him. The pale moon enhanced the shadows under her eyelids.

What was wrong with her? She hadn't spoken a single word since her sudden arrival a day ago. Her eyes, whenever he tried to engage them, appeared flooded to the brim, ready to breach the banks. Had Nawab Sharief carried the Jahanara tale to her as well? Oh no! Harfan shuddered at the thought of facing a hurt Jamilla. He had experienced her love and ecstasy, but this clouded look was new. He wasn't adept in handling such a situation.

Should he wake her up and tell the real story? Which story? The story of his real identity? His accidental involvement with Jahanara?

No. This wasn't the correct moment to present Jamilla with the harsh truth. His thought process frog-leapt to Alam's suggestion of getting involved with the airlifting operations. Not a bad idea! It might give him a spasmodic breather, until he hit upon a tunnel to bolt from Pakistan with Jamilla and Pervez.

What next? Facing the ISI hatchet men? Not yet. The ISI wouldn't find Triple X, a frozen dead rat, before he actually died. Death was the last item in his agenda. Prospects of trips to Dacca suddenly brought back to his memory the names of Major Anjum Mani of the Special Services Group and Wing Commander Ahsan Khondokar, a Bengali officer with the Eastern Command Pakistani Air force. The innumerable business contacts with them had flourished into a friendship. Things had been moving very fast and East Pakistan had become South Asia's new killing field. He ruminated over the thought briefly and fished out a peg in a remote corner of his mind to hang the faint hope of escaping to the safety of Dacca. He smiled. He was again gambling with destiny, and the Dacca plan was a long shot gamble, the chance of winning being 1:100.

The moon disappeared. The faint blue of the night lamp added new shades to Jamilla's pink limbs and Pervez, drawn to her bare bosom.

It was a heavenly piece of sculpture.

Harfan didn't have the heart to disturb the placid serenity of the frame. Perhaps he had forfeited the right to disturb Jamilla emotionally. The moment of truth was knocking his door. His real identity would surely shatter Jamilla's dream world. He wouldn't blame Jamilla for turning her face away. Would she be scared to see the real colours of his bones?

Perhaps, yes. May be, not.

Behind her frail frame and tender mind, Jamilla harboured a tensile courage. He had witnessed glimpses of that courage soon after their marriage, when he had tried to persuade her to dump the gold coins presented by Ramayani. She wasn't a Hindu, she said, but she was determined to preserve the coins. This was from a mother to a daughter, from one woman to another woman. What difference did it make if Ramayani was a Hindu?

How would he fill in her emotional scars, inflicted by his acts of treachery? Perhaps Jamilla's love for him would evaporate instantaneously. She wouldn't hesitate to wash him out of her existence, like she removed accidental specks of dust from her eyes, by simply splashes of cold water.

Would she really do that?

Harfan moved closer to his favourite window that opened to the forest greens which tapered down to the murmuring river. The distant rippling sounds and the moon hanging on the remote smoky horizon failed to soothe his ruffled emotions. Perhaps Alam was correct.

His love for Jamilla had transcended his cover identity, carefully crafted by Delhi. Ramendra Kaushal, the wild son of the wild king of Jhumra, had died long ago. His rebirth as Harfan was reshaped by destiny around Jamilla and Pervez. It wasn't the same Harfan Bukhari chiselled out of the factory of Bhagat and Maulana Rizwan. No. He could under no circumstances dupe Jamilla. He couldn't plan his life without them, at any cost.

Jamilla turned side on her bed. Harfan could see two silent drops of tears rolling down her cheeks. The wound, whatever it was, had hurt her and it was indeed deep. Her sphinx like silence tormented Harfan.

No. He wouldn't allow Jamilla to suffer silent agony. Her silence was cooler than sculpted ice on a frozen mountain spring. The waves were silent but eloquently resonant. Harfan closed the window, shifted to the drawing room, and over another cigarette remembered Alam's harsh articulation. Would he kill Jamilla and Pervez too? No. Not even Alam could arrogate that licence. He must survive the churning clouds of the impending typhoon and survive with his love and the essence of his new existence intact.

He was a better merchant of death and destruction. Harfan released his clasped fists and stretched out on the sofa. Alam wasn't correct. He couldn't kill a Kaushal at will, on his own or on Delhi's orders.

A spy reserved the right to live for another day, beyond his tomorrow. He could not be executed at the altar of patriotism and putrid animosity, which rooted back to the middle ages. These fanatics branded humanity by their rotten religion. No. He wouldn't allow either the ISI, or the NSI to have the pleasure of liquidating him and his love. Well! If his spy-cover weren't more tangible than a cobra's slough, he would discard it, at the appropriate moment. He knew the story, as they said back at Jhunjhunu. The cobra's venom turned more potent after every seasonal change of slough. Mian Alam Khan would find this new slough tougher than veritable steel armour.

Harfan switched off the hall lights and stretched his body on the sofa. He required some rest before cruising to Murree first thing in the morning. Mian Alam would have a free run of the house for electronic sanitising.

Harfan, lost in his thoughts, failed to co-ordinate the conflicting signals. Alam, ISI, Direction Finders, Nawab Sharief and the moist eyelids of Jamilla—the rush of past events rolled over fast against the canvass of his mind. A sudden black curtain dropped in to cut off his thoughts and Harfan simply dozed off. His brain had peaked to the brim and the circuit automatically switched off.

*

39

Alam carried out 'operation sanitisation' in a professional manner. It took him two hours to dismantle the HF wireless system along with the antenna and protective lead cover of the sunken chamber. Ibadat helped with minor masonry and painting jobs to hide the tool marks and other telltale signs. Alam examined the restoration job and suggested textured denting and soiling of vulnerable spots, which were likely to be examined by trained counterintelligence sleuths.

"Smear the underground pit with charcoal dust and kitchen grime," Alam instructed Ibadat, "and soak two leather shoes in warm water and place them below the pile of other shoes and used linen."

"What for?"

"That'd create an antique effect. The grime, charcoal and fungi mixture will make even the toughest investigator nauseous."

Ibadat went about his job meticulously and ended by burning the high grade OTPs (onetime cipher pads) and flushing down the ashes. Alam fished out several electronic spy gadgets from wall crevices and finally left for Hotel Royal Palace with two brief cases stacked with the incriminating evidence.

He slept well and woke up little before lunch to be greeted by Ibadat and a steaming cup of coffee. .

"Morning sir, it's time to get ready."

"Morning Ibadat. I'm as hungry as a wolf. Lay down my favourite Peshawari dish. Just allow me time for a nice steam bath."

Alam enjoyed the Peshawari meal, but his mind wasn't in it. He was engrossed, pondering over the daredevil traits of Harfan and the unexpected metamorphosis he had undergone. The valuable agent had started imagining the mirage as matter. He had donned the Jamilla cover like another layer of skin, which had developed parallel capillaries and vessels. His cover had started breathing in fresh flow of love, care and the dangerous symptoms of a desire to live. A hostile agent could transform to a double agent. Harfan's desire to live beyond his cover could endanger other operations in Pakistan. His own existence, Alam guessed, might face serious jeopardy.

Should Triple X be allowed to breathe freely?

Alam munched over the thought along with pieces of roasted beef. His head gave a decisive jerk. This high profile agent, Triple X, should be snuffed out at an appropriate moment, before the ISI closed in on him.

Should Delhi be taken into confidence?

Not necessarily, Alam concluded.

He would tackle this minor problem all by himself.

Alam smiled under his thick moustache. Starting with a small export-import venture at Khyber Bazaar, Jiwan Bahutule alias Mian Alam Khan, Delhi's Alamgir, had emerged as a respectable international trader, vital to Pakistan's defence quests.

His minions, operating in the international sub-ways of illegal arms peddling, procured weapons from pistols to tanks, missiles, and jet fighter-bombers to small naval crafts for the Pakistani armed forces. In the recent past, his services were used for clandestine procurement of uranium granules and red-mercury from East-European countries for Pakistan's infantile nuclear facilities.

The schemers of the Cold War used his services too. He had developed innumerable contacts in the predominantly Central Asian Muslim Republics of the Soviet Union and helped the CENTO allies to open up subterranean weapon supply channels to the Islamist rebels. The name of this patriotic Pakistani was well known to key US security and intelligence agencies. In Pakistan, he was respected and feared for his legendary connectivity to the top military and political leaders. He now controlled at least five resident agents, planted by the FIB and its inheritor, the NSI. He was India's one and only magnificent spymaster in Pakistan who enjoyed the authority of affixing and ejecting any talent from his orbit.

But, for how long!

An emotionally raw ram like Harfan could set off an avalanche of disaster. His second home in Switzerland, where his wife lived with their children, always allured him. Perhaps he too was getting tired with this cloak and dagger game. The onerous responsibility of mastering the art of living with multiple identities had started eating into his personality. Who was he in real life? Was he the same orphan from Maharashtra? Was he a Pakistani or an Indian? Was he a Hindu or a Muslim? He had forgotten his own self, Jiwan Bahutule, who had started from a modest background and who simply desired to have a secured job and a nice family. The endless game of deception he played on others had started deceiving him.

Should he call it a day? Should he wind up his tentacles and disappear into the salubrious climes of Switzerland?

No. He couldn't. For him there was no short cut to *nirvana* (beatitude). He was destined to live the cover, until he was caught or bumped off by the ISI or until Delhi decommissioned him.

He wondered which one would happen sooner.

*

"Sir, the ISI officers have taken several rounds of Jhumra in recent weeks. Some of them enquired about Harfan." Ibadat poured another beer and whispered. Alam didn't reply. Ibadat continued with the motion of pouring beer, while talking.

"Brigadier Barqat, the ISI team leader, was a guest in the hotel. He quizzed me," Ibadat added, "and my friend Karamat Suri and another cruel officer Arman Ali Niazi have been temporarily deputed to locally investigate our friend."

"Has anything special come to your notice?"

"General questions, about Harfan's place of origin, his workplace, in-laws, wife and friends."

"Proceed...."

"The ISI is probing his links with Jahanara. They suspect his amorous links with her. Karamat tells me that the ISI chief wants to stage another coup." Alam looked up at Ibadat and asked through corners of his eyes.

"Is he really involved with Jahanara?"

"Sir, she's a seductress. No virile young man can escape her. She either takes them to bed or destroys them. Harfan isn't a whoring philanderer."

"What gives you that feeling?"

"He loves his wife and child."

"How genuine are his feelings for them?"

"I think it's serious. He may do anything to save her and the child."

"Even sacrifice himself?"

"Possibly sir." Ibadat served Alam some mutton *biryani* (spiced rice).

"Look Ibadat," Alam negotiated a chunk of bony meat and spoke with a slurry drag, "I must share a secret with you. There's a possibility that Harfan is related to the former king of Jhumra. It is possible that he may resemble his late father. Have you heard any rumour about that aspect?"

"Sir," Ibadat feigned ignorance, "my mother could tell better."

"That does not help."

"Sir my mother is an illiterate woman. She is still glued to her past."

"Who else may be aware of his suspected linkages with the former king?"

"If you're correct sir," Ibadat spoke with feigned hesitation, "Ramayani is the only other person who may recognise him."

"Who is she?"

"A deranged woman from the remnants of the former royal retinue."

"Are you sure?"

"I guess I am correct."

"Is she safe?"

"No problem."

"Why don't you kill the lady before the ISI sleuths reach her? Can she withstand torture?"

"She appears to be a silent granite, doesn't react to anything around her."

"Keep me posted. You may have to eliminate her. Wait for my orders. Don't call the Quetta safe house number. Call Peshawar. Kill Harfan, if the ISI closes in. Keep this."

Alam passed on a .9 mm·automatic Colt, with a sawed off barrel.

"Use the weapon wisely. If it's too hot for you here, escape to Kabul. We'll rescue you from there. Hand over this cover to Harfan, personally. I expect an ISI raid soon. Conceal this carefully. If you can't hand it over, destroy it. Don't open. You know the cost of curiosity."

"Is it necessary to destroy Harfan?" Ibadat asked.

Alam looked up, wiped the beer froth with a napkin, and buried his teeth on a piece of mutton.

"Any objections? Look Ibadat, in our profession we strictly go by orders. If the decision is to kaput him, you carry out the order and ask no question." Alam finished his lunch leisurely, boarded his Toyota, and drove off towards Peshawar.

*

He was in a hurry. A firm date was to be kept with Israr Sharief. Before that, he should be able to talk to his friend Doug Chris, in Paphos, 150 km from Larnaca, the capital of Cyprus.

Doug Chris, his arms-bazaar friend, headed a chartered airline and flew in and out of the jaws of death, wherever there were wars, conflicts, and rancid odour of death. Doug, a one time lieutenant of the elite fighter squadrons of the Third Reich's Luftwaffe, administered the show with aid from an able partner, Vudurume, a South African of Indian origin.

Athena Air Lines, as the merchants of death liked to call their baby, operated in every theatre of proxy and dirty warfare. Often they hawked fiery hardware for and on behalf of the CIA, Mossad, SAS and the KGB; practically everybody. Doug and Vudurume worked for all conceivable clients, obviously for fat compensation packages often touching astronomical figures, all paid to numbered accounts in Switzerland. Their last big assignment, Alam recalled, was in a West African country, where they ferried weapons for CIA surrogates.

For Chris, war was another honourable business, the most profitable, and most eternal, more eternal than the stupid ideologies of emancipation, *nirvana,* and *moksha* (salvation) put together. The loonies invented these humbugs much later. Killing and war came first and would reign over human society, until Armageddon. Vudurume managed the birds' maintenance, flew sorties, and talked of teaming up with Nelson Mandela for dismantling the apartheid regime. He financially helped the African National Congress fighters and supplied them with small weapons. He loved South Africa but hated the system it followed.

Alam's thought process shifted from Doug and Vudu to Harfan. He was to attend another urgent call of duty, send a report to Nampoothiri. Harfan was on the edge of jeopardy. It was serious. The chances of his bumping against the ISI sleuths were real. What worried him most was Harfan's unconventional attitude towards his cover. The machine had developed a mind of its own. It would be too risky to allow Harfan to operate in Pakistan. He should be withdrawn or temporarily decommissioned. Changes in operational strategy and a midway course correction were overdue.

If these weren't found practical, and the ISI really closed in on Triple X, his physical neutralisation would be the most convenient route to safeguarding India's remaining operations in Pakistan. Some vital assets, including him, couldn't be compromised, because of the idiosyncrasies of an emotionally disturbed agent.

The decision had to be cruel. A surgeon couldn't help but amputate a gangrenous limb. Harfan had developed a serious infection. His mind and ideas were infected by love. Love could often be the most potent hemlock.

Alam wondered if Nawab could be the invisible conductor who had orchestrated ISI assault on Harfan's trail. It was possible. General Hyder was his personal friend and business partner. He would do anything to demolish Israr, now on the threshold of bagging a few hundred millions more out of the airlifting operation. To get at Israr, Nawab was sure to demolish his first shield, Harfan.

The picture presented a confusing collage.

Should he initiate 'operation neutralisation' on his own? No harm. Delhi was too far and their reaction time was often painfully slow. Alam breathed easy. The decision to neutralise Harfan was his own. Ibadat could well play the role of an executioner. Till then 'operation airlifting' should be the convenient dust cover. That should provide a breather and take the ISI off Harfan's trail. The days ahead, Alam felt, were likely to be gory. He smelled cordite and blood, and visualised the not too indistinct tentacles of the nemesis catching up with Triple X. That's when he'd signal Ibadat to pump the bullets in. Time was the essence of strategy. Alam steadied the wheel and accelerated. The Grand Trunk road started vanishing under his wheels like a celluloid reel, sans the arc lamps.

*

Harfan's Peugeot chugged along the asphalt snugly and whizzed past Lake Rawal. He slowed down as it started climbing the hills towards Murree and on to Nathia Gali. The asphalt below and the rushing air around orchestrated a rhyming sound, keeping pace with Harfan's pulsating heart...blip-blop-blip-blop.

His heart was in agony. It was in great pain.

Hazy uncertain future caused agony, and pain for Jamilla's silence. A sad mask shrouded her face with a pre-cyclonic ember glow. She hadn't talked since her unannounced appearance at Jhumra. Neither could he venture a guess, from her injured looks, whether the frozen cyclone was about to unleash torrents of snow or fire. Young Pervez, fast asleep on mother's lap, with a lavish black tuft of hair on his head and exquisitely curled up lips, looked simply like a miniature Kaushal, the disinherited potentate of Jhumra.

Harfan smiled. Yes, Pervez was the third generation claimant to the lost kingdom, perhaps a better claimant, being born to a Muslim Pakistani mother. What a funny quirk of fate!

Harfan played Jamilla's favourite Bade Ghulam Ali *thumris* (light classical music) in the car stereo. She ignored the lure.

Her eyes, not really fixed on any particular object, wore a vacant, remote look. She wasn't looking at Harfan, even from the corners of her eyes. Her elegant long and black eyelashes stood erect, like guards, not allowing the lids to close even for a second. Harfan was amazed to see her gaze, lost somewhere beyond the horizon! She looked like a sculpted image, except for her moist pupils. Accumulated tears were about to escape the brims of her eyes.

What was hurting her? Had she overheard his discussions with Alam? Good heavens! Harfan shuddered to imagine the portrait of an angry Jamilla. Their moments of togetherness left no space for anger and even feigned aloofness. The intense universe of their love transcended the finite space of physical proximity and, an invisible serene glow encapsulated them, in the charged clouds of the monsoon skies.

Jamilla looked different today. She covered herself with an impenetrable mysterious mesh. Harfan switched off the stereo, slowed the car down, and parked under the portico of a wayside motel.

"Shall we have some breakfast?" He asked, expecting Jamilla to respond.

"If you so wish," she replied without looking at Harfan, her eyes still scanning the horizon, "and Nanha Mian (Pervez) needs feeding." She alighted, collecting the folding pram.

Jamilla moved to a corner of the room to breast-feed Pervez. Harfan lighted a cigarette and ordered Jamilla's favourite dish of minced-meat-stuffed fried flatbread, served with mint and garlic sauce, followed by coffee.

Harfan broke the bread, garnished it with sauce, and took his fingers near Jamilla's mouth. Her eyes, an overflowing sea of tears, looked straight into Harfan's, quivered for a fleeting moment and breached the banks in uncontrollable sobs. Her body shook in wild spasm.

"What's my fault? Why are you punishing me?" Harfan took Jamilla gently into his arms and helped her to put Pervez on the pram. She continued sobbing with muffled sounds.

"You can't do this to me." Harfan lightly kissed her lips.

"Am I not beautiful enough? Have I lost my charm?"

"Why do you ask this? You're the essence of my life." Harfan wiped her eyes and cheeks with a handkerchief.

"Say what I hear about that ugly fat Malika is wrong." Jamilla again burst into tears.

So? The story had reached her as well.

Who could it be? The ISI crooks? Nawab?

Well! He'd figure that out later. Jamilla's doubts must be dispelled first.

"Absolute nonsense. The only time I met her was when I delivered some medicines on behalf of Nawab Sharief. You know him, Israr's brother. You shouldn't believe in rumours."

Harfan lied with slick smoothness, as if he was consciously duping a lie detector. He added a little dash of spontaneous emotion to what he had just said.

"*Allah kasam* (by God)?"

"*Allah kasam.* You're the highest truth in my life."

"Don't say that," Jamilla put her fingers on Harfan's lips, "why did Nawab call up father to say that he had chosen a wrong man for his daughter?"

"It's because of business rivalry Jami. You know this vengeful Sharief tribe. Ready to kill at the slightest provocation. Though they've lived in the Punjab for centuries, they haven't forgotten the wild Chingiside traits."

Harfan enlightened his wife in detail, the deeper implications of the business rivalry between Israr and Nawab, the latest one being the contentious arms lifting operations.

"That means you'll be flying to Dacca, braving Indian fighters all the way!" Jamilla closed in.

"I can't avoid that. Our company's committed. It's a national commitment." Harfan tightened his grip around Jamilla. The spontaneous heat accelerated his heartbeats.

Jamilla moved in closer, planted a kiss, a full thrust, and flattened him on the bed. This was one long kiss, Harfan felt, would never end.

"Let's eat. I haven't eaten for the last 24 hours." Jamilla broke the bread, laced it with the hot sauce, and put it in Harfan's mouth.

"Let's not waste time driving to Nathia Gali. Can't we go to a quieter place? Nathia is always crowded." Jamilla, back to her spirits suggested, as Harfan switched on the ignition for the final lap of the journey.

"Not a bad idea," said Harfan swerving the steering, "let's go to Taxila, only 45 km from here, say about an hour's drive. We can stay in the PTDC rest house next to the remains of Asoka's Palace. Being a Buddhist centre Pakistanis normally don't go there."

Jamilla pushed in the stereo button and her favourite Bade Ghulam Ali's voice filled her senses as nothing else could. Her world was again lost inside the man she loved.

*

After an enduring and satisfying session of love making, Jamilla covered her bare body with a pink sheet and moved closer to Pervez. It was time to feed him.

Harfan climbed out of bed, stood near the open window, and lighted a cigarette. His mind raced on another track.

Should he open up his heart to her? Tell Jamilla all about his real identity, his mission and discuss their future together? He could probably convince her of the compelling circumstances, which had made him succumb to the FIB blackmail. It wouldn't be difficult to convince her to leave Pakistan for a safer haven somewhere in mid-country USA. They could live an anonymous life, comfortably. Why not? It was possible. Should he unburden his heart, now?

Harfan's mind told him to reveal all, his heart sank in apprehension. No. Probably he couldn't take her back to the wild days of man-eater Ramendra Kaushal, who rampaged the Delhi University campus, peddled drugs, raped women, and killed unsuspecting friends. That simply wasn't her world. Certain truths should never surface. Harfan involuntarily shook his head and pushed the idea back, deep into the lowest strata of his medulla. Yes, the serpent should remain buried there, for all time to come.

He moved closer to the bed.

Jamilla was fast asleep. Pervez was busy playing with the locks of her hair and giggling out warm uncertain happiness. Harfan made a little space for him in the bed. Pervez was still busy throwing his limbs about in the air and making sweet sounds. His eyes recognised Harfan, his face lighted up in a broad smile.

That was an invitation to some heavenly pleasure. Harfan played with Pervez, the very games he had played in his mother's laps. Drops of tear rolled down his cheek. How could the kid Ramen, Ramu to his mother, transform himself to a criminal? When did he leave his mother's cradle and walk into the world of Ram Karan, Vidyasagar Suri and Matang Singh? Why did he kill that innocent girl? His father was not a criminal. Was it in his blood? Harfan wiped the teardrops and resolved that he would not allow such terrible things to happen to his son. He must live beyond Alam and the ISI to prove that he had performed penance for his mistakes. Only that could, he thought, give some solace and comfort to his mother Kasturi, who waited back at Jhunjhunu for her son to return from his foreign assignment.

The resolve helped Harfan to recompose his determination; and sleep finally enwrapped both, father and son.

*

40

The sight of blood, the most precious fluid, often invited depression. To certain creatures of the land and sea, blood excited hunger. The bright colour of blood often resembled the redness of the sun. Lt. Gen. Sarfaraz was not a hungry Hammerhead Shark, however, his black mood had partially brightened up when the footage of videos sent by General Tarakki reached him. Tarakki's troops and collaborators had swooped down on the Bengali traitors in Dacca and other major urban centres of East Pakistan. The valiant Punjabis and *muhajirs*, who made East Pakistan their homes after the partition, had joined the Islamist groups headed by the Rajakar, Ansar, Al Badr and Jamait-e-Islami activists. They fanned out to the riverine rural belts to mow down the treacherous Bengali Hindus and their Muslim collaborators.

However, most eligible women, Muslims and Hindus, were taken as war booty and distributed amongst the valiant warriors in pure Islamic tradition. Minor objections from the saner elements were scoffed off citing instances of similar war-booty-beauty distribution practices of the holy warriors of the Prophet Mohammad.

General Tarakki's tanks and armoured vehicles had mowed down thousands of Bengali traitors and Indian collaborators in front of the Dacca University and were given mass burial. Hundreds of dead bodies were thrown into the Buri Ganga and Shitalakshya Rivers. Sarfaraz agreed with Tarakki that Bengali blood would only strengthen the foundation of Pakistan. He appreciated the commendable work done by General Hyder in eliminating the leading troublemakers and the suspected Indian collaborators.

What worried him were reports of rebellious activities of the Bengali officers and men of the Army and para-military forces. More disturbing were the reports he received from Robert Armstrong, the Deputy Chief of the US embassy in Islamabad. The no-nonsense American diplomat was forthright in his assessment of the situation. The Indians had infiltrated the parochial and separatist movements in Sind and Baluchistan. He produced apparently convincing reports on two meetings between Sartaj Jamil and an Indian diplomat at a restaurant in New Jersey and a crucial meeting at Kabul between an identified Delhi based agent of the National Security India and Aliullah Mengel and Ashfaq Yusufzai, the rebellious Frontier leaders.

India, the US DCM cautioned Sarfaraz, had finalised plans to flood both, Sind and vulnerable tribal pockets in Baluchistan with sophisticated weapons through the land and sea routes. The State Department, he said, had decided to send a friendly demarche to the Indian Mission in Washington after consulting the CIA and the NSA. But the American action could only follow after some ground actions were taken by Islamabad and tangible proofs were produced.

The Bangkok station of the CIA, Robert Armstrong revealed, had also reported the visit of an Israeli mercenary, Yossi Dayan, to the Thai capital and some remote areas in Aranya Prathet in the north and Phuket in the south. A CIA agent trailed him to a nondescript Greek restaurant at Nana Road. A vital meeting between a senior Indian diplomat in Bangkok and Yossi was documented. However, the details of the transaction could not be recorded.

The CIA's archives had authentic documentation on Yossi's visit to Singapore thirty days ago and his involvement in supplying weapons and ammunition to various theatres of conflict. A consignment from Yossi to the Armenian terrorists, who fought against Turkey, was confiscated at a Black Sea port. The US, Armstrong warned Sarfaraz, had reasons to believe that India could have tapped Yossi for supplying weapons to the Bengali separatists through the sea route.

"You can bring pressure both on Tel Aviv and Bangkok to prevent Yossi from succumbing to the Indian allurement."

"The Tel Aviv government might agree. But I must warn you that there are several Jewish secret organizations, which support various anti-Semitic and anti-Islamist groups. The Israeli government has little control on them. These organisations headed by fanatic Rabbis and Hitler's concentration camp survivors are as fanatic as some of your Islamist *jihadis*."

"What about screwing up the Thai government? They can prevent Yossi."

Sarfaraz had argued with the US diplomat.

"I think Sarfaraz you're expecting too much from us. The Thai army is as faction ridden as yours is. General Prachanthakarno, who is known for thriving on arms and drug trade, controls the Aranya Prathet tract. My government wanted me to share this information with you and I've done my job. These are unsigned reports. The embassy wouldn't own up if you happen to leak to the media."

"What do you suggest?"

"Talk to our CIA station chief and ask your own Int. boys to follow up the leads."

"Our President would perhaps like to talk to Washington. These are very serious developments."

"I suggest Sarfaraz you first get into action and sound out Washington for further consultations. I've no other comment to make. Bye."

Robert Armstrong's visit had again thrown the Principal Staff Officer into a spin. The US DCM would not have visited him if the reports were not vetted and cleared by Washington. It meant real trouble. That bloody lady in Delhi was working on multiple strategies to encircle Pakistan from within. By *Allah*! His government was still sitting on haunches on the vital issue of airlifting weapons and men to Dacca. What the hell was happening? What was Hyder doing? Why did his intelligence machinery fail to gather these earth-shaking reports? What was General Naqibullah doing? That holy ghost of an advisor to the CMLA never took him into confidence, as if he ran a parallel government. He should have started off with the airlifting operations by now.

Sarfaraz dialled the number of General Naqi. The Defence and National Security Advisor to the President enjoyed a special relationship with the top man. Commissioned after 1947, Naqi had not been exposed to the secular traditions of the British Indian Army. A migrant from the Indian held Poonch in Kashmir, he hated the Indians much more than any other Pakistani did. He prayed five times a day and observed scrupulous fasting during the *Ramadan*. He conscientiously followed the prescriptions of the *Hadith*. He was perhaps one of the few officers who had pioneered the movement for allowing the officers and men of the armed forces to maintain long beard and moustache, as prescribed by the scriptures. Left to him, Sarfaraz shuddered to think, this zealot would one day revert Pakistan to the *Sharia* rules, no booze, no women and no fun. Naqi's idea of an Islamic Republic was modelled after the strict *fatwas* (edicts) from the Al Azhar of Egypt, the fanatic Sunni Wahabi fundamentalists of Saudi Arabia, and their nineteenth century Deobandi protagonists.

President Arif trusted him for reasons other than his religious proclivities. General Naqi was too junior to challenge the power brokers all by himself and being a Kashmiri, he lacked the vital networking amongst the Punjabi *biradari* (brotherhood). Additionally he was married to the daughter of General Naim, the PIB chief and elder brother of General Arif Khan. Naqi possessed another sterling quality. He and Jahanara were on excellent terms and the two satisfactorily and somewhat honestly worked as the proxy snouts of the President, in matters of extracting cuts and commissions from almost all the deals that involved more than Rupees 10 million.

*

General Naqi dropped in within ten minutes. He was a man in hurry. That's the impression he liked to throw all around.

"Anything urgent sir?" he asked Sarfaraz even before he took a seat.

"Yes Naqi. I've been informed by usually reliable sources that the Indians have started augmenting arms supply to the Bengalis and to some Sindhi and Baluch traitors. What are you doing to augment supplies to our eastern garrisons?"

"Well General, you know the situation very well. The Chinese supplies have piled up at Cairo and the American supplies are stocked in Turkey. The CIA flights are shifting these at Sargodha and Bhagatan. But the dirty Indians have stalled our CIA and German routes to airlift these to Dacca. The Sri Lankans are hesitant to allow our birds ferrying weapons. Some Tamil leaders have kicked up pro-Indian dust," Naqi opened up defensively, "we're now depending on the party hired by Alam. I believe this guy is a Cyprus based German."

"Have you met this guy personally?"

"Yes sir. I had a meeting with this fellow Chris and his partner, a South African of Indian origin, at London."

"Is it safe to have an Indian on board?"

"I don't think he is anything beyond a mercenary. His family had migrated three generations back."

"That's okay. When do you start the sorties?"

"My first consignment will leave Sargodha day after tomorrow. The delay has been due to some blockage at Colombo. I believe the old lady over there has finally relented after the US President spoke to her and assured a development grant of $ 900 million."

"Not a bad bargain. I believe Israr has won the contract."

"Correct. This man has wonderful reach to the top. And his excellent executive Mian Harfan will be our point man."

"Are you not attaching any other officer from the regular forces?"

"Oh yes sir. I have designated two liaison points. Brigadier Mustafa will be at Sargodha and Brigadier Saigol at Dacca. In fact, this fellow Harfan is a dust cover to convince peeping toms in Colombo and Dacca. Officially he represents the Red Crescent and is engaged in carrying relief materials."

"How many sorties will you require?"

"About 24 at the present estimate. It may be increased if more American supplies from Turkey arrive in time."

"Go ahead Naqi. Take care that the Indians and the rabid Bengalis do not create problems."

"The cover is watertight sir. These are experienced mercenaries. Additionally, I have talked to the Air Chief to provide some air cover, at least from the funnel of the Bay of Bengal."

"That's a nice additional precautionary step. Good luck Naqi."

"*Insha Allah.*" General Naqi saluted the PSO and marched out with his usual air of a man being in absolute hurry.

*

General Hyder Bux arrived pretty late. Nawab Sharief had almost bored him to death over a private luncheon at the Rawalpindi Club. The junior Sharief had a litany of complaints against elder brother Israr and his 'treacherous' executive, Harfan Bukhari. Why could Hyder not clinch the airlifting deal in his favour? He had paid a fat advance and was ready to pay more.

Hyder wanted to abort the frustrating discussion as politely as he could, and rush back to Sarfaraz. He was aware of the mischief potential of Nawab. The viper was sure to rush to his mentor, Izaz Afroz. Izaz, Hyder knew it well, would pretend to shed tears and assure his protégé the top chair in the Punjab after the general elections. Finally, both of them would whisper into the ears of some delicate media friends. And the media's thirst for juicy stories was unquenchable.

Hyder had pitched in for Nawab. Nevertheless, Israr clinched the deal after offering 11% commission to General Naqi, who fronted the President in all such deals. What else could he do?

"Look Nawab, I know you've been hurt. So am I. But certain things are beyond control."

"Don't cut excuses sir," Nawab retorted, "please try once more. I'm ready to match the amount paid by Israr."

"Listen carefully," Hyder spoke desperately, "I would surely try. But take care and don't talk to the media. This is a delicate matter of the state. I can't protect you if I'm asked to investigate the source of leakage."

"Are you threatening me?"

"No. I'm just reminding you that the Indians are on the prowl and we don't want this deal to sour."

"You've failed to take action against that Indian agent."

"Who?"

"Harfan. Are you not convinced that he is an Indian spy? I've given you the proof."

"Don't be silly Nawab. Your vengeful spite does not necessarily make him a spy. Rhetoric cannot sway me. I'm working on the leads and I'd take action at the correct moment. Hope you wouldn't pester me on this professional matter at least." Hyder finally left the Rawalpindi Club and directed his driver to take him to the office of the PSO.

"Ah Hyder, finally you're here."

"Sorry sir. It was very difficult to shake off that barnacle."

"Who's the brave heart to hold up the ISI chief?"

"It's that junior Sharief. He still cribs for the airlifting contract. Tell me how can I help? Issar paid a whooping 11% cut and bagged the loot."

"I know. The old man's appetite is insatiable."

"Yes, and Naqi and Jahanara have played their usual roles."

"Forget Hyder. Such things happen." Sarfaraz ordered special Darjeeling tea imported from London, "they take cut here, we'll take cut somewhere else. I want to share with you what I gathered from Naqi. He is using that fellow Harfan as a civilian cover for the Red Crescent. Hope you've no objection."

"Well! I don't want to put a spanner just now. Brigadier Barqat is investigating him."

"Please take care that the bitch is not ruffled."

"Leave the matter to me. He's after all a nonentity. It does not matter if he is neutralised today or after three months. We can hang him anytime it suits us. Now tell me what's cooking?"

"Too many broths, Hyder, are being cooked by too many cooks. I think I should consult you before we discuss the matters with the *Sadr*."

"Where is he?"

"At the usual joint. I've asked Munir to drag him out. *Insha Allah* we should have a session with him this evening."

Sarfaraz explained, over several cups of tea and nuggets of fried cheese balls, the details of his discussion with Robert Armstrong earlier in the day. India, he commented, was determined to strike both in the eastern and western theatres.

They might have even hired a Jewish mercenary to supply weapons to the People's League. Most vulnerable was the sea route between Indian Gujarat and the numerous islands in the vast estuary of the Indus and its tributaries.

Sarfaraz suspected that the unfriendly regime in Kabul was collaborating with India for pumping in supplies to Baluchistan and that the KGB was playing a vital role from its bases in neighbouring Tajikistan.

"What are your views Hyder? How should we proceed? Should this be discussed with the Chiefs of the three Services before we go up to the President?"

"I think that's the right course of action. It's better we meet the Chiefs at the earliest and examine the US inputs thoroughly. I've outlined some lines of action in my report. You must have seen those. I feel Naim should also be consulted."

"Okay."

Sarfaraz called his aide and directed him to convene a meeting of the NSMC (National Security Management Committee) at 5 p.m.

"Can't we request the CIA to identify the mercenary vessels around shallow waters of the Andaman in the east and Sir and Kori Creeks in the west?"

"No harm. But how do you stop these tiny country vessels?"

"Our helicopter gunship can strike and our naval patrol boats can chase them all the way."

"It's not feasible. India may retaliate by shooting down some of the choppers.

"Our presence in the blue waters is negligible. India and the USSR wouldn't allow massive US presence either. Let's consult the Chiefs."

"I think for the Indus estuary area we can request Zahoor to deploy his assets. He controls almost the entire *Mohana* fishing community. He's the uncrowned king of these low caste Muslims."

"Sounds good. What are your resources in that area?"

"Almost nil. We've paid attention to the land border across the Kachchh, especially after the last conflict. We've very minor resources in the disputed Sir and Kori Creek areas."

"Why don't you tap Zahoor?"

"That fellow Harfan is his son in law."

"I suggest go slow on that front. He can wait. Let's attend the burning issues first."

"I think you're correct. Where do we meet at five?"

"Here. And in the President's office if he graces us. Think over if we can do anything else in the East Pakistan." Sarfaraz suggested with a grave look.

"Well sir," Hyder jumped out of his chair and went over to the wall mounted maps and ran his index finger over a vast area in the estuary of the rivers Padma, Meghna and Brahmaputra, "I suggest we depopulate these islands, say from

Bhola and Sandeep to St. Martin. We evacuate the entire Bengali population from the minor ports around Chittagong and Cox's Bazaar. If you agree we can ask Tarakki to evacuate certain coastal villages of the districts of Comilla, Barisal and Noakhali."

"That's a brilliant idea Hyder. Let's call Tarakki right away. This action should brook no delay."

"This is a major strategic decision sir. Shall we wait for the NSMC meeting?"

"Decision making in Islamabad is not a matter of joke. The Indians would flood East Pakistan with weapons by the time our jokers finish scratching their baldpates."

Sarfaraz personally dialled the number of General Tarakki and told him that the ISI chief should be in Dacca tomorrow on a special mission. He should implement the orders carried by General Hyder in person.

*

The meeting of the NSMC was ultimately converted to a full-fledged meeting of the War Cabinet, presided over by General Arif Khan.

He was not spruced up, as he usually was, and was not even shaven and bathed. A pungent odour of stale beer escaped his mouth whenever he opened the trap and spoke through clouds of cigarette smoke. In fact, Col. Munir had almost physically helped him out of the pleasure den on the insistence of the Chiefs of the three Services. Sarfaraz had to list the assistance of the Chiefs, as the lady had consistently declined to connect him to the President. The Chief of Army Staff had conveyed a veiled threat that the President should not at all bother to come out from Jahanara's residence if he was not interested in presiding over the nation. Conveyed verbatim, the message had completely shaken General Arif. He couldn't risk the displeasure of the three pillars of his regime.

Sarfaraz placed the reports he had received from the American DCM and briefed the meeting about his discussions with the envoy. Finally, he outlined four scenarios for the War Cabinet to consider.

Scenario one: India's success in pumping in sophisticated weapons through the mercenary sources would deteriorate further the balance of logistics between the Pakistani forces and the combined forces of India and the People's League.

Action suggested by him to depopulate the likely drop-zones along the coastal area and deployment of some elements of the armed forces and large contingents of the patriotic volunteer forces of East Pakistan was accepted. The meeting also approved aerial surveillance of the area, seizure of all civilian boats and increasing river patrols.

General Hyder's idea to bomb the sparsely populated islands by the Pakistani Air Force was turned down on grounds of likely US disapproval.

General Arif listened to Sarfaraz with rapt attention and looked up to the three Service Chiefs.

"Do you agree?"

"Bombing of the villages will attract international criticism," replied the chief of Pakistan Navy.

"What are your views Hamid?" Arif Khan asked his Chief of Army Staff.

"Mr. President," General Omar replied rather officiously, "I can't disagree with the views of Sarfaraz. I'll like to go with him minus the bombing part."

"I agree," General Arif spoke firmly, "direct Tarakki to initiate immediate action."

"If you approve sir," Sarfaraz intervened without waiting for the Service Chiefs to join the issue, "Hyder may fly to Dacca tonight and supervise the operation."

"Approved."

General Sarfaraz advanced the second scenario and commented that Indian move to pump in weapons to the Sind partisans through the land and sea routes was bound to deteriorate internal security situation. He suggested the Navy to seize all mechanised civilian *dhows* (trawlers) and deploy those along the shallow waters between the Sir and Kori creeks and the strategic estuary islands and minor ports. The Navy chief agreed to deploy two frigates in the blue waters within the territorial waters of Pakistan bordering the Indian maritime zone.

On Hyder's suggestion the meeting agreed to requisition the services of Zahoor Chaudry to rally the civilian *Mohana* population.

President Arif, by now half asleep, nodded his head in agreement.

The joint operations by India and the USSR to pump in weapons to Baluchistan in collaboration with the hostile regime in Kabul could pose tough challenge to the internal security scenario. The security fault lines in Baluchistan, he added, were numerous and the Baluch tribesmen were more virulent fighters than the plain Sindhis. The meeting decided to redeploy the 7th Division at Quetta to thwart Indian threats. Sustained bombing of some selected villages inhabited by the rebellious Bugti, Mengel and Mazari tribes was approved. The Foreign Minister prevailed upon the meeting to approach Washington to neutralise the hostile attitude of Kabul. A second track diplomatic team should visit the Afghan capital to convey Islamabad's concerns.

"Agreed," General Arif suddenly raised his head and boomed out his concurrence, "what is your fourth scenario?"

"We augment our supplies to East Pakistan at breakneck speed and request our friends in Washington and Peking to symbolically move their forces towards the Indian borders."

"The Chinese have assured help," the secretary cabinet affairs, who was maintaining silence all the while opened his mouth, "I think the President may agree to depute Izaz Afroz to Peking for immediate consultations. Increased Chinese presence on the Indian borders will deter India."

"Not a bad idea. Sarfaraz, please request the Chinese ambassador to see me tonight. I think there is no need to involve Izaz at this point of time. But how do you expect the Americans to move in?"

General Arif looked up at the defence secretary.

"Sir," the white haired bureaucrat spoke with a peculiar North Indian accent, "I suggest you speak to the US President and explain the emerging scenario. India's design of creating another Bhutan type protectorate out of East Pakistan is very clear. We should offer military bases to the USA in East Pakistan."

"I agree Shafiq," General Arif endorsed the views of the veteran bureaucrat, "we'll deny that pleasure to India. But I want immediate US assistance."

"Sir we've to defeat Indian propaganda that millions of Bengali Pakistanis have been killed. The US should be made to see through the Indian smokescreen and ensure its naval presence in the Bay of Bengal."

"I think it is better you fly to Washington tonight. Take Izaz Afroz with you. They should be made to realise the orchestrated Indo-USSR design against the American and Pakistani interests in the region. Pakistan is a stable ally of Washington. Dismemberment of Pakistan will strengthen the Russian presence in Afghanistan and Iran. That would make the Cold War too warm for Washington."

General Arif stood up indicating that the meeting was over. He turned immediately back and moved to the head of the conference table.

"Gentlemen," he addressed the meeting in an impassioned voice, "our fatherland is under serious Hindu threat. We're not simply facing another war. It's a *jihad.* Tell me when our logistics in East Pakistan reach a viable point. I wouldn't hesitate to hit India first. I'd like to teach that widow a bitter lesson." Arif 's exhortation was greeted with thunderous applauses.

"When are you leaving for Dacca, Hyder?"

"I'd leave for Chak Lala airbase straight from here. The flight should take about sixteen hours."

"Wish you the best of luck. Ensure that the Indians don't find any human habitation in the coastal villages to drop weapons. Kill and dump them into the sea."

"It'd be a pleasure sir."

Hyder saluted and left for the airbase. He felt happy that the meeting by and large had approved the lines of action jointly worked out by him and Sarfaraz. In a tearing hurry to board the special flight to Dacca he forgot to leave instructions with Brigadier Barqat to defer his actions against Harfan Bukhari and to consult Sarfaraz before he contemplated proceeding against Zahoor Chaudry in any manner.

*

41

Brigadier Barqat's horde, herded by Jamanat Ali, the veteran counterintelligence sleuth, drove down to Jhumra at the wee hours of the same night and sneaked into the residence of Harfan Bukhari.

He was late by a couple of days, for his kill.

Jamilla, inundated and reassured by Harfan's love, was back to her Masti Gate niche. Mian Alam Khan had flown out of Pakistan to a European destination for scouting out new supplies of French ground to air missiles for the Pakistani Army. Harfan Bukhari, the all important sales executive of Israr International, was already on the wings of the Boeing 707 of Doug Chris's Athena Air Lines, piloted by Vudurume, Doug's partner and a South African of Indian origin.

Neither Jamanat nor Barqat were at fault for the delayed action. It took Barqat three days to convince the chief, General Hyder Bux, that a physical search of the residence of Harfan Bukhari was absolutely necessary to locate the clandestine trans-receiver. To cover up the raid a few more houses in the vicinity should also be searched.

The Direction Finders of the Joint Intelligence Signal Bureau and the Army Signal Corps had inexorably pointed the needle of suspicion at a cluster of buildings in Liaquat colony. Search of some selected houses didn't make them any wiser. Jamanat had insisted on searching the house of his prime suspect, Harfan Bukhari. He believed it was the proximate source of emission of the clandestine signals.

Hyder Bux had sounded a note of warning that the raid should appear like a precise and incisive clandestine housebreaking. His rationale was simple and pragmatic. Harfan represented an apex company that was associated with sensitive defence activities. He was married in a respectable family. Malika Jahanara treated him as a pussy pet. No indiscretion by Barqat's boys should ruffle her feathers again. There should be no repetition of the Lahore fiasco.

Jamanat had checked out the itinerary of Harfan, before he cobbled up his team, for the late night break in. Telephone tapping had confirmed his absence from Jhumra. The monitors gathered vague indications that the suspect was out on some assignment promoted by General Naqi. Brigadier Barqat's attempts at penetrating General Naqi's shield of secrecy had received silent rebuff. He failed to get into the depth of Harfan's itinerary. Israr Sharief declined to comment on the query.

Jamanat fretted and fumed for over three days, but vacillation at the top took the air out of his wings. General Hyder Bux ploughed over the bits and pieces of the intelligence inputs and took three precious days to give a hesitant clearance for a limited clandestine raid only for detection of the suspected transmitter. The decision came after prolonged deliberations with the DMI and the Joint Intelligence Signal Bureau, a top-secret signal-monitoring outfit of the ISI located at Malir Cantonment, Karachi.

The JISB chief wasn't sure if the intercepted signals were actually originated by a clandestine spy station. The electronic jamming beams operated by the Joint Intelligence North, another division of the ISI, also generated similar signals. These beams, oscillated from the ISI's powerful transmitters were aimed at the Indian radar formations along the western front.

The confusion was confounded by General Hyder's failure to amend his earlier order. He was sipping fragrant Ceylonese tea at the VIP lounge of Colombo airport when Jamanat broke into the Jhumra residence of his prime suspect. The ISI chief's mind was focussed on the task of depopulating the coastal villages and dumping two million odd Bengali rats into the blue waters of the Bay of Bengal. Harfan Bukhari and Zahoor Chaudry had slipped out of his memory bank.

*

Jamanat's men entered Harfan's Jhumra house late in the night, drenched like July ravens after braving a thunderstorm. Some lighted cigarettes and others hoped to discover a bottle or two of liquid fire from the ornate cellar of the business executive.

"Shut up you fools," Jamanat cursed the chattering ravens, "it's not a marriage party. Stop chattering. I don't want the entire colony tó wake up."

However, Jamanat was shocked to encounter Ibadat, sleeping in the outer living room. He hadn't expected any living soul, except cockroaches and lizards in Harfan's empty Jhumra residence. He had planned a silent break in, looking for the suspected HF transmitter and other telltale signs of a long-term resident agent.

"What the hell are you doing here?" He thundered at Ibadat.

"Who're you? Leave immediately or I'll call the police." Ibadat charged back with shallow bravado. He readily recognised Karamat Suri. In fact, Karamat had alerted Ibadat earlier in the evening about the impending raid. He was prepared for the show.

"We're from the Narcotics Control Bureau," Jamanat declared and produced an identity card, "we've orders to search the house."

"Show me the warrant."

"I don't require one." Jamanat brought out his pistol.

"Well, in case you represent the trigger end of the law, as you say, go ahead. Would you like to have some tea? It's so soggy and cold in here!"

"Don't mind. Are you the cook here?"

"In a way sir. Please give me five minutes and I'd get you the excellent tea in this town." Ibadat moved to the kitchen with nonchalant steps. He was mighty worried. Scratches from ISI paws, as they said in Pakistan, always ended in gangrene. The company wouldn't take minutes to strip Harfan off his skin and spirit away his remains to eternal oblivion.

Strange! Ibadat pondered as he stirred sugar granules in the teapot. The ISI never operated under a flimsy pretext. They visited like killer desert storms with accompanying thunder, lightening and sandblast. This couldn't be a low-key affair, some officer acting on his own. It must be a planned intelligence break-in, in search of incriminating electronic gadgets. Was it the fall out of the Direction Finder operations? Must be. They must be from the signal intelligence division of the ISI.

"*Janab* tea is ready." Ibadat served spiced tea, real Lahoria tea garnished with green cardamom and cloves.

"Excellent!" Jamanat relished the concoction and kept on directing his men. The junior sleuths, short of ripping the house to shreds, searched all possible nooks and corners. They hammered the walls with rubber truncheons and pried open every possible crevice of the wooden floor.

A constable finally hit the sunken chamber. With a disgusting grimace on his face, he pulled out used shoes, clothes and assorted soiled domestic items. His palms were blackened by charcoal powder.

"*Janab*," shouted the constable in excitement, "here's an underground chamber."

Jamanat rushed in and examined the sunken chamber with the intensity of a scientist scanning remote galactic dusts. He brushed his palm against the floor and walls and examined the soiled black dust. His expectations were belied. All that he could sniff out were sweaty, pungent, and husky odour. There were traces of charcoal too. Such chambers were essentially an adjunct to a fireplace for storing coal and chopped wood.

"Fool!" Jamanat Ali cursed.

He ordered an electronic scanning of the house for locating radiation from the tiniest electronic spy gadgets.

The signals proved sterile.

A frustrated Jamanat lost his cool, hot cups of tea notwithstanding. He summoned Ibadat and started interrogating him.

"Why the hell are you here?"

"Sir, the matter is very simple. Harfan sahib is our client. I guard his house, for a small fee, whenever he goes out of town. The entire town knows it. Even brother Karamat can testify that." Ibadat answered with a firm gaze in his eyes.

"Do you know him Karamat?"

"Yes sir. We're from the same locality and it's correct that he earns a few extra bucks by guarding the house of the suspect."

"Where has Harfan gone?" Jamanat turned to Harfan.

"How do I know sir?" Ibadat gave an expression of irritation, "you've to ask Israr Sharief sahib."

"Aren't you the son of that traitor Hamid, *bawarchi* (cook) of that *kafir* Hindu king?" A burly figure with a pockmarked face approached Ibadat, looking fiercely at him.

"Yes, but he was no traitor."

"How're you related to this fellow Harfan?"

"Who said that to you? I'm a hotel employee. Hope you don't grudge a poor man earning a few extra bucks."

"Don't act smart. I'd rip open your guts?" The pockmarked guardian of law shouted.

" Under what law you want to disembowel my guts?" Ibadat firmly accosted the bully.

He remembered the battered face of the middle-aged person. This was Arman Ali Niazi, who, as a kid of sixteen years, had severed the head of King Digvijay with a forceful blow of his scimitar. Arman, son of a dismissed soldier of the king, had avenged his father's humiliation. This very same killer had stabbed his father Hamid to death. What a surprise! The killer Niazi was now on the rolls of the ISI. How funny and small the world was!

Arman Ali grimaced ferociously, as if his looks were the sharpest scalpel, ready to perform a complicated operation on Ibadat's chest.

"Don't act funny with me," Arman Ali shouted, "talk straight, or I'll fry your brains for breakfast."

Jamanat pushed his lieutenant aside. The last thing he wanted was an ugly brawl and publicity. He took over the task of grilling Ibadat.

"Have you noticed any suspicious activity of Harfan Bukhari?"

"Sir, I'm your humble servant. I guard the house in his absence. How can I know his activities?"

"Don't try to be clever."

"Sir, I'm a poor man, trying to earn a few extra bucks. Come to the hotel and give me an opportunity to serve you. That's the job I know best."

Ibadat saluted Jamanat with all the humility he could muster.

Karamat Suri intervened in a slick move.

"I know this fellow sir. As I said, he lives in my *mohalla*. He is a mere cook in the hotel and does odd jobs to earn extra money."

"Fine. But you must work for me and keep me informed about this character."

Jamanat directed the words at Ibadat.

"That'll be my privilege sir. Being a Pakistani I feel proud to accept this task. You can depend on me."

Ibadat saluted again, this time almost prostrating on the ground and touching Jamanat's knee joint.

*

Next morning, after a lavish breakfast at Hotel Royal Palace Jamanat placed a call to Brigadier Barqat.

"Sir, the house was sterile. I think the DF readings were not precise."

"That's not possible Jamanat. The JIS and the Army Signals are pretty sure about their calculations."

"Can't help sir. I didn't even find any telltale evidence. It was a clear case of wrong identification."

"Do you feel he's clean?"

"I didn't say that. The transmitter issue isn't correct. It's necessary to find out his whereabouts. Shall I check with his office?"

"No harm. Do take care not to offend Israr sahib."

"Fine sir."

Jamanat and his troop marched out of the hotel for Sangla Hill.

Ibadat followed their exit with a phone call to Israr's office from a nearby public call office. He did not use the hotel phone.

"Can I speak to Israr sahib?"

"Who's calling?"

"I'm Ramzan from Jhumra, a neighbour of Mian Harfan Bukhari."

"Yes, Israr here. What can I do for you?"

"Janab I'm Ramzan Faroshi from Liquat colony, a neighbour of Harfan sahib. Last night a group of policemen had entered the empty house of Harfan Mian. They were probably looking for some radio set."

"Radio set? What do you mean by that?"

"Can't say *janab*. I repeated what I picked up from their conversations. I thought I'd keep you informed. Your man is so nice a chap."

"Thanks Ramzan sahib. Please keep a watch; the house is empty."

"My pleasure sir."

The deception worked well.

Israr was not surprised when a chit containing Jamanat Ali's name was shown to him. Jamanat entered with a flourish, offered a salute, and drew a chair for himself.

"What can I do for you?" Israr asked as politely as he could manage.

"I want to meet Mr. Harfan Bukhari."

"What for?"

"Ask a few questions."

"What about? Does the law want him? What for a police officer is in my office? Have you lost your mind?"

"Don't make hill out of a rye, sir. I'm from the ISI. It's a normal enquiry. We've been searching the general area of Jhumra for unauthorised radio transmission."

"Well Mr. Jamanat. I think you're exceeding your brief. Doesn't a Pakistani have the right to his privacy? I know there is a martial law in the country, but the least I expected was a call from your bosses about the radio transmission. Perhaps I've something to explain, not to you, but to your top boss in private." Israr did not lose his cool, but made it clear that Jamanat's break-in was totally exposed.

"Sir, you misunderstand me. I just want to know Harfan's whereabouts." Jamanat knew he was caught on a wrong foot.

Israr picked up the phone and called Major Gen. Naqibullah, Defence and National Security Advisor.

"Hello Naqi sahib," Israr could hardly conceal his irritation, "I've a man in front of me, who feels that my chief marketing manager Harfan Bukhari uses an unlicensed radio transmitter."

"Who's he?"

"He's from Hyder's company. He also wants to know Harfan Mian's whereabouts. What's happening in Pakistan? You know the job Bukhari is doing for us."

"Sorry friend," Naqi replied in a conciliatory voice, "let me talk to Hyder. Don't worry."

Jamanat's cortices suddenly fogged out, having lost neuronal connectivity in the labyrinth of high-sounding names. Did he commit a mistake by approaching Israr? Should he have left that job to Barqat? Nevertheless, mere movement check up was not an offence. He was simply doing his job.

The veteran intelligence bulldog begged to be excused and left.

"Karamat, check up if that Ibadat fellow had called up Israr."

"Janab, I know for sure Ibadad is a mere cook. He wouldn't dare calling a big guy like Israr sahib. You may like to check on the call lists of the day."

"Okay. Let's go."

Jamanat looked back at the events, as he travelled back to Bhagatanwala to catch a flight. It was Nawab Sharief who had insisted on a direct raid. What could his motive be? Destroying his brother's business empire? Were Barqat and the top bosses of the company taken for a ride by Nawab? Was the chief following a blind lead, only to embarrass Malika Jahanara. Was General Hyder conspiring against the President? Were they using the thin Harfan and Malika rope to hang the CMLA and justify a coup? A stink of conspiracy permeated the air in Islamabad. The President was indeed engulfed in the vortex of conspiracies. It was natural with the politicians in uniform.

Was the clock inside him slowing down? Was he chasing a shadow? Jamanat wasn't sure, which chefs were cooking up what kind of broth in whose kitchen?

Jamanat's reach didn't traverse the super orbit of the politicians and the uniformed rulers. He wasn't supposed to know the smoggy games of conspiracy played by the power mongers.

*

The Jhumra fiasco left many souls bruised and gory. Gentleman Israr hadn't found Jamanat's visit amusing. General Naqi's terse phone call sounded an alarm bell in the ISI's neuronal centres. The officiating chief alerted Barqat, in the absence of General Hyder, that some of his boys had treaded into the secret territories of General Naqi.

Jamanat entered Barqat's room even before he was summoned.

"Sir, I think we've a big problem on hand."

Jamanat clicked his heels producing a faint metallic sound.

"What happened? How did you bungle the raid?"

"The raid was clean. But as I said, the house too was clean. However, Israr sahib has taken exception to some of my enquiries about the suspect's whereabouts. Did you check up the hotel phone records?"

"Yes Jamanat. Your call to Israr's office, and a few calls to the US by an American guest, that's all."

"That's bad."

"Yes Jamanat. Perhaps we should have waited for concrete leads and not misguided by Nawab's inputs. I feel he's haunting that fellow. One of my reports has confirmed Nawab's talk to *mohtarma* Jahanara about medicines from India. He could as well use us to demolish his brother."

"I know sir. But his leads have pushed us to a blind lane."

"I agree Jamanat. Now I gather Gen. Naqi has commissioned Harfan for airlifting armaments to Dacca. Not many souls in Pakistan are aware of this. By *Allah* Jamanat, don't tinker with this operation."

Barqat shared some national secrets with Jamanat.

"That spells doom for me, sir. I don't want to retire with a blotch on my name."

"Don't panic, some damage control measures are necessary."

"Can anything be done sir?"

"It's difficult Jamanat. The boss is in Dacca."

He ordered tea and brooded over the scenario. Gen. Hyder Bux had cleared a silent break-in operation after long procrastination and had emphatically forbidden an overt raid. He wasn't likely to swallow the bitter pill without plucking out a star or two from his shoulder pips.

Barqat touched a religious charm, which hung around his neck, given by a *fakir* (mendicant). It acted as a shield against goblins, *jinns* and mortal enemies, and ensured victory over all hostile forces, human and ethereal.

Allah! He prayed, save me from this fool Jamanat and decided to lessen his burden by sharing the bad news with his second Allah, General Hyder.

The operator at Dacca end saluted Barqat and connected General Hyder promptly.

"Sir Barqat here. There is a minor problem in the Jhumra operation."

"What's the matter? Repeat."

"The Jhumra raid sir."

"By *Allah* Barqat! Did I not tell you to abort the raid?"

"No sir. I had seen you off at Chak Lala. You hadn't mentioned any change of plan."

"Me asshole. I was supposed to tell you that the matter should be deferred. That's what Naqi and Sarfaraz had pleaded for. We could conduct the raid after about a month."

"Well sir," Barqat wailed out on the line, "we've done it, and Jamanat has found nothing. Israr sahib is fuming."

"What should I do with you and Jamanat? Anyways, don't panic and create more complications. I've to carry a diverse team with me. Did Sarfaraz talk to you about visiting Zahoor Chaudry?"

"No sir. Should I ask him?"

"Leave it. I'll speak to Sarfaraz. Seal your mouth and ask your boys to plug their leaking cans until I return. I suggest you call on Israr and tell him that there was a mix up and you're sorry for it."

"I will do that right away sir."

Barqat hung up the line, relayed some terse orders to Jamanat and connected the Sangla line of Israr Sharief.

Barqat's brief visit and assurances did not assuage Israr's bruised feelings and the sense of insecurity. He surveyed the scenario and concluded that Nawab was not likely to rest on his haunches. He wouldn't hesitate to throw up more dirt. An urgent consultation with Mian Alam Khan was necessary. Israr Sharief picked up the phone and dialled Alam's Peshawar number. Alam was intrigued by the call.

He was more alarmed by a Live Letter Box alert from Ibadat, his Double X agent Qurban at Jhumra. This one local talent was highly professional. His coverage of activities of the Army and Air Force units at Jhumra, Mianwali, Sheikhupura and Bhagatanwala produced gold nuggets. He wasn't the type to make any frivolous call. That's what worried Alam most, not the panic call from Israr Sharief. He downed his usual evening Scotch and decided to drive down to Sangla Hills to have some business talk with Israr. He pondered over the scenario and formulated a strategic plan: to unify Israr, Jung Sher Khan, and his efforts to put pressure on the PSO and the ISI chief. Some back channel should be used to vitiate the ears of General Arif about Nawab's perfidious activities to scuttle the arms lifting operations.

Who could do the job for him?

Obviously Shazad Khan, executive editor of *Pakistan Mirror*. His paper always reserved space for paid and inspired news items and editorials. A news item on Nawab Sharief's unholy conspiracy to impede the war preparations in conjunction with some ambitious Generals accompanied by fat currency-stacks should do the job. Alam called the editor before he left for Sangla for a damage control trip.

Next morning he visited the office of General Naqi.

"Hello big man. Wherefrom?" General Naqi was surprised by the unannounced visit of the arms peddler.

"Have you seen this morning's *Pakistan Mirror*? It appears Nawab is after his brother's blood."

"I don't mind blood shedding by the Sharief brothers. What worries me is the secrecy of my arms lifting operations." Naqi did not suppress his annoyance.

" This viper is close to Hyder. I'm sharing Israr's concern with you General. I don't want Hyder's boys to advertise our use of the Third Reich and South African mercenaries."

"Well Alam," Naqi offered hot tea to the important arms bazaar scavenger, "I'm shocked too. I'll speak to Sarfaraz. I suggest you also speak to him."

"If you permit General. I'm risking my neck for you and Pakistan."

"Don't bother. I'm with you Alam."

*

42

Next morning's repeat front-page banner did not amuse Nawab and some sweating Generals, who worked for him on hefty retainer. It alarmed General Naqi and Sarfaraz.

Israr felt happy but failed to comprehend the paranoid compulsions of General Hyder in entrusting a delicate enquiry to a blundering junior cop! What could prevent the ISI to bring him under their scanner? Hyder could even push his *Allah* to amass riches. Or was he entangled with a parallel sabotage plan? Was he aiming at the President's jugular? That would mean a guillotine on his regime.

That was bad business news. He normally didn't agree with the suicidal policies, pursued by the CMLA bosses in East Pakistan. But the prospect of earning millions was more tempting than a few millions of Bengalis facing extermination.

Jung Sher Khan, an important member of Israr cartel, was perturbed too. It must be Nawab, they concluded. Nawab wasn't a lone ranger. He must have roped in General Hyder and Izaz Afroz. That again was bad business news. Hyder and Nawab were inseparable business partners. That called for an intervention by General Sarfaraz Lodi, the powerful PSO to the CMLA. He was the correct antidote.

General Sarfaraz wasn't amused by the prospect of receiving Israr Sharief, the weighty Pathan *sirdar* Jung Sher Khan and Alam Khan in his office. He was outraged and scandalised by the telephone tapping incident and the fact of his name figuring in it, as an importer of aphrodisiac from India. What could be more damning at this critical juncture of power struggle? Not even a Pakistani street dog would lick his dead skin, if it were tainted with Indian honey. What a bloody mess!

Why had Hyder failed to restrain his boys even after they had decided to the contrary only a couple of hours before the raid was conducted! Was it a case of deliberate amnesia? Not unlikely. The foxy ISI chief should've been sacked for bugging Malika Jahanara's bedroom. However, the fox knew too much of his mind. Their fingers were locked together in the same trigger, aimed against General Arif Khan's scalp. Antagonising him for the sake of a minor business executive wouldn't be a prudent decision. It was not a propitious time to be guided by the law books and the true interpretation of propriety.

Sarfaraz felt his tails were stuck in a cleft wood. Hyder could be conspiring with Izaz Afroz, the desperate demagogue and warmonger, bidding hastily and nastily for the highest chair.

The clever intelligence chief, Sarfaraz mused, was playing a double game. How could he eat the meatloaf and keep it too? Mustering the services of Zahoor and ordering a raid on Harfan's Jhumra home were as contradictory as mixing bitter drops in a glass of whisky.

How could he face Zahoor now?

He had not expected Hyder to commit such a silly mistake. It must be an orchestrated game to outsmart him.

Well! Sarfaraz, the scion of Amritsar's proud Lodi family, should now make a decisive bid for the throne. Why should he allow that pleasure to Izaz and Hyder? That Sindhi meteor should be smoked out of Pakistan's political firmament, permanently. The only way out was a putsch. But that was an uncertain and yet undefined game. The Air and Naval Chiefs weren't likely to support his move, just about when Pakistan was on the brink of another war.

The Yankees and the Chinese wouldn't welcome any change in Pakistan's political landscape. General Arif, they believed, was their diplomatic Point man. They would prefer doing business with General Arif, until India was thwarted in East Pakistan. The Big daddy wouldn't like to see India emerging stronger and drifting closer to the Red Bear.

This wasn't the time to agitate. This was a time for introspection and fathoming the waters around. He looked up at his aide de camp, whose smart salute suddenly snapped Sarfaraz's escape to his fantasy world.

"What's the matter?"

"Sir Mr. Israr, *Sirdar* Jung Sher Khan and Alam Khan are here."

"Please bring them in."

Sarfaraz stood up and opened the door himself. Jung Sher Khan was not only an important leader of the Pathan *jirga* (assembly), he was a trusted friend of the President. His followers in Baluchistan and the NWFP had wholeheartedly supported the military crackdown against the Indian inspired rebel forces. The Pathan *jirga*, headed by Jung Sher, had given a call for total cooperation with the military regime.

"Khan sahib," the PSO composed his reply rather cautiously, "smaller pinions often get stuck. Don't worry. There appears to be a mistake somewhere. Harfan is rendering valuable services to Pakistan, and we're proud of him."

"General sahib, I'm a true Pakistani and a Pathan. I know Harfan's uncle. I shudder to think what Hyder's people did to the boy. *Janab,* suspicion has the potential of multiplying fast. I don't know how to face Zahoor Chaudry."

"Oh no, Sirdar sahib, Zahoor is a personal friend. I'll call him straightaway and request to come over for a cup of tea. I need his services."

Sarfaraz asked his aide to connect Zahoor's Lahore number and picked up the handset as soon as he came on the line.

"Zahoor sahib, Sarfaraz this side. Why don't you come down to Islamabad? I have an urgent piece of business with you."

"I am flattered janab Sarfaraz," Zahoor replied, "but I've received a rather disturbing phone call from Nawab."

"What did he say?"

"It's regarding a raid at Harfan's residence. What's the matter? Is Hyder trying to ruin me?"

"I'm sorry Zahoor sahib. There has been a mix up. Some buffoons from Hyder's office have gone berserk. I'm ordering an enquiry into the matter. Please come over. I've some important matters to discuss with you about the defence of the *Mohana* area from possible Indian attack."

Sarfaraz sounded highly apologetic.

"That's fine *janab*" Zahoor replied with a wounded voice, "Nawab is out to destroy my family. Last time it was a rumour about Harfan's entanglement with *mohtarma* Jahanara, now he has engineered a raid on his home. I think I should request the *Sadr* to intervene."

"Please listen Zahoor sahib, I promise to pull up Nawab. Israr sahib is here. Please talk to him." Israr took the phone and patiently listened to Zahoor for good five minutes.

"I understand your problem Zahoor sahib. Convey our apologies to Jamilla and tell that her husband is an angel. Harfan is on his way to Dacca on the special mission. Sarfaraz here has promised to take all possible corrective action. I suggest you come and see him."

"I'm reassured Israr sahib. Nawab is seriously hurting my daughter. Please restrain your brother."

"You know him Zahoor sahib. Tell darling Jamilla that Nawab is a viper. We all have full faith in Harfan and he should be back to her arms in another two days."

"*Insha Allah*," Sarfaraz added, "no harm would reach Zahoor's son-in-law. I'll sort out the misunderstanding as soon as Hyder reaches Islamabad." The PSO adopted a defensive posture. He did not want to annoy the Pathan stalwart. He might require his help to neutralise Izaz Afroz. He would certainly require support from the Baluch and Pathan *sirdars*.

General Sarfaraz, the second most important uniformed bureaucrat in Pakistan, escorted the imposing Pathan *sirdar* and Israr Sharief to their cars and, as a rare gesture, clicked his heels. The metallic sound was clearly audible to their pleasing ears.

"Leave the matter to me." he reassured the visitors.

Back in his room, Sarfaraz called Salim Raizada, a senior editor of the *Frontier Post*, a powerful English, and Urdu daily.

"Salim sahib, Sarfaraz here. Please come for a cup of tea."

The invitation from the virtual number two was a big temptation.

"What's happening sir?"

"We've been thinking to send a delegation of the mainstream media to Dacca. Would you like to lead it?"

"That's an honour sir. I'll be with you right away."

The tea was sweet and so also the offer of a sponsored visit to Dacca via a stopover at Bangkok, as the leader of the media delegation. Salim Raizada was more than happy. Sarfaraz too felt happy. Salim had the key to approach the personal valet cum masseur of *mohtarma* Jahanara. He readily agreed to plant a very reliable story on the valet, as a personal favour to the PSO.

Sarfaraz could not allow an excellent opportunity to pass by. The ISI chief too should have some share of the dirt on his face. And valet Qader Shams was the most suitable person to whisper intimate gossips into Jahanara's ears, in exchange for fat considerations. Sarfaraz was sure that the wild lady would run amuck when Qader, while massaging her scantily clad body with imported Italian olive oil, would narrate the true story of the blasphemous activities of Hyder Bux and his officers.

Salim also agreed to plant a story, quoting sources close to Nawab, about the allegations of Jahanara having grabbed 11% commission from the arms lifting operations. Would she allow an unholy axis to develop between Izaz and Hyder? And what about that poor kid Harfan? Wasn't Nawab haunting him only to destroy his brother Israr? Wasn't Nawab a loyal crony of Izaz? Would the *mohtarma* allow the situation to slip out of her hand? Would she allow the *Sadr* to be hanged by the power grabbers?

Sarfaraz was convinced that a reasonably motivated Qader Shams was the right person to stir up the simmering cauldron of Jahanara's singed psyche. She was sure to initiate the domino action and he, Sarfaraz Lodi, would wait in the wings, to give a finishing touch to the end array of the cards.

*

Hyder's triumphant return from Dacca was followed by an orchestrated media cacophony about the heroic actions taken by the Pakistan army in shifting the entire population of the coastal islands of East Pakistan in anticipation of another severe cyclone, a fiercer one than the twister that had killed about half a million people a year ago. This was followed by another reporting outburst about the vicious Indian bombing and strafing of some of the coastal districts in the Great Estuary area of East Pakistan. The reports exhorted upon the international community to prevail upon India to desist from aiding and abetting the terrorists in East Pakistan.

New Delhi lodged a formal protest and presented a horrifying collage before the UN with evidences supplied by the People's League. The People's League and its allies managed to reach the foreign media with photographic evidence that there were no evacuation of population. The entire population of the estuary islands and over two score coastal villages were simply murdered and their bodies were either given mass burial or thrown into the sea. The planned pogrom is mass killing was intended to send a message of total genocide, much more tragic than what Hitler managed to do to the defenceless Jews. The international watchdog bodies, mostly tied to the apron strings of the USA, preferred to behave like the three monkeys of Mahatma Gandhi; they preferred not to speak, see, and hear, any evil.

Hyder and Tarakki's operation clean-up coastal area had not gone unnoticed in Delhi. Balachandran Nampoothiri had to carry out midstream course correction.

He alone could not take that decision. It required Prime Minister's clearance. However, he did not have to cool his heels in impotent anxiety. Rajinder Dewan's voice poured honey in his ears.

"Brother you're required here, now and immediately."

"What's on fire?"

"Important chestnuts, it appears. Only you can take it out and crack, for ma'am."

"Okay, give me ten minutes."

Nampoothiri was almost pushed into Manjira's teak panelled office room by Dewan.

"What's this report Balu?"

"Well ma'am, these are my reports on Pakistani crackdown in the coastal areas of East Pakistan."

"What's the tally?"

"About a million killed and five million forced out of their villages. The haggard villagers are escaping to Indian safety to the state of Tripura and West Bengal."

"I'm not pleased to here this. What about your Israeli friends? How're they going to drop weapons in the coastal areas?"

"We can't do that now. I've a plan to allow Yossi's small aircrafts to unload the supplies at an abandoned Second World War airstrip near Kakdwip in West Bengal. It's a sparsely populated area and adjacent to the Indian Sundarbans. Jainal's people can easily carry the loads in country boats."

"What's the news about Pakistani build up?" Manjira asked in anxious voice.

"They have stockpiled the US and Chinese supplies inside Pakistan and the Junta have employed a CIA front company to airlift the hardware to Dacca."

"Can we match their supplies?"

"Adequate. The Mukti Bahini requires effective medium and small weapons, demolition materials and plenty of firepower. Our drops from Thailand can take care of that."

"Have you consulted the Army chief?"

"If you clear the idea I will consult him and take assistance to facilitate the supply line from Phraet and Uttaradit airports in northern Thailand to Kakadwip."

"Can't the Pakis intercept these flights? Will the Thai authorities agree?"

"The area has several small airstrips used by the drug barons. Bangkok has no control over them. Theoretically, Pakistan can intercept the flights, but our stations in Shillong and Agartala can dominate the skies. Pakistan has hardly a squadron of F-28 in Dacca."

"Well Balu. Talk to both the Air and Army chiefs. Fly down to where you like and complete the deal. I give you only ten days."

"That's a good lead time ma'am." Nampoothiri complemented Prime Minister Manjira for the momentous decision and straight away drove down to the South

Block AHQ. The Air chief was in the next building and was not fussy to have a cup of tea with the NSI chief within the confines of the South Block.

*

In Islamabad, the felicitation parties, which tried to convey the message of victory of the Pakistani strategy against the perfidious Indian designs, could not rid Hyder of the nagging feeling of ground slipping away from under his feet. General Sarfaraz had not minced words to convey displeasure over the Jhumra incident and the likely existence of an unholy collusion between a section of the ISI officers and Nawab Sharief. Who was running the spy agency, Nawab or Hyder?

Neither *mohtarma* Jahanara had kind words to shower on Hyder. The explosive stories of the misadventure of the ISI at Jhumra were served to her garnished with plenty of pepper and spice. She enjoyed the nimble touches of masseur Qader Shams, but her intestines burned like they were on paraffin fire. She summoned her *habshi* and asked him to connect Hyder Bux.

"How're you dear Hyder?"

"I'm fine *mohtarma*. How have you been?"

"My well-being depends on you and the *Allah*. How're things in Dacca? I believe you were there to teach the Bengalis a lesson or two."

"The situation is grim. But we're trying our best," Hyder paused for a second and resumed the dialogue, "I believe ma'am there has been a minor indiscretion by my boys."

Jahanara chose not to react. She wanted to hear what the ISI chief had to say.

"It's that Jhumra incident. I presume you want to speak to me about that. There has been a misunderstanding and I want to come and explain to you. When can I come?"

"Yes Hyder. Sayeefa Zahoor had spoken to me. I wonder if you're the chief of the ISI Directorate or Nawab has taken over! Anyways, you're always welcome. I only hope Hyder," Jahanara injected the venom in her final sting, "the intelligence and security of the country haven't been mortgaged to people like Nawab Sharief!"

"Things are under control. I'd like to see you this evening if you're free."

"I'm told you've information about an 11% commission taken by me."

"Don't believe in the yellow press ma'am. They're playing nasty games. They want to destroy the country. I can explain the dirty game people play to malign the *Sadr*. When can I come?"

"Well Hyder, you better explain these to the *Sadr*. Begum Sayeefa is regretfully hurt. You should talk to her."

"Your advice is well taken. I'd do the needful. Can I come this evening?"

"You're welcome Hyder. The best cookies in town are waiting for you."

Jahanara's words did not sound sweet like Karachi *halwa* (sweetmeat). A brave soldier, Hyder was not struck by panic, but his heartbeat surely escalated by a few beats and caused a strange discomfort in his stomach. Historical whores and mistresses often changed courses of countries and history.

*

43

Brigadier Barqat was, for obvious reasons, panic hit. His professional élan was deflated by the Jhumra faux pas. Jamanat's all muscle and brawn approach had put a dirty blob on his reputation. For the first time he felt, he was standing bare-chested before Hyder's barrel. General Hyder, a veteran of many wars, did not fail to understand the circumstances that had led to the fiasco. He should have put a cork on the Jhumra operation before emplaning for Dacca. Barqat had simply carried out his earlier order that was necessitated by the overwhelming SigInt reports.

He decided to brave the difficult situation. The crocks in the power-poodle of Pakistan were gunning for his scalp. But he could not bow out of the ring simply because some sensitive feathers had been ruffled. He had let Barqat off with a stern warning. He had not failed to mention that addition of a few more stars on his pips depended on defter handling of operational affairs.

Barqat wasn't essentially a political player, like most of his peers were, in the fellowship in uniform. He listened the homily patiently and managed to say 'yes sir' on each operational point spelt out by Hyder Bux.

Hyder dismissed his India Counterintelligence Division chief with a faint smile. He knew, he too was caught in the whirlwinds of politics of succession and couldn't force an important establishment ally to abandon Operation Rosewood, the coverage of *mohtarma* Jahanara. This sex kitten wielded several keys to the inner chambers of the CMLA.

Hyder's damage control mechanism was activated after he physically turned up at the residences of Jahanara and Sayeefa Zahoor and shared kebabs and tea with them followed by solemn assurances of a high level enquiry into the matter and adequate punishment to the blundering baboons in his department. This was not an easy exercise for the mighty chief of the ISI. Who in Pakistan would imagine the indignity of the secret service chief lowering his cap before two circumstantially reputed women? In his Jat brotherhood, such acts are treated as blasphemous. However, Hyder consoled himself by reasoning that current history was not essentially the permanent history of Pakistan. Two women could not decide the fate of the nation, which he was ordained to preside over sooner than later. As a soldier, he treated the move as an act of defensive aggression.

Barqat, however, couldn't escape Jamanat Ali's gravitational pull. The sword-sharp intelligence operative had something extra in him, a special capability to chase shadow and catch ghosts out of moonless mists. He had successfully netted many counterintelligence operations by chasing shreds of suspicion, from fragile leads to smoking gun proof. Perhaps, his handling of the Harfan affair was premature, but surely not irrelevant.

He did not bother about the pink blushes on the cheeks of the top bosses. His guts told him he was on the right trail, but he did not yet have the right evidence. His mistake was trying to pull off an intelligence coup by applying traditional brawl and muscle tools of the ISI. Harfan Bukhari, he finally digested the message, was a key operator and to nab him he would require superior tradecraft.

*

That's what precisely happened, when Barqat, with Jamanat in tow, appeared before the high level committee, appointed by General Sarfaraz, following a subtle hint from Hyder. The committee was to examine two issues: alleged bugging of Jahanara's phone and interference in the sensitive matter of airlifting of emergency supplies to Dacca by some unscrupulous business houses; a transparent hint to Nawab Sharief.

Barqat pressed the talisman hard against his chest and resigned to his fate.

"Sir, I may have gone wrong marginally. But the Direction Finders weren't wrong." Jamanat Ali conveyed his assessed views to the committee chaired by General Sarfaraz.

"Aren't you imagining too much Jamanat?" The ISI chief made the comment casually.

"Sorry sir," Jamanat replied, still standing at a respectable distance, "the DF operations were conducted by the JIS."

"But why did you search Harfan's home?" Gen. Naim, the PIB chief asked.

"Sir, we checked about 30 homes in the area," replied Jamanat, "his was in the arc of triangulation."

"Well Mian Jamanat," added Gen. Naim, "Intelligence is a game of possibilities and probabilities. But in this instance we require more specifics." General Naim, present in one of the very rare inter-agency briefing sessions, confronted the veteran ISI sleuth.

Jamanat's wasn't a new face to him. Their families hailed from Dera Ghazi Khan and they enjoyed common family ties. But today's meeting was a special one, ordered by the PSO. There was no room for any personal powwow.

"Why are you silent?" Thundered the DMI.

Brigadier Barqat intervened, but was silenced by Gen. Naqi. He asked Jamanat to explain his thesis. HumInt should have buttressed the technical inputs and the hypothetical suspicion of the location of the suspected transmitter.

"Sir, our technical reports were precise, indicating the location of the clandestine station within half a mile of the suspect's residence."

"Was it supported by HumInt?"

"No. We thought of conducting a discreet search, but something went wrong and 1we couldn't back out." Jamanat explained his point forcefully.

"How do you narrow down your suspicion on this character Harfan? What are his antecedents?" asked Gen. Naim.

"There is no chink in his armour. We didn't single him out. We searched a number of homes."

"Why don't you arrest and interrogate Harfan?" Asked the DMI.

"We don't have any positive evidence. In fact, we haven't arrested any one. It was a routine search prompted by JIS findings."

"Here I agree," intervened General Hyder Bux, "Israr has been operating a wireless set, of course with the approval of General Naqi. It was but natural for the boys to check with him. Comparison of the operational frequencies and schedules was necessary. The boys should've taken clearance from the D&NS Advisor. I'll take care of this minor problem."

"I think your SigInt boys have bungled. Signal radiation can be caused by several factors, including solar eruptions and atmospheric interference. Often direction finders go bonkers. Possibly your JIS boys have picked up signals from Israr's set." Lt. Gen. Naim made an indirect dig at the ISI chief.

"We know that Naim," replied Hyder, "there has been a minor operational indiscretion. I can't hang the boys for this. Neither can we hang Nawab Sharief."

"From what I learn, I feel there's no tangible evidence against this character Harfan." Commented Gen. Naqi, the Defence and National Security Advisor.

"The last thing I want is to convey to the President that someone somewhere has been trying to put a spanner in the arms lifting operation. I think Nawab has to be cautioned, and if necessary blacklisted for future defence contracts. Let's bury the skeleton here and let's pacify the important lady. And I've taken care of the ruffled feelings of Zahoor sahib." Lt. General Sarfaraz talked in a conciliatory voice.

The PIB chief nodded silently, which meant both agreement and disagreement. He wasn't in a mood to berate Jamanat, his village pal, and a former PIB hand. What could a small cog like him do? The ambitious ISI chief was responsible for the sordid affair. He was definitely trying to sully brother Arif's image and his friend, Begum Jahanara.

The meeting dismissed Barqat and Jamanat and reverted to the next agenda.

"To start with," General Naqi initiated the discussion, "I don't think we can pin down any particular business house. Shall we ask the Defence Secretary and the Deputy CMLA, in charge of the Supply Corps, General Hussain, to go into the matter and submit a report?"

"I think that's the correct approach. I feel no business house was behind engineering the Jhumra raid. It was a professional approach, though handled crudely. The second item on the agenda will require some in-depth investigation and this meeting can't do that."

General Sarfaraz tried to bail out his senior colleagues. They were all involved with some business house or the other. He did not want to pin down Nawab Sharief for tactical reasons. Such a move would have antagonised Hyder and he did not want to annoy the person who was being projected as the next chief minister of Punjab.

"So we decide that we've no problem with Harfan Bukhari and as Hyder says, there has been no tapping of the phones of Malika Jahanara and we refer the other item to a committee of technical experts."

Sarfaraz read out the decisions adopted in the meeting.

"You're correct sir. I can swear by Allah that there has never been any tapping of the phones of *mohtarma* Jahanara. Our telephone lines depend on vulnerable co-axel cables. Under the circumstances, cross connections cannot be avoided. I recommend that we should go for electronic exchanges and optic fibre cables."

"I've noted this. This will be forwarded to the secretary communication for preparing a project report."

"You're correct sir. But we should appoint a joint team to analyse and investigate the SigInt data." Naim widened the circumference of his grin. It was a cosmetic gesture. General Naim wasn't disinclined to offer in charity the intestines of Hyder, to the Himalayan condors. However, the existing power equation in Pakistan tilted in favour of the troika of three Generals plus the Sindhi jackal.

The ISI chief too didn't harbour a profound affection for Gen. Naim. His slit-eyed glance that swept across the table threw a glint of disdain at the PIB chief. He should thank *Allah* that he happened to be the elder brother of the boss. Otherwise, Hyder exhaled a deep breath, he would have him incarcerated at the Badr interrogation centre and disembowelled his intestines.

He managed to display a cute grin and said, "I think the PIB and the ISI should set up a joint team and pursue the SigInt puzzles." Gen. Hyder Bux declared.

"It's fine with us. You two tackle the matter. Draw some support teams from the Army Signals Corps," Gen. Naqi said conclusively. He was relieved to get past this sticky situation. He couldn't afford to ground the flights to Dacca.

"So," Sarfaraz commented, "the problem has been identified and isolated. We put up a joint front and brief the President. Agreed?"

"I don't say that you move away the needle of suspicion from any particular target," commented General Naim, "but our approach should be based on the accepted principles of counterintelligence operations. We can't afford to throw the country into a spin, simply because one Nawab Sharief insisted on guillotining his business rival."

"Not exactly...," Gen. Hyder grudgingly demurred, "our initial lead came from SigInt." General Hyder managed to throw up a shrivelled smile.

"Fine, let's dissect the details. We've formulated our recommendations to the President. I repeat, Sarfaraz read out the formulation once again, "No monitoring of *mohtarma* Jahanara's phone was intentionally done. Some foolish telephone lineman had mixed up the junction box wires that connected the Indian High Commission to our juice boxes. And some boys of the company had walked into

Harfan Bukhari's house inadvertently, instead of searching a neighbouring house. It was a genuine mistake. The third agenda has been referred to the committee of experts. Do you all agree?" The big bosses present in the meeting nodded their heads in agreement. It was indeed a great deliverance.

"Thanks brother officers. I'm seeking a personal audience with the President to explain the accidental breach. Perhaps the ISI chief will like to accompany me." Hyder looked at the PSO over the shoulder of General Naqi and displayed a smile of concurrence.

The meeting ended with practised smiles on the faces of the wary veterans and daggers unsheathed a few more centimetres. The gentlemen in uniform were simply short of jumping at each other's jugular. Their silent dispersal was louder than the grinding and shearing sounds of sharp edged saws cutting up anything that came its way. No ground was lost. No ground was won.

*

44

Jamanat wasn't amused to see the veterans gnashing teeth at each other, instead of allowing the intelligence professionals to pursue delicate leads. What was so great about a small mistake? When did Pakistan don the mantel of a transparent democracy? Had the government machineries surrendered their institutional privileges to the idiosyncrasies of a few individuals and their bed warmers? Were not the moneyed men, hot women, and paranoid Generals running Pakistan?

A counterintelligence expert, he understood the intricacies of tradecraft and deep penetration-defensive and forward-intelligence operations. He fumed at the dramatics of the Generals, who arrived at a consensus only to grab power at an opportune moment. Did any one of those bother about the honour of Pakistan?

"I won't spare that bastard." Jamanat blew his top, once out of the high-powered committee room.

"Patience Jamanat Ali." Counselled Barqat.

"They have buried the issue."

"Patience Jamanat, the present phase is perilously transient. No one, except *Allah,* can now stand between these blind Generals and Balkanisation of Pakistan." Barqat spoke in a whisper, as if he was delivering a final commandment. The tinge of pain in his voice didn't escape Jamanat.

"Sir, I'll superannuate soon. Don't hesitate calling me. I won't rest until these Indian *kafirs* are defeated. The flag of Islam must fly again over the Red Fort."

"Wait Jamanat. We'll live beyond these bosses and see better days. Islam is on the march. No one, not even the USA, can stop it."

Barqat kept on talking in a pensive mood, as they walked along the winding corridors of the ISI headquarters.

"It's strange sir," Jamanat was still unable to escape the churning of the whirlpool of frustration within, "one becomes important in today's Pakistan by simply fucking a whore."

"That's the irony of the moment. You'll have your chance. Take only five trusted officers and continue with the operations."

"That's a tall order sir," added Jamanat, "give me a few experienced hands."

"Fine. Select real professionals. If your Harfan is a spy, he'll simply not end up in stealing our secrets. He must've allies inside Pakistan. If we can't catch him at the far end of his contacts inside Pakistan, we should be able to get good leads from his communications." Barqat reassured his veteran subordinate, respected as a legend in the Pakistani intelligence fraternity.

"You can't keep this operation official now, not after this meeting."

"I know. I'll take it off the unit office. Report to me directly. But, Jamanat," Barqat sounded a note of warning, "in the intelligence game, sixth sense is important, but we can't move an inch without solid proof."

"Yes sir. I'll now concentrate on digging his past out. A live man can't travel without leaving footprints. There must be some leads somewhere in India, Umerkot, Hyderabad and Karachi. Grant me some secret service fund and allow me the digging operation."

"Okay Jamanat. Now you're on the right track. Keep the lid down. Concentrate on HumInt, until you can peel off his cover. That's the most important asset of any resident agent." Barqat counselled his junior.

"Fine sir. *Insha Allah*, we'll rip apart his cover, very soon. Rest assured."

"*Insha Allah*," Barqat nodded in agreement, "start with Karachi, and I'll ask Delhi station to trace this man's background in India. He must be having traces back there, if he is a plant. It's a lengthy process, but the tradecrafts do really work."

"I refuse to digest the story that this impostor is a patriot." Jamanat left after offering a hesitant salute and without clicking his heels. He normally reserved the sharp heel-clicking protocol of salutation for more buoyant occasions.

*

Jamanat had a date to keep with Karamat Suri, his inspector, and Jaffar Tyrewala, a retired colleague, now living in a Karachi suburb. His mind worked fast. Karamat Suri had successfully stationed a Resident near Jullandhar airbase and was still handling him for obtaining intelligence on military matters. Jaffar Tyrewala, a veteran Parsi, had the entire Sind on his palms. He had spent thirty years in the province, rose through the ranks and retired as a deputy superintendent. Both were capable investigators, though Karamat suffered from the habit of talking beyond his brief.

Jamanat's perception was clear about three main routes of infiltration by Indian intelligence agents. Gujarat channel was preferred because of linguistic, religious, and cultural affinity of the people on either side of the border. The Rajasthan desert tract was sparsely used because of inhospitable terrain and hostility between the Pakistani supporters of Pir Pagara and tribal Hindu border smugglers. The other area that concerned Jamanat was the Punjab and Sri Ganganagar tract of Rajasthan. This tract was heavily exploited by the Indian and Pakistani agencies for infiltrating intelligence agents.

He narrowed down the spatial thought to the probable point of entry of Harfan Bukhari, if he at all infiltrated from India. He must have used the Gujarat tract for accessing the Karachi route with the help of obliging smugglers. To appear in Karachi one wouldn't take the trouble and risk of entering through Punjab.

He summoned Jaffar Tyrewala to Islamabad at government expense.

"Jaffar *bhai*, there is a job for you." He offered usual courtesy to the retired officer in a ISI rest house.

"Jamanat sahab, I've dedicated my life to the services of Ahur Mazda. I run an orphanage and look after destitute elderly people."

"I know Jaffar *bhai*. You're a known and recognised social worker. However, there is a thing called paying back the salt of the nation, when the nation requires it." Jamanat titillated the patriotic fervour of the retired intelligence operator.

"What can I do for the *quam*? If the nation wants I'll again take up the sword."

"No need doing that. I want a few enquiries done at Mithi, Umerkot, Nagar Parker, and Hyderabad. Here is a brief. It may take you a few months. Start with the border crossers and smugglers, zero in on the Indian Consulate and Shamim Bukhjari. That should give you enough meat."

"Why don't you engage serving people?"

"Jaffar *bhai*, this country is no more as it were in your days. Now the dogs in uniform are biting away portions of the country as they please and can afford. I can't trust these army chaps. You and I are old school friends. We love Pakistan and can die for it." Jamanat Ali spoke in flowery Urdu to drive in the message of patriotism in the veteran police officer.

"Okay Jamant *bhai*. *Watan se bara koi nahin* (nothing is higher than the country). It's a deal. Look after my material needs and don't involve your local boys over there."

"Fine. It's a deal. Keep this envelope. You'll get more as and when you require. However, it should be a quiet job."

"Don't bother. My NGO has a vast network in Sind. Give me easy time to breathe."

Next target was Karamat Suri. He had put on years of service at Rahimyar Khan in lower Punjab and at the ISI forward post at Phullarwar near Lahore. Despite his blabbermouth, he was an efficient agent launcher and handler.

"Come Karamat. What's your report about the Karachi enquiry?"

"*Janab* (Sir) some good lead has emerged. A man called Irfan Cowasji, a Parsi driver employed by the Indian Consulate, handled most Indian agents. If your suspect entered through Sind he must have been filtered through Cowasji."

"That's very good. But how many people know this?"

"*Janab*, I'm not irresponsible. I know how to guard a trade secret."

"Well Karamat, you like to spin stories."

"*Janab*, there's difference between *kahani* (story) and *khas jasoosi baat* (exclusive spy story). I don't mix private and professional lives."

"Don't take offence Karamat. I'm joking. You're a great operator. Would you like to check up the Punjab border contacts to eliminate the possibility of this *harfanmaula's* (jack of all trades) infiltration from that corridor?"

"You mean Harfan Bukhari? I think sir he's a spotless goat. Why are we trying to sacrifice him?" Karamat gave a story telling touch to his comment.

"Well Karamat. Only a spotless goat should be offered for Id sacrifice. Isn't it?" Jamant's repertoire was not less poetic.

"As you order sir. In any case, I must add that this one goat must have intruded from Sind area, if he is an intruder. Nevertheless, I'll activate my men in the Punjab tract. Give a few weeks."

"Go ahead Karamat. I assure you two full stars on your shoulder if you break this case."

"*Insha Allah* and by your grace, this will be done. If there is a bud it must bloom to the touch of Karamat."

"Well said. You should have been a *shair* (poet)." Jamant spent a friendly pat on Karamat's back and said *shabba khair* (good night).

Having done what he had to do Jamanat activated Shauqat Ansari, his personal channel in Delhi, a journalist with an Urdu daily, and arranged a meeting at Dubai. Shauqat's paper *Yeh Duniya* (this world) was financed by Jamanat's agency and the dough was regularly transferred through a Dubai based *hawala* trader.

Jamanat had taken permission from Barqat to fly down to Dubai. Barqat reviewed the scenario and concluded that there was no harm if distant and remote enquiries were conducted about a security suspect. His unit was not needling the VIP suspect that could irritate big bosses and sexy bumps.

*

45

Harfan Bukhari wasn't blind to the gathering clouds and not too distant thunders. His focused eyes and ears ceaselessly monitored the impulses and dissected the anatomy of the threat to his person, his loved ones and his mission. The intelligence sleuths, he was aware, had picked up his scent and he expected them to close in, eventually. The airlifting operation came as a good reprieve, albeit temporarily. That smoke screen, he presumed was quite thin. That wouldn't deter the ISI sleuths from homing in on their target. The probable scenarios fleeted past his mind's eye as he gravely but vaguely looked at the complicated instrument panels manipulated by the pilot of the mercenary chartered flight, cruelly christened: Lady of the Light.

He was escorting yet another sortie to Dacca.

The Lady of the Light, a Boeing 707 of Athena Air Lines, owned by Doug Chris & Associates, was painted with a convincing International Red Crescent logo. It flaunted an IATA approved call sign. Flying at 35,000 feet the silvery bird was on autopilot. Vudurume, the pilot, a South African of Indian origin, was busy discussing the peculiarities of the new route and the mission with Harfan Bukhari. His company had never flown in this new theatre of conflict.

Vudurume, a derivation from the hackneyed eastern Uttar Pradesh Hindu name, Buddhu Ram, Rama the Fool, had plethora of dreams stored up in his mind, about his forefather's homeland.

Vudu's great-grandfather, Faltu Ram, Rama the Insignificant, a bonded indigo plantation slave, was tied up with a few hundred other indentured labourers by the *Company Maharaj* (the British East India Company) and was dumped somewhere near Cape Town, at the tip of the dark continent. Some luck and some genetic and inherent trait of survival of the Homo sapiens in the most hostile environment, and the process of natural selection had helped him in rearing up a family of slaves.

From a sugarcane crusher Faltu Ram had graduated to a cook, in the household of a Huguenot Boer family, and had migrated north, after the British occupation of the Cape of Good Hope. Converted to Christianity, Faltu managed to impart good education to his children. Vudurume's father, Mitha Ram, Rama the Sweet, had climbed up the social ladder further, by qualifying as one of the rare coloured auto-drivers, of Indian descent.

From a slave to a jet pilot was a tortuous and bitter journey for Vudurume, a quantum jump for any member of the Ram family. Vudurume belonged to the generation of post-Mohandas Karamchand Gandhi coloured Indians, who gathered courage and voiced their existence as fellow human beings; a little higher in the ladder of evolution, than the intelligent African ape, the Chimpanzee. The messianic Afrikaners and the self-righteous British had grudgingly accepted their rights to breathe and live, as a slightly higher species than the gutter insects, the aboriginal black Africans.

Vudurume had managed to go to school and enlist in the South African Air Force, during the Second World War. He had flown with distinction, as a fighter sergeant pilot in the North African campaign. It was a rare break for a coloured sub-human being.

Wars are great levellers. The Second World War was no exception. It ushered in the collapse of many barriers. In a sense, its visitation was marked by a new era of liberation and mapping of a new political and social geography. In South Africa, Nelson Mandela, another landmark in human history, had encouraged Vudu to claim a better deal for his children.

Vudu had earlier pulled off a miracle of sorts by marrying a white girl, a German Jew, who had managed to survive another perverse human laboratory—Hitler's concentration camp. His story of drifting into mercenary flights formed an integral part of dirty shenanigans of the white skins ruling over a land, which they considered as the special gift of the Lord, the God in the Dark Continent.

Vudurume was an unwanted intruder in the last bastion of white supremacy. His biggest crime was his marriage to a white woman and assertion of rights for his children to study in exclusive white schools. He fought a battle for justice. His seditious doggedness had provoked the white masters, and ultimately he was sacked on a trumped up charge of collaboration with the African National Congress.

To Harfan the story was fascinating.

No. Harfan hastened to add, he had nothing much to say about his life history. He was the only member of his family to survive yet another perverse laboratory experiment of the white masters—the partition of India, and the communal holocaust during hasty escape by the British Empire. They had escaped leaving the Hindus and Muslims to bathe in blood and play Xylophone with human bones, generating a tune they preferred to call their respective national anthems.

"Did they kill everyone?" Vudu asked in utter shock.

"Well, not exactly. Even Hitler couldn't exterminate all the Jews he wanted to. But I lost my immediate family."

"That's awful Mr. Bukhari." Vudurume sympathised with Harfan's personal tragedy.

"Call me Harfan," Harfan replied, "don't worry. Killing is the most honourable human trait. Thousands have been killed in East Pakistan, where you and I are flying this deadly sortie."

"Do you regret it?"

"Well! All of us have to work to earn our bread. It's not important if you earn bread by killing people or serving them. At the end of the day, it is bread that is important. And officially, we're flying in mercy supplies for the cyclone victims and our sponsors are the International Red Crescent." Harfan parried Vudurume with a curt but philosophical reply. Another Greek aviator, Alex Onasis, Vudu's co-pilot and a Sicilian soldier of fortune, walked up the aisle.

"Hi Cap, look left. That's your India, the blessed land." He drew Vudu's attention to the tip of the Indian peninsula, as their plane crossed the Palk channel between India and Ceylon.

"Thanks Alex." Vudurume disengaged from Harfan and peered down the window. It was his land of dreams. He must visit one of these days. But who'd give a visa to a South African national, in this segment of human civilisation? Not India, in any case.

While Vudu and Alex were busy with the contours of Indian coastlines Harfan looked at the arrays of aluminum pallets containing deadly weapons. He was carrying death for the East Pakistan Bengalis.

What a big fun!

Vudurume didn't feel any guilt-pang anywhere in his psyche. Not any more, after the white masters had placed him in the same cage with his 99% jungle cousin, the Chimpanzee. For him these mercenary flights were important to support his kids pursuing higher studies in Paris on the meagre income of his wife, a schoolteacher of sort.

"Mr. Bukhari." Vudurume walked in and took a seat next to Harfan.

"Anything for me Captain?"

"We're approaching Colombo," Vudu said, "hope there won't be any hassles there!"

"There were none with the last three flights," Harfan replied, "I expect the Pakistan International Airlines and High Commission officials to be on the tarmac."

"How many people know of this operation down the line?"

"Don't worry Captain. The Ceylonese are not in love with India. The two big ladies aren't on the best of terms and the islanders have scores of problems with the Tamils of Indian origin." Harfan comforted a jittery Vudu.

"I would like to visit India once." Vudurume lighted a cigarette and offered one to Harfan.

"For sight seeing?"

"Yes. I'd like to go to Ballia, somewhere in *Utterprades* (Uttar Pradesh) to dig out my family roots. I'm told my father's cousins are still there."

"Fine Captain. I'd also like to visit Ludhiana, my native place. Let this war business be over. It'll be a pleasure travelling with you."

"Hope so," Vudurume shrugged, "wars never end. I know very well. I've been supplying fuels to innumerable war theatres. I know, wars can't end, especially when hatred is the main building block of human character. The Hindus, Christians, and Muslims, all like wars. We live by killing."

Vudurume sounded philosophical and bitter. He sounded tired too.

"Perhaps you're correct Captain. We've inherited a fractured legacy. History had initiated the process of assimilation, but the civilisational conflict caught up with us. We're divided within and without."

"What a pity. I hope the madness will subside soon."

"History travels slowly on the arrow of time, Captain. God alone knows, when we'll learn to live together in harmony."

"Beg your pardon, Mr. Bukhari. There's some turbulence ahead. Let me handle the controls." Vudurume excused himself and concentrated on the landing procedures.

*

The Lady of the Light, flight AAL-X-356 entered the wild delta funnel of the Indian subcontinent, which drained trillions of cusecs of waters of the Ganges, Brahmaputra, Meghna and scores of other rivers, into the Bay of Bengal.

The sleek bird dropped altitude and followed the contours of Cox's Bazaar and Chittagong. It banked to the left to avoid Indian airspace over Tripura and banked right shortly after charting a course towards Bhairab Bazaar. Destination Kurmitola airbase was just twenty minutes away.

At 28,000 ft, the Boeing 707 was in steady radio contact with Dacca air control, seeking guidance for landing procedure.

Vudurume saw them first, flying from 3 o'clock, two small sparrow like Gnat fighters. The birds were probably loitering at 25,000 ft, the Captain guessed. The Indian Air Force logos on their fuselage shone bright in the blazing mid-day sun. He asked Dacca control to advise the intruders to descend to a safer altitude. They were flying too dangerously close to the Lady of the Light, the International Red Crescent mercy flight. Weren't they violating Pakistani air space?

The Dacca tower crackled into the international civil aviation frequency.

"Intruders, you're too close to a civilian flight. Clear the skies of Pakistan."

The Indian Air Force radar at Shillong, the central hub of the Eastern Air Command, was monitoring progress of the strange flight, flaunting on its fuselage and tails the logo of the International Red Crescent. In a warlike situation, the Geneva central office of the International Red Cross should've normally kept Delhi informed, about one of its flights ferrying supplies to Dacca. The IRC flights were permitted to over fly Indian airspace. Why did it take the Colombo route?

Previous such flights had evoked Indian suspicion. The IRC was yet to reply to Indian queries. Were these a part of the humanitarian succour for the victims of the violent orgy and genocide by Pakistani armed forces? No international agency had so far sounded the government of India about these flights. In the absence of any worthwhile intelligence input, the civil aviation mandarins were at a loss to understand the true nature of these flights.

That's why the midget sized Gnats were still dogging the flanks of the Boeing 707. They were instructed to harass the flight and escort it to a nearby Indian airport, if possible at Shinger Beel airfield on Sylhet-Tripura border.

"Clear Pakistani air space. You're violating the Montreal Agreement 1966, by obstructing a civilian cargo flight."

Dacca tower warned the Indian fighters.

The Indian version of the Folland Gnats, with 4,500 lb. Rolls Royce Orpheus 701-01 turbojet engines, were armed to the teeth–each with two 30 mm Adam Mk 4 canons, two bombs and six rockets.

Like big Amazonian mosquitoes, they crisscrossed the flight path of AAL-X-356, disturbing its IAS, Intended Air Speed, on the descent manoeuvre. Shillong was in no mood to relent.

"You're endangering an authorised international flight," Vudurume's voice crackled heavily on the radio, "move out. This is the Lady of the Light, a ICRC mercy mission."

"You're finally warned to vacate Pakistani air space," Dacca tower warned angrily, "you've two minutes, before our missiles zoom in on you."

Delhi's Directorate of Air Intelligence exchanged quick notes with the DMI and NSI. These flights had become regular features. AAL-X-356 couldn't be a holy ICRC flight, they agreed. There was no confirmation from any quarter.

Should it be shot down? The AHQ sought clearance from the Prime Minister's office.

Balachandran Nampoothiri intervened vigorously. He knew the secrets of these flights. The PM too was clear in her mind. She had overruled any provocative action, which could trigger world condemnation. She did not want to offer a leeway to the USA to jump into the fray.

No... . The Prime Minister's office shrieked. No tampering with the ICRC flights. The country couldn't afford another international scandal and give Pakistan a propaganda relay-baton.

Shillong, in constant touch with Delhi's Air Force Headquarters, signalled the Gnats to disengage and return to Shingar Beel base, off Agartala, capital of the Indian State of Tripura.

Vudurume looked out.

The Gnats, now accompanied by two MIG 21s made a rhythmic loop manoeuvre, went past the Boeing 707, about 1000 feet below and levelled up again. The Indian pilots grinned at the worried facial expressions of the International Red Crescent flight commander. Vudurume waved back with a matching grin. He was too hardened a veteran of treetop flying, to be cowed down by some intimidating hot-blooded pranksters.

The Lady of the Light took a slight detour to avoid the airspace over Dacca city, which was under virtual control of the paramilitary and civilian police forces loyal to Sheikh Jainal. Some of the freedom fighters, fondly called *Mukti Bahini* by the Bengalis, had acquired medium machine guns and light anti-aircraft guns (LAA). These were capable of sniping at low flying aircrafts landing at Kurmitola Air Force base. They had shot down two helicopters in last thirty days.

"Hang on, escorts will guide you." ATC Dacca advised AAL-X-356.

Vudurume hovered over Buri Ganga River. Two helicopter gunship, armed with rapid-fire machine guns and air-to-ground rockets levelled up and fired, rather indeterminately, at some of the near and distant villages. These village clusters, around the suburban town Tungi were strong bastions of the freedom fighters. The helicopter gunships peeled off, as the tarmac showed up, enabling flight AAL-X-356 to make a smooth landing.

*

46

The communication protocol for Double X agent Qurban was cleverly designed by the ODQ (Operations Desk Q) at the NSI central hub. This agent was designated to accept tasking from Alamgir. He was operationally architectured to report on the deployment of Army and Air Force units and other defence related matters, as well as to achieve penetration in Pakistan IB and ISI through lower conduits. Delhi had tasked him to map and photograph the underground hangers at Khushab, an extension of the Sargodha base, which housed three squadrons of F 28 fighter bombers, acquired from the USA and medium range missiles supplied by China.

Ibadat, a Double X asset, nom de plumed Qurban, was raised by Alamgir very back in 1960. He primarily handled this local agent of intermediate stature. Ibadat was permitted to communicate directly to Delhi only during grave emergency and during Alamgir's prolonged absence from Pakistan. His independent channel of communication was well defined. He could, on rare occasions, contact a designated diplomat in the Indian consulate in Jalalabad or pass on his message through a Live Letter Box in Lahore.

His role was slightly modified after Harfan Bukhari, the Triple X agent, was housed at Jhumra. Ibadat was tasked to help the new asset to grain himself smoothly into the grooves of his deep cover and to keep a watch on his security status.

However, Ibadat did not know when Harfan Bukhari, the Prince of Jhumra, had started driving roots into his mind. A mixed bag of reasons, Ibadat had reasoned, were responsible for driving him closer to Harfan and his wife Jamilla. He often felt that the seeds of old family loyalty had re-germinated. He had started liking the man, whom Alamgir did not consider anything more than another expendable intelligence agent.

That sense of caring had resurfaced during his meeting with Karamat Suri at his *mohalla* Rajora residence. Suri was back to Jhumra on a brief furlough, in fact, for attending his own *sagai* (engagement) ceremony. He was getting married to a girl from the same village.

Karamat called aside his childhood friend Ibadat after several bottles of country liquor, dozens of roasted fowl and bowls of *biryani* (rice fried with chunks of meat) were downed.

"I'm scared."

Karamat lighted a cigarette and offered one to Ibadat.

"What for? Is anything wrong at your work place?"

"No brother. I'm coming to that later. I am afraid of the girl I'm getting married to."

"Why should you be afraid? She is a nice neighbourhood girl."

"I've never been close to any girl."

"Shit! You're an army officer. Face the girl like you face bullets."

"Brother facing a bullet is easy. Facing a woman is like putting your nose in the barrel of 125 pounder. Never faced them. Give me a lesson or two. I don't have time. I go back again to Phullarwan area near Lahore."

"What's happening there?"

"Oh dear brother!" Karamat found back his confidence, "I'm assigned to investigate that fellow Harfan. He is suspected to be an Indian agent. I hope you know that employee of Israr sahib."

"No brother, not very well. To me he is another customer. I'm happy to earn a little extra money from him. As I was telling, you should be very kind when you seduce your wife... ." Ibadat used the diversion wilfully. He knew that the slightest obstruction infused waves of surge in Karamat. He was a compulsive talker and that compulsion was always compounded after he downed a few ounces of intoxicants.

"Wait brother. I was talking about that Harfan fellow. The Director General has rebuffed Jamanat sahib for his raid on Harfan's house. There was nothing in it. But Jamanat sahib feels that there is something fishy in that fellow and he may have been a petty criminal, before he took up Israr sahib's employment."

"I'm damned confused Karamat."

"Brother Ibadat," Karamat raised his voice slightly, "he was a smuggler sort of criminal with linkages in India."

"Is he a *jasus* (spy)?"

"You can't rule out that possibility. Most smugglers are *jasus*."

"I think that will be another wild goose chase," Ibadat tried to disengage himself, "as I was telling you, brother Karamat, a newly married wife is just like a fresh rose bud. Handle her carefully. Don't try to force her to bloom overnight. Patience helps in the germination of love and respect."

"You talk big things brother. I want to embrace and kiss her, but I feel shaky."

"Wake up Karamat. You're a hotblooded man. You can do it."

"How do I embrace her?"

"We'll talk again. We've too much of food and drink in our stomach. Let's sleep well."

"But I leave for Lahore tomorrow."

"We shall meet on your return. *Shadi* (marriage) is thirty days hence."

*

Ibadat left his Rajora residence surreptitiously in the melting morning darkness, and boarded the 4 a.m. Peshawar Express for Lahore. He intended to contact Alamgir through his Peshawar Live Letter Box telephone. Karamat's story had reconfirmed what he had earlier gathered from a contact in the office of the CMLA, a telephone operator, who manned the special area exchange. Broken pieces of information from him had vaguely indicated that a high level meeting had discussed a security suspect named Harfan Bukhari. But the contact was not sure of the context. He, however, produced a transcript of the telephonic talk between Brigadier Barqat and Captain Amin, aide d'camp to the PSO. The brief intercept had given a broad indication about the ISI's deep suspicion on Harfan Bukhari. Both the officers had, however, agreed that Harfan should not be disturbed until completion of the airlifting operations to Dacca and till such time Barqat was not able to dig out culpable evidence.

The Peshawar LLB telephone was attended by a familiar voice, but he informed Ibadat that his master had gone for *umra* (pilgrimage) to Mecca. He would return after a week. The code word *umra* was used for Alamgir's trips to foreign destinations. Ibadat did some quick calculations and entered the narrow lanes of the Anarkali market. After an hour-long survey, he selected a miniature soapstone replica of the Lahore Fort and settled down for breakfast in an exclusive restaurant, often frequented by the backpack foreign tourists. He carved out a hollow under one of the minarets with the help of a pocketknife and secured a document, along with a small piece of iron nail deep inside the cavity. He covered the cavity with layers of plaster of Paris. He felt happy with the camouflage and hoped that the drop would safely reach its destination.

Ibadat boarded a cycle rickshaw after a leisurely breakfast and asked the puller to take him to *gali kabaarian* (lane of the scrap dealers), the main trading centre of the solid waste recycling vendors.

Momin Ansari, a veteran *kabaari* (scrap dealer), conducted his family business from a small front shop with a sprawling makeshift shed at the backyard. Momin, a weaver by caste, had inherited the business from his father, who owned a flourishing business at *gali bhistiwalan* (lane of the water carriers) at the back of the historical Jama Masjid of Delhi. Part of the extended family had migrated to Lahore on the eve of partition and had set up business at Anarkali market. Momin's brothers and cousins still operated from the backyards of the walled city of Delhi.

The secret behind Momin's wealth had very little to do with his scrap business. It was a front for another flourishing business that dealt in *hawala* (unofficial) transfer of money between India and Pakistan at a high premium. Momin controlled another shady business, the illegal *sawari* (smuggler-passenger) traffic between India and Pakistan. His *sawaris* operated on both sides of the international border and smuggled in and out contraband items. The *sawari* business had flourished more in the recent years, following the 1965 war and the present tense situation.

Momin was an all rounder. His network operated all over India and the important urban pockets in Pakistan. His genius did not go unnoticed by the intelligence agencies of the two feuding countries. The PIB and the ISI tapped his *sawaris* for gathering shallow penetration intelligence from India and the Indian FIB and the NSI too tapped his talents for similar purposes. It was a free for all game, and Momin, seated in his ramshackle shop at the backyard of *gali kabaarian* controlled his multifaceted financial empire.

"Hello Mian Idris." Momin greeted Ibabat, "haven't seen you for a long time. *Sab khairiyat hai* (hope things are well with you)?"

In and around *gali kabaarian* Ibadat was known as Idris Ahmed, a smuggler, who once in a while availed of the services of Momin, for transferring money to Delhi. He normally paid 3% of the total amount as commission.

"*Salam alaikum janab*," Ibadat greeted the aged tycoon, "I'd been to Dubai for a while. I hope you're doing well too."

"No son. Business is no more attractive. The war clouds have dampened the market."

"How is the *sawari* business? I hope you're accepting consignments for India."

"It's very risky these days. These Indian and Pakistani *jasus* (spies) and police officers trouble me a lot. These days they are asking for 7% commission. How can an honest business be run if you've to dole out 7 to 10 % to the spies and the cops?"

"That's correct *chacha* (uncle). I've a small gift to be delivered to my *chacha* in Delhi. I hope there wouldn't be any problem."

"There are problems. This time you've to pay 5% extra. Days are very bad."

"That's too high *chacha*. I can offer only 4%."

"Okay Idris sahib. I'm doing the favour only because you're a trusted customer. Give me your uncle's address in Delhi."

"It's Mirza Hafiz Qadri, Gali Kabristan, Turkman Gate, Delhi."

"Is he your *dargahwala* (custodian of a holy shrine) uncle?"

"Yes *chacha*. It should reach him quickly."

"Don't worry. My *sawari* is leaving for Delhi today. Your uncle will receive it tomorrow. Check up with him on phone. Momin Ansari is the most reliable trader in this line."

"I know that *chacha. Khuda Hafiz*."

Ibadat paid the commission amount and noted down the name of the female *sawari*, who was supposed to carry the miniature replica of the Lahore Fort to Delhi. It was a trusted channel. He moved over to the Inter State Bus Terminal, made a call to a designated Delhi number, and boarded a midday bus for Jhumra.

*

Israr International's Mercedes picked up Harfan from Lahore airport. His favourite chauffeur, Latiff Masih, a virtual chatterbox, was on the wheels.

"Take me to Zahoor sahib's place." Harfan ordered.

"Sir, it's necessary to meet Israr sahib first at Sangla Hills." Latiff insisted.

"What's the matter Latiff? What's the big deal?" Harfan asked in a tense voice.

"*Sahib*, you've been busy flying to Dacca. Plenty of water has flown by the Ravi since then. The plague had visited your house at Jhumra." Latiff spoke in his usual flowery and fenugreek flavoured Kasuri dialect.

"What the hell do you mean?"

"They say, I mean some people say, that the Narcotics Bureau people had raided your house. Israr sahib is very upset. He met several military officers. They suspect you.... I believe."

"What else?"

"They searched your house, and people say, unearthed sacs full of US dollars."

"You believe in that shit!"

"No *sahib*, nobody believes in it. People know that Nawab Sharief is after your life, simply for destroying his brother's business. This arms lifting contract has enraged the viper. What you see outside isn't real. Nawab wants political power and he thinks Israr is his main rival in Punjab."

"But, they're brothers."

"Forget it sir. They're archenemies."

Latiff kept on narrating the family secrets of the Shariefs. Harfan didn't reply. He lowered the windowpane and lighted a cigarette. He tried to comprehend the scenario that might have taken shape in his absence.

Scenario one: Would Nawab go to that extent, simply because he was beaten in the airlifting bid?

The ambitious Nawab was mighty inscrutable and unscrupulous. He wouldn't hesitate erasing Harfan's name from the face of the earth, simply to hurt Israr. Nawab was capable of committing any mischief.

Scenario two: The ISI must have dug up the entire place and stumbled upon some of the electronic devices. These electronic darlings of the intelligence community weren't supposed to be decoration pieces in a business executive's house. He wondered if Alam had removed all the incriminating evidence.

It was possible that he had. Possibly he hadn't.

Scenario three: The ghost of his association with Jahanara was still haunting him and the Direction Finders must have zeroed in on his living room fireplace. It was eminently feasible.

A chilling shiver almost paralysed the pumping muscles of Harfan's heart. Well! He was as good as a dead scarecrow now. Instead of rotting in the ISI dungeons and being shot through his skull, he should make good his escape. But how was he going to pull off the vanishing trick? Crossing over to India through the land border was impossible. If not the Rangers, the Indian security forces were sure to make fine mince of his meat, bone, and tissue. Could Bhagat smuggle him back to India? Unlikely.

His visa was still valid for the UK and Canada. Perhaps he could take a chance and disappear from Pakistan.

Without Jamilla and Pervez?

How could he think of that? Harfan's body chemistry instinctively responded to the absurd thought. He shifted position and lighted another cigarette. No. Life wasn't worth escaping the ISI dragnet without Jamilla and Pervez.

Could he disappear into East Pakistan, taking help from his friends, Major Anjum Mani of the SSG and Ahsan Khondokar, a wing commander in Pakistan Air Force? The freedom fighters might not find it difficult to push him and Jamilla across the Indian border. Harfan chewed on the cigarette butt, spat it out, and lighted another. The idea appeared to be remote and absurd.

Could he count on Alam? He didn't expect Alam or anyone else from the Indian agency to rescue him. His last encounter with Alam, a free and frank one, had helped Harfan to crawl out of the cocoon of false security he was assured by Delhi. The message was loud and clear; Delhi didn't retrieve its soured agents. Alam was correct. An inexpensive bullet was the final reward for a compromised spy. Harfan smiled silently. The damn fool that he was!

Anger did not seize Harfan. Perhaps his foolish romanticism had benumbed his reasoning. Perhaps he was just caught up in the trap of a vague revenge mindset, woven by the FIB psy-war experts. He'd just fallen into their trap. But what would he do about the dream mission of avenging his father's assassination? Had Jamilla's arrival in his life and this latent threat dissolved his resolution?

No, yes and perhaps.

No. He could by no means identify Jamilla with Pakistan. His love for her in no way impeded his mission.

Yes. He had lost himself in the neo-realities of Jamilla and Pervez. His love for them had transcended the pseudo-reality of his cover, fabricated by the intelligence experts.

Perhaps he was scared of the possibility of walking down to the Badr interrogation centre. Perhaps he was afraid of dying the death of a frontline soldier.

No one was going to immortalise him in ballads and nursery rhymes. He wasn't another patriotic soldier, falling down to enemy bullets. He was a simple spy, a shadowy creature; no one was ready to own him up. His today was uncertain and his tomorrow might not even dawn.

Had he developed cold feet? Was he trying to formulate a philosophy to support his escape strategy?

The ridiculous thought kept on plaguing Harfan.

Hell with Delhi! Harfan lighted another cigarette.

Why was he weighing the possibility of bolting from Pakistan? Jhumra was his destiny. He would stay put to fight his personal war. He wasn't going to bolt from Pakistan before he liquidated his father's assassins. This one precious life, bestowed on him, Harfan mused, wasn't going to be offered to the scimitars of the NSI and ISI cheerleaders. Why should he? He wouldn't.

Harfan clenched his fist and banged the back of the driver's seat. The Jhumra war was a personal mission. This was one war, Harfan resolved, he must fight to the last bullet. Someone must pay with blood, for spilling his father's blood. Harfan's eyes suddenly detected the piercing eyes of Latiff intently scanning him through the rear view mirror. Was he a suspect in his eyes too? Or did he act abnormally in a fit of shadow boxing?

"We're here sir. Your servant is never late."

The screeching sound of tyres and Latiff 's voice brought Harfan out of his woolly thoughts. His car was already inside the factory gates. Israr Sharief stood at the top of the stairs, flanked by General Naqi and Captain Ayub. Was it the end of his game?

Harfan's presumption wasn't correct either. Gen. Naqi and Ayub weren't there to escort him to jail. They were emerging out of a meeting with Israr Sharief, the Managing Director of Israr International.

Naqi was on an urgent visit. A sensitive piece of intelligence, presumably originated by a Delhi based agent, had made the CMLA and the President lose his cool. The Indian forces were in battle readiness, in the eastern front; the probable D-day was November 20-21 night, the day of the holy Id (Muslim religious festival). CIA's U2 spy photographs and station operators in Delhi and Dacca had independently corroborated the input. The message from Pentagon was loud and clear. The Indian forces were foxtrotting to launch an attack all along the eastern front. It had virtually encircled East Pakistan by deploying six divisions with supporting arms. Defending East Pakistan was a greater strategic need for Washington, if not for Islamabad. The US interest in South East Asia could not be surrendered to India, a Moscow surrogate. The White House couldn't allow East Pakistan to become an Indian protectorate.

The Chinese ambassador, wantonly sweet and sour, added to Islamabad's worries. Peking, he said, wasn't in a position to roll their forces down the Himalayas. The Russian Bear had been growling menacingly along Mongolian borders, across River Usuri. Peking's fighters and bombers were tied up against the renegade, bourgeoisie, and reactionary forces of Moscow. Some fifth columns of Moscow were busy promoting counter-revolution. The ambassador, however, assured Islamabad that the great Peoples' Republic of China would step up military hardware supplies, of course in lieu of appropriate compensation in hard US currency.

The Chinese somersault was counterbalanced by the generous under the sleeve offers from Washington. Pakistan wouldn't starve for military hardware, though there was an official embargo on arms supply. The secret tunnels to NATO supplies would be opened up via Riyadh, Amman, and Istanbul routes.

Gen. Naqi came calling to explore the possibility of pressing in a few more mercenary chartered flights to augment the airlifting operations at breakneck speed. The dough, the visiting Under Secretary of State, Jim Baxter, had whispered, would come from Fort Knox. All he expected Islamabad to do was to reinforce the airlifting operations by the CIA approved Athena Air Lines.

"*Adab arj* (salutation) Mian Harfan." Gen. Naqi was mighty pleased to see the daredevil *muhajir.*

"How was your mission?" Asked Israr.

"Harrowing. The Indian fighters are in total command of our airspace. Two of their Gnats buzzed us for about five minutes, before we were allowed to land. It's risky to fly these machines there." Harfan briefly described his latest air adventure to Dacca.

"Interesting. Come sometime. I'd like to get a firsthand account of your adventure with the Bongs. I've to rush. Ayub will be with you for plugging in the remaining holes."

"But sir, it's risky all the way. I'm afraid whether my boys can live up to your expectations." Israr replied.

"Keep trying and that's all we can do, besides praying."

"Don't you think that the Americans should get directly involved? They can't allow the dismemberment of Pakistan." Israr Sharief asked.

"We've plenty of indications that the rattling sounds from Peking are empty, and they've belied our expectations." Naqi blurted out his bitterness over the alleged Chinese betrayal.

"I'm talking of direct US intervention." Israr added.

"No. They won't. They're afraid of the possible Russian response," Naqi added, "The US President has directed his Jewish trouble-shooter to divert more military hardware from Jordan and Saudi. You know very well Israr, our friends are pressurising the Security Council to restrain India, and the 7th Fleet may be ordered to move to the Bay of Bengal."

"Hope Washington won't abandon Pakistan." Israr commented, echoing the fervent expectations of fellow Pakistanis.

"That's our only prayer. Only *Allah* and America can save our skins." Naqi briskly walked down to the waiting chopper and asked the pilot to send at GHQ helipad at Islamabad. He had a meeting with the PSO in mind.

"*Allah* shall not betray his faithful," Israr added. He turned to Harfan and said, "I know it's cruel. But please spend a little time and get a detailed briefing from Capt. Ayub, on the latest inventory."

"I'd like to discuss a few points with you." Harfan tried to convey the urgency of his proposition.

"Let's talk it over dinner. There's no emergency, I hope. Please get going. I've to locate Alam and hire a few extra chartered flights. The situation is getting desperate." Israr left for his executive suite.

*

Harfan winked at Ayub to follow him.

"So, how have you been?" Asked Ayub.

"Spare me a minute." Harfan dialled Jamilla's Lahore number.

She picked up the phone.

"You didn't call from Dacca." she complained.

"I couldn't darling. There were problems. How have you been? How's my Pervez?" Harfan flooded Jamilla with all the questions he could shoot out in one single breath.

"Talk to your *farishta* (angel)." Jamilla put the receiver in front of the bubbling and gurgling infant.

For a few moments, Harfan was lost in utter bliss, in the meaningless sounds from Pervez and Jamilla's sweet inviting voice. He must visit Lahore at least for a day. She missed him and she wanted him very much, very warmly and intimately. Harfan could disconnect only after conceding a promise to visit her by the weekend.

"Sorry friend," Harfan apologised, "I hope you understand."

"No problem *dost* (friend). Such problems are elixirs of life, nobler than carrying weapons to Dacca." Ayub echoed Harfan's sentiments.

"You appear to have changed views since we met last!"

Harfan ordered tea and some onions and aubergine fried in batter.

"How reliable is this highly placed intelligence?" Asked Harfan.

"Can't say *yar*," Ayub crunched on the delicate snacks and replied, "it's perhaps a reliable agent report."

"He appears to be a popular spook in Pakistan."

"Well! I hear some bosses swear by him."

"Then his days should be numbered." Replied Harfan.

"How do you say that?"

"You don't run a marathon with a leaking oil can. It spoils your relay race." Ayub smiled rather meaninglessly and opened his Pandora's box–the new shopping list of the Armed Forces.

"Tell me what's the new wish list." Harfan reverted to the contents of Israr's briefing.

"Your company has to hire three more cargo planes and expedite the airlifting operations. To avoid complications the birds may fly non-stop to Dacca."

"What about refuelling?"

"Washington has agreed to loan two aircrafts for mid-air refuelling."

Ayub paused for a while and suddenly lowered his voice to a feeble modulation.

"Perhaps this is my last meeting with you."

"Why? Are you reverting to your Signals unit?" Harfan asked the probing question expecting Ayub to blurt out additional information on the Direction Finder episode.

"Oh yes!" Ayub obliged, "Recall that DF story? We'd pinpointed the suspected radio station to Jhumra. Aren't you from there?"

"No. I happen to live there."

"That's it. The ISI had raided a few houses and drawn a blank. I believe they visited your house too."

"Don't tell me, I don't deserve this after all that I'm doing."

"Don't despair. The ISI has queer ways of needling their suspects. General Naqi knows all about it and he has pulled up General Hyder." Ayub tried to console a visibly upset Harfan.

"So you're on to the front? What about your lady love?"

"Yes *yar*. I'm too junior to be a permanent fixture in the CMLA office. My unit, as I told you, has been shifted to Jessore in East Pakistan. I've received the marching orders." The young captain stood up, put on his cap, and saluted.

Harfan embraced Ayub, with an overwhelming and surging lump in his throat. The poor fellow, just married, might not return home, to the tolling of welcoming bells. His body might not even be retrieved by the retreating troops. Perhaps he wouldn't even receive a decent burial.

"It's a pity that our wives haven't met," Harfan took out his wallet and carefully fished out a photograph of Jamilla, "look, here's my soul mate."

Ayub intently looked at the charming photo of Jamilla and instinctively brought out his wife's photograph.

"Here's Reshma, my wife. She's just twenty. Isn't she beautiful?"

"Heavenly!"

A sudden flood of pity and sadness overwhelmed Harfan, for Ayub, for himself, Jamilla, Pervez and Reshma. Perhaps all of them would be offered at the altar of hatred. There was no escape from the crunch of distorted history, crafted by wily politicians, on either side of the border.

"See you soon. *Khuda Hafiz*." Harfan wished the departing Captain.

"*Insha Allah*, if I return from the front."

"Most of us live in some kind of front Ayub. All of us fight some kind of war, mostly for the survival of the vested interests. We sacrifice our today for their tomorrow. But we shall survive." Harfan replied.

"I'm a soldier and I know better when to expect a bullet. I can already sniff cordite in the air."

"Hope and pray for the best."

"See you brother."

"Sure. Don't get upset. Convey my *salaam* to Reshma." Harfan escorted Ayub to his vehicle. Harfan was amazed by Ayub's brief outburst. He was a braggart. But sometimes he talked sense. There must be somewhere in him some trace genes of a desert troubadour, the irresistible emotional ballad singer.

Caught in between the cleft edges of two religions Harfan hardly said his prayers. But, today he raised his hands and prayed for Ayub's safe return, to the warm embraces of Reshma.

*

47

The dinner meeting at Hotel Royal Palace started on a tense note.

Harfan spoke in a hushed voice and didn't hide his wound and apprehension.

"I'm sorry Harfan. There has been some terrible misunderstanding." Israr responded on a sympathetic note.

"Why should you be sorry? I think I should resign. This has landed me in a heap of social garbage." Harfan spoke with simulated hurt in his voice. Israr Sharief, his shield, should be used to maximum advantage.

Israr obliged. In a low decibel monologue, he narrated his encounters with the PSO and other top brass. They were convinced, Israr added, that a junior officer had bungled all the way. He was probably misguided by some erratic electronic signals. Harfan's wasn't the only house searched by the ISI. Probably, he hastened to add, Nawab had planted some stories against him.

"That's no insurance against the ISI. Hungry tigers don't simply kiss their supper. They eat it."

"Oh Harfan!" Israr spoke in a flattering voice, "your Urdu is poetic. But don't get upset. I'm there to protect you. You'd better get going with the job."

"You know your brother better. I believe he's a partner of General Hyder."

"That's correct. And that's why the ISI is on a demolition operation against me. You're just a front. I'm the target. However, I've Sarfaraz and Naqi with me. And Jahanara is our good friend."

"That's the problem Israr sahib. She's in the eye of the storm of political conspiracy and I've been sucked into it just for the heck of it."

Harfan explained his position.

"I understand. All of us are entangled with one or the other arm of the vicious twister. We'll take care. Please get going with the flights."

"I would like to take a day off."

"Lahore?"

Harfan didn't reply.

"Just take my car after dinner and drive down to Lahore. Latiff will drive you. Return by midday. I'm expecting Alam *sahib*. He'll help in contracting the additional charters." Israr handed over another fat envelope to Harfan.

"What's this?"

"Keep this. It's a small portion of your share of the profit. The airlifting operations are going to get us millions. This is for your wife and kid."

"But sir," Harfan added, "money can't repair the damage done by Hyder's people. I don't know how can I show my face to Zahoor sahib."

"Don't worry. Sarfaraz has spoken to him. In fact, Zahoor sahib is helping out the government in lower Indus areas."

"What's he doing there?"

"I believe the Indians are trying to pump in weapons to some Sindhi parochial groups through the sea route. He is mobilising a volunteer force in aid of the navy and the border rangers."

"It's a news to me. I did not know that he had that kind of influence over the *Mohana* people."

"He's the uncrowned king of the *Mohana* area. Don't wreck your head over that small incident. Zahoor understands the intricacies of the situation. *Khuda Hafiz.*"

As Israr left on a hopeful note Ibadat closed in with a pot of coffee.

"Spare me a bit of your time."

"Sit down."

"No. Not here. Your mind is in Lahore. Take this cover, read the contents on your way. Follow the disposal instructions. Memorise the contents before destroying it. Meet me before you go on next errand."

Ibadat took out a cover from inside his hotel livery, handed it over and said good night.

*

The reading light in the Mercedes emitted adequate illumination. Harfan opened the envelope. The unsigned and typed letter was from Alam. He had inscribed instructions for disposal on top of the letter.

"These papers are edible and the ink is non-toxic. Chew and gulp it down with your favourite whisky."

It was one of the standard prescriptions in the intelligence community. Harfan lighted a cigarette, moved closer to the reading light, and unfolded the pages.

"Read carefully. In your job, you won't survive even a slight mistake. This is your last *chance, Insha Allah*....

"I've dismantled the HF trans-receiver and removed all ElInt (electronic intelligence) equipment. Be sure, they won't find any trace. The raid has been a blind one. The top bosses have closed the chapter, but it's being pursued by a dedicated group of professionals....I should say that you're yet to be badly scratched....

"Your communication channels have been restructured. Pick up a DLB from beneath the foyer of Sangla Hills Baptist Church. You'd find the drop inside a Petunia flower pot, third from the left. Dig slightly and recover the plastic vial. It contains details of all fresh DLBs and LLBs....

"You shall drop your written reports in a pre-selected DLB and disappear. Don't bother about clearance....

"For brush communication: Walk along Egerton Road on the second Sunday between 3 and 3.30 p.m.; attend *namaj* on the third Friday at Wazir Khan mosque; the fourth bench on the northern side of Bagh-e-Jinnah should be used on the third Tuesday....

"Safest LLB: Under the portico of Roshni gate, leading to the tomb of Maharaja Ranjit Singh, look for an old leper beggar. Deposit your dispatch with him. Code: offer one half of the ten-rupee note enclosed. The other part will be with him. Match the numbers, contours, and edges before passing on any document to him. Use a new note every time or fix your own code. New LLBs will be developed later....

"Keep up a brave face. Avoid Ramayani. Observe all anti-surveillance techniques and all security tradecrafts."

"Latiff, how far are we from Lahore?"

"Another 30 minutes *janab.*"

"Faster friend."

"Don't worry. We'll be there before 11."

Harfan took out a flask, poured a drink, and put the papers in it. The rice paper dissolved, leaving a few bubbles on the surface. Harfan sipped the drink and silently thanked Alam for sanitising his house well before the ISI reached there. What about Ramayani? Why was Alam worried about her? Was the agency using her too?

Probably she had been guarding, deep in her chest, too many secrets of the former royal family. The ISI wouldn't have any qualms about cracking her bones, if that helped neutralising an Indian resident agent. She was indeed a weak link in the chain. What should he do with her? Kill her?

No. It wasn't possible. He wouldn't allow any harm to a friend of his mother.

The car screeched to a halt and Latiff sounded the horn twice.

"Sir it's 11 p.m. and we're here." He declared proudly.

"Thanks a lot *dost* (friend). Park the car and rest in the usual room. We start at 9 a.m. sharp."

Jamilla ran. The sound of two familiar honks, and the footsteps sent signals of recognition streaming into her veins. Pounding heart made her legs wheel faster to the door.

Harfan landed straight into her arms and before he could close the door behind, she implanted a high voltage kiss on his lips. The invitation to a sleepless night was very warm, warmer than the churning heat in a galactic core.

Harfan slithered out of Jamilla's embrace late in the night, entered the toilet, and took out an electronic pocket encoder. He composed a report in convertible numerical code, selecting each group carefully from the generated figures. Delhi would use a mainframe computer to break the code. The FIB and the Joint Cipher Bureau experts had taught him this emergency coding technique.

To say *al vida* (adieu) to Jamilla and Pervez wasn't an easy job. The young angel shook his head incessantly and simply refused to release Harfan's collars. His innocuous biological tools to prevent papa from boarding the car seemed to be more powerful than a mighty tow-crane.

Harfan flooded his young angel with kisses and reluctantly asked Latiff Masih to drive straight to Sangla factory, with a small diversion by Roshni Gate. The old leper LLB was there. His limbs were amply bandaged, with oozing blood marks all over. Harfan casually walked down to the leper, after directing Latiff to fetch a packet of cigarettes.

The beggar examined the finely scissored ten-rupee note, brought out the other half, and passed it on to the stranger, with a rather uncertain look in his eyes. Harfan matched the two halves and passed on a neatly secured polyethylene bag. It contained a detailed report on weapons ferried to Dacca and Chittagong and the cipher message encoded last night.

"Some of the papers are... ." Harfan couldn't finish the sentence.

"Don't talk." The beggar whispered and started screaming, "*Allah* is omniscient. He knows your inner wishes and will fulfill your desires."

The LLB noticed Latiff crossing over from the other end of the road and started canting in a wailing voice, "*Allah* shall give you hundred fold, give ten rupees to the *kori* (leper)."

Harfan took out two halves of a ten-rupee currency note, passed on one half to the leper, and put the other half in his purse.

"Sir, you shouldn't go near these *koris* (lepers). *Allah* alone knows why they allow such dangerous animals to roam free. They should either be shot dead or thrown into the Ravi."

Latiff indignantly emptied his mouth of *paan* (betel leaf) juices, directing the liquid spittle hardly inches away from the leper. That was his social reaction to an ostracised leprosy patient, begging on the roadside.

"Don't be so unkind to this unfortunate fellow. It's a curable disease." Harfan tipped the beggar lavishly and followed Latiff to the car. He was satisfied with the LLB arrangement, an excellent cover, and a sure-fire conduit. He admired the tradecraft expertise of Alam.

Harfan's mind raced back to his workplace. The next few days, he presumed, would be tough and his survival would depend on the whims of the Indian fighter jets and the ISI sleuths.

What a choice it was! A nutty Hobson's choice!

Harfan's neurons resumed emitting cross signals as Latiff concentrated on driving and beating the winds. Contradictory waves kept on rocking him. The situation was far from comfortable. Neither of the agencies was engineered to shower mercy. He was a lone ranger in this jackal's game. Could he out-fox the master jackals!

The conflicting cross currents started sinking into his brain, like paralysing tarantula toxin, sending signals of numbness through his limbs. Harfan jerked off the sinking feeling with a deliberate motion, cranked his cortices, stretched limbs, and lighted a cigarette. To hell with the paralysing feeling of a fatalist! That was a trash philosophy. He was the master of his destiny. He was prepared to play the game immaculately, according to his own rules. He would live, Harfan vowed, beyond the copybook regulations of the NSI and the ISI.

Nevertheless, the creeping fear of being bumped off by an assailant's bullets still kept haunting him. He wondered if the hot lead would come first from the Indian or Pakistani barrels. He was, Harfan concluded, vulnerable to both, the barrels of the Indians and Pakistanis, sandwiched between the two killer agencies.

Latiff screeched the car to a halt in front of the factory and announced, "Sir, it's twelve and we're at Sangla."

Harfan shrugged off the shadow of death stalking his thoughts. How stupid could he get? Harfan smiled to himself.

"Thanks *dost*, for the excellent drive."

"Sir, your servant can beat the wind."

"Sure you can."

Harfan climbed the stairs silently.

Yes. He had in him the capability of banishing the dark thoughts haunting him. The nuclear fission inside was still capable of exploding in deadly eruptions and blinding the forces of death. He could beat the mighty intelligence machines. That power was within him. Why should he be afraid of the lurking shadows? The sun was sure to rise tomorrow and many more tomorrows for him, Jamilla and Pervez. He should better look towards that 'disc' of eternal 'energy' rather than counting the dark footsteps of death.

Harfan remembered and recited slowly but resolutely the couplets from *Yajurveda* (one of the *Vedas*), he had learnt from his mother: O Sun God! Your golden disc hides the face of Truth. Uncover that, O Sun, in order that I, the worshipper of Truth, may see your eternal flame.

Harfan took a deep breath and mustered the courage to kiss the brazen face of truth. He must beat the stalking truth of death and reaffirm his own truth, the truth of love and life.

*

48

It was another bad morning indeed.

Balachandran Nampoothiri was simply caught up in a sticky web of confusion. Two stiff coffees and the endearing Havana didn't help dissolving the fog. It still appeared to be seeping inside the crevices of his cranium. He drew open the curtains and looked down at traffic zooming past the streets below. From his eleventh floor window, they looked like toy buggies. He looked yonder, towards the watery glimpses of the river Yamuna, which was virtually a sewer drain of India's capital. His mind was behaving like that clogged poodle, the dirty Yamuna. It wasn't flowing in any direction.

Three topsecret red folders were on his table. Nampoothiri had been leafing through the pages for the last two hours. He couldn't make up his mind. The thinner red folder with a distinctive marking of the cipher section was on top of the pile. This was yet another message from Triple X, received a few hours back, through the Kabul diplomatic bag. It contained another bombshell. His specific information on the Pakistani mole, suspected to be Aftab, was crystal clear. Kabul input was fortified by a document recovered from the custody of Vidyasagar Suri, Karan's hotel manager. It contained photocopy of the Cabinet decision authorizing the Armed Forces to cross the Rubicon on Nov 20-21 night. A few twists and tuners on his body by Bhagat & co stimulated Suri to sing the name of Brigadier Iskandar of Pakistan Embassy, who already possessed a copy of the top secret government paper. His recorded voice clearly spelt the name of Ram Karan in Queen's alphabet. It was Ram Karan Prasad all the way. He was Islamabad's Aftab, Operation Sun, in simple English.

Only eight people were privy to the vital Cabinet decision. Nampoothiri had examined threadbare all the names, including that of Shankar, the impetuous son of the PM. Manjira wasn't a novice. She had no doubt, put Shankar on probation, but he was yet to take over control of the thinking neurons of his mother. The involvement of the Generals was ruled out.

Nampoothiri was determined to push the Aftab case with convincing evidences. Manjira, when confronted with the vital agent inputs and technical evidences, maintained enigmatic silence. She listened to Nampoothiri with stony eyes and a frozen face. The issue, she averred, was politically explosive and she would handle it politically. It was not a simple spy case.

"I'm convinced Balu. Ram is the most plausible source of leakage. He can't play with my Lotus scheme. From your position, you can suggest immediate dropping him from the cabinet and action under the law. I can't do that. Politically it'll be a disaster. The information has leaked and we've to control the damage. Ram will face the fire shortly."

Nampoothiri was disheartened but not dispirited. He appreciated Manjira's concern. He continued with briefing on other aspects of Triple X's cipher, which had catalogued details of weapons supplied by China and through the US Turkish, Jordanian, and Saudi conduits. The Langley had funded the hiring of additional Athena Air Lines' chartered aircrafts. The sharing of aerial photographic intelligence between the CIA and the ISI was yet another chilling evidence of the extent of collaboration. The White House was tinkering with the idea of positioning the 7th fleet in the Bay of Bengal. Nampoothiri's analysis impressed Manjira. Her views concurred on the probable Chinese and American designs in the sub-continent. She would take care of these concerns, she assured her chief spymaster.

"Shall we shoot down some of their mercenary planes?" Asked Shankar, Manjira's younger son seated across his mother's table.

"That won't be prudent," Nampoothiri hastened to add, "we don't want to provoke the Americans."

Manjira nodded in silent agreement. She pushed a button and summoned her secretary.

"Dewan, inform the Foreign, Home, and Defence secretaries, and request the three Chiefs to come here, in another 20 minutes sharp. Tell my Special Secretary and Mr. Taploo to join."

She turned to Nampoothiri and spoke in a murmuring tone.

"Give me a quick status report on the US and Chinese deployment in our vicinity. Alert your sources in the Straits of Malacca. I want a precise time count of the probable appearance of the Seventh Fleet in the Bay of Bengal, and the exact headcount of the Chinese troops and aircrafts across our borders."

Nampoothiri walked out of the PM's room with mixed satisfaction. Bilious rage and confusion about Ram Karan episode confounded him. His concern about the US and Chinese moves verged on acute anxiety. Well! He finally shrugged and rationalized the encounter as a true professional black screen; he often faced with strong willed politicians. The Prime Minister had the prerogative to reserve decision on any delicate matter of the state. He returned to his den, closed the Triple X cipher folder, and pressed the buzzer for Amrita.

"Yes sir." Amrita came on the intercom.

"Call Robin." He opened the other folder that was received from Alam via Kabul station, on the heel of the Triple X message.

The other red cover worried Nampoothiri most. It contained a cipher from Alamgir that astutely analysed the security status of Triple X. The third cover, which contained another interesting report from Double X Qurban, supplemented the cipher from Alam. Harfan's penetration was unique, Alam's report added, and he possessed the rare qualities of charming his targets with electrifying impulses.

However, he exhibited the characteristics of a comet, burning brightly no doubt, but leaving blazing trails behind. A clandestine operative couldn't afford to leave behind smoky trails. Contradictory psychological traits had made him vulnerable. A thorough nationalist and patriot, Triple X was committed to his profession. But his marriage to Jamilla had transformed the intelligence robot into a human being. He could perhaps die, for his love, but not for the mission.

Alam's analysis charted out three probable courses of action that Harfan could adopt when caught in the ISI net: rot in a Pakistani jail; turn over and serve the ISI as a double agent, with a view to saving his wife and child; and defect to a third country.

The possibility of his neutralisation by the ISI wasn't imminent. The process had just started. Permanent silence of the valuable asset, Alamgir recommended, would spare the agency and India severe embarrassment. His silence would ensure the continuity of at least ten other deep penetration agents.

What did Alam mean by permanent silence, assassination or venue shift after radical disengagement?

Nampoothiri didn't share agent Qurban's message with his desk officer. It had offered more tactical details of the operational mechanism of the ISI. Though officially buried, a dedicated team of counterintelligence experts was pursuing Operation Salamat, ISI's nom de plume of the investigations against Harfan.

An extraordinary disclosure by Qurban had rattled Nampoothiri. He had noticed escalating symptoms of hostility between Alamgir and Harfan. The bridge of trust between the two had collapsed. Alamgir, he suspected, was of the view that Harfan should be physically neutralised before the ISI caught up with him. This contemplated action, Qurban averred, could vitiate the ambience of confidence essential for survival in hostile environment.

Nampoothiri weighed the arguments proffered by Alamgir and Joint Secretary, Robin Achariya. These were textbook arguments, taught in espionage schools all over the world. He wasn't convinced. There was something in Qurban's message that required careful evaluation.

For a while, he weighed the feasibility of a smooth separation process, a final golden handshake with Triple X. The separation process, particularly from an important and sensitive agent, was often complicated. Nampoothiri knew the drill. Each step required perfect calibration.

By late evening Nampoothiri managed to descend to the bottom of his thought process. Triple X should have a fair chance to explain his position. The NSI should know what had really gone wrong. The disease could not be diagnosed by remote control. The ISI was indeed suspicious of Harfan's linkages with certain key personalities in Pakistan. But they had no proof of his NSI connectivity. The clandestine radio was decommissioned well in time and even Alam couldn't pin a sticker on him for any major tradecraft lapse. Harfan, if not seen through the Alam prism and offered to Robin scimitar, deserved a personalised debriefing and rehabilitation. He was still a productive agent and the time had not come for giving him a quiet burial.

Balachandran Nampoothiri summoned Jatadhari and asked him to seal and stack away the Alamgir folder in his personal safe, secured by a time lock. He pressed the intercom button and asked for Dhiren Bhagat.

"How long would you take to activate the River Channel?"

"For Triple X?"

"Yes."

"Isn't it better to go via Kabul or Jalalabad?"

"No. I prefer the River Channel."

"Give me two hours sir."

Dhiren Bhagat returned around 6 p.m. He had plenty of news to share.

Triple X was conscious about the ISI sniffer dogs. But, he was unable to disengage from airlifting operations. River Channel did not suit him. He could spare a few hours in Colombo, next Friday, two days hence, at Hotel Tathagata International, room 1406.

Nampoothiri ruled against Bhagat's meeting Triple X. Bhagat, a visible north Indian Hindu, would stink like rotten fish. Col. Khaliq, the ISI station chief in Colombo, was a logged subject of the NSI. He could be under orders to mount surveillance on Harfan Bukhari.

Maulana Rizwan figured as a natural choice.

He was, as part of his cover, scheduled to visit Colombo to attend a congregation of the *Alami Tabligi Jammat Ijtema* (worldwide proselytising conference). The meeting, convened by Saudi based *Rabita-al-Alam-al-Islami* (World Muslim League), was supposed to voice concern against nefarious Indian aggression against Pakistan. The choice of Colombo was symbolic of the security concern of India's smaller neighbours.

Nampoothiri briefed Maulana Rizwan on all possible aspects of the meeting. Safety of several NSI operations in Pakistan depended on a balanced debriefing of the asset, who was under a cloud. He must get at the root of the problem. Having done, what he thought he should do, Nampoothiri felt slightly relaxed.

*

49

Nampoothiri, however, was not aware that the boat so carefully crafted by him could also leak at several joints. Minor and major joints were equally vulnerable. One such minor leaking joint was Satya Dev Brahmbedi, fondly called SD. He was a team member of Unit Helix of the NSI. The Helix team covered the city beat in Delhi and scrounged out information from suspected front operators and organisations of foreign intelligence agencies. The print media was the proud host of several such front personalities, who, besides filing reports to their desk editors traded information on the slight with foreign diplomats and nodal reception points created by them.

Raghu Chawla was not only a listed and categorized front media personality, but he was also a double-edged operator. Scroungers like Satya Dev Brahmbedi presumed that by rubbing skin with talents like Chawla they had penetrated peripheral operational areas of targeted foreign embassy. In reality, hunters like Raghu managed to steal more information from such scroungers by pretending to share great secrets about task-specific foreign embassies. This was a funny and witty game of deception, often played with trader's precision of balancing of gain and loss estimates at the end of the day. It was a speculative equity market situation, each one trying to invest less and harvest more.

Satya Dev selected a clever rendezvous to meet his 'friend' at Madras Café, Delhi's watering hole for intellectuals, gossipmongers, and political conspirators.

"What's so urgent, Mr. Brahmbedi?"

"The matter is grave. I believe an important minister is likely to be dropped for his alleged connection with Pakistan." SD pretended to throw a lure at his subconscious 'friend'.

"No idea dear," the subconscious 'friend', more conscious than the unconscious NSI scrounger was evasive, "have you heard any name?"

"That's what I want you to confirm. People say Ram Karan Prasad is a Pakistani mole."

"Must be a bogus guess. He's so powerful a minister. I don't think Manjiraji can afford to alienate him when the country is facing a war." Chawla buried his teeth on a juicy chicken drumstick.

"My information isn't vague. Please have a check. You've lots of diplomat friends." SD finally footed the bill and left with a sense of satisfaction that his important bit of inquiry was registered with the most knowledgeable person in Delhi's English media.

Raghu walked out of the joint, lighted a cigarette, and cursed Ram Karan.

Satya Dev Brahmbedi was a junior operator of the NSI. Someone at the middle formation of the agency must have been tasked to scrounge out information on Ram Karan. The agency had correctly zeroed on him, an identified crony of Ram.

It was time to play safe. How could he escape the nutcracker if Ram Karan was pressed in the mill?

Raghu gulped down a glass of water and picked up the phone.

"Karanji," he whispered, "can we meet?"

"Come for dinner, say at ten."

"Can't it be earlier?"

"Sorry friend, I'm receiving a Nepalese delegation at eight. The guests may linger on."

Ram Karan wasn't really receiving any official delegation from the neighbouring Hindu kingdom. His business partners in flesh and drug trade had landed in Delhi on a mission to rescue two of their operators, nabbed with a consignment of Nepalese women from a west Delhi transit shack. Ram Karan had intervened, but the rogue police officer had refused to relent. To add to the minister's worry he brought in some women's rights protagonists to highlight the shameful flesh-trade scam.

Ram Karan was in the midst of giving final touches to the rescue plan, which involved a hold up of the police van escorting the prisoners to a trial court. General Kalua, with two professional killers in tow, was to execute the operation.

Raghu Chawla, unaware of the gravity of Ram Karan's immediate priority banged the phone on its cradle. He uttered a curse. The jackal had got him entangled in the espionage net. He had survived the Col. Zaved episode by the skin of his teeth. It was high time he disengaged from Ram's quagmire. By his own right, Chawla mused, he was now a recognised figure in the tricky world of print media. Another 50 million in his pocket, he should be able to launch his own newspaper, *Indian Mirror*. He should now be out of this game of peddling information. Now was the time to don long hair, a goatee, and other props of an intellectual. The leaking boat, Ram Karan, could be conveniently jettisoned. That scum had outlived his utility.

He lighted another cigarette and dialled the number of Shankar.

"Morning sir. Are you free?"

"Hi Chawla, your editorial this morning on Bangladesh is superb."

"Sir, we try to reflect the truth and only the truth."

"Don't shit. I know what kind of truth you sell. Tell me if there's anything special."

"Yes sir," Chawla spoke in a spirited voice, "some people are keen to organise mass rallies in support of the PM's East Pakistan initiative."

"Spell out the details."

Raghu's scheme was simple. The PM had caught imagination of the nation and international community, by boldly supporting the East Pakistan Bengalis. Ram Karan Prasad had come out with a novel idea. He wanted to organise mass rallies all over the country with a view to galvanise the people behind the PM. A few hundred millions could be raised from these rallies, for national defence.

"That's a grand idea Raghu. How many millions do you expect?"

"The country is ready to pay. It's collection time. Just don't forget your loyalist servant."

"Let me consult mom. She'll sure be pleased. Let's go ahead with it." Shankar thanked Raghu for the brilliant idea.

*

Chawla's next stop was New Delhi's Saturday Club, an exclusive preserve of the diplomats, to which he was a permanent invitee. The diplomats of the rank of Minister, Counsellor and First Secretary were the institutional members of this exclusive club. It welcomed the new arrivals, bade adieu to the departing friends and provided a placid pool for information hunting and intelligence angling. Some bottom pinching and bossom brushing were accepted as gracious *coup de foudre.*

"You appear to be jittery." Commented Brig. Iskandar, Minister, and Military Attaché of Pakistan High Commission, as he drifted in with a beer mug for his friend.

"Yah, for good reason. Ram has been compromised." Raghu whispered in Iskandar's ear.

"What's fresh? His last tip was rated very high in Islamabad. It was a real hot piece of information."

"That's okay. But the agencies are after him, you, and me. "

"Really?"

"It's very real Iskandar sahib. I learn Ram is talking like a canary to the intelligence bosses." Raghu whispered.

"What else?"

"You and I can be sacrificed by him. He has reneged. He is organising rallies all over the country to kick up anti-Pakistan hysteria. You know Iskandar, he has tremendous influence on the low caste Hindus and Muslims of East Pakistan."

Chawla donned a mask of acute anxiety on his face, as he spoke.

"It doesn't matter. Bengali Muslims aren't real Muslims."

"It is not so simple Iskandar," Chawla tried to hammer in the fear of God into Iskandar, "Ram was interrogated by the NSI. And I'm told he has compromised your identity."

"You aren't joking, I hope." Iskandar reacted sharply.

"I'm a serious Jhangi (a district in Pakistani Punjab) trader. Being a fellow Punjabi from Sialkot, you should know that I may poke a woman here and there, but I never crack a joke on serious matters. Ram Karan is surely in the NSI net. I feel you aren't safe. The Indians may declare you PNG (persona non-grata) any moment." Raghu Chawla gestured towards a waiter for a refill of his glass.

Brig. Iskandar sipped his beer in silence and slowly placed his left hand on Raghu's shoulder, guiding him to a corner.

"Are you sure? I hope it's not a trick."

"*Ma kasam* (swear by my mother). You should take care and also take care of this poor journalist."

"Thanks pal. Our boys will take care of Karan. My man will see you in your office. It's better that way. Pay my regards to Ram."

"Won't you like to brief him personally?"

"It's not necessary. I hope you won't ditch me!" Brig. Iskandar uttered the words, as if he was chanting requiem for an old friend.

"I'm a reliable trader. Protect my interests."

"Sure. Our relationship will continue."

Raghu Chawla, happy over his performance, picked up the whiff of a fair and young first secretary of the USSR embassy, who was passing by and drifted towards the fluttering Freya of the diplomatic corps.

The major part of the day was well spent. He looked forward to a nice and meaningful dinner with Ram Karan.

*

Ram Karan too felt mighty relaxed. The rogue police officer had fallen to the killers' bullets. His Nepal business partners and the rescued pimps had taken a flight to Bangkok. The killers were back to their holes with a handsome bounty. General Kalua, as he usually did after every victorious engagement, had another close shave of his head and went for a brief worship of the carrier of the Lord Ganesha, the divine rodent.

The permanent minister in the Indian cabinet was ready at hand to greet Raghu. Nobody had ever blamed Ram Karan for tardy hospitality. The dinner and drinks were lavish, served by bearers wearing starched livery. As usual, Kalua supervised their discreet movement.

"Kalua." Ram Karan shouted.

"Yes sir, *hukum karo* (order me)." The castrated rat-eating tribal bowed in front of his master.

"You bloody Bhangi (night soil carrier)," Ram Karan shouted, "how could you forget to serve the fried *hilsa* fish (Clupea Alosa) eggs, specially flown in from Calcutta, only for Raghuji?"

"Pardon sir, I'm not a Bhangi. I'm a Mushahari. The fish eggs are ready."

Kalua bowed out and came back with a plateful of delicate *hilsa* eggs, batter fried with garlic, ginger, and a dash of green coriander and chilly.

"Heaven's here Raghuji, in these fried eggs." Ram Karan placed the plate in front of Raghu.

"I'm honoured Ramji. Heaven is like a shifting desert dune. It's here now and moments later it may lie between the thighs of a cute belle. Isn't it?"

"You charlatan!"

Ram Karan complimented his friend for mirroring so truly his own philosophy of life. Heaven, he always felt, didn't exist beyond money, women, wine and good food. He often boasted that God was discovered by deprived people, as an amorphous replica of the powerful and muscled mortal master, who raped their women, looted their belongings and occasionally allowed them to breathe.

"I'm facing tremendous problems from the Pakis, Karanji."

"It's a professional risk. You're as good a friend of Iskandar as I am. You're paid for these tasks. Use your discretion."

"Are you disowning me?"

"Come on Raghu," Ram Karan poured another whisky for his friend, "we've been together for all these years. How can I desert you? You can't desert a boat without a life jacket. Moreover, you won't like to have a bullet hole in your skull."

"Are you threatening me?"

"No. I'm just projecting the possibilities and suggesting a pragmatic way out."

"What's that?"

"Ask Iskandar to disengage. We have had enough of that business. Neither you nor I require that connection any more."

"You're wonderfully correct Karanji. I wonder how you keep your wisdom so well concealed!" Raghu's eyes rained fire and hatred, but he picked up another morsel of fried *hilsa* eggs and hastened to add, "oh my dear! I missed the main story of the day."

"What's so important?"

"It's very important Karanji. Shankarji wants you to organise a series of rallies, all over the country, supporting the PM's initiative on East Pakistan. He expects you to raise funds for national defence."

"Hope you aren't pulling another fast one."

"*Ma Kasam*. Shankarji wants something spectacular to be done. You're his nominee, to lead the campaign. It's a great honour."

"Raghuji, the goat nearest to the priest is the dearest and most convenient sacrificial beast. Closeness to Shankar can often be dangerous. Anyways, if Shankar so desires, I can't probably escape the rallies." Ram Karan enlightened Raghu Chawla with another nugget of his hidden wisdom.

"In fact, I've told Shankar that you've already started preparations for the rallies."

"You're great Raghu. Any compensation for this favour?"

"I'm not that mean Karanji. I'm a patriot too."

"All of us are, but business comes first."

"Business can wait, while we fight the enemy."

"Wrong, you're wrong again. Look at the British. They established empires, while trading, and we fucking Indians will destroy our national independence, because we don't allow honest trading."

Ram Karan, high on whisky, kept on cracking prophetic pronouncements.

"When do we meet Shankar?" He continued.

"At the earliest."

*

Shankar was thrilled over the idea of organising rallies in support of his mother. He bubbled with enthusiasm and disturbed his mother in the midst of a strategic meeting with a senior officer.

Manjira smiled indulgently and buried her head in the files. She didn't have time for rallies. She didn't require them. However, indulgent as she was to her younger son, Manjira didn't think that a few more straws on her wagon would matter much. Shankar's efforts should be able to generate a mass hysteria, in favour of her surgical operation against Pakistan. It could as well bring unity between the Hindus and the Muslims, who were yet to support her fully. Manjira gave a casual nod and asked her son to get along with the proposed rallies.

The mass rally, in support of the historic handling of the Bangladesh tangle, was planned on a grand scale. Never before had Delhi witnessed such a gala rally, not even on the eve of India's Independence or during the mammoth funeral procession of Mohandas Karamchand Gandhi. For the first time Hindu India was on the verge of humiliating a Muslim power, a power that had subjugated and occupied *Bharatvarsha* (India) about eleven centuries ago. It was a time to rejoice, it was time to reassert Hindu claim on the timeless mass of land, chronicled in mythology as *Jambudwipa,* the Jambu island. Some Hindu leaders had described Manjira as the mother goddess Durga, the supreme *Shakti* (power) that had destroyed the demons and restored the heavens to the gods.

People came from all conceivable directions, courtesy government resources, dressed in colourful regional apparel they could afford. After all, they had been brought to Delhi to see the daughter of Amritlal, granddaughter of Mahatma Gandhi (they believed) and a living incarnation of Mother Durga, invoked with a thousand names by devoted Hindus. The festive crowd, accommodated in huge tented mini-cities, thronged around the wonderful city of the Pandavas, Mughals and the British and that of Manjira Mai (mother). They used the sprawling lawns of India Gate as open-air lavatories and kitchenettes, with the green canopies serving as a natural cover.

October 20th dawned with a surge of human waves thronging the ramparts of the Red Fort. Manjira arrived precisely at 09.45, dressed in a white sari with a golden border, a golden blouse, and a coiffeur in traditional Indian style. She exuded the looks of a mother goddess. She surveyed the crowd of 1.5 million from atop the rostrum and spoke briefly on the threat from Pakistan and other foreign forces.

"I've precise information that the military demon in Pakistan is preparing for an all out war against India. They've got weapons from China, America and other sources." Manjira tried to touch the raw chords of the crowd.

"But, your daughter, whom you've given a strong mandate, shall not fail your expectations. You're members of my extended family and the people of Bengal, now being killed in millions, are my brothers and sisters. I shall protect you all with the last drop of my blood. Our armed forces are much stronger now. We shall emerge victorious." Spontaneous claps and roaring greetings reverberated with thundering echoes from the walls of the historic Red Fort.

"Evil forces inside and outside the country are bent upon assassinating me. I'm not afraid of such threats. I vow to fight the enemies of the nation to the last drop of my blood....

"Even at this venue enemy agents are on the prowl with deadly weapons. Ram Karanji, our veteran freedom fighter, who was a colleague of two former Prime Ministers and a worthy representative of the toiling masses, will be with you, to recount the harrowing tales of genocide by Pakistan."

Manjira, followed by son Shankar and members of her entourage, left the rostrum, amidst thunderous applause and slogans.

Ram Karan Prasad, in a rare realisation of self-fulfilment, started addressing the gathering. He invoked the names of Mahatma Gandhi and other leaders, who had guided the destiny of the nation from darkness to light. He was a small spark from those galactic events, Ram Karan added. He assured the roaring crowd that his small spark would add up to the blazing torch of freedom, democracy, and secularism, carried by Manjira on her shoulders. Goddess Durga, nemesis of all evil would be victorious, he had no doubt.

"*Bolo* Manjira *Mai ki jai*.... (Hail mother Manjira)... ."

Ram Karan Prasad's words instead of being blared out through the loudspeakers were suddenly shattered down to inaudible low decibel sound fragments. A sudden flash and fire, followed by a big bang threw the rostrum high up into the air. Ram Karan Prasad, the veteran freedom fighter and a permanent fixture in the union cabinet, was hit directly by an explosive charge, hidden below the specially built podium. Ram Karan wasn't alone in death.

The media described the gory and pathetic death of 50 others including a few security personnel. A devastating fire triggered off a menacing stampede, leading to the death of another sixty villagers, who were huddled into Delhi to have a glimpse of the city of the Mahabharata, Mughals, Maharani Victoria and Manjira Mai. Manjira loudly attributed the incident to the evil designs of foreign hands. She reminded the media of her speech, just before the explosion, which had shredded Ram Karan to bits and pieces. She ordered a high level judicial commission to enquire into the dastardly assassination of a national figure.

Media reports, however, quoted unnamed official sources, to put the blame on the Inter Services Intelligence of Pakistan. Raghu Chawla, in a front-page obituary described Ram Karan as the first Indian soldier martyred in the struggle for freedom of Bangladesh. His was a poetic and sentimental tribute from an old associate.

Brigadier Iskandar didn't wait for a formal farewell from the Saturday Club. He stealthily boarded a Cathy Pacific flight to Bangkok. His last assignment in Delhi was a roaring success.

*

50

The bang that killed Ram Karan was loudly heard all over the subcontinent. The media added to waves of speculation. While most eminent grey commentators articulated on sudden departure of an important diplomat of Pakistan High Commission, some linked it to Pakistan intelligence agencies, which aimed at sabotaging Ram Karan's valiant contribution to the freedom struggle in East Pakistan. Some commentators and analysts directed the needle of suspicion at the NSI and the FIB.

Nampoothiri did not join, generally wide off the mark, Delhi's professional analysts' club. It was not his duty to investigate an act of crime. Satisfaction came to him from closure of the historic file and an internal evaluation of the incident that killed Ram. It was a Pak job, he jotted in the margin.

He was more worried about his prized agent in Pakistan, Triple X. Mapping the precise contours of the depth of the psychological and situational quagmire, in which Triple X was just about to sink, was a specialised task. Nampoothiri had no better choice than Maulana Rizwan. He was known for his superb navigational acumen. Nampoothiri's expectation climaxed with Amrita's tinkle announcing Maulana's return from Colombo.

*

It wasn't customary for Nampoothiri to visit a nondescript hotel to meet a deep-cover agent. The top boss didn't customarily involve himself in minor operational tasks. But this was an unusual case. The usual NSI premises were out of bounds for Maulana Rizwan. Moreover, Nampoothiri didn't want his desk officers to debrief the Maulana, after completion of his Colombo mission.

Rizwan, by pre-arrangement, had checked into a little known inn. The seedy establishment, fronted by a charming lady, an off the roster secret service funded employee of the NSI, was very sparingly used for delicate agent meetings. Jatadhari Garo chauffeured the car and Nampoothiri, donning a beard and a mosque cap to match, visited the inn at the wrong side of midnight. He tapped the door using Morse language, read correctly by discerning Rizwan: BOSS.

"Welcome sir."

"Well Purohit, I need coffee first and tell me what's your report."

Rizwan's briefing enthralled Nampoothiri. Triple X was candid and open, the ace trainer disclosed. His cover was still intact. But a single act of indiscretion, though not a voluntary one, had put the ISI sleuths on his trail. The ISI hunters had started at the Jahanara end of the thread, but the signal intelligence boys were more skewed up by the mysterious emissions from his clandestine HF station. Rizwan estimated that usual security parameters were probably not observed while installing the trans-receiver. Harfan had no control over it. A technical expert should have done the job. That was the cardinal mistake. Nampoothiri digested the dig silently.

The later developments, like the induction of an Infantry Division to Jhumra and the presence of the Chinese radio transmission facility at the Bhagatanwala airbase had also narrowed down the signal security parameters against Harfan.

He was sure, Rizwan added, Triple X's incidental foray into the political minefield of Pakistan had created an explosive situation. He was accidentally drawn into the cross-conspiracies of the ambitious Generals. They were more anxious to give a dirty burial to General Arif than fighting a war with India.

"Any other special developments?"

"There are two. His employer's brother Nawab Sharief is after his blood, and he did not vibe well with Alamgir from day one."

"Triple X didn't give me any hint of it." Nampoothiri was happy to receive a confirmation of the report of Qurban from his most trusted officer.

"The moral of the story is," Rizwan tersely commented, "we simply can't afford to have an intermediate master in important remote operations."

"But we've a system of controlling such operations through our Mission based operators."

"That's fine sir. However, the clash of idiosyncrasies is a personalised matter. Their entire chemistry misfired."

Nampoothiri noted the pregnant observation. Rizwan was too veteran an intelligence artist and scientist to be ticked off. This nugget of advice received from Rizwan required microscopic examination.

"Is his cover still intact?"

"Yes and no. The ISI hasn't been able to crack his cover. But sir, you know the intelligence professionals. They won't take years to penetrate Harfan." Rizwan spoke in his usual flowery style.

"Well said Purohit. Have all the equipment been removed?"

"No problem. Alam has taken care of it, but…" Rizwan abruptly stopped.

"What's the problem?"

"Arms ferrying is a transient cover for Harfan. I think they've chosen him out of compulsion."

"You mean he's a disposable tissue!"

"I suspect so."

"What's your suggestion?"

"There's one more point."

"Come clean Purohit."

"I feel Triple X and Alam have developed not merely temperamental but functional incompatibility. Harfan has perceived whiffs of burning hostility ... perhaps, professional jealousy, from Alam's behaviour."

Rizwan explained the most delicate part of the briefing. He was aware of the special relationship between Nampoothiri and Alam.

Nampoothiri didn't respond. He lighted a Havana and asked for another coffee.

"Would you suggest neutralisation? What're the chances of his defecting to the other side? Can he betray us?" he made anxious enquiries.

"How did you get that impression? I've trained him. I know he won't do that." Rizwan asserted.

"Don't be emotional Rizwan." Nampoothiri mildly chided his expert.

"Pardon sir," Rizwan came out frankly, "a spark flies to extinction. I feel Harfan is guarding the fire under his chest. He is not a spark. He loves his job and family."

"That's the problem. I wouldn't like his wife to become a part of his life. She's a cover, nothing more, nothing less."

"I get you sir. I suggest you deactivate the operation. Let him temporarily hibernate in a new station. In the meantime he should be advised to observe anti-surveillance measures, protect his cover and use communication channels sparingly."

"Any other psychological change in him?"

"He's suffering from anxiety. Didn't open up on his future plans. He maintains a sullen silence whenever Alam's name is mentioned."

"Has he developed hostility towards him?"

"Better say, distrust."

Nampoothiri gave an imperceptible nod. Yes, he could visualise the debris of the bridge of trust.

"Thanks Shyam," Nampoothiri stood up, "you're excellent, as usual. Let me think over the inputs."

"One final request." Rizwan followed the boss to the door.

"Be frank."

"Handle the situation yourself. Don't allow Alam to decide Triple X's fate. And do it as early as possible sir."

Nampoothiri nodded approvingly. He understood the gravity and sensitivity of the situation. The Triple X affair had suddenly thrown up important issues, threatening a total operation collapse in Pakistan. He would have to take a fine chiselled decision. Perhaps Triple X could be relocated, albeit temporarily, in a safer station

*

Back to his hole, Nampoothiri closed the door and asked Jatadhari and Amrita Bhalla not to disturb him, unless calls were from the Prime Minister and stations

Zebra and Cobra–the headquarters of the Provisional Government of Bangladesh in Calcutta and Jessore respectively.

Nampoothiri opened the electronically controlled safety vault, took out a numerical cipher pad, specially designed for Triple X individual agents abroad. The message was simple. *Operation Retrieval* was set in motion: Triple X should shift to London immediately and await fresh instructions. He should take a particular foot track to cross over to Afghanistan, from where he would be flown to Moscow and London. Kabul would have his latest diplomatic travel documents. His family could join him later.

Nampoothiri sealed the communication in a tamper-proof hollow capsule, resembling a piece of broken edged brick. He buzzed the intercom.

"Yes sir!" Amrita entered promptly.

"There's a small job dear. Send this to Kabul by A category diplomatic bag."

"Anything else sir?"

"Yes dear. Originate a cipher and ask Kabul station chief to personally hand over the packet to Alamgir."

"Done sir."

Amrita walked out gracefully with the packet.

The drill devised by Nampoothiri was ingenious. Alamgir would place the drop at a pre-determined Dead Letter Box. He would direct Triple X to pick up the drop and adjust his needle in accordance with the new instructions direct from *Behest.* This, he would understand, was the final signal for him to vanish; another piece of Indian rope trick.

*

Vanishing wasn't exactly what churned inside Harfan. His world had changed, in its entire connotation, since Vudurume's flight landed at Bhagatanwala, a subsidiary airbase of Sargodha. Israr Sharief's soothing nonsense notwithstanding, he could hear the alarm bell ticking away, somewhere deep inside of him. The animal in him whispered loudly that its primordial radar had picked up signals of a rumbling quake.

Harfan, seated in a corner of Imperial Plaza, a special dining room in Hotel Royal Palace, maintained a cultivated brave face. Dinner served by Ibadat was usually superb.

"How do you like the food sir?" Ibadat's question snapped his chain of thought.

"Excellent, straight from heaven. How have you been?" Harfan applied delicate pressure on a chunk of prawn and enquired.

"Fine. How're Jamilla *bhabhi* (sister in law) and Pervez?"

"They should be fine. Haven't met them for two weeks."

"I've something special to talk." Ibadat whispered while pouring water.

"Let's take a stroll, the rooms may not be safe."

"There's a problem. Place order at the front counter for home delivery dinner. Expect me at 8 p.m."

Ibadat collected the plates and moved away behind the pantry curtain. Harfan ignited his car engine for the next thirty minutes' journey to Sangla. His thoughts hovered over a scattered spectrum.... Jamilla-Pervez.-the ISI dragnet-Alam and his latest encounter with Maulana Rizwan.

He was convinced that the end of the road was just around the corner and that time had come for taking a firm decision, a joint decision with Jamilla, for a life beyond the ISI and the NSI. A spy was bonded to the ethics of his profession, if there were any, but he surely had a right to his life and liberty. Ignoble death was not the *produit m fini* of his life.

Harfan's broken collage of thoughts was snapped by a queer spectacle. Two Toyotas were piloting and escorting him, in a sandwich mobile surveillance format. The Mosur (mobile surveillance) teams maintained a studied distance of about 50 yards, at either end. This was a known surveillance pattern, caging the suspect in between the sandwich. Yes. Ibadat wasn't behaving funnily. He was living up to his tradecraft training. His hints simply reflected the truth that the noose around his neck was tightening up. Who could they be? The ISI nemesis!

By God! Harfan felt a shiver travelling through his spine. Chain reactions burnt spontaneously in the psyche of some intelligence professionals. They hardly slept. Some people in the dreaded agency didn't sleep at all.

Israr's assurances were playroom palliatives. The poor good soul! The false assurances from General Sarfaraz had swayed him. General Hyder and the ISI weren't likely to miss their kill, simply because an expendable *muhajir* was helping them out in the arms lifting operations. Somewhere, some determined sleuths were keeping the pendulum swinging, silently but inevitably.

That was a bad news indeed.

Harfan didn't make any effort to dodge the surveillance vehicles. He maintained a steady 60 km. and drove straight to Israr's factory. The Mosur officials baffled by total lack of concern of their target, peeled off, half a kilometre short of the factory gate. The Toyota on Harfan's tail took a right turn, exposing a full profile of the surveillance officer. It was an evil looking, pockmarked face, with a deep furrow on the forehead, resembling a carpet-bombed battle terrain. The eyes looked cool and fierce, ready to pump out burning lead. Harfan couldn't focus his gaze straight on that killer face. Yes. The nemesis was closing in. Counterintelligence was a game of endless reflecting mirrors. Its vista stretched the captured image to infinity, until the eternal crunch finally smashed the suspect to ionised particles.

Harfan didn't take long to perceive the ultimate peril closing on him. He was captured inside the dark mirrored chamber. But, why the killer looks? Harfan tucked the idea deep inside as he walked into Israr's office. Israr wasn't alone. Alam, seated on the right end of the table, was sipping coffee and General Naqi, with a Brigadier in tow, was busy discussing some papers.

"You needn't send a slip in," Israr fondly admonished Harfan, "even when I'm not alone. You know all, I presume."

"I'm Harfan Bukhari." He extended his palm to greet the Brigadier.

"I'm Zia, Brigadier Zia-ul-Haqqani, from 9 Azad Kashmir Regiment. Glad to meet you. I'm an upgraded version of your old friend Captain Ayub. You're a legend by now. Doing extremely well, I hear."

The Brigadier heaped praises on Harfan, while speaking through his protruding incisors. His deep sunken eyes, almost lost below bushy brows, emitted different signals.

Harfan noticed the masked laughter and disguised daggers in his eyes. It was a brand butcher's look.

Atmospheric and static noises of a radio trans-receiver disturbed the monotony of the meeting. The sounds came from a cubicle next to Israr's toilet. Alam's station was busy, Harfan presumed. Business as usual, eh!

"We've worked out the broadsheet of supplies delivered so far. Ten sorties are over, eight more to go before November tenth." Israr tossed the papers at Harfan.

"There're problems," Alam intervened, "my contacts in Cyprus are fidgety over dangerous buzzing by Indian fighters. Capt. Vudurume has serious reservations. Other pilots are unwilling to fly."

"What do you say Harfan?" General Naqi asked.

"Alam sahib is correct. You can even see the Indian pilots grinning at us," Harfan replied, "without protective air cover it's a touch and go affair."

"You all know the problem best. We can't expose our Air Force birds to the Indians, not at this stage." General Naqi added.

"*Bandish* (code for Doug Chris) has jacked up rates by an additional 4%," Alam commented stoically.

"Bastard," swore Brig. Zia menacingly, while pushing up his drooping moustache, "the dogs are demanding more than they can chew. Do we have to pay that much?"

"It's blackmailing." Alam walked towards the anteroom and closed the door behind him. He emerged out in five minutes, with a paper in hand.

"What's new?" Israr asked.

"Station *Bandish* is negative. We've to cough up an additional 4%, towards the cost of increased insurance fees. Else, we can fuck off. That's a clear message."

"That's not my cup of tea," General Naqi, the Defence Advisor, threw up his hands, "only the top man can decide. Let's go Zia. We'll be in touch." He left, a disappointed man.

"Are you home tonight?" Alam asked Harfan.

"I presume not, may go to Lahore. Any urgent business?" Harfan sounded dry and formal.

"Nothing special." Alam stood up and gestured to Harfan to follow him in the transmission room.

"I feel the noose is tightening around you." Alam whispered.

"Thanks for the information." Harfan smiled back, rather nonchalantly.

"It's time for you to wind up, if you want to avoid the bullets."

"Whose bullet Alam sahib? Don't frighten any more. Tell me if you can help. Remember, if I'm pushed to the gallows, you're sure to walk the plank."

"You can't betray the country."

"That's the last thing I'd do, be rest assured. But, the country can't write me off either. I'm not a bad debt."

"It's better you pull up your guard. The ISI is ruthless, when it comes to firing at Indian targets." Alam's naughty wink pained Harfan.

"Thanks for the tip. Tell me something better." Harfan replied mechanically.

"Bravado won't pay Harfan. In our job, we take well-considered decisions. Wait for fresh instructions." Alam shifted his gaze, uncomfortable with Harfan's opaque looks.

"Thanks." Replied Harfan coolly.

Alam's departing dead-fish looks scared Harfan. He looked like a frustrated hangman stepping out of the planks with knotted ropes tucked behind, his mission unfulfilled. Alam gave an effusive jerk as he shook Israr's hand. He didn't look back at Harfan.

"Don't disappoint me Alam sahib." Israr pleaded.

"The disappointment will be mutual brother Israr. It'll be a national disappointment, if Doug reneges."

"Try your best to get him on our terms."

"Oh sure, I'd. And my friend Harfan would take care of the rest." He threw a dry smile and left.

*

Momentarily Harfan was lost in his dark thoughts.

Was Alam planning a nasty trick, his own brand of operation elimination? Or was there a rat race between the NSI and the ISI for reaching his jugular?

"Where are you? Lahore?" Israr's words brought Harfan's thoughts back to the present, "have patience and you can zoom down to your *mehbooba* (lover), tonight itself."

"How're things in the East?" Israr added without waiting for Harfan's reaction to his innocent joke.

"Hopeless. The Bengalis feel cheated and they're not ready to co-habit with us.

"Bangladesh appears to be a reality." Harfan replied.

"Is it safe for the sorties?"

"No, not really. But I'm ready for whatever is expected of me. Can't betray the country."

"That's like Mian Harfan."

Getting down to business talks Harfan explained that, if Alam's party was asking for 4% more, Israr should as well demand an added 3%. The risk factor was enormous.

"I think I should. In this business, your share is well above rupees five million. You can take it any time." Israr made a generous offer.

"Please transfer the money to my off-shore account. I don't like the tax people troubling me again."

"That's fine with me. In the meantime, sort out the pending inventory of weapons. I would be out to Karachi."

"How much are you paying Alam?" Harfan asked.

"I don't pay him. Probably he has an arrangement with Doug. Perhaps Naqi takes care of it. Why ask?"

"Don't you think Doug's additional 4% is pretty high?"

"What can we do? Anyways, the money flows up, I mean subterranean, the Indus from the Potomac. I don't have any qualms if Alam makes few extra bucks in the bargain." Israr disengaged and left Harfan to complete the paper work.

Inside Israr's empty office Harfan worked out the data, took a print out and explained the intricacies to Israr's secretary.

His mind was not completely occupied by Israr's business calculation. A vast vacant corner was occupied by Jamilla, Pervez and the churning twister of threats from the ISI. Lifting weapons was a priority but ensuring safety of his family and escaping the ISI nutcracker were on top of his agenda. Harfan lighted a cigarette, instructed the office staff to close the shop, and boarded the car with expectations and trepidations clashing inside like thunder bearing clouds.

*

With Latiff behind the wheel, Harfan concentrated on the surveillance tails. He didn't have to look back. A small pocket cosmetic mirror helped him keeping track of the tails cruising in a pair formation. One of them was falling back, once in a while, giving a chance to his colleagues to go ahead. They played a funny game, like young monkeys trying to climb up a greased pole, under the cover of assumed trees and bushes where there were none. The fools!

Harfan asked Latiff to press more gas in and to take care of the fleet of trucks rushing in from opposite direction. The ISI Mosurs didn't expect the sudden surge of the Mercedes, already cruising well above 100 km. Their mothballed cars faded away in Harfan's mirror and he was well within sight of his Jhumra home a few minutes later. He anxiously waited for dinner. Not so much for the food, but for Ibadat. The old loyal had whispered in the morning about a special message. Ibadat's special talks often turned out to be prophetic.

Harfan was not worried about the Mosurs anymore. He wasn't even anxious about the Tesurs (technical surveillance). He had seen their faces, understood their intentions and expected them either to fire from their stunted barrel .38 colts or spirit him away to one of their torture chambers.

He wasn't ready to oblige the ISI hunters yet. It didn't matter any more, if the lunatics in Delhi and Islamabad preferred to lock their horns in another mutual suicide pact. The fools were capable of doing that.

Shit! There was no fun in serving these zombies, the hay and clay stuffed politicians and bureaucrats, any more. He had had enough of patriotism! Fine! The underlying philosophy had crystallised. But how could he forget his father's assassins? That was his personal agenda. He could not renege on that resolve.

How could he ascertain the identity of his father's assassin? Was he still around? The vague idea of avenging his father's killers could not be achieved without ascertaining the identity of the killers. He was not on a mission to declare war on Pakistan and its people. Who was he to do that? Harfan Bukhari was a mere minor tool in the abominable war machine.

The debate shredded Harfan into pieces.

Harfan sat facing the fireplace after a quick shower, with his favourite choice of whisky. He dialled the Lahore number and reached Jamilla. She was, Harfan mused, the most proximate and important person in his life, whom he could face frankly and boldly at any moment of truth. That moment was there, and would vanish into past with his bones and ashes. He could discern the footsteps of destiny catching up with him. Jamilla should know the truth, from his mouth and not from the rumour mills.

Ibadat's footsteps broke the serpentine rhythm of his thoughts. Harfan declutched and looked out. A lone foot-watcher was still lurking at the entrance alley of his home, taking cover behind a cluster of dwarf pines.

Ibadat didn't look at the burly Multani with a rustic ambience and a massive moustache on his bloated face. He was almost a permanent fixture, standing there from 2 p.m. until 12 p.m. to the dot. His bulging loin betrayed the presence of a pistol and a VHF communication set.

Fools! Ibadat mused. They should have the common sense of changing the faces at random. What was the fun in ritually positioning that fat blob in front of Harfan's gate?

"Have you noticed that guy?" Ibadat asked.

"Yah. I've smelt him more."

"How come?"

"He uses the pine bush as his urinal. The whole place stinks." Harfan laughed.

"You haven't drawn the curtains and the TV is off." Ibadat wasn't happy to see Harfan in a contemplative and depressed mood.

"What difference does it make?"

"Lots," Ibadat arranged the curtains, increased the television volume and continued, "you should take care of voice activated vibration recording devices, which pick up and transmit wave modulations."

"How do you know that? Who're you?"

Ibadat didn't reply. He silently went about his chores.

"Food is ready." Ibadat announced.

"Go to hell, you and your food," Harfan stood up in an aggressive mood, "You haven't replied me."

He emptied his glass into the faint embers of the fireplace. The tongues of flame momentarily shoot up licking the stale air. Harfan's gaze, fixed on the fire, reflected his inner turmoil. Ibadat looked squarely into Harfan's eyes and displayed a cross sign with his index and middle fingers.

Harfan stepped back in surprised recognition of the code taught by Dhiren Bhagat. It meant that Ibadat was something special. They were on the same side of the fence. Ibadat wasn't a small time agent of Alam. A Double X agent of the NSI, he had direct links to Delhi, most probably through Station Kabul, with an independent communication channel.

"Perhaps you'd like to wash." Ibadat silently led Harfan to a toilet and closed the door behind.

"You're required to keep a date at point Chinar, at the battered Mughal time west wall of *Shalimar* Gardens on October 30th, and pick up an important drop." Ibadat whispered.

"Is this room safe?"

"Yes. See that blue lamp? It's an infra ray vibrator, oscillating at 240 cycles and creating a sub-sonic noise, not audible to human ears. It's capable of driving all electronic listening devices crazy. To ordinary eyes it's nothing but an insect repellent."

"What're the timings?"

"Read this. Don't ask questions aloud. The enemies are on the prowl. Act according to new instructions. My instructions are to declutch from you. Henceforth, we'll meet only in the hotel. Don't visit Ramayani."

"Why?"

"She's on the ISI hit list. She knows your real identity and may buckle down under pressure. Don't fiddle with her."

"Can't she be spirited away to India?"

"Not now. Let the storm-clouds blow over. We shall try."

"What're the chances?"

"It's still fifty-fifty in your favour. They're professionals and won't give up easily."

They emerged out of the toilet and ate dinner amidst small talks about Pervez, Jamilla and Harfan's risky job of ferrying weapons to East Pakistan. Ibadat tuned on the television and started talking in a low voice.

"Listen carefully. I'm not a great guy, but I've my ears to the ground. Your mission is almost over."

"Is the old lady safe?" Harfan abruptly asked.

"Think of yourself and your mission. Leave the rest to us." Ibadat almost admonished Harfan.

"Tell me the identity of my father's killers." —Harfan wrote down on a piece of paper.

"Why?" —Ibadat too scribbled.

"Do me this favour." —Again a silent scribble.

"The pockmarked battered-moon face, the one on your tail. He's Arman Ali Niazi, an employee of the ISI. He's the killer. Take care. He shoots before asking questions." —

Ibadat scribbled back.

"Thanks for the good dinner, brother Ibadat. Another question. What are your orders? To kill me?"

"No comments. Be sure that your father's salt still runs in my veins. I won't fire the first shot." Ibadat scribbled back and stood up.

Harfan opened the door for him and said *Khuda Hafiz*. He turned back to the fireplace, threw the paper pellets on the dying tongues of fire, which were still emitting the mellow fragrance of pine resin.

*

51

Mian Alam Khan's dark-alley diplomacy, Israr Sharief's treasure chest, and favourable winks from General Naqi finally clinched the issue of chartering additional flights from the CIA short-listed Athena Air Lines. General Sarfaraz and the Chief of Army Staff too had pitched in. The American ambassador and the CIA station chief in Islamabad had facilitated their task. Their boys had crosschecked with Doug Chris and vetted the genuineness of the enhanced '*risk factor cost.*' Washington, Alam boasted, had gladly signed on the dotted line, approving an additional expenditure of $ 500 million. Islamabad couldn't have any reservations, if Washington had none. The hardware was sure to reach Dacca before the mid-November deadline and the coffers of whoever mattered in Pakistan were sure to be filled to the brim.

It was indeed a time to celebrate.

But Nawab Sharief had very little to celebrate. He had failed yet again to reach the source of the supply bonanza. His coterie of Generals and politicians, no less illustrious than the Sarfaraz-Naqi faction, had failed to have their way with the Americans, and of course with the CMLA. The top boss and his ladylove developed neuronal flu whenever the name of Nawab figured in talks with Hyder Bux and other Generals. That evil fungus, Jahanara openly blurted out in one of the meetings, was poisonous.

General Hyder Bux, a profound admirer of Nawab Sharief 's business acumen and political penetration, finally threw up hands. He got a clear message that General Arif wouldn't touch Nawab with a bargepole. Washington wasn't willing to change its horse midway. The same Cyprus based company, an established CIA surrogate, had bagged the contract. That meant an addition of more than rupees 100 million to Israr's coffer. To hell with it!

Nawab stormed into his Volvo and shouted at the chauffeur to drive straight to General Hyder's residence.

Merry hell! Hyder wasn't there. Of all places, Hyder's batman informed, his boss had gone to the *jama masjid* at Ramna-6 for offering *eshan* prayers (last prayer of the day). Nawab's car screeched to a halt in front of the *jama masjid.* He removed his shoes, performed the ritual oblations, and walked up to the prayer hall.

General Hyder, standing in the last row of the gathering of the faithful, with a mosque cap on his head looked entirely lost in his prayers. Nawab crawled up and joined the General after placing a mosque cap on his scalp.

"Sir..." he tried to open up a dialogue.

"Shh..." Hyder bent down with the rest of the faithful, his eyes still closed.

"There's a big problem..."

"Not here..." Hyder concentrated on his prayers.

"Your prayers can wait. My problem can't."

"Shh! Follow the rituals." Hyder whispered back.

The prayer assembly dispersed after about twenty agonising minutes. Nawab finally cornered General Hyder near the foyer of the *hujra* (room of the chief *mullah*)

"It's a blatant betrayal General. I've been let down."

"Can't get you Nawab." Replied General Hyder Bux.

"I'm talking about the airlifting contract. I paid two million in advance, yet the fresh contract has been awarded to brother Israr."

"Sorry Nawab. I'd pitched in with Naqi and the COAS," Hyder shrugged, "but you know I'm not the final authority in Pakistan."

"Why don't you remove that imbecile Arif and rape his woman? Pitch in with Izaz and I assure you a top slot in the new dispensation."

"Have patience Nawab. We shall have our day."

"What about my money?"

"You can take back my share of it, but I can't stand guarantee for the rest." Hyder started walking towards his car.

"You mean that whore would decide our fate and that bloody Harfan would keep on fucking her! What're you doing about that lousy Indian agent?" Nawab gave vent to his frustrations in a rather loud voice.

"Shh," Hyder advised caution, "Not so loud."

"Why can't you hang him?"

"Nawab sahib, have patience. Don't make wild allegations. We're not ameatures," General Hyder started walking down the steps, "we're on the job."

"Should I approach the Director Military Intelligence? You're taking the matter very lightly. Are you afraid of that whore?"

"Nawab sahib, enough of your shit," Hyder replied in a grim voice, "I don't serve under the MI. Don't mix up your business rivalry with matters of the state. I'm the spymaster. I know who fucks whom in Pakistan. I know who all are your beaus in Pakistan and London. Shall I get a list published in the *Dawn*?"

"You're wrong Hyder sahib. I fuck beaus at my own cost. Who doesn't in darn Pakistan? The army alone doesn't own this country," Nawab protested vehemently, "it's not my business I'm referring to. I'm talking about Pakistan's security."

"Leave that to us, we're the professionals. Don't interfere with what Harfan is doing now. And don't stretch the elastic beyond a point. Paying advance goodwill money doesn't guarantee any contract. You know the system."

"But I've invested."

"That's risk money. You often lose it. And Nawab, we in the ISI aren't pusillanimous about people badgering us."

Hyder asked his driver to accelerate to the office of the Chief Martial Law Administrator. He was supposed to be present in an inter-services briefing to the President.

*

Nawab sulked for a while under the arch of the mosque, and hurled abuses at General Hyder, for milking him of rupees two million.

Once inside his Volvo, Nawab picked up his car phone and dialled the number of General Naim, the PIB chief.

"Hi General, how's life? Can I drop in? There's something hot that's come up and it's related to our national security."

"Come on, if you're so keen." General Naim didn't like to offend the most poisonous viper in Pakistan. Hanging precariously on to his position at the mercy of brother Arif and Jahanara, he had discovered to his charm, that patience paid. These politicians were strange animals and democracy was a curse to the humanity. Tomorrow this bloody Nawab could dump him in the garbage bin. And vipers like Nawab kissed sweetly once in a blue moon, if it served their business and political interests.

Nawab switched on the engine and added his anger to the fuel. The Volvo kicked up a cloud of dust and raced towards General Naim's residence. He had made up mind to share with the PIB chief some sensitive secrets concerning Israr and Harfan. The celebrity brother must also be made aware of the conspiracy hatched by General Hyder and Sarfaraz. He had in his pocket a few transcripts of the telephone conversations between the ISI chief and the PSO. That should give clinching proof of their evil designs. He had enough colour in store to paint Harfan as an Indian spy.

Nawab lighted a cigarette, spat out a curse directing Israr and Harfan to the abyss of roaring hell. He must bag this contract at any cost.

*

Harfan Bukhari was out on his own errands.

The new contract and the additional flights sounded good. However, he wasn't sure of the ground below him. The smiling faces and the bulging pockets couldn't lull the scratched psyche of the injured jackal.

The thought of fathoming the waves of the swirling tsunami about to hit his coastline struck him as he drove leisurely along Lahore's busy market place. Tailed by the Mosur he swung the Toyota Corolla into the highway. The surveillance vehicle was determined to shadow Harfan bumper-to-bumper, afraid of losing his tail. Harfan sighted the pockmarked face and muttered a silent curse. The tail deserved some twisting. The beast must pay for his crime.

Harfan's priority was to shake off the leech, as quickly as possible. He required some free space and time to drop a DLB to Delhi on the latest contract with AAL and to be with Jamilla and Pervez at the earliest.

The decision to dodge the ISI tail electrified his Delhi campus chemicals. Harfan swung his car again, and guided the wheels towards General Naqi's office. He'd like to buy some time, share his thoughts with Jamilla and work out a strategy. He couldn't allow the Mosur to trail him to Jamilla's bedroom.

Harfan sped along Circular Road and entered Anarkali market. He cut through a lane across Nasir Road and emerged at Montgomery. The Mosur car, cruising along the narrow lane, lost control, hit a few handcarts vending vegetables. An angry mob instantly surrounded the occupants. The pockmarked face took out a pistol and fired in the air. The mob pounced on him and the frenzy left Arman Ali Niazi bruised and battered. Harfan accelerated for the Cantonment area. Poor chap! He felt sorry for the battered face with a drooping moustache. His canvas was often painted with rotund face with deeps and peaks, which often licked lips, like a hungry hyena on prowl.

The DLB, an unsealed streetlight junction box, was about a kilometer from General Naqi's office. He secured the small packet in the mesh of wires and suddenly remembered that Brigadier Zia Haqqani, the jackal with rodent teeth and sunken eyes, had replaced Ayub. Why not sound that coin? What excuse could he proffer for visiting the ubiquitous officer from Jullandhar in Indian Punjab?

Why not discuss Vudurume's latest met-report! He had called from Karachi to share the US satellite reports about a swirling cyclone hanging over the funnel of the Bay of Bengal. It wouldn't be safe to fly for another two days, unless the wild swirling low altitude demon took an unexpected turn towards the Indian coast.

Harfan's visit, an unannounced one, surprised Zia. He liked surprises, only when he could spring one upon his rivals. He detested the reverse traffic. His drooping moustache moved up and down, and his thick eyebrows twisted in all conceivable directions conveying surprise and displeasure. Zia sucked his sunken cheeks in, displayed his rodent teeth, and made a grunting sound. It was supposed to be a sort of smile.

Harfan had no plausible excuse to be there.

His next flight to Dacca was scheduled for 25th October, and Harfan's brief was to join Capt. Vudurume at Sargodha. He wasn't supposed to visit this office. Not many were welcome to this hole. Many in Pakistan weren't even aware of the clandestine airlifting of Chinese and NATO weapons to Dacca and Chittagong, using the services of internationally infamous mercenaries. Harfan was a mere *kurta* on display in the boutique of General Naqi. Efficient he was, but very expendable. There'd be no tears, no epitaph, and no requiem, if his flight disappeared from the East Pakistan skies. He was just another mercenary, a means to an end. Why should he show up his asshole here?

"What brings you here Harfan?" Zia didn't suppress his anxiety, if not annoyance.

"Well Brigadier!" Harfan drew a chair and thrust himself on the puzzled officer. He enjoyed Zia's not too opaque discomfiture, "I've a message from Capt. Ram."

"Who's bloody Ram? We don't know any by that damned Hindu name."

"I mean Vudurume. You know he is a Hindu of Indian origin." Harfan enjoyed the dancing of the eyebrows of the Brigadier.

"He doesn't exist for me. He's your baby." Brigadier Haqqani replied in his accented Jullandhar Punjabi.

"That's not the point," Harfan replied in Lahoria Punjabi, "the pilot says that the depression hanging over the Andamans is travelling North East and may hit the East Pakistan coast any time. Storm cloud level is 30,000 feet. He won't fly till the churning storm clears up."

"Have you informed the General?"

"I'm on two days' furlough. Perhaps you'd favour me if you inform the General. You're the boss."

"Have a coffee."

"Thanks boss. I must move. Wish to see a movie. The Delight is screening an old Raj Kapoor starred movie."

"How can they show an Indian movie?"

"Sir, I'm an ordinary Pakistani. I'm not well informed on such complicated matters." Harfan winked at the distorted furrows on Zia's face and threw him a twinkling smile, as he left the room.

He didn't completely bluff the seasoned Jullandhari. He had just exaggerated the preliminary report received from Vudurume. October-November was the usual time for cyclones and typhoons in the delta funnel of the Ganges, Meghna and Brahmaputra, which often penetrated deep inland, carrying apocalypse in their trails. The Bengalis, living on either side of the vast delta, dreaded, hated, and worshipped these churning weather demons and gods. They worshipped the storm deities with more fervour than they observed the Islamic rituals, to the serious consternation of the better-trained Muslims.

Needling Brigadier Zia was a pleasure. Harfan didn't take a liking to his rattail moustache and python eyes. His rodent smile did not remind him of Bugs Bunny, the ever-funny cartoon. In Zia he smelt another military ruler in the making. Harfan didn't like to take a chance with the sucker-climber.

He knew his spin would travel far and long. The Defence wouldn't take seconds to cross check with Alam. Doug Chris would be consulted and it would finally bounce back to the Karachi camp of Vudurume. He was a stickler for the rules of the skies and safety of his bird. It was better to keep him in the picture.

Harfan decided to get back to Israr and Vudu and give them an account of his encounter with Naqi's deputy. First, he called Israr and advised him to remain in touch with Naqi. Next, he called Vudu.

"Hello Captain, have you anything on the latest met report?"

"Twisters over the Bay?"

"Yes. We call it a cyclone, often deadlier."

"Yeah, the WSAT predicts intensification of the cyclone. It is likely to hover over the delta for another two days and hit the East Pakistan coast with a speed of

250 miles per hour. Cloud ceiling is 35 to 45,000 ft. I don't like the idea of being sucked into the eye of the cyclone. Relax, and my best wishes to your queen and crown prince." Vudu replied.

"I happened to visit Brigadier Zia. Shared the info with him and Israr."

"Fine. Take care of your lovely lady."

"I need the wings of your prayers to be there with them. Thanks pal." Harfan disconnected the line and steadied the wheel towards Lahore.

*

52

After a warm and satisfactory togetherness Jamilla had gone to sleep, her body covered with a fine embroidered tribal Baluchi rug. Harfan had purchased this precious piece from Karachi's Zainab market, Pakistan's best address for carpets and rugs. Pervez was fast asleep in his cradle.

Harfan walked over to the window, opened a panel, and lighted a cigarette. The silhouettes of the minarets of the Mosque of Maryam Zamani looked eerie in melting opaque darkness. The grey sky, still clinging to a few departing stars, provided an infinite and expectant panoramic canvass.

A pale reddish hue momentarily gleamed on the white marble dome of the mosque. A slice of moon, still hanging reluctantly behind the tallest minaret of the house of God, reminded Harfan that the sun was about to make its inevitable appearance as it had been doing for over last four billion years or so.

The *muezzin* (mosque-crier) was about to remind the faithful, over his loudspeaker, of the greatness of the God—*Allah-hu-Akbar*. It was time for the believer to say *fajr namaj* (morning prayer).

"Come to bed." Jamilla whispered.

Harfan extinguished the cigarette and turned back.

"I want to say something."

"Come closer."

Harfan didn't move. His bare upper body glistened with sweat, not because of the volcanic convulsions of conjugal encounter that had lasted nearly two hours. This was usual with Jamilla. She extracted the last drop of Harfan's energy and still yearned for more. This early morning sweat was due to nervousness and anxiety. Harfan faced the silhouette of the mosque and said a silent prayer, *Bismillah-ar-Rehman-er-Rahim*.

"I want to say something." He advanced towards the bed.

Jamilla pulled the rug around her and sat up.

"What's bugging you dear? Any problem at workplace?"

"No. Pardon me for betraying your holy trust."

"I never said anything about that Jahanara witch."

"It's not that. Let me have my say. This is the best time to face the truth. This is the time for saying the payers and facing the *Allah*."

Harfan continued.

"I'm not a Pakistani and not a born Muslim, though I was in a way converted. I'm in Pakistan to spy for India." Harfan spoke fast, the words overlapped and produced a whispering effect, as if his lung was emptied of oxygen.

"You're a spy! Of all things you're a spy!" Jamilla looked with disbelief and moved away from Harfan.

"Listen my story. You've the right to do whatever you like after you hear me out. Be sure, I'm true to you and Pervez. I love you both. Without you my life has no meaning."

Harfan spoke haltingly, narrating the essentials of his story and the threat he was now facing from the Inter Services Intelligence and the National Security India's station boss, Mian Alam Khan. They were bound to catch up with him, sooner or later.

"Harfan, you married me only because you wanted a shield, a believable cover?"

Jamilla tightened the rug around her body.

"No. You're not a part of the mission. At the Lahore Fort, I lost my way in your eyes. The blue eyes had mesmerised me. My love has nothing to do with my profession. Yes, I'm a spy. A real spy doesn't care for emotion and love. I could've disappeared, leaving you two behind. I'm here because I love you."

"And you're the Prince of Jhumra! You came to avenge your father's assassination and destroy Pakistan in the bargain!"

"A Prince I could have been. Thank *Allah*; I'm not one. Yes, I want to square up with the killers of my father. I'm not an enemy of the people."

"How can you love us Harfan, me and Pervez, when you're propelled by hatred?"

"I was, when I was launched, as a tool of destruction. My love is my life now. In your love, I've lost the keys to my steaming storehouse of hatred. All of us have been victims of deceit, prejudice, and perverse political manoeuvres. I want to live with you and Pervez." Harfan gently put his hand on the covered shoulder of Jamilla and applied a slight squeeze.

Jamilla tightened the rug, and momentarily disappeared to the toilet. Harfan gently tapped on the door and begged her to come out.

"Listen. My love is mine, only mine. I confess my faults. Please come out. I've very little time left. Listen to me."

Jamilla, now fully dressed, opened the door.

Muezzin's distant voice recited—'Praise be to *Allah*, unto Whom belongeth whatsoever is in the heavens and whatsoever is in the earth.'

She walked straightaway to the cradle, stirred the milk for Pervez, and started feeding him.

"I suspect my cover is about to be blown up. The ISI is closing in."

"Harfan, I feel cheated, not because you're a spy. You're a pawn in the power game between our two stupid countries, a prop in the hands of the professional killers. I've nothing to do with your politics and espionage." Jamilla's facial muscles relaxed. Tears cascaded down her cheeks.

"You should understand how they killed my father and forced my mother out. I came to take revenge."

"On whom? All Pakistanis? I'm a Pakistani too. Why this drama of love? Why don't you kill this Pakistani first! Killing doesn't solve problems. Wars can be fought by peace. Jihad is not the solution to ills around you." Jamilla spoke in a choked voice.

"Jami, the truth can be seen only when the debris settle down. Truth is a layered onion, you keep on peeling, and finally you get lost. Now I understand, my love is my truth. I stand by you and Pervez as a loving husband and father. That's my truth. It can't be peeled." Harfan spelt out truly felt and believed in.

"What do you expect of me?" Jamilla asked.

"Your options are open. If you like call the ISI and hand me over."

"How could you say that? How can you doubt my love?" Jamilla replied with a calm and composed voice.

"I've only three options before me." Harfan moved over to Pervez's cradle.

Jamilla didn't react.

"I escape from Pakistan alone, with you and Pervez; I get caught in the ISI net, or Alam's bullets get me. Finally, I've the option of swallowing the capsule."

Jamilla looked up in silence.

"What's that?"

Harfan brought out two blue cyanide capsules from a tiny steel container tucked in his purse and placed them on his palm.

Jamilla looked at the capsules and asked.

"Poison?"

"Yes, cyanide. Death is instantaneous."

Jamilla looked up. Tears rolled down in torrents.

In a sudden move, she snatched the capsules away from Harfan's open palm and rushed into the toilet.

"Jami, *Allah kasam* (by God), don't swallow the capsules. Don't leave me and Pervez alone." Harfan kept on lightly banging on the toilet door, crying in miffed voice. There was no response from Jamilla.

"If you don't come out I'll pump bullets into my head. I'll count five." Harfan started counting loudly.

Jamilla opened the door.

"Now you've only two options left. Choose any one you like. Don't talk of death, talk of life. I can't die, leaving you and Pervez all alone." Jamilla spoke in a soft steely voice, still sobbing.

Harfan, benumbed and frozen by Jamilla's sudden action, involuntarily dropped the loaded pistol on the carpeted floor. A cool sigh escaped his chest, with an audible sound.

"Where are the capsules?"

"Don't bother, I've taken care. If these are capable of killing, by this time millions of insects and microbes down the gutter must have perished." She concentrated on feeding Pervez.

Harfan heaved a sigh of relief. Thank God! She hadn't swallowed the capsules. Obviously, she hadn't. His heart had almost stopped beating and the legs were glued to the floor. Slightly relaxed, he attempted lighting another cigarette.

"Don't smoke, Pervez can't stand it." For the first time she objected to his smoking.

"What's your decision?" Jamilla asked, looking straight into Harfan's eyes.

"I've told you everything. I'll go by your decision." He put his shirt on and sat on the edge of the bed.

"Harfan," Jamilla spoke in a straight and steady voice, "I'm neither a Muslim nor a Hindu. I believe in God, I believe in man and love. Mummy has taught me the intrinsic values of life and nature. I'm your woman, take me wherever you can, ensure that our son remains unharmed."

Jamilla's words, spoken in soft syllables, penetrated deep into Harfan's heart. He seemed to have lost his power of speech. He burst into tears and sobbed loudly. Jamilla's compassion and love engulfed Harfan in the fragrant juices of love and life. Her intrinsic strength transmitted in him a strong desire to fight back, like his father did, in the face of insurmountable odds. Fight he must, against the ruthless machines of India and Pakistan.

Unsuspectingly he recited, perhaps for the first time, —*'La Illaha illa 'llah Muhammad-ur-Rasulu 'llah'.*

Jamilla was surprised too, to hear Harfan reciting the holy verse. She had never bothered about religion and rituals. Like her mother, she had grown up as a free soul. It didn't bother her if Harfan said his prayers five times a day and kept the Ramadan fast. She never observed it anyway.

She gathered Harfan's head in her hands, kissed his cheeks and wiped tears away.

"Destiny is an inescapable force. However, I won't be tricked by that cruel time machine. I'm your woman, you decide. This isn't the time to cry. We must live on."

Jamilla's warmth transmitted a sudden surge of excitement in Harfan. A fresh life force ignited the molecules in his brain, and new chemical droplets started creeping under his skin, giving him goose pimples. The new *mantra* warmed up his soul. Harfan raised his head, walked down to the window, looked at the new sun. It looked like a giant red hibiscus. The new sun, he knew, as they said in the *Upanishads*, washed away all past sins. He folded his palms and saluted the maker of the new day, all days, and all nights.

"We'll escape, we'll escape from these vicious vipers. We'll escape to live in the future."

"Where and how?"

"Be ready. Something is germinating in my mind. I won't be able to give you enough notice. Don't bother about money, I've plenty. Let me tie up the loose ends. Do you drive?"

"Yes. Why?"

"Keep a car ready, no driver," Harfan kissed Jamilla and Pervez and said, "the spy in me is dead. To me India and Pakistan don't exist any more. Let them fight and exterminate each other. I've only one more job to accomplish and I've more stories to tell."

Harfan ducked his head under a pillow and felt he was walking above the clouds amidst the exploding galaxies. He was ready for his third birth. They said in India a Brahmin was a *dwija* (twice born), once from his mother's womb and again when he underwent the thread ceremony.

Harfan felt that he was transcending into the third dimension of his life, totally submerged in Jamilla and Pervez's love. This new life was holier than the life of the twice born Hindu Brahmin, Ramendra Kaushal, son of Digvijay Kaushal, Raja of Jhumra and a spy in jeopardy. He felt like he was being sucked into the core of a delightfully bright and swirling fiery cloud. Suddenly a silken tunnel opened up, Jamilla stood at the far end, with hands outstretched, waiting to embrace him.

Harfan realised before he lapsed into sleep, that he had just stepped into a new phase of life, a crucial third birth. The sea of love inundated him. He felt safe and secure after a long time. The scared Harfan was dead. There was no place for Bhagat, Nampoothiri and Alam in this new galactic tunnel.

No Pakistan, no Hindustan. No war, no espionage.

It was his own small world, Jamilla and his Pervez.

He must protect that world, at any cost.

*

53

With Jamilla at the steering, Zahoor Chaudry's brand new Toyota Corona chugged along the Grand Trunk Road with a monotonous rhythmic sound. Harfan, ostensibly engrossed with Pervez, diligently monitored the single Mosur vehicle, a Nissan, which was piloted by the terra Moon-faced ISI operative.

Harfan advised Jamilla to drive straight, at a steady speed of 60. That was the ideal speed to drive through the maddening traffic of trucks, military vehicles and assorted kaleidoscope of camel, bullock, and horse carts.

Driving was really frustrating, especially for the ISI tail.

Arman Ali Niazi was foxed to see a lady driving the car and his subject blissfully playing with a child, no anxiety on his face. The ISI briefing room had counselled him about the extremely sensitive nature of his target. Conscious about tails, he usually adopted anti-surveillance measures. Only the other day he happened to taste the vagaries of tailing a conscious fidgety target in a narrow lane off Lahore's Anarkali market.

The lady driver too displayed studied unconcern. She should've noticed the persisting Nissan and made some evasive manoeuvres. She didn't. That's what foxed the trained Mosur team.

"Cee Aarr (Control Room), this is *musafir* (traveller)," Arman Ali spoke on car radio, "the target is going to the Shalimar Bagh, probably with his wife and child."

"Cee Aarr to *musafir*. Follow at any cost. Don't miss as you did the other day."

"No sir, it won't happen again. I'm just behind him. He can't play footsy any more."

Arman Ali was disappointed. The unexpected move came suddenly. Jamilla avoided the main entrance to Shalimar Bagh and swung the car left, and hit a dirt road, which wound through the congested localities.

Arman Ali faced a major technical problem. Mosur teams were instructed not to mother their subjects, chaperoning the fledging under their wings. He decided to flout the copybook. Determined not to miss the target he surged forward and almost tail ended Jamilla's Toyota.

"Take care. He's aggressive. Don't be nervous."

"Don't worry. I'll take care."

Jamilla didn't betray nervousness. She followed Harfan's instructions and piloted the Toyota to an opening, along the remnants of the historic western wall of the garden. She parked the car under a *chinar* (maple) tree and helped Harfan unload the picnic materials, a foldable mattress, eats, playthings, and Pervez's special basket. They leisurely walked past a few dwarf bushes, entered the garden through a breach, and selected an isolated spot, next to a dilapidated Mughal period wall. It faced an open lawn, well manicured, and studded with flowerbeds and ornamental bushes.

The Mosur tail encountered a series of problems. Instructions had cautioned him not to park next to the suspect car.

Fine. Arman Ali followed the rulebook and parked his car at a distance of about 50 meters. He lighted a cigarette and set the car stereo to a loud pitch, hoping to generate congenial ambience noise.

What next? Join the picnic party?

Arman Ali and his partner negotiated the breach, hurriedly walked into the garden, and parked themselves behind a Chinese bamboo bush. Harfan's picnic party was clearly visible through a maze of yellow bamboo leaves and stocks. Harfan and Jamilla ate their lunch leisurely and stretched out on the garden greens. Pervez wasn't in any mood to make small talks. He toddled on the grass with a broken, uneven, and uncertain rhythm.

It was a sure invitation to an exciting afternoon. Harfan gently pushed a multicoloured inflated plastic ball towards the broken wall. Pervez followed it. Jamilla walked along guiding and guarding him.

Point Chinar was just another five feet away.

Harfan pushed the ball gently and invited Pervez to take it, by gesturing with hands and making encouraging sounds. Jamilla helped the toddler by gently holding his fingers.

Hai Rabba!

The Mosur team felt enormously befuddled.

A troupe of giggling, prancing and singing lasses, dressed like unislamic fluttering butterflies suddenly descended near the bamboo bush. Arman Ali grimaced furiously. These fluid pretty creatures, though good in bed, had no respect for the law and established order. Weren't they responsible for all the apocalyptic catastrophes in human civilisation? For all the wars men had fought? For all the thrones, they had lost or grabbed? Hadn't the *sharia* excluded them from all such frivolous activities? The best place for such volatile characters, Arman Ali thought, was the secured corners of homes and behind the veils. They should derive all heavenly pleasures, as prescribed by the *alems* (learned teachers), from cooking dinners and delivering children at regular intervals.

Arman Ali, the Mosur captain, uttered a loud curse and spat out at the belles. He lighted another cigarette and asked his mate to crawl closer to Harfan's location.

By the time the Mosur team could place themselves behind another transparent bush, Harfan's plastic ball had reached *Point Chinar*. Pervez and Jamilla followed the ball. Harfan picked up a small briquette, placed in a hollow of the old Mughal wall, and put it in his trouser pocket.

Toddling like a lump of sugar Pervez reached the ball and kicked it to a considerable distance, towards the bamboo bush. One of the giggling lasses picked up the ball, brought it back to Pervez, and hugged him fondly.

Jamilla thanked the girl, picked up Pervez, and flooded him with kisses. The Mosur moved in closer, as Harfan approached the car to pick up a cane basket that contained a coffee-flask and Pervez's feeding bottle. It was time for his drink and early afternoon nap.

Jamilla followed a pre-set drill. She occupied the front-passenger seat and started breast-feeding Pervez. Harfan concealed the briquette in a cavity, behind one of the speakers of the music system. Arman Ali peeped in and spontaneously stepped back. His cultural education told him that it was not in good taste to pry on a mother breast-feeding her child.

The sly spy, immensely happy with the copybook pick up, lighted a cigarette and whistled a popular film tune. He signalled Jamilla and jumped into the Toyota. The car accelerated to 100 km, even before the Mosur could react. Arman Ali jumped out, dashed past the screaming college girls, tumbled a few, and scrambled into the Nissan. He picked up the radio handset.

"Cee Aarr, this is *musafir*, target on way to Lahore."

"What has he been doing all these hours?"

"Family picnic sir."

"Shit! Follow and don't miss."

Harfan drove leisurely keeping a steady vigil on the rear view mirror and allowing the Mosur to pick up his trail. He slowed down behind a truck and captured the gushing eyeballs of Arman Ali. They spewed out anger, hatred, and murder at him. Here were the eyes of his father's killer. God willing, he shouldn't miss the opportunity to empty a full magazine on his chest.

Harfan swerved right, surged ahead of the truck, and pressed on the accelerator.

Arman Ali again missed him.

*

Back to Lahore, Harfan pried open the plastic capsule, shaped like a piece of broken brick. The coded message was short. Harfan decoded it with the help of a pocket computer, generating groups of numerical keys, buried deep in its memory. Jamilla tiptoed behind Harfan and placed her hands around his neck.

"What's my spy doing so attentively?"

Harfan placed the decoded message in front of Jamilla.

"Behest November 10. In the absence of usual communication link Sparrow has chosen this DLB mechanism. Read carefully and comply....

"YOUR COVER BLOWN. WITHDRAW AND PROCEED TO RIVER. FOLLOW GIVEN ROUTE. GOOD LUCK."

"What does it mean?" Jamilla was really intrigued with the calculations littered on a piece of paper.

"Don't mind my smoking?" Harfan walked down to the window, "this is my withdrawal warrant, from my bosses in India. They want me to escape to London and wish me good luck."

"London is a good idea."

"No doubt. But the ISI surveillance is total. I'm allowed to fly to Dacca, because I'm the convenient fall guy. Delhi has dumped me and Islamabad is about to shoot. A very fine situation indeed! No Jami, General Hyder's men won't allow me to fly out of Pakistan, by PIA or any other foreign carrier."

"How do you escape otherwise?"

"It's a no-win situation, Jami. Delhi is gracious. But I doubt if Alam would spare my life."

"Don't feel down and out. *Allah* is with us. Have you planned anything for escaping from the ISI noose?" Jamilla tightened her hands around Harfan's shoulder.

"Don't worry. We shall overcome; we shall be victorious. We shall live for Pervez and for ourselves, not for India and not for Pakistan. Do you recall Edmund Burke's famous line: 'to make us love our country, our country ought to be lovely'. I can't say our countries are lovely enough, beyond what nature has gifted them." Harfan collected the scraps, burnt, and flushed down the ashes. He carefully wiped out the pocket computer's memory and stacked it away under a pile of used clothes, in Jamilla's personal closet.

"Why is Delhi so insensitive to your welfare?"

"They call it professional risk, a soldier's right to die, because he has no better option to earn his bread." Harfan encircled Jamilla's waist with his hand.

"You mean they're not responsible for your safety!"

"I should thank my stars that they've given me a final disengagement message. It means they're worried, not about my safety, but about other assets in Pakistan. I know too much."

"Have they disowned you?"

"Yes. If I don't clear out quick enough, they may silence me, permanently."

"Will they kill you?"

"Yes. If they fail, the ISI will carry out the sacrificial ritual."

"*Allah*!" Jamilla pressed closer to Harfan.

"Poor *Allah* has nothing to do with these mundane things. Men spin circumstances and the fabric of time wraps them up. The *kaafan* (shroud) is now ready for me. They think I should don it, now." Harfan lifted up Jamilla and took her to bed.

"Come. Let's drink the nectar while it's still there. They can't be wiser jackals. The two of you'll live to see me foxing both the Indian and Pakistani killers. I'm a jackal of the Chenab marsh, more cunning than the NSI and the ISI professionals put together. I'm the knight of all these jackals."

"That's a grand knighthood. I like it. But what's your game plan?" Jamilla fastened her grip around Harfan.

"Perhaps, we'll fly out of this mess. May be we'll fly to Dacca."

"That's one hell of a place to go," Jamilla whispered.

"That's a new horizon Jami, a nation in birth pangs, and all births are painful. Our mothers understand that truth better; you know it all. Let's enjoy these few precious moments, in our infinite love together. Destiny may or may not give us another chance." Jamilla smiled and yielded.

Together they had seen the face of death and decided to escape into the realm of love, a proven medicine to defeat death.

*

54

Some breeds of intelligence jackals never sleep. Their neurons keep ticking and clicking, like the inevitable galactic clock, until the needle of suspicion punctures the membranes of doubts and reaches the core, called truth.

Jamanat Ali, one such irrepressible jackal, entered Barqat's room with a flourish. Inner ecstasy made his mighty moustache twitch involuntarily.

"So, Jamanat, where are we?"

Brigadier Barqat asked his intelligence bulldog, who just entered his room with a mighty clicking of heels, a trade mark of his very happy frame of mind.

"Almost near the bull's eye. I've narrowed down the circle of suspicion. I'm waiting for a few more check points on his background in India."

Jamanat bubbled out his frothy disclosures.

"Wait Jamanat. Allow me to digest your frothy recipe." Barqat offered coffee to his junior colleague.

"As I was telling sir, my men are going crash on the job. I've no doubt that this man Harfan is a real *harfanmaula*, a jack-of-all-trades. There are important leads in Jhumra. I want your permission to lift a few suspects for interrogation. With no police meddling."

"There's no hurry, friend. Let's chop this piece of meat with finesse. Give me the names of your suspects and allow me a day or two. We've to be extra cautious. The bugger is well connected and I don't want the Indian NSI becoming any wiser."

"He might escape our net."

"He can't. The borders are sealed. He can't board any foreign flight."

"What about the flights to Dacca?"

"He won't dare defect to the Bongs. They'd eat him up like *machher jhol* (fish curry)."

"But sir, we should hurry, he's a sly fox."

"The name of the game is hush-sh-sh, till we choke the jugular of that bastard. One fish isn't good enough Jamanat; we've to haul up the entire Indian network in Pakistan. As of now, we don't know the extent and depth of Indian penetration. A hasty move may alert the hidden shoal."

"Sir I've no personal axe to grind. I seek the truth."

"Fine Jamanat, I understand. The game rules demand that we unearth the entire network. Killing a mocking bird will scare away other Indian assets. I don't see any reason to go crash driving. Would you not like to haul up the entire conspiracy? He can't escape our net. Give the names of the suspects you want to lift."

Jamanat scribbled the names of Ibadat and Ramayani on a piece of paper and handed it over to Barqat.

"What do you expect from that old lady?"

"Sir," Jamanat puffed in a few quick breaths, like a fish starved of air, "you know our Mosur chap, Arman Ali?"

"Perhaps. That cratered face?"

"Yes sir. His father was in the employment of the former Raja of Jhumra. He had personally beheaded that *kafir* despot. He knows the secrets of Ramayani. And this man Harfan, if Arman's to be believed, resembles the former king."

"Aren't you stretching it too far?"

"It sounds odd. But sir, there was a Hindu king and this lady was a concubine of that sacrilegious *kafir*. Please allow me to get to the bottom of the well, the juice is down there." Jamanat pleaded.

"Okay," Barqat shrugged, "I'm doubtful though. Don't worry, I'll swim along old boy, as long as you don't commit another faux pas."

"And sir..." Jamanat stopped midway.

"Don't hesitate. There's no shortage of secret service funds. Take as much as you require."

"It's not money sir. Our man Jaffar Tyrewala has been able to dig up a few fresh skeletons."

"Please Jamanat, spare me the chaste Urdu. Who is this Tyrewala?"

"Sir he is our retired officer at Karachi. I'd sent him to Umerkot and Karachi for inquiry. His stool pigeons inside the flesh and drug trade rings have given valuable leads. Perhaps Harfan's Umerkot records are forged. Tyrewala knows a man, who used to chauffeur the Indian embassy cars in Karachi. We can locate him. He knows a lot about these bloody Indians."

"Do you mean your target was infiltrated more than half a decade ago?"

"Long term agents are embedded carefully. Karamat, our junior officer, has drawn blank from usual Punjab infiltration routes. I think the Umerkot route is most probable."

"Well Jamant, please don't jump into conclusions. Proceed carefully."

"Please have faith in me sir," Jamanat pleaded with folded hands, "I've the experience of busting a ten-year-old Indian ring in Lahore-Sialkot area. I've thirty-eight years of experience of working with the legendary CIB and PIB bosses."

"I don't doubt your professional integrity Jamanat. Please don't get me wrong."

"A few pieces of my information have been corroborated by Nawab Sharief too. He has a vast network in Sind, courtesy his closeness to Izaz sahib."

"Best of luck Jamanat. But lick Nawab's salt with dashes of honey." Barqat sounded a note of caution about Nawab's conflict of interest status.

*

Jamanat hadn't received the affirmative nod even after a week. Hyder Bux was not disinclined to net the catch. Nevertheless, he deferred the decision after a media friend wizened him about President's foul mood. The intimate masseur of Jahanara had dropped an authentic story about an unholy conspiracy between Hyder and Nawab to scuttle the airlifting operation.

Was it a coup inspired by Israr International or another dirty trick by Sarfaraz? Hyder greased his way to a personal meeting with the *Sadr* after fattening the pocket of Col. Munir.

Jahanara was not amused by his presence and was surprised when Hyder brought up the subject of Harfan Bukhari. General Naim had thrown vague hints about ISI operations against Harfan. He had also added that the unholy duo of General Sarfaraz and Hyder was more interested in implicating the Malika and slinging mud on the President. She should, Naim had pleaded, thwart Hyder for at least a couple of weeks. That should give him sufficient time to assimilate the intelligence collage and decide if the ISI was using the spy-charade to defame her and topple the President.

"I agree Hyder." Jahanara started on a conciliatory note, "this fellow could be a competitor of that fat lout Nawab, I mean your friend Nawab. But how do you say that he's a spy? Where's the proof? Do you want to hang a devoted son of Pakistan only because some intelligence officers don't like his face and a certain Nawab Sharief demands his blood?" Malika Jahanara winked at the President.

"Mr. President sir," Hyder Bux argued, "we should be allowed to pick up some of the suspects for interrogation. That's a part of our investigation process."

"Do you want to pick up Sayeefa's son in law?" Jahanara intervened.

"Well Hyder," the President finally spoke, "this business of arms ferrying is complicated. Our Chinese and US friends apart, some delicate friends in the Islamic fraternity are keen on keeping their names under wraps. A South African mercenary and a Third Reich thug aren't the most beautiful tunes to hit their ears."

"Perhaps you may like to entrust Nawab Sharief with this task." Hyder added. The un-dissolved salts of the younger Sharief were still rubbing against his bruised conscience.

"No Nawab business. He's an enemy of the country." Jahanara roared out like a irritated lioness.

"You keep out of it dear," the President waved his hands at her, "I can't change horses at the last lap Hyder. And I believe Nawab is spreading canard against me. I hope you boys aren't blind to these dirty tricks of the junior Sharief." The President made his intentions clear.

"I'm sorry that you have this impression. Nawab is under our scanner. Can I add a small point sir?" Hyder demurred peevishly.

General Arif moved his thick eyebrows and twitched a signal of affirmation.

"Nawab has the support of a few important Generals. Perhaps we can't ignore him."

"Well put Hyder," Gen. Arif burst into a rare loud laughter, "they too want to join the looting, eh?"

"Not exactly sir...."

"Tell them that with the lion around the jackals don't have any right to the kill. The CIA, so also the Athena Air Lines, have cleared Israr. I can't undo this without consulting them." Gen. Arif requested Jahanara to light a cigarette for him.

Hyder measured up the President's mood and quickly changed the track.

"I agree sir. There're too many fragile linkages," commented General Hyder Bux, "Izaz Afroz would be the first to embarrass your Excellency. And you know sir, the PSO is in cahoots with him."

Hyder pelted the stone into the disturbed pool of Arif's mind with a delicate calculation. This was a propitious opportunity to generate waves of doubt in the bubbling psyche of the instable man. Barqat, Jamanat, and their case against Harfan could wait for a while. The *Sadr* of the country wasn't in a hurry.

"Are they plotting against me?"

"Excellency, I'll like to brief you on the details. They're too ambitious. And sir, General Sarfaraz and Izaz have roped in Air Chief Rahmat Khan."

"How dare these jackals do that?" Jahanara pitched in with a shrill voice.

"Quiet darling," General Arif mildly admonished his pleasure queen, and continued, "Is that son of a low caste Hindu woman, I mean Izaz, really involved?"

"My reports are fairly accurate sir."

"What's their timeframe?"

"Any time sir."

"You didn't warn me earlier. How can I believe you?"

"Please consult the American ambassador. The CIA is aware of the conspiracy." Hyder Bux pumped in more adrenaline into the President.

"Do you suggest that I arrest and intern them?" General Arif lighted a cigarette and asked for a whisky.

"I think we should watch out for a few more days. In the meantime," Hyder continued, "I suggest your Excellency may like to mobilise the loyal officers. Perhaps you may summon all the Corps Commanders for consultations and assess the situation."

"I can't disturb the battle command now. The Armed Forces have started the reverse counting after the last input from Aftab. All the formations are set for action before November 20th."

"In that case sir," Hyder came out with a novel suggestion, "pit both Izaz and Sarfaraz against the Bengalis. Let them be busy with the dirty job."

"That's okay. But Izaz won't mind a crushing defeat in Dacca. He wants at any cost to be the ruler of whatever is left of Pakistan." General Arif shrugged, as he nervously sipped whisky.

"Your humble servant is ever present Excellency. I'm ready to die for you and the country." Hyder made a deliberate effort to touch the most sensitive chord in General Arif Khan.

"Thanks Hyder. Watch Izaz and Sarfaraz. Remain in touch. You should be my Chief of Staff. Wait for my return from Dacca and keep the powders ready. Anyways, is this fellow Harfan a security threat?"

"Not really," Hyder hastened to add with a broad smile thrown at Jahanara, "we're still probing. He can't escape. All the exit routes have been plugged."

"Carry on your investigation, but let that fellow continue with the airlifting. Zahoor is putting his best in the estuary area. I can't do without him. Harfan is a small matter. You can always share your thoughts with Malika sahiba. I'm with you." General Arif dismissed the briefing engagement with a warm handshake. General Hyder Bux saluted smart, bowed wantonly at the virtual first lady and left with a glint of a smile in his eyes.

Holy hell! Was he going to learn a lesson or two on intelligence from that whore?

Never. He would kick out the balls of that small time *muhajir* at his own pleasure. Hyder felt happy that he had succeeded in squeezing in enough venom into the boss' veins. He hoped that the toxic effect of the story planted by Sarfaraz had been neutralised. The standoff with India could wait. Sheikh Jainal could rot for a few more months at Muree guesthouse. Harfan and Jamanat could wait until he consolidated his position and shredded Sarfaraz and Izaz to dirty rags.

His destiny, Hyder calculated, as he stepped out of *Aiwan-e-Sadr* (President's palace), was beckoning him with the stars and insignia of the Chief of Staff of the Pakistan Army. He would require only a few more paces from that slot to reach the throne of Pakistan.

What was his name? Harfan Bukhari? Anyways, he was a useful slave. What was the harm if he was allowed to breathe fresh air for another couple of days! His personal agenda was more important, incarcerating Sarfaraz and Izaz to a convenient dungeon and arranging a coffin for Arif Khan. The joint visit to Dacca by Izaz and Sarfaraz should expedite that process. It shouldn't be difficult for him to persuade General Tarakki to coincide their visit with a blood bath on Dacca streets. That should be the precise time for him to march along with his supporters to the throne room of the *Aiwan-e Sadr*.

The holy land of Pakistan rightfully belonged to him. Yes, it was within his reach.

*

Brigadier Barqat felt happy to see General Hyder alighting from car, whistling a gutsy film tune. Hyder's cathartic mood, Barqat knew, could arise from two sublime factors: a satisfactory encounter with his latest *hum-bister* (bed partner) or a fruitful fishing with the CMLA. Five in the evening wasn't the usual time for a romantic trip to his latest obsession—Cambridge educated wife of a prominent politician.

This orgasm must have been caused by a successful encounter with the President.

Barqat was right and wrong. Right about the fishing expedition and wrong in assessing the catch.

"Hey Barqat," the chief greeted his junior with a jovial tone, "what's the latest from Dacca?"

Barqat fumbled with his words.

"Sir, did you expect any special report from Dacca?"

"Oh Barqat, don't be stupid. Dacca is the most important point on earth for we Pakistanis. Mobilise your media contacts and plant stories about demands made by the People's League leaders for direct dialogue with Izaz Afroz and Lt. General Sarfaraz Lodi."

"Any other coordinate sir?"

"I want to see them on the streets of Dacca at the earliest possible. No bouquets, only brickbats. Bullets better. Ask our EP Division to produce a couple of reliable reports about the need for direct talks between Izaz and the leaders of the People's League. Ask your stooges in the PL to voice similar public statements. You're authorised to spend half a million rupees for creating a media symphony and reliable agent reports."

"Fine with me sir. You sure want brickbats not bullets?" Barqat again struggled for the correct words. He couldn't decipher the strategic meaning of the strange instructions. Was the boss aiming at an immediate coup?

"Take it easy boy. I want slime and grime on their faces and plenty of Bengali blood on the streets. See you soon. Get going with the task."

"I need a clarification sir. Should we proceed with the lifting and interrogation of the suspects in Operation Salamat?"

"Oh no Barqat. You haven't understood my priority. Get going with the Dacca stuff. No hurry about Salamat," advised Gen. Hyder Bux, "Let that salesman Harfan continue with the operations for another two weeks or so."

"We should listen to Jamanat, sir. He has a solid case." Barqat pleaded.

"The case is solid. But Jamanat's impatience can kill the operation. You can arrest, interrogate, torture, and liquidate the suspect without deciphering the depth and spread of Indian penetration. You know certain people never breach the banks of patience. Tell him to see these ramifications?" Hyder sounded genuine but not convincing.

"I agree sir," Barqat argued, "but I presume, the collated clues are strong."

"I don't disagree Barqat. In the ISI we shoot first and invent a story later. This guy has good links. In a fragile nation, raw nerves can unleash havoc. What about your journalist friend in Delhi?" Hyder referred to Pakistan's important asset in India, Raghu Chawla.

"He's a sleeper now, after Aftab's death in that blast."

"It was time for Aftab to go. The blighter was buttonholed by the NSI."

"How come sir?"

"No details please. It's over. Anyways, ask Delhi station chief to energise Chawla. Offer him as much as you want and gather relevant feedback." Hyder dismissed the meeting and hoped that he had sufficiently obfuscated his subordinate.

"Feedback on what?" Barqat pressed in his point.

"How would Delhi react if there is a regime change in Islamabad?" General Hyder looked up, with a final twinkle of disengagement in his eyes.

"Do you foresee one?"

"Who knows what *Allah* wants? When it happens, you'll be my staff officer Major General. Get going with what I want." Hyder picked up the broken whistling tune and left for his room.

*

Barqat felt mighty disenchanted. What the hell was happening to Pakistani top guns? Why were they plunging on a suicide course? Well! He wasn't the messiah to retrieve the calamitous events. But he was not a born loser either. His inner passion always propelled him to reach the marker. Jamanat was sailing with the right current.

They interpreted Hyder's acts of obfuscation as another smoke-signal of an intense power struggle. Hyder was one of the foremost bidders for the highest seat in Pakistan.

"Pakistan is in for worse days sir." Jamanat lamented with a prophetic gesture.

"I can't agree less Jamanat. But we can't help." Brigadier Barqat added philosophically.

"What do I do with that *harfanmaula*?"

"Don't disturb him, that's what the boss wants. Investigate the side characters," Barqat advised Jamanat, "drag the net in quietly. Avoid headlines. There is no one to throw the line to rescue you and me, when deluge hits us."

"That means I can chop the lamb." Jamanat wasn't too happy with the decision.

"Cut it very fine and no blood please." Barqat added.

"My Delhi friend Shauqat Ansari has started sending in bits and pieces of the mosaic. There're several gaps. I'm sure, his skeletons are buried shallow, back there, somewhere in Delhi." Jamanat tried to cheer up his boss.

"I can't agree more Jamanat. Twist the tails of some of the minor characters. Let's see what *ghazals* (form of music) they sing."

Jamanat nodded in silent agreement.

"Why not start with Ramayani?" He suggested.

Barqat looked up and acquiesced. There was no harm if Jamanat had a quiet go at that friendless lonely soul. The hungry hound had been straining at the leash for too long.

"Don't involve the Badr interrogation centre. Keep things informal." Barqat gave him a final okay.

"Don't worry sir. I'll depute a crack team to take her to one of our innocuous safe houses."

"It's better that way."

Jamanat left with a mighty click of heels and a smart salute. He was happy with the orders. Ramayani, he was sure, would sing pretty when put under the nutcracker.

*

55

Jamanat's men arrived almost ceremonially, three of them, dressed in Pathan suits, mehndi-pink beard, and chewing tobacco flavoured beetle leaves. As they entered the front portico of Hotel Royal Palace, their Vietnam vintage jeep fretted and fumed enormously.

"Hey you there, park our jeep." One of the sleuths shouted at Ibadat.

"Yes sir." Ibadat read their faces and instantly placed them in their correct slots in the company, junior commissioned army officers, seconded to the ISI.

"We want rooms, and where's your manager?"

"Sir, he's off to Bhagatan for the day. Anything can I do?" Ibadat asked politely.

"Here's my card, we're from the ISI. Hope you give good cuts to our company?"

"Sir for you there's a 25% discount on food and beverages." Ibadat led his guests to the front office and helped the desk clerk to note down their names and designations.

"What would you prefer for dinner sir?" Ibadat asked while scanning the high sounding names of the ISI agents, headed by a middle-aged subaltern, Allahdin.

"We want room service, in the Kaptan's (Captain) room." one of them said after glancing respectfully at the team leader.

Ibadat served a five-course meal, typical Punjabi fare, *sarson da saag* (mulled green mustard leaves fried in butter), *makki di roti* (baked maize flour bread), beef tenderloin, chicken kebab, and fish fried in Amritsari style.

"Excellent!" Allahdin was effusive in his praise for the food, "how did you know we're Punjabis?"

"Sir," Ibadat submitted with a trained stammer, "I'm from Mianwali. A Punjabi should know his clan. And sir, this bottle of Royal Salute is with the compliments of the manager."

"That's great," whistled the Kaptan, "sit down. I've a few questions."

Ibadat had anticipated the moment, but felt relieved that he wasn't their target. Their visit might have something to do with Harfan. He took a seat next to the subaltern.

"What do you know about this Ramayani? What's this lone Hindu lady doing here?"

"Sir, I don't have answers to all your questions. She's believed to be a companion of the former queen. Our *Ghazis* killed her husband, during the partition turmoil. She didn't migrate to India."

"Who all live with her?"

"She lives alone, with goats, a cat and a dog. She performs Hindu rituals and worships the family deity of the former royal family."

"What're her connections with this character Harfan?" the captain asked in a hushed tone.

"Seems no connection. This Harfan fellow works at the Sangla factory of Israr sahib. I often carry food to his house."

"Why shouldn't we treat you as his accomplice?"

"Sir, you're the master. I'm at your mercy. But sir, your servant is a true Pakistani and I'm a friend of Karamat Suri. Very often I help him in his professional work."

"He's in the clear Kaptan." One of the officers came to his rescue.

"Okay. I take it that you're helping our company. But, have you lately noticed anything fishy?"

"No *janab*. This old lady is treated as a part of the vegetation," Ibadat carried the team along with his studied innocence, "she lives in her own fantasy world. And appears to be imbalanced."

"Ha! Once she faces our interrogation she'll forget her gods and dreams." Allahdin and his colleagues loudly licked, cracked the chicken drumsticks, and reached for the bottle.

"Fine. You guide us to her place tomorrow morning, say at about nine." One of the officers said.

"Would you like to go now?"

"Get more whisky. It's whisky time after good food. Come at nine tomorrow."

"I'll be here at nine sharp. But sir," Ibadat bowed in Japanese style and continued the dialogue with a seducing hiss, "your humble servant suggests you have a comfortable breakfast before moving out. We specialise in *keema paranthas,* (fried flat bread stuffed with minced meat), pure Sheikhupura style."

"As I said, get another on-the-house bottle." The subaltern gestured with drooping eyes and slurred voice.

"It's our pleasure sir." Ibadat returned in minutes with another bottle of Royal Salute and wished *Khuda Hafiz.*

*

Two bottles of Scotch had numbed Allahdin and fellow ISI operatives to a dreamless stupor. That's what Ibadat waited for. He slipped out and ran towards Ramayani's hut, finding his way through the frozen darkness. His mind raced before his steps. She must be isolated from the ISI sleuths. The silent safety-vault of many secrets of the royal family wouldn't survive the dirty tricks of the interrogators. Their tradecraft ranged from the absurd to the gory often involving the application of burning cigarette butts in private parts to hanging upside down for hours on end. She should not face the ISI.

Ibadat was surprised to see Ramayani in her worship room. He wasn't aware that she was insomniac. The goddess of sleep had deserted her, since the horrible night, when Digvijay Kaushal was decapitated and her own husband was cut into pieces. Their only daughter Durga was kidnapped by one of the Niazi *sirdars* (chief).

Ramayani was seated in front of the deity whose four hands wielded weapons and assorted totems. She was busy reciting *sutras* (stanzas) from the Hindu scripture *Chandi.* Ibadat removed his shoes to enter the room. He did not think it prudent to wait for her rituals to be over. He wanted to pre-empt the ISI nemesis.

His steps froze, as Ramayani pricked her finger with a sharp needle and smeared a few drops of blood on the protruding tongue of the deity, simultaneously reciting some *Sanskrit verses.*

"Wait, don't come in," Ramayani woke up from her trance, as if she had smelt Ibadat's silent breath, "I'd a premonition that you'd come with the inevitable bad news. The Mother had told me that. Is the Prince safe?"

"Can't say for sure. The police are investigating. They suspect he's an Indian spy. Shall we go in?"

Ibadat tried to prod her to the adjoining hut, near the palace compound, silhouetted by heavy vegetation.

"I wanted to tell him all the while that what's lost was lost. Who got him here?"

"That's a different story. I've bad news. The police suspect your involvement with the Prince and believe you've evidence. The police goons are here to investigate and interrogate you." Ibadat squatted on the steps of the room.

"Are you frightening me?"

"No. To tell you the truth, you're only six hours away from death. They'll not only interrogate you, but inflict severe torture to extract confession."

"That means they'd search my room."

"Anything is possible."

"Wait." Ramayani went inside and came out with a bulky photo album and two oil paintings.

"Take these away. Destroy these. The Prince has a striking resemblance to his father. Police won't take time to get to his roots."

"And keep these," Ramayani took out a thick bunch of letters, "these are from the *maharani* (queen). She's been in touch, ever since we parted company. In one of the envelopes you'll find some photographs of the Prince."

This was bad news indeed, explosive enough to blow up Harfan's cover. Lousy! He thought. The entire operation was damn lousy. How could Delhi push him to an unexplored black hole?

Ibadat's silence puzzled Ramayani.

"And will you do me a favour?"

"Just order." Ibadat replied in whispering tone.

"Keep this jewel box. There are diamonds and gold ornaments in it. Can you reach it to my daughter Durga?"

"How do I get to her?"

"You can reach her at Pannu, at the house of Sardar Allahbux Niazi. She has been renamed Ayesha Begum."

"You got her married to a Muslim!"

"No. She was kidnapped the night the king, my husband and your father were killed by the Niazi chiefs."

"I'm sorry to hear that."

"Don't feel sad. She's alive and well and is the mother of four kids. Promise that you'd give the jewels to her?"

"Sure, you've the promise from a true Mussalman."

"How real is the danger to my son?" she asked.

"Did you say your son?"

"I mean the Prince."

"Very real. The police are on his trail." Ibadat's frankness sounded fearsome.

"That's bad. I must protect him."

The old lady, on the verge of a violent death, stood like a gleaming sword before Ibadat. Her looks didn't betray passion and pain. Ibadat couldn't meet her eyes. A sense of guilt gripped his conscience. He was here tonight as a cruel messenger of death. She must die, before the ISI caught up with her. He wasn't left with any choice.

"The police are coming for you in a few hours," Ibadat continued, "it's better you don't face them."

"I've the courage." She stood firm with her lips drawn in.

"We can't take chances. Your arrest will expose the Prince. You're a vital link." Ibadat felt the cool steel of the pistol in his pocket. A single bullet through her head would be good enough. He withdrew the hand on second thoughts. The bullet would kill this frail old lady. But the sound waves from the .38 revolver were sure to betray his presence.

"Do you suggest that I escape?" Ramayani asked.

"You don't have the time."

"You mean I've to die and you, our cook's son, want to kill me!" Ramayani's gaze looked moist, even in the thick darkness of the room.

"*Khuda kasam* (by God)," Ibadat brought out a tiny steel snuffbox from his pocket, took out a capsule and held it on his palm, "I've no intention of killing you. But the road ends here and now."

"What's this?" She glanced with a detached look at the death pill on Ibadat's palm.

"Poison. Take it and you'd die peacefully. Hope you aren't afraid of death."

"Ibadat," Ramayani spoke in an icy voice, "I've had a long journey. Your father knew I've been living with death, ever since I came to Jhumra. I consider death to be the ultimate cure for a disease called life."

"What do you mean by that?"

"Read these letters. Protect my son. Your father was loyal to the king. He knew all my secrets, my happiness, and my shame. Hope you won't betray the king's son, my son?" Ramayani opened a tin suitcase and brought out a faded black and white photograph and a silver box.

"What's this?"

"Give it to our son, the Prince of Jhumra. The photograph is for him and the box is for his wife. The blue diamond in it used to adore the neck of the former queen, my *saheli* Kasturi. You're here to dispense death; I give you the essence of life, a life you were never aware of; your father was. Give me the tablet of death."

Ramayani extended her palm.

"Pardon me, mother. Your death can save the Prince. If they close in on me, I've the pills for my own death as well. Our family shall never betray the king." Ibadat handed over two capsules to Ramayani and picked up the jewel box, the album, letters, and the paintings.

"Take care. *Allah* shall be with you in your final journey."

He turned back on her frozen figure and walked in doubles, in the direction of the Chenab waters. He must destroy the incriminating evidences by burning. He selected a secluded spot down the riverbanks and settled down under the flowering hazel and lilac groves. He carefully read the letters, under faint beam of a pencil torch.

Allah! His bones rattled.

Harfan, whatever his Hindu name might have been, was born from the womb of Ramayani, the queen's companion. That's what had prompted the moving stone to remain rooted to the relics of the bygone kingdom! That's what motivated her to receive Harfan and Jamilla in that queer Hindu fashion!

He examined the faded photo positive. Ramayani, with a suckling child in her arms, flanked the king, seated on an ornate chair. This was perhaps the only evidence of her legal status as Harfan's blood-mother. The legal mother indeed she was, in a queer way, as prescribed by the Hindu scriptures.

Damn Harfan! The jackal on espionage mission should know the truth before something drastic happened to his blood mother. No. He couldn't be the harbinger of death to this noble soul. *Allah* wouldn't pardon him for this abominable crime. No. He wouldn't play by the rules of the other sinister jackal, the wily Alam Khan. Ibadat climbed the slopes and ran along the tracks to Ramayani's hut. She hadn't exaggerated; he realised, when she had talked of death being the ultimate medicine of her life. Her life had hung, all these years, on a frail twig of hope, the hope of embracing her son, at least once in her lifetime.

*

Ramayani, after her fatal encounter with Ibadat, was not left with any illusion. She gave a last contemplative look at the silhouette of the old palace and coolly entered the worship room. She changed into her decades old clothes, a red gold-threaded Benarasi sari, the one she was made to wear on the eventful night of her first and last conjugal bliss with the king, in a secret chamber of the palace. A *mantra*-chanting priest had escorted her, for the eventful ritual.

Ramayani stood in front of a broken mirror, in dim candlelight, and put on a few pieces of heritage jewellery and the *mangal sutra* (a symbol of a married Hindu woman). She squatted on the ground, in *padmasana* (a yogic posture), lit the oil-lamp and a few incense sticks, and started reciting *slokas* (stanzas) from the Hindu scripture *Chandi*. She ended by appealing to the mother goddess to protect her son, his wife, and his line.

What a cruel joke! Her drop of blood turn up after two decades and shake her failing emotions and frail frame. Perhaps she should have gathered courage and told him the truth, the secret of his birth. However, the sacred vow, taken in front of the holy sacrificial fire, stood as an insurmountable barrier between herself and her son. What cruel game was fate playing again?

Who was responsible for this cruel joke? Why should her son be in Pakistan, married to a Muslim, and living a shadowy life? Why should the police be after his blood?

Ramayani didn't find answers to her questions. Her goddess watched in mute silence. Perhaps her death was the final wish of the Mother, a mechanism to shield her son.

Ramayani etched the fairy like face of Jamilla, her son's bride, in her inner canvass, and uttered a blessing—*Aum*. The Mother is perfect; this tiny girl is perfect. She has been born from the perfect Mother. *Aum shantih, shantih, shantih* (peace, peace, peace).

In a final act of obeisance, she prostrated before the image, now glistening faintly against the feeble oil-lamp and re-positioned herself in the *yogic* posture. She controlled her breathing, by alternately closing and opening her nasal orifices and tried to achieve equilibrium within herself. She felt an ethereal aromatic air entering her inner crevices, in an even and sustained flow.

Her supra-conscious mind was now aligned with the rays reflected from the benign eyes of the Mother. There was a sure invitation, for the eternal journey, to her lap. Ramayani looked straight into the fiery and kind eyes of the deity and swallowed the capsules. Her frail body slumped on the oil-lamp. The old ornate dress caught fire, which spread fast with roaring and crackling sounds. Ramayani's body received a holy cremation at the feet of her deity, the granite statue being a mute witness to the spectacle.

*

Ibadat ran as fast as he could through frozen darkness, but arrived a little too late.

Ramayani's hut was reduced to a few kilograms of ashes.

A lump of emotion and guilt stuck in his throat and silent tears came streaming out. He was responsible for her death. It was unfair to Harfan. The lump dissolved soon. The distant horizon was becoming transparent with the promise of another day. Ibadat checked his wristwatch. It was about time that he returned to his quarters.

No. He shouldn't allow his emotions to run riot! Ramayani's death was the safest insurance for Harfan. She was born to suffer. Death had delivered her from the disease, often called life.

Ibadat secured the jewel box, placed the letters, saving four, the album and the paintings on the dying embers of funeral fire. This was perhaps an eternal fire, preserved in the wicks of the oil-lamp. Death, her ultimate cure, came soaring on the fiery wings of the same fire. Perhaps she had always wanted to embrace death that way. Ibadat silently saluted the remains of Ramayani and hurried back to his Rajora residence.

*

After a steaming bath, groomed and dressed in crisp hotel livery, Ibadat knocked the Captain's door.

"It's nine, I'm ready sir."

"Your food and whisky were excellent."

"My pleasure, sir. I shall feel obliged if your honour gives more opportunities to serve you." He bowed in Japanese style.

The walk from the hotel lobby to the far end of the palace compound took about fifteen minutes. The ISI contingent reached the ashes of what used to be Ramayani's hut after wading through a small crowd of curious onlookers.

She was gone, forever, leaving behind a few grams of ash, bone, and charred tissue. One of the onlookers, on order from the officers, scrounged the debris and took out, what appeared to be the remains of the umbilical sinews, a few pieces of bones and tiny lumps of gold.

"*Reham karo Khuda* (oh God be merciful)." A former subject of the Kaushal king covered the scrawny remains with a piece of cloth and stepped back.

"She was a pious lady." Commented another.

"We're here to arrest her. How the hell did she die?" Thundered Allahdin.

"*Janab,* you can't travel to the land she has transcended to. Let *Allah* give peace to her." The villager raised his hands in prayers.

The ISI officials pushed back the small crowd and ordered another search of the rubble, hoping to decipher Ramayani's secrets.

"The fucking old whore. She couldn't have died at a worse time." One officer muttered scornfully.

"Bullshit!" cursed another officer, "what do we say to our bosses? There appears to be a conspiracy, an attempt to hide the trail."

"Nope." Allahdin uttered a final judgment, "it must have been an accidental fire."

"Perhaps her worship room caught fire. She was in the habit of worshipping late into the night." Commented a villager.

The officer nodded in agreement.

"Perhaps you'd like to go back to the hotel sir, and enjoy our *keema parantha* (minced meat stuffed flat bread)."

Ibadat invited the ISI team with a trained bow.

"Sure. Hope you've some of the English stuff left." The leader winked expectantly.

"Sure sir. It's a pleasure." Ibadat led the way, praying and hoping that the Jhumra trail was convincingly buried with the ashes of Ramayani.

That should give Harfan a breather.

He tried to guess the likely next move of the ISI.

"Sir, can you send Karamat down to me?" He spoke to the team leader in a conspiring tone.

"Why?"

"I believe her daughter is married to a Niazi *sirdar* at Pannu. Perhaps she can throw some light."

"No brother Ibadat. That's not what we propose to do. This bugger's uncle lives at Karachi. And there're other leads. Let's consult the boss." Allahdin thanked Ibadat and occupied the front seat of the jeep.

"One more point," he said, directing his fingers at Ibadat, "I am enrolling you as an agent of my company. I expect regular feedback on Harfan, our main suspect."

"It'll be an honour, sir, to serve you and the company." Ibadat bowed profusely as the jeep kick started with a plenty of noise and acrid smoke.

*

56

Brigadier Barqat, a rugged Punjabi from Sialkot, wasn't known for his love for music. But, he was in a rare ecstatic mood today. He softly whistled a *ghazal* (light music) tune by Begum Noorjehan, the empress of classical melody. He felt good and buoyant. There was real good news to celebrate. His company had made a significant breakthrough and had unearthed valuable clues on Harfan Bukhari.

Bits and pieces from Shauqat Ansari, editor of Delhi's prime Urdu daily, *Nai Watan*, Jaffar Tyrewala and Karamat Suri were substantiated by Raghu Chawla, Islamabad's newest Operation Sargam.

These assets had done a grand job out of shadows of doubt spun by veteran Jamanat. They had dug out the roots of the Bukhari family. Harfan, son of Maqdoom Bukhari and Shamina Begum of village Faqira, Ludhiana, and nephew of Jubaida Khatoon of the walled city of Delhi did exist. Agent enquiries in remote Ludhiana villages, markets, and lanes of Amritsar and Delhi established the facts. However, Harfan, Maqdoom's minor son, had, in all probability, perished in the communal riots. He was roasted alive way back in 1947.

Indian Intelligence Bureau had used those grains of fact and built upon it the entire cover for their long-term resident agent. It was indeed a very clever ploy.

"A wonderful copybook operation, if it is correct." Jamanat added.

"*Insha Allah*, it's correct Jamanat. We've to take a conscious and cautious decision. I'm waiting for conclusive corroboration. The NSI network is big, and we should haul up all the eels and pikes, buried deep under mud." Barqat's effervescence spilled over his usual cautious approach.

"Let's talk to the chief. He can't put off a decision. Hope the *Sadr* and Malika won't stand in the way." Jamanat's ebullience matched that of Barqat.

"We've cast-iron proof now. It won't take time to convince the boss, and it's my job now to convince others." Barqat warmed up to Jamanat's bubbling effusion.

"But Jamanat," he applied the brake, "Wait for a few days. We require untying all the knots; the real Gordian knots this time. I wouldn't like any last minute hiccup."

"But sir..." Jamanat stopped in mid sentence.

"Don't worry," Barqat assured him, waving his hand. "We've plenty of time to fill in the Umerkot, Ludhiana and Karachi mosaic."

"These enquiries are almost over sir. I'm yet to confirm his links with the Indian Consulate in Karachi," Jamanat added, and confronted Barqat with an embarrassing question, "would you please tell me why the bosses are dithering on a minor counterintelligence issue?"

"The matter isn't minor where from you got it Jamanat. The suspect is well connected and his mother-in-law is a friend of Jahanara. Many big heads like Israr, Jung Sher and a couple of others would come tumbling down. Let's be clear, we don't want to trigger off a violent cascading effect that can threaten the regime."

"That's not my intention, sir. However, I am sure that the Indian agency had infiltrated him through the Nagar Parkar route. Mian Farooq Rathore, the drug baron of yesteryears and now an important leader of Izaz Afroz's party, had collaborated with the Indian side."

"That's good news. Now try to explore the links between Harfan and the Indian Consulate at Karachi. There must be a fifth column somewhere, who had betrayed Pakistan."

"I believe at that point of time one Irfan Cowasji, a Pakistani national used to chauffer the Ambassador's car. Jaffar Tyrewala has confirmed this. He can probably throw some light."

"Locate him first and then go for Shamim Bukhari. Let's guard these nuggets carefully. And give me a few days to brief the boss, when you're ready with all the details." Barqat wrapped up the small private meeting with great élan, by offering a full bottle of Scotch to Jamanat. It was celebration time, he said and his old bones deserved some cooling.

*

The same ghost that often overawed Sarfaraz afflicted General Hyder. He was not in a mood of celebration.

Belligerent People's League leaders, who reiterated that a national government could only be formed with Sheikh Jainal as the Prime Minister, greeted Izaz Afroz's visit to Dacca with stones, mud-balls, and shoes. Neither Afroz nor Sarfaraz was melted by democratic paeans of the East Bengal leaders. Izaz valued democracy that verged corners with the democracy of Adolph Hitler. Queen's democracy was not his ball of meat.

General Sarfaraz's meeting with the military commanders and patriotic vigilantes were highlighted by passionate speeches, reiteration of the holy spirit of Pakistan and consumption of tons of flesh and spirit. Their visit was heralded by another raid on Dacca University and several villages in and around the city, which resulted in dumping of more Bengali bodies in the Buri Ganga and Shitalakshya rivers. In absence of civilian sweepers, the fire brigade jets washed off blood from the university campus.

They returned home with a good harvest.

Izaz, before emplaning for Karachi, had advised General Tarakki that General Nuruddin, the chief of the Eastern Command, should be directed to decimate the incorrigible Bengalis. Imitating the cheroot puffing Churchill he declared that he would never be a party to handing over the nation on a platter to Sheikh Jainal, the

Indian agent. Tarakki did not wait for Nuruddin, a conservative military officer. He fulfilled the desire of the Prime Minister in waiting with jihadi zeal. The Reuter reported about a few thousand more body bags and three suspected mass-graves.

Brigadier Barqat's secret coffer had influenced some of the leading newspapers to highlight the developments in Dacca and to blame Izaz for the political impasse. Some oblique mentions were also made about Sarfaraz's suspected involvement in the latest act of genocide. Some media columns cried like opera sopranos for the distressed democratic Bengalis.

Nevertheless, General Arif, even after perusal of two executive intelligence summary submitted by Hyder, refused to buy the story that Izaz and Sarfaraz duo had acted against the interest of Pakistan. The country, General Arif had pointed out, required committed soldiers like Izaz and Sarfaraz. The Bengalis deserved death if they defied the mandate of 1947. The *Ummah* was one and that was the political philosophy of Pakistan. It was the protector and guardian of the Muslims in the subcontinent and in the proximate region.

A deflated Hyder's discreet parley with the Corps Commanders of Sialkot and Multan proved equally frustrating. They were not ready to accept him as the leader of a new junta. They had declined to embark on an uncertain adventure on the eve of another war with India. They advised Hyder to mind his own job, the job of generating intelligence about the war plans of the Indian forces.

Hyder did not like to be pushed to the walls. He normally didn't react violently against his opponents. He was trained to store all his frustrations in an exclusive pouch of his mind and recycle these unpleasant ingredients into powerful explosive devices. He preferred to demolish his competitors mercilessly, in his own inimitable way, by focusing his total energy against them.

He sincerely believed that he was the rightful owner of Pakistan and Izaz and Sarfaraz were the stumbling blockades. Should he use the ultimate weapon of secret assassination to get rid of his opponents? The blame could easily be passed on to the Bengali renegades and the Indian agents.

Just when the acid drops of frustration inflamed Hyder, General Naim walked in for an informal discussion. Hyder was piqued, if not embarrassed, by the bombshell thrown by the IB chief. He claimed to have solved the major riddles concerning Harfan Bukhari. How did this imbecile bumblebee develop a sting and steal a march over his boys?

"That's not your area of operation, Naim."

"Perhaps you've forgotten the charter of 1962 devised by Zafarullah Committee. Counterintelligence in Pakistan is my area of responsibility."

"You should've kept me informed, Naim. How authentic are your boys?" Hyder asked rather casually.

"No Hyder, you're mistaken again. Don't forget that my IB is responsible for internal security as well. My men have carried out detailed investigation and the results are stunning." General Naim said.

"Would you like to compare with my findings?"

"Why not? Start with your bugging of Malika's rooms, and monitoring the phones of the *Sadr*. You'd started with a mission to demolish the President by demolishing that *mohajir*. My boys have found out a different tunnel altogether." General Naim lighted a cigarette and released a cloud of smoke as if he was releasing his long suppressed frustration.

"Well Naim," Hyder toned down his voice, "we do often put phones of important persons on the hook for security reasons. No record is kept and no transcription made. You can't hang me for doing what I'm supposed to do to thwart foreign designs against the person of the *Sadr*. I concede you've a territory to protect. We can do that jointly. Can't we?"

"Why not? Let's place our cards straight."

"When do you want to sit?"

General Naim examined his pocket engagement book and after a good pause spoke through his teeth.

"My daughter's marriage is on the twelfth of this month. The President is visiting our ancestral village. I should be free by the fifteenth. Can we sit then?"

"No problem, Naim. I hope I figure in the guest list."

"Oh brother! Let professional matters not stand in our social relationship. We Peshawris are the most chivalrous people. However, keep in mind that we're yet to find out a few pieces of the mosaic of Harfan riddle and the President is keen to complete the airlifting operations as quickly as possible."

"I agree, Naim. Let him fly for a few days more. I want his custody first."

"We can talk, Hyder."

General Naim left like a frontline soldier. Had he scored a rare victory over his all-powerful ISI rival?

Hyder couldn't instantaneously clear up the foggy mirror. His efforts to place Naim in an appropriate slot eluded a solution. Was this upstart of an intelligence novice trying to foul up his high voltage game, the game of staging a coup? Was Naim trying to hijack Operation Salamat for protecting Jahanara and his brother? A dead Harfan was sure to divert media attention and give opportunity to the CMLA's acolytes to lionise their sinking hero. But that scenario would deprive him of a valuable tool, the tool of using the Harfan affair to defame Jahanara and General Arif.

Like massive hailstones bureaucratic wrath too follow the law of gravity, the very way Sir Isaac Newton had calculated. Hyder pressed the buzzer hard. He wanted his anger to be heard along with the electric sound wave.

"Call in Barqat." He ordered the uniformed attendant.

Barqat rushed in only to be hit by flaming pieces of volcanic stone and pumice.

"How is it that Naim knows everything about Operation Salamat?"

"No idea, sir."

"Well Barqat, if you don't have any idea about who moves with leaking cans in your office you better go back to your village and push the plough." Hyder thundered like a fresh exploding jet of magma.

"Would you mind clarifying, sir?"

Hyder toned down and sipped in a part of his anger with a glass of chilled water. He narrated verbatim the humiliating experience he had a couple of minutes back.

"Pardon, sir," Barqat took a seat and spoke in an even voice, "General Naim could break our walls through several points: *Mohtarma* Jahanara, the discussions you had in the high level committee meeting and parallel watch and surveillance. I fully trust Jamanat."

"Do you think he'd carry the tales to Jahanara and the President?"

"I don't think he would just now. Before he does, he has to establish a conspiracy theory. I don't think he has any."

"Thanks, Barqat. Sorry, I lost temper. This lout Naim is so irritating! Do you think he has the grey matters to be the chief of the PIB?"

"Sir, he has connections. And wants to protect his turf."

"Well said. Shit with his turf. I don't think the PIB should exist. Anyways, go-slow on Salamat."

"There has been a minor problem."

"Jamanat again?"

"No, sir. This old lady at Jhumra died a few days back in an accidental fire. We couldn't interrogate her."

"Anyways, she wasn't that important. Investigate Irfan Cowasji. He could be a vital link."

"We're yet to locate him. He's probably adopted a dervish's life, serving in a dargah."

"Doesn't matter. Break his bones. A traitor's prayers aren't heard by the *Allah*."

"We're on the job, sir."

Barqat left with a smart salute and lots of laughter under his chest. The boss went almost naked before him. The furrows of panic on his face showed up like the dried up channels on Mars. He would, in all probability, stoop down before the *Sadr* and *Malika* to prove that he was more loyal than Naim.

Poor uniformed foxes of Pakistan!

*

57

The modest and cool bearings Sarfaraz could hardly conceal the bushfire burning inside, fanned by accumulated frustration. The needles of his intentions and decisive action were not coinciding at the final take off point.

Was it his cowardice? Or were it his spiked stars? Sarfaraz could not buttonhole the precise cause and effect relativity. Was his failure due to *naïveté* or *effete*? No. He was neither a fool nor was he a spent force.

The crown of Pakistan was, in fact, lying there just for the grab. Why should he, the Principal Staff Officer to the Chief Martial Law Administrator, not pick up the crown? The fire inside had been pushing him inexorably to the Presidential throne. He had secured support of three top Generals and at least two important Corps Commanders. The elite Special Services Group could be mustered for a determined assault on the presidential palace. General Mukhtiar Ghori, the SSG chief, was beholden to him for an out of turn promotion and a possible court martial. Admiral Shauqat, the Naval chief, a misfit in General Arif's court, could be bullied to submission.

He could tackle the COAS General Omar and Air chief Rahmat Khan. The people who gave him creeps were the wily Izaz Afroz and General Hyder. General Tarakki, an Izaz crony, was sure to lend support to his Sindhi foster father.

The clicking of heels and the swish of a smart salute disrupted Sarfaraz's journey through the wild maze of his neurons.

"Sir, General Hyder Bux is here." Announced his aide d' camp.

"Oh yes." Sarfaraz sported a weary smile, "send him in, please."

General Hyder Bux's visit, one of his infrequent ones, was specific to Operation Salamat, neutralisation of the suspected Indian agent, Harfan Bukhari. He couldn't sit tight any more, especially after an unsavoury encounter with the PIB chief. On second thought, he decided to take Sarfaraz into confidence. He required that shield to ward off any adverse reaction from Jahanara and Israr's powerful lobby.

Hyder Bux came straight to the point. He requested permission for immediate interrogation of Mian Alam Khan followed by Zahoor Chaudry. Barqat was ready to lift the senior Bukhari from Karachi and transfer him to the Badr interrogation centre.

General Sarfaraz didn't disagree. Intelligence was Hyder's business and he was best suited to brand any suspect as an Indian virus. But he politely reminded Hyder of the importance of being Alam Khan. He enjoyed confidence of several heads of West Asian Islamic countries. Pakistan's most illustrious hunter in the arms bazaar had access to the corridors of the White House, State Department, and Langley. He was a vital link to the mercenary operators, who airlifted direly needed men and weapons to East Pakistan. His good offices had helped in securing additional flights and crucial aerial refuelling facilities from Diego Garcia base.

General Hyder Bux, apparently apologetic, pointed out that it shouldn't be the usual dark-chamber interrogation. It would be done, if feasible, at the level of the PSO. If not Barqat could be tasked with a detailed interrogation brief.

"We can't sit over the issue any longer. Naim has come up with claims of breaking Harfan's cover. He may upstage us by influencing his brother, and you know the consequences we may face, if he manages to replace me." Hyder argued.

"That's a valid point. Why don't you arrange an accident for him?" Sarfaraz sounded out Hyder on the possibility of a discreet liquidation.

"That's not easy," Hyder replied, "we have two intelligence poles. Izaz and the *Sadr* use Jahanara and Naim for most of their secret political manoeuvres. That's what explains his closeness to them."

"It means they don't trust you!"

"Sir, I'm, like you, a suspect in their eyes."

"It's better we purify the air from time to time. That's essential for ensuring our good health and would prevent our detractors from pumping in poison in our oesophagus. Izaz can meet an accident," Sarfaraz replied evasively.

"I agree. But keeping Izaz alive suits us, he's schizophrenically anti-Bengali and he alone can preserve West's preponderance," Hyder added, "you'd better call the big man Alam and talk informally. We should sort out this minor pinprick. Now Naim has ganged up. The real problem isn't this spy. It's a deliberate sabotaging of our establishment by the CMLA and some imbecile cronies around him."

The calibrated release of emotion eased Sarfaraz. It was a deliberate effusion for sounding out Hyder's reaction.

"You're correct sir. And the Sindhi fox is even ready to preside over a truncated Pakistan. Let's move fast and frustrate his evil designs. As long as we Punjabis are around a Sindhi or a Bengali can't be trusted with the fate of the nation." Hyder suggested.

"I agree. How can we Punjabis trust the son of a low caste Hindu woman?"

"Correct sir. I don't think we should give this buffoon the pleasure of donning the mantle of the second father of our nation." Hyder added.

"He's no buffoon Hyder. He's a ruthless manipulator."

Sarfaraz suggested caution. The people wouldn't accept an aborted coup at this critical juncture. He pleaded for time. Perhaps the post-war situation would bring favourable tidings. The people would appreciate a lightening push, once

Pakistan was stuck in the East. Two of them, Sarfaraz spoke with a luscious smile, could hang General Arif and Izaz Afroz leisurely, at least ensure a quasi-judicial hanging, if not orchestrate their assassination in a midnight shooting spree.

Sarfaraz's exposition convinced Hyder that his supposed collaborator was a dreamer and not a performer. Brave heart leader of the fighting forces could only stage a successful coup. He was the one to lead the nation to another level of change and not Sarfaraz.

He made a move to disengage from the sterile discussion.

"Are you in a hurry?"

Sarfaraz commented with a bland look at his apparently bored partner.

"Not exactly."

"I find you're too eager to conclude your Operation Salamat. I've a suggestion."

"You're welcome, sir."

"Why don't we shoot down his next sortie somewhere over the Bay of Bengal? We can kill several birds in one stone."

"Please clarify, sir."

"You get rid of Harfan and we're relieved of the contradictory directions from the CMLA and his girl friend. This should be done just before the President's scheduled visit to Dacca, for final round of talks with the Bongs. Cook up a few reports highlighting the possibilities of such dastardly attacks by the Indians on Pakistani flights carrying important personalities. We can blame Delhi and request the USA for intervention."

"Are you sure the White House would purchase this story?"

"The Yankees are a gullible lot. You can sell them land on Mars."

"That's okay. But, where would you get the missiles to bring down the giant jet? You can't trust the Air chief."

"We've a couple of ground to air missile batteries at Cox's Bazaar and Feni. Tarakki can take care of the logistics."

"Are you sure that he'd cooperate?"

"He's a taxi. You can hire him any time for the correct fare plus a decent tip. Offer him the sky."

"I think sir," Hyder finally stood up, "your suggestion requires serious consideration. At the end of the day, General Arif and Izaz shouldn't get away with our heads and play soccer."

He saluted the PSO and left with grave thoughts etched all over his face. The two conspirators parted company with trained smiles on their faces, daggers hidden under their respective sleeves. General Hyder was happy that the PSO had accepted his agenda of informally interrogating Mian Alam Khan.

Sarfaraz, on his own account, was keen for an informal chat with Pakistan's best-known wheeler-dealer. He had his own agenda to pursue.

*

Mian Alam Khan had anticipated the move.

Double X Ibadat's LLB message about Ramayani's death had sent in thousands of crawling caterpillars in his cortices. Ibadat had averted a great disaster. The ISI was expected to widen its net. And he, Mian Alam Kahn, was the biggest Indian whale in Pakistan's murky water.

He had his own telescope trained on the gathering clouds around Triple X. He nursed no illusion that sooner than later the ISI would tap him for a few gentle questions, initially, followed by the big crunch. They were, he estimated, about to drag the net in for the big counter-intelligence catch. He knew what they were up to.

The realisation gave him peace and anxiety. Peace came from the resolution to liquidate Triple X. The drilling anxiety emanated from the shaken foundations below his feet. This meteor of Delhi was about to vaporise his own existence by a sudden thunderous impact. Sacrificing one Harfan wouldn't bleed his conscience. He should be able to protect the intelligence network, which he had helped casting far and wide over two decades. It was all the more important to save his skin and soul. How could he neglect the illusory business empire he had built up and the fortune he had stashed away in Switzerland?

Sharp telephone rings disrupted his thought. Mian Alam picked up the phone and replied in a submissive voice.

"I'm honoured sir. It's a privilege to have coffee with you." He readily accepted the invitation to coffee from General Sarfaraz, the second most important pinion in the Pakistani establishment.

"I know you're a busy person Alam sahib. Spare at least an hour for me." Sarfaraz sounded extra sweet on the phone.

Alam took a deep breath and allowed his mind to sweep the surface and crevices of the panorama of events that could have prompted the PSO to invite him. He shuffled his strategic arguments that he could deftly use to befuddle the seasoned General and boarded his sterling silver Mercedes.

*

"We've no chance of winning this war, without direct support from America and China." Sarfaraz initiated the discussions over a cup of coffee.

"The Yankees are fooling us. Their arms-pushing exercises from Phuket ended in a fiasco. And I think, all these talks about their Seventh Fleet coming to our rescue are too vague."

Alam very gingerly warmed up to the dialogue. He was still circumspect about the invitation to coffee.

"I'm told the CMLA has a direct line to Washington and that the White House is committed to preserving Pakistan's unity." Alam intended guiding the dialogue to Sarfaraz's Achilles' heel—the grim security situation and his burning ambition.

"He must be Alam. But Washington is more worried about Russian nuclear missiles than a Pakistan falling apart. What do you think of the power sharing scenario, if we get a beating in the war?"

Sarfaraz directed a probing question to gauge Alam's depth of knowledge of strategic thinking in Washington. It's the White House, which would decide the contours of fresh political alignment in post-war Pakistan.

"*Janab*," Alam harvested the hint and titillated Sarfaraz's dream theme, "you're the man of destiny. Why wait for a defeat in Dacca? Strike now. But sir, take care of the ISI and PIB chiefs. They aren't your well-wishers."

"Thanks Alam. Careful, not so loud," Sarfaraz cautioned his visitor, "a defeat in Dacca is bound to take its toll and I depend on good wishes of friends like you. You know how the old man is wasting himself!"

"*Janab*, I've a submission to make," Alam scaled down his tone, "open a discreet dialogue with Jainal at Muree, before Izaz taps him. Suggest a loose federation. Plug on to the White House, Pentagon, and the CIA. They should know you're the man of destiny. They should deal with you and not that flunky Sindhi orator. Demonstrate you can handle Jainal better and ensure Pakistan's integrity."

"That's a great idea, Alam. I require your help. Activate your conduits in the State Office and the CIA. Hyder gives me the creeps. He has direct linkages with the CIA."

"Any time, General. The Deputy Assistant Secretary of State and the Under Secretary for Defence are my good friends. I suggest you've a free and frank dialogue with the Secretary of State." Alam assured the worried PSO.

"That Jew isn't dependable."

"I know. A Jew can't be a friend of Islam. They'd even betrayed our Prophet. But in today's US he matters. He's rabidly anti-Indian and hates PM Manijra's guts."

"Can I pay off some key Congressmen?"

"Possible. I've to sound Senator O'Leary and Congressman Jacque Perry. They've the ears of the White House."

"Tell me when you require money transfer. There's a small point Alam. This blighter Hyder isn't able to get out of paranoid fixation about Harfan. Hyder has been influenced by Nawab."

"He's doing a fine job in the airlifting operations. Anything wrong?" Alam asked in an innocent tone.

"Nothing serious. Someone in Hyder's company wants to verify a few points about him and wants to talk to you. Hope you don't mind."

"Why should I? I'm ready, if it helps Pakistan." Alam finished the coffee without raising his eyes.

"Has he any suspected Indian link?" Sarfaraz asked.

"Not that I know. Jung Sher Khan, a business associate of Harfan's uncle, referred him to me. I don't mind Hyder probing the frequent flyer," Alam paused, "the coffee is excellent. Can I have one more?"

"My pleasure." The PSO pushed the buzzer and ordered another round of coffee.

"I'll be out to Paris and London for a few days. The unofficial NATO supplies of multi-barrel rocket launcher batteries are to be airlifted, from bases in Turkey. These are special supplies for our western front. You can tell Hyder to get in touch with me, say in another four days time."

"That should be fine. Give him a call. Don't forget to talk to your friends in Washington. Perhaps you may like to cross the Atlantic from Istanbul and meet your friends. Don't bother about the funds." Sarfaraz pleaded.

"Rest assured General," Alam replied, "I'd activate the correct circuits. You'd better activate the US ambassador here. His views will carry weight. Do you know this fellow, Hansen Lindsey, the CIA station chief? It's better if you carry him along."

"What about the British?"

"It's good that you've raised the point. The High Commissioner is a personal friend of Izaz Afroz. They served together in the UN. Better, not activate him. My friends in MI6 can be of better use to us."

"Know any one in that company?"

"Yeah. Michael Brandon, the deputy chief of South Asia desk, is a personal friend."

Alam paused a little to finish the coffee.

"Anyways, General thanks for the coffee and I'd be in touch with the US and Brit friends. You take care of Jainal, Izaz Afroz and Hyder. *Allah* shall light up your skies."

"Amin." Lt. General Sarfaraz repeated.

*

58

Alam turned the car towards Jhumra Valley.

Sarfaraz was sweet. However, it was foolish to expect him to come to his rescue when Hyder's scimitar slit his jugular. Moreover, why should he risk his neck for a two-penny Triple X agent? No. He wouldn't. It was about time he eliminated the major irritant. He should direct Qurban to liquidate Triple X before he boarded the flight for Istanbul. That was the easiest way to escape the jam. A dead Harfan wasn't going to serenade Hyder's spooks. That would firewall the pathway of the twister.

There was no need to consult Delhi.

Who would keep track of a small road accident?

For the first time Alam felt, he was facing the wall of doom—the firing squad, with fingers on the triggers. It was now a personal war. Sacrificing Harfan was the best way out. Alam gulped a dash of whisky, straight from the silver canteen and lighted a cigarette.

Millions of insects of anxiety and suspicion had started scratching his intestines. But his resolution to liquidate Harfan firmed up. Triple X couldn't be allowed to face ISI interrogation.

*

Ibadat hadn't expected Alam. He entered Alam's room with a salver of tea, light snacks, and took a seat.

Alam didn't disappoint him.

"Well done so far," Alam referred to Ramayani's death, "a good job done. Now it's time to eliminate the main threat."

"Who's that?" Ibadat asked.

"Mian Harfan Bukhari. He should die, before the ISI closes in on him."

"Why should he die? We can spirit him out." Ibadat spoke as he poured tea.

"Nope, Mian Ibadat. His death is important, for our lives."

"We can push him back to India."

"Leave aside your emotional secretions. When does Harfan return?" Alam sipped tea with relish.

"Perhaps tonight," Ibadat replied, "this is his eighth consecutive sortie."

"The ISI sleuths are closing in, Harfan has to be eliminated."

"You told me."

"I'm here to convey Delhi's orders."

Alam took out a piece of paper and sketched a route map between Jhumra and Sangla. His pen stopped at a major crossing, a north south highway intersecting the Grand Trunk road.

"The truck should naturally speed up from this road. Nothing should be left to chance. It should be a hit and run case. Pay the driver heavily. And ensure that he vanishes." Alam spoke coolly, like a hardened butcher, for whom killing was a part of daily bread.

"Is that the only option? Can't we push him to Kabul?" Ibadat asked.

"*Mian*," Alam spoke through his teeth, "why don't you understand? In our business we carry out orders and don't ask questions."

"What's wrong with discretion? Our objective is to protect the system, not to kill."

Alam stood up with an impatient gesture, walked up to the window, and whipped out a .25 Spanish automatic Astra, which snuggled nicely in the pan of his palm.

"I always carry this in my pocket." He pointed the pistol at an unspecified corner of the ornate colonial ceiling.

"My own life is just micro millimetres away, between this barrel and skins on my temple. My trade is more important than my life. Don't ever betray me, you won't even know when the hot bullets kiss you. My people are everywhere."

Ibadat shuddered in his bones. The chill of death brushed past his soul. He hadn't seen Alam earlier in this frame. The suave, sweet, and charming businessman had just disappeared behind the burning silhouette of a professional killer. He again looked at the pistol, barely visible, behind Alam's thick fleshy palm Its greyish blue tinge looked like a cobra's forked tongue.

Perhaps most spies ended this way, quietly, often violently, kissing the lips of death.

Why had Alam spun a story to kill Harfan? He doubted if Delhi would opt for operation elimination. Was it Alam's personal agenda?

"Where are you lost?" Alam placed the Astra back in his pocket.

"I've an idea!" Ibadat faked a deliberate suggestion, "I know some army drivers who operate between Jhumra and Lahore. Perhaps one of them can be tasked. The ISI tails would take the event as a genuine accident."

"A bright idea indeed!" Alam placed a briefcase on the table, "keep this, there're two grand in it. Spend wisely. His death should be sure and certain. We're safer that way."

As Ibadat bent down to pick up the brief case, Alam tapped his shoulder and gave him a gentle squeeze.

"Don't mind the tough talk. It's all part of the game. In our profession, our dearest consort is death. We accept it when it comes, like one goes to bed with a faker femme. We dwell uncertainly between life and death. I didn't wish to hurt you."

"What do we do with his wife and kid?"

"Nothing!" Alam shrugged wantonly, "she can take another husband under the Islamic law. And Zahoor has enough money to support them." Ibadat returned a feeble smile, not knowing what would exactly please Alam.

"These are small things. What happens to my wife if I die today? What happens to your mom? She will cry a bit and then get going with her life. That's the law of nature."

"That's correct sir."

"Don't delay. We don't have time to squander, and I feel the ISI is just a couple of steps ahead of us. I'll be out for a few days and I must rush to catch the early morning flight." Alam reinforced his pleading by gently squeezing Ibadat's shoulder and asking him to place his car under the porch.

*

Ibadat left Hotel Royal Palace, soon after Alam's car zoomed out kicking a trail of dust. He boarded a Lahore bound train. Out in the dung-littered parking lot, he hired a rickety horse cart and asked the driver to proceed to Masti Gate. The driver, a resident of the walled fort settlement, offered free commentary on the various landmarks of the historical city. Ibadat silently suffered the friendly but unsolicited comments and dismounted about a kilometre short of Masti Gate. He followed a service lane to reach Zahoor Chaudry's house.

Jamilla wasn't expecting Harfan at this time of the night. His special flight was supposed to land either at Jhang Maghiana or Bhagatanwala airbase late next evening. Jamilla paused briefly.

Who could it be? The Police, the ISI sleuths?

Were they here to pick up Harfan?

She partly opened the security latch, peeped out, and was surprised to see Ibadat. She liked him no doubt, but never expected an unsolicited visit from him.

"*Walai-kum-assalam*," she returned Ibadat's greetings, covered her head with the scarf, and enquired, "hope things are fine at Jhumra."

"Fine, absolutely fine. I'd been to Lahore on business and thought of looking you up and enquiring about brother Harfan and dear nephew Pervez." Ibadat's feeble efforts to justify his visit didn't convince Jamilla.

"Please be seated." She disappeared behind the fine muslin curtains and returned with Pervez.

"Any news from brother Harfan?" Ibadat asked.

"No idea." Jamilla wasn't in a mood to talk. She had promised not to betray any hint of their escape plans, not even to her parents.

"Any message for him?" Jamilla tried to fathom Ibadat's intention.

"Nothing. Just thought I'd look you up. You haven't been to Jhumra for months."

"So kind of you. A little more tea?"

"Don't mind having some," Ibadat had one more serving of *jelebis,* "there has been a terrific accident at Jhumra." He tried to drag the dialogue on.

"So sorry to hear," she poured tea and pretended to be unconcerned, "hope there hasn't been much damage to the fine hotel."

"It's not the hotel. Remember the old Hindu woman? She died in an accidental fire in her worship room. Poor soul, there was nobody around to save her."

For a moment, Jamilla's eyes twitched involuntarily. She tried to recall Harfan's suspicions; the old woman had perhaps recognised him, as the son of the former king. Yes, how could she forget the coins, minted by one of the kings of Jhumra! These were still with her, kept as talisman, a totem of good luck.

Was Ibadat conveying an indirect message? Were the nets around Harfan closing in? Did the Pakistani police kill her? Or, was it a mere accident?

"Let *Allah* give peace to her soul." Jamilla lowered her eyes to avoid Ibadat's prying looks. The fellow was trying to analyse her looks and reactions. He wasn't behaving normally.

"*Allah-hu-Akbar*," repeated Ibadat, "please tell brother Harfan to see me urgently, in case he happens to visit you first."

"Anything wrong?" The words escaped Jamilla's mouth involuntarily, betraying her anxious looks.

Ibadat walked up to the window, looked around for the possible presence of static surveillance. There were none.

"Has he told you anything?"

"About what? Anything specific?"

"About the ISI." Ibadat pinned the point and waited for Jamilla's reaction.

"Anything to do with Ramayani's death?" Her eyes twitched again with an expression of anxiety.

"Possible. Tell him that very little time's left and he must do whatever he can. Give this cover to him, he'll understand. Take care, *Khuda Hafiz.*" Ibadat passed on a closed envelope and got up to bid adieu.

"Tell me all you know," Jamilla demanded.

"And keep this box. It's for you. But open in the presence of brother Harfan."

"What's in it?"

"A surprise gift."

"You aren't coming out clean," she insisted.

"All that I can say, brother Harfan is in danger," Ibadat turned towards the door and suddenly wheeled back, "I think it would be better if you come down to Jhumra. Better be by his side."

"How can I help?"

"He needs your help. Brother Harfan is in danger and you alone can help. He requires you."

Ibadat said *adaab* and closed the door behind.

Jamilla followed and bolted the latch.

She walked over to the window, looked up at the minarets of the mosque, and kneeled down in prayer.

"*Bismillah-ar-Rehman-ur-Rahim,*" she continued to pray, "save him and the child from all evils. I shall observe complete *roza* (Ramadan fast), and offer the best sacrifice in your name."

Jamilla concentrated on the faces of Harfan and Pervez and focussed her will force to the united-field around the aura of the *Allah.* She tried to imagine the presence of a supreme heavenly face hanging brightly through clusters of galaxies. As a Muslim, she was never trained to imagine a material body of the Creator. However, at this moment of crisis she felt like touching the creator and deriving his blessings.

She prayed for Harfan and Pervez's safety. No, she wouldn't allow either the Indian or Pakistani evil machines to harm them. The benediction of the *Allah*, the wonderful benign Supreme Being, would save them. Harfan was her man, a much-wronged person and she wouldn't allow the political butchers to harm him. There was space for them beyond the soils of India and Pakistan—two foolish countries bleeding each other. The hangmen of scarred history couldn't choke their life force off.

*

59

The Lady of The Light, Athena Air Line's Boeing 707, dropped altitude to 29,000 feet, as it crossed the skies over Karachi. It followed the Indus, which appeared, in the golden fading light, like a fluttering blue ribbon on a naughty maiden's head, just swept free by the wild westerly wind. The river's vast winding course was girdled by a flood of yellow and grey hues—yellow of the first flush of flowering mustard plants and the golden grey of the almost mature, ready to harvest paddy fields.

Vudurume followed ATC instructions, banked right, and took a north-easterly course from Muzaffargarh.

Harfan, seated behind the pilot, looked down the front windshield. Dera Ghazi Khan's faint lights on the left were blooming up in ones and twos, and some faint clusters of lights in Multan were glistening and pulsating like distant galactic debris.

"Anxious for Jamilla!" Vudurume asked while levelling the plane.

"Vudu, you know the causes of my anxiety," Harfan spoke in a hushed voice, "I'm doing my best to serve the country. But some power hungry jackals don't want us to win this war against India. They think I'm an important cog in the CMLA juggernaut, close to the President. I smell a coup in the air."

"It's a pity. Hope I'm done with this assignment before you people jump at each other's throat. I fly because it's my profession, not for war. That's your business." Vudurume again dropped altitude and aligned the plane to the railway track below, traversing north.

"I'm sick of this mission and want a break. I've flown to most scary joints in Africa and South America, but your flunkies are real screwed up. Anyways," he shrugged, "I want to be with my kids before Christmas. How're your lovely wife and kid? You Muslims don't like to take your wives out of their veils! Isn't it?"

"Don't be silly," Harfan helped himself to a cigarette, "Jami is a modern girl. We've been damn busy flying these horrible death machines. You must meet her this time."

"Pity I can't go to your town. My contract doesn't allow."

"Why bother? I'll request her to come down to Bhagatan. It's not far from her home."

"Why wait, call now. What's the exchange telephone number?"

Harfan shared with him the number of Zahoor Chaudry.

Vudurume picked up the handset, dialled and asked the operator to patch Zahoor Chaudry's number.

"Who is it?" Jamilla's anxious voice sounded faint.

"It's me, Jami."

Jamilla took a fraction of a second to recognise Harfan's voice, slightly distorted by the noise of mechanical patching.

"Hi Jami, it's me. How're you? And Pervez?"

"Hai *Rabba*! (Oh God)," Jamilla recovered her composure immediately, "your voice is faint. Are you calling from Dacca?"

"No darling, just from the air, not far from you. We're landing at Bhagatan. Can you come down there with Pervez? Perhaps, I won't be able to go to Lahore this time. There's another job ahead."

"Sure. When do you expect me to be there?"

"Darling every minute is precious. I miss you. Get at the wheel and you'll be there in two hours flat. Take a driver. Come straight to hotel Nishat."

Harfan's excitement infused a churning in Jamilla's surging emotions. She replied in the affirmative, brushed aside Sayeefa's protests, and hit the road in fifteen minutes, with Pervez by her side.

*

What Jamilla hadn't expected and noticed was a battered Ford, which followed her at a safe distance with Ibadat at the wheels. Ibadat was intrigued by Jamilla's sudden move. He had expected her to drive straight to Jhumra. He felt vexed when her car followed a different trail altogether towards Sargodha. What was she up to? Was she in touch with Harfan? Were the Bukharis double-crossing him and escaping from Pakistan?

Chasing Jamilla was not easy. She was propelled by love, and Ibadat by mere gasoline. Her Toyota suddenly swerved from the main Sargodha road and headed towards Bhagatan town.

Was she going to meet Harfan? Had they kept him in the dark? Why not? He had not expected Harfan to trust him. A cornered boar did not trust its own shadow. Poor fellow! From day one, Harfan's biological and intellectual vibes hadn't clicked well with that of Alam. Two inflated egocentric individuals were in perpetual conflict. Poor Delhi! All their meticulous calculations went haywire. Ibadat chuckled.

He tried to make an intelligent guess. The mercenary flights operated from Bhagatanwala, Jhang Maghiana and Mianwali, under supervision of the Air Traffic Control, Sargodha. These non-strategic airports were taken over by the Air Force and civilian traffic was diverted.

Was Harfan landing at Bhagatan this evening?

Ibadat's irritation squirmed up caustic juices in his guts. If Jamilla was going to meet Harfan, the ISI stool pigeons shouldn't be far behind. They must be following her too. He adjusted the rear view mirror. No. There was no sign of any Mosur vehicle following her, not even the terra-Moon faced Arman Ali Niazi. He accelerated, keeping pace with Jamilla's car. Ibadat steadied his steering and adjusted his speed to maintain a steady hundred-meter distance from Jamilla's Toyota.

*

Vudurume felt irritated and exhausted. Fatigue of non-stop flying from Dacca was furrowed into his face. To top it Sargodha ATC just radioed, as he was on the descent mode, to hang on for a while. All air lanes in the vicinity were closed down.

He banked right, took a south-west tangent, leaving the Sargodha main base at far left, reduced speed, released the elevators and prepared for a landing.

"ATC, Lady of The Light here. Aligned to land."

"AAL 356, hang on. Climb to 20,000 ft. A VIP flight is scheduled at Sargodha in 10 minutes. All air lanes are embargoed." The ATC came in sharp in the Boeing's cockpit.

"Fucking hell! Why didn't you warn me?"

"Fly southward and approach after fifteen minutes." The ATC, conversant with Vudurume's tantrums, replied in a cool flat voice.

Vudurume cursed the ATC supervisor, swerved down south, and gained altitude. He swore choicest appellatives, which came in loud and clear in the tower terminals.

The foul-up was due to an unscheduled landing of a presidential flight at Sargodha. Bad weather had resulted in closing down of the Chak Lala airport. General Arif and his US Congressional guests, therefore, had decided to land at the strategic Air Force base, on their flight back from a forward formation. Pakistan could not afford to expose a mercenary flight to Congressmen, most of them hostile to the White House.

Vudurume was blissfully ignorant of the complicated nerve wrecking games played by the sub-continental political players. He was neither concerned with the blatant US tilt nor the open Chinese interference in the Indo-Pakistan stand off. He flew the death machines for his keeps.

The ATC clearance came well after thirty minutes. Vudu approached the runway from its southern funnel, following the course of a tributary of Jhelum. He released the under gear and asked Harfan to fasten seat belt.

A red-light-flashing military police car guided Vudu to a remote apron, camouflaged from the rest of the airport by well-landscaped curtains of vegetative growth. Vudurume and crew were driven down to hotel Nishat.

Harfan followed them in a taxi.

He braved the mid-November chill and waited behind the shadows of a jasmine vine. His eyes were riveted to the main approach, anticipating Jamilla and Pervez. His knowledge of the working ethos and modus operandi of the intelligence agencies exacerbated his anxiety. His company, the National Security India, was capable of bumping off its useless and estranged agents.

Jamilla's car screeched to a halt under the portico of hotel Nishat, before Harfan could notice its passage through the main entrance. His eyes, though open, were lost in the imaginary gorge with Jamilla's gored body rolling down its slopes.

"Hi darling." Jamilla waved as she alighted.

Harfan opened the door and helped Jamilla pick up her night bag. Pervez giggled loudly and jumped into Harfan's hands.

"Go to room 627, while I park the car."

Harfan asked the driver to move the car to a covered garage and park himself in a nearby low cost hotel.

Vudurume ambushed them near the second floor landing.

"Hi prince charming," he waived out, "now you can't escape."

"Meet my wife Jamilla and our prince Pervez." Harfan introduced Vudurume.

"Holy Christ! You're a lucky dog," the South African pilot whistled, "what do you say, *namaste,* oh no! It must be *salaam* with you. Pardon me ma'am. You know, my parents were Hindu and I don't really know what I am."

"*Adaab*." Jamilla replied while covering her head with a white scarf.

"Be my guest for dinner." Vudurume invited Jamilla with an expansive gesture, like a banquet floor manager.

Dinner wasn't a big do, but the cuisine of the small hotel was characteristically Lahori. Vudurume added the romantic touch by producing rare Toulouse champagne from his personal cellar.

"You must fly one of these days with me," he poured the frothy champagne for Jamilla, "hope you've been in one of these jumbo crafts."

"Not really." Jamilla replied in a hushed voice.

"You must come. Bring her one of these days, Harfan. It'll be my privilege to fly them."

The South African pilot was in an expansive mood.

"My wife Janice, a German lady, is a teacher."

"Is she from proper Germany?" Jamilla enquired.

"No, Austria. Her entire family, all Austrian Jews, were stuffed into a train and fed as fodder to Hitler's gas chamber at Auschwitz by the Nazi psychopath Joseph Mengele. She alone survived the war in a concentration camp, serving the maniacal Aryans and was rescued by the Allied forces. A brave lady indeed."

"Please tell me more about Janice and your family." Jamilla demanded in a low voice.

"There's nothing great to tell. A coloured South African can't have much to say. Harfan knows the story. In simple language I was hounded out of the Air Force for pressing my children's right to study in an all white school." Vudurume tried to cut short the dialogue.

"Please tell me more." Jamilla insisted.

"The inheritor of a bonded labourer can't protest in South Africa, even if you're married to a white woman. That itself is a crime." Vudu replied and continued...

"Janice, I mean my wife and Ralph and Ramie, our sons, live in Paris. And my dear," Vudu paused, "I want to retire and move to Paris, as soon as the boys finish their courses in medicine and engineering. That's the short story of a sort of a long journey over three generations, from Ballia, an unknown corner in India. From a bonded labourer to a jet pilot, isn't it a big jump?" Jamilla's liquid eyes drew Vudu's attention.

"Oh dear!" He lifted Jamilla's wineglass by the stem and put it near her lips, "don't weep. We've wept for generations. Now it's time to fight back. I can't be a Gandhi or a Mandela. But fight we must and fly to our freedom."

"I wish I could join in your fight. I've read a lot about Mandela." Jamilla spoke in a hushed voice.

"Come to my flight to freedom."

"Well Captain," Harfan added, "don't insist. We may just accept your offer, one of these days."

"Don't challenge a bush-flyer. Bring this little angel too. Come in the next flight."

Vudurume's voice hoarsened with hidden emotion.

*

60

Harfan and Jamilla sat around a coffee table in the confines of their room. Burning with curiosity and anxiety Harfan opened up his mind.

"Did Ibadat say Ramayani died in an accidental fire?" Harfan asked.

"He didn't elaborate. All he said was that her death had something to do with your safety. He sounded nervous, edgy, and hesitant. Better, read the letter. He said it's urgent." Jamilla took out Ibadat's letter and the small box from her night-bag.

Harfan opened the box first. The blue diamond shone translucently under the fluorescent lamps.

"What's this?" Jamilla looked intently at the gem.

Harfan picked up the stone and examined it against light. He could not make any sense out of it.

"Here's something." Jamilla picked up a chit from the box and started reading it.

"This rare blue diamond, Neel Kamal (Blue Lotus) is for the *bahu* (daughter in law) of my son and the son of the king of Jhumra. This is an heirloom of the Kaushal kings. Tradition says this diamond belonged to the Pandavas of Indrapasth. A descendant of Nadir Shah, who had pillaged Delhi mercilessly, last possessed it. The second Kaushal king had retrieved the diamond in one of his campaigns, on behalf of the British, against the Afghan tribes in Kandahar region. Protect it."

"What's the meaning of this?" The short note baffled Jamilla.

Harfan opened the envelope rather hesitatingly.

Ibadat couldn't probably carry any message from Delhi. Nampoothiri's earlier message was clear; they had washed their hands off him with all the perfume of Kanauj (Indian town famous for perfumes). His name was probably scratched off from their honour rolls. Harfan smiled. No mercy could be expected from Delhi.

Had he reached, what the French called, *fin de ligne,* end of the line? Perhaps he ran too fast. Perhaps intelligence agents should behave like arrows in a quiver and remain passive observers.

What should he do?

What does an animal do when cornered by a dogged hunter?

Defend yourself fool! Harfan's soul screamed out.

The NSI must have given the order to eliminate him, Operation Elimination Triple X. They would be more interested in protecting their existing assets in Pakistan. They wouldn't care for retrieving a daredevil resident agent, who had been milked white with no juice left for the suckers in Delhi.

"What're you thinking?" Jamilla brought Harfan back to his senses.

"Yah." He gingerly shelved the agonising thoughts and opened the envelope. He quickly glanced through the contents and looked up at Jamilla with an ashen pale face. Perspiration appeared in visible droplets on his forehead.

"Any problem? Are you okay?" Jamilla placed her hand on his forehead, *"Hai Rabba!* You're absolutely cold."

"I'm fine, don't panic. Read this aloud."

He passed on the letters to Jamilla, placed his head on her lap, and burst into loud sobs.

The first page was in Ibadat's hand:

"Brother Harfan. Or shall I salute the Prince of Jhumra! I don't recall the name given to you on the sixth day of your birth, according to Hindu rituals....

"By now you know that you're not a born Muslim. Leave the preliminaries. You can't get back your kingdom. These small things in life aren't important. I wonder if you should consider such grandiose plans when you're inside the nutcracker....

"The most important truth in your life shouldn't frighten you. Face it. Queen Kasturi isn't your blood-mother. She wasn't capable of bearing any child, because of an operation she had undergone soon after her marriage. The truth must be told ....

"Ramayani, the queen's *saheli* (friend), by common consent and religious edict, nursed in her womb the seeds of your father and gave birth to you, behind the super-secret royal walls. It's an ancient Hindu practice, I'm told....

"Seconds after your birth, you were separated from your real mother and were brought up by the royal mother....

"Your two mothers were in correspondence. I've burnt all those letters, except four. Keep the rare photograph of your father and real mother snapped together. Read these carefully. You shall know how fortunate you've been to be blessed by two mothers and how they were concerned with your wild ways of life....

"Don't forget to tell Jamilla, how happy they were to know about your marriage to her. Ramayani had recognised you and had blessed your wife in a peculiar Hindu way, when you had brought her to the palace for the first time. Remember that... .

"The blue diamond is a gift from your amma to your wife... .

"Coming back to business, I must tell you that the ISI has completed their investigations. They hesitate because of your connections, and your frontline utility. You're the proverbial canary, taken down the mineshaft, for testing the carbon monoxide levels. You die to save your masters....

"Alam has issued your execution orders, that's what the Big Man has ordered me to do. I'm supposed to carry it out. Take care while on the road. His hands are long and we can't expose him...

"Sorry for gate crashing the other day on Jamilla *bhabhi*. Perhaps we shall not meet again, hence this letter. Take care. *Khuda Hafiz*."

Jamilla stopped. She was too stunned to speak. What a quirk of fate! She was just in the midst of a royal intrigue. She was caught in the crossfire of a sinister proxy war between India and Pakistan. Destiny had placed her in the arms of an Indian intelligence agent, son of a former king, now facing bullets from his supposed friends and foes.

"Read the other two letters." Harfan, now more collected, requested Jamilla. Jamilla read out the letters, one from Ramayani and the other from Kasturi. The contents confirmed in vivid detail her own visits to the former palace and the first meeting with Ramayani. The unfortunate old lady was mighty glad to meet her! She had, in fact, accepted Jamilla as her daughter-in-law.

Jamilla secured the letters and the diamond in her vanity case. No. She wouldn't allow the sacrifices of two mothers to be consumed by the fires of betrayal and hatred. She must preserve the old coins and the fabulous blue diamond, symbols of good luck and links with the legendary royal family. She must preserve the rare photograph.

"Better destroy these by burning. These are solid evidence against us."

Harfan advised Jamilla.

"Destroy Ibadat's letter. I'd keep the others. *Allah* willing, I'd carry these with me."

Jamilla's voice sounded stubborn.

"Where do we go from here?"

"Don't despair dear. Closing of one window doesn't mean we're shut off from the world." Jamilla replied in a buoyant mood.

Harfan didn't dare contradicting her. He silently burnt Ibadat's letter, poured the ashes into the toilet bowl, and flushed it down. Gurgling water carried down some of his secrets to an unknown abyss.

Harfan walked over to the window. His mind raced out to the red, blue, and white beams of light from Bhagatan ATC tower, which pierced the dark night in lightening flashes.

What should he do now? Stay put for taking revenge? Avenge his father's assassination and the gruesome murder of his mother? The thought bounced back from hollow crevices of his mind. He didn't get the correct replies, though his thoughts kept on flashing through the darkest alleys of his mind, like the ATC signal beams.

Jamilla kept on stirring coffeé she had just brewed. Tears rolled down her cheeks.

"What do we do now?" She asked.

Harfan lifted her head tenderly.

"Don't weep. My life is a wreck. Why don't you leave me? Let me surrender to the ISI. Let me face the consequences."

"No," Jamilla stoutly protested, "you won't do that. You can't desert Pervez and me. We'll do everything together, whether it is in life or in death."

"I'm not worthy of your affection."

"You alone can't take that decision. You can't end up in front of an assassin's bullet." Jamilla spoke in a firm and resolute voice.

"I'm not worried about my life. I'm worried about you and Pervez."

"Don't be afraid of life. Mummy says life is like a flowing river. Every moment it assumes new character and new properties. Death isn't the final medicine for the problems of life. You can fight these ailments with your life force. Life has still many wonders to offer."

Jamilla moved closer and planted a light kiss on Harfan's lips. Harfan suddenly felt a surge of energy flooding his entire existence. He clasped Jamilla firmly against his chest, returned her kiss, this time a hot and passionate one.

"You're correct, Jami. For a moment, I had lost myself in the blind alleys of my own misdeeds and misadventures. I forgot that there is more to life than being a spy. I'm a son, a husband, and a father too. Above all, I'm alive and kicking. I can't be paralysed. Let's live together."

He guided Jamilla to the bed.

*

61

Harfan called Israr Sharief around five in the morning. The sun was yet to cross the misty golden ribbon of the horizon.

"Boss, sorry for the early call."

"It's okay. When did you land?"

"Last night. There's a small problem boss."

"What's new? Hope the Indians aren't firing rockets."

"It's not the Indians, boss. It's a minor problem of the heart." Harfan narrated the romantic escapade of Jamilla to Bhagatanwala and spending the night with him. He didn't want her to go back to Lahore. The next flight to Dacca should take off in another 24 hours, from Bhagatan itself.

"Can we spend a few hours in your Bhagatan guesthouse?"

"Still the eternal love birds?" Israr asked indulgently, "no problem, you're welcome. Listen, I've an urgent piece of business. Come to office, say around nine. It's super secret."

"Anything special?"

"Presume so. Naqi has a surprise packet for Dacca."

"Fine boss. See you in the office."

Harfan disconnected and called Zahoor Chaudry to inform Jamilla was with him and she would stay on for another two days. They wanted privacy and no one should be given their address.

At daybreak, Harfan walked down and called Jamilla's driver.

"Salam Fardin *bhai*," he pushed a wad of notes in his hand, "aren't you from Shukran village?"

"Yes sir. It's only five miles from here."

"Take a break. Jami wouldn't require you for the next 48 hours. Report back day after tomorrow. Have a nice time."

"But sir...."

"Come on Fardin! Go home and spend some time with your *begum* (wife) and kids. Give me the keys."

Fardin obliged hesitatingly. Harfan rushed back to the hotel. By seven, he planted a kiss on Jamilla and kicked off the accelerator. The nascent idea of escaping from Pakistan started rolling inside and sprouted spontaneously. The letters from his mothers helped in the magical growth of the beanstalk. The befuddled Jack that he was, he could climb that fragile beanstalk and reappear at a safer place. No. He had no desire to reach the other end of the world. He simply wanted a cosy, safe home for Jamilla and Pervez.

Yes. Vudurume was his beanstalk and he could easily climb and vanish beyond the clouds.

For a while, Harfan was lost in his thoughts. However, he didn't fail to notice a car tailing him. He adjusted the rear view mirror and concentrated on the occupant of the car behind. He expected the pockmarked face of Arman Niazi. The other face surprised him. There was no mistaking. It was Ibadat, following him at a safe distance. Was he there to pump in a few lethal bullets? Why should he follow him stealthily? He could have taken a pot shot at him long back and didn't require some lonely stretch of road to carry out Alam's orders.

Why was he tailing him?

Harfan took out a .38 colt with sawed off barrel and tucked into his belt. But, Ibadat suddenly stirred his car to a narrow left lane. The emerging contours of Sangla factory and Ibadat's sudden peeling off made Harfan to press the break, to avoid a head on collision with a truck. Perhaps Ibadat wasn't the messenger of death, deputed by Alam. He liked to believe Ibadat wouldn't betray him. If he were, where was the need for that lengthy sentimental letter? Why should he caution him? Why should he chaperone him in like a mother goose?

Harfan heaved a sigh of relief, as he alighted from the vehicle. He could now coolly plan a new operation, the daring 'Operation Escape.' The galactic watch ticking inside kept telling him that the correct time had come. It was time for the Jackal of Jhunjhunu, or say Jhumra, to borrow the wings of destiny and fly... Well! Fly where? Into the uncertain blues? Would he be able to land with Jamilla and Pervez well tucked under his wings? He uttered a silent prayer. The power of love and life should enable him to make a perfect landing.

Where was he to land? Harfan smiled. The last gamble of the Knight of the Jackals was yet to be unfolded.

*

62

Jamanat Ali stormed in, in double marching order, clicked his heels with a piercing sharp metallic sound, and saluted with a stiff but shaking palm. Brigadier Barqat looked up, anticipating another ecstatic outburst from the veteran sleuth. He must be bubbling to the brim with information. The sharpest metallic sound ever produced by Jamanat's heels and the swishing salute was indicative of the Quranic revelations to come. He appreciated Jamanat's tenacity. A near perfect counterintelligence officer, who never said die, was in the habit of doggedly pursuing even the thinnest shred of evidence. Failures helped in honing up his spirit and determination. Only a month away from superannuating, Jamanat espoused two pre-retirement ambitions: netting Harfan Bukhari, the Indian spy, and *Insha Allah*, a final visit to Phillaur, his alma mater and his maternal *nana*'s (great grandpa) village near Fatehgarh Churian, both in Indian Punjab.

"*Janab, Allah meherban* (God is merciful)," he spoke in a booming voice, "I've all the crucial evidence in my pocket."

"Evidence of what?"

"That bloody Harfan. He's an Indian spy. My evidence is incontrovertible." Jamanat took out a folder and placed it carefully before the Brigadier, "please read. There's everything in it."

"*Shukria* (thanks) Jamanat sahib. Please sit down. Would you like to have some tea?"

"I wouldn't mind some, sir."

The meticulously compiled report contained a complete profile of Harfan Bukhari, his family history in undivided India, total annihilation of the lineage of Maqdoom Bukhari in communal riots, and his uncle Shamim Bukhari's migration to Karachi. Young Harfan Bukhari, according to the report, was hurled into a blazing infernal fire by the marauding Hindu-Sikh mob and burnt alive with his parents and two sisters. His uncle had seen him last, a few days before the orgy of violence, when he was a five-year-old toddler, learning Urdu alphabets from the village *madrassa* (religious school).

Shamim's sister, married to a Delhi trader, died around 1952, two years after her husband was assassinated in another communal violence in 1950. Her husband's immediate family had migrated to Lahore.

"You mean this Harfan didn't live to grow up at all! He didn't exist!"

"A Harfan did exist till he was killed by Hindu rioters. The Indian FIB picked up the name of the dead boy and retextured his family history in order to weave a cogent cover for their long-term resident agent. A good cover indeed, I must admit sir. The FIB and now the damn NSI has blistered our eyes and senses successfully." Jamanat sipped the tea with relish.

"That's a classic tradecraft strategy, Jamanat."

"An excellent one at that it must be the handy work of Dutta sahib."

"Who is he?"

"The legendary Director of the Indian FIB sir, Rabindra Narayan Dutta. I've seen him functioning from close quarters."

Jamanat replied with an air of nostalgia.

"What about his documentation?"

"All forged. Some have been procured with the help of Irfan Cowasji, who was in the employment of the Indian Mission in Karachi. And the rest were obtained by greasing palms of Pakistani officials."

"Wait, wait," Barqat pleaded, "not so fast. How did you get these materials? Our station in Delhi appears to be efficient."

"Pardon me sir," Jamanat spoke in an ingratiating voice, "the attached note gives details of friend Shauqat's inputs and our new Operation Sargam."

"You mean Chawla?"

"Yes sir."

"Congratulations. The PIB boss tells me that his boys have collected valuable details. Is there any leakage?"

"No sir. They've their own ways to pursue a suspect. Their reports should corroborate our materials." Jamanat narrated the detailed reports collected by Jaffar Tyrewala, Karamat Suri and other operatives.

"Wonderful, Jamanat!"

Jamanat had done a fabulous job. The devil had hooked two whales with one harpoon, busting the cover of Harfan Bukhari and reviving the dormant Project Magnet as new Sargam. No doubt, Raghu Chawla should, in due course, replace Operation Aftab, Pakistan's most successful intelligence project.

Hai Rabba! How could he have overlooked the transparent evidence! Perhaps the bosses were too obsessed with that pugnacious insignificant courtesan, the supposed first lady. How could the ISI succumb to her fleshy whims! Jamanat was correct all the way.

"Sir, I'm not bothered by the delay. I request you to scrutinise the mechanism our enemy agencies have adopted to infiltrate and house this forward agent with almost a fool-proof cover."

"What do you mean by that?"

"We still don't know how he was infiltrated, who his Pakistani collaborators are! I've picked up Hassan Rathore of Umerkot, a notorious smuggler and partner of Aftab, a specialist in the narcotics and flesh trade."

"Was he responsible for Harfan's infiltration?"

"No sir. Amrik Singh, a front paw of Aftab, had approached Rathore. But the Indian FIB didn't use that channel. We don't know why."

"Was that feudal Soda Rajput chieftain of Ramsar involved in sheltering him?"

"No sir, we're yet to hit the correct tunnel."

Jamanat explained the role of the key dramatis personae, Irfan Cowasji, the Pakistani driver of the Indian Mission in Karachi. Now retired, the driver worked as a *khidmatgar* (voluntary worker) at the shrine of Abdullah Shah Ghazi, a *Sufi dargah* (mausoleum) above Clifton Viewpoint hilltop. He didn't require much persuasion. A few routine twists on his old bones had opened up the rusted reeds, and he revealed the fascinating details of induction and baptism of Harfan Bukhari in his treacherous trade inside Pakistan.

Shamim Bukhari, Jamanat explained, was a victim of his love and longing for the soil, he had left behind. This was peculiar to all the *muhajirs.* A little scratch often ripped open stored memories of the walled city of Delhi.

He wasn't adamant. He came out clean and his wife, half his age, and two young brothers-in-law were more than cooperative. They blamed the old haggard for claiming a stranger as his nephew. What they didn't mention was that, they invoked the *Allah* in their daily *namaj*, to call the old haggard to His services, at *behest* (heaven) or *dozakh* (hell), whatever slots His Angels had reserved for the fool.

The rest of Harfan's contacts came through open business connections, Jamanat opined. Jung Sher Khan, Alam Khan and Israr Sharief, all pure Pathans and Punjabis, were not conscious players in the Indian drama. The wily fellow, this Harfan, was an efficient charmer and knew the tricks of climbing the correct ropes.

"What about his marriage?" Barqat asked.

"*Janab*, it appears to be a case of love at first sight. Jamilla's father, Zahoor Chaudry, an estuary tribal from a low caste fishing community, is an inferior Muslim. He married a nautch girl, not exactly a whore, but a famous *mujrewali* (professional singer) from Lucknow. Supposedly close to Malika Jahanara, she doesn't strictly believe in the tenets of Islam. Born of such parents, Jamilla isn't expected to be a puritan in her religious views. She's well educated and loves her husband."

No. She could not be called a committed Pakistani, but she wasn't a *na-pak* (impure) Pakistani either. She was one of those enlightened unislamic socialites, who impertinently questioned the wisdom behind social practices prescribed by the *Hadith* and the *Sharia.* Such blasphemous people should have no place in the land of the pure, Pakistan, Jamanat asserted forcefully.

"You've an iron cast case, Jamanat. I'm fully convinced. Nevertheless, Zahoor is helping the government in a big way. His people in the delta areas have already neutralised five weapons landing efforts by India. Don't you think he would intercede on behalf of his son-in-law?"

"That's a valid point sir. But I don't think he would be delighted to know that his son-in-law is not even a Muslim."

"Let me think over the matter. Give a little time to plan out the operation. You have done a fine job."

Barqat complimented his junior colleague.

"We should pick him up, now. We've put our fingers in too many holes and the reptile must have been alarmed. And sir..." Jamanat hastened to add, "I doubt this fellow Ibadat as well. His behaviour is suspect."

"I agree. Pick him up," Barqat advised his colleague, "but I must discuss with the Chief and the Operations Appraisal Committee. And Jamanat, you know the sensitivity of this case. It's better we carry the bosses with us."

"But, sir..." Jamanat fumed like a wounded bison.

"Keep cool, Jamanat. I'm with you. This time we aren't talking in the air. The evidences are conclusive. Just give me two or three days. I'll take full responsibility. Let me prepare an executive summary for the chief and the PSO to the CMLA. You better pick up Ibadat and be in town for consultations."

"Hope we don't have to wait for a presidential consent." Jammat was still not convinced that his immediate bosses were serious.

"No Jamanat. It's an open and shut case, the biggest catch we've ever had so far. Let's play cool." Barqat pacified his junior's ruffled feelings. "Unmasking of the biggest Indian wizard, Jamanat, in fact, is entirely a one-man *jihad.* You should be recommended for a top national honour, say the Nishan-e-Pakistan."

"I want no extension of service sir," Jamanat mumbled, "after forty years of slogging I want peace and time to remember the *Allah.*"

Jamanat stood up, again clicked his heels, and made a smart about turn. He felt extremely happy today. His lifelong ambition of neutralising a top Indian resident agent in Pakistan was about to be crowned with success. He would prefer to have a deep sleep, only after bringing a few shining Pakistani heads under the chopper. What better reward could a superannuating intelligence officer dream of!

*

63

Israr International's Bhagatan guesthouse was located on a midget sized hillock, locally known as Laluwali *tikri*, a landmass jutted into a tributary of the river Chenab. The river looped around the hillock isolating the small colonial bungalow, which once served as the official residence of the British agent to the nearby Shahpur Nawabdom. There was an old world charm to it.

Harfan had chosen the guesthouse not merely for its idyllic location and scenic beauty. The grand isolation of the bungalow had an added advantage. It was just about four kilometres from Bhagatan airbase. It had other strategic advantages as well.

Harfan wasn't asleep. His mind hovered between the super and supra conscious levels of cerebral cortex. Eyes closed, he was mixing, like an editor in darkroom, forward, backward, and multi-directional images of the immediate past events and rushes of probable forthcoming clips.

Israr Sharief 's briefing floated on top of his mind. The next flight, he said, would carry a consignment of highly confidential load—nerve gas artillery shells. The deadly chemical weapons were procured from a delicate US source. Probably these were Vietnam surplus WMD (weapons of mass destruction).

Harfan had protested on moral grounds. How could he carry the deadly chemical weapons meant for killing innocent millions in East Pakistan and probably India? Israr overruled him. It was a simple business transaction. It did not matter if the junta killed innocent millions by conventional or chemical weapons. The orders were from the top, he added.

There would be no meddling by the Supply Corps personnel. General Naqi had given specific instructions for safeguarding secrecy of this particular consignment. The CMLA and his small coterie of advisors did not want any leakage of Pakistan's WMD capability. The US sources had imposed strict conditions for storing, airlifting, and war field use. Pakistan could use these weapons only after obtaining clearance from the USA.

Harfan breathed slowly, listened to Israr like a disciplined soldier, and quickly ran over the scenarios hitting his psyche with accelerated particles. Yes. Why not? He visualised Jamilla's dream window opening up, through which he could fly to freedom, with Pervez and his love by his side.

Harfan rolled over in the bed...the debate within stabilised. His left hand lightly rested on Jamilla's bosom, and the fingers of his right hand were locked with those of Pervez.

Their soul-vibes, Harfan wished to believe, were running through his blood stream and strengthening his determination. His own warmth and confidence, his steely-will to protect the family, Harfan imagined, were seeping into their existence. Impregnated impulses from their unified life forces created a unique protection field. It was a regeneration process, injecting driblets of strength in him with fresh life force, and transferring particles of hope and love into them.

Another elemental wave, however, knocked his supra conscious senses.

Dot-dot-dash, dot-dash-dot—

The Morse sounds were hitting his trained eardrums in faint broken waves.

Harfan's mind slowly correlated the sound waves.

Yes. The pattern was clear.

I—B—A—D—A—T. O—P—E—N. U—R—G—E—N—T.

What was the blighter doing here?

Harfan again listened to the faint sounds produced by finger strokes on the door panel. Who could it be? What if some one had faked the signals? The ISI interrogators could have cracked Ibadat and he may have spilled the beans.

Perhaps Alam had hired a killer to execute him.

Nothing surprised him anymore.

Harfan opened eyes and tried to fathom the depth of darkness enveloping him. He gradually discerned the contours of the room. His glances traversed past the figures of Jamilla and Pervez.

Harfan removed his hands carefully and felt the loaded pistol under the pillow. The warm metal gave him confidence. He slithered out of bed, the warm colt in readiness, and stealthily stepped on the floor like a dragon lizard and proceeded towards the source of the signal. He held his breath and placed his right ear on the door panel. The Morse code was still piercing through the wooden barrier. He tried to sniff the smell of the stranger.

Damn! Harfan breathed out a curse.

Who could it be? The ISI would not have offered the courtesy of a wakeup call with sophisticated Morse signals. Alam's killers could've broken in through one of the windows. Harfan collected his breath.

It could be Ibadat. He tiptoed to a side window that opened onto the balcony and climbed out. His gaze pierced the veil of darkness, and located the slight figure of Ibadat. Harfan hit his knee joints in a quick karate move, flooring and immobilising him.

"Free me. You'll wake up the entire guesthouse." Ibadat hissed out in anguish.

Harfan relaxed his grip and helped Ibadat stand up.

"Wait. Let me open the door."

Harfan slithered back into the room and opened the door. Ibadat squeezed past the opening and closed the panels behind.

"Why are you stalking us? I've seen you following me from Lahore. What's the game? Do you want to kill us?" Harfan asked, his pistol still aimed at Ibadat's head.

"Remove the gun and sit down. I'm not here to kill you. I need urgent consultations."

Ibadat pushed aside Harfan's loaded hand and made a move towards the sofa.

"I'm not stalking you Harfan. Don't mix up reflexes. You're in a dark tunnel. Fly like a bat. Sharpen your radar. You require it now more than you ever did." Their excited whispers ruined Jamilla's sleep. She carefully turned on her side and switched on the bed lamp.

"What's the matter?" she demanded an answer from Harfan.

"Put the light off. Nothing to worry." Harfan whispered.

They sat around the coffee table, while Jamilla prepared black coffee.

"Pardon me, for disturbing you at Laluwali," Ibadat sipped the invigorating brew, "I'd no other option. I can't afford to be seen with you anymore. Tell me what're your plans."

"What's this Alam up to? Why does he want me dead?"

"That's his problem," Ibadat replied, "you know what the last instructions from Delhi are. It asks for a simple disengagement. The top boss wants you out to Kabul and London."

"Has Alam been sold to the Pakis?"

"Most unlikely. He's trying to insulate himself, by offering you as the sacrificial goat. He doesn't forgive, and I don't expect mercy from him. I want you back in India, with Jamilla *bhabhi* and Pervez. Another mother is waiting for you. What's your plan?"

"Nothing in particular," Harfan replld, "I fly to Dacca in another couple of hours and Jamilla goes back to Lahore."

"Don't kid. You know what I mean," Ibadat pushed the cup forward and requested another fill, "you're caught in a crossfire. This is no time to hedge."

"How near are we from death?" Jamilla asked while pouring coffee, in the darkness, spilling some, her hands shaking slightly.

"Very near, in fact, in front of you." Ibadat took out a gun, tucked near the crevice of his spine.

"I've Alam's orders to eliminate Harfan. And if I don't do the job before the ISI catches up, I'm shot. It's as simple as that. The other fascinating way of executing Alam's order is to smother Harfan under the wheels of a speeding truck. Sounds charming! Doesn't it?"

"How can he give that order?" Jamilla asked.

"Don't ask me that *bhabhi*. Both of us are caught in the whirlpool of destiny. Most of the agents disappear that way."

"What's this darn job?"

"They call it espionage. One of the oldest trades, a refined form of knowing what cooks in the neighbour's pot." Ibadat laughed heartily.

"Strange are the ways of politics." Jamilla commented.

"You know better. Politics and intelligence are the oldest bedmates. They're the hinge stones of the power structures that fashion our destiny." Ibadat heaved a philosophical sigh.

"Couldn't you save my real mother? Why did you not tell me the truth earlier?"

Harfan asked Ibadat with a pain stricken voice.

"Believe me brother. I had no other option. The ISI would have killed her anyways, perhaps after inflicting plenty of pain and humiliation. I faced the moment of truth much later. Perhaps you would've also offered her the grains of graceful poison, to save her from indignity. The Hindu ladies are known for their valorous *zahar* ceremony (mass suicide by poisoning to escape indignity)." Ibadat embraced Harfan to pacify his feelings.

"Destiny has played a cruel joke with me Ibadat. What a quirk of fate! I land up at Jhumra and fail to recognise my real mother! Did you find her nervous, afraid of dying?"

"On the contrary," Harfan tightened the embrace, "she welcomed death as a cure for all her sufferings."

"She really suffered, silently and nobody told me about it."

"Preserve these finer sentiments, brother. Life isn't a programmed magic box. Take it as it comes. Your priority is to escape the ISI and Alam's dragnet, very fast. You don't have more than two days, before they pick you up." Ibadat walked up and opened a window at the far corner of the room.

"Tell me, what's your plan?" Ibadat asked.

"Nothing whatsoever." Harfan wasn't ready yet to share his strategy, still half-baked, audacious, and absurd, and the contours of which were still in its foetal form, in his imagination.

"As I said, you've precisely two days to dodge the ISI and Alam. My moles in the company say that Brigadier Barqat and Jamanat have pieced together all the missing links. Your full profile is now complete. The only thing they don't know is the secret behind your birth."

"How good is your source inside the ISI?"

"Good, at the cutting edge level," Ibadat spoke cryptically, "and they'll give you only that much freedom, as essential to their operational needs with no extra bonus. Jamanat's people are everywhere, looking for you."

"I know. Options are limited."

"Why don't you escape to Dacca in tonight's flight?" Ibadat whispered, "they're not aware of your return and the CMLA hasn't restricted these special flights. General Naqi is very secretive too."

"That's the correct decision." Jamilla intervened.

"I agree Jami. But there're many imponderables." Harfan added.

"When do you fly next?" Ibadat asked.

Harfan looked at his watch and smiled.

"Its three now. Just in another fifteen hours. We're supposed to take off at eighteen hundred. Loading should start at eleven hundred hours."

"Are you taking off from Sargodha?"

"No, from Bhagatan. Sargodha isn't used for these flights."

"That makes it easier, brother Harfan," Ibadat commented in a relaxed tone, "Bhagatan is a small place. Take the flight, if you've any chance of getting lost in Dacca. Crossing over to India from there won't be difficult."

"Thanks for the suggestion," Harfan looked up with a derisive smile, "I won't move out an inch, if I can't take Jami and Pervez with me."

"They can join later. They can perhaps fly to London when the dust settles down."

"Yah! After they're salted, roasted, and peppered by the ISI! I won't take any chance. Not any more. I've lost my mother and I would hate to leave them at the mercy of the vultures." Harfan replied with a tone of finality.

"I appreciate your sentiments," Ibadat replied, "you're entitled to fashion your destiny, but your approach is impractical. Learn to leave some aspects of your life to *Allah*." Ibadat tried to convince Harfan with a persuasive smile.

"Calculate straight, Harfan," Jamilla added, "what happens when we land in Dacca and cross over to India is a different matter. We can quietly go back to Jhunjhunu and start afresh."

"How do I get you two out?"

"Talk to Vudu, accept his invitation," Jamilla intervened forcefully, "I'm in favour of the gamble, if you can manage to put us in the flight."

"Wonderful," Ibadat jumped to his feet, "I like the idea. We can't wait for the ISI torture chambers and the final dispatch to some insignificant jail. A security prisoner in Pakistan has no official recognition. Indian spies are left to rot and die in isolation. Most of them are injected with opium extracts, turning them insane."

A shiver ran down Harfan's spine. He lighted a cigarette, went over to the window, and reflected on the daring suggestion. It wasn't Ibadat's unique brain wave. He had planned it out as the only viable alternative. Escaping the ISI noose was on top of his mind. He had lost all manoeuvrability in Pakistan, Harfan reasoned. The magic mirror, he had assiduously crafted, had started cracking up. All his attempts to project a coherent collage of his thoughts had broken into uneven pieces. Perhaps Ibadat and Jamilla were correct. He was being unnecessarily emotional and cautious.

He should take the plunge.

"Well, you're possibly correct," Harfan turned back, "can you help me?"

"Brother Harfan, my veins carry the blood of a man who was loyal to the last drop of his blood. He died defending his king. Tell me what can I do? I'll like you,

Jamilla *bhabhi* and Pervez to clear off, in another couple of hours." Ibadat spoke in an emotion-choked voice.

"I've a plan. Listen."

Harfan's scheme sounded simple, ridiculous, and audacious. The absurd perpetual gambler had scripted a daring escape to Dacca, in the next flight of Vudurume. For him to disappear in Dacca and cross over to India wouldn't be a big deal. The Tripura border was just 80 km away and highly porous. A few hundred bucks would be good enough substitute for legal travel documents.

However, the biggest catch was boarding the Lady of The Light. The ground staff, military police wouldn't allow any unauthorised passenger. The passenger's manifest required their clearance. He wouldn't have any chance of taking Jamilla beyond the VIP lounge. The ISI, he reasoned, might not even allow him to board the flight. Perhaps these were his last few hours of freedom.

"I suggest you talk to the pilot. He may not have the tunnel vision, we're suffering from." Ibadat added.

"There is perhaps a way out," Harfan stood up in excitement, "another cup of coffee, please Jami."

"What's that?" Jamilla asked.

Harfan narrated the story of his encounter with Israr earlier in the day. They had discussed airlifting of six special crates. Maj. General Mukhtiar Ghori brought this super secret hardware in a special flight from Oman. Israr was summoned by General Naqi to discuss the top-secret merchandise. His next charter flight was assigned to carry 60 nerve gas shells. The mercenary pilot, Naqi had warned, shouldn't be taken into confidence.

"What's special about these crates?" Asked Ibadat.

"These are special artillery shells, which can hit targets beyond 30 kilometres. The toxic gas can kill thousands in minutes. The warheads contain deadly nerve gas, called either VX aerosol or Sarin, may be Tabun. I'm not an expert on these weapons of mass killing." Harfan shrugged.

"You mean Pakistan is going to kill the Bengalis by using these toxic nerve gas shells!"

"I've no precise idea about the targets. They could be fellow Pakistani Bengalis or Indians as well. Who cares?" Harfan's comments sounded bitter and cynical.

"Are you going to carry these to the conflict zone?" Ibadat asked.

"Do I have any option? I don't care. These crates can help me out. The weapons of death for the unknown Pakistani Bengalis and Indians can bring luck and life to me and my family, and even you."

*

Harfan explained his plan.

Loading of conventional military hardware would start by eleven in the morning. He would personally load the special crates around 1700 hrs. The doors would be armed for take off, precisely at 1750 hours. The kernel of his plan, Harfan explained, would be to pack Jamilla and Pervez in one similar looking crate, minus the artillery shells. This would be the seventh crate, one extra than the packages delivered by General Ghori. The military police did not normally check the cargo manifest. They merely provided physical security. It would not be difficult to hoodwink them. A few bottles of Scotch that he had saved from the last trip could seal their eyes and ears. Once out of Pakistani airspace he would unpack Jamilla and Pervez. The other crewmembers, one Greek, and the other a Cypriot could create a fuss. However, Vudurume was trustworthy and sympathetic. He would understand the intricacies and seriousness of the problem.

While in Dacca, Jamilla and Pervez could be passed off as Khondokar's Punjabi wife and child, visiting from Lahore. Wives of some top army officers generally availed of special PAF carriers to visit their husbands. Khondokar's wife, related to a two-star General in the CMLA headquarters, was expected to receive preferential treatment in Dacca. The airbase security personnel weren't likely to lift her *hijab* for an identification parade.

"It's an audacious plan, Harfan. Do you think it will work?" Ibadat asked.

"I've stopped thinking. It's a gamble and let's hope we'd win," Harfan smiled enigmatically, "can you give Pervez something to eat and administer half a tablet of barbiturate? That'll induce sleep for at least four hours and prevent detection by the security staff and ground crew." Harfan looked at Jamilla expectantly.

"Do you think it's safe to be packed like sardines for hours with those highly toxic shells? Won't it harm Pervez?" Jamilla looked pale and concerned.

"I'll take care to pack you two as comfortably as possible. I'd place soft foam padding and cotton lining. There won't be any shell in your crate. Are you ready for the gamble? This is the only option left to us."

Harfan reassured Jamilla by placing his hands around her shoulder.

"Well! We'd at least live or die together, in a brave and dignified way. I'm game", she turned towards Ibadat, "are you coming?"

"No *bhabhi*. I've to stay back. That's my fate. Get ready for the great escape. I shall be around. Don't panic."

The loud cock-a-doodle-doo of a rooster pierced the fading dark veils of the night. Ibadat stood up. He slowly lifted a corner of the curtain and measured up the intensity of the early morning light. The cover of darkness had started wilting, as the piercing arrows of light, travelling through the ethereal void, painted the waves and layers of clouds with indeterminate strokes.

Ibadat never claimed to be a devout Muslim, a believer in rituals. But the fast changing colours on the clouds, the chirping of birds and the soft aroma rising out of the soggy grounds enchanted him. He hadn't noticed before that the *Allah's* universe was so beautiful and full of love–unique love, exemplified by Harfan and Jamilla's desire to live and die together.

"I must go now. Work on the plan. I'd pick up Jamilla and Pervez and join you at the warehouse, well in time."

Ibadat embraced Harfan and briefly prayed by cupping his palms in the usual *namaj* format. He recited *La Ilaha Illa 'llah Muhammad-ur-Rasulullah*, and closed his eyes. Finally, he said *Khuda Hafiz* and placed his caressing palms on sleeping

Pervez. Harfan cautiously opened the door, peeped out to survey the corridor. Ibadat slithered out and in a second disappeared in the morning mist.

"That's the only option we have Jami. Get ready. I know you can do it. At least it gives us a fair chance. I don't think they can bring down the flight once Vudurume is airborne. We intend to accept his invitation."

"*Hai Rabba*! You've planned the great escape just like that!" Jamilla looked at Harfan with wide disbelief writ large in her eyes.

"I've been floating in air of uncertainty all these years. *Insha Allah*, Vudu will help. You forget one thing, he's a big gambler himself."

"You're incorrigible Harfan, a born gambler, *Allah jane* (God knows)," Jamilla threw up her hands, "let me get the things lined up. Hope your gamble will pay off."

"It's time for me to report to Israr. I'd call you up, say in two hours time, once the packing crate is ready. Please wait for Ibadat. If he fails to turn up, drive down yourself. Take the car inside the warehouse and park it at the rear. The gate-man won't stop. I've tackled him."

"Can we trust Israr?" Jamilla asked.

"No problem. See you. I've to load the crates, marked **UNICEF EMERGENCY MEDICAL SUPPLIES**. That's how they've decided to deliver death to East Pakistan, or may be to India."

Harfan planted a quick kiss on Jamilla's lips and on Pervez's forehead.

"Synchronise your watch darling. It's ten past six, 19th November 1971. Okay? You've to act in absolute precision. Don't get nervous."

"So, it's our last day in Pakistan?"

"Yes darling. Tomorrow will be another day and if I'm not incorrect India and Pakistan would plunge at each others throat on that historic tomorrow."

Harfan gave a weary smile, ran down the stairs, switched on the ignition, and zoomed out of sight.

*

64

Brigadier Barqat was giving final touches to Operation Salamat, hauling up a major Indian espionage network, spearheaded by Harfan Bukhari. Operations Briefing Room (OBR), the virtual heart of the India Counterintelligence Section of the Joint Intelligence Miscellaneous, was packed to the capacity. This holy corner, an exclusive preserve of the surveillance and enquiry cells of the division, was solely devoted to cracking the Indian intelligence penetration in Pakistan.

Jamanat Ali lorded over the unit, which specialised in counterintelligence.

The OBR walls were decorated with photographs of Indian agents neutralised during the last 10 years. A small paragraph below the photographs explained the essentials of each case study.

Photographs of suspected Indian Federal Intelligence Bureau and National Security India agents, posted in Pakistan under diplomatic cover, were featured on another frame on the wall. Jamanat's boys regularly updated the data boards from Indian civil lists, departmental telephone directories, information obtained from friendly foreign agencies and Pakistan's own sources in embassies abroad. Linear charts elaborated the connectivity between Indian agents and their Pakistani contacts.

The habitual trans-border smugglers and their Pakistani and Indian master handlers occupied another proud corner of the room. Each group was clubbed under the operational linkages of cartels on either side of the border. However, Jamanat wasn't allowed to display the names and identities of the drug barons and their collaborators in the Armed Forces. The holy camels of Pakistan were above the law.

The expectations of trapping a big catch had pushed up ambience biological temperature by a few degrees. Barqat, seated at the head table, addressed a group of 40 officers of the 'S Division.' This was a mandatory practice, before trained sleuths were deployed on sensitive operational tasks. It could be any task from surveillance, breaking in, raids, and agent interception to application of dirty tricks that often included assassination, bomb explosions, and mass destruction in enemy territories.

Barqat switched on the slide projector. Harfan Bukhari's profiles from different angles were flashed on the screen at regular intervals of three minutes, allowing the agents to memorise the features.

"Memorise the photographs carefully," Barqat spoke in a commanding tone, "his assumed Muslim name is Harfan Bukhari. We're not sure of his Hindu name." He flicked the switch on. A full frame of Harfan standing on the stairs of the CMLA headquarters and talking with Capt. Ayub flashed in. The clandestine photo, taken with a tele-lens captured the sharp frontal features of the suspect.

"Concentrate on the subject, ignore the Pakistani Captain. He's fighting the infidels at the war front. The Indian pigeon is 6 ft. plus, fair, sports black hair; backcombed and sports a thick growth of bushy beard. Look at his eyes. He doesn't have the features, either of a Punjabi or a Pathan. He looks like a Hindu Pundit." Barqat spoke in studied short sentences, in chaste Punjabi.

"I'll now request Mian Jamanat Ali to brief you about the agent's activities and the task on hand."

Jamanat took the microphone and continued the briefing in chaste Urdu, often falling back on Punjabi, his mother tongue.

He expounded the importance of the task of physically apprehending Harfan Bukhari and his associates. He was, perhaps, the first Indian resident agent to penetrate deep inside the system, right into the core around the Presidency. He had caused tremendous damage to Pakistan by stealing super-sensitive secrets. Jamanat, in his own brazen way, blamed the top brass for being gullible and trusting a foreign agent with the super-secret task of Pakistan's war preparations against India.

"Have you memorised the physical features of the spy?"

The officers nodded in silence. Jamanat continued in the same monotonous tone.

"I don't expect you to commit any mistake. Look at these photos, Harfan Bukhari without a beard and a moustache."

He clicked on the slide projector.

"We're deploying four teams. The Karachi team will act independently, raid his uncle Shamim Bukhari's house and search other places. One team headed by Karamat Suri will raid the house at Jhumra." Jamanat continued.

"The Lahore team, headed by Khaleq, will leave immediately by a special flight and raid the suspect's in law's house in order to detain his wife. She'll require a thorough interrogation."

"What's your report from Lahore? I'm told your watchers haven't seen his wife for the last 38 hours. Hope she hasn't gone underground." Barqat intervened.

"You're correct sir. Enquiries around Zahoor indicate that the girl is suffering from fever and hasn't stepped out for two days," replied Jamanat, "my men have rechecked and confirmed the report."

"As I was saying," Jamanat continued, "I'll lead the team to the Sangla complex of Israr Sharief. We've inside information of his suspected involvement with the Indian agency."

"Regarding Israr," Barqat intervened, "we've to take the allegations with a pinch of salt. He'd require interrogation though."

"But sir...." Jamanat tried to contest the views of his senior.

"Are you sure that Harfan is at Sangla? I was told by Brigadier Zia that he'd gone over to Dacca with the special flight." Barqat enquired.

"Sir, that's our weak link. The CMLA's office and the office of General Naqi are too secretive about these flights. They refuse to share any information. They ignore the ISI in matters of national importance. Why don't you speak to them again?"

"Well Jamanat," Barqat winked, "I've done that. Probably he's returning late tonight. That's what Zia said. Find out if the target is at Sangla."

"Fine sir." Jamanat took the hint and dialled a Sangla number, spoke briefly and turned to Barqat, "sir, my contact says Bukhari is returning this night."

"Why don't we nab him at the airport?" Asked a junior officer.

"Sorry boy," Barqat replied, "we can't be rash. When he sings, many important heads will roll. We're not only trying to catch a spy, we're chasing a national scandal."

"We've placed surveillance teams at Sargodha, which is the normal operating terminal of these special flights. They'll ambush and lift Bukhari on his way home. No one should utter the name of the Company. The whole operation should be handled in total secrecy." Jamanat added and explained the modalities of radio contact between different teams and the operations control room. There should be no use of firearms against the target, he warned. The subject would have to be captured alive, at any cost.

"We call this 'Operation Salamat.' Mosurs have been designated as Salamat 1, 2, etc. Your team captains have the details. Use codes during radio conversations. The call sign for the Ops Control Room is Shamsher 1 and Shamsher 2 for me. All teams barring the Lahore and Karachi ones will move simultaneously at 17.00 hrs today, four hours from now. Is that clear?"

Jamanat watched reactions of the team members and was pleased to see them tilting their heads in affirmation.

"Are we sure about the timings?" Arman Ali Niazi boomed out from a far corner of the room.

"Yes boy," Jamanat replied reassuringly, "we've tied up all loose ends. We don't want to be late for the catch."

"One final point," Barqat said in a cool voice, "all teams to note. No harm should come to the subject. I want him in one piece. There could be no leakage whatsoever to any other agency, be it the PIB or office of the CMLA. Take him to the Badr. Okay?"

Badr was the code name for the ISI's top-secret interrogation centre, located in the basement of 'Deeni Publications', a front company that published and marketed religious books.

"Everybody has to keep his trap shut, understand!" Jamanat added.

"It's a controlled operation. No one takes unauthorised initiative, no shooting from the hip." Barqat reminded the gathering.

"But sir, how do we tackle unforeseen developments?" Arman Ali Niazi asked.

"Good question Arman," Barqat lifted a hand held VHF communication set, "each unit will have these sets and standby batteries. You'll simply ask for directions. Hope things are clear and there's no confusion."

Barqat wished them good luck and left the briefing room. He was expecting a call from Alam Khan, the most important cog in the complicated wheel. The PSO had indicated that the top arms hunter and peddler had returned from foreign jaunt and was ready to help out the ISI. General Hyder had designated Brig. Barqat to debrief him. The level of interaction was pegged high, keeping in view the stature and connections of the man.

*

65

Alam Khan panicked.

The powwow with General Sarfaraz was a kid stuff. It wasn't difficult to sell dreams to the scheming Islamabad Generals. Each one of them pretended to be worthy successor to the gallant invading horsemen from the northwest, the Ghoris, the Lodis, the Khans and the Mughals. Pakistan, a relic of the past Islamic empire in India, they thought, was bequeathed to them by destiny like the Biblical land in Palestine was gifted to the Jews by the western powers. The men in uniform were licensed to plunder it like their predecessors on horseback had plundered numerous temples and treasure troves of golden *Bharatvarsha*.

Alam rubbed shoulder with the Generals but not for expressing feline love. It was a part of his profession. However, facing Brigadier Barqat, a seasoned ISI officer, was a different ball game. He wanted to avoid the encounter. Interrogation process, he knew for sure, was an endless labyrinth. Barqat's elegantly furnished front room could, in no time, lead to the dreaded basement bunkers of the Badr.

To add to his misery Ibadat had just disappeared. Hotel Royal Palace at Jhumra returned a stock reply. Ibadat was on short leave and didn't leave behind a forwarding address. He should be back in a couple of days.

Harfan Bukhari was still alive. That's what Israr Sharief had indicated on the phone. How could Qurban, the Double X asset, flout his orders? Had this son of a cook ganged up with the prince charming? Had he overrated Ibadat? Was he playing the old loyalty tune? Perhaps he was.

Alam rued his decision to expose Ibadat to Harfan Bukhari. It wasn't a prudent move. This was one mistake, Alam thought, was definitely going to explode on Delhi's face. Delhi's face? No. It's his face.

To hell with Delhi!

It shouldn't explode on his face. That's what he prayed for. Alam's efforts to rationalise the situation generated intellectual smog. The screw drilled deep down into his mind, inside the primordial chemical and electrical impulses of his brain. The serpent, hidden below his medulla started hissing. No. He wasn't ready to face the ISI interrogators. He couldn't destroy his cover, built assiduously over the last 23 years. He had generated vital human intelligence assets in several target areas of Pakistan. He must prevent the ISI from destroying the super-structure crafted by him painstakingly, brick by brick.

How could he prevent visiting his nemesis, the ISI interrogator? What diversionary tactic could he adopt? He must invent some excuse to obfuscate the imminent urge of the ISI to interrogate and categorise him. His own survival was of cardinal importance. Delhi wouldn't be able to run its forward paws in Pakistan in his absence. His own exposure would spell disaster for his family too. The ISI was sure to get to his wife and kids in Switzerland, kidnap and liquidate them.

Alam burnt a couple of cigarettes and concluded that his foremost priority was to locate Harfan and Ibadat and destroy both of them. They couldn't be allowed the luxury of breathing freely. Their continued intake of oxygen could spew fire for him. Moreover, Ibadat had forfeited his right to life. A rogue agent deserved only a one-way journey to the mortuary. Ibadat deserved the first shower of bullets. He knew more about him than Harfan did.

*

Alam picked up his phone and called a Mochi Mohra area number of Islamabad and contacted Rayees, a Mengel tribal from Zhob, Baluchistan, and a Darra Adam Khel based arms smuggler and hired killer.

"*Salaam* brother Rayees, Mian Alam here."

"*Janab,* hearing you after ages," the other end replied in effusive response, "what's the order?"

"There's a special job."

"*Janab*, business is dull. The Baluch *sirdars* have donned *burkas*. It seems that they've lost appetite for fighting. You haven't ordered new consignments for ages. Fresh supplies of Kalashnikov from Mazar Tepe (Tajikistan) are expected in three days, with cheap spares."

"That's encouraging news, Rayees *bhai* (brother). Is it 74 or 56?"

"Both are available. I can offer Avtomat Kalashnikova 100 too, 7.62x39 calibre. Five magazines bonus."

"Excellent. I'll require 5000 pieces of AK100. Organise a demo. But there's an urgent personal job here."

"*Janab* order me and the job's done." Rayees replied in a genie-of the-lamp style.

Alam reverted to dialogues better understood by hired killers like Rayees. The job was simple. A friend of his, Alam elaborated, suffered from insomnia and required sleeping pills. Rayees, he said, should personally deliver it in the next 24 hours at the given address.

Yes, he was ready to pay the usual price. In dollars? Fine, no problem; he could take the entire amount in advance.

The dialogue over, Alam lighted a cigarette.

Well! Rayees was a sure shot. He never missed his target. That should take care of Ibadat.

Should he arrange Harfan's capture by tipping off his contacts in the CMLA and the ISI? Could that be self-defeating? What if Harfan betrayed in turn? Would he sing like a pacific parrot? That would be too risky.

Alam tossed the critical dilemma over in his mind and gulped in liberal doses of cognac. Yes. Harfan should be eliminated. For him the ISI shooters were the best executioners. The combination of Rayees for Ibadat and Hyder for Harfan sounded absolutely fine.

Now he should provide Hyder with a steady target. And that required locating Harfan.

*

"Hello, Israr sahib," he dialled Israr's Sangla office, "how have you been?"

"Where have you been?" Israr responded warmly, " I'm oxygen starved."

"Where's my precious nephew?"

"Perpetually airborne. At Bhagatan, flying out late tonight."

"Where's his angel, I mean my cute daughter Jamilla?"

"At Bhagatan only. Mian you've to see this couple to believe it. They're ideal lovers." Israr laughed loudly.

"A perfect match." Alam readily agreed and managed to add a faint laughter.

"Come down. There're some business discussions that you must be in on."

"Keep it tomorrow, *Khuda Hafiz*."

Alam wasn't in a mood to listen to Israr's deliria. He seethed in anger and burnt in the churning fire of revenge. What was Jamilla doing at Bhagatan? The gambler must be planning something spectacular. Was he planning a quiet escape from Pakistan? Must be. Otherwise, why should his wife and child be at Bhagatan airbase?

No. He couldn't allow Harfan to escape.

Alam dialled Zahoor Chaudry's Lahore number and after exchanging meaningless small talk entered into a business like dialogue.

"How are darling Pervez and Jamilla?"

"Oh dear brother!" Zahoor replied in a jovial tone, "they're new generation kids. She has gone to spend a few days with Harfan at Sangla. She was missing him."

"I know, it's so cruel of us, all of us, to push nephew Harfan so hard. You know all about these special flights to East Pakistan." Alam feigned a genuine concern for Harfan.

"I know. In fact, the other day General Sarfaraz made a special mention of Harfan's valuable contribution to our defence preparedness. I'm proud of him." Zahoor replied.

"Me too. When do you expect her back?"

"Can't say. Possibly by tomorrow."

"Sweet of you Zahoor sahib. I'd like to drive down, may be in another two days, for business talks and for looking up Pervez."

"Welcome Alam sahib. Jamilla and Sayeefa will be very happy to receive you." Zahoor extended a cordial invitation to Harfan's distant uncle.

"My pleasure," Alam replied in a delightfully mechanical voice, "convey my regards to *mohtarma* (madam) Sayeefa."

"My pleasure," replied Zahoor, "come over one of these days. Let's have a meal together."

"*Insha Allah*!" Alam disconnected and immediately dialled the number of General Naqi.

"How're you General? *Kaise mizaj* (how is the mood)?" Alam asked General Naqi, who normally carried with him bags full of idiosyncrasies.

"Fine. Thanks for calling," Naqi replied, "hearing you after ages."

"Yes friend. I'd been to Istanbul and Riyadh. How're your flights? Hope there hasn't been any hiccup." Alam wanted the dialogue to stretch.

"No problem. The President appreciated the exigencies. Your nephew's doing a fine job," Naqi added.

"Oh Naqi! He's not my nephew, by any stretch of imagination. I happen to know his uncle, and that's how he calls me uncle."

"Anyways," Naqi replied, "He's doing a fine job."

"Where could I reach him?"

"He's at Israr's Bhagatan guesthouse. Here's his number." Naqi readily obliged Alam.

"What time does he take off?"

"Not sure. May be late midnight or before the daybreak." Naqi replied evasively. He didn't want to share the flight details of this special sortie.

"I want to talk to him urgently."

"Well! Try your luck. Zia knows the details. But he is at Chak Lala in connection with the President's visit to Dacca."

"Aren't you seeing off the President?"

"Oh yes. I was about to hit the road."

"Thanks, General. I'll try my luck." Alam replied curtly and hung up.

*

Alam smelt the vapour of burning cordite running through his intestines. He expected an explosion, a devastating one. Harfan was definitely working on a super-secret escape plan. Should he allow him to clear out from Pakistan? Alam tossed the idea over for a while and discarded it. Liquidation of Harfan was the best prescription. He lifted the handset, dialled the Bhagatan guesthouse number, and requested the operator to connect him to Jamilla Bukhari.

"Who's speaking?" the operator insisted on disclosure of the caller's identity.

"It's me brother, Harfan Bukhari." Alam replied closely faking Harfan's voice. The operator obliged.

"Hello, who's there?" Jamilla was surprised to hear Alam's voice.

"Hello, dear Jamilla, Alam uncle this side. How're you, Pervez and dear nephew Harfan? Where is he?"

Jamilla hadn't expected the call. Alam wasn't supposed to call Harfan. Instead, she expected him visiting the mortuary, to see his frozen naked body. She gathered herself in seconds and replied in broken words and sentences

"I believe...I don't exactly know. He may fly out early morning tomorrow. Can't you stop these flights uncle?"

"It's a national duty dear. I'm happy that you are there to give company. The poor boy's really hard pressed."

"That's the problem uncle. He's totally wedded to his work, more than to me." She tried to break into a small laughter, trying to prolong the talk and fathom Alam's intentions.

"I know dear Jami. It's in the family. He burns himself out. How can I get to him?"

"You may call Sangla around ten thirty, when he's expected to meet Israr sahib. I intend to leave for Lahore in minutes. Come down to Lahore uncle. You haven't been with us for months."

Jamilla disconnected the line and called Harfan at the warehouse.

"I'm driving down now."

"Wait for Ibadat."

"No, I can't. Alam had called and I doubt his intentions. He's sure to get you killed. I didn't like his vibes."

"How did he get the number?"

"No idea. He must have sniffed us out. Receive me at the gate."

"Don't panic. Ibadat should call any time."

"Fine, but I won't wait indefinitely."

Jamilla disconnected and started packing Pervez's milk bottle and some foodstuffs.

*

Alam's trained mind could discern the fine emotional and mechanical strains in Jamilla's otherwise effervescent voice. She always bubbled with life. Her untrained mind wasn't reacting spontaneously to his questions. She had hesitated for precious seconds, before spinning out the words. There was hollow whisper in her laughter. Alam admired her courage and presence of mind, but was convinced that the fairy queen of Harfan wasn't a good liar. The cordial invitation to Lahore and nonsense nothings had convinced Alam that the chic couple was planning a cute vanishing trick. The excellent opportunity offered by Harfan should be used to maximum advantage. That should be his valid excuse to avoid appearing before the ISI Brigadier.

Yes. That was the easy way out.

Alam planned and executed another shrewd call.

"Pardon me Hyder sahib, I hope I haven't disturbed you." Alam's next call was to General Hyder Bux, the ISI chief.

"Sweet surprise! Where have you been all these days?"

"Mostly around the Mediterranean and at the SOL."

"What's SOL?"

"Statue of Liberty Hyder sahib. We must meet one of these days. The Pentagon corridors are abuzz with rumours that your friend, I mean, the boss in the CMLA's office, is the hot favourite of the White House." Alam dangled the most attractive carrot in front of Hyder.

"You mean Sarfaraz! Alam sahib, I can assure you, that this nincompoop carries rotten balls between his thighs. How can he carry the country on his shoulders?" Hyder spat out venom against his rival.

"You're the fittest person General. I told so to George Kenney, deputy chief of the CIA, and Mike Stalbot of the NSA." Alam spoke in a seductive voice.

"What did they say? Can you really span a bridge?"

"It's a pleasure, General. Can I come down for some urgent talks? There's something wrong with this fellow, I mean Harfan Bukhari."

"I'm in a jam, Alam sahib. I've to rush to Chak Lala Cantonment and accompany the President to Dacca. Be brief."

Alam breathed deep, composed his thoughts, and shared with the ISI chief, in chaste Punjabi, the most shocking piece of information. By the grace of *Allah,* Alam added, a British diplomat happened to narrate the story of a KGB agent neutralised by the MI6. The Russian spy had spilled the beans to MI6 interrogators about existence of a deep penetration Indian resident agent in Pakistan. He had, the interrogators revealed, learnt about this agent from his station chief in Delhi.

The sketch and accounts narrated to him by the UK diplomat perfectly matched Harfan Bukhari. It was the most shocking information, almost unbelievable. But the truth was always stranger than fiction. Wasn't it?

His British friends, Alam whispered, had burrowed tunnels into the pockets and conscience of some NSI operators. They had corroborated the basic ingredients of Harfan's cover story.

Alam's theatrics and general contours of the information struck the right chords in General Hyder Bux. He had gone through the Operation Salamat broadsheet, prepared by Barqat and Jamanat and had consciously decided to neutralise the Indian agent. Alam's controlled leak sounded highly feasible. The patriotic Pakistani, Hyder presumed had picked up the story correct.

The spymaster, however, paused for a few seconds. Should he seek corroboration from the CIA and MI6 liaison officers in Islamabad?

"Are you on the line Hyder sahib?"

"Are you sure that the story is reliable?"

"Sir," Alam modulated his voice to the sweetest possible decibel, "I'm hundred percent convinced. And I've a nasty feeling that Harfan is trying to escape from Pakistan."

"Well Alam sahib, I'm happy to know that the British have corroborated what we already know. I'm just about to leave for the airport. You'd better rush to Barqat and tell him the details. See you on my return from Dacca."

"Right General."

"One more point Alam. Talk to your friends in Washington immediately. Time's running out."

"You're my only priority Hyder sahib. Your job will be done. You're surely the next occupant of the presidential palace. Kindly leave a message with Barqat, *Khuda Hafiz.*"

Hyder, in a hurry to reach the airport for joining the presidential entourage to Dacca, took a mental note of the urgency of an exclusive meeting with Alam after his return from Dacca. This arms peddler was the right person to build bridges with right quarters in Washington and London. The remote vision of the bridge, as spanned by Mian Alam Khan, had clouded up Hyder's earlier resolution to get the sensational information vetted by the Islamabad based CIA and the MI6 liaison officers. For a few precious moments, the intelligence officer in him was overtaken by the vision of the ornate high chair in the presidential palace.

*

Alam hastily disconnected the line, in doubles climbed down the stairs, and asked the driver to head for Brigadier Barqat's residence.

He quickly glossed over the turn of events. Well manoeuvred! Indeed well orchestrated! Alam congratulated himself. God willing, Rayees should take care of Ibadat, and Harfan should be a piece of cold meat in another couple of hours. An obliged Barqat should be eager enough to strike the machete, straight at the jugular of the prize catch.

Alam smiled, a sweaty butcher's smile, and lighted another cigarette. The scenario wasn't as bleak as it had appeared a couple of hours ago. He was shaken to his bones by the crafty jackal Harfan. The young cub should have known that lion Alam had the infinite capability to turn and twist events and personalities in Pakistan. Nampoothiri was far removed from ground zero to realise what had gone wrong with Triple X and Double X. He was sure to accept a plausible story dished out by his most trusted friend in Pakistan.

Hyder, the scheming ISI chief, should continue to be beholden to him. Why not? His job was to build bridges. What was wrong if he helped in building bridges between General Hyder and the White House, the CIA and the Pentagon? Sarfaraz could wait or return to his village, produce wheat, or cotton, whatever he wanted for a living. The planned coup by Hyder wouldn't be the last one. Pakistan was destined to witness more coups. Well! Let the Generals be bogged down in the intractable and un-fordable marsh of power politics. Let them commit hara-kiri; let them screw up the unfortunate people of Pakistan. That suited him, perhaps Delhi too. At the end of the day, Alam chuckled the bucks were well secured in his Swiss account.

Nevertheless, one unsolved mystery continued to haunt him. He was foxed by the mysterious chessboard moves of Harfan and Ibadat. The presence of Jamilla at Bhagatan was putting pressure on the mercury flow of his coronary barometer. He smelt a rat, a rotten one at that.

Harfan must have worked out an escape plan in one of the special flights. He knew the daredevil pretty well. A born gambler, he would like to fly on the wings of hope and risk everything. He had been lucky all these years and could as well pull off one bigger gamble, the biggest in his life.

Barqat felt rather fidgety to see Alam at the oddest possible hour, Hyder's call notwithstanding. He had wasted a good three hours waiting for the celebrity arms peddler. He hadn't turned up at the appointed time. The ISI had been working on a tight time schedule for concluding 'Operation Salamat'. Alam's interrogation was expected to provide important inputs. But the big gun played truant.

Barqat glanced at his Swiss quartz, 17.25. It was time for him to drive to the airport, to show his face to the President and the CMLA, who was flying to Dacca, heading a high-powered team. The West Pakistani power brokers as well as the international observers had pinned high hopes on this visit, perhaps the final one by the head of the state. General Arif 's failure to persuade the Bengali leaders to accept the compromise power-sharing formula would mean end of the road. Pakistan's ugly civil war would explode into a disastrous fireball of war between India and Pakistan.

"Hello Alam sahib, anything urgent? I expected you a couple of hours ago." Barqat didn't hide his displeasure.

"I'm sorry for the delay Brigadier sahib," Alam apologised profusely, "some unexpected events had held me up. I've something very explosive to share. It's a matter of state security, you can say. I didn't want to talk on the phone."

"Yes, the boss was telling me something. Jump into my car." Barqat boarded his Toyota and gestured Alam to ask his driver to follow. What a bloody time to be disturbed! The drive to Chak Lala airport would take over 30 minutes. That would leave him with barely five minutes to seek out his slot in the bon voyage row. He would hate to miss the chance of showing face to the President. The top man was scheduled to sign his promotion file, making him a Major General and assigning him the coveted post of the Director General SSG, replacing Gen. Mukhtiar Ghori.

"Speed up, Bashir," Barqat prodded his driver, "and Alam Sahib, tell me what's so important."

Alam opened his treasure chest exposing rare intelligence nuggets concretising his suspicions about Harfan being an Indian spy. His sources of information, he added, were crucially located in London, in the CIA and MI6.

"I'm told that this snake is a Hindu. He was given the cover of a Muslim from Ludhiana, and was infiltrated soon after the '65 war."

Alam released bits of information from his treasure chest and convinced Barqat that his story was genuine, which fitted into the mosaic already put together by the ISI.

"That's not all Barqat sahib. This viper has compromised most sensitive military secrets to India. What a great chameleon he is! I wonder why this spy is still allowed to ferry weapons to the East."

"I believe you had recommended him." Barqat quipped.

"That's an old story. Indeed I'd suggested his name, because General Naqi didn't want to deploy regular army reps." Alam replied without batting an eyelid.

"Aren't you a little too late Alam?" Barqat retorted back, "you didn't reveal anything to the PSO."

"Nothing happens without it being willed by the *Allah*," Alam raised his hands in prayer, "I was totally guided by the recommendations of Jung Sher Khan, a business associate of Shamim Bukhari, Harfan's uncle."

"When did you discover his seamy activities?" Barqat's voice seemed to be serious.

"Just 24 hrs ago. My London friends tipped me off and I took the first available flight here. I just made two calls to ascertain Harfan's location and rushed to you."

"Why do you suspect him to fly out with his family?"

"She's lodged in a guesthouse near Bhagatan airbase. It is really odd and adds up to the fact that they have hatched a plan to escape together. I have received a corroborative information from my MI6 friend in London."

Alam finished the sentence and breathed heavily, as if he was still gasping under a heavy shock, with the tragedy of betrayal by his close associate.

"As a loyal and patriotic Pakistani, I can't allow this scoundrel to endanger our national security," Alam added, "my London based CIA friends feel that Harfan is carrying some microfilms on our nuclear projects."

"I should be back from Chak Lala, as soon as the President's flight takes off. What time are they flying out tonight?"

"Probably late tonight, that's what Israr told me."

"Surprise!" Barqat muttered inaudibly.

"Are you surprised?"

"Not exactly. I was working on a different time schedule altogether."

"No Brigadier sahib, we've to act fast and get him at Bhagatan itself. That's a good three hours drive. Can you arrange a chopper for me? I can help in identifying the rascal." Alam threw another bait and Barqat swallowed it, hook, line, and sinker.

"Shamsher 2 to Shamsher 3." Barqat spoke into the handset. Odd, damn odd! His static observers at Lahore were wrong. Jamilla wasn't confined to her bed. This damn Pakistani girl was mesmerised by the Indian spy.

"Shamsher 3 here. Getting you fine, sir." Jamanat came on air instantaneously.

"Shamsher 3, your target is at Bhagatan, the old Political Agent's bungalow near Laluwali *tikri*. Your bird is flying out late tonight with microfilms containing sensitive national secrets."

"If it's Bhagatan sir, I should be suffering about 90 minutes handicap. I'm halfway near Sangla." Replied Jamanat.

"I know. Rush your teams to Bhagatan. Prevent him from boarding the flight. Listen, his wife and child should be in the guesthouse. Send out a separate team and arrest them. Shoot them, if it becomes absolutely necessary to immobilise Harfan. Don't kill. I want him alive. Keep Shamsher 1 informed."

Barqat's orders were crisp and categorical.

"Roger, Shamsher 1."

"Shamsher 3, Listen. Mian Alam is flying down to Bhagatan in a chopper. He knows the details of the microfilms. Help him out."

"Roger sir. Ask him to team up at the Mangni-Bhagatan T-junction."

"Okay. Let *Allah* bless your mission. I'm on air and should be in my office in another 45 minutes. Over and out."

"Roger and out." Jamanat Ali switched on a reserve frequency and directed the Lahore team to rush to his aid. His own team took a sharp U-turn and accelerated for Bhagatan.

Alam thanked Barqat profusely and parted company short of Chak Lala Cantonment gate. His Mercedes followed a service road and drove straight to the heliport, three miles south of the airbase.

*

66

Rayees Sikander was one of his kinds. He was above the law, government control and even beyond the reach of the ISI. Normally he kept the law and order in his pocket and smoked occasionally when he needed to smoke out the law of the land. He ran a parallel administration all over Pakistan with the help of his vast mafia network. This shadow administration thrived on drug monopoly, trans-border smuggling and arms merchandise. The military administration normally winked at his activities as an entrepreneur like Rayees contributed significantly to the tottering economy of the country. Their forward and backward trading linkages brought in plenty of dollars from all conceivable nook and corner of the globe. The Army bosses used his services for engineering unrest, communal carnage, and sectarian killings, in the absence of any other institutionalised arrangement. They preferred to follow, at that historical point of time, the Sicilian formula of running a second track administration. Rayees enjoyed his unique status in the putrid Pakistan of the day.

Rayees wasn't a magician, but he knew a few tricks to find his way out even in the dark back alleys of Lahore's Dabbi Bazaar. Jabbar Pathan, his Man Friday in Lahore, came up with confirmed information about Ibadat's whereabouts. He wasn't at Jhumra and hadn't visited his home for last six days.

"He can't disappear into thin air. What car does he use?" Exploded Rayees.

"A battered Ford, which carries a Mianwali number plate."

"He can't go far. Alert our boys in Lahore, Karachi, and Sargodha. He might team up with Harfan Bukhari." Rayees Sikander passed on the orders while removing a strand of hair from his nasal cavity, with great care and research.

A thin lead came from his scouts at Bhagatanwala. They had noticed Ibadat's Ford parked behind the bushy undergrowth, next to a Sikh *Gurudwara* (temple).

Gurudwara Bhagatan was a small affair.

Rayees jumped into his Volkswagen Passat with five armed goons by his side. The old Ford was there, parked behind assorted bushes. The advancing footsteps of nature overwhelmed what was once a pleasant garden, in the backyard of the Sikh temple. The trees and bushes, neglected for over two decades, had grown into giant proportions. The green undergrowth had covered up most of the dilapidated remnants of human touch. Wild nature had reoccupied with vengeance what was snatched away from her.

"Drag out the *Granthi* (priest)." Rayees ordered.

His armed goons entered the dilapidated temple premises and literally dragged out its only occupant, an aged Sikh, who merged well with the wild vegetation around.

"What's your bloody name?" Thundered Rayees.

"Sardar Kirpal Singh. I'm the chief priest of the *Gurudwara*."

"Where's that bastard Ibadat?"

"Who?"

"Ibadat-ud-Daula Khan, owner of the car, parked on your land."

"*Wahe Guru*," Replied the priest, "I'm the only human soul who lives here. The nearest human habitat is about 3 km away."

"How come the car is parked here?"

"*Janab*," Kirpal Singh added, "all sorts of animals, drug smugglers and criminals use the garden. I've no control on them."

Rayees wasn't convinced. He ransacked the temple premises and after a good one-hour was convinced that Kirpal was the only occupant of the deserted Sikh shrine.

"*Ustad* (captain) shall we burn this *kafir's* temple?" asked an accompanying goon.

"No. That won't help. Let's talk to the police chief. He should know what to do."

"It's a new place *Ustad*. Should we get involved with the local police?" asked another goon.

"No harm. My law runs everywhere. The local police should know if the joker has been moving the streets of this town." Rayees replied.

He wasn't far from the truth.

Ibadat had abandoned his car behind the bushy growth and hired a taxi for his local movement. He had anticipated the ISI sleuths to move into the area, following Jamilla's trail. And he didn't like the idea of carrying her and Pervez to the airport in his branded car, which was known to Arman Ali's Mosur teams.

The police officer, a rusty Punjabi, wasn't unaware of the name and fame of Rayees Mengel. Men of means and money as well as the law enforcing agencies were painfully aware of the charismatic underworld don. He ran his own government from his Peshawar Fort capital, in addition to the one supposedly run by the men in uniform from Islamabad.

"What can I do for you sir?" The SHO (Station House Officer) asked with all the humility that he could muster.

"Have your men seen this character in town?" Rayees produced a photograph of Ibadat.

"Abdul." Shouted the SHO.

Abdul, a pot-bellied constable, appeared gingerly.

"Have you and your men seen this character in Bhagatan?" Abdul looked at the photo and looked back at his boss, simultaneously extending his palm.

"Stupid," shouted the SHO, "Mr. Rayees is our honourable guest. Don't expect gratis from him."

"Look up hotel Aasman." Abdul peevishly pulled back his palm and replied in a flat tone.

"Come with me. You'd be adequately compensated."

"Don't march up with the entire gang sir. Hotel Aasman is a small place, located in a crowded market place, next to Naaz cinema hall. We don't want a big story in the morning's news papers." The discerning SHO advised.

"No problem. You all wait here," Rayees ordered his gang, "I should be back in half an hour. It's a small job."

Hotel Aasman, literally speaking hotel sky, offered a birds eye view of the street that led to its stairs. Ibadat noticed the pot-bellied constable and Rayees from his first floor room. Rayees had in his hand a machine carbine.

Why should a potentate of law and an armed person, who could only be an ISI storm trooper, rush up to his hotel?

Ibadat collected his Belgian Kahr MK9 pistol and spare magazines and climbed down a rain water pipe, which landed on an open gutter. He followed the drain, hailed a horse cart, and ordered the driver to take him to the nearby mosque.

Rayees stormed up the stairs, the menacing machine carbine in his hand and kicked open the door. The hotel manager lodged a meek protest and was silenced by a burst from the carbine. Crowds from the nearby cinema hall and busy marketplace thronged the hotel approach. Abdul, the police officer, strutted his baton, made way for frustrated and abusive Rayees, and guided him back to the police station.

Ibadat performed the ritual ablutions and joined a gathering of *namajis*. The prayers over he called the *Imam* to a corner.

"Can I use your phone? My mother is seriously ill."

"Sure. Pay the charges."

"No problem." He pushed a ten-rupee note in Imam's palm.

Jamilla came alive on the line.

"Don't wait for me," Ibadat spoke in a collected voice, "there're problems here. Go by yourself. I shall be at your final destination."

"What's the problem? Is anything wrong with Harfan?"

"No. It's with me. Be on time. That's important. I shall be there."

"Alam had called." Jamilla spoke in a shaky voice.

"That's dangerous. Rush and board the flight."

"What about you?"

"I'll be there. Don't wait for me."

Ibadat thanked the *Imam* profusely and hurried down the stairs.

He did some quick thinking.

Back at Hotel Aasman, it wasn't the ISI. They didn't appear with a lone police pilot openly with arms in their hands.

Could the carbine-wielding man be Alam's hired executioner?

Must be.

Well, not bad! He could still make it to the airport and provide a buffer to Harfan and Jamilla, if the carbine-wielding goon was a part of Alam's private war. He wondered if Alam and the ISI were working in tandem.

Ibadat hailed a passing cab and zoomed for the airbase.

*

67

Ibadat's call to Laluwali guesthouse and his inability to escort Jamilla triggered off Harfan's sensory alarms. Something had gone wrong. Ibadat had failed to befuddle the sniffing canines and perhaps the ISI and Alam were on hot pursuit.

Harfan did not like praying. It was no prayer time. He stirred the automated loader tractor towards the fuselage of the Lady of The Light. Determination to load the precious 7th crate and take off at the dot prodded him.

Harfan hadn't expected Ibadat, of all places, at the special apron, restricted to authorised personnel and special flights like the one operated by Athena Air Lines. This exclusive part of the apron connected the parking bay to the arrays of over and underground hangers. The Army and Air Force police controlled access to the exclusive aprons with a massive drop-gate and galvanised iron sheet doors. An eight feet high barbed wire fence, covered with a thick creeper growth, segregated the rest of the airport, both administrative and technical areas.

Ibadat had positioned himself behind stacked containers, scribbled with Arabic and Chinese letters. Harfan had become familiar with these metal boxes that ferried arms and ammunition from destinations in China and the Middle East.

Harfan paused for a while. Two Air Force police officers inspected the cargo-crate meticulously and gave thumbs up sign. Harfan heaved a sigh of relief. Thank God! The final barriers were crossed and it was just seconds before he forklifted the most precious cargo to the fuselage. Two precious pieces of his life were inside the nondescript wood and metal packing. Flight AAL-X-356, technically serviced, fuelled for a non-stop flight to Dacca, and stocked with in-flight supplies was ready to take off at eighteen hundred hours sharp.

Vudurume waited impatiently for the last crate to be loaded. His chief co-pilot Antichopoulas stood near the front door and signalled Harfan to speed up.

The Air Traffic Control repeatedly reminded the pilot, amidst loud crackling and static noises that he had only ten minutes to take off. The tower wouldn't allow any craft to be airborne, half an hour before and after the scheduled VIP flight from Chak Lala. The air space over the landing and takeoff approaches would be embargoed.

Harfan slowed down the forklift tractor as he neared a curb next to the crouching figure of Ibadat.

"What the hell are you doing here?"

He stepped down from the forklift and asked Ibadat in an anguished voice.

Ibadat was all ears as his VHF set crackled loudly.

"Have you finished loading?" Ibadat asked, still listening to some agitated conversation on the handset.

"This is the last one. But, how did you manage entry into this bay? No civilian is allowed here."

Ibadat pointed his finger at a foxhole-sized gap in the fence, covered by ivy growth. He gestured at Harfan to listen to the loud exchange of messages, often interrupted by static and squelching noises.

"Have you put *Bhabhiji* and Pervez in the plane?"

"They're just about to be loaded. Aren't you coming with us?"

"No. Be quick. Jamanat Ali and Alam are chasing you. Take off immediately."

"You come too."

"Don't be silly. Get going."

*

"How far are you from Bhagatan Jamanat sahib?" Harfan could identify Alam's voice on Ibadat's handset.

"Just 50 km short. When are you landing?"

"*Insha Allah*, in another 20 minutes…The Indian agent is taking off anytime. That's what Chak Lala told me. He should be prevented from boarding the aircraft." Alam's voice was distorted by static noise, caused by disruption of the line of sight contact by intervening hills.

"Order Bhagatan air traffic to stop the 707 flight…surround the airport, your suspect is trying to escape." Alam's voice boomed in.

"So Alam is the double agent?" Harfan asked.

"No. He's trying to save his asshole more than securing Delhi's intelligence assets in Pakistan."

"At my cost, I presume." Harfan quipped back in anger.

"Dead men don't tell tales, brother Harfan. This jackal is more ferocious than his master, back in Delhi. Run and take off."

"I regret I can't pump bullets into Arman Ali's chest, the killer of my father."

"Leave that to me. Alam's silence is more important. The ISI won't take time to turn the heat on him. His film of deception is thin." Ibadat spoke in a steely voice.

"You can't do that without Delhi's orders."

"Leave it to me. I know what I'm doing."

"I'll miss you Ibadat."

"We shall meet, Allah willing. Run and take off."

*

"Don't allow him to take off...That's the order of Brigadier Barqat and your chief....

"Shoot him, if you can't take him alive." Alam's voice shrieked out from the set.

"Roger Alam sahib, be quick..." Jamanat's voice came in louder, indicating the fast approach of his chopper to Bhagatan.

"Has Sargodha directed Bhagatan TC to abort this flight?"

"No. There're some problems. My pilot says that Bhagatan tower has directed the flight to clear the skies in another few minutes." Alam conveyed in a nervous voice.

"Has there been a change in the schedule?"

"I can't say. It appears we're misinformed about the timings. There's some VIP movement from Chak Lala. All civil and air force flights have been suspended. They're keeping radio links to the minimum."

"Why don't you alert the air force and the airport security people?"

"I can't. There's a frequency incompatibility. My pilot has radioed Sargodha to alert the Military Police."

"Oh hell! I'm rushing. I'll blow up the plane if need be."

Jamanat pressed the accelerator hard.

*

"Don't waste time, rush and take off," Ibadat pushed Harfan towards the forklift tractor, "I'll take care of Jamanat and delay his entry into the tarmac." Harfan embraced Ibadat, said *Khuda Hafiz,* and turned the tractor towards the rear door of the fuselage.

"I leave with two regrets," Harfan said as he mounted the trolley, "I couldn't save my mother and kill this character Arman Ali, my father's killer."

"Accept things courageously that you can't change. Somewhere you've to concede defeat gracefully. Leave that serpent to my care. Keep these papers. It's a report on Pakistan's plan for an Israeli-type air blitzkrieg on Indian airports, military installations, and targets in Delhi. Call Delhi as soon as you make it to Dacca."

"Have the military bosses gone mad?"

"Read the letter leisurely. Run and take off..go..go..."

Ibadat pushed Harfan out. He crouched behind a massive container and took out the loaded pistol and eight spare magazines from his waistband.

The loading over, Harfan parked the tractor at a safe distance, climbed the ladder and signalled for the ground crew to peel off.

"Close and arm all doors and take to your stations." Vudurume's voice boomed in from the intercom.

Alexis Onasis and another flight assistants complied as Harfan took his seat next to the crates of cargo.

The Lady of The Light, a Boeing 707/C135A modified Stratolifter; all four Pratt

& Whitney 157-PW-59W turbo jets revved up, wing flaps fully down, lurched towards the take off marker.

"AAL-X-356, ready to take off." Vudurume aligned the plane along the mid-marker.

"ATC to AAL-X-356. You're cleared to take off. Bank west, avoid Chak Lala, and follow the charted ATR (Air Traffic Route). Climb to 15,000 ft, steer towards Lahore, climb 20,000 ft, bank right and expect instructions from Lahore ATC."

Bhagatanwala tower heaved a sigh of relief. These spooky flights usually scared them. It was especially bad today with Sargodha breathing fire down their neck. The VIP DC10 was ready to take off at 19.00, for a non-stop flight to Dacca. The sleepy, puffy eyed and fatigued assistant air traffic controller, a stubborn Pathan, was glued to the radar screen. He felt annoyed when the red hot-line phone rang sharply. What's the problem? The Air Headquarters and the Directorate of Civil Aviation Security rarely used that phone.

"Yes please, ATC Bhagatan here." He leisurely responded.

"Abort the Boeing 707 flight. It shouldn't take off under any circumstances," shouted an angry voice.

"Who is it?"

"Jamanat Ali, Superintendent ISI. I order you, on the authority of the CMLA. Stop that flight."

"Sorry sir, the bird is already airborne," the ATC assistant replied, "I require orders from General Naqi's office to abort this special flight. I don't take orders from the ISI." He switched on the desk tape recorder in disgust. How funny, he scowled! These police chaps had now turned to controlling air traffic too!

Jamanat shouted some expletives and screamed his head off, directing the ATC to abort the flight.

"Sorry sir, I don't take orders from the ISI. Please get the appropriate authority to call me. I'm under orders to clear this flight immediately."

"You traitor," Jamanat erupted on the phone, "you'll be hanged for betraying Pakistan."

"Sorry sir, I can't obey your orders. Sargodha has already cleared this priority flight. Talk to them or General Naqi's office."

Jamanat, now accompanied by Alam, in a last minute desperate move turned towards the wicket gate. The Air Force and Military Police, M-16 assault rifles slung on shoulders straps, stopped Jamanat and his cavalcade of mixed ISI and police officials.

"You can't get in. Show us your ID." The zombie faced security commander ordered Jamanat.

"To hell with you." Jamanat flaunted his ISI identity card.

"That's not valid for this airport. You require a yellow ID card from the Air Force."

"Hell with your red and yellow cards. I'm going in. Call Brigadier Barqat and get your damn orders." Jamanat pushed aside the guard commander, whizzed past the gate, and turned towards the runway.

Alam picked up Jamanat's mobile phone, dialled Gen. Hyder Bux and hurriedly filed a situation report. He requested immediate aborting of flight 356.

"Alam, you've called at a critical moment. The President's cavalcade has just arrived, and I can't leave this place, you know that." General Hyder replied.

"But it's important to stop the Indian spy."

"What're you doing there? I suppose it's your baby. You abort it."

"He's not my baby. I've explained that to you General. An enemy of Pakistan is making good his escape. Please do something." Alam cried out in frustration.

"Are you sure you're on the right track? Where do you think he can take the plane?"

"*Allah kasam* (swear by the *Allah*) Hyder sahib," Alam replied, "he's escaping with his family, to Delhi."

"Don't be silly. How can he take this aircraft to India? We can get him in Colombo, if not at Dacca. Why panic?"

"What prevents him from diverting the flight to India? The pilot is an Indian too. Why take a chance? Please order the Air Force to intercept the bloke. He's carrying lots of Pakistani secrets." Pleaded Alam.

"Alam sahib," Hyder almost scolded the reputed arms peddler, "it's you who had hired these chartered flights. I had to ditch Nawab. What's biting you?"

Hyder was surprised over Alam's choice of time for proclaiming an emergency. The smart guy, he thought, was acting rather funny. He decided against pushing the panic button and walked down to the ceremonial gate to receive President General Arif Khan. Alam or no Alam, he should not be seen missing from the ceremonial celebrity gathering.

His presence rather than his performance was important in the new dispensation.

Barqat, standing near the gate, saluted smartly, as the chief approached him.

"Hey Barqat," he asked, "what's eating this character Alam?"

Barqat didn't expect Hyder to ask this awkward question, moments before the arrival of the President.

"We're concluding 'Operation Salamat', as you know sir."

"That's fine. But how does Alam figure in it?"

Barqat explained his eventful tryst with the celebrity arms peddler.

"Why the hell are you here then? Rush to the tower and stop the flight. Alam says, that bugger Harfan is escaping, with lots of national secrets. Hurry."

"Yes sir." Barqat rushed for the ATC tower, at a considerable distance from the ceremonial lounge. He cursed Alam for activating the live wire at an embarrassingly odd time.

Hyder spotted General Mukhtiar Ghori puffing a cigarette frantically. An inveterate smoker he wished he could finish the fag before President Arif Khan arrived in his ceremonial cavalcade.

"Hi Ghori," Hyder spoke loudly, "there's an emergency. Talk to Barqat and ask your SSG boys to join my men at Bhagatan."

"What's the great problem?"

"Barqat," Hyder shouted, "take Ghori with you. Tackle the situation. Keep in touch."

*

"AL-X-356, abort your flight. Return to base," General Ghori shouted at the pilot of the Boeing 707, "I'm Director General SSG ordering."

"What does it mean pal?" Vudu replied in a perplexed voice.

"I'm the SSG chief. Obey my orders."

"Sorry, I can't abort my flight. Sargodha has closed its airspace."

Vudurume ignored Ghori's orders, banked left, and kept ascending.

"Land at Lahore." Barqat shouted.

Vudurume glanced back at Harfan standing near a crate and supporting it with a tender hand. He smiled, whistled a Bach tune, set the altimeter to 15000, and kept climbing.

"What the hell's happening?" Vudurume turned towards Harfan and asked.

"Sorry Captain," he replied, "as I told you earlier, we've accepted your invitation. My wife and child are your passengers."

"Really? Where are they? I don't see them."

"In one of those seven crates." Harfan pointed his finger at the deadly consignment.

"ATC Lahore, this is the Lady of The Light. I'm facing turbulence and want to gain altitude. Suggest a safe cruising height."

"You blighter, return to the base." Shouted Barqat.

"Sorry pal. Facing turbulence." Vudurume switched off the radio.

"What's the matter? Why have you packed your family like sardines?"

"Captain, you know the problem. Please don't abort the flight. They'll kill my family and me. The ISI blokes are after my blood. They suspect that I've leaked out vital information to India, about Islamabad's mad men ferrying nerve gas shells to Dacca, for another round of genocide."

"What? Did you say nerve gas shells? Which gas?"

"Not sure captain. May be Vietnam surplus."

"I wasn't told by Naqi's men."

"Sorry boss. There're 60 shells in these crates, enough to kill ten million."

"Holy Christ! I haven't carried such deadly weapons even to the primitive war zones in Africa. My wife and kids won't pardon me, specially my wife, after having survived Hitler's gas chambers. I refuse to carry these death chamber gas of the Fuehrer of Washington."

"Well Captain, that's the truth for you. And that's why I'm hounded."

"Where have you packed your wife and child?"

"In this crate."

"Damn fool," Vuduiume shouted, "don't you know that these shells emit toxic fumes. Hell of a guy you are! Take them out, quick. Antico," he signalled at the co-pilot, "help this rascal."

He grinned, whistled his favourite tune from The Sound of Music, and notched the altimeter to 28,000 ft.

*

Jamanat's men faced their first obstacle while negotiating a stationary array of gas tankers. The airport police shouted at them, for violating air-traffic security and speeding on the tarmac. Two security teams joined the fray with cars flashing red lights and blaring shrill hooters. A helicopter of the SSG headquarter detachment joined the cavalcade of the security staff. It flew dangerously low over his car as Jamanat shouted back in impotent rage and sped along the runway, sharply turning corners, which housed container stacks, barely missing an accidental impact.

Ibadat fired first, in short bursts and punctured two tires of Jamanat's Toyota. The occupants jumped out, took positions behind a pile of containers, and returned Ibadat's bullets.

Ibadat aimed at the fuel tank of the front car and set it ablaze. The occupants crawled out and took cover behind an array of containers.

Ibadat fired again, setting ablaze the second car. He ignored the ISI and SSG contingent firing and inching forward to his position. Ibadat crawled up behind a wall of containers as the helicopter flew in his direction. He sighted Alam and Jamanat through the firing sight of his Kahr MK9. They were advancing, inch-by-inch, on their knees and elbows. Arman Ali armed with a M-16 rifle covered their flanks.

He noticed, in the fading saffron light, the profile of Alam and shouted, "Alam sahib, *Khuda Hafiz.*"

Alam twisted his body to the right and saw Ibadat aiming at him from a cool range of 30 feet. Ibadat steadied his grip, aimed, and fired, this time in the automatic mode, emptying the magazine. Alam's mouth gaped open in disbelief and terror and before he knew, Ibadat's bullets hit him on the chest. He slumped like an ice encapsulated frozen twig. Death came even before he hit the ground.

"*Allah kasam* Arman," Ibadat shouted, "these bullets are for killing the king and my father. Jamanat sahib, take care. I'm coming for you, next." Ibadat took calibrated aim and fired at Arman Ali Niazi, emptying an entire magazine. Ali's head cracked open with a loud sound and red and yellow matter splattered out of the bony cage.

Ibadat kept on firing at Jamanat, in raging fury, swaying between the dream of a martyr and the anger of an avenger. All his magazines empty, he shook the pistol with a luminescent smile on his face and stood firm like a sculpted figure.

Jamanat picked up Arman's M-16, took deliberate aim, and perforated Ibadat's torso like a sieve.

Ibadat mumbled the name of his God, *'Bismillah... '* and collapsed.

Jamanat jumped over Alam's body, skirted past the burning cars and rushed towards the runway. He looked helplessly at the minuscule silhouette of the Boeing 707, now a disappearing saffron dot in the evening sky.

Someone fired from an M-16 in the direction of the distant dot.

"Stop it fool," Jamanat shouted, "the jackal has escaped."

*

68

Vudurume turned the radio on, turned the frequency and adjusted the earphones. A new command came over with slowly punctuated precision.

"AAL-X-356. This is Air Vice-Marshal Rahim. I give you two minutes to descend to 10,000 ft. Prepare for landing at Lahore." The voice sounded cool and menacing.

"Don't talk rubbish. I'm at 28,000 ft, can't descend that fast like a dead bird."

Vudurume replied coolly.

"Look out, you've company."

Vudurume leaned out towards the right first and left next. He wasn't really alone. Two F-104 Starfighters, their slim fuselage faintly gleaming in the saffron light of the setting sun, skimmed the skies at his flanks. The gleaming darts flew just 500 metres apart, maintaining a vulnerable distance.

Vudurume wasn't a stranger to these deadly US multi-role fighter bombers, which carried 9 weapon stations under the fuselage and short-span thin wings—Sparrow and Sidewinder air-to-air missiles and a 20 mm M-61 Vulcan multi-barrel canon. These deadly flying machines supplied by the USA, through the Saudi conduit, constituted the striking fulcrum of the Pakistani Air Force.

So, this small adventurer Harfan was indeed a big guy! The Pakistani Air Force wouldn't have scrambled up its prestigious fighters just for saying bon voyage to a renegade salesman. They must be gunning for a big guy, Harfan.

Vudurume looked out again. The F-104 formation was still escorting him. He imagined their grim faces and their fingers softly placed on the missile release buttons.

"Turn back, in two minutes." Voice of one of the F-104 pilots crackled in.

"Sorry pal. Nice birds you guys fly. I wish I could fly one. Our times were different, flying those damn beautiful old dames, slower but delightful. Don't you like slow rhythmical move of a maiden?" Vudurume chuckled jokingly. He signalled Harfan to make his wife and child comfortable in a passenger seat and directed one of the crew to serve them coffee and milk.

"There's no fun in suffocating them. The Pakis in any case have scent of you skunk. Strange are the ways of you fellows. What are you? A spy? A big guy, defecting to the Indians?"

"Stop joking, you bloody shit. You've only a minute to descend," came in the muffled voice of the F-104 fighter, "descend to 10,000 ft, and follow me."

"Sorry chum," Vudurume replied, "I don't take orders from you." He set the altimeter at 33,000 ft and changed cruising course due east.

"I give you exactly thirty seconds, that's final," Air Vice-Marshal Rahim's voice came in sharply, "after that my boys have the orders to shoot you down."

"Sorry Marshal," Vudurume replied, "you definitely won't do that, I know for sure. I'm carrying VX nerve gas artillery shells, enough to kill the population of half of your Punjab province. The choice is yours."

"Don't bluff," Rahim's voice sounded menacing in the cockpit, "I'll count up to 30, and you're responsible for the rest."

"Don't rush Marshal, talk to your bosses, I'm carrying these shells to Dacca, and these are gifted by Washington. Instead of killing Bengalis and Indians, you'd be killing fellow Pakistanis. I propose to bring down the bird on the most crowded part of Lahore. What do you call it? The Fort market or Bazaar Anarkali?"

Vudu's whistle irritated Rahim.

"Stop joking you bloody gunk. Be ready for the consequences."

"Don't rush Marshal. Suggest you call your bosses. No doubt, one of your indiscreet arrows would kill me. But the entire world would know that, you mad men in Pakistan, are dishing out death to the Bengalis and Indians, with American supplied nerve gas shells."

"Nobody would know."

"Don't hurry Marshal. Our voices are recorded by many agencies...may be Indians too." Vudurume heaved a loud sigh and silently prayed that the gamble would pay off.

"Stop blackmailing us. We know how to evaporate you scum in the air." Rahim threatened.

"Better ask your President, if he'd like to make the world wiser about his decision to resort to an unilateral chemical war on the defenceless Bengalis. Even your American friends had found the going tough in Vietnam. Remember Agent Orange?"

Air Vice Marshal Rahim's silence emboldened Vudurume. He made the plane steady at 35,000 ft and asked Antichopoulas to chart out the ARP (air-route map) to the nearby airports in India, capable of taking a Boeing 707 Stratolifter.

"We can land at Paattaankot (Pathankot) or Odaampore, (Udhampur), both have adequate ground facilities." Antoc made a quick check of the air map and replied.

"Set me the bearing and contact the nearest tower." Vudu directed his co-pilot.

"Are we going to land in India Cap?" Antoc gasped in disbelief.

"What's wrong with that?"

"We aren't legal. The Indians won't roll out the red carpets for us."

"Who cares? I may be an angel of death, but I refuse to carry these Nazi weapons of mass murder. My life and time have suffered the ghastly perfidies of the mad men of the Third Reich. I can't be a party to another Nazi crime against innocent people." Vudurume grinned gingerly.

"The Indians will impound our bird and put us behind bars, for war crime, Cap."

"Don't worry. Le'mme do the bargaining with the Indians. I'm carrying a surprise cache for them. They should thank their stars.."

"What about Doug?"

"Antoc," Vudurume replied, "le'mme do the thinking. Have faith in me. I've been your Captain for ten years, I guess."

He leaned forward and looked out ahead.

The F-104 Starfighters gained speed, zoomed past ahead of the 707, climbed up vertically and peeled off. Their gas trails floated behind like spiralled white garlands.

"Do you get me, Marshal?" Vudurume addressed Lahore ATC, "what's your decision? Do I bring down my bird on Lahore?"

"You son of Satan," A faint voice cursed from Lahore end, "get lost. We shall take care of you, anyways."

"Fine chum. It should be a pleasure doing business with you again, when you require to dump weapons of death in Sind or Baluchistan." Vudurume spoke, punctuating his words with soft whistles in between.

"Cap, I've raised Odaampore. Please talk." Alex Onasis increased the volume.

"Hello Odaampore, This is Captain Vudurume, flying the Lady of The Light, Boeing 707, a special flight from Bhagatanwala, destination Dacca. We want permission for an emergency landing."

"We've been reading you AAL 356, rather the Lady of the Darkness. You're already within 20 km. of Indian airspace." A voice boomed in from Udhampur control room.

"Sorry pal. Hope you don't mind the infringement."

"Yes. We mind. You've a funny name for your bird."

"It's the Lady of The Light. You know the lady who had brought hope to the hopeless victims of war."

"But you're carrying death."

"Not really. I bring hope and love to you."

"Stop the rhetoric. Your identification is inadequate. Please give us proper identification or turn back. A Pakistani aircraft isn't allowed to overfly the Indian airspace."

"I'm not flying Pakistani flag," Vudurume replied in his characteristic jovial voice, "I'm a flagless mercenary. Allow me to land at Paataankot or Odaampore."

"Captain, can I identify myself and request my boss to be at the airport?" Harfan interjected.

"Better help the crew and serve some coffee. Le'mme take care of the situation. Attend Jamilla and Pervez."

"AAL-X-356, descend to 20,000 ft and identify the flag you're flying." Udhampur Air Force Tower kept on tracking the mercenary flight.

"Squadron ZV-036 and squadron SS-001 do you read me?" A new voice came into the air.

Vudurume adjusted his earphones.

"036 and 001 scramble two Gnats and two Maruts, level up with the intruder and wait for orders."

"A nice welcome team pal. Anyways, guide me along the landing corridor. I'm carrying extra fuel." Vudurume stretched his neck to locate the Gnats and Maruts. He had encountered the Folland Gnats on the East Pakistan skies. These Amazonian mosquitoes gave him stomach cramps.

The Maruts, technically known as HF-24 Marut MK 1, were as deadly as any other aircraft flown by Pakistan. Each one of them carried four 30 mm Aden MK 2 canon, fifty 68 mm SNEB air-to-air rockets and four 1000 lb. bombs.

Vudurume adjusted his on board radar screen to keep track of the climbing Indian fighters.

"Hello AAL-X-356," a voice from one of the Gnats came in, "I'm Wing Commander Blair of the Indian Air Force. Identify yourself and follow me. I'm 500 knots ahead of you at 23,000. You're flanked on all sides, follow instructions."

"Roger. This is AAL-X-356. I'm at 20,000, following your instructions. Guide me to the nearest airport." Vudurume acknowledged the warning sounded by the Gnat pilot.

"Identify yourself. You've just got another two minutes," Udhampur ATC warned the pilot of the Boeing 707, "I've orders to shoot you down. Are you having a special bomb bay? What other weapons do you carry?"

"This is Captain Vudurume here, formerly a Squadron Leader with the South African Air Force, now flying for Cyprus based Athena Air Lines, a chartered company."

"What the hell are you doing in Indian air space? You can't take this route to Dacca."

"The flight to Dacca is aborted. I'm carrying 30,000 Kgs of weapons, including deadly VX nerve gas shells."

"What're you doing over Indian air space?"

"I'm a hired mercenary flyer, now flying from Sargodha to Dacca. I'm carrying, repeat, carrying VX nerve gas shells of US origin. I don't want to fly these Nazi weapons of mass killing. I want to terminate my flight in India. Require dumping of extra fuel before landing. Suggest location and direction." Vudurume explained the situation succinctly.

"This is Delhi ATC, elaborate weapons holding." Boomed in another new voice.

"Ditto as I said. Nothing new to add."

"Hang on."

Delhi ATC faded out.

69

Vudurume wasn't aware of the flutter and fright his flight had caused in Delhi. India's capital was in a spin mode. The riddle of flight AAL-X-356 was as formidable and earth shattering as the sighting of UFOs by nutty stargazers.

The Joint Crisis Management Committee (JCMC) that drew members from three wings of the Armed Forces, Civil Aviation, FIB, NSI and other security outfits, were camping at Palam airport and monitoring the minute-to-minute developments. The Cabinet Secretary, India's topmost bureaucrat, led the gang.

The new voice that sounded in Vudurume's cockpit was from the Director of Military Intelligence, Major General Gilani.

"I can't hang on indefinitely. We've plenty of time to talk. Allow me to land,"

Vudurume replied.

"Avoid funny manoeuvres. Talk sense." The DMI shouted back.

"No tantrums friend," Vudurume replied, "how come you're a Muslim and the Indian DMI?"

"It's India. Religion is not a trademark. Answer straight."

"Well! As I said, I hold nearly 60 VX nerve gas artillery shells, capable of killing a couple of million people. Guide me for offloading extra fuel and to land. We can have a nice chat later. I don't mind sharing a coffee with you."

"Why do you seek emergency landing facility? Any technical problem?" Delhi asked.

"No technical problem, the problem is of the heart, my heart and the hearts of your son and daughter-in-law," Vudurume chuckled, "and if you're information hungry, here it is. I repeat: it's an Athena Air Lines bird, a mercenary company, owned by a former Luftwaffe colonel. It's CIA funded, hired by Pakistan; and carrying Chinese weapons, including CIA supplied nerve gas shells. This is my thirteenth sortie to Dacca. Any more dope required?" Vudurume chuckled on the microphone.

The JCMC huddled together and went into frantic consultations. The security luminaries threw about conflicting views on the unprecedented contingency. Some advised against landing of the flight on Indian soil. That could invite a retaliatory attack from Pakistan. Finally, they agreed on the formulation of a capsule executive summary for the Prime Minister, who was in constant touch over the UHF (Ultra High Frequency) radio channel, from her South Block office.

"Hope you read me clear!" Vudurume continued, "one more point. Please inform your NSI chief. He has a guest in the flight. He may like to receive personally."

"Identify the guest." Delhi ATC demanded.

Vudurume maintained silence.

"Speak up 356."

"Harfan. He has an important messages for the chief. Don't miss informing him, it's vital for your national safety." Vudurume replied in a commanding tone.

Delhi ATC came alive after a brief silence.

"Who's this bloody Harfan? Elaborate."

"Tell your NSI chief. He'd understand and I don't think you require further information."

The Joint Crisis Management Committee huddled their heads together again. Some of the members demanded an explanation from Balachandran Nampoothiri.

"Who's this character Balls?" the Cabinet Secretary demanded.

"I'll explain later. Perhaps we can divert the plane for dumping excess fuel and consult the Prime Minister." The NSI chief made it clear that he wasn't willing to discuss Harfan with them.

"Is this pilot an agent of your company?" Asked a security expert.

"I refuse to comment. Please do as I say." Nampoothiri returned a curt reply.

The JCMC relapsed into silence.

"Hi friends," Vudurume's voice came in, "I can't hang on indefinitely. What's your decision? Should I crash over Delhi?"

"Turn 12 O'clock, follow the Air Force birds, and jettison extra fuel. Keep reserve for two hours and follow landing instructions." The JCMC decision was conveyed by the ATC, after brief but hectic consultations.

Their decision was hastened by Nampoothiri's intervention. His argument was impeccable. Harfan was his liability and that wasn't going to rain death over Delhi. But the VX nerve gas shells could if the funny pilot decided against hanging over Delhi skies or his bird developed technical snag.

*

The Gnats banked right, signalled the Boeing 707 to ascend to 35,000 ft and follow for dumping extra fuel over the Himalayas.

The Delhi tower used a reserved digital channel to direct the Air Force to escort the Boeing 707 for landing at Hindon Airbase, about 70 km north of Delhi. Two factors, the deadly weapons load and the presence of the mysterious passenger, a guest of the NSI, influenced the decision. Palam was too close to the capital and was easily accessible to the national and international media.

The Joint Crisis Management Committee, usually comfortable with bureaucratic indecision hustled up their act, prodded by a call from the PMO. They flew in a MI8 chopper and landed on the green turf of the National Stadium, which stood at the end slope of the once imposing Raisina Hills, and now Lutyens' Viceroyal palace, renamed Rashtrapati Bhavan.

The Foreign Secretary, otherwise a docile happy-go-lucky diplomat, scurried in with his colleagues for a hurried meeting with the Prime Minister. Her South Block office was just at the other end of the elegant stretch of the Kings Way, renamed Raj Path. The mercenary flight, he suspected, could be part of a rogue intelligence operation by the National Security India. He had as much faith on Nampoothiri as fellow bureaucrats had on his diplomatic skill.

The Cabinet Secretary, when the chief foreign office mandarin whispered the suspicion into his ears, just managed to display a dry grin on his emaciated face. The very idea, his eyes conveyed, was ridiculous.

"Don't be silly." He managed to comment.

"It's real. It's copied from one of those CIA sting operations." The Foreign Secretary insisted.

"Let's see. We'll cross the bridge when it comes."

"Balls require some fixing."

"Do you've a lathe machine to reshape him? Leave the matter to the PM."

*

Prime Minister Manjira seated behind the massive table, looked like an ivory sculpture. Her face looked stony and devoid of emotion. She was lost in the depth of unfathomable contemplation, dissecting the minute threads of the crisis.

Another war cloud was looming low and dark on the horizon. Was she guiding the country to another military stand off, like the one in 1965? She glossed over the games she had played when her predecessor, Jung Bahadur had accepted the UN brokered peace deal, in the wake of the drawn 1965 war. It had been a child's play to instigate some ministers and members of parliament against that rustic hinterland leader.

In less than six years, she had manoeuvred the country into the vortex of another whirlwind, another war. Had she pushed the country to the present eyeball-to-eyeball stand off?

No. Manjira shook her head. She hadn't.

Pakistan had bargained for this punishment by systematically and irrationally pursuing the so-called unfinished agenda of the Great Partition, twice in the Vale of Kashmir and with the ceaseless meddling in India's internal security concerns, by unleashing a proxy war in the North East.

Its misadventures and acts of genocide in East Pakistan had inundated India with a flood of human migration from the ravaged eastern wing of Pakistan. One way or the other India was sure to collapse, either by the onerous responsibilities of feeding and accommodating 20 million refugees, or by another round of war.

This war between India and Pakistan had become a historical necessity. In fact, an undeclared war was already raging in the eastern front. The war of attrition between the Pakistani forces and the combined forces of the Indian irregulars and the *Mukti Bahini* were ravaging the riverine East Pakistan.

"Ma'am." Rajinder Singh Dewan rattled his throat cautiously to draw the PM out of her trance.

"Yes." She imperiously turned her neck, not really meeting the eyes of her aide.

"The JCMC members are here; they request an urgent audience. It has something to do with a Pakistani plane."

"Yes Dewan. What were they saying about a guest of the NSI being in the Pakistani flight?"

"Some Harfan, they said, was carrying important defence related information."

"Call in Nampoothiri first."

*

The NSI chief, tossed between unknown and half-known facts about his prized agents in Pakistan, briefly apprised the PM of the identity of Harfan Bukhari and the essentials of Operation Triple X.

He hastened to add that the events had taken him by total surprise. The NSI wasn't in a position to offer the Prime Minister a cogent and rational explanation of the events leading to an intrusion by the mercenary flight.

"I presume it's the same fellow who is giving us a running commentary of the weapon and armament induction in East Pakistan!"

"Yes ma'am."

"I hope Balu," Manjira asked with a squinted look, "it's not one of your sting operations!"

"That's what Pakistan would like the world community to believe," Nampoothiri replied with a straight face, "our sting operations are also closely monitored by the Security Advisor to the PM."

"I believe the pilot has nearly 60 nerve gas shells in his cargo bay. What are the security implications? Are we equipped to face a major chemical or biological attack by our enemy?"

"The implications are simple ma'am. The USA had used similar shells in Vietnam with devastating consequences. Our defence forces and the civil defence machineries have no contingency plan to cope with such attacks."

"I think your X fellow has done a great job. Take it easy. Talk to me before he is interrogated. Isolate him and other members of the crew. Now I've some nice Xmas gift for the White House."

A smile flashed over Manjira's face.

"Rajinder, call in others, order tea, and some light eats." She collected herself, looked down at her reflected image on the glass table top, combed back her unruly hair, shuffled her *sari* and asked Dewan to summon the Defence and External Affairs Ministers.

*

Seated around the table, the dozen seasoned bureaucrats, responsible for key areas in national life, stared blankly at the PM, as if they were disciples of Buddha under the Wisdom Tree, waiting for the message of *nirvana*.

"So, what's this drama in the skies?" Manjira asked, as if she wasn't aware of what acts were being unfolded in the sky.

The Cabinet Secretary, Chairman of the JCMC, narrated the story, in his Oxonian English, not forgetting to make a subtle dig at the NSI chief, for his stubborn refusal to disclose the identity of his guest.

Manjira, amazingly unruffled, offered tea and snacks to the assembled officials and kept on surveying their faces.

"Anything else?" She asked.

"Ma'am," Balachandran Nampoothiri cleared his throat and reported in a low tone, "it's better if we keep my guest out of this discussion. We should be able to interrogate the other players in the drama in another few hours."

"Is it a case of hijacking?" the PM asked in an amused tone.

"It doesn't appear to be one." Nampoothiri replied peevishly. A piqued and worried man, he wasn't in a position to share the details of the aborted Operation Triple X. He silently regretted Harfan's comet like appearance over the skies of Delhi.

"What's your assessment of the weapons carried by the plane?" She asked the Military Intelligence chief.

"In fact ma'am," the fiercely mustached DMI responded in a squeaky voice, "we've been kept updated by the NSI and other sources, about the induction of conventional weapons to East Pakistan by some of these chartered mercenary aircrafts."

Manjira didn't respond. She kept on tossing a pencil on the glass top and moving her head gently. The people sitting across again went back to the yogic posture of receiving the *nirvana* message.

Finally, she dropped the pencil with a deliberate motion of her hand.

"And Chief," she glanced at the Air Chief, "how do you expect Pakistan to react?"

"My intelligence and inputs from friendly sources indicate that Pakistan has moved eight squadrons of advanced fighter bombers to Sargodha, Multan, Lahore and two other minor airbases. The modified F-14 and Mirage squadrons are capable of striking at our strategic bases, at the shortest possible notice." Replied the Air Chief.

"Thanks Chief. Natarajan..." she addressed the Cabinet Secretary, "Prepare a handout for a media briefing. It should state that a Pakistani mercenary cargo flight, carrying loads of dangerous weapons, including nerve gas artillery shells of Chinese origin has defected to India."

"US origin, ma'am, as the pilot says." The Cabinet Secretary mumbled.

"Make it *'probably Chinese origin.'* I'd like to dangle the knot around Washington's neck at an appropriate time. And you," she turned to the Foreign Secretary, "summon heads of the diplomatic corps and give them the same briefing. Collect additional materials from Nampoothiri, if necessary. However, no mention is to be made about the identity of the mercenary pilot, his crew and the guest of the NSI. Do I make myself clear?"

The wise men of Delhi nodded their heads in robotic synchronisation.

"Dewan," She turned towards her secretary, "connect me Moscow, London, Washington, Paris and Tokyo, as soon as the flight lands."

"Yes ma'am."

"I'd like to meet the War Cabinet, in another twenty minutes. And connect me to the *Rashtrapatiji* (the President). I'd like to call on him, after the War Cabinet meeting."

"And Nampoothiri," she again picked up the pencil, "I hope you'll receive your guest suitably. There should be no conclusive action without my knowledge. And rush me the special message from him. I'm curious."

"Yes ma'am. I've positioned special communication posts both at your office and residence. They will keep you informed of the latest developments at Hindon." Nampoothiri bowed in compliance.

"I want an immediate assessment and appraisal of the information carried by your guest, at your personal level. I don't want mindless meddling with the sensitive guests. Protect them well. Insulate them from media. Pakistan should have no access to them."

"Yes ma'am."

Nampoothiri silently cursed Triple X for upstaging him in the most unexpected manner. He should have been in a London safe house by now. He wondered why Alam had failed to execute his last order and why he was dead silent for over 72 hours. Well! He would require plenty of patience. Agent Triple X had indeed surprised him and India by delivering a dreaded consignment of nerve gas shells. There couldn't be a better birthday present for the PM, which was just two days hence, the nineteenth day of November.

The PM beckoned at the retreating hoard as the ministers and officials dispersed.

"Examine the feasibility and probability of Pakistan launching pre-emptive air strikes. They would like to avenge the humiliation and bad publicity once our press handout is released. That man in Islamabad appears to be losing his shirt."

"We've made full preparations to meet all possible Pakistani threats." Replied the DMI.

"Are our radar formations capable of intercepting the aerial blitzkrieg by Pakistan?"

"Not really ma'am. Our radars can't detect tree-skimming aircrafts." The Air Chief added.

"I'm not glad to hear that Chief," Manjira spoke with overt efforts to control the involuntary twitching of her right eyelid, "I want foolproof measures. I can't afford to send a message that Pakistan enjoys air superiority over us. Alert all your formations and order all air defence units to prepare for any eventuality."

"But we've an edge over Pakistan in missile technology. Our SAM batteries can take care of their advanced American fighter bombers." The Air Chief added.

"That's your headache. I don't want their birds to penetrate our skies." Manjira dismissed the meeting.

"Dewan," she buzzed him on the intercom, "are we ready for the War Cabinet meeting?"

"Yes ma'am, they're waiting in the next room."

"Keep me informed of the developments at Hindon."

Manjira closed her eyes and switched back to the deep meditation posture. She tried to envision the proceedings of the next meeting, which she had summoned to take a momentous decision. War was finally knocking at the door and she had to have the stamp of the War Council and order the Indian troops to officially enter East Pakistan. She smiled and pressed the button summoning Rajinder Singh Dewan.

"Call the cabinet members in."

She looked into the glass top again and readied herself for the epoch making meeting. A mysterious smile lingered on her face as she greeted the senior cabinet colleagues and top brass of the Armed Forces.

*

Five shifting blinks gradually emerged brighter on the airport pulsed radar screens. The echo pulses, converted to video signals, indicated that the Gnats and the Maruts flying in a close V formation were chaperoning the Lady of The Light at 8000 ft.

"Approach from the southeast, runway at 2 O'clock. Do you get 356?"

"Loud and clear," Vudurume whistled and replied, "hi pal, before you bundle me out to your prison, I hope, you'd allow me a visit to Ballia in Utterpraades. My roots are there."

"Concentrate on your gears and instruments." The ATC mildly rebuked the pilot.

"Fine friend, be my guest for a nightcap, don't disappoint me. I hope you've alerted the emergency services and the fire tenders. I'm carrying volatile materials." Vudurume advised Hindon ATC.

"That's our headache. Prepare for a safe touch down."

Vudurume whistled for a while, before releasing the under carriage. He banked right, aligning the plane for a landing, his first on Indian soil.

"What's that fascinating tower pal?" He asked Harfan.

"That's the Qutub Minar Captain, a tower built by a Muslim ruler on an old Hindu edifice."

"Hope I get to see this wonderful ancient place. Be my guide, if I'm not put behind the bars straightaway."

Vudurume shifted his eyes to the blinking panel consoles and the grounds below, which presented a dusty barren and battered look with ugly yawning mine holes dotting the carpet.

The Maruts whistled past the Boeing and disappeared into the horizon. The Gnats peeled off, climbed up vertically, and proceeded to nearby Sarsawan base.

"Await for parking instructions at the special bay. Follow the blue light flashing pilot car." Delhi ATC, familiar with the daredevil voice by now, advised Vudurume.

"We've a lady and a child in the flight; arrange a vehicle for them and a nice place for their stay."

Vudurume came in, as the wheels screeched against bitumen and flared out tongues of fire and smoke.

"Who are they?"

"Your daughter-in-law and grand child." He giggled rather loudly.

"Take a right turn, follow the ground pilot." The ATC guided Vudurume to a remote corner of the technical area.

"Did you say your daughter?"

"Mine yes, and yours too. Daughter-in-law of India."

"What? What nonsense are you talking?" The Cabinet Secretary asked.

"As I said daughter-in-law and a grand son too. Surprised?"

"Talk straight."

"Ask your NSI chief." Vudurume whistled loudly, broke into a soft humming of his favourite song, and brought the plane to a halt.

He looked out and was impressed by the motley reception crowd; a dozen vehicles of the armed forces, a phalanx of fire tenders, couple of ambulance vans, and two white unmarked cars. Helicopter gun ships whizzed past just a 100 meters above the fuselage of the Boeing 707.

The distant silhouettes of truck-mounted ground to air missiles with mobile radar in tow didn't surprise him. Delhi wasn't taking any chances against possible retaliatory air raid by the Pakistani fighter-bombers.

"Elaborate, about the lady and the child." A member of the Joint Crisis Management Committee demanded.

"A big surprise pal! Wait. Hope you've ritual sweets to welcome her." Vudurume laughed, as he applied the brakes.

"Don't talk rubbish."

"Ask your NSI chief, as I said. ATC, please order the ladder and requisite ground facilities. Advise a very delicate and expert handling of the volatile cargo, if you don't want a nasty accident."

He switched the powerful engines to idling position and asked the crew to disarm the doors.

Vudurume wasn't aware of the other drama being enacted by the Indian Air Force and the crack contingents of 8th Grenadiers, a specialised force that handled emergencies like the one created by the landing of the Lady of The Light.

About half a dozen MIGs encircled over the Hindon airbase for intercepting surprise intrusion by Pakistani aircrafts. A couple of MI8 gun ships hovered over the flanks of the base with orders to shoot down intruders.

A few batteries of vehicle mounted SAM missiles, synchronized with the radar formations were positioned at Hindon and at several vulnerable places and installations in and around Delhi.

The Northern Air and Army Commands were put on the highest alert, ready to move against Pakistan in a few minute's notice.

Four columns of the Grenadier commandos rushed in and took positions under the fuselage and wings of the plane, as Vudurume stepped out. Pervez Bukhari, wrapped up in white linen was on his lap. Jamilla followed him, a white scarf drawn on her head. Harfan trailed her shadow.

The South African pilot whistled a popular tune from *The Sound of Music*… . Climb Ev'ry Mountain…as he trotted down the stairs. The haunting musical, portraying indomitable courage and a pining for freedom always excited the reeds of his mind.

Finally freedom it was. This was his final redemption from another bondage, at the end of a long journey through a dark winding tunnel. This was his final tryst with mercenary flights. He would fly back to Paris and join his wife and kids. The city of liberty, equality, and freedom beckoned him. It was far removed from the daggers of Doug Chris and the jaundiced white skins of Johannesburg.

The merchants of death wouldn't be able to follow his furrow to the green pasture of peace. There wouldn't be any Pakistan, any India, and any merchandise of death. Enough! He had seen enough of the deadly tangoing of the hungry marsh jackals, jumping at each other's throat over pieces of rotten flesh.

Vudurume squeezed Harfan's shoulders and gently placed Pervez on Jamilla's lap.

"Thanks Captain." Harfan embraced Vudurume tightly.

"Thank you pal. I'm indebted to you and baby Jamilla. You've taught me afresh, the meaning of life and love. No more plying of the ferry of death. I'll rest on my oars. I too will go home, to my wife and kids. I hope people in Delhi won't detain me here for the rest of my life."

Vudurume walked straight into the waiting car, flanked by armed commandos. Nampoothiri quietly walked past the JCMC members and approached Harfan, standing under the sprawling wing of the Boeing 707.

"Follow me. Come dear."

Jamilla stepped out hesitantly with Pervez clutching her neck. Her white scarf softly fluttered in the cool mid November breeze.

Pervez, enormously excited by the meaningless hustle and bustle around him, waved his tiny hands about and giggled loudly, trying to capture the colourful beams of light from the control tower that momentarily lighted up his bewildered face and imagination in multicoloured hues.